Readings and Conversations in Social Psychology

Psychology
Is Social

Second Edition

Readings and Conversations in Social Psychology

Psychology Is Social

Second Edition

Edward Krupat

Massachusetts College of Pharmacy and Allied Health Sciences

Scott, Foresman and Company **Glenview, Illinois**

Dallas, Tex. Oakland, N.J. Palo Alto, Cal. Tucker, Ga. London, England

In Memory of My Father

Library of Congress Cataloging in Publication Data
Main entry under title:

Psychology is social.

Includes bibliographies and index.
1. Social psychology—Addresses, essays, lectures.
I. Krupat, Edward.
HM251.P84   1982   302   81-23347
ISBN 0-673-15382-7 (pbk.)   AACR2

2 3 4 5 6 - KPF - 86 85 84

Preface

My initial goal in preparing the first edition of this book was to introduce social psychology to students in a way that would capture their interest—to show that in addition to being an interesting *academic* subject, social psychology is alive with concepts and ideas that might enlighten and expand our understanding of everyday personal experiences. I was gratified to learn from students and instructors alike that they found the book to have a large store of "good reading" as well as "good learning," and therefore my goal in revising the book remains the same. The means for achieving interest that I have chosen also remain the same: 1) the introduction of each section via a conversation with a leading social scientist in the particular subject area and 2) the selection of articles from a variety of sources and perspectives.

The second edition of *Psychology Is Social* contains two new sections. One, "Loving and Liking," deals with a traditional and basic interest of social psychologists, interpersonal attraction and social relationships; the other, "Health and Illness," explores a new, rapidly expanding, and highly relevant research interest, the topic of health and health behavior. My thanks go to Zick Rubin of Brandeis University and to George Stone of the University of California at San Francisco for giving me their time and offering their opinions and insights on these newly added topics. In addition, there are two other new conversations in this edition—with Rhoda Unger of Montclair State College in the section "Male and Female" and with Robert Baron of the National Science Foundation in the section "Aggression and Violence." My thanks go to them as well.

Over 70 percent of the articles in this second edition did not appear in the first. I have, however, attempted to maintain the same balance and variety as before. I have tried to include the most current and up-to-date research without being subject to mere fads. In addition, I have included a number of classic research pieces so that students can read these in the original. I have included both field and laboratory research and reports of single studies, as well as reviews of a whole subject area. I have tried to strike a balance between covering basic and applied issues and between presenting objective accounts of research and subjective commentary on it as well. As in the first edition, many of the articles taken from professional journals in this edition have been slightly abridged. For the most part, these abridgments have been made in the "results" section of articles, where references to statistical tests and various technical issues have been omitted for purposes of readability and brevity. I have attempted to do this while maintaining the basic integrity of these articles and thank the authors for allowing me to edit them.

I would like to thank a number of people at the Massachusetts College of Pharmacy and Allied Health Sciences, especially Carol Feldman, David Fedo, and Sumner Robinson for their warm support during the course of this project. They have made me know that a social psychologist can feel very much at home in something other than the traditional liberal arts college. At Scott, Foresman, thanks to Katie Steele, who helped carry this revision through. Also, I would like to express my appreciation to the faculty and students in the Health Psychology program at the University of California at San Francisco for providing me with such a satisfying environment in which to complete work on the book during my year's stay there. And, Nancy Snyder deserves thanks for her efforts in typing and other such tasks.

Last (and, as they say, not least), my deepest thanks go to my wife Barbara and my sons Jason and Michael, whose own attitudes, perceptions, influence, and love have provided me with food for thought as well as personal nourishment.

EDWARD KRUPAT

Massachusetts College of Pharmacy
and Allied Health Sciences

Contents

4 Loving and Liking   154

5 Aggression and Violence   200

6 Altruism and Aid   244

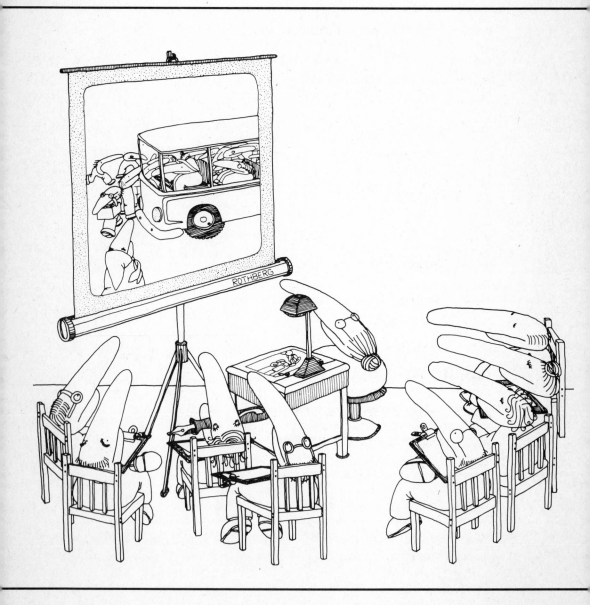

Introduction

Social Psychology as a Perspective on Behavior

The very first question that a book on social psychology should address itself to seems a rather simple and straightforward one: Just what is social psychology? The problem with answering that question is that there is no *one* generally accepted definition—even among social psychologists. This was demonstrated to me as I personally asked for a definition from a number of social psychologists at the end of the conversations we held about the topics in this book, and I compared their answers to certain textbook definitions. The different answers that I got offer a glimpse of some of the broad characteristics of this field, but also demonstrate the differing emphases which differing social psychologists place on a number of issues.

Philip Zimbardo defines social psychology in the broadest sense as being at "the core of the psychology of behavior." He states that whenever we deal with questions of human behavior, we are dealing with social psychology "insofar as the behavior of individual organisms is under the control of or is influenced by other people." He adds that there are "relatively few situations—and they tend to be more trivial ones—which demonstrate that a given behavior is purely individual behavior." Zimbardo's definition is expanded upon and formalized in the definition offered by Robert Baron in his textbook with Donn Byrne. They define social psychology as "the scientific field that seeks to investigate the manner in which the behavior, feelings or thoughts of one individual are influenced or determined by the behavior and/or characteristics of others" (Baron and Byrne, 1977, p. 4). Another recent text, while referring to the same general areas, offers a somewhat different emphasis, stating that social psychology is "the study of how people organize, evaluate and respond to their social experience" (Schneider, 1976, p. 2). The authors of a third text (Jones, Hendrick, and Epstein, 1979) are not very different in their orientation, but offer as their key element of emphasis "the study of social relationships."

1

While these individuals and texts are able to offer a broad view of the field of social psychology, I found that some of the people I interviewed were reluctant to refer to even these general outlines. Richard Nisbett felt that until the early '60s, "social psychology could have been pretty easily defined—it was the study of attitudes, social influence and group interaction." Now, however, he believes that the most important thing that social psychologists have to offer tends to emphasize more individual or intrapsychic processes such as questions involving self-perception rather than the perception of others.

John Darley was reluctant to give a definition at all, saying that he had given up trying to do that both for himself and for his students because "if I gave you any sort of answer, it would somehow limit my freedom to look at problems as and where I choose." Referring to the research orientation of social psychologists, he said that "we're different in certain ways. We have been trained in using as tight experimental methods as possible in research that still preserves the real complexities which we know to occur in human beings. We work with the whole person, accept the reality of that, and do what we can in investigating the problems that we are interested in."

ELEMENTS OF A DEFINITION

When we look back at this set of definitions and try to find some areas of agreement, one such area is so obvious that it is likely to be overlooked. That is, the social psychologist deals with the *individual*. Now, this statement may seem trivial until we look at how it helps us distinguish social psychology from a field such as sociology, with which it is often confused.

Understanding and Explaining the Individual's Social Behavior

Sociological explanations very often tend to "lose" the individual: to submerge the individual in describing groups, social structures, and patterns of social organization. Social psychologists in no way mean to deny the strong effects of culture, religion, position in the class hierarchy, etc., except for the fact that our interest is not in dealing with the class structure itself, but rather in understanding the effects of any and all of these variables on the *individual's social behavior*.

But then, how does social psychology differ from any other type of psychology, such as experimental or clinical psychology? As for experimental psychology, the answer lies in the fact that while social psychologists want to ensure that the individual is not *lost*, we also want to be certain that the individual is *maintained*. That is, social psychology, as John Darley says, deals with the behavior of the whole individual in all of the complex settings and under all the multiple influences of existence. We prefer not to segmentalize or break the individual into reaction times, learning curves, and knee jerks, but to look at the individual in normal settings and roles as friend, as lover, as parent, etc.

Then, how does the social psychologist differ from the clinical psychologist, who also works with the total individual? The answer to this question lies, first of all, in the fact that social psychology deals with everyday or "normal" processes rather than with pathological ones, and, secondly, in that the social psychologist tends to emphasize the nature of the individual's relationship to the *external* environment, while clinical and personality psychologists more often look toward the *inner* dynamics of individuals in order to explain their behavior.

Using Knowledge to Predict Behavior

Then, after all this, how does social psychology differ from good old common sense? What does a social psychological explanation add to the layman's understanding of human behavior? The problem with common sense is that it is capable of explaining anything *after the fact*. For the man who delays asking a girl to marry him and loses her to another, there is always "He who hesitates is lost"; but should it have been that as a result of waiting, things worked out extremely well, common sense still offers "Look before you leap." Everyone knows that "You can't judge a book by its cover"—or is it that "Clothes make the man"? Social psychologists not only attempt to understand and explain behavior, but they also attempt to *predict* it *before* the fact on the basis of their accumulated knowledge. And, in attempting to predict, we look at individuals in terms of the normal internal *and* external pressures operating upon them on an everyday basis.

Now, how far have we progressed toward a definition? First, we have said that social psychology is concerned with the individual, both whole and normal. To this, we add the social environment and the individual's interaction with that environment. To social psychologists, life is a contact sport. People influence others and are influenced by them in return. Each response one person makes is the stimulus to another person's next reaction. It is not even necessary for people to be aware of their own influence, nor do others have to be physically present to affect them. Yet, whether the pressures and expectations of others are explicit or implicit, people are clearly *social* beings.

You would be justified to ask whether this definition of the *content area* of social psychology isn't quite imperialistic and self-centered. So far, the matter appears all too simple: Social psychology deals with all that is interesting about human behavior, and other fields can simply study whatever else is left. It seems as if I am saying that we exist at the center of the universe and the other "satellite" fields revolve around us. (See Figure 1.)

NEED FOR A DIFFERENT DEFINITION

According to what has been said so far, just what is *not* social psychology? It is true that when we try to define the subject matter of social psychology, we tend to be too inclusive. For this reason, we seem to need a different type of definition, a definition which sees social psychology not in terms of *content*, but in terms of *perspective*.

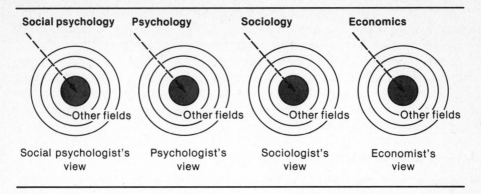

| Social psychology | Psychology | Sociology | Economics |

| Social psychologist's view | Psychologist's view | Sociologist's view | Economist's view |

FIGURE 1.   The universe as often seen by different social scientists.

What I am suggesting is that social scientists and professionals of all sorts tend to think along specific tracks; they tend to seek explanations only from a limited set of professionally relevant directions. The economist often tends to explain wars on the basis of trade deficits, and laws of supply and demand; the historian often looks to past conflicts between people and smoldering, age-old animosities; the sociologist seeks explanations in terms of the differing social structures of the warring societies; and some psychologists see innate, aggressive urges as the root cause of violence in general and wars in particular. The social psychologist (hopefully) is eclectic—feeling that the explanation and prediction of behavior can best be done by taking into account all of the relevant intrapersonal, situational, and structural factors that can be accommodated.

Zick Rubin, whom I talked with in Section 4, has suggested that social psychology should not be considered a discipline, as are economics, history, sociology, and psychology, but believes it should be thought of as an "interdiscipline" (Rubin, 1973). However, while this term does catch the breadth of the social psychologist's approach, perhaps social psychology could simply and more accurately be called a *perspective*, a particular outlook on the understanding and interpretation of human behavior. This choice of terminology reflects the idea that even the most basic social acts have numerous determinants and require a great deal of knowledge (and many different types of knowledge) to answer the question "why?"

This concept of social psychological perspective follows the very simple formula offered long ago by the social psychologist Kurt Lewin (1951):

$$B = f(P, E).$$

That is, behavior *(B)* is a function of both the person *(P)* and his or her environment *(E)*. I am suggesting that we take this sort of perspective because it is unwise to attempt to pull all of our answers out of only one hat. Furthermore, until we seek answers both in the individual *and* in his or her social environment, it is likely that we will disregard very many good answers to abstract questions and very many good solutions to practical problems.

AN EXAMPLE: SUICIDE

Let us make this point a little more concrete by taking a social phenomenon, suicide, and seeing how it has been explained by some classical sociological and psychological thinkers. Emile Durkheim, the French sociologist, looked at the sociocultural factors which he believed determined suicide rates. He investigated records of suicide in different historical periods and in different countries, and found that people in various class and religious categories, and living under certain political conditions, were more likely to commit suicide than others (Durkheim, 1897). However, while it is clear that social conditions do affect suicide rates, Durkheim still has not fully explained the "why" of suicide. And although it is likely that various societal conditions do make people feel less involved with others, Durkheim's explanation does not demonstrate why, given identical social situations, some people *did* commit suicide while others *did not*. His explanation leaves out the individual and the subjective impact of the social situation upon the individual. This type of explanation can only predict that suicide *rates* will vary in different *groups*. In addition, while Durkheim's explanation does take into account those factors which may disturb and upset individuals, it does not clearly show why they should go out and commit *suicide* and not *homicide*.

In direct distinction to a purely sociological explanation of suicide, we have the purely psychological one. But while it is different, it also is lacking in certain critical respects. The classical Freudian explanation of suicide is that it represents a case of aggression turned against the self, an extreme instance of *intro*punitiveness. Some of the personality characteristics associated with suicide are extreme depression, a lack of good interpersonal relationships, and the feeling of being a burden to someone else, which are attributed to problems in the individual's early developmental stages. This approach has what the sociological one lacks, a personal description of the feelings and experiences of the suicidal individual, but it lacks what the sociological one has. That is, it emphasizes the importance of individual problems and early childhood experiences, but it tends to ignore the complexities of the social and cultural forces working on both parent and child. In addition, while some people may occasionally *feel like* committing suicide, various cultural norms may largely determine how likely they are to actually do it, and *how* they will do it. The unhappy, depressed American is very unlikely to end up as a kamikaze, nor is he likely to burn himself as a public protest as have some Buddhist monks. To more fully explain the various aspects of a phenomenon such as suicide requires that social psychology becomes that interdiscipline mentioned above; it requires that we adopt a social psychological perspective and combine the knowledge available from psychology, sociology, and the other social sciences.

A MORE MUNDANE EXAMPLE AND SOME DATA

The case of suicide is admittedly out of the mainstream of our everyday lives. For the sake of illustrating how we may apply the social psychological perspective with things a little closer to the everyday, let's say for the moment that we are advertisers with a product to sell. That is, we are people who are interested in studying attitudes and applying our knowledge in an effort to bring about attitude change. And, by the way, you don't have to be an advertiser or a social psychologist to want to study and change attitudes. Any student who has ever tried to talk an instructor into raising the grade on a term paper, or anyone who has asked someone else for a date has tried to assess and change attitudes. If we are interested in selling our product, maybe we can get some hints from real advertising campaigns. For instance, just before writing this, I was told on my TV that I am probably a safe driver, a good middle-class family man, and if I want insurance I will be "in good hands with Allstate." Yesterday I was told by another company that "Liberty Mutual stands by you." They showed some gruesome scenes from an auto accident, and they assured me that if and when I die, they will pay for the funeral and take care of the kids when I am gone.

On another subject, I've seen quite a few ads from the American Cancer Society lately. Sometimes they show cartoons and jingles, and suggest people would be happier if they "kicked the habit." But a few years ago they used a very different approach. I remember seeing a commercial made by an actor who announced that he was really about to die from cancer. He said smoking had been the cause of his problem and he wanted to let others know so they could quit before it was too late for them, too.

These two sets of sales appeals clearly reflect a divergence of opinion over which works better—a high-fear or a low-fear campaign. If we want to get people to change their attitudes and behavior, which kind of campaign is more effective? Is the only way to get people aroused and thinking about your product to scare them into action, or would that be only likely to turn them off and scare them off? Maybe it is better to mildly coax and gently prod. You don't run the risk of having people reject you and your message, but you do run the risk of not moving them enough to get them to change the ways they are used to doing things.

This question of attitude change via fear appeals has been researched extensively by social psychologists as well as people in the advertising and market research business. Their research has spanned over twenty years, and it is not my intention to attempt to summarize their findings. The answer to this matter of fear appeals, like any other question about social behavior, is not simple.

In one study, Irving Janis and Seymour Feshbach (1953) tried to get subjects in three experimental groups to change their toothbrushing habits. They gave different lectures to the three groups, with all of the lectures containing the same factual information and the same recommendations. However, along with the lecture the first group saw slides of basically healthy gums and were threatened only in the most minimal way; a second group saw slides of moderately severe gum problems; and the third group was shown pictures of diseased, decayed gums which were extremely unpleasant and fear-arousing. Janis and Feshbach found that they got the most change from the group with the least fear. However, in other research Howard Leventhal and his associates have demonstrated that they achieved the greatest amount of change on both toothbrushing and safe-driving campaigns with high-fear campaigns (Leventhal and Niles, 1965; Leventhal and Singer, 1966). What shall we do? Whom shall we believe?

It is possible to reconcile such conflicting research conclusions by looking at the absolute levels of fear aroused in the subjects during the different studies or by seeing whether recommendations for change were offered to the subjects, but to gain the most complete explanation we must adopt a social psychological perspective. While it is important to be highly aware of all of the factors relevant to the "situation" or the "message," it is also important to know a good deal about the characteristics of the audience. We must add personality and situation together to see how the two interact.

When Janis and Feshbach (1954) reanalyzed the results of their study by classifying their subjects as high or low on anxiety, they found that although low-fear messages seemed to work best overall, this result could be accounted for by the fact that the anxious subjects responded very well to the low-fear message, but hardly at all to the high-fear appeal. At the same time, however, the nonanxious subjects responded slightly better to the high-fear campaign. Further studies by Michael Goldstein (1959), as well as by James Dabbs and Howard Leventhal (1966), have looked at other measures of personality, such as coping style and self-esteem; and their findings have also demonstrated that it is not necessarily that one type of appeal may generally work better than others, or that some people may generally be easier to convince than others, but that to be able to predict attitude and behavior change, we must take into account the interaction of both personality and situation. To put it another way, we come back to Lewin's $B = f(P, E)$.

PEOPLE AND SITUATIONS

Numerous other examples could be cited to demonstrate the need to consider both personality and situation. But after it has been said a few times, it starts becoming hard to think why it hasn't been done all the time. However, in their attempts to explain behavior, psychologists have tended to focus upon concepts such as need, habit, and attitude to such a great extent that they have not bothered to look beyond these concepts. Recently, we have been greatly impressed by some very dramatic demonstrations such as the shock-obedience studies of Stanley Milgram[1] (discussed in Meyer, "If Hitler Asked You to Electrocute a Stranger," Section 3) and the mock-prison study of Philip Zimbardo et al. (Section 5) in which people acted in ways which were very different from what we would have predicted, based on a knowledge of their personalities.

When the results of these studies show that people delivered electric shocks of up to 450 volts to another person when ordered by an experimenter, or that college students became harassing guards who degraded fellow students acting the role of prisoner, our first tendency is to think what sorts of awful people they must be. Yet, when it becomes clear that there is no reason to believe that those people were any different from the rest of us, then we must begin to focus on the nature of the situational pressures acting on them. We must begin to ask just how difficult it is to say, "No, I refuse" to a scientific experimenter, or how a guard feels when he is taunted by a prisoner. We are now becoming very much aware of the powerful effects of situations upon people, yet we have to be careful not to move to the other extreme and disregard the importance of the individual and individual dispositions.

A SIMPLE MODEL

We can simplify our discussion up to this point with a model. Let us assume that there is a world "out there" which consists of people, places, and various interpersonal communications, expectations, and pressures. This is the *objective reality* within which the individual works. To some extent we are involved in creating this world, having a degree of choice over selecting the situations in which we will interact and the people with whom we deal. But more than that, we are an active rather than a passive element in interpreting that world—we select, accentuate, and act upon certain messages while disregarding or completely missing others. This personal image of the world provides a *subjective reality* that the person may be expected to act upon. Even then, however, the person's behavior may or may not be consistent with these perceptions of objective reality because the form of behavior taken will also depend on another set of factors: the individual's abilities, beliefs, or needs as well as characteristics of the specific situation that may encourage or reinforce certain types of behavior while discouraging or punishing others. (See Figure 2.)

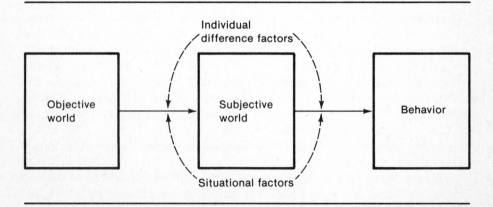

FIGURE 2. A simple model of the influences on social behavior.

What we can conclude from all this is not that the situation accounts for X percent of social behavior and the person accounts for Y percent; this sort of debate has been unproductive. Nor do we have to play the game of "chicken and egg" to determine whether person or situation logically comes first.

Instead, we can say that the subject matter of social psychology may be *anything* of interest concerning human behavior; the technique of social psychology is to analyze and observe behavior in terms of the dynamic interaction between individuals and the situations they are in. Social behavior may be a contact sport, but the "game" is a very complex one, in which the players and the rules are continuously modifying one another.

A NOTE ABOUT THE ORGANIZATION OF THIS BOOK

The rest of this book is divided into nine sections, each on a different topic. Yet, in the preceding pages, I have stated that social psychology should be defined in terms of a "perspective" rather than in terms of a set of "topics." My intention in bringing together this collection of readings and conversations is still to reflect that perspective, but to reflect it within the context of a set of topics that most social psychologists will recognize.

The focus of this book moves from topics traditionally considered the realm of basic laboratory-oriented experimental psychologists to those dealing with more applied field-oriented and even policy-oriented interests. This distinction, however, is not really a neat one for one of the very reasons that makes social psychology such an interesting and constantly evolving field. That is, much of the best research dealing with applied topics such as sex discrimination, causes of societal violence, the quality of life in the cities, and relations between doctors and patients relies upon and contributes back into the pool of knowledge on *basic* interpersonal processes. So that much of the best basic research has real practical applications, while much of the best applied research illuminates and extends our thinking about basic interpersonal processes.

Sections 1 and 2 begin with the topics attribution and social perception and attitudes and attitude change. The first is probably the most currently researched issue in the field while the second represents the very cornerstone upon which scientific social psychology was built. Some people have criticized social psychology's current interests in these two topics, suggesting that they both refer to *individual* rather than *social* variables. After all, attitudes and attributions are something that exist *within* the person's head— how are they social? Yet attitudes and attributions tie us to other people and other things. How we feel toward another person (attitudes) and what we believe motivated his or her actions (attributions) directly determine how we will behave toward that person and as such they link us to the world outside, to the social environment. In Section 1 we deal with the way in which we perceive others and their intentions and how biases in our perceptions and attributions may lead to interpersonal problems. In Section 2 we consider why and when we change our attitudes and the ways in which attitudes are related to our behaviors.

Sections 3 and 4 expand our scope, specifically to aspects of interpersonal relations. Section 3 on conformity and social influence points to the strong yet sometimes subtle social pressures that are exerted on us every day to go along with the decisions, requests, and judgments of other people. While this aspect of social relations is a very important one, Section 4 on interpersonal attraction and social relations focuses on the general nature of social linkages; why people are attracted to one another, how they come together, and how we can distinguish between superficial and deep relationships, between liking and loving.

While in one sense, the nature of interpersonal relationships represents a basic issue, in another sense, social psychology's entrance into the topics of love and attraction represents a step into the realm of applied problems and practical issues. The same can be said of Section 5 on aggression, and Section 6, on helping behavior. That is, while the study of why humans help or hurt others may be relevant to understanding something very basic about interpersonal orientations, answers to such questions as what effects TV violence has on children and when people will donate effort or money for a cause are important to lawmakers and activists as well. In taking a social psychological perspective on aggression and altruism, Sections 5 and 6 focus on the environmental and situational factors which combine to instigate and inhibit violent actions between people or to make people more or less likely to come to the aid of someone in need.

The final three sections deal most directly with topics that have grown out of the personal and professional commitments of social psychologists to apply their knowledge to decisions in the "real world". Section 7 deals with the issue of sex roles. The articles in this section consider how early socialization and current expectations differ for males and females and what the consequences of these are. Section 8 deals with urban life and the consequences of living in an environment that is densely peopled but can also be highly impersonal. The articles illustrate how the physical environment affects people and how we adapt to the demands of urban living. The final section on health and illness represents one of the newest and potentially one of the most important interests of social psychologists. Here we deal with how health may be affected by life-styles and social orientations, and also how a particular social relationship, the one between patient and practitioner can affect the course of diagnosis, treatment, and recovery.

It should be noted that these topics are not in any way meant to define or limit the scope of interest of the social psychologist. Wherever there are issues of importance that can be explained in terms of individual and situational influences, that is where you will find social psychologists. In this book, I simply offer these nine topics as a starting point and I hope that you will expand your interests and understanding well beyond.

NOTE

1. An important issue with which you will be confronted concerns the use of deception on subjects who take part in social psychological research. This issue has been widely discussed from the point of view of experimental validity as well as the ethical implications of deception. This debate has focused upon such research as the shock-obedience studies of Stanley Milgram, which have been condemned by some (e.g., Baumrind, 1964) as violating the rights of the subjects, and praised by others (see Milgram, 1964) for offering a startling and necessary revelation about social behavior. In reading the accounts of such research, it is vital to consider why deception was used, and what were the potential gains in knowledge from its use as compared to the potential harm to the people involved. Secondly, it would be well to consider alternative methods of studying social behavior which will preclude the need to deceive or distress the subjects who serve in future studies.

REFERENCES

Baron, R. A., & Byrne, D. *Social psychology: Understanding human interaction*. Boston: Allyn & Bacon, 1977.

Baumrind, D. Some thoughts on ethics of research: After reading Milgram's "Behavioral study of obedience." *American Psychologist*, 1964, **19**, 421–423.

Dabbs, J. M., Jr., & Leventhal, H. Effects of varying the recommendations in a fear-arousing communication. *Journal of Personality and Social Psychology*, 1966, **4**, 525–531.

Durkheim, E. *Le suicide: Étude de sociologie* (Trans. *Suicide: A study in sociology*). Paris: Alcan, 1897.

Goldstein, M. J. The relationship between coping and avoiding behavior and response to fear-arousing propaganda. *Journal of Abnormal and Social Psychology*, 1959, **58**, 247–252.

Janis, I., & Feshbach, S. Effects of fear-arousing communications. *Journal of Abnormal and Social Psychology*, 1953, **48**, 78–92.

Janis, I., & Feshbach, S. Personality differences associated with responsiveness to fear-arousing communications. *Journal of Personality*, 1954, **23**, 154–166.

Jones, R. A., Hendrick, C., & Epstein, Y. M. *Introduction to social psychology*. Sunderland, Mass.: Sinauer, 1979.

Leventhal, H., & Niles, P. Persistence of influence for varying durations of exposure to threat stimuli. *Psychological Reports*, 1965, **16**, 223–233.

Leventhal, H., & Singer, R. Affect arousal and positioning of recommendations in persuasive communications. *Journal of Personality and Social Psychology*, 1966, **4**, 137–146.

Lewin, K. *Field theory in social science*, D. Cartwright (Ed.), New York: Harper, 1951.

Milgram, S. Issues in the study of obedience: A reply to Baumrind. *American Psychologist*, 1964, **19**, 848–852.

Rubin, Z. *Liking and loving*. New York: Holt, Rinehart, and Winston, 1973.

Schneider, D. J. *Social psychology*. Reading, Mass.: Addison-Wesley, 1976.

Perceptions and Attributions

The way people know the world is through their senses. But if we are to account for the way people perceive and relate to others, we must go well beyond sensory data to look at the ways people process and organize the stimulation available to them. On the one hand, there is far too much information out there in the world for anyone to deal with it all. As a result, people must filter, sort, and process that information into a form that is manageable. Sometimes people see and experience only what they "want" to see. That is, they select and accentuate certain aspects of people and events and cognitively interpret them within the framework of their own needs, expectations, and past experiences.

But at the same time that they use only part of the information potentially available to them when perceiving others, people also go well *beyond* the information and make inferences about other people and the motives behind their actions. Whenever we take a person's actions and ask the question "why"—whether as a psychologist or as an everyday person—we are dealing with the process of making *attributions*. For instance, when someone fails an exam we can ask: Was the exam difficult, was the student too busy studying for other exams, was the student upset at having lost a boyfriend or girlfriend recently, or is that person just not very bright? Clearly, there are any number of potentially correct answers to the issue of why. As social psychologists, we are interested in knowing how we come to choose certain types of attributions over others.

More than any other single area of research, attribution, which is concerned with the question of how we use information to make causal inferences, has captured the interest and imagination of social psychologists over the past decade. Richard Nisbett, Professor of Psychology at the University of Michigan is one of the major contributors to the literature in this area. Together with Edward E. Jones, David E. Kanouse, Harold H. Kelley, Stuart Valins, and Bernard Weiner, he has published a series of papers on the subject in the book *Attribution: Perceiving the Causes of Behavior* (1972). In our conversation, Dr. Nisbett explained some of the "whys" of his own interests in the attribution process and how attribution theory is useful—personally and professionally. He suggested that we can avoid potentially inaccurate conclusions about others if we take into consideration the situational pressures acting on them rather than merely attributing their acts to something which lies in their own dispositions.

A CONVERSATION WITH RICHARD NISBETT

The University of Michigan

KRUPAT: *If we are going to talk about how people perceive others and how others are perceived, what shall we call our topic? Shall we call it* person perception *or* social perception—*or what label would you prefer?*

NISBETT: I guess I am interested in what we might call *causal perception,* the process by which individuals infer causes about the behavior of others.

KRUPAT: *I assume then that you are implying that when the object of your perceptions is a person rather than something inanimate, there are additional considerations that you must take into account. Is that the difference between this and other aspects in the general topic of perception?*

NISBETT: Yes, the main difference I can think of is that if something is alive (it's not so much that it be human, but only *alive*) we are inclined to think of it as a nexus of causality, as a source of causes. And I think that, to a degree, we are all subject to a general illusion about cause whenever another organism is involved. For some reason it is very plausible to us to imagine that if something is alive and it does something, that it *wanted* to do it, that it was motivated to do it, or that doing it was an expression of something inside itself.

KRUPAT: *I think I see what you mean. There's no doubt why that rock hit me. We know it had no intentions—but its thrower did. I might think the other* *person was an enemy who was aiming at me, or I might infer that it was merely an accident. This is the same kind of question as that dealt with by Hastorf and Cantril in this section—where the spectators thought they knew why the other side was playing dirty. Where do you get into such an issue of how attributions differ? Do you talk about motives behind those attributions or reasons for the distortions?*

NISBETT: Actually, the thing that has also fascinated me about an attribution theory approach is the perverse joy of going through phenomenon after phenomenon, showing how it can be explained *without* resort to a motivational concept of any kind other than the desire to *know*. Sometimes it's a very useful way of looking at things.

KRUPAT: *Could you give me an example of what you mean by this?*

NISBETT: For example, we all know that most people, with rare exception, tend to think that their own group is better than others, the thing we call *ethnocentrism*. I believe that this ethnocentrism may often result from simple, honest, information-processing error. Let me illustrate this with a personal experience. A couple of years ago, after my wife and I had been in Europe a couple of months, we met someone on a bus who turned out to be not only Jewish, but also from Brooklyn—so is my wife. They had an animated conversation, just a wonderful time, and later my wife said to me (as she has said under various circumstances), "Jewish people are so nice."

Actually, by the time we'd been in Europe that long we tended to find all sorts of desirable qualities in any American we met. But you don't have to be in Europe for this sort of pleasurable recognition to occur. When two people find themselves facing each other, they are likely to try to find some common ground, a basis for exchange of information. What I am implying is that whenever there is the possibility of an entree to this kind of relationship, you are going to reveal something of yourself, you're going to have a more animated conversation, and you're going to think better of that person. You are less likely to have a pleasant experience with someone with whom you do not have something in common, whether it's my country, my religion, or my group. That would explain ethnocentrism to me in a very satisfying way without resort to any belief motivated by something on the order of "I'm good, therefore my group must be good."

KRUPAT: *OK, but it seems you are suggesting that the initial knowledge "Gee, I'm from Texas, you're from Texas" leads us to believe that we are both likely to be good people. Why shouldn't that situation just as often result in the recognition that "Gee, people from Texas aren't all that good after all"?*

NISBETT: People are inclined to put on a good impression. People in our society generally try to be pleasant, especially if you're thrown together on a bus ride or if you're introduced at a cocktail party. Given that people try to be neutral and pleasant, it should make all the difference whether we can find a common topic of conversation which allows you to do your pleasant, charming, relaxed thing.

KRUPAT: *The other thing which I assume is important in this process is that if you and another person get along, you perceive, believe, infer that it is the nature of the* person *rather than the nature of the* situation *which is contributing to the fact that you are getting along well.*

NISBETT: Yes, and that relates back to what we were saying before about intentionality, that everything that a person does is a manifestation of his inner being. And so, if we find people behaving pleasantly, we tend to assume it's because they are pleasant people, rather than because the *situation* demanded it. I think we can be very quickly conned into believing that our behavior is a manifestation of ourselves, no matter what the situation.

Let me give you some examples as suggested to me by Lee Ross and Barry Collins. They believe that sensitivity groups have a great impact on people precisely because they are able to create the illusion that the behavior which is really situationally determined in the group is in fact dispositional— an expression of the inner nature of the person. The most extreme example of this that they give is of a sensitivity group session they went to where the participants were provided with soft plastic bats, and then entered a room with loud, high-tension music on the stereo. And although nothing is *explicitly* said that aggression is expected, here is jungle music, here they have plastic bats—and sure enough, before long they are swatting each other and mayhem breaks loose. Afterwards, people come away shaken by this. They say they had no idea they had so much aggression *in them*.

Well, is it true or not? I think you can tell almost anybody he has almost any kind of disposition and get away with it. But again, the point is that there is a strong tendency to attribute our behavior to our dispositions rather than the situations we are in.

KRUPAT: *But, when we as individuals are trying to understand an event such as this bat-swinging sensitivity group, there is a whole lot of information available to us. In order to properly perceive and interpret what's happened, we must have to filter the information, to accept and emphasize some pieces of information and reject others. What is the* process *by which we infer causes or intentions?*

NISBETT: I think in general there is a very primitive and lazy thing we do. If you do "X," then I say you have "X" tendencies. It is very easy to do that because the adjectives we have for people are very easily arrived at; we have the same root in the adjective to describe the *person* as we have to describe the *behavior*. You *aggressed* against that guy, so I guess you are an *aggressive* person. It's very primitive and easy. And for those things that are not all that important to us in life, nothing requires us to really think about other possible reasons. It's only when we have strong reasons for processing and picking up more of the facts (the person is very important to us or the behavior is a very significant one) that we do a little more work. And one thing I've discovered is that if you start probing at all, at least with bright college students, you find that with more thought people will *situationalize* their behaviors.

KRUPAT: *But, even if we generally see other people acting because of their internal dispositions rather than the external circumstances, we can still perceive a number of different reasons behind their behavior. For instance, take a fellow who is saying nice things about me. Is he saying those things because he's a nice guy who tells the truth, or is it because he's a flatterer? How does an individual decide? Does it then depend on circumstantial evidence or situational factors?*

NISBETT: I guess I would say that the question of the perception of what the behavior was and the reason for it are completely bound up together. They do happen simultaneously. Whether I say he's a nice guy or a flatterer is completely dependent on what the other cues tell me this person is trying to accomplish. One thing, of course, that lets you decide is whether you happen to have some other dispositional evidence about this person. Once, for instance, I was interacting with a particular student who was constantly saying flattering things about me. I marveled at the perceptiveness of these things that the student was able to see that other people in my environment were so likely to miss about me. But then I happened to overhear him at a party saying the very same complimentary things about another faculty member whom I did not regard so highly.

KRUPAT: *And at that point you knew it was flattery.*

NISBETT: And I will say it was one of those rare occasions that I must admit that motivated processes were going on. It was more than the "desire to know" which made me take so long to question his "motives."

KRUPAT: *Let me ask you a different sort of question. So far we've been discussing the perception of social aspects of our environment from an attributional point of view. One recent criticism of work such as this involves the matter of the "relevance" of such research and thinking. Some people might say, "Where does this attributional explanation get us? What practical applications does it have?" How do you relate to something such as this?*

NISBETT: Well, I'm reminded of Kurt Lewin's statement that there is nothing as practical as a good theory. Personally, ever since the day in 1967 when I read Harold Kelley's attribution paper* I've looked at the world a lot differently. I'm sure that eventually we're all going to see things a lot straighter because of an attribution way of thinking.

KRUPAT: *In what ways, for instance?*

NISBETT: I think one effect could be to make us a little more charitable than before. If you come to really believe that we are subject to an *illusion* of seeing other people's behavior as dispositionally caused, then we might be less likely to jump to conclusions, especially unpleasant conclusions, about people. Our inclination might be to see the cause of the behavior in the situation rather than in the person.

Let me give a very concrete example. A few years back I was working on an attribution theory paper. At the time, my wife and I were living in an

*Kelley, H. H. Attribution theory in social psychology. In D. Levine (Ed.), *Nebraska symposium on motivation*. Lincoln: University of Nebraska Press, 1967.

apartment which was on the top floor of an old three-family house, and the people who lived below us were an older couple. They had control of our thermostat, and also our fuses were attached to theirs. In a way, they controlled our fate. There were times we would come into the house and it would be absolutely freezing because they had changed the thermostat, or it would be sweltering because they had opened their windows while painting and turned up the thermostat to compensate. Or their fuse would blow and they would turn all of the lights off to change it without telling us. My wife, who is quite charitable and pleasant most of the time, got to hating these people downstairs. Whereas for me, living through this while writing the article, I tried to imagine the situation as it existed for them. I'm sure we were hardly a part of their life space at all. If a person is in the middle of cooking dinner for guests and the lights blow, the last thing he is going to think about is if the people upstairs are there and if they might be similarly inconvenienced by his actions. For my part, I was able to stop and look at the situational determinants of their behavior.

I really believe that situational explanations are generally more correct than dispositional ones. And even if they are wrong, pragmatically we'd be better off if we believed them.

KRUPAT: *It would seem that in all sorts of conflict situations we might be better off looking at the factors which constrain people and make them act in certain seemingly unpleasant ways rather than condemning the other side because they are "bad" people.*

NISBETT: There is a study which Kelley and Stahelski have done which deals specifically with that point. They have two subjects, one the buyer and the other the seller. Just as is usually the case in real life, each does not know the profit margin of the other. In one case the profit margins barely overlap, so that there is only a very narrow range where both can possibly come out ahead. And, in the other case the profit margins overlap a great deal, leaving a wide range of possible joint profits. Then Kelley and Stahelski let their subjects go through the bargaining process and ask them how they feel about each other. Where there is a widely overlapping profit margin, each thinks the other is very reasonable and says it's a shame real businessmen aren't as pleasant and accommodating. But under the barely overlapping condition, they hate each other and say, "What a skinflint!" Of course, neither party bothers to pay attention to the situational determinants of the other's behavior.

KRUPAT: *I see what you mean. And haven't you even suggested that personal, psychological problems, as well as interpersonal situations, can be analyzed from a self-perception, attribution point of view? Could you explain how therapy and treatment can be related to this type of social perception process?*

NISBETT: Yes, and I believe that psychotherapy and even standard medical situations may be the best opportunities for the use of an attributional analysis. Just about every newspaper in the country has at least one psychologist giving advice to his readers. They tend to make dispositional diagnoses on the basis of the information people give in their letters. First of all, as you know by now, I believe they should be directed toward the situation. Secondly, the advice they give is not only usually wrong advice, but it is damaging. People don't usually write in about good things, and if they take the advice, they make negative inferences about themselves, which I think is very unfortunate. It is very important to prevent people from making such inferences, of giving themselves the label of incompetent, neurotic, or bad. Once that happens, then enormous damage has been done.

KRUPAT: *Do you mean that there should be a columnist writing about situations and how they affect people?*

NISBETT: Exactly. I saw such a piece recently on the depressions that result from moving. I had been convinced before I read this that there is a very typical response to changing the setting where you live—involving depression, anxiety—a lot of the things we might call neurosis. That's pathology, there's no denying it, but if it is *typical*, then you are going to look at it very differently. You are likely to say "Gee, I'm in a bad situation, one that often makes people feel terrible." If instead you attribute the feelings to your own *unique* reaction you're likely to say, "I don't seem capable of handling my new environment. What kind of person am I that I need the old familiar routine to function?"

KRUPAT: *And if you perceive that you are the* cause *of the problem, I assume this leads to further complications.*

NISBETT: Yes; perhaps a final personal example might demonstrate how important this is, even in the field of medicine. I had an appendectomy a couple of years ago, and like most people, I knew very little about what was involved. In addition, I did not know that the hospital I was in did not have a recovery room on Sundays. This means that I was awake within five minutes after the last stitch went in. I was just barely conscious enough to make out shapes, but the pain was intense. Now, making constant attributions may be an academic's disease (although I think everybody has it), but I quickly made the inference that if I am so out of it that I can't even see straight and if I am having pain like this, something must have gone wrong. Now, in a way I was right, something had gone wrong. The hospital had run out of money and couldn't afford the recovery room, and therefore I was waking up two hours earlier than people ordinarily do. In fact, had I awakened two hours later it would not have been that painful.

Actually I had made the wrong causal inference based on the correct perception of the data; that is, I was experiencing too much pain. As a result, I probably screamed and shouted for more Demerol than I would have otherwise, but had I been a more hysterical personality I might have caused real complications in my situation. The second thing is that from day to day I had no idea what to expect. I was astonished at how long it took me to recover. The second or third day after the operation people would come in and talk to me and I would find that a fifteen-minute conversation exhausted me. I was not prepared for this and I worried about the progress of my recovery, which probably didn't do my physical condition any good. I later found out that the course of my recovery was normal, but I should have been told from the outset what to expect.

KRUPAT: *But how can we deal with your perceptions and attributions as well as your pain? Is there a cure for that dread disease, attributionitis?*

NISBETT: Very simple, by giving information. There ought to be simple mimeographed sheets for people, outlining what will definitely happen, what usually happens, what may go wrong and whether it is anything to worry about, and what you should tell your physician—as simple as that. I think the amount of grief that could be avoided is enormous. Sometimes, instead of just performing my laboratory experiments, I feel I ought to be out crusading among medical practitioners that the nature of their patients' perceptions and attributions may affect their recovery—that they are not just treating a body, but the mind is clicking away, too.

AN INTRODUCTION TO THE READINGS

In the first article, Edward E. Jones reviews some of the basic issues and important experiments in attribution theory. In particular, Jones deals with the proposition that people make different kinds of attributions depending on whether they are explaining the causes of their own behavior or that of another person. He presents a good deal of research evidence demonstrating that when we explain our own behavior we tend to focus upon its situational determinants ("I fell because the street was slippery"), while an observer of the same behavior tends to focus on the personal or dispositional factors as its cause ("He fell because he is not very coordinated"). Citing research both inside and outside of the laboratory, he notes that the tendency for actors and observers to interpret the causes of behavior differently sows the seeds for a number of interpersonal problems and misunderstandings.

In the next paper, while David Rosenhan does not refer directly to attribution theory, he presents a vivid illustration of the ways in which individuals making hasty attributions can be the source of many problems. Rosenhan asks the question: "If sanity and insanity exist, how shall we know them?" In order to answer his question, he had eight normal people ask to be admitted to a mental hospital, each claiming to hear voices. Except for revealing this one symptom, which they immediately discarded once they were admitted, they acted as they normally would at all times. Each one was admitted with a rather severe diagnosis. The major observation of the study was that once the "patient" was given a dispositional label (i.e., *crazy*) all of his or her actions were seen to be derived from the presumed pathology. For instance, all of the pseudopatients took extensive notes as part of the study. Their "writing behavior" was noted by the staff, who merely assumed that it was part of their problem. One pseudopatient was pacing the halls with nothing else to do. The staff automatically inferred that this was due to nervousness, a dispositional cause, rather than merely to boredom, a situational cause.

Finally, while the first two articles deal with the different inferences made by actor versus observer, the last paper, a classic study by Albert Hastorf and Hadley Cantril demonstrates how two sets of observers may interpret an event differently depending on their point of view. The authors point out that the perceptions of any individual in a given situation are unique because what the person "brings" to the situation is also likely to be unique. They illustrate this point with a study of a real-life incident, a football game between Princeton and Dartmouth. The game was marked by extremely hard hitting; and in it, Princeton's All-American star was injured along with two of Dartmouth's players. In regard to how the game was perceived by people on different sides of the field, the data show that there was not *one* game going on, but there were *two*—one as seen by the Dartmouth fans and one as seen by the Princeton people. In response to a questionnaire, over half of the Dartmouth students characterized the game as "fair" whereas only 3 percent of the Princeton raters were that charitable. And even at a later point, when subjects were shown a film of the game, the two sets of perceptions still varied greatly.

Together, these three papers demonstrate that the process of social perception and the making of causal inferences is a complex one. It suggests that we should be cautious about drawing conclusions about people and their motives because while each of us is sure that his or her perception of reality is accurate and true, there is likely to be another person out there who is equally sure, but whose perceptions and attributions are quite different.

EDWARD E. JONES

How Do People Perceive the Causes of Behavior?

Finding the causes for behavior is a fundamental enterprise of the psychologist. But it is an enterprise he shares with the man on the street. Our responses to others are affected by the reasons, or *attributes*, we assign for their behavior. At least this is the basic assumption of the attributional approach in social psychology, an approach that concerns itself with phenomenal causality—the conditions affecting how each of us attributes causes for his own and others' behavior. The hope is that if we can better understand how people perceive the causal structure of their social world, we can better predict their responses to that world. If *A* attributes *B*'s anger to the fact that *B* has lost his job, *A* is less likely to reciprocate. If a teacher attributes a student's poor performance to lack of motivation, he is more likely to express open disappointment than if his attribution were to lack of ability. A supervisor's appreciation of a subordinate's compliments is more or less alloyed by his attribution of ulterior motives.

The attributional approach (Jones et al. 1972) is essentially a perspective, or a framework, rather than a theory. The perspective owes much of its current prominence to the seminal writings of Fritz Heider. However, propositional statements have been spawned within the framework, and there are some identifiable theoretical positions. Davis and I outlined a theory of *correspondent inferences* in 1965 which is especially concerned with inferences about the dispositions and intentions of a person drawn from observing his behavior in particular contexts. Simply put, the theory states that causal attribution will be made to an actor to the extent that he is not bound by circumstances and is therefore free to choose from a number of behavioral options. If a person has choice, and if his actions depart in any way from expectations, the perceiver-attributor should gain information about his motives and personality. Under these conditions, we might say that the person reveals himself in his actions. We can make a correspondent inference that ties an act to a causal disposition: "He dominated the meeting because he is dominant"; "He cries because he is in pain"; "He voted for ERA because he believes in full civil liberties for women."

Two years later, Kelley proposed a comprehensive theory of *entity attribution* which was the complement of correspondent-inference theory. Whereas Davis and I

"How Do People Perceive the Causes of Behavior?" by Edward E. Jones from *American Scientist*, vol. 64, 1976. Reprinted by permission of *American Scientist*, journal of Sigma Xi, The Scientific Research Society.

wanted to explain how attributions to the person can be made by ruling out environmental explanations, Kelley wanted to show how we decide whether an actor's response is caused by the entity to which it is directed rather than by some idiosyncratic bias on his part. Both approaches accepted the division of person and situation as reflecting the terms in which the naive attributor is supposed to make his causal allocations.

In 1971, Nisbett and I rather recklessly proposed that actors and observers make divergent attributions about behavioral causes. Whereas the actor sees his behavior primarily as a response to the situation in which he finds himself, the observer attributes the same behavior to the actor's dispositional characteristics. This proposition had grown out of a number of informal observations as well as a sequence of experiments on attitude attribution. Let me digress for a moment to summarize briefly this line of research.

LABORATORY EXPERIMENTS

Nine separate experiments were run within the same general paradigm with college undergraduates from widely separated universities. Each followed a procedure in which subjects were given a short essay or speech favoring a particular position and were asked to infer the underlying attitude of the target person who produced it. In one experiment the statement was presented as an answer to an examination question; in another it was identified as the preliminary statement of a debater; in still others the statement was attributed to paid volunteers recruited for personality research (cf. Jones and Harris 1967). The statements used in each experiment involved a particular social issue such as the viability of Castro's Cuba, marijuana legalization, desegregation and busing, liberalized abortion, or socialized medicine.

The experimental conditions were created by varying whether the target person could choose which side of the issue to write or speak on, and whether or not the side was the expected or popular position. Some subjects were informed that the target person was assigned to defend a particular side of the issue (by his instructor, the debating coach, or the experimenter). Others were told he had been free to choose either side. The statement itself took one or the other side of the issue. In the typical experiment, then, there were four experimental groups: pro-position with choice, anti-position with choice, pro-position with no choice, and anti-position with no choice. For any given sample of subjects, one of the sides (pro or anti) was more popular or expected than the other.

All of the experiments showed remarkable stability in supporting the predictions one would make from correspondent inference theory. Attitudes in line with behavior were more decisively attributed to the target person in the choice than in the no-choice condition, but degree of choice made a greater difference if the essay or speech ran counter to the expected or normative position. This is illustrated in Figure 1, which presents the results from an early study (1967) dealing with attitudes toward Fidel Castro. Subjects read an essay presumably written as an opening statement by a college debater, but actually it was scripted beforehand as an unremarkable pro or anti summary, the kind of thing an undergraduate debater might write after minimal study of the issue. The subject was also told either that the

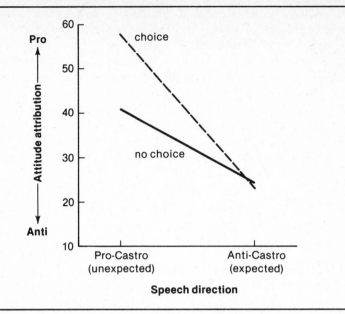

FIGURE 1. In this attitude-attribution experiment, target persons presented short speeches either for or against the Castro regime in Cuba. Some were said to have chosen which side to support (choice condition); others were said to have been required to take the position endorsed (no choice condition). Observers then rated what they felt was each target person's true attitude toward Castro; the possible range was from 10 (extreme anti) to 70 (extreme pro). Observers rating pro-Castro target persons in the "choice" condition saw their true attitude as more decisively in favor of Castro than observers rating Castro supporters in the "no choice" condition. Choice was a negligible factor when the speech opposed the Castro regime. At the time the experiment was conducted, most subjects — both target persons and observers — held anti-Castro views. Data from Jones and Harris (1967).

target person had been directed by the team advisor to argue a specific side of the debate or that he was given his choice of sides.

After digesting the essay and noting the context in which it was produced, each subject was instructed to rate the target person's true attitude toward the Castro regime. From Figure 1 it is apparent that choice has an effect, but only in the pro-Castro condition, where the debater's position was not in line with the expected attitude of a college student in the late sixties.

For our present purposes, what is most interesting is a finding that could not have been predicted by correspondent inference theory: even in the no-choice conditions, subjects tended to attribute attitudes in line with the speech. They seemed to attach too little weight to the situation (the no-choice instructions) and too much to the person. Although several alternative explanations quickly suggested themselves, these were effectively ruled out by additional experiments (Jones et al. 1971; Snyder and Jones 1974). I became and remain convinced that we are dealing with a robust phenomenon of attributional bias and that persons as observers are all too ready to infer underlying dispositions, like attitudes, from behaviors, like opinion statements, even when it is obvious that the statements are produced under constraint.

Although these results were compatible with the hypothesis that actors and observers have divergent perspectives, they said nothing, of course, about the actor. But there is abundant evidence from other social psychological experiments that actors do not adjust their attitudes to make them consistent with their behavior if they are required (given little or no choice but) to defend the opposite of their initial position on an issue (cf. Aronson 1969; Bem 1972). Their behavior can be adequately explained by an attribution to the situation.

Nisbett and his associates (1973) set out to test the actor-observer proposition more directly. They found in a questionnaire study that people assign more traits to others than to themselves, a finding quite consistent with the notion that observers see personal dispositions in others but believe their own behavior depends primarily on the situation. Nisbett and his group also conducted an experiment in which some subjects were turned into actors and some into observers. The actors were asked to volunteer to take distinguished visitors around the Yale campus, while observers monitored the actors' responses to the volunteering request. Actors who volunteered were judged by the observers to be more likely to agree to canvass for the United Fund (an instance of response generalization implying a ''volunteering trait'') than those who did not volunteer. There was a slight reversal in this trend when the actors themselves were asked whether they would volunteer to canvass. By inference, then, the observers assumed that someone who volunteers in one setting will volunteer in others—they attributed a volunteering disposition to the actor.

Nisbett and I (1971) incorporated these data and tried to elucidate some of the reasons why the actor-observer divergence might occur. As a starting point, it may be helpful to consider the observer's orientation. In the attitude-attribution paradigm, and in the volunteering experiments, we confront the observer with a brief sample of behavior produced in a particular setting. The actor is aware of a history of his prior actions in similar settings and is likely to compare the present behavior to previous behavior. Differences in his behavior over time can readily be attributed to the situation. The observer, on the other hand, is typically ignorant about details of the actor's history and is likely to take a cross-sectional, or normative, view, asking himself, ''How do this person's reactions differ from those I would expect from others, from the average, from the norm?'' Thus the observer's orientation is individuating; he seeks out (and exaggerates?) differences among people, perhaps because this gives him a feeling of control against the unexpected. His error seems to lie in failing to see the situation as a completely sufficient cause of the behavior observed. Heider (1958) must have had something similar in mind when he talked about the tendency for behavior to ''engulf the field.'' Behavior belongs to the person; the ''field'' acts on everyone.

In addition to the observer's relative poverty of information, it is also true that the same information will be processed differently by actors and observers. For the observer, in general, action is dynamic, changing, unpredictable, and therefore *salient*. In the attitude-attribution paradigm, the essay appears to stand out as the unique product of the writer. It must, since it is the only concrete information the perceiver has about the writer, reflect the writer's characteristics in a number of ways. That is what "the experiment" is about: the subject is in the position of wondering how good he is at estimating a person's true attitudes. The actor who writes a counterattitudinal essay has faced situational pressure and succumbed to it. The observer knows in some intellectual sense that the pressure was there, but he is so drawn to the essay as the focus of his judgment task that he infers too much about the individual and his uniqueness.

There is good evidence, finally, that *perceptual focusing* leads to attribution (Duncker 1938; Wallach 1959). Of special relevance here is a study by Storms (1973). He set out to investigate whether observers and actors could be induced to exchange perspectives with the aid of videotape replay. As in the case with most important experiments, the design was elegantly simple. Two experimental subjects (actors) held a brief get-acquainted conversation while two other subjects were each assigned to observe a different actor. Television cameras were pointed at each actor, but after the conversation the experimenter appeared to notice that only one had been working properly.

During the next phase of the experiment, all subjects observed the intact videotape replay of the conversation (focusing on one of the actors) and then made a series of attributional judgments. Thus, one actor had the same orientation toward the other actor that he had in the conversation—he was looking at the other on the video replay. The other actor was looking at himself on the replay. He had become a self-observer. When asked to account for the target person's behavior in terms of the contributions of personal characteristics and characteristics of the situation, the actors observing themselves were much more inclined to attribute their behavior to dispositional influences. Attributions by the two observers varied depending on their new orientation. The original observer of the nontaped actor was asked to account for his target person's behavior after looking at the other actor. In this changed orientation, he attributed his target person's behavior to situational factors. The other observer, who watched the taped subject originally as well as in phase . two, assigned much greater dispositional influence to his target person.

To summarize these findings, then, attribution seems to follow along with perceptual focus, or perspective. It appears that we attribute causality to whatever or whomever we look at, at least when we are asked. The implications of this fact for persistent interpersonal misunderstandings are obvious. In a persuasive communication setting, for example, the communicator thinks he is describing reality, whereas the target person thinks he is expressing his personal biases.

The results of Storms's experiment also suggest that seating arrangements might be extremely important in a discussion group. In fact, this has been demonstrated by Taylor and Fiske (1975). In their experiment, subjects observing a two-person "get-acquainted" discussion between two confederates of the experimenter were seated in such a way that some faced one discussant, some faced the other, and some observed both from a 90° angle. These differences in literal perspective strongly affected the observer-subjects' attributions of causality for various aspects of the conversation. Specifically, the discussant directly in the observer's line of sight was assigned greater personal causality. When the discussants were both observed from the side, equal personal causality was assigned.

In an even more subtle manipulation of perspective, Hansen et al. (unpublished) presented videotaped shots of a person solving a jigsaw puzzle or playing chess. The shots either viewed the puzzle or chessboard from the point of view of the actor or from an angle perpendicular to that of the actor. Once again, the observer focusing on the actor attributed greater behavioral causality to him. The observer with the same angle of vision as the actor attributed the game outcome to the situation.

These experiments essentially converted observers into actors by letting them literally see what the actor saw. Could the same result be achieved by a shift in *psychological* perspective? Regan and Totten (1975) showed college women a videotaped "getting-acquainted" discussion, telling half of them to empathize with discussant A (the target person) and to try to imagine how A felt as she engaged in the conversation. The remaining subjects were given no such instructions. Using the same measures that Storms had used, Regan and Totten confirmed their hypothesis that empathy-inducing instructions produce a shift toward attributing behavior causation to the situation. This was especially true in a condition where the subject could see only the target person on the tape, though she could hear the other discussant as well. Thus, the authors argue, the divergence of perspective between actors and observers is founded in more than differences in available information. It derives, at least in part, from differences in the ways in which the same information is processed.

Arkin and Duval (1975) have also found that the subjects' attention can be manipulated to affect their causal attributions. Actors in a picture-judging experiment attributed their preferences more to various features of the situation than to themselves (whereas observers were more inclined to attribute the preferences to the actor as a person). However, these differences were reversed when actors felt that they were being videotaped. The self-consciousness induced by the presence of a TV camera apparently shifted the causal assignment from the situation to the self. This is quite in line with the Duval and Wicklund (1972) theory of *objective self-awareness*, which suggests that an actor's causal attributions are a function of whether or not his attention is focused on himself.

FIELD STUDIES

It is quite apparent that something interesting is happening here, and the evidence that perceptual perspective influences causal attribution seems reliable and replicable. But, the reader might demur, is this one of those hothouse laboratory phenomena that is overwhelmed by other variables in the more chaotic and complex natural environment? Obviously, we should not expect to find a quick answer to this question, but a recent study by West et al. (1975) shows the predicted basic pattern of actor-observer differences in a dramatic field experiment simulating the Watergate burglary attempt.

Undergraduate criminology majors at a state university were contacted by a man whom they knew as a local private investigator. He arranged a meeting with each subject at which detailed plans of a business burglary were presented. The subject was asked to participate in breaking into the offices of a local firm to microfilm a set of records. In one condition of the experiment, the subjects were told that a competing local firm had offered $8,000 for a copy of designs prepared by the first firm. The subjects were told that they would be paid $2,000 for their participation in the crime. In other conditions, the experimenter presented himself as working for the Internal Revenue Service and said that the records would allegedly show that the firm was trying to defraud the U.S. government. Of the subjects exposed to the IRS cover story, half were told that they would receive immunity from prosecution if caught; the other half were told that there would be no immunity. After an elaborate and convincing presentation of the plan, subjects were asked to come to a final planning meeting. Their assent or refusal was the major dependent measure of the experiment. Once the subjects either agreed or did not agree to participate in the burglary, the experiment was then over and they were given extensive debriefing concerning the deceptions involved and the purpose of the experiment. (Readers interested in the ethical problems of this experiment will find a considered view presented by West and his colleagues, 1975, and comments by Cook, 1975, who tries to place the experiment in the more general framework of ethical problems in psychological research.)

Not surprisingly, whether the subject thought he or she would be granted immunity if caught was a crucial determinant of the frequency of compliance. Nearly half (45 percent) of the subjects in the immunity condition agreed to attend the final planning session. It is somewhat surprising that only 1 out of 20 subjects in the IRS no-immunity condition complied, whereas 4 out of 20 subjects in the reward condition agreed, although this difference was not statistically significant.

In addition to the involved subjects, a large sample of role-playing "observers" were asked to imagine themselves in the situation of the subject. They were given a very detailed description of experimental events in the condition to which they were assigned and asked whether they would or would not comply. About 18 percent of these observer-subjects said that they would have agreed, and there was no difference as a function of the various conditions. Of special interest in the present context, all subjects (actors and role-players) were asked to explain *why* they did or did not agree to move closer toward the burglary. Whether the actors were compliers or noncompliers, they attributed their decision to environmental factors more than to personal dispositions. The role-playing observers, on the other hand, were much more likely to attribute the decision to dispositions in the actor. This was true whether they were asked to explain the decision of a complying or a noncomplying actor. Thus the actor-observer divergence in this case is not simply a matter of the actor's being inclined to rationalize his "criminal" behavior by blaming the situation.

In another, less dramatic, field study, McGee and Snyder (1975) followed their hunch that there are interesting attributional differences between those who salt before and those who salt after tasting their food. Restaurant patrons were approached after placing themselves in one of these two categories by their salting behavior, and were asked to rate themselves on a series of polar adjectives like realistic–idealistic, cautious–bold, and energetic–relaxed. Each adjective pair was followed by another option, "it depends on the situation." As predicted, the before-tasting salters tended to check more traits as characteristic of themselves than the after-tasting salters, who were much more inclined to check "it depends on the situation." (It should be emphasized that none of the traits made any reference to eating behavior, taste, and so on.) When asked why they salted their food, the two types also diverged: the before-salters explained their behavior in terms of personal characteristics, whereas the after-salters tended to refer to the food.

Snyder and Monson (1975) have also shown that subjects classified as high "self-monitors" expect themselves to behave variably across different hypothetical situations. Low "self-monitors," on the other hand, expect to show greater cross-situational consistency. The authors classified their subjects by means of the score attained on a self-descriptive questionnaire where they were asked to check as true or false such statements as "I'm not always the person I appear to be" and "I may deceive people by being friendly when I really dislike them." On another questionnaire, describing different hypothetical situations, low self-monitors expected their behavior and environment in these different situations to be much more stable than did the high self-monitors. There is some evidence, then, that Nisbett's and my proposition must be qualified: *some* actors tend to attribute their actions to themselves, whereas others—more faithful to the proposition—typically make situational attributions.

There are other experimental results which seem more drastically at odds with our proposition. Most of these studies (e.g. Wolosin et al. 1975) involve the perception of behavioral freedom as the main dependent variable. Under some conditions, at least, actors will rate themselves as freer of situational influence than observers would rate them. Thus, if the attributional question is phrased in terms of whether the situation has *required* the actor to behave in a certain way, or if it strongly implies the giving up of his freedom and control, actors will claim greater freedom and responsibility whereas observers will see them as relatively constrained. If the question is more neutral with regard to relinquishing control, however, actors will see their behavioral decisions as responses appropriate to the opportunities and constraints of the environment (cf. Bell 1973).

There is an important philosophical distinction between "reasons" and "causes" (discussed at length by Beck, 1975) that is relevant here. Apparently, under most conditions, actors do not like to think that their behavior is *caused* by either the environment or the personality. At the less deterministic level of *reasons*, however, they are more likely to attribute their behavior to situational rather than to personal factors, though to some extent we all realize that both factors are involved.

Monson and Snyder (unpublished) raise a caveat that deserves to be mentioned. They point out that most actor-observer studies have been laboratory experiments in which the actor's behavior is, in fact, "controlled" by a situational manipulation. Thus, Nisbett and his colleagues (1973) induced actors to volunteer to lead sight-seeing tours by offering to pay them. In such a case, it is not surprising that the actor—who, most would agree, is more sensitive to situational variations— tends to attribute his behavior to the setting. He is right. The monetary incentive was "responsible" for his behavior. On the other hand, Monson and Snyder point out that in the natural environment people are not placed in situations so much as they choose them. Or, as Wachtel (1973) has argued, the situational forces to which actors respond are often of their own making. To the extent that this is true, actors may see their behavior, even though it varies from situation to situation, as dispositionally caused, whereas observers who see only the variation with situations may, if anything, underestimate the dispositional role.

This is an intriguing point, and it has some support in empirical data. For example, experimental evidence supports the fact that actors attribute their choice *among* situations to personal, dispositional factors. Once in the situation, however, they see their behavior as controlled by its salient cues (cf. Gurwitz and Panciera, 1975). It remains true, however, that even in the natural environment we often find ourselves in situations which we may have long ago selected but which we do not control in any detail. We should be wary of an easy translation from the laboratory to real life, but we should be equally careful not to assume that the laboratory is some irrelevant microcosm.

WIDER IMPLICATIONS OF THE THEORY

I think the balance of the evidence provides rather remarkable support for our "reckless" proposition. To say that actors attribute to situations what observers assign to dispositions is obviously not a law of behavioral science. But it is a useful guiding hypothesis that holds under a surprising range of conditions. The proposition can be subverted by special motivational factors (such as wanting to claim personal responsibility for a success) or by special knowledge on the part of the actor that he selected among many situations the one to which he now exposes himself. In the absence of these special conditions, however, our proposition seems to be robust and quite general. The proposition derives its validity in part from differences in perceptual perspective and in part from differences in the information available to actors and observers.

The major implication of the observer bias in attitude-attribution studies is that such a bias sows the seeds for interpersonal misunderstandings. It seems reasonable to assume that the more two people get to know each other, the more capable they become of taking each other's perspective; there should be a gradual merging of actor-observer orientations. In more transient interactions, however, we may all be victims of a tendency to misread role for personality. If our research has any generalization value at all, it is very likely that we assign to another's personality what we should be viewing as a complex interaction between person and situation. Particular roles within society or within an organization may call for certain patterns of behavior that are then used as a clue to what the role player is really like. What the reviewed research shows is that people make some allowance for the determining significance of roles and other situational pressures, but the allowance undershoots the mark. As a consequence, people who may be arbitrarily assigned to a group role, or assigned to a role on the basis of some initial response to strong environmental pressures, may have attributed to them a set of unwarranted personality characteristics to explain the role-induced behavior. Furthermore, once the group members make these attributions, their behavior toward the target person may constrain him to meet their expectations by "taking on" the personality they have assigned him. This is in the nature of a self-fulfilling prophecy: I expect John to behave in a certain way, and I give off subtle cues to ensure that he does.

In recent years a number of social scientists have pointed to and commented on the tendency in the field of psychology toward overattribution to the person. Mischel (1968, 1969) has essentially argued that there is not enough personal consistency across situations to warrant the personality psychologist's confident attribution of traits and attitudes to individual subjects or clients. Anthropologists D'Andrade (1974) and Shweder (1975) have also criticized individual difference psychology, claiming (with supportive evidence) that personality impressions follow the conceptual logic of the perceiver but do not fit the behavior of the persons being judged. The present research results point in the same direction by at least hinting at the pervasiveness of personal overattribution.

One final question might be raised: If such a pervasive attributional bias does exist, how come we get along as well as we do in the world? And how come the tendency doesn't get corrected by feedback and eventually drop out? One answer to the first question is, Maybe we don't get along so well. The Peter Principle (1969) is a striking example of attributional bias. A man gets promoted to his level of incompetence because the manager doesn't realize that a good performer in one setting may be incompetent in another. There may be other human costs incurred by the person who is misread by others, costs associated with the strain of meeting false expectations.

Perhaps one reason the bias persists uncorrected is that predictions from personality often overlap with or converge on predictions from situations. Much of our social life is more highly structured than we realize. Because we often see particular others in a restricted range of settings, cross-situational consistency is not an issue. Furthermore, we as observers are always a constant in the situation, which gives a further impetus to behavioral consistency. In situations restricted to a standard setting, it makes no difference whether the prediction of behavioral continuity is based on attributions about personality or perceptions of situational requirements. There is no opportunity for corrective feedback. It is also the case that social behavior is notoriously ambiguous as feedback, and many an observer can tailor his perceptions of behavior to previously made personality attributions. We are probably all rather adept at maintaining trait inferences in the face of disconfirming behavioral evidence. When practiced by some psychoanalytic writers, the maneuvering can be truly breathtaking.

REFERENCES

Arkin, R. M., and S. Duval, 1975. Focus of attention and causal attributions of actors and observers. *J. Exp. Soc. Psych.* 11:427–38.

Aronson, E. 1969. The theory of cognitive dissonance: A current perspective. In *Advances in Experimental Social Psychology*, vol. 4, Leonard Berkowitz, ed. N.Y.: Academic Press, pp. 1–34.

Beck, L. W. 1975. *The Actor and the Spectator*, New Haven: Yale University Press.

Bell, L. G. 1973. Influence of need to control on differences in attribution of causality by actors and observers. Ph.D. dissertation, Duke University.

Bem, D. J. 1972. Self-perception theory. In *Advances in Experimental Social Psychology*, vol. 6, Leonard Berkowitz, ed. N.Y.: Academic Press, pp. 2–62.

Cook, S. W. 1975. A comment on the ethical issues involved in West, Gunn, and Chernicky's "Ubiquitous Watergate: An attributional analysis." *J. Pers. Soc. Psych.* 32: 66–68.

D'Andrade, R. 1974. Memory and the assessment of behavior. In *Measurement in the Social Sciences*, Hubert M. Blalock, ed. Chicago: Aldine.

Duncker, K. 1938. Induced motion. In *A Sourcebook of Gestalt Psychology*, Willis D. Ellis, ed. N.Y.: Harcourt, Brace, pp. 161–72.

Duval, S., and R. A. Wicklund. 1972. *A Theory of Objective Self-Awareness*. N.Y.: Academic Press.

Gurwitz, S. B., and L. Panciera. 1975. Attributions of freedom by actors and observers. *J. Pers. Soc. Psych*. 32:531–39.

Hansen, R. D., D. J. Ruhland, and C. L. Ellis. Actor versus observer: The effect of perceptual orientation on causal attributions for success and failure. Unpublished manuscript.

Heider, F. 1958. *The Psychology of Interpersonal Relations*. N.Y.: Wiley.

Jones, E. E., and K. E. Davis. 1965. A theory of correspondent inferences: From acts to dispositions. In *Advances in Experimental Social Psychology*, vol. 2, Leonard Berkowitz, ed. N.Y.: Academic Press, pp. 219–66.

Jones, E. E., and V. A. Harris. 1967. The attribution of attitudes. *J. Exp. Soc. Psych*. 3: 1–24.

Jones, E. E., D. E. Kanouse, H. H. Kelley, R. E. Nisbett, S. Valins, and B. Weiner. 1972. *Attribution: Perceiving the Causes of Behavior*. Morristown, N.J.: General Learning.

Jones, E. E., and R. E. Nisbett. 1971. *The Actor and the Observer: Divergent Perceptions of the Causes of Behavior*. N.Y.: General Learning.

Jones, E. E., S. Worchel, G. R. Goethals, and J. Grumet. 1971. Prior expectancy and behavioral extremity as determinants of attitude attribution. *J. Exp. Soc. Psych*. 7:59–80.

Kelley, H. H. 1967. Attribution theory in social psychology. In *Nebraska Symposia on Motivation*, David Levine, ed. Lincoln: U. of Nebraska Press, pp. 192–240.

McGee, M. G., and M. Snyder. 1975. Attribution and behavior: Two field studies. *J. Pers. Soc. Psych*. 32:185–90.

Mischel, W. 1968. *Personality and Assessment*. N.Y.: Wiley.

Mischel, W. 1969. Continuity and change in personality. *Am. Psych*. 24:1012–18.

Monson, T. C., and M. Snyder. Actors, observers, and the attribution process: Toward a reconceptualization. Unpublished manuscript.

Nisbett, R. E., C. Caputo, P. Legant, and J. Maracek. 1973. Behavior as seen by the actor and as seen by the observer. *J. Pers. Soc. Psych*. 27:154–65.

Peter, L. J., and R. Hull. 1969. *The Peter Principle*. N.Y.: Morrow.

Regan, D. T., and J. Totten. 1975. Empathy and attribution: Turning observers into actors. *J. Pers. Soc. Psych*. 32:850–56.

Snyder, M., and E. E. Jones. 1974. Attitude attribution when behavior is constrained. *J. Exp. Soc. Psych*. 10:585–600.

Snyder, M., and T. C. Monson. Persons, situations, and the control of social behavior. *J. Pers. Soc. Psych*. 32:637–44.

Storms, M. D. 1973. Videotape and the attribution process: Reversing actors' and observers' points of view. *J. Pers. Soc. Psych*. 27:165–75.

Shweder, R. A. 1975. How relevant is an individual difference theory of personality? *J. Pers*. 43:455–84.

Taylor, S. E., and S. T. Fiske. 1975. Point of view and perceptions of causality. *J. Pers. Soc. Psych*. 32:439–45.

Wachtel, P. 1973. Psychodynamics, behavior therapy, and the implacable experimenter: An inquiry into the consistency of personality. *J. Abnormal Psych*. 82:324–34.

Wallach, H. 1959. The perception of motion. *Sci. Am*. 201:56–60.

West, S. G., S. P. Gunn, and P. Chernicky. 1975. Ubiquitous Watergate: An attributional analysis. *J. Pers. Soc. Psych*. 32:55–65.

Wolosin, R. J., J. Esser, and G. A. Fine. 1975. Effects of justification and vocalization on actors' and observers' attributions of freedom. *J. Pers*. 43:612–33.

DAVID L. ROSENHAN

On Being Sane in Insane Places

If sanity and insanity exist, how shall we know them?

The question is neither capricious nor itself insane. However much we may be personally convinced that we can tell the normal from the abnormal, the evidence is simply not compelling. It is commonplace, for example, to read about murder trials wherein eminent psychiatrists for the defense are contradicted by equally eminent psychiatrists for the prosecution on the matter of the defendant's sanity. More generally, there are a great deal of conflicting data on the reliability, utility, and meaning of such terms as "sanity," "insanity," "mental illness," and "schizophrenia." Finally, as early as 1934, Benedict suggested that normality and abnormality are not universal (1934). What is viewed as normal in one culture may be seen as quite aberrant in another. Thus, notions of normality and abnormality may not be quite as accurate as people believe they are.

To raise questions regarding normality and abnormality is in no way to question the fact that some behaviors are deviant or odd. Murder is deviant. So, too, are hallucinations. Nor does raising such questions deny the existence of the personal anguish that is often associated with "mental illness." Anxiety and depression exist. Psychological suffering exists. But normality and abnormality, sanity and insanity, and the diagnoses that flow from them may be less substantive than many believe them to be.

At its heart, the question of whether the sane can be distinguished from the insane (and whether degrees of insanity can be distinguished from each other) is a simple matter: Do the salient characteristics that lead to diagnoses reside in the patients themselves or in the environments and contexts in which observers find them? The belief has been strong that patients present symptoms, that those symptoms can be categorized, and, implicitly, that the sane are distinguishable from the insane. More recently, however, this belief has been questioned. Based in part on theoretical and anthropological considerations, but also on philosophical, legal, and therapeutic ones, the view has grown that psychological categorization of mental illness is useless at best and downright harmful, misleading, and pejorative at worst. Psychiatric diagnoses, in this view, are in the minds of the observers and are not valid summaries of characteristics displayed by the observed.

Gains can be made in deciding which of these is more nearly accurate by getting normal people (that is, people who do not have, and have never suffered, symptoms of serious psychiatric disorders) admitted to psychiatric hospitals and then determining whether they were discovered to be sane and, if so, how. If the sanity of such pseudopatients were always detected, there would be prima facie evidence that a sane individual can be distinguished from the insane context in which he is found. Normality (and presumably abnormality) is distinct enough that it can be recognized wherever it occurs, for it is carried within the person. If, on the other hand, the sanity of the pseudopatients were never discovered, serious difficulties would arise for those who support traditional modes of psychiatric diagnosis. Given that the hospital staff was not incompetent, that the pseudopatient had been behaving as sanely as he had been outside of the hospital, and that it had never been previously suggested that he belonged in a psychiatric hospital, such an unlikely outcome would support the view that psychiatric diagnosis betrays little about the patient but much about the environment in which an observer finds him.

This article describes such an experiment. Eight sane people gained secret admission to twelve different hospitals. Their diagnostic experiences constitute the data of the first part of this article; the remainder is devoted to a description of their experiences in psychiatric institutions. . . .

PSEUDOPATIENTS AND THEIR SETTINGS

The eight pseudopatients were a varied group. One was a psychology graduate student in his 20s. The remaining seven were older and "established." Among them were three psychologists, a pediatrician, a psychiatrist, a painter, and a housewife. Three pseudopatients were women, five were men. All of them employed pseudonyms, lest their alleged diagnoses embarrass them later. Those who were in mental health professions alleged another occupation in order to avoid the special attentions that might be accorded by staff, as a matter of courtesy or caution, to ailing colleagues. With the exception of myself (I was the first pseudopatient and my presence was known to the hospital administrator and chief psychologist and, so far as I can tell, to them alone), the presence of pseudopatients and the nature of the research program was not known to the hospital staffs.

The settings were similarly varied. In order to generalize the findings, admission into a variety of hospitals was sought. The twelve hospitals in the sample were located in five different states on the East and West coasts. Some were old and shabby, some were quite new. Some were research-oriented, others not. Some had good staff-patient ratios, others were quite understaffed. Only one was a strictly private hospital. All of the others were supported by state or federal funds or, in one instance, by university funds.

After calling the hospital for an appointment, the pseudopatient arrived at the admissions office complaining that he had been hearing voices. Asked what the voices said, he replied that they were often unclear, but as far as he could tell they said "empty," "hollow," and "thud." The voices were unfamiliar and were of the same sex as the pseudopatient. The choice of these symptoms was occasioned by their apparent similarity to existential symptoms. Such symptoms are alleged to arise from painful concerns about the perceived meaninglessness of one's life. It is as if the hallucinating person were saying, "My life is empty and hollow." The choice of these symptoms was also determined by the *absence* of a single report of existential psychoses in the literature.

Beyond alleging the symptoms and falsifying name, vocation, and employment, no further alterations of person, history, or circumstances were made. The significant events of the pseudopatient's life history were presented as they had actually occurred. Relationships with parents and siblings, with spouse and children, with people at work and in school, consistent with the aforementioned exceptions, were described as they were or had been. Frustrations and upsets were described along with joys and satisfactions. These facts are important to remember. If anything, they strongly biased the subsequent results in favor of detecting sanity, since none of their histories or current behaviors were seriously pathological in any way.

Immediately upon admission to the psychiatric ward, the pseudopatient ceased simulating *any* symptoms of abnormality. In some cases, there was a brief period of mild nervousness and anxiety, since none of the pseudopatients really believed that they would be admitted so easily. Indeed, their shared fear was that they would be immediately exposed as frauds and greatly embarrassed. Moreover, many of them had never visited a psychiatric ward; even those who had, nevertheless had some genuine fears about what might happen to them. Their nervousness, then, was quite appropriate to the novelty of the hospital setting, and it abated rapidly.

Apart from that short-lived nervousness, the pseudopatient behaved on the ward as he "normally" behaved. The pseudopatient spoke to patients and staff as he might ordinarily. Because there is uncommonly little to do on a psychiatric ward, he attempted to engage others in conversation. When asked by staff how he was feeling, he indicated that he was fine, that he no longer experienced symptoms. He responded to instructions from attendants, to calls for medication (which was not swallowed), and to dining-hall instructions. Beyond such activities as were available to him on the admissions ward, he spent his time writing down his observations about the ward, its patients, and the staff. Initially these notes were written "secretly," but as it soon became clear that no one much cared, they were subsequently written on standard tablets of paper in such public places as the dayroom. No secret was made of these activities.

The pseudopatient, very much as a true psychiatric patient, entered a hospital with no foreknowledge of when he would be discharged. Each was told that he would have to get out by his own devices, essentially by convincing the staff that he was sane. The psychological stresses associated with hospitalization were considerable, and all but one of the pseudopatients desired to be discharged almost immediately after being admitted. They were, therefore, motivated not only to behave sanely, but to be paragons of cooperation. That their behavior was in no way disruptive is confirmed by nursing reports, which have been obtained on most of the patients. These reports uniformly indicate that the patients were "friendly," "cooperative," and "exhibited no abnormal indications."

THE NORMAL ARE NOT DETECTABLY SANE

Despite their public "show" of sanity, the pseudopatients were never detected. Admitted, except in one case, with a diagnosis of schizophrenia,[1] each was discharged with a diagnosis of schizophrenia "in remission." The label "in remission" should in no way be dismissed as a formality, for at no time during any hospitalization had any question been raised about any pseudopatient's simulation. Nor are there any indications in the hospital records that the pseudopatient's status was suspect. Rather, the evidence is strong that, once labeled schizophrenic, the pseudopatient was stuck with that label. If the pseudopatient was to be discharged, he must naturally be "in remission"; but he was not sane, or, in the institution's view, had he ever been sane.

The uniform failure to recognize sanity cannot be attributed to the quality of the hospitals, for, although there were considerable variations among them, several are considered excellent. Nor can it be alleged that there was simply not enough time to observe the pseudopatients. Length of hospitalization ranged from 7 to 52 days, with an average of 19 days. The pseudopatients were not, in fact, carefully observed, but this failure clearly speaks more to traditions within psychiatric hospitals than to lack of opportunity.

Finally, it cannot be said that the failure to recognize the pseudopatients' sanity was due to the fact that they were not behaving sanely. While there was clearly some tension present in all of them, their daily visitors could detect no serious behavioral consequences—nor, indeed, could other patients. It was quite common for the patients to "detect" the pseudopatients' sanity. During the first three hospitalizations, when accurate counts were kept, 35 of a total of 118 patients on the admissions ward voiced their suspicions, some vigorously. "You're not crazy. You're a journalist, or a professor [referring to the continual notetaking]. You're checking up on the hospital." While most of the patients were reassured by the pseudopatient's insistence that he had been sick before he came in but was fine now, some continued to believe that the pseudopatient was sane throughout his hospitalization. The fact that the patients often recognized normality when staff did not raises important questions.

Failure to detect sanity during the course of hospitalization may be due to the fact that physicians operate with a strong bias toward what statisticians call the Type 2 error (Scheff, 1966). This is to say that physicians are more inclined to call a healthy person sick (a false positive, Type 2) than a sick person healthy (a false negative, Type 1). The reasons for this are not hard to find: it is clearly more dangerous to misdiagnose illness than health. Better to err on the side of caution, to suspect illness even among the healthy.

But what holds for medicine does not hold equally well for psychiatry. Medical illnesses, while unfortunate, are not commonly pejorative. Psychiatric diagnoses, on the contrary, carry with them personal, legal, and social stigmas. It was therefore important to see whether the tendency toward diagnosing the sane insane could be reversed. The following experiment was arranged at a research and teaching hospital whose staff had heard these findings but doubted that such an error could occur in their hospital. The staff was informed that at some time during the following 3 months, one or more pseudopatients would attempt to be admitted into the psychiatric hospital. Each staff member was asked to rate each patient who presented himself at admissions or on the ward according to the likelihood that the patient was a pseudopatient. A 10-point scale was used, with a 1 and 2 reflecting high confidence that the patient was a pseudopatient.

Judgments were obtained on 193 patients who were admitted for psychiatric treatment. All staff who had had sustained contact with or primary responsibility for the patient—attendants, nurses, psychiatrists, physicians, and psychologists—were asked to make judgments. Forty-one patients were alleged, with high confidence, to be pseudopatients by at least one member of the staff. Twenty-three were considered suspect by at least one psychiatrist. Nineteen were suspected by one psychiatrist *and* one other staff member. Actually, no genuine pseudopatient (at least from my group) presented himself during this period.

The experiment is instructive. It indicates that the tendency to designate sane people as insane can be reversed when the stakes (in this case, prestige and diagnostic acumen) are high. But what can be said of the 19 people who were suspected of being "sane" by one psychiatrist and another staff member? Were these people truly "sane," or was it rather the case that in the course of avoiding the Type 2 error the staff tended to make more errors of the first sort—calling the crazy "sane"? There is no way of knowing. But one thing is certain: Any diagnostic process that lends itself so readily to massive errors of this sort cannot be a very reliable one.

THE STICKINESS OF PSYCHODIAGNOSTIC LABELS

Beyond the tendency to call the healthy sick—a tendency that accounts better for diagnostic behavior on admission than it does for such behavior after a lengthy period of exposure—the data speak to the massive role of labeling in psychiatric assessment. Having once been labeled schizophrenic, there is nothing the pseudopatient can do to overcome the tag. The tag profoundly colors others' perceptions of him and his behavior.

From one viewpoint, these data are hardly surprising, for it has long been known that elements are given meaning by the context in which they occur. Gestalt psychology made this point vigorously, and Asch (1946; 1952) demonstrated that there are "central" personality traits (such as "warm" versus "cold") which are so powerful that they markedly color the meaning of other information in forming an impression of a given personality. "Insane," "schizophrenic," "manic-depressive," and "crazy" are probably among the most powerful of such central traits. Once a person is designated abnormal, all of his other behaviors and characteristics are colored by that label. Indeed, that label is so powerful that many of the pseudopatients' normal behaviors were overlooked entirely or profoundly misinterpreted. Some examples may clarify this issue.

Earlier I indicated that there were no changes in the pseudopatient's personal history and current status beyond those of name, employment, and, where necessary, vocation. Otherwise, a veridical description of personal history and circumstances was offered. Those circumstances were not psychotic. How were they made consonant with the diagnosis of psychosis? Or were those diagnoses modified in such a way as to bring them into accord with the circumstances of the pseudopatient's life, as described by him?

As far as I can determine, diagnoses were in no way affected by the relative health of the circumstances of a pseudopatient's life. Rather, the reverse occurred:

The perception of his circumstances was shaped entirely by the diagnosis. A clear example of such translation is found in the case of a pseudopatient who had had a close relationship with his mother but was rather remote from his father during his early childhood. During adolescence and beyond, however, his father became a close friend, while his relationship with his mother cooled. His present relationship with his wife was characteristically close and warm. Apart from occasional angry exchanges, friction was minimal. The children had rarely been spanked. Surely there is nothing especially pathological about such a history. Indeed, many readers may see a similar pattern in their own experiences, with no markedly deleterious consequences. Observe, however, how such a history was translated in the psycho-pathological context, this from the case summary prepared after the patient was discharged.

> This white 39-year-old male . . . manifests a long history of considerable ambiva-
> lence in close relationships, which begins in early childhood. A warm relationship
> with his mother cools during his adolescence. A distant relationship to his father is
> described as becoming very intense. Affective stability is absent. His attempts to
> control emotionality with his wife and children are punctuated by angry outbursts and,
> in the case of the children, spankings. And while he says that he has several good
> friends, one senses considerable ambivalence embedded in those relationships
> also. . . .

The facts of the case were unintentionally distorted by the staff to achieve consistency with a popular theory of the dynamics of a schizophrenic reaction. . . . Clearly, the meaning ascribed to his verbalizations (that is, ambivalence, affective instability) was determined by the diagnosis: schizophrenia. An entirely different meaning would have been ascribed if it were known that the man was "normal."

All pseudopatients took extensive notes publicly. Under ordinary circumstances, such behavior would have raised questions in the minds of observers, as, in fact, it did among patients. Indeed, it seemed so certain that the notes would elicit suspicion that elaborate precautions were taken to remove them from the ward each day. But the precautions proved needless. The closest any staff member came to questioning these notes occurred when one pseudopatient asked his physician what kind of medication he was receiving and began to write down the response. "You needn't write it," he was told gently. "If you have trouble remembering, just ask me again."

If no questions were asked of the pseudopatients, how was their writing interpreted? Nursing records for three patients indicate that the writing was seen as an aspect of their pathological behavior. "Patient engages in writing behavior" was the daily nursing comment on one of the pseudopatients who was never questioned about his writing. Given that the patient is in the hospital, he must be psychologically disturbed. And given that he is disturbed, continuous writing must be a behavioral manifestation of that disturbance, perhaps a subset of the compulsive behaviors that are sometimes correlated with schizophrenia.

One tacit characteristic of psychiatric diagnosis is that it locates the sources of aberration within the individual and only rarely within the complex of stimuli that surrounds him. Consequently, behaviors that are stimulated by the environment are commonly misattributed to the patient's disorder. For example, one kindly nurse found a pseudopatient pacing the long hospital corridors. "Nervous, Mr. X?" she asked. "No, bored," he said.

The notes kept by pseudopatients are full of patient behaviors that were misinterpreted by well-intentioned staff. Often enough, a patient would go "berserk" because he had, wittingly or unwittingly, been mistreated by, say, an attendant. A nurse coming upon the scene would rarely inquire even cursorily into the environmental stimuli of the patient's behavior. Rather, she assumed that his upset derived from his pathology, not from his present interactions with other staff members. Occasionally, the staff might assume that the patient's family (especially when they had recently visited) or other patients had stimulated the outburst. But never were the staff found to assume that one of themselves or the structure of the hospital had anything to do with a patient's behavior. One psychiatrist pointed to a group of patients who were sitting outside the cafeteria entrance half an hour before lunchtime. To a group of young residents he indicated that such behavior was characteristic of the oral-acquisitive nature of the syndrome. It seemed not to occur to him that there were very few things to anticipate in a psychiatric hospital besides eating.

A psychiatric label has a life and an influence of its own. Once the impression has been formed that the patient is schizophrenic, the expectation is that he will continue to be schizophrenic. When a sufficient amount of time has passed, during which the patient has done nothing bizarre, he is considered to be in remission and available for discharge. But the label endures beyond discharge, with the unconfirmed expectation that he will behave as a schizophrenic again. Such labels, conferred by mental health professionals, are as influential on the patient as they are on his relatives and friends, and it should not surprise anyone that the diagnosis acts on all of them as a self-fulfilling prophecy. Eventually, the patient himself accepts the diagnosis, with all of its surplus meanings and expectations, and behaves accordingly (Scheff, 1966). . . .

It is not known why powerful impressions of personality traits, such as "crazy" or "insane," arise. Conceivably, when the origins of and stimuli that give rise to a behavior are remote or unknown, or when the behavior strikes us as immutable, trait labels regarding the *behaver* arise. When, on the other hand, the origins and stimuli are known and available, discourse is limited to the behavior itself. Thus, I may hallucinate because I am sleeping, or I may hallucinate because I have ingested a peculiar drug. These are termed sleep-induced hallucinations, or dreams, and drug-induced hallucinations, respectively. But when the stimuli to my hallucinations are unknown, that is called craziness, or schizophrenia—as if that inference were somehow as illuminating as the others.

THE EXPERIENCE OF PSYCHIATRIC HOSPITALIZATION

The term "mental illness" is of recent origin. It was coined by people who were humane in their inclinations and who wanted very much to raise the station of (and the public's sympathies toward) the psychologically disturbed from that of witches and "crazies" to one that was akin to the physically ill. And they were at least partially successful, for the treatment of the mentally ill *has* improved considerably over the years. But while treatment has improved, it is doubtful that people really regard the mentally ill in the same way that they view the physically ill. A broken leg is something one recovers from, but mental illness allegedly endures forever. A broken leg does not threaten the observer, but a crazy schizophrenic? There is by now a host of evidence that attitudes toward the mentally ill are characterized by fear, hostility, aloofness, suspicion, and dread (Nunnally, 1961; Sarbin, 1967; Sarbin & Mancuso, 1970). The mentally ill are society's lepers.

That such attitudes infect the general population is perhaps not surprising, only upsetting. But that they affect the professionals—attendants, nurses, physicians, psychologists, and social workers—who treat and deal with the mentally ill is more disconcerting, both because such attitudes are self-evidently pernicious and because they are unwitting. Most mental health professionals would insist that they are sympathetic toward the mentally ill, that they are neither avoidant nor hostile. But it is more likely that an exquisite ambivalence characterizes their relations with psychiatric patients, such that their avowed impulses are only part of their entire attitude. Negative attitudes are there too and can easily be detected. Such attitudes should not surprise us. They are the natural offspring of the labels patients wear and the places in which they are found.

Consider the structure of the typical psychiatric hospital. Staff and patients are strictly segregated. Staff have their own living space, including their dining facilities, bathrooms, and assembly places. The glassed quarters that contain the professional staff, which the pseudopatients came to call "the cage," sit out on every dayroom. The staff emerge primarily for caretaking purposes—to give medication, to conduct a therapy or group meeting, to instruct or reprimand a patient. Otherwise, staff keep to themselves, almost as if the disorder that afflicts their charges is somehow catching. . . .

I turn now to a different set of studies, these dealing with staff response to patient-initiated contact. It has long been known that the amount of time a person spends with you can be an index of your significance to him. If he initiates and maintains eye contact, there is reason to believe that he is considering your requests and needs. If he pauses to chat or actually stops and talks, there is added reason to infer that he is individuating you. In four hospitals, the pseudopatient approached the staff members with a request which took the following form: "Pardon me, Mr. [or Dr. or Mrs.] X, could you tell me when I will be eligible for grounds privileges?" (or " . . . when I will be presented at the staff meeting?" or " . . . when I am likely to be discharged?"). While the content of the question varied according to the appropriateness of the target and the pseudopatient's (apparent) current needs the form was always a courteous and relevant request for information. Care was taken never to approach a particular member of the staff more than once a day, lest the staff member become suspicious or irritated. In considering these data, remember that the behavior of the pseudopatients was neither bizarre nor disruptive. One could indeed engage in good conversation with them.

. . . Minor differences between these four institutions were overwhelmed by the degree to which staff avoided continuing contacts that patients had initiated. By far, their most common response consisted of either a brief response to the question, offered while they were "on the move" and with head averted, or no response at all.

The encounter frequently took the following bizarre form: (Pseudopatient) "Pardon me, Dr. X. Could you tell me when I am eligible for grounds privileges?" (Physician) "Good morning, Dave. How are you today?" (Moves off without waiting for a response.)

It is instructive to compare these data with data recently obtained at Stanford University. It has been alleged that large and eminent universities are characterized by faculty who are so busy that they have no time for students. For this comparison, a young lady approached individual faculty members who seemed to be walking purposefully to some meeting or teaching engagement and asked them the following six questions.

1. "Pardon me, could you direct me to Encina Hall?" (At the medical school: " . . . to the Clinical Research Center?").
2. "Do you know where Fish Annex is?" (There is no Fish Annex at Stanford).
3. "Do you teach here?"
4. "How does one apply for admission to the college?" (At the medical school: " . . . to the medical school?").
5. "Is it difficult to get in?"
6. "Is there financial aid?"

Without exception, all of the questions were answered. No matter how rushed they were, all respondents not only maintained eye contact, but stopped to talk. Indeed, many of the respondents went out of their way to direct or take the questioner to the office she was seeking, to try to locate "Fish Annex," or to discuss with her the possibilities of being admitted to the university.

Similar data were obtained in the hospital. Here too, the young lady came prepared with six questions. After the first question, however, she remarked to 18 of her respondents, "I'm looking for a psychiatrist," and to 15 others, "I'm looking for an internist." Ten other respondents received no inserted comment. The general degree of cooperative responses is considerably higher for these university groups than it was for pseudopatients in psychiatric hospitals. Even so, differences are apparent within the medical school setting. Once having indicated that she was looking for a psychiatrist, the degree of cooperation elicited was less than when she sought an internist.

POWERLESSNESS AND DEPERSONALIZATION

Eye contact and verbal contact reflect concern and individuation; their absence, avoidance and depersonalization. The data I have presented do not do justice to the rich daily encounters that grew up around matters of depersonalization and avoidance. I have records of patients who were beaten by staff for the sin of having initiated verbal contact. During my own experience, for example, one patient was beaten in the presence of other patients for having approached an attendant and told him, "I like you." Occasionally, punishment meted out to patients for misdemeanors seemed so excessive that it could not be justified by the most radical interpretations of psychiatric canon. Nevertheless, they appeared to go unquestioned. Tempers were often short. A patient who had not heard a call for medication would be roundly excoriated, and the morning attendants would often wake patients with, "Come on, you m----- f-----s, out of bed!"

Neither anecdotal nor "hard" data can convey the overwhelming sense of powerlessness which invades the individual as he is continually exposed to the depersonalization of the psychiatric hospital. It hardly matters *which* psychiatric hospital—the excellent public ones and the very plush private hospital were better than the rural and shabby ones in this regard, but, again, the features that psychiatric hospitals had in common overwhelmed by far their apparent differences.

Powerlessness was evident everywhere. The patient is deprived of many of his legal rights by dint of his psychiatric commitment. He is shorn of credibility by virtue of his psychiatric label. His freedom of movement is restricted. He cannot initiate contact with the staff, but may only respond to such overtures as they make. Personal privacy is minimal. Patient quarters and possessions can be entered and examined by any staff member, for whatever reason. His personal history and anguish is available to any staff member (often including the "grey lady" and "candy striper" volunteer) who chooses to read his folder, regardless of their therapeutic relationship to him. His personal hygiene and waste evacuation are often monitored. The water closets may have no doors.

At times, depersonalization reached such proportions that pseudopatients had the sense that they were invisible, or at least unworthy of account. Upon being admitted, I and other pseudopatients took the initial physical examinations in a semipublic room, where staff members went about their own business as if we were not there.

On the ward, attendants delivered verbal and occasionally serious physical abuse to patients in the presence of other observing patients, some of whom (the pseudopatients) were writing it all down. Abusive behavior, on the other hand, terminated quite abruptly when other staff members were known to be coming. Staff are credible witnesses. Patients are not.

A nurse unbuttoned her uniform to adjust her brassiere in the presence of an entire ward of viewing men. One did not have the sense that she was being seductive. Rather, she didn't notice us. A group of staff persons might point to a patient in the dayroom and discuss him animatedly, as if he were not there.

One illuminating instance of depersonalization and invisibility occurred with regard to medications. All told, the pseudopatients were administered nearly 2100 pills, including Elavil, Stelazine, Compazine, and Thorazine, to name but a few. (That such a variety of medications should have been administered to patients presenting identical symptoms is itself worthy of note.) Only two were swallowed. The rest were either pocketed or deposited in the toilet. The pseudopatients were not alone in this. Although I have no precise records on how many patients rejected their medications, the pseudopatients frequently found the medications of other patients in the toilet before they deposited their own. As long as they were cooperative, their behavior and the pseudopatients' own in this matter, as in other important matters, went unnoticed throughout.

Reactions to such depersonalization among pseudopatients were intense. Although they had come to the hospital as participant observers and were fully aware that they did not "belong," they nevertheless found themselves caught up in and fighting the process of depersonalization. Some examples: A graduate student in psychology asked his wife to bring his textbooks to the hospital so he could "catch up on his homework"—this despite the elaborate precautions taken to conceal his professional association. The same student, who had trained for quite some time to get into the hospital, and who had looked forward to the experience, "remembered" some drag races that he wanted to see on the weekend and insisted that he be discharged by that time. . . .

THE SOURCES OF DEPERSONALIZATION

What are the origins of depersonalization? I have already mentioned two. First are attitudes held by all of us toward the mentally ill—including those who treat them—attitudes characterized by fear, distrust, and horrible expectations on the one hand, and benevolent intentions on the other. Our ambivalence leads, in this instance as in others, to avoidance.

Second, and not entirely separate, the hierarchical structure of the psychiatric hospital facilitates depersonalization. Those who are at the top have least to do with patients, and their behavior inspires the rest of the staff. Average daily contact with psychiatrists, psychologists, residents, and physicians combined ranged from 3.9 to 25.1 minutes, with an overall mean of 6.8 (six pseudopatients over a total of 129 days of hospitalization). Included in this average are time spent in the admissions interview, ward meetings in the presence of a senior staff member, group and individual psychotherapy contacts, case presentation conferences, and discharge meetings. Clearly, patients do not spend much time in interpersonal contact with doctoral staff. And doctoral staff serve as models for nurses and attendants.

There are probably other sources. Psychiatric installations are presently in serious financial straits. Staff shortages are pervasive, staff time at a premium. Something has to give, and that something is patient contact. Yet, while financial stresses are realities, too much can be made of them. I have the impression that the psychological forces that result in depersonalization are much stronger than the fiscal ones and that the addition of more staff would not correspondingly improve patient care in this regard. The incidence of staff meetings and the enormous amount of record-keeping on patients, for example, have not been as substantially reduced as has patient contact. Priorities exist, even during hard times. Patient contact is not a significant priority in the traditional psychiatric hospital, and fiscal pressures do not account for this. Avoidance and depersonalization may. . . .

THE CONSEQUENCES OF LABELING AND DEPERSONALIZATION

Whenever the ratio of what is known to what needs to be known approaches zero, we tend to invent "knowledge" and assume that we understand more than we actually do. We seem unable to acknowledge that we simply don't know. The needs for diagnosis and remediation of behavioral and emotional problems are enormous. But rather than acknowledge that we are just embarking on understanding, we continue to label patients "schizophrenic," "manic-depressive," and "insane," as if in those words we had captured the essence of understanding. The facts of the matter are that we have known for a long time that diagnoses are often not useful or reliable, but we have nevertheless continued to use them. We now know that we cannot distinguish insanity from sanity. It is depressing to consider how that information will be used.

Not merely depressing, but frightening. How many people, one wonders, are sane but not recognized as such in our psychiatric institutions? How many have been needlessly stripped of their privileges of citizenship, from the right to vote and drive to that of handling their own accounts? How many have feigned insanity in order to avoid the criminal consequences of their behavior, and, conversely, how many would rather stand trial than live interminably in a psychiatric hospital—but are wrongly thought to be mentally ill? How many have been stigmatized by well-intentioned, but nevertheless erroneous, diagnoses? On the last point, recall again that a "Type 2 error" in psychiatric diagnosis does not have the same consequences it does in medical diagnosis. A diagnosis of cancer that has been found to be in error is cause for celebration. But psychiatric diagnoses are rarely found to be in error. The label sticks, a mark of inadequacy forever.

Finally, how many patients might be "sane" outside the psychiatric hospital but seem insane in it—not because craziness resides in them, as it were, but because they are responding to a bizarre setting, one that may be unique to institutions which harbor nether people? Goffman (1961) calls the process of socialization to such institutions "mortification"—an apt metaphor that includes the processes of depersonalization that have been described here. And while it is impossible to know whether the pseudopatients' responses to these processes are characteristic of all inmates—they were, after all, not real patients—it is difficult to believe that these processes of socialization to a psychiatric hospital provide useful attitudes or habits of response for living in the "real world."

SUMMARY AND CONCLUSIONS

It is clear that we cannot distinguish the sane from the insane in psychiatric hospitals. The hospital itself imposes a special environment in which the meanings of behavior can easily be misunderstood. The consequences to patients hospitalized in such an environment—the powerlessness, depersonalization, segregation, mortification, and self-labeling—seem undoubtedly countertherapeutic.

I do not, even now, understand this problem well enough to perceive solutions. But two matters seem to have some promise. The first concerns the proliferation of community mental health facilities, of crisis intervention centers, of the human potential movement, and of behavior therapies that, for all of their own problems, tend to avoid psychiatric labels, to focus on specific problems and behaviors, and to retain the individual in a relatively nonpejorative environment. Clearly, to the extent that we refrain from sending the distressed to insane places, our impressions of them are less likely to be distorted. (The risk of distorted perceptions, it seems to me, is always present, since we are much more sensitive to an individual's behaviors and verbalizations than we are to the subtle contextual stimuli that often promote them. At issue here is a matter of magnitude. And, as I have shown, the magnitude of distortion is exceedingly high in the extreme context that is a psychiatric hospital.)

The second matter that might prove promising speaks to the need to increase the sensitivity of mental health workers and researchers to the *Catch 22* position of psychiatric patients. Simply reading materials in this area will be of help to some such workers and researchers. For others, directly experiencing the impact of psychiatric hospitalization will be of enormous use. Clearly, further research into the social psychology of such total institutions will both facilitate treatment and deepen understanding.

I and the other pseudopatients in the psychiatric setting had distinctly negative reactions. We do not pretend to describe the subjective experiences of true patients. Theirs may be different from ours, particularly with the passage of time and the necessary process of adaptation to one's environment. But we can and do speak to the relatively more objective indices of treatment within the hospital. It could be a mistake, and a very unfortunate one, to consider that what happened to us derived from malice or stupidity on the part of the staff. Quite the contrary, our overwhelming impression of them was of people who really cared, who were committed and who were uncommonly intelligent. Where they failed, as they sometimes did painfully, it would be more accurate to attribute those failures to the environment in which they, too, found themselves than to personal callousness. Their perceptions and behavior were controlled by the situation, rather than being motivated by a malicious disposition. In a more benign environment, one that was less attached to global diagnosis, their behaviors and judgments might have been more benign and effective.

NOTE

1. Interestingly, of the 12 admissions, 11 were diagnosed as schizophrenic and one, with the identical symptomatology, as manic-depressive psychosis. This diagnosis has a more favorable prognosis, and it was given by the only private hospital in our sample. On the relations between social class and psychiatric diagnosis, see Hollingshead and Redlich (1958).

REFERENCES

Asch, S. E. Forming impressions of personality. *Journal of Abnormal and Social Psychology*, 1946, **41**, 258–290.

Asch, S. E. *Social psychology*. New York: Prentice-Hall, 1952.

Benedict, R. Anthropology and the abnormal. *Journal of General Psychology*, 1934, **10**, 59–82.

Goffman, E. *Asylums: Essays on the social situation of mental patients and other inmates*. Chicago: Aldine, 1961.

Hollingshead, A. B., & Redlich, F. C. *Social class and mental illness: A community study*. NewYork: Wiley, 1958.

Nunnally, J. C., Jr. *Popular conceptions of mental health*. New York: Holt, Rinehart & Winston, 1961.

Sarbin, T. R. On the futility of the proposition that some people be labeled "mentally ill." *Journal of Consulting Psychology*, 1967, **31**, 447–453.

Sarbin, T. R., & Mancuso, J. C. Failure of a moral enterprise: Attitude of the public toward mental illness. *Journal of Clinical and Consulting Psychology*, 1970, **35**, 159–173.

Scheff, T. J. *Being mentally ill: A sociological theory*. Chicago: Aldine, 1966.

ALBERT H. HASTORF
HADLEY CANTRIL

They Saw a Game: A Case Study

On a brisk Saturday afternoon, November 23, 1951, the Dartmouth football team played Princeton in Princeton's Palmer Stadium. It was the last game of the season for both teams and of rather special significance because the Princeton team had won all its games so far and one of its players, Kazmaier, was receiving All-American mention and had just appeared as the cover man on *Time* magazine, and was playing his last game.

A few minutes after the opening kickoff, it became apparent that the game was going to be a rough one. The referees were kept busy blowing their whistles and penalizing both sides. In the second quarter, Princeton's star left the game with a broken nose. In the third quarter, A Dartmouth player was taken off the field with a broken leg. Tempers flared both during and after the game. The official statistics of the game, which Princeton won, showed that Dartmouth was penalized 70 yards, Princeton 25, not counting more than a few plays in which both sides were penalized.

Needless to say, accusations soon began to fly. The game immediately became a matter of concern to players, students, coaches, and the administrative officials of the two institutions, as well as to alumni and the general public who had not seen the game but had become sensitive to the problem of big-time football through the recent exposures of subsidized players, commercialism, etc. Discussion of the game continued for several weeks.

One of the contributing factors to the extended discussion of the game was the extensive space given to it by both campus and metropolitan newspapers. An indication of the fervor with which the discussions were carried on is shown by a few excerpts from the campus dailies.

For example, on November 27 (four days after the game), the *Daily Princetonian* (Princeton's student newspaper) said:

> This observer has never seen quite such a disgusting exhibition of so-called "sport." Both teams were guilty but the blame must be laid primarily on Dartmouth's doorstep. Princeton, obviously the better team, had no reason to rough up Dartmouth. Looking at the situation rationally, we don't see why the Indians should make a deliberate attempt to cripple Dick Kazmaier or any other Princeton player. The Dartmouth psychology, however, is not rational itself.

Slightly abridged from "They Saw a Game: A Case Study" by Albert H. Hastorf and Hadley Cantril in *Journal of Abnormal and Social Psychology*, Vol. 49 (1954), pp. 129–134. Copyright 1954 by the American Psychological Association. Reprinted by permission.

The November 30th edition of the *Princeton Alumni Weekly* said:

> But certain memories of what occurred will not be easily erased. Into the record books will go in indelible fashion the fact that the last game of Dick Kazmaier's career was cut short by more than half when he was forced out with a broken nose and a mild concussion, sustained from a tackle that came well after he had thrown a pass.
>
> This second-period development was followed by a third-quarter outbreak of roughness that was climaxed when a Dartmouth player deliberately kicked Brad Glass in the ribs while the latter was on his back. Throughout the often unpleasant afternoon, there was undeniable evidence that the losers' tactics were the result of an actual style of play, and reports on other games they have played this season substantiate this.

Dartmouth students were ''seeing'' an entirely different version of the game through the editorial eyes of the *Dartmouth* (Dartmouth's undergraduate newspaper). For example, on November 27 the *Dartmouth* said:

> However, the Dartmouth-Princeton game set the stage for the other type of dirty football. A type which may be termed as an unjustifiable accusation.
>
> Dick Kazmaier was injured early in the game. Kazmaier was the star, an All-American. Other stars have been injured before, but Kazmaier had been built to represent a Princeton idol. When an idol is hurt there is only one recourse—the tag of dirty football. So what did the Tiger Coach Charley Caldwell do? He announced to the world that the Big Green had been out to extinguish the Princeton star. His purpose was achieved.
>
> After this incident, Caldwell instilled the old see-what-they-did-go-get-them attitude into his players. His talk got results. Gene Howard and Jim Miller were both injured. Both had dropped back to pass, had passed, and were standing unprotected in the backfield. Result: one bad leg and one leg broken.
>
> The game was rough and did get a bit out of hand in the third quarter. Yet most of the roughing penalties were called against Princeton while Dartmouth received more of the illegal-use-of-the-hands variety.

On November 28 the *Dartmouth* said:

> Dick Kazmaier of Princeton admittedly is an unusually able football player. Many Dartmouth men traveled to Princeton, not expecting to win—only hoping to see an All-American in action. Dick Kazmaier was hurt in the second period, and played only a token part in the remainder of the game. For this, spectators were sorry.
>
> But there were no such feelings for Dick Kazmaier's health. Medical authorities have confirmed that as a relatively unprotected passing and running star in a contact sport, he is quite liable to injury. Also, his particular injuries—a broken nose and slight concussion—were no more serious than is experienced almost any day in any football practice, where there is no more serious stake than playing the following Saturday. Up to the Princeton game, Dartmouth players suffered about 10 known nose fractures and face injuries, not to mention several slight concussions.
>
> Did Princeton players feel so badly about losing their star? They shouldn't have. During the past undefeated campaign they stopped several individual stars by a concentrated effort, including such mainstays as Frank Hauff of Navy, Glenn Adams of Pennsylvania and Rocco Calvo of Cornell.
>
> In other words, the same brand of football condemned by the *Prince*—that of stopping the big man—is practiced quite successfully by the Tigers.

Basically, then, there was disagreement as to what had happened during the "game." Hence we took the opportunity presented by the occasion to make a "real life" study of a perceptual problem.[1]

PROCEDURE

Two steps were involved in gathering data. The first consisted of answers to a questionnaire designed to get reactions to the game and to learn something of the climate of opinion in each institution. This questionnaire was administered a week after the game to both Dartmouth and Princeton undergraduates who were taking introductory and intermediate psychology courses.

The second step consisted of showing the same motion picture of the game to a sample of undergraduates in each school and having them check on another questionnaire, as they watched the film, any infraction of the rules they saw and whether these infractions were "mild" or "flagrant."[2] At Dartmouth, members of two fraternities were asked to view the film on December 7; at Princeton, members of two undergraduate clubs saw the film early in January.

The answers to both questionnaires were carefully coded and transferred to punch cards.

RESULTS

Table 1 shows the questions which received different replies from the two student populations on the first questionnaire.

TABLE 1. Data from First Questionnaire.

Question	Dartmouth students (N = 163) %	Princeton students (N = 161) %
1. Did you happen to see the actual game between Dartmouth and Princeton in Palmer Stadium this year?		
Yes	33	71
No	67	29
2. Have you seen a movie of the game or seen it on television?		
Yes, movie	33	2
Yes, television	0	1
No, neither	67	97
3. (Asked of those who answered "yes" to either or both of above questions.) From your observations of what went on at the game, do you believe the game was clean and fairly played, or that it was unnecessarily rough and dirty?		

Question	Dartmouth students (N = 163) %	Princeton students (N = 161) %
Clean and fair	6	0
Rough and dirty	24	69
Rough and fair*	25	2
No answer	45	29
4. (Asked of those who answered "no" on both of the first questions.) From what you have heard and read about the game, do you feel it was clean and fairly played, or that it was unnecessarily rough and dirty?		
Clean and fair	7	0
Rough and dirty	18	24
Rough and fair*	14	1
Don't know	6	4
No answer	55	71
(Combined answers to questions 3 and 4 above)		
Clean and fair	13	0
Rough and dirty	42	93
Rough and fair*	39	3
Don't know	6	4
5. From what you saw in the game or the movies, or from what you have read, which team do you feel started the rough play?		
Dartmouth started it	36	86
Princeton started it	2	0
Both started it	53	11
Neither	6	1
No answer	3	2
6. What is your understanding of the charges being made?**		
Dartmouth tried to get Kazmaier	71	47
Dartmouth intentionally dirty	52	44
Dartmouth unnecessarily rough	8	35
7. Do you feel there is any truth to these charges?		
Yes	10	55
No	57	4
Partly	29	35
Don't know	4	6
8. Why do you think the charges were made?		
Injury to Princeton star	70	23
To prevent repetition	2	46
No answer	28	31

*This answer was not included on the checklist but was written in by the percentage of students indicated.
**Replies do not add to 100% since more than one charge could be given.

TABLE 2. Data from Second Questionnaire Checked While Seeing Film.

Group	N	Total number of infractions checked against Dartmouth team Mean	Princeton team Mean
Dartmouth students	48	4.3	4.4
Princeton students	49	9.8	4.2

Questions asking if the students had friends on the team, if they had ever played football themselves, if they felt they knew the rules of the game well, etc., showed no differences in either school and no relation to answers given to other questions. This is not surprising since the students in both schools come from essentially the same type of educational, economic, and ethnic background.

Summarizing the data of Tables 1 and 2, we find a marked contrast between the two student groups.

Nearly all *Princeton* students judged the game as "rough and dirty"—not one of them thought it "clean and fair." And almost nine-tenths of them thought the other side started the rough play. By and large they felt that the charges they understood were being made were true; most of them felt the charges were made in order to avoid similar situations in the future.

When Princeton students looked at the movie of the game, they saw the Dartmouth team make over twice as many infractions as their own team made. And they saw the Dartmouth team make over twice as many infractions as were seen by Dartmouth students. When Princeton students judged these infractions as "flagrant" or "mild," the ratio was about two "flagrant" to one "mild" on the Dartmouth team, and about one "flagrant" to three "mild" on the Princeton team.

As for the *Dartmouth* students, while the plurality of answers fell in the "rough and dirty" category, over one-tenth thought the game was "clean and fair" and over a third introduced their own category of "rough and fair" to describe the action. Although a third of the Dartmouth students felt that Dartmouth was to blame for starting the rough play, the majority of Dartmouth students thought both sides were to blame. By and large, Dartmouth men felt that the charges they understood were being made were not true, and most of them thought the reason for the charges was Princeton's concern for its football star.

When Dartmouth students looked at the movie of the game they saw both teams make about the same number of infractions. And they saw their own team make only half the number of infractions the Princeton students saw them make. The ratio of "flagrant" to "mild" infractions was about one to one when Dartmouth students judged the Dartmouth team, and about one "flagrant" to two "mild" when Dartmouth students judged infractions made by the Princeton team.

It should be noted that Dartmouth and Princeton students were thinking of different charges in judging their validity and in assigning reasons as to why the charges were made. It should also be noted that whether or not students were spectators of the game in the stadium made little difference in their responses.

INTERPRETATION: THE NATURE OF A SOCIAL EVENT

It seems clear that the "game" actually was many different games and that each version of the events that transpired was just as "real" to a particular person as other versions were to other people. A consideration of the experiential phenomena that constitute a "football game" for the spectator may help us both to account for the results obtained and illustrate something of the nature of any social event.

Like any other complex social occurrence, a "football game" consists of a whole host of happenings. Many different events are occurring simultaneously. Furthermore, each happening is a link in a chain of happenings, so that one follows another in sequence. The "football game," as well as other complex social situations, consists of a whole matrix of events. In the game situation, this matrix of events consists of the actions of all the players, together with the behavior of the referees and linesmen, the action on the sidelines, in the grandstands, over the loudspeaker, etc.

Of crucial importance is the fact that an "occurrence" on the football field or in any other social situation does not become an experiential "event" unless and until some significance is given to it: an "occurrence" becomes an *"event"* only when the happening has significance. And a happening generally has significance only if it reactivates learned significances already registered in what we have called a person's assumptive form-world (Cantril, 1950).

Hence the particular occurrences that different people experienced in the football game were a limited series of events from the total matrix of events *potentially* available to them. People experienced those occurrences that reactivated significances they brought to the occasion; they failed to experience those occurrences which did not reactivate past significances. . . .

In this particular study, one of the most interesting examples of this phenomenon was a telegram sent to an officer of Dartmouth College by a member of a Dartmouth alumni group in the Midwest. He had viewed the film which had been shipped to his alumni group from Princeton after its use with Princeton students, who saw, as we noted, an average of over nine infractions by Dartmouth players during the game. The alumnus, who couldn't see the infractions he had heard publicized, wired:

> Preview of Princeton movies indicates considerable cutting of important part please wire explanation and possibly air mail missing part before showing scheduled for January 25 we have splicing equipment.

The "same" sensory impingements emanating from the football field, transmitted through the visual mechanism to the brain, also obviously gave rise to different experiences in different people. The significances assumed by different happenings for different people depend in large part on the purposes people bring to the occasion and the assumptions they have of the purposes and probable behavior of other people involved. . . .

In brief, the data here indicate that there is no such "thing" as a "game" existing "out there" in its own right which people merely "observe." The "game" "exists" for a person and is experienced by him only in so far as certain happenings have significances in terms of his purpose. Out of all the occurrences going on in the environment, a person selects those that have some significance for him from his own egocentric position in the total matrix.

Obviously in the case of a football game, the value of the experience of watching the game is enhanced if the purpose of "your" team is accomplished, that is, if the happening of the desired consequence is experienced—i.e., if your team wins. But the value attribute of the experience can, of course, be spoiled if the desire to win crowds out behavior we value and have come to call sportsmanlike.

The sharing of significances provides the links except for which a "social" event would not be experienced and would not exist for anyone.

A "football game" would be impossible except for the rules of the game which we bring to the situation and which enable us to share with others the significances of various happenings. These rules make possible a certain repeatability of events such as first downs, touchdowns, etc. If a person is unfamiliar with the rules of the game, the behavior he sees lacks repeatability and consistent significance and hence "doesn't make sense."

And only because there is the possibility of repetition is there the possibility that a happening has a significance. For example, the balls used in games are designed to give a high degree of repeatability. While a football is about the only ball used in games which is not a sphere, the shape of the modern football has apparently evolved in order to achieve a higher degree of accuracy and speed in forward passing than would be obtained with a spherical ball, thus increasing the repeatability of an important phase of the game.

The rules of a football game, like laws, rituals, customs, and mores, are registered and preserved forms of sequential significances enabling people to share the significances of occurrences. The sharing of sequential significances which have value for us provides the links that operationally make social events possible. They are analogous to the forces of attraction that hold parts of an atom together, keeping each part from following its individual, independent course.

From this point of view it is inaccurate and misleading to say that different people have different "attitudes" concerning the same "thing." For the "thing" simply is *not* the same for different people whether the "thing" is a football game, a presidential candidate, Communism, or spinach. We do not simply "react to" a happening or to some impingement from the environment in a determined way (except in behavior that has become reflexive or habitual). We behave according to what we bring to the occasion, and what each of us brings to the occasion is more or less unique. And except for these significances which we bring to the occasion, the happenings around us would be meaningless occurrences, would be "inconsequential."

From the transactional view, an attitude is not a predisposition to react in a certain way to an occurrence or stimulus "out there" that exists in its own right with certain fixed characteristics which we "color" according to our predisposition (Kilpatrick, 1952). That is, a subject does not simply "react to" an "object." An attitude would rather seem to be a complex of registered significances reactivated by some stimulus which assumes its own particular significance for us in terms of our purposes. That is, the object as experienced would not exist for us except for the reactivated aspects of the form-world which provides particular significance to the hieroglyphics of sensory impingements.

NOTES

1. We are not concerned here with the problem of guilt or responsibility for infractions, and nothing here implies any judgment as to who was to blame.
2. The film shown was kindly loaned for the purpose of the experiment by the Dartmouth College Athletic Council. It should be pointed out that a movie of a football game follows the ball, is thus selective, and omits a good deal of the total action on the field. Also, of course, in viewing only a film of a game, the possibilities of participation as spectator are greatly limited.

REFERENCES

Cantril, H. *The "why" of man's experience*. New York: Macmillan, 1950.
Kilpatrick, F. P. (Ed.) *Human behavior from the transactional point of view*. Hanover, N.H.: Institute for Associated Research, 1952.

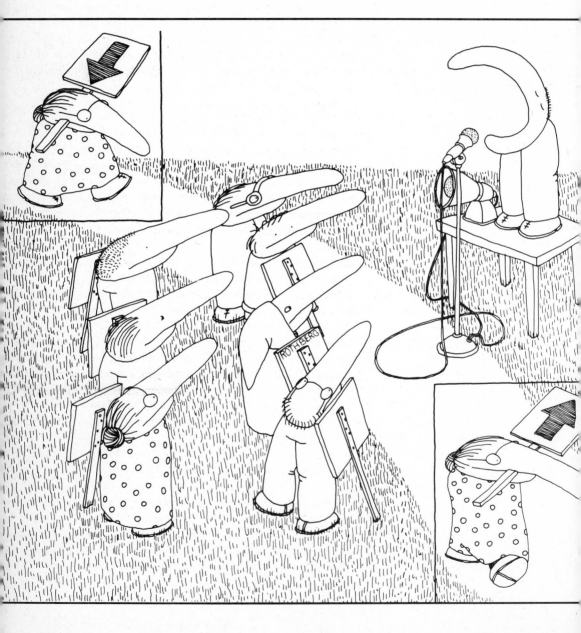

2

Attitudes and Attitude Change

When some people think of social psychologists, they get a mental image of poll takers and attitude surveyors, like the people who come to your door or stop you on the street wanting to know if you like Ted Kennedy, what you think of J.R. Ewing, or if you eat Krispy-Krunchies. And, while the field of social psychology encompasses far more than simply the description and measurement of attitudes, dealing with and understanding people's attitudes is, nonetheless, a cornerstone of our trade.

For example, we study how young children derive their attitudes, opinions, and values from their social environment, because we know that children are not born with the beliefs and preferences they exhibit as adults. We also study how attitudes are organized, because attitudes do not exist in isolation but are associated with whole sets of similar and interrelated beliefs and opinions. And we study how attitudes can be changed, because people are subject to change as the result of communication, direct attempts to influence them, and the need to maintain internal consistency among their attitudes and between their attitudes and behaviors.

The conversation that introduces this section was conducted with Philip Zimbardo, Professor of Psychology at Stanford University and coauthor of *Influencing Attitudes and Changing Behavior* (Zimbardo and Ebbesen, 1969), a lively introduction to the study of attitudes. Dr. Zimbardo's own attitude is that psychology ought to be exciting, and his research—consistent with that position—has been stimulating, flamboyant, and controversial. (See, for example, his report elsewhere in this book of a prison-simulation study.) In our conversation, Dr. Zimbardo suggested a very important point which many students and professional social psychologists seem to lose sight of. That is, the study of attitudes is important and relevant only as long as we remain aware of the relationship of attitudes to *behavior*. In addition, he noted that we most often change our attitudes not simply to maintain congruence among them, but rather because we need to appear to ourselves and other people as sane, rational, not-too-different, and consistent in our words and deeds.

A CONVERSATION WITH PHILIP ZIMBARDO

Stanford University

KRUPAT: *I think that if we're going to talk about attitudes and why they change or how they stay consistent, we ought to know just what we mean by the term. Just what is an attitude, anyway?*

ZIMBARDO: The traditional definition of an attitude usually gets framed in terms of three components. They have been described as an affective or emotional component, a cognitive or belief component, and an action component. Now, what that means is that typically an attitude consists of some idea, some proposition, about a given object or class of objects. These ideas can be simple or they can be complex; they can be based on very little information or a great deal of it. Apparently, what makes a belief system into an attitude is when, in addition to the knowledge involved in the belief, you also have some degree of affective involvement in maintaining the system, and also some potential for acting upon the belief-affective proposition.

KRUPAT: *OK, as you've defined it, it seems as if an attitude is something that is* inside *the person. If this is true, it seems strange to think that much of social psychology is built around this concept. What makes this thing called attitude* something that is "social"?

ZIMBARDO: Well, a long time ago Gordon Allport pointed out the study of attitudes as *the* distinguishing feature of social psychology. Essentially it was the study of attitudes which made social psychology appear to be "scientific."

Now, I personally think that the reason for that early emphasis on the study of attitudes and attitude change came from the desire to find some element or some process *within* the individual which you could use to predict his or her *social* behavior. By the way, I believe that the concept of the personality trait in psychology has the same functional value as does the concept of attitude; namely, as an inferred disposition to action. Just as clinicians have been interested in personality, social psychologists have been concerned with attitudes. Why? Because they'd like to find a cheap and dirty way to be able to predict behavior. It would be a great economy if we could simply get somebody to check off on a piece of paper a set of attitude statements or self-description statements, and on the basis of that we could predict whether he or she is going to become a juvenile delinquent or a good parent, whom he or she is going to vote for, or whether or not such people will allow Sicilians to move into their neighborhood. Attitude measurement would be a very useful tool if we could accomplish this.

KRUPAT: *Then, if that's the reason for studying attitudes, the next question has to be: Does it work? Haven't an increasing number of social psychologists questioned the one-to-one relationship between attitudes as we measure them and the behavior people express which "ought" to be based on them?*

ZIMBARDO: Yes, that's true. There's very little evidence that attitudes and personality measurement have the external validity that their proponents claim. In fact, one of the most reliable and disappointing findings in the area of attitude change is the fact that attitude change appears to be completely uncorrelated with behavior change. It appears to me that although initially or conceptually the interest was in studying attitudes as an inferred mediating process in order to predict significant social behavior, somewhere in the process many social psychologists simply lost sight of that goal, that end product, and have settled for a check mark on a piece of paper.

KRUPAT: *And yet we have evidence as far back as LaPiere in 1934 that a verbally expressed statement of prejudice or discrimination and the actual acting out of that "attitude" are not necessarily going to be the same. If this is so, then let me go one step further and ask: Why aren't they the same?*

ZIMBARDO: At this point, I'd say that a behaviorist analysis would indicate that overt behavior is controlled by a great many contingencies which are not part of the controlling process of covert attitudes. To put it more simply, there are lots of things you might believe or think that you wouldn't say in the presence of just anyone, or just anywhere, or just under any circumstances. Your perception of the *consequences* of uttering certain kinds of statements will change your overt behavior; whether making that statement will get you thrown in jail, or hurt someone's feelings, or lose you your job. You don't tell your boss that you think this is a crumby job when there are no other jobs available and you think the overt expression of your attitude will get you tossed out. You might even smile most of the time. Or a much simpler example—let's call it our spy model of attitude expression—is that if you were a good American spy and hated Communism, you would never allow any overt expression of your underlying attitude. Here it's quite obvious; any expression of the attitude might get you killed, or might simply get you fired because you weren't a very good spy. Well, these same types of considerations enter into the expression or inhibition of any of our attitudes, and help account for the lack of relationship between the two.

By the way, I should mention that in some cases where attitudes are *very* strongly held, they may predict to behavior. That is, if you feel so strongly about something that you don't care about the consequences, there would be a higher predictive value from knowledge of such attitudes. If you got people who were out-and-out racist in their attitudes, it would only be under rare circumstances that they would behave tolerantly. I don't mean, then, to say that attitudes may not predict behavior at all, but that they do so only when there is enough affect involved so you become less concerned about the full range of circumstances and impression management. Unfortunately, most of the attitudes social psychologists have studied in their research are those that have been rather weakly held.

KRUPAT: *Then, if we come full circle back to my question about what makes attitudes "social," it would seem as though attitudes connect us, at least in terms of feelings and beliefs, to objects in our social environment, and that attitudes get expressed or acted upon as a function of the social setting.*

ZIMBARDO: Yes. Instead of thinking about attitudes as predispositions to act, if you think about attitudes as cognitive structures which relate individuals to other individuals and groups, then indeed they can be the basis for social psychology. But now one of the things which we haven't considered yet, which may be developing from what we are saying, goes off in a slightly different direction.

I think that one of the most critical attitudes a person can have is the attitude toward maintaining his or her own self-image. Individuals organize and utilize information in order to perceive certain kinds of relationships between themselves and other people, and each of us attempts to maintain a given image, a given self-attitude, or to enhance our attitude of ourselves. Every time people act in a certain way, they are aware of the response of others to their behavior, and continually modify attitudes to define themselves in relationship to the environment. And, it's important for individuals to see themselves as rational, reasonable, consistent human beings. That doesn't mean that people go out actively seeking consistency, as some people would say, but that if they are made aware of the fact that they are behaving inconsistently, irrationally, or unreasonably, I think they are motivated to give themselves and others the impression that this is not the case. People desire to see themselves and be seen as people who do what is normative or appropriate in a given situation.

KRUPAT: *It seems that by way of introducing attitudes about self, you are suggesting a basis by which we change or maintain our attitudes. Yet the basic principle of Festinger's theory of cognitive dissonance [which is discussed in the Aronson article] merely states that we are motivated to* *change our attitudes when two cognitions disagree or when our behavior and attitudes don't follow from one another. Where exactly does the concept of self-image fit into the idea of attitude change?*

ZIMBARDO: The reason that dissonance theory works, as far as I'm concerned, is that individuals observe themselves making commitments which do not fit in with the attitude—cognitive-belief structure that they have; and therefore they are behaving in ways which are unreasonable, which they would not predict for themselves. And so, my orientation is that the attitude change which results is always in the direction of enhancing one's own self-image. What you will do is to change your attitudes, change your cognitive structure, or change the way you behave so that both you and other observers of your behavior will see you as a sane, rational, and consistent individual.

KRUPAT: *I assume, then, that if you can alter some aspect of the attitude system you will find the person changing other aspects of it to maintain an image of consistency and reasonableness. It would seem that you're saying that we can best hope for self-acceptance or social recognition when we maintain this consistency.*

ZIMBARDO: One of the very best studies to support this idea is one by Milton Rosenberg where he created inconsistencies between feelings and beliefs. I remember the study very well because I was one of his research assistants. By means of hypnosis he was able to get people to feel very strongly about a given attitude object. For example, he took medical-school students at Yale and suggested that the thought of living in Los Angeles would fill them with delight or disgust, or that the thought of socialized medicine would fill them with joy. So, what he did was to change the *affective* component of the attitude for people who had previously described a set of cognitions which were inconsistent with that feeling. And that's *all* he did. Now it was up to them to resolve this discrepancy between feeling very strongly *negative* about something and having a whole set of prior beliefs which should support a very *positive* feeling.

What he found was that since he had anchored the negative affect, subjects changed their *beliefs* very dramatically, and in a very short time, to fit this new affect. Remember, this is without any persuasive communication about beliefs, without any additional informational input. I think this study is about image maintenance. That is, it is irrational to have affect and cognitions which are that inconsistent. Also, it's not clear, if you did have such inconsistency, just how you would behave. If you felt strongly about someone—if you really hated somebody but had a set of beliefs which supported the facts that this is a wonderful person that you and everybody else ought to like—then either your behavior would be inconsistent, or you would feel hypocritical, or you would be confused, not knowing how to act.

KRUPAT: *That sounds like quite a substantial finding, but you still have to wonder about the total impact of such a lab manipulation. Did it have a long lasting effect?*

ZIMBARDO: Well, let me tell you some interesting sidelights on that.

Rosenberg had very complete and thorough debriefings of his subjects after the study was over, in which he explained the whole procedure to his subjects. But, in follow-ups of these people over a month later, there was still significant retention of the attitude change.

KRUPAT: *I'm impressed. But still, as you yourself said before, how about that all-important link between attitudes and behavior? I ask this barely seriously, but how many of your young Yale doctors moved out to California or petitioned for socialized medicine?*

ZIMBARDO: It's funny you should ask that. I was there on a Friday afternoon running a subject with Rosenberg. We had a medical student who had just been told that the thought of living in Los Angeles filled him with delight and euphoria who then changed his beliefs to indicate why Los Angeles was a cultural mecca and land of opportunities and so forth. But the student kept checking his watch and Rosenberg thought he was concerned about going to dinner at the dorms, or something like that. He said to him, "Don't worry, we'll finish up before six," so he could get out and have dinner at the medical-school dormitory.

And the student said, "No, we've got a long weekend coming up. We don't have any classes on Monday and I always wanted to go to Los Angeles. I was thinking this might be a good time to do that."

And he was dead serious about this. We had to sit him down and literally talk him out of it.

KRUPAT: *That effect is fascinating to me, not only because of its apparent strength, but because it highlights the relationship of affect or emotion to cognition or belief. Yet, hasn't much of the emphasis in consistency theory, especially cognitive dissonance theory, been on demonstrating how compliance, a change in action, can affect attitudes?*

ZIMBARDO: The question concerning dissonance has been: Under what circumstances will the attitude or value change to fit the behavior? But I think the mere act of compliance which you referred to is not sufficient. Take a study I did a number of years ago where I induced subjects to try eating grasshoppers. In our grasshopper study we got half the subjects to eat fried Japanese grasshoppers even though they said they hated them, even hated the thought of them. Now, after making this public compliance, did their attitudes change? Well, from that and all the other research I've done, my conclusion is that attitudes will change only under conditions where the individual cannot totally justify the discrepant behavior in terms of external situational forces. The reason is very simple. When we can say, "The devil made me do it," the causality is external to yourself and does not affect your image maintenance. It's only when to your self-monitor or some other reference person you cannot generate sufficient *external* sources of causation (for instance, he was holding a gun to my head, or I'd have lost a hundred thousand dollars if I didn't) that you have to accept that your behavior was caused internally, and therefore change your attitude. Only *then* do you have to change your attitudes and values to fit the compliance to appear consistent and rational.

KRUPAT: *So, if I recall that study, when a nice supportive guy asked them to eat grasshoppers, they did it as a favor, but they didn't come to like the food any more than before. They had sufficient justification for their compliance because they did it as a favor.*

ZIMBARDO: But if they were asked by an abusive, negative person and complied, then they could not justify their acts in terms of the qualities of the person they were doing it for. So their behavior was seen as inconsistent and they reasserted their consistency, maintained their image as rational thinkers by saying, "I ate them because I *like* them." I think this process is fundamental and critical, and is an important social psychological process because the most relevant source of feedback for our self-image is the evaluation of other people. So, to the extent that any individual is concerned about the social acceptance and recognition of other people, he or she will attempt to maintain an appearance of normality; in addition, such a person will want to know the cause of his or her behavior, and act and believe according to reasonable rules of causation (which is the rational component of thought and action). For me, that is a very simplistic but effective way of thinking about all of the consistency theory type of research.

KRUPAT: *But if we accept the idea that our attitudes and behaviors are all tied to an image we have of ourselves, how is it that individuals are often so poor at predicting what they would do in certain situations? How is it that we can be made to act in ways which are inconsistent with our beliefs, attitudes, and values in the first place?*

ZIMBARDO: One of the reasons why the premeasurement of attitude often does not predict behavior in a given situation as well as you think it might is that, typically, individuals underestimate the power of the *social* forces in any given situation; and they overestimate the controlling influence of their own internal states—that is, attitudes, values, motivations, etc.

For instance, look at a number of the most interesting studies in social psychology: Asch's conformity study, Milgram's obedience study, and even the experiment I and my students did on simulating a prison.* For each of these studies, an individual observer looking at the behavior of other subjects assumes that he or she would *not* have acted in that particular way. Observers feel they would not conform, would not deliver strong electric shocks on command, would not become a violent prison guard, or a passive prisoner. People assume this on the basis of inspecting their own positions on these things: their personal attitudes and values. And they attribute to themselves much more—let's call it dispositional power—than they really have. That is, they perceive that they have more invulnerability than they really do. They underestimate or are unaware of the subtle but powerful forces in the social situation being brought to bear on themselves as subjects.

Now, we can say this only because when you take those people and put them into that experimental situation, then it can be shown that they will behave in that very same way. The power of the group pressure, the pres-

*See Section 5 for the prison study.

sure toward unanimity, the pressure to be liked, the pressure to be accepted, the pressure to appear consistent and rational, your concern for survival first instead of your concern for altruistic goals—all of these things which operate only in the immediacy of the situation—very often dramatically change people's behavior. They can make people conform, make them aggressive, or even make them brutalize other people.

KRUPAT: *If I understand what you're leading to, it would seem as though you're saying that we are very much controlled by social forces, but that the process is such that our attitudes change as our behaviors change, and vice versa. And, as a result, the two constantly appear to be in line.*

ZIMBARDO: I think that what we're saying is that we have a two-faced process. In the first place, individuals can be made to do things that they believe they could not be made to do—things which are against their attitudes and belief systems. However, *after* they do this, it will produce changes in their attitudes and values such that individuals will say, "The situation had nothing to do with it. I changed because I *now* believe it was better to have done so." So that *after* the fact, after engaging in a behavior which is totally contrary to what you stood for, you can now readjust your cognitions so you can *justify* what you did. This aspect, this incredible facility to change our attitudes to justify any behavior at all, is another aspect of the dissonance-attitude change research that fascinates me.

KRUPAT: *Let me ask you a final question which perhaps may lead from your last set of statements. I'm wondering if at the extreme you are suggesting a "straw in the wind" model of man. Are humans far more malleable than we ever thought they were? If we chose to, could we induce all sorts of attitude and behavior changes permanently in people as we pleased?*

ZIMBARDO: The problem is, I could answer that one either way. One answer says "Yes"; your extreme conclusion is correct insofar as we look around us and see the range of different people that have developed from infancy, given the relatively narrow range of genetic, physiological differences within a given culture or species. When you see this incredible range of differences, you say yes, people can be made into anything for which there is enough social support or pressure.

Now, on the other hand, we are talking here about the development of individuals starting from a relatively plastic, moldable state. This is contrasted with how much of an effect a given manipulation can have on an adult. At that point, the magnitude of the impact really depends on the nature of the supporting system around it in terms of other related values, the feedback from other people, and institutional supports. In our prison-simulation study, we were amazed how within days college students placed in the role of prison guard could become brutes, and active intelligent people put in the role of prisoner could become passive sheep. Still, for almost everyone, because the effect was so specific to the situation, the negative impact was transient.

Still, if you are dealing with nontrivial psychological variables, then the subject has to be affected in some permanent way as a consequence of being in any experiment. No amount of debriefing can change that. You can make the subjects feel less upset, but you cannot change the self-knowledge of what they've done. And this knowledge has the potential to lead to further changes in attitudes and behavior as people attempt to justify their actions and maintain their own self-image.

AN INTRODUCTION TO THE READINGS

The articles in this section, while concerned with the structure of attitudes and how and why attitudes change, focus additionally on how attitudes and behavior are related to one another. The first one, by Russell Weigel and Lee Newman, addresses itself to what has come to be known as the attitude–behavior controversy. That is, if attitudes are important because they are a good index of someone's tendency to act in one way or another, then why is it that much research has demonstrated that there is only a weak relationship between attitudes and behavior? While some people have argued that we ought to discard the attitude concept, Weigel and Newman point out that there are other alternatives. They suggest that we must design attitude measures more carefully and consider how these are related to the behavioral measures which we use. Their research shows that while attitudes accounted very well for a single behavior, they were related more strongly to a comprehensive measure of people's activity.

The second article, by Elliot Aronson, further addresses the issue of attitude-behavior consistency from the perspective of cognitive-dissonance theory. As implied by Philip Zimbardo in our conversation, Aronson notes that in order to seem rational we often change our attitudes to bring them in line with our actions. People living on the San Andreas fault, he points out, are unlikely to allow themselves to believe that an earthquake is imminent. Aronson reviews a considerable body of research from the way in which individuals justify efforts to join a new group to the consequences of a decision to act immorally to the effects of insufficient rewards—all of which demonstrate the pervasive influence of dissonance in our everyday lives.

The final study in this section is one of a series of classic studies looking at the effect fear may have on inducing changes in attitudes and behavior. In this research, Leventhal, Singer, and Jones attempted to change attitudes toward tetanus inoculations as well as to get students to have the shots. They found that both could be affected, but by differing variables. Greater fear was associated with a positive change in attitudes. However, in order to get people to act, the most important issue was whether or not the subjects were offered a plan of action. This, like the other papers in this section, notes that attitudes and behavior are related, but in complex ways that make both important topics of study.

RUSSELL H. WEIGEL
LEE S. NEWMAN

Increasing Attitude–Behavior Correspondence
by Broadening the Scope
of the Behavioral Measure

The frequent reports of low or nonsignificant correlations between attitude measures and behavioral criteria (e.g., Wicker, 1969) clearly challenge the proposition that attitudes are precursors of action (i.e., predispositions to respond to an object in a consistently favorable or unfavorable manner). It is a challenge that has provoked a variety of reactions ranging from profound disenchantment with the utility of attitudes for understanding human activity (Deutscher, 1966; Wicker, 1969) to phenomenologically oriented defenses of the attitude concept (Brandt, 1970; Kelman, 1974). Other authors have responded to the accumulated evidence of attitude–behavior inconsistency by suggesting conceptual and methodological refinements intended to increase the likelihood of correspondence between attitude and action. These refinements represent a shift in the focus of research efforts; a shift from examining whether or not attitudes are related to behavior to examining the conditions under which attitudes and behavior covary. In particular, more recent research has displayed recurring interest in both the effects of other personal and situational variables which, when operative, could counteract and obscure the impact of attitude on behavior (Bowers, 1968; Ehrlich, 1969; Frideres, Warner, & Albrecht, 1971; Insko & Schopler, 1967; Schofield, 1975; Warner & DeFleur, 1969; Wiegel & Amsterdam, in press) and the degree to which the attitude measure specified the behavioral criterion employed (Crespi, 1971; Davidson & Jaccard, 1975; Fishbein, 1966; Heberlein & Black, 1976; Wiegel, Vernon, & Tognacci, 1974; Weinstein, 1972; Wicker & Pomazal, 1971).

Fishbein and Ajzen (Ajzen & Fishbein, 1970, 1972, 1973; Fishbein, 1967, 1973) have presented a carefully articulated conceptual model which simultaneously addresses both the "other variables" and specificity issues. First, they suggest that attitude measures should focus on the respondent's beliefs and feelings about engaging in particular behaviors (i.e., attitude toward the act) rather than on the respondent's beliefs and feelings about particular objects. That is, instead of asking about respondents' general attitudes toward black people as a group, researchers should assess their attitudes toward the act of working with blacks, living in a desegregated neighborhood, participating in a civil rights demonstration, and so on. Consistent with the specificity notion, the likelihood of engaging in a particular action should be better predicted by one's attitude toward the act itself than by one's attitude toward an associated object or class of objects. The second suggestion advanced by Fishbein and Ajzen represents an attempt to specify the other variables which should be measured along with attitude toward the act to facilitate behavioral prediction. At various times in its development the nonattitudinal variables incorporated into this model included the personal and social norms pertinent to the behavior in question and the person's motivation to comply with these norms. Variables not incorporated into the model, then, are assumed to influence behavior only if they affect attitude toward the act or one of these nonattitudinal predictor variables.

Although a number of studies have provided empirical support for Fishbein and Ajzen's conceptual model (see Ajzen & Fishbein, 1973), some concerns also have been expressed. Schwartz and Tessler (1972), for example, pointed out that since a wide array of extraneous variables could affect the attitude–behavior relationship (e.g., competing attitudes and motives, activity level, expressive style, demographic characteristics), the model's selective focus is not sufficient to eliminate the necessity for sampling further from these other potential antecedents of behavior. Indeed, because the number of potentially important other variables is essentially infinite, the logic of this approach confronts attitude researchers concerned with the behavioral implications of their measures with the formidable task of attempting to anticipate and independently assess the full range of variables that might disrupt attitude–behavior correspondence.

Schwartz and Tessler also noted the limitations of reliance on attitude toward the act. While their research indicated that attitude-toward-act measures improved prediction of a given behavior, the authors caution that attitude toward the act is limited to the prediction of only very specific behaviors in particular situations, "while researchers often wish to use attitudes to predict a range of presumably related behavior across a variety of situations" (Schwartz & Tessler, 1972, p. 235). Indeed, when evaluating the wisdom of employing attitude-toward-act measures, it seems reasonable to ask whether or not the attitude concept has become somewhat sterile in evolving from a concept representing a relatively stable underlying disposition capable of mediating a variety of object-related behaviors to a concept which seems to equate attitudes and behaviors under specified situational circumstances. Certainly as Cook and Selltiz (1964) have pointed out, "if validly distinguished, a dispositional concept has, by its very nature, a wider range of situational relevance—including projectability into relatively novel situations" (p. 36). Without contesting the power of attitude-toward-act measures for predicting a specific behavioral response, then, we feel that the proposition that traditional attitude-toward-object measures can capture broad, enduring dispositions with strong and diverse behavioral implications merits further investigation. While this view stands in marked contrast to the bulk of the currently available findings revealing nonsignificant correlations between attitude-toward-object measures and overt behavior, two lines of argument raising questions about the adequacy of the methodology and behavioral criteria employed in these studies can be developed which suggest the wisdom of renewed inquiry.

THE METHODOLOGY PROBLEM

Although Wicker's influential review of the attitude–behavior literature (Wicker, 1969) indicates that traditional attitude-toward-object measures rarely have been able to account for as much as 10% of the variance on overt behavioral measures, serious methodological problems cast doubt on the quality of much of the research cited. Indeed, when Dillehay (1973) critically reexamined the most frequently referenced investigations reporting low correspondence between attitudes and actions, he concluded that these studies (Kutner, Wilkins, & Yarrow, 1952; LaPiere, 1934; Minard, 1952) were irrelevant to the attitude–behavior issue for a variety of reasons. For example, Dillehay points out that in both LaPiere's (1934) widely cited study and a similar investigation conducted by Kutner et al. (1952), it was quite likely that the subjects who provided the behavioral data were *not* the same people from whom the attitude data were obtained.

A pervasive problem which prompts further suspicions about the credibility of much of the past attitude–behavior research is the widespread lack of concern with establishing the reliability and validity of the attitude measures employed. The point is simple, important, and frequently overlooked: One reason why a low correlation between attitude and behavior might obtain in a given study is that a poor quality attitude measure was used. In hopes of examining this possibility further, we managed to recover 42 of the 47 original papers cited in Wicker's (1969) tabular summary of the attitude–behavior literature. Our purpose was to determine the effect of variation in the quality of the attitude measure (i.e., whether or not data documenting the reliability and validity of a measure had been collected) on the magnitude of the attitude–behavior correlations observed. This effort was abandoned because in the vast majority of the cases the attitude measures employed were not described in sufficient detail to permit such an appraisal. The absence of this information in these published studies is revealing in itself, however. That is, it seems reasonable to demand that investigations purporting to examine the relationship between attitudes and actions should explicitly provide evidence of the internal consistency of the attitude measure for the current sample as well as some evidence of the measure's validity derived from an independent sample. Without these data the question of how frequently poor quality attitude measures have been responsible for low attitude–behavior correlations remains unanswered but provocative.

THE BEHAVIORAL CRITERION PROBLEM

Attitude measures should be expected to predict only behaviors that are appropriate to the attitude under consideration. It would follow, then, that measures assessing attitudes toward a highly specific object or behavior should predict behavioral responsiveness to that particular object or the likelihood that the individual will engage in the behavior specified. As previously noted, this specificity hypothesis has received empirical support in a number of studies. On the other hand, when the attitude object is a general or comprehensive one (e.g., black people, the environment, the government), then the behavioral criterion should be equally general or comprehensive. An adequate test of attitude–behavior consistency under these circumstances would demand the use of several independent measures of behavior designed to adequately sample the universe of action implications engaged by the attitude measure.[1]

This latter point has been articulated repeatedly (Calder & Ross, 1973; Doob, 1947; Fishbein, 1973; Thurstone, 1931; Tittle & Hill, 1967a) but largely ignored in past empirical research. In elaborating these arguments, Fishbein (1973) has emphasized that while two people may hold equally favorable attitudes toward a given object, their specific actions with respect to that object may vary considerably. Taken together, however, their behaviors will be similar in revealing the same degree of favorableness toward the object. Hence, Fishbein concludes that scores on traditional attitude-toward-object measures should not be expected to predict an isolated single act, but should predict "multiple-act criteria" (single or multiple observations of *different* behaviors reflecting the overall pattern of the person's actions with respect to the attitude-object).

The only empirical evidence related to this claim has been generated quite recently. Fishbein and Ajzen (1974) had 62 undergraduates check which of 100 religious behaviors they had performed as well as complete five traditional attitude measures assessing beliefs and feelings about religion. Results indicated that scores on all five attitude scales were highly correlated with the total number of different behaviors performed whereas the correlations between the attitude scales and single behavioral self-report items were low and nonsignificant. Although these findings support the proposition that attitude-toward-object measures can predict multiple-act criteria, the data remain vulnerable to criticism on two grounds. First, the authors rely on retrospective behavioral reports rather than on direct observation of behaviors in constructing their multiple-act measure. In view of the evidence that self-reports often contain substantial error (Brislin & Olmstead, 1973; Tittle & Hill, 1967b), this reliance remains disconcerting despite the counterarguments noted by Fishbein and Ajzen. Second, not only were many of the activities part of the regular experience of the subjects but the attitude measures apparently were taken immediately after the behavioral self-report measures were completed. Given this state of affairs, the high correlations may have resulted from a tendency for subjects to infer their attitudes from the frequency with which their past behavioral choices—choices made salient by the data-gathering procedure—implied a given attitude (Bem, 1967).[2] Insofar as these difficulties tend to limit the confidence which can be placed in Fishbein and Ajzen's findings, they serve to underscore the need for further inquiry with respect to the capacity of attitude-toward-object measures for predicting broad configurations of object-relevant behaviors.

The hypothesis of the present study was tested under the following conditions. The study utilized an attitude scale measuring concern about environmental quality. The scale's content ranged broadly across conservation and pollution issues, and evidence of the measure's reliability and validity had been previously established.

Because of the broad focus of the attitude measure, a fair test of attitude–behavior relationships demanded that subjects be presented with a diverse array of opportunities to manifest in their overt behavior variation in their concern about environmental protection. Consequently, a variety of behavioral measures was employed, and scores on the attitude scale were compared with scores on these measures. These separate measures also were combined to form a more comprehensive behavioral index intended to encompass a behavioral domain of comparable breadth to the attitude domain assessed. Under these conditions, we hypothesized that attitude scores reflecting broadly focused concerns about environmental quality will be highly correlated with scores on the comprehensive behavioral index but not with performance or nonperformance of each of the separate behaviors from which the index was derived.

METHOD

Subjects

A survey of attitudes toward a variety of social problems (about 20% of the items focused on environmental issues) was administered to 91 residents of a medium-sized New England town. These 91 respondents represented 87% of the total number of subjects designated by the original random sample. In order to reduce the number of subjects to a manageable size with respect to our capacities for behavioral follow-up, a subsample of 50 individuals was selected on a random basis. The 3-month interval between the administration of the initial attitude survey and the first follow-up contact generated some attrition: Four persons could not be contacted because they had moved away from the area during the interim, one person could not be contacted because she was on vacation for the entire summer, and one other was dropped from further consideration because he was in the process of moving during the summer, which precluded the possibility of obtaining the full range of behavioral data from him. The final subject pool, then, consisted of 44 persons including 25 males and 19 females.

Procedures

Beginning 3 months after the survey data had been collected, the subjects were contacted three times during the ensuing 5-month period and offered opportunities to participate in a variety of organized ecology projects. First, a confederate solicited signatures on the three petitions described below in the Behavioral Criteria section. The confederate had previously participated in an intensive training program which included the learning of a standardized script specifying how to approach the subjects, role-playing procedures designed to anticipate potential questions and develop a standard set of responses, and 10 practice interviews with persons in a neighboring town not included in the present study. The confederate was given a randomized list of names and addresses. He was not given any information as to how the subjects had responded to the initial survey and was instructed not to probe for the general level of interest in environmental issues.

Instead, the importance of approaching each individual on the list in the same manner was emphasized repeatedly. Approximately 6 weeks later, a second confederate contacted the subjects soliciting their help in a series of roadside litter pick-ups. After another 8-week interval, a third confederate contacted the subjects soliciting their participation in a recycling program. Both of these latter activities are described more fully in the Behavioral Criteria section. The order in which subjects were to be contacted was varied for each confederate to ensure that a given subject would not be uniformly contacted early or late with respect to all three activities. The same types of training and blinding procedures were employed for the second and third confederates as for the first.

Each of the three confederates claimed to be a member of an environmental protection organization comprised of local citizens. This pretext was necessary to provide a credible cover story which would minimize the likelihood of suspicion about being contacted repeatedly with respect to the petition, litter pick-up, and recycling enterprises. None of the subjects expressed any suspicions about the legitimacy of the organization nor did any subjects question whether the confederates were associated with the survey that they had taken previously. With respect to the ethical implications of these deceptions, it should be noted that the organization did in fact fulfill all promises made to the subjects: Signed petitions were forwarded to the specified congressman, roadside litter pick-ups were conducted as scheduled, and bottles and papers were collected on a weekly basis and delivered to the local recycling center. When the recycling project was concluded, each participating subject was contacted personally. It was explained that because of time commitments and financial considerations, the recycling program could not be continued. In general, subjects indicated that they regretted the termination of the recycling program but were appreciative of the time and effort required making the program difficult to manage on a volunteer basis. Thus, while subjects were never informed about the full nature of the experiment for fear of undermining their future responsiveness to environmental organizations, pains were taken to ensure that all subjects were treated with dignity and that all our obligations to provide environmental programs in which they could participate were honored.

The Attitude Measure

The environmental concern scale, a measure focusing on the level of attitudinal concern about a variety of conservation and pollution issues, was embedded in the initial survey. The measure was composed of 16 items, 9 of which were negatively stated and 7 of which were positively stated. Subjects rated each item along a 5-point Likert dimension ranging from strongly agree to strongly disagree. Each item was scored from 0 to 4, allowing the summed score across items for a given respondent to range from 0 to 64, with high scores indicating greater concern about protecting environmental quality. The environmental concern scale exhibited excellent internal consistency with respect to the responses of the 44 subjects included in the present study. The highly satisfactory level of interitem consistency was not surprising because preliminary evidence of the reliability and validity of the environmental concern scale had been established previously. The items comprising this scale were selected from a pool of 31 items used by Weigel et al. (1974) in the prediction of subjects' responsiveness to requests for help in Sierra Club activities by members of that organization. The 16 items chosen were those which were the best predictors of the behavioral criterion employed in the Weigel et al. investigation. . . .

The items included in the environmental concern scale employed in the present investigation, then, were selected on the basis of previously collected data suggesting their utility in terms of both forming a homogeneous attitude scale and demonstrated ability to predict behavioral variation. With respect to the considerations about attitude–behavior relationships raised in the introduction, the present investigation employed an attitude measure which had evinced both internal consistency and validity on a separate sample. What remained was to use this promising instrument to put the present hypotheses regarding attitude–behavioral relationships to an appropriate test. Such a test required the establishment of a set of behavioral criteria that specified a configuration of behaviors of sufficient breadth that they corresponded to the broad attitudinal focus of the environmental concern scale.

The Behavioral Criteria

Behavioral measures were employed which (a) were relatively novel with respect to the subjects' past experience, (b) were clearly related to environmental issues, and (c) would provide a number of independent opportunities to display the intensity of one's behavioral commitment to protecting environmental quality. Three general types of behavior, each involving a set of distinct actions, were assessed.

Petitioning. Three petitions were brought door-to-door by the first of the trained confederates. All three petitions were presented in a single trip and always in the following order: (a) a petition opposing oil drilling off the New England coast, (b) a petition opposing construction of nuclear power plants, and (c) a petition proposing more stringent regulation and punishment of those who remove air pollution devices from their automobile exhaust systems. Each petition had places for four signatures, but no names appeared on the petitions when presented to any given subject. This procedure was intended to standardize the presentation of petitions and to control for any differential sensitivity to conformity pressures resulting from previous accumulation of names. Each subject received a rehearsed explanation of the rationale for each petition and was told at the outset that the petitions would be sent to the congressman for the district. All subjects, regardless of whether or not they signed petitions, were asked if they would circulate the petitions to family or friends who might be interested in signing them. Subjects who accepted the blank petitions to circulate to friends and family were also given a preaddressed, stamped envelope in which to mail back signed sheets. An innocuous number in the upper right-hand corner of the "circulation" petitions enabled subject identification when the petitions were returned. Although 16 subjects refused to sign any petitions, and only 17 signed all three petitions, all but 2 subjects agreed to circulate extra copies to friends and family. Thus, while not all of the subjects who agreed followed through on their promise, nearly all of them were exposed to the opportunity to circulate not just at the door but by actually having blank petitions in hand. Petitioning behavior, then, was comprised of four separate acts: signing or not signing each of the three petitions and returning or not returning circulated petitions with at least one signature. Performance of a given act was scored 1 and nonperformance was scored 0.

Roadside litter pick-ups.   Six weeks after the initial follow-up contact, a second confederate solicited the subjects' aid in a roadside litter pick-up program being conducted in nearby areas in the town. Subjects who agreed to participate gave the confederate their home phone number, specified whether they would prefer to work on weekday evenings or weekends, and were asked to recruit a friend or family member to participate as well. In a subsequent phone call, each subject was given a choice of three separate times to participate in the pick-up program. Subjects who indicated that they could participate at one of the three scheduled times were reminded of their promise in a second phone call the night before the scheduled date. Behavioral participation in the roadside litter pick-up program, then, involved two separate acts: participating or not participating on one of the three dates and recruiting or not recruiting at least one other person as the confederate had explicitly encouraged each subject to do. Performance of a given act was scored 1 and nonperformance was scored 0.

Recycling.   Approximately 8 weeks later, subjects were contacted again by a third confederate. They were asked if they were willing to take part in a recycling program in which they would bundle their papers, remove metal rings from their bottles and put the recyclables outside where these materials could be picked up on a regular weekly route. Papers and bottles were then picked up every week for 8 weeks and delivered to a local recycling facility. In this instance a similar action (placing recyclable materials in the appropriate place at the time agreed upon) could be either performed or not performed on eight different occasions. Performance on a given occasion was scored 1 and nonperformance was scored 0.

Comprehensive behavioral index.   It should be obvious that these 14 distinct behaviors were not selected capriciously. Rather, they were chosen because they provided a means of operationalizing the intensity of subjects' responses to the petitioning, litter pick-up, and recycling projects. For example, summing across the separate actions associated with the petition drive yielded a behavioral commitment scale with scores ranging from 0 to 4: one point for each petition signed and one point for returning circulated petitions. Similarly, summing across the separate actions associated with the litter pick-up and recycling projects yielded scales scored 0–2 and 0–8, respectively. These three scales, then, represented organized sets of actions—relatively independent avenues through which the attitude under consideration might seek behavioral expression. All three scales were incorporated into a more comprehensive behavioral index in order to further articulate the contours of a behavioral domain comparable in breadth to the attitude domain assessed. . . .

RESULTS

Consistent with the arguments presented in the introduction, it was hypothesized that scores on the environmental concern scale would be highly correlated with scores on the comprehensive behavioral index but not with performance or nonperformance of each of the separate behaviors from which the index was derived. The attitude–behavior correlations pertinent to this hypothesis support the hypothesis of the present study; attitude–behavior correspondence increases as the scope of the behavioral measure is broadened. Although the attitude scores made good predictions of a few of the single act criteria, and two thirds of these correlation coefficients were significant at the .05 level of confidence or better, the magnitude of the average correlation with the 14 single behaviors was quite modest. Combining the single behaviors into three general categories yielded behavioral scales reflecting the intensity of the subject's responsiveness to the petitioning, litter pick-up, and recycling projects. The average correlation between attitude scores and scores on these three behavioral scales was considerably stronger. As hypothesized, the correlation between scores on the comprehensive behavioral index and scores on the environmental concern scale was higher than the correlations between attitude scores and scores on any of the component behaviors. The meaning of these differences is underscored when one notes that while attitudinal variation, on the average, can account for less than 10% of the variance on the single behavioral measures, the amount of shared variance between attitudinal concern and the overall pattern of environmentally oriented actions is 38%.

DISCUSSION

The present study was designed to minimize the methodological and behavioral criterion problems which compromise the value of much of the past research on the relationship of attitudes and actions. The results indicate that a substantial attitude–behavior correlation can obtain when an attitude measure of established quality is employed in conjunction with behavioral measures that map out an action domain of comparable breadth to the attitude domain assessed. Attitude scores representing broadly focused concerns about environmental quality made only modest predictions of performance or nonperformance of the 14 separate actions observed in this study. However, the correlation between scores on the attitude measure and scores on the comprehensive index combining these separate actions was much more pronounced.

These data seem compelling for a variety of reasons. First, the behavioral criteria utilized in this study were all overt behaviors, thereby eliminating the problems associated with using self-reports of past activities. Second, the field setting and noncollege sample avoids the heavy reliance on undergraduate subjects that is characteristic of past research. Third, since the behavioral data were collected several months after the attitude measure was administered, the magnitude of the correlation observed suggests both the enduring character of attitudes and their continuing relevance for understanding actions with respect to the attitude object. Finally, the correlation characterizing the relationship between scores on the attitude scale and scores on the comprehensive behavioral index (.62) is much stronger than has generally been reported in previous research. As Wicker (1969) pointed out, attitude–behavior correlations "are rarely above .30 and often near zero. Only rarely can as much as 10% of the variance in overt behavioral measures be accounted for by the attitudinal data" (p. 65). By contrast, variation in environmental attitudes accounted for 38% of the variance in the overall behavioral configuration in the present study. Aside from documenting strong attitude–behavior correspondence in this instance, these findings suggest that future research examining the behavioral implications of attitude-toward-object measures should employ several independent measures of behavior designed to adequately sample the universe of object-relevant actions.

The strong attitude–behavior relationship observed in the present study is particularly impressive in that it emerged even in the absence of any attempt to take systematic cognizance of the effects of intervening personal and situational variables operating to attenuate the relationship. This outcome seems especially encouraging for attitude research because of the practical impossibility of anticipating all of the variables which might disrupt attitude–behavior correspondence for a given subject in a given situation. A single example from the present study illustrates this point. A subject who scored high on the environmental concern scale initially agreed to participate in the litter pick-up project but later reversed her decision. In reneging on her offer, she told the confederate that she would have liked to participate, but her husband had asked her not to do so. She explained that her husband opposed her participation because he had hopes of organizing the Boy Scouts in a similar project and felt that the current project could undermine the realization of those hopes. In this case, pressure from the husband represented a situational variable which prevented the subject's participation in the litter pick-up program despite her proenvironment attitude. The effect of this idiosyncratic situational variable in disrupting attitude–behavior consistency was neutralized, in part, by assessing other environmentally oriented behaviors in which this situational pressure was not operative. Although the accuracy of such anecdotal information cannot be evaluated with precision, its implication remains provocative: The inordinate difficulty involved in attempting to anticipate and measure the effects of a potentially large number of extraneous variables may be circumvented by using multiple behavioral criteria.

In sum, the present data indicate that a high-quality attitude measure focusing on a general or comprehensive attitude–object can make strong predictions of behavioral variation when that behavioral variation is sought in the context of patterned sets of actions rather than in a single act. These findings stand in marked contrast to the predominantly pessimistic assessment of the utility of the attitude concept apparent in much contemporary social psychology literature. While this previous literature has been useful in inhibiting cavalier inferences about the meaning of attitude data, it also seems to have generated some unnecessary and unfortunate overkill. In the past when inconsistency occurred between attitudes and behavior, the tendency was to question the wisdom of conceptualizing attitudes as underlying dispositions mediating a variety of behaviors rather than to question either the quality of the particular attitude measure or the appropriateness of the behavioral criteria employed. When these latter considerations are taken into account, the present data suggest that attitudes will exhibit a robust capacity to influence the direction that behavior will take. These data do not obviate the need for caution in claiming that a given study of attitudes is socially significant merely because the attitude–object is socially significant (Wicker, 1969). However, they do suggest that carefully developed attitude-toward-object measures will continue to be valuable tools in psychological research—tools capable of complementing both direct behavioral observation and highly specific, behaviorally focused attitude measures by assessing dispositions with enduring action implications across a variety of situational contexts.

NOTES

1. Despite the logic of this argument, 85% of the 42 studies we recovered from Wicker's tabular list utilized behavioral criterion measures which could be characterized as a single or repeated observation of only one type of action. By contrast, those investigators who included a number of distinct object-relevant behaviors in their criterion measures all found evidence that attitude scores were significantly related to at least some of the behavioral criteria employed in each study (Bernberg, 1952; Carr & Roberts, 1965; Fendrich, 1967; Goodmonson & Glaudin, 1971; Heron, 1954; Potter & Klein, 1957; Tittle & Hill, 1967a).
2. Schwartz and Tessler (1972) raise a similar objection with respect to two other studies conducted by Ajzen and Fishbein (1969, 1970). They argue that relatively novel behavioral criteria should be utilized to preclude the possibility that past performance is the primary determinant of both attitude scores and behavioral reports.

REFERENCES

Ajzen, I., & Fishbein, M. The prediction of behavioral intentions in a choice situation. *Journal of Experimental Social Psychology*, 1969, **5**, 400–416.

Ajzen, I., & Fishbein, M. The prediction of behavior from attitudinal and normative variables. *Journal of Experimental Social Psychology*, 1970, **6**, 466–487.

Ajzen, I., & Fishbein, M. Attitudes and normative beliefs as factors influencing behavioral intentions. *Journal of Personality and Social Psychology*, 1972, **21**, 1–9.

Ajzen, I., & Fishbein, M. Attitudinal and normative variables as predictors of specific behaviors. *Journal of Personality and Social Psychology*, 1973, **27**, 41–57.

Bem, D. Self-perception: An alternative interpretation of cognitive dissonance phenomena. *Psychological Review*, 1967, **74**, 183–200.

Bernberg, R. E. Socio-psychological factors in industrial morale: The prediction of specific indicators. *Journal of Social Psychology*, 1952, **36**, 73–82.

Bowers, W. J. Normative constraints on deviant behavior in the college context. *Sociometry*, 1968, **31**, 370–385.

Brandt, L. W. The behaviorist's leap: An inquiry into what attitude researchers measure. *Journal of Social Issues*, 1970, **52**, 163–166.

Brislin, R. N., & Olmstead, K. H. An examination of two models designed to predict behavior from attitude and other verbal measures. *Proceedings of the 81st Annual Convention of the American Psychological Association*, 1973, **8**, 259–260.

Calder, B. J., & Ross, M. *Attitudes and behavior*. Morristown, N.J.: General Learning Press, 1973.

Carr, L., & Roberts, S. O. Correlates of civil rights participation. *Journal of Social Psychology*, 1965, **67**, 259–267.

Cook, S. W., & Selltiz, C. A. A multiple-indicator approach to attitude measurement. *Psychological Bulletin*, 1964, **62**, 36–55.

Crespi, I. What kinds of attitude measures are predictive of behavior? *Public Opinion Quarterly*, 1971, **35**, 327–334.

Davidson, A. R., & Jaccard, J. J. Population psychology: A new look at an old problem. *Journal of Personality and Social Psychology*, 1975, **31**, 1073–1082.

Deutscher, I. Words and deeds: Social science and social policy. *Social Problems*, 1966, **13**, 235–265.

Dillehay, R. C. On the irrelevance of the classical negative evidence concerning the effect of attitudes on behavior. *American Psychologist*, 1973, **28**, 887–893.

Doob, L. W. The behavior of attitudes. *Psychological Review*, 1947, **54**, 135–156.

Ehrlich, H. J. Attitudes, behavior and the intervening variables. *American Sociologist*, 1969, **4**, 29–34.

Fendrich, J. A. A study of the association among verbal attitudes, commitment and overt behavior in different experimental situations. *Social Forces*, 1967, **45**, 347–355.

Fishbein, M. The relationship between beliefs, attitudes, and behavior. In S. Feldman (Ed.), *Cognitive consistency*. New York: Academic Press, 1966.

Fishbein, M. Attitude and the prediction of behavior. In M. Fishbein (Ed.), *Readings in attitude theory and measurement*. New York: Wiley, 1967.

Fishbein, M. The prediction of behaviors from attitudinal variables. In C. D. Mortensen & K. K. Sereno (Eds.), *Advances in communication research*. New York: Harper & Row, 1973.

Fishbein, M., & Ajzen, I. Attitudes toward objects as predictors of single and multiple behavioral criteria. *Psychological Review*, 1974, **81**, 59–74.

Frideres, J. S., Warner, L. G., & Albrecht, S. L. The impact of social constraints on the relationship between attitudes and behavior. *Social Forces*, 1971, **50**, 102–112.

Goodmonson, C., & Glaudin, V. The relationship of commitment-free behavior and commitment behavior: A study of attitude toward organ transplantation. *Journal of Social Issues*, 1971, **27**, 171–183.

Heberlein, T. A., & Black, J. S. Attitudinal specificity and the prediction of behavior in a field setting. *Journal of Personality and Social Psychology*, 1976, **33**, 474–479.

Heron, A. Satisfaction and satisfactoriness: Complementary aspects of occupational adjustment. *Occupational Psychology*, 1954, **28**, 140–153.

Insko, C. A., & Schopler, J. Triadic consistency: A statement of affective-cognitive-conative consistency. *Psychological Review*, 1967, **74**, 361–376.

Kelman, H. C. Attitudes are alive and well and gainfully employed in the sphere of action. *American Psychologist*, 1974, **29**, 310–324.

Kutner, B., Wilkins, C., & Yarrow, P. R. Verbal attitudes and overt behavior involving racial prejudice. *Journal of Abnormal and Social Psychology*, 1952, **47**, 649–652.

LaPiere, R. T. Attitudes versus actions. *Social Forces*, 1934, **13**, 230–237.

Minard, R. D. Race relationships in the Pocahontas coal field. *Journal of Social Issues*, 1952, **8**, 29–44.

Potter, H. W., & Klein, H. R. On nursing behavior. *Psychiatry*, 1957, **20**, 39–46.

Schofield, J. W. Effect of norms, public disclosure, and need for approval on volunteering behavior consistent with attitudes. *Journal of Personality and Social Psychology*, 1975, **31**, 1126–1133.

Schwartz, S. H., & Tessler, R. C. A test of a model for reducing measured attitude–behavior discrepancies. *Journal of Personality and Social Psychology*, 1972, **24**, 225–236.

Thurstone, L. L. The measurement of attitudes. *Journal of Abnormal and Social Psychology*, 1931, **26**, 249–269.

Tittle, C. R., & Hill, R. J. Attitude measurement and the prediction of behavior: An evaluation of conditions and measurement techniques. *Sociometry*, 1967, **30**, 199–213. (a)

Tittle, C. R., & Hill, R. J. The accuracy of self-reported data and prediction of political activity. *Public Opinion Quarterly*, 1967, **31**, 103–106. (b)

Warner, L. G., & DeFleur, M. L. Attitude as an interactional concept: Social constraint and social distance as intervening variables between attitude and action. *American Sociological Review*, 1969, **34**, 153–169.

Weigel, R. H., & Amsterdam, J. T. The effect of behavior relevant information on attitude–behavior consistency. *Journal of Social Psychology*, 1976, **98**, 247–251.

Weigel, R. H., Vernon, D. T. A., & Tognacci, L. N. The specificity of the attitude as a determinant of attitude–behavior congruence. *Journal of Personality and Social Psychology*, 1974, **30**, 724–728.

Weinstein, A. G. Predicting behavior from attitudes. *Public Opinion Quarterly*, 1972, **36**, 355–360.

Wicker, A. W. Attitudes versus action: The relationship of verbal and overt behavioral responses to attitude objects. *Journal of Social Issues*, 1969, **25**, 41–48.

Wicker, A. W., & Pomazal, R. J. The relationship between attitudes and behavior as a function of specificity of attitude object and presence of significant others during assessment conditions. *Representative Research in Social Psychology*, 1971, **2**, 26–31.

ELLIOT ARONSON

The Rationalizing Animal

Man likes to think of himself as a rational animal. However, it is more true that man is a *rationalizing* animal, that he attempts to appear reasonable to himself and to others. Albert Camus even said that man is a creature who spends his entire life in an attempt to convince himself that he is not absurd.

Some years ago a woman reported that she was receiving messages from outer space. Word came to her from the planet Clarion that her city would be destroyed by a great flood on December 21. Soon a considerable number of believers shared her deep commitment to the prophecy. Some of them quit their jobs and spent their savings freely in anticipation of the end.

On the evening of December 20, the prophet and her followers met to prepare for the event. They believed that flying saucers would pick them up, thereby sparing them from disaster. Midnight arrived, but no flying saucers. December 21 dawned, but no flood.

What happens when prophecy fails? Social psychologists Leon Festinger, Henry Riecken, and Stanley Schachter infiltrated the little band of believers to see how they would react. They predicted that persons who had expected the disaster, but awaited it alone in their homes, would simply lose faith in the prophecy. But those who awaited the outcome in a group, who had thus admitted their belief publicly, would come to believe even more strongly in the prophecy and turn into active proselytizers.

This is exactly what happened. At first the faithful felt despair and shame because all their predictions had been for nought. Then, after waiting nearly five hours for the saucers, the prophet had a new vision. The city had been spared, she said, because of the trust and faith of her devoted group. This revelation was elegant in its simplicity, and the believers accepted it enthusiastically. They now sought the press that they had previously avoided. They turned from believers into zealots.

Living on the fault. In 1957 Leon Festinger proposed his theory of *cognitive dissonance*, which describes and predicts man's rationalizing behavior. Dissonance occurs whenever a person simultaneously holds two inconsistent cognitions (ideas, beliefs, opinions). For example, the belief that the world will end on a certain day is dissonant with the awareness, when the day breaks, that the world has not ended. Festinger maintained that this state of inconsistency is so uncomfortable that people strive to reduce the conflict in the easiest way possible. They will change one or both cognitions so that they will "fit together" better.

Consider what happens when a smoker is confronted with evidence that smoking causes cancer. He will become motivated to change either his attitudes about smoking or his behavior. And as anyone who has tried to quit knows, the former alternative is easier.

The smoker may decide that the studies are lousy. He may point to friends ("If Sam, Jack and Harry smoke, cigarettes can't be all that dangerous"). He may conclude that filters trap all the cancer-producing materials. Or he may argue that he would rather live a short and happy life with cigarettes than a long and miserable life without them.

The more a person is committed to a course of action, the more resistant he will be to information that threatens that course. Psychologists have reported that the people who are least likely to believe the dangers of smoking are those who tried to quit—and failed. They have become more committed to smoking. Similarly, a person who builds a $100,000 house astride the San Andreas Fault will be less receptive to arguments about imminent earthquakes than would a person who is renting the house for a few months. The new homeowner is committed; he doesn't want to believe that he did an absurd thing.

When a person reduces his dissonance, he defends his ego, and keeps a positive self-image. But self-justification can reach startling extremes; people will ignore danger in order to avoid dissonance, even when that ignorance can cause their deaths. I mean that literally.

Suppose you are Jewish in a country occupied by Hitler's forces. What should you do? You could try to leave the country; you could try to pass as "Aryan"; you could do nothing and hope for the best. The first two choices are dangerous: if you are caught you will be executed. If you decide to sit tight, you will try to convince yourself that you made the best decision. You may reason that while Jews are indeed being treated unfairly, they are not being killed unless they break the law.

Now suppose that a respected man from your town announces that he has seen Jews being butchered mercilessly, including everyone who had recently been deported from your village. If you believe him, you might have a chance to escape. If you don't believe him, you and your family will be slaughtered.

Dissonance theory would predict that you will not listen to the witness, because to do so would be to admit that your judgment and decisions were wrong. You will dismiss his information as untrue, and decide that he was lying or hallucinating. Indeed, Elie Wiesel reported that this happened to the Jews in Sighet, a small town in Hungary, in 1944. Thus people are not passive receptacles for the deposit of information. The manner in which they view and distort the objective world in order to avoid and reduce dissonance is entirely predictable. But one cannot divide the world into rational people on one side and dissonance reducers on the other. While people vary in their ability to tolerate dissonance, we are all capable of rational or irrational behavior, depending on the circumstances—some of which follow.

Dissonance because of effort. Judson Mills and I found that if people go through a lot of trouble to gain admission to a group, and the group turns out to be dull and dreary, they will experience dissonance. It is a rare person who will accept this situation with an "Oh, pshaw. I worked hard for nothing. Too bad." One way to resolve the dissonance is to decide that the group is worth the effort it took to get admitted.

We told a number of college women that they would have to undergo an initiation to join a group that would discuss the psychology of sex. One third of them had severe initiation: they had to recite a list of obscene words and read some lurid sexual passages from novels in the presence of a male experimenter (in 1959, this really was a "severe" and embarrassing task). One third went through a mild initiation in which they read words that were sexual but not obscene (such as "virgin" and "petting"); and the last third had no initiation at all. Then all of the women listened to an extremely boring taped discussion of the group they had presumably joined. The women in the severe initiation group rated the discussion and its drab participants much more favorably than those in the other groups.

I am not asserting that people enjoy painful experiences, or that they enjoy things that are associated with painful experiences. If you got hit on the head by a brick on the way to a fraternity initiation, you would not like that group any better. But if you volunteered to get hit with a brick *in order to join* the fraternity, you definitely would like the group more than if you had been admitted without fuss.

After a decision—especially a difficult one that involves much time, money, or effort—people almost always experience dissonance. Awareness of defects in the preferred object is dissonant with having chosen it; awareness of positive aspects of the unchosen object is dissonant with having rejected it.

Accordingly, researchers have found that *before* making a decision, people seek as much information as possible about the alternatives. Afterwards, however, they seek reassurance that they did the right thing, and do so by seeking information in support of their choice or by simply changing the information that is already in their heads. In one of the earliest experiments on dissonance theory, Jack Brehm gave a group of women their choice between two appliances, such as a toaster or a blender, that they had previously rated for desirability. When the subjects reevaluated the appliances after choosing one of them, they increased their liking for the one they had chosen and downgraded their evaluation of the rejected appliance. Similarly, Danuta Ehrlich and her associates found that a person about to buy a new car does so carefully, reading all ads and accepting facts openly on various makes and models. But after he buys his Volvo, for instance, he will read advertisements more selectively, and he will tend to avoid ads for Volkswagens, Chevrolets, and so on.

The decision to behave immorally.   Your conscience, let us suppose, tells you that it is wrong to cheat, lie, steal, seduce your neighbor's husband or wife, or whatever. Let us suppose further that you are in a situation in which you are sorely tempted to ignore your conscience. If you give in to temptation, the cognition "I am a decent, moral person" will be dissonant with the cognition "I have committed an immoral act." If you resist, the cognition "I want to get a good grade (have that money, seduce that person)" is dissonant with the cognition "I could have acted so as to get that grade, but I chose not to."

The easiest way to reduce dissonance in either case is to minimize the negative aspects of the action one has chosen, and to change one's attitude about its immorality. If Mr. C. decides to cheat, he will probably decide that cheating isn't really so bad. It hurts no one; everyone does it; it's part of human nature. If Mr. D. decides not to cheat, he will no doubt come to believe that cheating is a sin, and deserves severe punishment.

The point here is that the initial attitudes of these men is virtually the same. Moreover, their decisions could be a hair's breadth apart. But once the action is taken, their attitudes diverge sharply.

Judson Mills confirmed these speculations in an experiment with sixth-grade children. First he measured their attitudes toward cheating, and then put them in a competitive situation. He arranged the test so that it was impossible to win without cheating, and so it was easy for the children to cheat, thinking they would be unwatched. The next day, he asked the children again how they felt about cheating. Those who had cheated on the test had become more lenient in their attitudes; those who had resisted the temptation adopted harsher attitudes.

These data are provocative. They suggest that the most zealous crusaders are not those who are removed from the problem they oppose. I would hazard to say that the people who are most angry about "the sexual promiscuity of the young" are *not* those who have never dreamed of being promiscuous. On the contrary, they would be persons who had been seriously tempted by illicit sex, who came very close to giving in to their desires, but who finally resisted. People who almost live in glass houses are the ones who are most likely to throw stones.

Insufficient justification.   If I offer George $20 to do a boring task, and offer Richard $1 to do the same thing, which one will decide that the assignment was mildly interesting? If I threaten one child with harsh punishment if he does something forbidden, and threaten another child with mild punishment, which one will transgress?

Dissonance theory predicts that when people find themselves doing something and they have neither been rewarded adequately for doing it nor threatened with dire consequences for not doing it, they will find *internal* reasons for their behavior.

Suppose you dislike Woodrow Wilson and I want you to make a speech in his favor. The most efficient thing I can do is to pay you a lot of money for making the speech, or threaten to kill you if you don't. In either case, you will probably comply with my wish, but you won't change your attitude toward Wilson. If that were my goal, I would have to give you a *minimal* reward or threat. Then, in order not to appear absurd, you would have to seek additional reasons for your speech—this could lead you to find good things about Wilson and hence, to conclude that you really do like Wilson after all. Lying produces great attitude change only when the liar is undercompensated.

Festinger and J. Merrill Carlsmith asked college students to work on boring and repetitive tasks. Then the experimenters persuaded the students to lie about the work, to tell a fellow student that the task would be interesting and enjoyable. They offered half of their subjects $20 for telling the lie, and they offered the others only $1. Later they asked all subjects how much they had really liked the tasks.

The students who earned $20 for their lies rated the work as deadly dull, which it was. They experienced no dissonance: they lied, but they were well paid for that behavior. By contrast, students who got $1 decided that the tasks were rather enjoyable. The dollar was apparently enough to get them to tell the lie, but not enough to keep them from feeling that lying for so paltry a sum was foolish. To reduce dissonance, they decided that they hadn't lied after all; the task was fun.

Similarly, Carlsmith and I found that mild threats are more effective than harsh threats in changing a child's attitude about a forbidden object, in this case a delightful toy. In the severe-threat condition, children refrained from playing with the toys and had a good reason for refraining—the very severity of the threat provided ample justification for not playing with the toy. In the mild-threat condition, however, the children refrained from playing with the toy but when they asked themselves, "How come I'm not playing with the toy?" they did not have a superabundant justification (because the threat was not terribly severe). Accordingly, they provided additional justification in the form of convincing themselves that the attractive toy was really not very attractive and that they didn't really want to play with it very much in the first place. Jonathan Freedman extended our findings, and showed that severe threats do not have a lasting effect on a child's behavior. Mild threats, by contrast, can change behavior for many months.

Perhaps the most extraordinary example of insufficient justification occurred in India, where Jamuna Prasad analyzed the rumors that were circulated after a terrible earthquake in 1950. Prasad found that people in towns that were *not* in immediate danger were spreading rumors of impending doom from floods, cyclones, or unforeseeable calamities. Certainly the rumors could not help people feel more secure; why then perpetrate them? I believe that dissonance helps explain this phenomenon. The people were terribly frightened—after all, the neighboring villages had been destroyed—but they did not have ample excuse for their fear, since the earthquake had missed them. So they invented their own excuse; if a cyclone is on the way, it is reasonable to be afraid. Later, Durganand Sinha studied rumors in a town that had actually been destroyed. The people were scared, but they had good reason to be; they didn't need to seek additional justification for their terror. And their rumors showed no predictions of impending disaster and no serious exaggerations.

The decision to be cruel. The need for people to believe that they are kind and decent can lead them to say and do unkind and indecent things. After the National Guard killed four students at Kent State, several rumors quickly spread: the slain girls were pregnant, so their deaths spared their families from shame; the students were filthy and had lice on them. These rumors were totally untrue, but the townspeople were eager to believe them. Why? The local people were conservative, and infuriated at the radical behavior of some of the students. Many had hoped that the students would get their comeuppance. But death is an awfully severe penalty. The severity of this penalty outweighs and is dissonant with the "crimes" of the students. In these circumstances, any information that put the victims in a bad light reduces dissonance by implying, in effect, that it was good that the young people died. One high-school teacher even avowed that anyone with "long hair, dirty clothes, or [who goes] barefooted deserves to be shot."

Keith Davis and Edward Jones demonstrated the need to justify cruelty. They persuaded students to help them with an experiment, in the course of which the volunteers had to tell another student that he was a shallow, untrustworthy, and dull person. Volunteers managed to convince themselves that they didn't like the victim of their cruel analysis. They found him less attractive than they did before they had to criticize him.

Similarly, David Glass persuaded a group of subjects to deliver electric shocks to others. The subjects, again, decided that the victim must deserve the cruelty; they rated him as stupid, mean, etc. Then Glass went a step further. He found that a subject with high self-esteem was most likely to derogate the victim. This led Glass to conclude, ironically, that it is precisely because a person thinks he is nice that he decides that the person he has hurt is a rat. "Since nice guys like me don't go around hurting innocent people," Glass's subjects seemed to say, "you must have deserved it." But individuals who have *low* self-esteem do not feel the need to justify their behavior and derogate their victims; it is *consonant* for such persons to believe they have behaved badly. "Worthless people like me do unkind things."

Ellen Berscheid and her colleagues found another factor that limits the need to derogate one's victim: the victim's capacity to retaliate. If the person doing harm feels that the situation is balanced, that his victim will pay him back in coin, he has no need to justify his behavior. In Berscheid's experiment, which involved electric shocks, college students did not derogate or dislike the persons they shocked if they believed the victims could retaliate. Students who were led to believe that the victims would not be able to retaliate *did* derogate them. Her work suggests that soldiers may have a greater need to disparage civilian victims (because they can't retaliate) than military victims. Lt. William L. Calley, who considered the "gooks" at My Lai to be something less than human, would be a case in point.

Dissonance and the self-concept. On the basis of recent experiments, I have reformulated Festinger's original theory in terms of the self concept. That is, dissonance is most powerful when self-esteem is threatened. Thus the important aspect of dissonance is not "I said one thing and I believe another," but "I have misled people—and I am a truthful, nice person." Conversely, the cognitions, "I believe the task is dull," and "I told someone the task was interesting," are not dissonant for a psychopathic liar.

David Mettee and I predicted in a recent experiment that persons who had low opinions of themselves would be more likely to cheat than persons with high self-esteem. We assumed that if an average person gets a temporary blow to his self-esteem (by being jilted, say, or not getting a promotion), he will temporarily feel stupid and worthless, and hence do any number of stupid and worthless things—cheat at cards, bungle an assignment, break a valuable vase.

Mettee and I temporarily changed 45 female students' self-esteem. We gave one third of them positive feedback about a personality test they had taken (we said that they were interesting, mature, deep, etc.); we gave one third negative feedback (we said that they were relatively immature, shallow, etc.); and one third of the students got no information at all. Then all the students went on to participate in what they thought was an unrelated experiment, in which they gambled in a competitive game of cards. We arranged the situation so that the students could cheat and thereby win a considerable sum of money, or not cheat, in which case they were sure to lose.

The results showed that the students who had received blows to their self-esteem cheated far more than those who had gotten positive feedback about themselves. It may well be that low self-esteem is a critical antecedent of criminal or cruel behavior.

The theory of cognitive dissonance has proved useful in generating research; it has uncovered a wide range of data. In formal terms, however, it is a very sloppy theory. Its very simplicity provides both its greatest strength and its most serious weakness. That is, while the theory has generated a great deal of data, it has not been easy to define the limits of the theoretical statement, to determine the specific predictions that can be made. All too often researchers have had to resort to the very unscientific rule of thumb, "If you want to be sure, ask Leon."

Logic and psychologic. Part of the problem is that the theory does not deal with *logical* inconsistency, but *psychological* inconsistency. Festinger maintains that two cognitions are inconsistent if the opposite of one follows from the other. Strictly speaking, the information that smoking causes cancer does not make it illogical to smoke. But these cognitions produce dissonance because they do not make sense psychologically, assuming that the smoker does not want cancer.

One cannot always predict dissonance with accuracy. A man may admire Franklin Roosevelt enormously and discover that throughout his marriage FDR carried out a clandestine affair. If he places a high value on fidelity and he believes that great men are not exempt from this value, then he will experience dissonance. Then I can predict that he will either change his attitudes about Roosevelt or soften his attitudes about fidelity. But, he may believe that marital infidelity and political greatness are totally unrelated; if this were the case, he might simply shrug off these data without modifying his opinions either about Roosevelt or about fidelity.

Because of the sloppiness in the theory, several commentators have criticized a great many of the findings first uncovered by dissonance theory. These criticisms have served a useful purpose. Often, they have goaded us to perform more precise research, which in turn has led to a clarification of some of the findings which, ironically enough, has eliminated the alternative explanations proposed by the critics themselves.

For example, Alphonse and Natalia Chapanis argued that the "severe initiation" experiment could have completely different causes. It might be that the young women were not embarrassed at having to read sexual words, but rather were aroused, and their arousal in turn led them to rate the dull discussion group as interesting. Or, to the contrary, the women in the severe-initiation condition could have felt much sexual anxiety, followed by relief that the discussion was so banal. They associated relief with the group, and so rated it favorably.

So Harold Gerard and Grover Mathewson replicated our experiment, using electric shocks in the initiation procedure. Our original findings were supported— subjects who underwent severe shocks in order to join a discussion group rated that group more favorably than subjects who had undergone mild shocks. Moreover, Gerard and Mathewson went on to show that merely linking an electric shock with the group discussion (as in a simple conditioning experiment) did not produce greater liking for the group. The increase in liking for the group occurred only when subjects volunteered for the shock *in order to* gain membership in the group—just as dissonance theory would predict.

Routes to consonance. In the real world there is usually more than one way to squirm out of inconsistency. Laboratory experiments carefully control a person's alternatives, and the conclusions drawn may be misleading if applied to everyday situations. For example, suppose a prestigious university rejects a young Ph.D. for its one available teaching position. If she feels that she is a good scholar, she will experience dissonance. She can then decide that members of that department are narrow-minded and senile, sexist, and wouldn't recognize talent if it sat on their laps. Or she could decide that if they could reject someone as fine and intelligent as she, they must be extraordinarily brilliant. Both techniques will reduce dissonance, but note that they leave this woman with totally opposite opinions about professors at the university.

This is a serious conceptual problem. One solution is to specify the conditions under which a person will take one route to consonance over another. For example if a person struggles to reach a goal and fails, he may decide that the goal wasn't worth it (as Aesop's fox did) or that the effort was justified anyway (the fox got a lot of exercise in jumping for the grapes). My own research suggests that a person will take the first means when he has expended relatively little effort. But when he has put in a great deal of effort, dissonance will take the form of justifying the energy.

This line of work is encouraging. I do not think that it is very fruitful to demand to know what *the* mode of dissonance reduction is; it is more instructive to isolate the various modes that occur, and determine the optimum conditions for each.

Ignorance of absurdity. No dissonance theorist takes issue with the fact that people frequently work to get rewards. In our experiments, however, small rewards tend to be associated with greater attraction and greater attitude change. Is the reverse ever true?

Jonathan Freedman told college students to work on a dull task after first telling them a) their results would be of no use to him, since his experiment was basically over, or b) their results would be of great value to him. Subjects in the first condition were in a state of dissonance, for they had unknowingly agreed to work on a boring chore that apparently had no purpose. They reduced their dissonance by deciding that the task was enjoyable.

Then Freedman ran the same experiment with one change. He waited until the subjects finished the task to tell them whether their work would be important. In this study he found incentive effects: students told that the task was valuable enjoyed it more than those who were told that their work was useless. In short, dissonance theory does not apply when an individual performs an action in good faith without having any way of knowing it was absurd. When we agree to participate in an experiment we naturally assume that it is for a purpose. If we are informed afterward that it *had* no purpose, how were we to have known? In this instance we like the task better if it had an important purpose. But if we agree to perform it *knowing* that it had no purpose, we try to convince ourselves that it is an attractive task in order to avoid looking absurd.

Man cannot live by consonance alone. Dissonance reduction is only one of several motives, and other powerful drives can counteract it. If human beings had a pervasive, all-encompassing need to reduce all forms of dissonance, we would not grow, mature, or admit to our mistakes. We would sweep mistakes under the rug or, worse, turn the mistakes into virtues; in neither case would we profit from error.

But obviously people do learn from experience. They often do tolerate dissonance because the dissonant information has great utility. A person cannot ignore forever a leaky roof, even if that flaw is inconsistent with having spent a fortune on the house. As utility increases, individuals will come to prefer dissonance-arousing but useful information. But as dissonance increases, or when commitment is high, future utility and information tend to be ignored.

It is clear that people will go to extraordinary lengths to justify their actions. They will lie, cheat, live on the San Andreas Fault, accuse innocent bystanders of being vicious provocateurs, ignore information that might save their lives, and generally engage in all manner of absurd postures. Before we write off such behavior as bizarre, crazy, or evil, we would be wise to examine the situations that set up the need to reduce dissonance. Perhaps our awareness of the mechanism that makes us so often irrational will help turn Camus' observation on absurdity into a philosophic curiosity.

HOWARD LEVENTHAL
ROBERT SINGER
SUSAN JONES

Effects of Fear and Specificity of Recommendation Upon Attitudes and Behavior

Information alone seldom provides sufficient impetus to change attitudes or actions toward a given object (Cohen, 1957; Klapper, 1960; Rosenberg, 1956). The information must not only instruct the audience but must create motivating forces which induce attitude and behavioral change. Janis and Feshbach (1953, 1954) were among the first to explore the effects of information which arouses fear or avoidant motivation on the changing of attitudes. Their results indicated that high fear arousal produced less adherence to recommendations, presumably because high fear produced responses of defensive avoidance. Support for the finding of less persuasion with high- than with low-fear communications has also been presented by Goldstein (1959) and by Janis and Terwilliger (1962). However, in other recent studies evidence has accumulated which suggests the need to reevaluate the relationship between fear arousal and persuasion.

First, Berkowitz and Cottingham (1960) have demonstrated that, at relatively low levels, increments in fear may produce increased attitude change especially for subjects for whom the communication was less relevant. Leventhal and Niles (1964), and Niles (1964) have also found that fear arousal increases persuasion. They obtained a positive correlation between reported fear and intentions to act (Leventhal & Niles, 1964), and increases in intentions with increasingly powerful communications (Niles, 1964). These effects were found using stimuli considerably more vivid and frightening than those used in any of the earlier investigations. Thus, these experiments suggest that fear functions as a drive which promotes the acceptance of recommended actions, and, regardless of the absolute level of fear arousal used in any study, the communication which arouses more fear will be more persuasive.

There are a number of incidental factors that may account for the different results in these studies: for example, Janis and Feshbach's topic was dental health while lung cancer was the topic for Leventhal and Niles (1964) and Niles (1964); Janis and Feshbach (1953) used high-school students, Leventhal and Niles used people attending the New York City health exposition, and Niles used college students. However, while these factors could be responsible for the different outcomes, one variable which seems of particular importance is the availability of the recommended action. In their study, Janis and Feshbach (1953) suggested that fear arousal could lead to increased persuasion if the action was immediately available. In the Leventhal and Niles study, action was immediately available to all groups of subjects; that is, they could get an X ray, and, while stopping smoking may require concerted effort over a long period of time, it can be initiated immediately. In the Niles experiment the arousal of fear increased desire to take action principally for subjects who do *not* see themselves as v ulnerable to disease. Subjects who feel vulnerable to disease showed relatively small increases in willingness to take preventive action when made fearful. Their greater resistance to persuasion seemed to be related to their tendency to judge the recommendations to prevent lung cancer as ineffective. In addition, subjects high in vulnerability scored low on a scale of self-esteem that relates to seeing oneself as able to cope with the environment (Dabbs, 1962; Leventhal & Perloe, 1962). The findings suggest that when environmental conditions or the subject's dispositional characteristics make action seem highly possible and effective, fear will promote action and attitude change.

The present study was designed to provide additional data on this question. Fear-arousing and non-fear-arousing communications were used recommending a clear action (taking a tetanus shot) which is for all intents and purposes 100% effective. Thus, in line with our earlier findings (Leventhal & Niles, 1964; Niles, 1964), it was predicted that more attitude change and more action would be produced by the high-fear conditions. Second, an attempt was made to experimentally manipulate the perceived availability of the recommended action by giving some subjects a *specific plan* to guide their action. It was hypothesized that adherence to the recommended act would be greater among subjects possessing a specific plan. Finally, an interaction was expected between fear and specificity: highly motivated subjects, that is, those exposed to the fear-arousing materials, were expected to show the greatest attitude and behavioral compliance when a clear plan for action was given to them.

Another question which was raised with regard to these divergent findings was the kind of emotion evoked by the stimulus. Careful attention has been given to discriminating levels of fear arousal, and to the possibility that fear-arousing communications arouse aggression as well as anxiety (Janis & Feshbach, 1953; Robbins, 1962). Other studies in the current program (Leventhal, Jacobs, & Trembly, 1963 unpublished) suggest that fear may be experienced with many other emotions. Therefore, several items were used to assess emotional arousal with the hope that these would provide added information on the nature of the fear associated with persuasion.

METHOD

Design and Subjects

The experimental design incorporated two levels of fear and two levels of information on the availability of the recommended action. Additional control groups were run to clarify questions unanswered by the factorial design. These are described in the Results section. Booklets were used to present the fear-arousing stimuli and to deliver the recommendation for inoculation. A questionnaire was completed after reading the booklet.

All subjects were seniors at Yale University and were selected by taking every other name from the class list. Initial contacts were by mail, and specific appointments for the experimental session were made by phone. No inducements were offered for participating in the study and subjects only knew that they were to evaluate a public health pamphlet. All contacts with the subjects were made by using the name of the John Slade Ely Center and the University Department of Health.

Subjects were run individually and in a building 2.5 blocks away from the University Health Service. Conducting the study in the University Health Building would have made it far too simple for subjects to get shots. When a student entered the experiment, he was given a pamphlet and told: "Would you please read this pamphlet carefully. When you are finished, please bring it back to me and I will give you a questionnaire to fill out about it." After reading the pamphlet and filling out the questionnaire the students departed. There was minimal conversation with the experimenters.

Experimental Manipulations

The booklets were composed of two sections: a "fear section," dealing with the causes of tetanus and including a case history of a tetanus patient; and a "recommendation section," dealing with the importance of shots in preventing the disease. There were two forms of each section: high fear and low fear, specific recommendation and nonspecific recommendation, making four pamphlets.

Fear manipulation. The same facts about the disease were present in both fear levels. Three devices were used to manipulate fear: coupling frightening or nonfrightening facts with basic information on tetanus; emotion-provoking or emotion-nonprovoking adjectives to describe the causes of tetanus, the tetanus case, and the treatment of tetanus; and including different kinds of photographs to illustrate the pamphlet. For example, in the high-fear booklet the incidence was described as being as high as that for polio, and the bacteria were described as "under your finger-nails, in your mouth" etc., and as literally surrounding the reader. The low treatment simply stated these facts in a nondramatic way. The aim of the high-fear booklet was to create a strong feeling of personal vulnerability.

A case history, constructed from reports in medical journals, was presented to make vivid the severity of the disease. In the high-fear condition, the wording was constructed to create a clear image of the patient's symptoms (convulsions; his back arched upwards, his head whipped back, mouth slammed shut, etc.). Photographs were also included which showed a child in a tetanic convulsion and bedridden patients. Three of the photographs were in color. One illustrated a gaping tracheotomy wound, the others depicted patients with urinary catheters, tracheotomy drainage, and nasal tubes. The treatments illustrated are actually used in the therapy of severe cases of tetanus. They proved to be quite startling to the subjects.

In the low-fear condition, colored photographs were omitted as were the pictures of the hospital patients and equipment. Two photographic copies of drawings of the facial expressions found in tetanus were included. The case history was described in unemotional terms and, whereas the patient died in the high-fear booklet, he survived in the low-fear case. Otherwise, the booklets were factually identical and were approximately of equal length (7 mimeographed pages).

Plan for action. After the presentation of the case history, all pamphlets contained identical paragraphs on the importance of controlling tetanus by inoculation. This point was illustrated by statistics which clearly demonstrated that shots are the only powerful and fully adequate protection against the disease. In addition, it was stated that the University was making shots available free of charge to all interested students.

For the high availability treatment additional material was included urging the students to take a shot and providing a detailed set of suggestions as to how he could do this within the context of his daily activities. The points made can be paraphrased as follows: The University Health Service expressed the hope that all students would take the necessary action to protect themselves, the location of the University Health Service was described and the times that shots were available were listed, precisely where to go and what to do to get a shot was indicated, a map was presented of the campus with the University Health Building clearly circled, and a request was made that each student review his weekly schedule to locate a time when he would pass by the University Health so that he could stop in to be inoculated. The specific recommendation, then, is essentially a detailed plan to make the subjects rehearse the various steps needed to take the suggested action. Thus, the low availability groups are told of the effectiveness of shots and that shots are available. The high availability groups have this information plus additional material helping them to plan and to review the specific steps needed to take shots. It should be made clear, however, that since the subjects were seniors, they *all* knew the location of student health, and it is extremely likely that they had all visited the building at some time in the past. The plan, therefore, would simply make salient that which is *already* known rather than providing new information.

Response Measures

Two types of responses were observed for all subjects participating in this experiment. Immediately after the communication all subjects completed a questionnaire on which they reported their attitudes, feelings, and reactions to the experimental setting. In addition, a record was obtained of all subjects taking a tetanus inoculation.

Questionnaire measures. The questionnaire included items on: prior inoculation against tetanus; intentions to be inoculated; attitude regarding the importance of inoculation; judgments of the likelihood of contracting tetanus and its severity *if* contracted; emotions experienced while reading the communications; and reactions to, and interest in, the communications. The items used will be reported in the Results section.

Behavioral measures. The records of all participants were checked by student health authorities and a count was made of the subjects in each condition who were inoculated. The dates for inoculation were also obtained. Those students who were inoculated at the close of the semester, more than 1 month *after* the study termination, were not included in the inoculation count. It is common practice for students taking trips abroad to receive inoculations at the end of the semester.

The questionnaire also included a variety of items on many diseases besides tetanus. The items were included principally to suggest to the subject that the investigation was on *health,* rather than an attempt to coerce him into taking an inoculation. Thus, items asked about prior shots for polio, typhoid, and flu, and feelings of susceptibility to and the severity of six other diseases.

RESULTS

Fear Arousal

. . . The fear manipulation was highly successful. Subjects report feeling greater fright, tension, nervousness, anxiety, discomfort, anger, and nausea in the high- than in the low-fear treatment.[1] Incidental observations indicated that the high-fear booklets were indeed distressing. All subjects were extremely intent and focused on the materials; some appeared pale, others shaken and many made other sounds and gestures indicating distress. These treatment effects were significant whether or not subjects had been inoculated against the disease. . . .

Attitudes. A general question ("How important do you think it is to get a tetanus shot?"—13-point scale) was used to assess the degree of importance which subjects attached to tetanus shots. Another question was used to assess his intentions to avail himself of inoculation ("Do you intend to get a tetanus shot?"— 13-point scale). Regardless of prior inoculation, subjects in the high-fear conditions feel that shots are more important than do subjects in the low-fear conditions. . . .

For the intention question, there were two important trends. First, subjects who had had a shot within the last 2 years scored lower than those who had not had a shot. In addition, there was a trend for subjects in the high-fear treatment, regardless of inoculation status, to express stronger intentions to get shots than did subjects in the low-fear condition. . . .

Action. During the 4–6 week period between the experimental sessions and the end of classes 9 of the 59 eligible subjects went for shots. Of the 9, 4 were in the high fear specific, 4 in the low fear specific, 1 in the low fear nonspecific, and none in the high fear nonspecific. A comparison between the 27.6% of specific takers and the 3.3% of nonspecific takers is significant. Subjects in the specific condition were more likely to get shots. Thus, attitudes and actions appear to be affected by different factors. While a low fear nonspecific communication has little influence on either attitudes or actions, fear-arousing messages affect attitudes regardless of specificity of plan, and recommendations using specific plans affect actions regardless of the level of fear.[2]

Recommendations-only control. Because the specificity factor did not interact with arousal as predicted, it was unclear whether the arousal of fear was a necessary condition for action. Specific information may be a sufficient condition for the occurrence of action. To test this possibility a control group was run of subjects exposed only to specific information. This group was run the following year and a time difference is involved which was absent in the other comparisons.

The procedures for contacting and dealing with subjects were identical to those used in the four experimental groups. Of the 30 eligible subjects in the group not one availed himself of the opportunity to obtain an inoculation. Thus, specific information alone does not seem to be sufficient to influence actions or attitudes. . . .

Action base line. The date of tetanus inoculation for a sample of 60 students was also obtained to record the base rate of inoculation seeking during the experimental period. None of the students (eligibles or ineligibles) were inoculated during that period. Therefore, while the rate of shot taking was not high in the specific experimental treatments (27.6%), it is obviously greater than the base rate.

Mediating Factors

Variables associated with attitude change. In addition to the fear measures, several other measures of reported feelings varied in the same manner as did attitudes toward tetanus inoculations. Subjects in the high-fear condition felt that tetanus was more serious than did subjects in the low fear treatments. Subjects in the high-fear conditions also reported more concern about getting tetanus, more worry about the way they had treated cuts, and reported more irritation directed at the photographs than did subjects in the low-fear condition. High-fear subjects were also more certain than low-fear subjects that the pictures used enhanced the pamphlet. These effects were significant regardless of the subject's prior vaccination history. As with the prior measures of emotional arousal, being vaccinated is no protection against the distressing emotions which appear to be elicited by the pamphlet per se. It is also interesting to note that the arousal of aggression (anger and irritation) occurs in the same conditions as opinion change. Therefore, either the annoyance and irritation prompted by the communication and the illustrations does not minimize their effectiveness or was not of sufficient strength to arouse resistance to persuasion.

Variables associated with action. In examining data relating to action, we shall compare the means only for those subjects *eligible* for vaccination. Subjects receiving specific recommendations tended to report stronger feelings of susceptibility to tetanus. . . .

Subjects receiving the specific recommendation reported feeling *less* nauseated than those getting the general recommendation. Thus, while nausea was increased by the high-fear booklets, it was depressed by the specific recommendation. In addition, the specific subjects reported more interest in the communication. It seems, therefore, that the correlates of action are a greater interest in the outer environment and a lessening of what may be potentially inhibiting visceral reactions, though fear itself is high.

Takers versus nontakers. The analyses to this point appear to indicate that fear arousal is sufficient to influence attitudes while both arousal stimuli and specific recommendations are needed for action. Since an increase in the level of fear does not increase the rate of action taking, it may appear that actions and attitudes are no longer related to one another. To obtain further evidence on this question a post hoc comparison was made of takers and nontakers on the questionnaire measures. The only values that approached significance were for anxiety, fright, importance of shots, and feelings that the illustrations enhanced the pamphlet. Thus, shot takers, who are mainly in the specific recommendation condition, not only differ from nontakers in the *general* recommendation condition in the ways discussed before, but they *also* show higher scores on the above measures. Attitude and arousal are related, therefore, to action.

DISCUSSION

The data lend mixed support to the hypotheses. As in the earlier experiments (Leventhal & Niles, 1964; Niles, 1964) fear-arousing communications increased attitudinal acceptance of the recommendations, in this case, favoring tetanus inoculations. Supporting evidence for the facilitating effect of fear on attitude change can also be found in Weiss, Rawson, and Pasamanick (1963) where high scores on dispositional anxiety facilitated opinion change. However, these results are contradictory to the data reported in two studies of acceptance of recommendations for dental hygiene (Goldstein, 1959; Janis & Feshbach, 1953) where increases in fear level appeared to be associated with resistance to the recommendation. As suggested earlier (Leventhal & Niles, 1964; Niles, 1964), the discrepancy between the experiments may relate to differences in the perceived effectiveness of the recommended actions. Thus, tetanus inoculations are far more effective as a preventive measure for tetanus than toothbrushing is for dental disease. No matter how one cares for his teeth, he is still likely to have some cavities. On the other hand, the incidence of tetanus is practically zero for protected people, and for lung cancer, the incidence is extremely low for nonsmokers. Therefore, when fear is aroused it may be critical to present an extremely effective (or effective-appearing) recommendation to minimize the possibility that subjects will leave the communication setting still in need of reassurance and thus open to counterpersuasion.

It has also been suggested (Weiss, et al., 1963) that fear will have opposite effects upon attitude change depending upon the subjects initial position. When subjects hold competing opinions, the increased drive level could be predicted to strengthen the incorrect responses more than the correct ones (e.g., Farber & Spence, 1953). In the present experiment, it is clear from the control-group data that subjects are initially favorable toward shots. It is possible, however, that subjects in the dental hygiene study (Janis & Feshbach, 1953, 1954) were negative toward some of the recommended practices and that fear strengthened the "incorrect" responses. However, this argument loses some strength as smokers in the lung cancer studies also showed more acceptance of recommendations with high levels of fear (Leventhal & Niles, 1964; Niles, 1964). Still, the actions recommended in the current setting are preventive, simple to take, and relatively painless.

Of greater interest, however, is that specific plans for action influence behavior while level of fear does not. But specific information alone is insufficient as action is influenced only when specific information is combined with one of the fear-arousing communications. The group exposed only to specific information is generally quite similar to an unexposed control for reported emotions and very similar to the unexposed control's attitudes concerning the importance of shots. Therefore, while emotional arousal is necessary for attitudinal and behavioral change, it seems to be sufficient for the former and only necessary for the latter. Does this mean that behavior and attitudes are entirely independent of one another? In our first study on lung cancer (Leventhal & Niles, 1964) a very high correspondence was found between intentions to get X rays and actually having one taken. In addition, X-ray takers reported more fear than nontakers. In the present study, the comparisons of takers and nontakers revealed a similar effect, that is, the takers regarded shots as more important (though intentions were *not* stronger) than the nontakers, and the takers had higher scores on some of the fear indices. Neither of these experiments shows significant differences between fear treatments for the action measures. If one reexamines the setting for the lung cancer study, it soon becomes apparent that subjects in all conditions were given a highly specific plan for taking X rays; that is, while delivering the recommendation for X rays, "the experimenter pointed directly at the X-ray unit which was down the corridor from the 'theatre.' The unit was clearly visible to all *S*s . . . [Leventhal & Niles, 1964, p. 462]." Therefore, the effects on action are extremely similar in both studies and both studies produced a relationship between attitude and actions, though the relationship is weaker in the present experiment.

Although there is a positive relationship between attitudes and behavior, the present data show that the independent variables have different effects upon attitudes and actions. Specific information for taking action does not in itself produce favorable attitudes but does establish a link between attitude and action. What is the nature of this link that permits the attitude to be translated into action? In certain situations, for example, those where the action is immediately possible, specificity may entail the elimination of barriers to action (Leventhal & Niles, 1964). However, in situations such as the present, where the actions were carried out several days subsequent to the communication, other aspects of the manipulations, for example, rehearsing the action, making a decision to act, as well as simple information on how to make the response, could be responsible for the link. An examination of questionnaire effects associated with the specificity manipulation tentatively suggests that specificity altered the subject's emotional state. Thus, subjects receiving the specific plan for action were somewhat more interested in the materials and reported significantly less nausea which can be interpreted to mean that the specific information eliminated various inward-turning inhibitory features of the fear state. Several authors have distinguished between inhibitory or depressive fear states and excitatory fear states (Bull, 1962; Kollar, 1961; Shands, 1955) and have associated striving and protective activity with the latter. However, while it is clear that these affective states can be distinguished in communication studies (Leventhal et al., 1963 unpublished) the study of their relationship to persuasion and action has just begun. The present data do suggest, however, that providing a clear possibility or plan for action can reduce the inhibitory properties of certain fear states.

Regardless of the exact process by which specific information links the evaluative and action components, it is still puzzling why more action did not occur in that condition where the attitude change was greatest. There is a very simple hypothesis that can be suggested to account for this. If the effects of fear dissipate rapidly with time, then it may be that the failure to find more action in the high-fear treatments reflects the fact that attitudes were measured *at* the time of exposure while action took place *after* the fear-induced attitude effects had been dissipated (Leventhal & Niles, 1965). If this is the case, no relationship between attitude change and behavior could possibly be expected.

NOTES

1. The self-reports of emotion were obtained by asking "While you were reading the pamphlet did you find that you had any of the following feelings?" A series of adjectives with 21-point scales followed this statement.
2. Seven additional eligible subjects took shots following the close of classes. These were distributed as follows: four specific (two high and two low) and three nonspecific (two high and one low). Adding in these cases gives 41% specific, 13% nonspecific taking shots. Among the ineligible subjects two in the high fear nonspecific conditon took shots. It appears that most of these subjects were receiving shots as part of a series in preparation for travel.

REFERENCES

Berkowitz, L., & Cottingham, D. R. The interest value and relevance of fear arousing communications. *Journal of Abnormal and Social Psychology*, 1960, **60**, 37–43.

Bull, Nina. *The body and its mind: An introduction to attitude psychology*. New York: Las Americas, 1962.

Cohen, A. R. Need for cognition and order of communication as determinants of opinion change. In C. I. Hovland et al. (Eds.), *The order of presentation in persuasion*. New Haven: Yale Univer. Press, 1957. Pp. 79–97.

Dabbs, J. Self esteem, coping and influence. Unpublished doctoral dissertation, Yale University, 1962.

Farber, I. E., & Spence, K. W. Complex learning and conditioning as a function of anxiety. *Journal of Experimental Psychology*, 1953, **45**, 120–125.

Goldstein, M. J. The relationship between coping and avoiding behavior and response to fear-arousing propaganda. *Journal of Abnormal and Social Psychology*, 1959, **58**, 247–252.

Janis, I. L., & Feshbach, S. Effects of fear-arousing communications. *Journal of Abnormal and Social Psychology*, 1953, **48**, 78–92.

Janis, I. L., & Feshbach, S. Personality differences associated with responsiveness to fear-arousing communications. *Journal of Personality*, 1954, **23**, 154–166.

Janis, I. L., & Terwilliger, R. F. An experimental study of psychological resistances to fear arousing communications. *Journal of Abnormal and Social Psychology*, 1962, **65**, 403–410.

Klapper, J. T. *The effects of mass communications*. New York: Free Press of Glencoe, 1960.

Kollar, E. J. Psychological stress: A re-evaluation. *Journal of Nervous and Mental Disease*, 1961, **132**, 382–396.

Leventhal, H., & Niles, P. A field experiment on fear-arousal with data on the validity of questionnaire measures. *Journal of Personality*, 1964, **32**, 459–479.

Leventhal, H., & Niles, P. Persistence of influence for varying durations of exposure to threat stimuli. *Psychological Reports*, 1965, **16**, 223–233.

Leventhal, H., & Perloe, S. I. A relationship between self-esteem and persuasibility. *Journal of Abnormal and Social Psychology*, 1962, **64**, 385–388.

Niles, P. Two personality measures associated with responsiveness to fear-arousing communications. Unpublished doctoral dissertation, Yale University, 1964.

Robbins, P. R. An application of the method of successive intervals to the study of fear-arousing information. *Psychological Reports*, 1962, **11**, 757–760.

Rosenberg, M. J. Cognitive structure and attitudinal effect. *Journal of Abnormal and Social Psychology*, 1956, **53**, 367–372.

Shands, H. C. An outline of the process of recovery from severe trauma. *American Medical Association Archives of Neurology and Psychiatry*, 1955, **73**, 403–409.

Walker, Helen M., & Lev, J. *Statistical inference*. New York: Holt, 1953.

Weiss, R. F., Rawson, H. E., & Pasamanick, B. Argument strength, delay of argument, and anxiety in the "conditioning" and "selective learning" of attitudes. *Journal of Abnormal and Social Psychology*, 1963, **67**, 157–165.

Every man, wherever he goes, is encompassed by a cloud of comforting convictions, which move with him like flies on a summer day.

Bertrand Russell

From *Sceptical Essays*, p. 28, published by W. W. Norton & Company, Inc., 1928.

Conforming and Nonconforming

Every day, each one of us is confronted by such decisions as whether to go along with the group we're in, whether to act in the same way that a friend is acting, and whether to comply with the demands of a boss, teacher, or political leader—in short, whether or not to conform. Much of the time, we prefer not to appear terribly different or deviant from those around us; we simply prefer to go along and get along with the people we are associated with. Nonetheless, there are other times when we feel the necessity of resisting the pressures and going it alone.

When individuals find themselves in conflict with another individual or a group they belong to, they must find a way of resolving the conflict between what they believe is right and the way others would have them act. They may choose to be different and remain independent of the group's actions, they may reject the group and act in the very opposite manner, or they may yield to the group and thereby conform to the pressures upon them. But, even if they conform, they may do so for many different reasons—perhaps to avoid looking different or foolish, perhaps because they believe that the group is trustworthy, or perhaps because they simply believe that the others' information is better or more reliable. Whatever decision is made, social psychologists have come to realize that this process of deciding is not a simple one; the issues involved concern the very basis of the individual's relationship with the social environment.

The conversation that follows is with Herbert C. Kelman, Professor of Social Ethics at Harvard University. Dr. Kelman is a social psychologist widely known and respected for his social activism. Our conversation began with a discussion of general issues concerning the nature of social influence, especially Dr. Kelman's model of the three processes of influence. From there, we proceeded to speak about obedience to authority and the place of individuals in following or questioning the pressures and demands placed upon them by political systems.

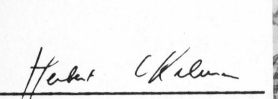

A CONVERSATION WITH HERBERT C. KELMAN

Harvard University

KRUPAT: *Let me begin by asking you to react to some rather strongly worded statements I've seen used in psychology textbooks. How do you feel about statements such as "Man is a straw in the wind" or "People are putty in the hands of others"?*

KELMAN: I guess I would consider these to be incomplete statements, for two main reasons. One is that I don't subscribe to the idea that there is simply a one-sided relationship between the individual and his social environment. When we think of a human being, we think of an interaction between the self and various social forces, various kinds of social influences. It is not a one-sided interaction, but one in which the person is trying to express and become something and is developing himself in relationship to those external forces. So, I view the statements as incomplete because they imply a totally passive, empty organism which is then written upon and molded by outside forces, whereas I think much more in terms of a process of interaction and negotiation between the person and society.

My second reason for considering these statements incomplete is that social influence is typically a reciprocal process, not only between self and society in general, but also between the different people involved in any given interaction. In every influence situation, not only is A influencing B, but B is also influencing A. Now, there are differences between situations depending, for instance, on the status of the individuals involved, their personality characteristics, the kind of influence being used, or the context of the interaction. There are some interactions that are much more one-sided than others, and these may well be captured by the metaphors you cited. But, these are special cases; they are not necessarily the governing reality.

KRUPAT: *OK, given this reciprocal process, just why does one individual* choose to accept influence from another? What motivates the person to conform rather than nonconform?

KELMAN: I shall use *conformity* in the broadest sense—in the sense of going along—for whatever reason—with the influence a person is being subjected to, meeting the demands, requests, or suggestions conveyed to him, or following the socially expected behavior. I suppose the most natural way for me to answer is in terms of my own work in which, as you know, I have tried to distinguish three processes of social influence: compliance, identification, and internalization. The three processes can be seen as representing three different types of motives or types of concerns, although the *specific* motivations underlying conforming behavior or the acceptance of social influence in each case may cover the entire range of human motives one could think of.

In the case of compliance, the person's concern is with achieving a particular kind of social effect which is controlled by the other, that is, by the person or group exerting influence over him. In this case, the person presumably conforms or, in other words, accepts influence, as a way of manipulating the response of the other person or the group—as a way of assuring that he will get the reward or approval he wants to get, or will avoid the punishment or disapproval he hopes to avoid. The specific motives might be quite different, depending on the nature of the rewards and punishments at issue. They might be connected with basic motives such as food, survival, or sex, or they might be related to certain status or security concerns.

KRUPAT: *So, compliance gets us something which may be quite material: a raise in pay, a pat on the back, or a kiss on the cheek. What, then, is involved with identification?*

KELMAN: As I've put it, and I'll explain this a bit more clearly, the person accepts influence here to establish or maintain a satisfying self-defining relationship to the other. Basically, the person is concerned not so much with what the other can directly give him or withhold from him, but with maintaining a particular kind of relationship to the other; conforming or accepting influence, in the case of identification, is a condition for maintaining that relationship. The relationship may be one that I call *classical identification*, where it is important for the person to be like the other—for instance, when the child identifies with the parent or when a person identifies strongly with a group that has personal meaning for him. Alternatively, the relationship may be one that I call *reciprocal-role identification*, which involves a more instrumental kind of process. In this case, it's not so much that the person wants to be *like* the other, but that he wants to meet the expectations of another person in order to maintain a reciprocal-role relationship that matters to him.

KRUPAT: *So, in compliance you are concerned about reward or punishment; in identification you are concerned about your relationship to the other; then, how about internalization?*

KELMAN: The process I call *internalization* refers to a situation where a person conforms, or let me use the more neutral-sounding term "accepts influence from another," because he finds the particular content of the behavior or attitude being offered to be consistent with his own values. That is, he finds this behavior congenial to his own self-image or congruent with his own value system. The person sees the other as essentially a source of information, useful from the point of view of maximizing the achievement of his own values.

KRUPAT: *Let me stop you a second and ask you something before we go any further. Almost every time you've used the word* conformity *you've said "or accepts social influence." There seems to be something about that word that makes you rephrase it. As you've described all three of your processes of influence, they seem quite rational and reasonable for any person. But then, why does the word* conformity, *which applies to these processes, seem to carry such a negative connotation?*

KELMAN: The reason why I stop and rephrase it each time is related to my own experience with the term *conformity*. I originally referred to my "three processes of influence" as "three processes of conformity." I later decided that this was not the ideal term and changed it. The reason for doing so was that the word *conformity* has acquired certain special connotations, particularly in common usage, but also to a certain extent when used by social psychologists. It carries the connotation of conformity for conformity's sake, or else of conformity as a personality characteristic describing "a person who doesn't have a mind of his own." To some extent, what I've described as the process of identification comes closest to carrying that connotation. Some people may see this process as reflecting a *need* to conform, or an overconcern with being like others or not deviating, although this was not my intention.

KRUPAT: *To me, there has always been the implication that in "conforming" the person would be willing to do something wrong, to say something he knows to be incorrect, just to go along with the group—almost a "blind" conformity.*

KELMAN: I agree. This is, of course, true in some, but not in all, influence situations. Therefore, I prefer to use a term which is more general, one that would include this situation, as well as other situations in which a person goes along for an entirely different set of reasons.

KRUPAT: *I assume you mean that accepting influence in no way diminishes the individual. He is not necessarily less of a person; he has lost no integrity when he, in the broadest sense, conforms to others.*

KELMAN: Exactly. In and of itself, it certainly does not diminish him. A great deal depends on what the circumstances are, how he conforms, and so on. This holds true for each of the three processes I've described, even though the descriptions inevitably carry differential value implications. This is very hard to avoid; internalization sounds like the most mature kind of process, and compliance sounds, in a sense, very opportunistic.

KRUPAT: *It certainly does sound much more acceptable to be seeking knowledge than to be seeking money or approval.*

KELMAN: Yes, I would say that the *capacity* to engage in internalization is something that does represent a higher developmental stage, but even when one has reached that stage, the necessity of engaging in compliance and identification remains a fact of life. One cannot exist in society without complying; it's just a matter of how and when one does it.

KRUPAT: *Even though you say that it's a matter of how and when, I do think that many people are quite upset at the extent of conformity we find in laboratory studies. We place the person in the lab, set up a situation in which he disagrees with a group, or is ordered to do something against his beliefs by an authority, and then we see how he reacts. And, what we find is that he goes along to an extent greater than many would have believed.*

KELMAN: Let me first respond to that statement from a methodological standpoint. The model of research you describe is quite typical; it is one that implies a passive individual only able to react to outside forces without being able to influence them. This is a popular model because it's very difficult to do research in which you allow a truly reciprocal process to take place; reciprocal kinds of processes create problems from the point of view of experimental control. But, one of the consequences is that we may not be simulating reality very well, or we may be simulating only a special kind of reality. It can be argued, of course, that the way society is structured, people really are heavily controlled under most circumstances and are really very passive. I don't think this is universally true but, insofar as it is true, one could argue that what happens in the lab does not provide that distorted a picture of a great deal of social life.

But even so, there is still another issue: What about the potentiality for other kinds of social behavior? In terms of human potentiality, the problem is that much of what goes on in the laboratory does not represent the full range very well. We need to develop different kinds of research models that allow for greater spontaneity in subject behavior, greater initiative, and a greater degree of reciprocity than our current lab models permit.

KRUPAT: *I agree with you, but couldn't one argue that once the subject is in the lab, he still has the option of going along or not, which he has the right to exercise? The opportunity may be limited, but he is allowed to talk back; he is allowed to send messages. In the obedience research of Milgram, which is discussed in the readings in this section, subjects are ordered by the experimenter to shock another individual, even though that individual appears to be in great pain and distress. It would seem as if the option to refuse and walk out is there, but that people have difficulty availing themselves of it. Do you feel that a laboratory situation such as Milgram's represents a sort of reality?*

KELMAN: This is an issue about which there is considerable debate. My own feeling is that the Milgram experiment does adequately simulate certain kinds of social relationships—namely, relationships between authorities and subordinates—and that these are fairly common and certainly very important relationships. So I do think that there are real-life counterparts to the kind of situation Milgram developed. Now, within this situation, as within any kind of authority situation, there is the option for the individual, as you say, to refuse to obey. But, the situation is so structured that to do so is very difficult. To disobey in a situation in which you are dealing with legitimate authority requires a readiness on the part of the individual to challenge the legitimacy of the authority. As long as the authority is legitimate, the individual feels *obligated* to obey him and feels that the other person has the *right* to expect his obedience.

The case of the Milgram experiment differs from the case of political authority in the sense that the experimenter has a very limited authority; it exists only insofar as the individual is willing to subject himself to it. But, within this limited laboratory context, the subject has, in a sense, made a contract with the experimenter and, according to the terms of that contract, the experimenter calls the shots and tells the subject what he wants him to do. So, in that situation, to say "I won't do this" is equivalent to saying "I'm going to break my contract," and the subject can do that only by challenging the wisdom of the experimenter's judgment, the legitimacy of his demands— in short, his authority. And that is something which is difficult for anyone to do, and it is more difficult for some people than for others.

KRUPAT: *But, in fact, when you nonconform in any situation, aren't you really challenging the source of those pressures? It may not be the legitimacy of the source; it may only be the validity of the information. It would seem that in any situation to disobey or to nonconform requires one to say, "I choose to challenge you. I choose to reject."*

KELMAN: There is a difference, and this has to do precisely with the distinction between *nonconformity* and *disobedience*. The term *obedience* implies an obligation. When a holdup man comes to you with a gun saying, "Turn over your money," and you do, one might say you're obeying, but I think that would be an imprecise use of the term. You are complying with his coercive demands because it just would not be smart to do otherwise, but you are not obeying.

The term "obedience to law," for example, implies that you have an obligation to obey, an obligation to follow. You're not just going along because you've decided it's wiser to do so; you're doing it because the other has the right to make certain demands and you have the obligation to meet them. By contrast, the more standard kind of conformity or influence situation is one in which we are dealing with preferential choices.

Even in the holdup situation I described, the person complies because he *prefers* to do it in the sense that, while he has every right to refuse, it's in his best interest not to refuse. Now, what makes an authority situation different is that it is one in which a nonchoice element predominates. And, therefore, the kind of challenge it takes to say "No" is in many ways a more fundamental challenge. You are really challenging the basic way in which the other has presented himself. He has said he is an authority and you say, "No, you're not an authority; you don't have the right to tell me to do that." In other cases, I agree, there are also challenges involved, but they are more specific. When you challenge the way a person has presented himself, it requires a complete redefinition of the situation.

KRUPAT: *Now that I think of it, my sixth-grade teacher never did say to* *me "How dare you nonconform!" She always said "How dare you dis-obey!" But then, where does obedience begin; why do individuals accept a person's legitimacy in the first place? Is there something inherent in the relationship between a parent and a child, a citizen and his government, which makes them obey, makes them feel they have no choice? Is this the type of "blind" conformity we were talking about before?*

KELMAN: My answer to that has to be a bit long and complicated. To begin with, I want to distinguish between authority and legitimacy, on the one hand, and unquestioning obedience to authority, on the other. I happen to believe in the importance and necessity of authority in any kind of social system, but I do not believe in *unquestioned* authority. So I do not want to identify accept-ance of authority with this kind of blind or unquestioning obedience. This may be one way of reacting to authority, and we have evidence that it is a fairly common way, but it is not necessarily the *only* way.

A major reason why authority exists in social systems is that it would be difficult to run a system without it. Take the political system, for example. In order to administer complex institutions effectively, to allocate resources and adjudicate competing interests equitably, and to manage international rela-tions dependably, the government must be able to assume that its demands—within certain specified limits—will be met, even if they do not correspond with the short-term preferences of every citizen. This, in turn, implies that the authorities must be trusted—which is really, to a large extent, what is meant by *legitimate* authority. If the system is to operate smoothly, a certain degree of credit or trust must be extended to people in responsible positions, and these people can then proceed, within limits, to make demands upon others without having to persuade or coerce them at every step. This lends a degree of predictability, a degree of stability to the social order. But, that trust has to be earned, and so does the continuation of that trust. Once someone has been put in a position of authority, he has to act within certain constraints in order to maintain the trust of system members. *Legitimacy* implies the use of power within specified limits, rather than in arbitrary fashion. If a leader abuses his authority, if he goes beyond the limits of what he is allowed to do by virtue of his position, he must be held accountable. And this clearly calls for a readiness, among system members, to question authority—to challenge policies and demands that exceed the bounds of legitimacy.

KRUPAT: *Yet, as you've said, the evidence is that for a great many individuals authority goes unquestioned. Where and how does the indi-vidual come to both respect, and also potentially to question, authority?*

KELMAN: From the point of view of the individual, this is something that has to be learned. Acceptance of authority itself presupposes a fairly advanced stage of moral development, which recognizes the need for certain kinds of rules and mechanisms in the society that make it possible to balance the interests of individuals in various segments of the society, and to coordi-nate complex social processes so that everyone's rights will be protected and needs will be met. But questioning of authority calls for a *higher* stage of moral development, which recognizes that—even though there is a need for such rules and mechanisms, which imply delegating authority to certain people and the obligation of individuals to obey laws and meet authoritative demands even when they are not personally convenient—these rules and mechanisms cannot be justified as ends in themselves. They have to be justified by reference to certain higher principles, which means essentially that the person also has an obligation to evaluate and question authority.

Now, disobedience of laws or authoritative demands is something that, in my view, ought not to be undertaken lightly; it ought not to be done simply because you find a particular law inconvenient or uncongenial to your own interests. But, under special circumstances, when you feel that a higher principle demands it, the right to disobey—in fact, the *duty* to disobey—is in my opinion a very crucial one.

KRUPAT: *It's interesting to see how we've started off discussing issues surrounding individual conformity on a small scale and now we've moved to questions of disobedience between an individual and his government. Is it possible for us to tie these different issues together at this point?*

KELMAN: In my own thinking about social influence, I have moved from initially looking at it largely from the point of view of interpersonal influence to looking at it from the point of view of the relationship of the individual to larger social systems. My model of social influence, which we talked about earlier, was originally concerned with the direct influence of A over B, but more and more I have come to see it as conceptualizing the way in which an individual relates himself to the various social systems to which he belongs. In fact, I have increasingly come to regard social influence as a concept that is precisely designed to bridge the two levels of analysis which social psychology is intended to bridge, the individual and the social system levels. As my scheme has developed, I have come to see the three processes as corresponding to different components of the social system through which the person is integated in it. Compliance corresponds to the *rules* of the system, identification to the *roles* of the system, and internalization to the *values* of the system. One can then distinguish, as I've been trying to do in my recent work, among three different patterns of orientation to the system focusing, respectively, on system rules, roles, or values.

I think that we can now come back, from this point of view, to the question of blind conformity and unquestioning obedience. I have said before that compliance *per se* is not a bad thing; to comply under certain circumstances is both a necessity and an element of maturity; it becomes an issue only when the person is unable to resist compliance where it would be inappropriate. In the same sense, being oriented toward rules and being respectful of rules is an important feature of membership in any kind of social system. As I said earlier, I think rules are necessary, and it's important for the health of a system that people accept them and feel an obligation to obey them.

But, I am concerned when people's orientation to the system is entirely at the level of rules. I am speaking of people who see the rules as something totally external to them, something not subject to their own control or capable of being questioned. They see a sharp separation between the authorities who set the rules and the individuals who must live up to them. I feel this is an undesirable pattern of relationship between the individual and the political or any other kind of social system. By contrast, we have the individual who also extends legitimacy to the authorities, but for whom the perception of legitimacy depends on the degree to which the authorities live up to certain underlying values which he personally shares and on which the system is built. This is an individual who would feel a right and obligation to evaluate authoritative demands, to question them, on occasion to challenge them, and under extreme circumstances to disobey them.

KRUPAT: *It's not very difficult for me to infer that you believe that we could do with some more healthy independence when it comes to accepting influence in general. As a final matter, to what do you think the person's ability to question authority is related, and how can we bring about more of it?*

KELMAN: To me, the degree to which the person is able to question authority depends on his sense of personal efficacy, on his feeling of personal power and control. This, in turn, tends to be related to the person's position in society. People in lower social classes have generally been socialized in a way that leads them to expect little control over their lives and to be passive in relation to authority. But, of course, it's not simply a matter of socialization; it's also a matter of the realities they confront. People with limited education and lower occupational status, in fact, do not have power and control within our society. They are not in a position to really play an active role or influence policy. Social class is only one of the factors that determines a person's relationship to authority. Clearly, there are many people with relatively high education and socioeconomic status who have little sense of personal efficacy and tend to obey authorities without question; conversely, there are many lower-class people who manifest a high degree of efficacy and independence. To account for these differences, we would have to look at personality characteristics and at socialization patterns and life experiences that are not directly class-linked.

What I would like to see happen is that we create within the society, both through changes in socialization patterns and through changes in social structure—through changes not only in psychological conditions but in *real* conditions as well—a widespread sense of personal efficacy and power which would be conducive to a more independent, questioning relationship to outside influences.

AN INTRODUCTION TO THE READINGS

The first article in this section deals with the three processes of social influence about which Dr. Kelman spoke in our conversation—compliance, identification, and internalization. In testing the validity of his model, Kelman presented different groups of subjects with a tape-recorded interview designed to persuade them to change their attitudes about a specific issue.

While the *content* of the message was the same for all groups, each group of students believed that the *source* of the message was different. One group believed the communicator was a man with great control over the university's financial status; the second group thought they were listening to a well-liked and respected student; and the third group believed they were listening to a highly knowledgeable professor of history. Kelman's expectation was that the three different sources would affect the subjects' attitudes via different influence processes, and therefore that the extent and permanence of change would vary among the experimental groups. The results of this research were found to strongly support the model, with compliance-based change being the most temporary and internalization-based change the most permanent.

In the second article, Robert Cialdini and his colleagues also discuss compliance, but from a different point of view. They ask the question: What should we do to get someone to comply with a request of ours? One suggestion which they refer to is known as the "foot-in-the-door" technique— to ask a small favor which is easy to do first and then to ask the favor you *really* want done. However, they suggest that by doing just the opposite, using the "door-in-the-face" technique, we may get equally good results. That is, first ask a much larger favor, one which very few people would be willing to do, but then reduce the request to the one you really want done. In a series of three field experiments, the authors demonstrate how compliance can be gained by this method, and suggest a number of advantages of using this technique.

In the next article of this section, Philip Meyer reports on the research of Stanley Milgram in which subjects were faced with a very different type of influence attempt. In his obedience research, Milgram set up a situation which placed subjects in a difficult predicament: should they follow the experimenter's orders and possibly do serious harm to another person or should they, as Kelman has mentioned, challenge the very authority of that person to make such a demand. Meyer notes that all of us are likely to imagine that we and all other "reasonable people" would defy the experimenter rather than yield to his request, yet Milgram's findings indicate that a majority of the subjects did obey the experimenter rather than defy his authority. Meyer suggests that before we go around labeling the obedient subjects "sadistic" or "spineless," we ought to recognize just how difficult it is to say "no" to a legitimate authority—and that each of us should wonder what *we* would have done in the same situation.

In the final paper in this section, Charlan Nemeth presents a recent and important extension of the literature in social influence. She suggests that in considering group relations we have tended to phrase our questions too narrowly. That is, we have looked at how the majority exercises *social control* over the minority, but not at how those in the minority can lead the majority to reconsider their opinions—thereby creating *social change*. She reviews a number of studies showing how minorities can be effective. In doing so, she demonstrates that the influence process is quite complex and points out directions deserving of further study.

HERBERT C. KELMAN

Compliance, Identification, and Internalization:
Three Processes of Attitude Change

A crucial issue in communication research relates to the *nature* of changes (if any) that are brought about by a particular communication or type of communication. It is not enough to know that there has been some measurable change in attitude; usually we would also want to know what kind of change it is. Is it a superficial change, on a verbal level, which disappears after a short lapse of time? Or is it a more lasting change in attitude and belief, which manifests itself in a wide range of situations and which is integrated into the person's value system? Or, to put it in other terms, did the communication produce public conformity *without* private acceptance, or did it produce public conformity coupled with private acceptance? (Cf. Festinger, 1953; Kelman, 1953.) Only if we know something about the nature and depth of changes can we make meaningful predictions about the way in which attitude changes will be reflected in subsequent actions and reactions to events.

These questions about the nature of attitude changes are highly significant in the study of international attitudes. For example, we may have observed changes in opinion toward certain international issues—e.g., aspects of foreign policy, international organization, or disarmament—among the population of a given country. The implications that we draw from these changes will depend on their depth and on the psychological meanings that can be assigned to them. Let us assume that we find an increase in favorable attitudes toward the United Nations among the population of the United States at a particular juncture. This change in attitude may be due primarily to recent pronouncements by high-placed figures and may thus represent an aspect of "social conformity." On the other hand, the change may result from a series of international events which have led large segments of the population to reevaluate American foreign policy and to ascribe a more central role to the UN. Depending on which of these *motivational processes* underlies the change in attitude, we would make different predictions about the manifestations and consequences of the new attitudes: about their durability, about the number of different

Abridgement of "Compliance, Identification, and Internalization: Three Processes of Attitude Change" by Herbert C. Kelman from *The Journal of Conflict Resolution*, March 1958, vol. 2, no. 1. Copyright © 1958 by Sage Publications, Inc., by permission of the publisher, Sage Publications, Beverly Hills.

The experiment reported here was conducted while the author was at Johns Hopkins University as a Public Health Service Research Fellow of the National Institute of Mental Health.

attitudinal areas that will be affected by them, and about the ways in which they will be translated into action and will determine reactions to international events. Similarly, our predictions about the subsequent history of the new attitudes will depend on their *cognitive links*, i.e., the particular attitude structure within which the new attitude toward the UN is imbedded. For example, Americans may have become more favorable toward the UN because an important resolution sponsored by the United States delegate has been accepted. The new attitude toward the UN is thus an aspect of attitudes toward one's own nation and its prestige and international success. On the other hand, favorableness toward the UN may have increased because UN action has successfully averted war in a very tense conflict situation. In this case, the new attitude toward the UN is imbedded in an attitude structure revolving around the whole question of war and effective means of preventing its outbreak. Again, we would draw different implications from the changed attitudes, depending on which of these attitude areas was primarily involved in the occurrence of change.

The same considerations apply when we interpret the effects of international communications. For example, if we find changes in the way in which nationals of different countries perceive one another, it would be important to know at what level these changes have occurred and to what motivational and cognitive systems they are linked. These questions are important not only for the analysis of changes in attitude toward various international issues, objects, or events which may have occurred as a result of various kinds of communication or experience but also for the development of propositions about the conditions for change. In international relations, as in other areas of social behavior, one of our ultimate concerns is the exploration of the conditions under which lasting changes occur, changes which are generalized to many situations and which represent some degree of value reorganization.

In the present paper I should like to describe briefly an experimental study which is concerned with some of the conditions that determine the nature of attitude changes produced by communications on social issues. The specific content of the attitudes that were investigated in this study was in the area of race relations rather than international relations. The hypotheses refer, however, to general processes of attitude change, irrespective of the specific attitudinal area. Relationships found should be equally applicable, therefore, to the analysis of international attitudes.

I. THEORETICAL FRAMEWORK

The experiment reported here grows out of a broader theoretical framework concerned with the analysis of different processes of attitude change resulting from social influence. It is impossible to present this framework in detail in the present paper, but I should like to outline its main features.[1]

The starting point of the theoretical analysis is the observation discussed in the preceding paragraphs, i.e., that changes in attitudes and actions produced by social influence may occur at different "levels." It is proposed that these differences in the nature or level of changes that take place correspond to differences in the *process* whereby the individual accepts influence (or "conforms"). In other words, the underlying processes in which an individual engages when he adopts induced behavior may be different, even though the resulting overt behavior may appear the same.

Three different processes of influence can be distinguished: compliance, identification, and internalization.[2]

Compliance can be said to occur when an individual accepts influence because he hopes to achieve a favorable reaction from another person or group. He adopts the induced behavior not because he believes in its content but because he expects to gain specific rewards or approval and avoid specific punishments or disapproval by conforming. Thus the satisfaction derived from compliance is due to the *social effect* of accepting influence.

Identification can be said to occur when an individual accepts influence because he wants to establish or maintain a satisfying self-defining relationship to another person or a group. This relationship may take the form of classical identification, in which the individual takes over the role of the other, or it may take the form of a reciprocal role relationship. The individual actually believes in the responses which he adopts through identification, but their specific content is more or less irrelevant. He adopts the induced behavior because it is associated with the desired relationship. Thus the satisfaction derived from identification is due to the act of conforming as such.

Internalization can be said to occur when an individual accepts influence because the content of the induced behavior—the ideas and actions of which it is composed—is intrinsically rewarding. He adopts the induced behavior because it is congruent with his value system. He may consider it useful for the solution of a problem or find it congenial to his needs. Behavior adopted in this fashion tends to be integrated with the individual's existing values. Thus the satisfaction derived from internalization is due to the *content* of the new behavior.

The three processes represent three qualitatively different ways of accepting influence. A systematic treatment of the processes might, therefore, begin with an analysis of the determinants of influence in general. These determinants can be summarized by the following proposition: The probability of accepting influence is a combined function of (*a*) the relative importance of the anticipated effect, (*b*) the relative power of the influencing agent, and (*c*) the prepotency of the induced response. A variety of experimental findings can be cited in support of this proposition.

Compliance, identification, and internalization can each be represented as a function of these three determinants. For each process, however, these determinants take a qualitatively different form. Thus the determinants of the three processes can be distinguished from one another in terms of the *nature* of the anticipated effect, the *source* of the influencing agent's power, and the *manner* in which the induced response has become prepotent.

In other words, each process is characterized by a distinctive set of *antecedent* conditions, involving a particular qualitative variation of a more general set of determinants. Given the proper set of antecedents, then, influence will take the form of compliance, identification, or internalization, respectively. Each of these corresponds to a characteristic pattern of internal responses (thoughts and feelings) in which the individual engages while adopting the induced behavior.

Similarly, each process is characterized by a distinctive set of *consequent* conditions, involving a particular qualitative variation in the subsequent history of the induced response. Responses adopted through different processes will be performed under different conditions, will be changed and extinguished under different conditions, and will have different properties.

Since each of the three processes mediates between a distinct set of antecedents and a distinct set of consequents, the proposed distinctions between the three processes can be tested by experiments which attempt to relate the antecedents postulated for a given process to the consequents postulated for that process. The present experiment was designed to vary one of the antecedents—the source of the influencing agent's power—and to observe the effects of this variation on one of the consequents—the conditions of performance of the induced response.

Power is defined as the extent to which the influencing agent is perceived as instrumental to the achievement of the subject's goals. The sources of the agent's power may vary (French, 1956). The following hypotheses are offered regarding the variations in source of power:

1. To the extent to which the power of the influencing agent is based on means-control, conformity will tend to take the form of compliance.

2. To the extent to which the power of the influencing agent is based on attractiveness, conformity will tend to take the form of identification.

3. To the extent to which the power of the influencing agent is based on credibility, conformity will tend to take the form of internalization.

Now let us look at the consequent side. One of the ways in which behaviors adopted through different processes can be distinguished is in terms of the conditions under which the behavior is performed. The following hypotheses are offered regarding the conditions of performance:

1. When an individual adopts an induced response through compliance, he tends to perform it only under conditions of surveillance by the influencing agent.

2. When an individual adopts an induced response through identification, he tends to perform it only under conditions of salience of his relationship to the agent.

3. When an individual adopts an induced response through internalization, he tends to perform it under conditions of relevance of the issue, regardless of surveillance or salience.

II. PROCEDURE

The subjects in this experiment were Negro college freshmen in a border state. The experiment was conducted in the spring of 1954, just prior to the announcement of the Supreme Court decision on desegregation in the public schools. The social influence situation to which the students were exposed consisted of a fixed communication designed to change their attitudes on an issue related to the impending Court decision. Specifically, each of the communications employed in the study presented essentially the following message: If the Supreme Court rules that segregation is unconstitutional, it would still be desirable to maintain some of the *private*

TABLE 1. Design of the Experiment and Predictions.*

Experimental groups: Variations in communicator power	Questionnaires: Variations in conditions of performance		
	Questionnaire I Surveillance Salience Issue-Relevance	Questionnaire II Nonsurveillance Salience Issue-Relevance	Questionnaire III Nonsurveillance Nonsalience Issue-Relevance
High power, based on means-control	H	L	L
High power, based on attractiveness	H	H	L
High power, based on credibility	H	H	H
Low power	L	L	L

*H = high probability that attitude will be expressed; L = low probability that attitude will be expressed.

Negro colleges as all-Negro institutions, in order to preserve Negro culture, history, and tradition. Preliminary testing indicated that a large majority of the subjects would initially oppose the message presented in the communication.

The communications were tape-recorded interviews between a moderator and a guest (the communicator). They were presented to the subjects as recordings of radio programs which we were interested in evaluating. By varying the nature of these communications, it was possible to manipulate experimentally the source and degree of the communicator's power, while keeping the message of the communication constant. Four different communications were used, as can be seen from Table 1, which outlines the basic design of the experiment (see left-hand column).

In one communication the attempt was made to present the communicator in such a way that he would be perceived as possessing high means-control. He was introduced as the president of the National Foundation for Negro Colleges. In the course of the interview it became evident that his foundation had been supporting the college in which the study was being conducted; that he had almost complete control over the funds expended by the foundation; and that he was the kind of person who would not hesitate to use his control in order to achieve conformity. He made it clear that he would withdraw foundation grants from any college in which the students took a position on the issue in question which was at variance with his own position.

In the second communication the communicator was presented in such a way that he would be perceived as possessing high attractiveness. He was introduced as a senior and president of the student council in a leading Negro university. He was also chairman of his university's chapter of an organization called Student Poll, which recently did a study on the attitudes of Negro college seniors on issues relating to the Supreme Court decision. He presented the same message as the first communicator, but he made it clear that he was presenting not simply his own opinions but the overwhelming consensus of opinion of the college students represented in the polls. He was portrayed as a representative of one of the subjects' reference groups and as a person who was in a position to supply valid information on the group norms.

In the third communication the communicator was presented in such a way that he would be perceived as possessing high credibility. He was introduced as a professor of history in one of the country's leading universities. In the course of the interview, it became evident that he was one of the top experts on the history and problems of minority groups; that he was highly respected both by his colleagues and by members of minority groups; and that he had a profound concern for the welfare of the American Negro community. He presented the same position as the other speakers, but he made it clear that this position was based on his research and on the evidence of history.

For purposes of comparison, a fourth communication was used in which the communicator was presented in such a way that he would be perceived as possessing low power, that is, as being low in means-control, attractiveness, *and* credibility. He was introduced as an "ordinary citizen," who had no control over the subjects and no special knowledge about the topic. His attractiveness and credibility were further undermined by the fact that he was portrayed as a white man with a southern accent, who had recently come from Mississippi and who did not clearly dissociate himself from a pro-segregation point of view.

Each of the four communications was presented to a different experimental group. There was also a control group, which was not exposed to any communication at all. This group provided a base line for post-communication attitudes, since we did not obtain before-scores from the experimental subjects.

After exposure to the communication, the subjects in each experimental group filled out attitude questionnaires, designed to measure the extent of their agreement with the communicator. The questionnaire consisted of eighteen statements which were directly or indirectly related to the central message of the communication. Subjects were asked to respond to each item on a six-point scale. Scores for each item ranged from 1 for extreme disagreement with the communicator's position to 7 for extreme agreement (the score of 4 was not used, since the scale did not contain a neutral position). A total score for each subject was computed by adding up the individual scores on the 18 items. Thus the range of possible total scores was from 18 (complete disagreement) to 126 (complete agreement).

To vary the conditions of performance, we presented these eighteen statements to each subject on three separate questionnaires. As can be seen from Table 1, it is assumed that issue-relevance was present on all three questionnaires, since the attitude items dealt with the issues involved in the communication. The questionnaires differed, however, with respect to surveillance and salience.

Questionnaire I was completed under conditions of salience and surveillance. In order to maximize the salience of the communicator and the communication, the questionnaire was administered immediately after the communication. In order to maximize surveillance by the communicator, it was made clear—both by the appearance of the questionnaire and by the instructions—that this questionnaire was being administered at the communicator's request and that he would see each subject's answers. Moreover, the subjects were asked to sign their names and to give other identifying information.

Questionnaire II was completed under conditions of salience and nonsurveillance. In order to maximize salience, the questionnaire was administered immediately after Questionnaire I, so that the relationship between the questionnaire and the communication was still clearly apparent. In order to minimize surveillance, Questionnaire II was anonymous, and it was made clear to the subjects that their responses would not be seen by the communicator or by anyone other than the research staff.

Questionnaire III was completed under conditions of nonsalience and nonsurveillance. In order to minimize the salience of the communicator and the communication, the questionnaire was administered from one to two weeks after the communication session, in a different place, under different auspices, and by a different experimenter. The questions were embedded in a large number of other attitudinal items; and no mention of the communication was made. In order to minimize surveillance, Questionnaire III was anonymous and was in no way tied in to the communication.

III. HYPOTHESES

The specific hypotheses that were tested were as follows:

1. Attitudes adopted from a communicator whose power is based on means-control will tend to be expressed only under conditions of surveillance by the communicator. The mediating process postulated here is compliance.

The specific prediction can be noted in Table 1. In the means-control group there will be a greater amount of acceptance of the communicator's position on Questionnaire I than on Questionnaires II and III, since Questionnaire I is the only one completed under conditions of surveillance. There should be no significant difference between Questionnaires II and III.

2. Attitudes adopted from a communicator whose power is based on attractiveness will tend to be expressed only under conditions of salience of the subject's relationship to the communicator. The mediating process postulated here is identification.

Specifically, it is predicted that in the attractiveness group there will be a smaller amount of acceptance of the communicator's position on Questionnaire III than on Questionnaires I and II, since Questionnaire III is the only one completed under conditions of nonsalience. There should be no significant difference between Questionnaires I and II.

3. Attitudes adopted from a communicator whose power is based on credibility will tend to be expressed under conditions of relevance of the issue, regardless of surveillance or salience. The mediating process postulated here is internalization.

The specific prediction for the credibility group is that there will be no significant differences between the three questionnaires, since they were all completed under conditions of issue-relevance.

IV. RESULTS

Before proceeding to examine the data which bear directly on the hypotheses, it was necessary to check on the success of the experimental variations. Did the subjects really perceive each of the variations in communicator power in the way in which we intended it? To provide an answer to this question, Questionnaire II included a series of statements about the speaker and the communication to which the subjects were asked to react. An analysis of these data indicated that, by and large, the experimental manipulations succeeded in producing the conditions they were intended to produce, thus making possible an adequate test of the hypotheses.

TABLE 2. **Effects of Variations in Communicator Power on Acceptance of Induced Attitudes Under Three Conditions of Measurement.**

Groups	N	Mean attitude scores		
		Quest. I	Quest. II	Quest. III
Means-control (compliance)	55	63.98	60.65	58.04
Attractiveness (identification)	48	56.81	55.94	49.67
Credibility (internalization)	51	59.51	56.39	56.10
Low power	43	49.33	50.58	53.35

The findings which are directly relevant to the hypotheses are summarized in Tables 2 and 3. Table 2 presents the mean attitude scores for the four experimental groups on each of the three questionnaires. All subjects who had completed the three questionnaires were used in this analysis.

It can be seen from the summary of the significance tests that all the experimental predictions were confirmed. In the means-control group, the mean score on Questionnaire I is significantly higher than the mean scores on Questionnaires II and III; and there is no significant difference between the scores on Questionnaires II and III. In the attractiveness group, the mean score on Questionnaire III is significantly lower than the mean scores on Questionnaires I and II; and there is no significant difference between the scores on Questionnaires I and II. In the credibility group, there are no significant differences between the three questionnaires.

While these results are all in line with the hypotheses, examination of the means in Table 2 reveals that the findings are not so clear-cut as they might be. Specifically, we should expect a relatively large drop in mean score for the means-control group from Questionnaire I to Questionnaire II. In actual fact, however, the drop is only slightly higher than that for the credibility group. This might be due to the fact that the analysis is based on *all* subjects, including those who were not influenced by the communication at all. The hypotheses, however, refer only to changes from questionnaire to questionnaire for those people who *were* initially influenced.

It was not possible to identify the subjects who were initially influenced, since there were no before-scores available for the experimental groups. It was possible, however, to approximate these conditions by using only those subjects who had a score of 60 or above on Questionnaire I. If we make certain limited assumptions (which I cannot spell out in this brief report), it can be shown that the use of a cutoff point of 60 "purifies" the experimental groups to some degree. That is, the subsamples selected by this criterion should have a higher ratio of influenced to uninfluenced subjects than the total groups from which they were selected. It was anticipated that an analysis based on these subsamples would provide a better test of the hypotheses and would yield more clear-cut results. This did, in fact, happen, as can be seen from Table 3.

Table 3 presents the mean attitude scores for the three high-power groups, using only those subjects who had scores of 60 or above on Questionnaire I. Examination of the means reveals a pattern completely consistent with the hypotheses. In the means-control group, agreement with the communicator is relatively

TABLE 3.   Effects of Variations in Communicator Power on Acceptance of Induced Attitudes Under Three Conditions of Measurement.*

Groups	N	Mean attitude scores		
		Quest. I	Quest. II	Quest. III
Means-control (compliance)	30	78.20	70.76	67.56
Attractiveness (identification)	23	71.30	69.57	59.70
Credibility (internalization)	26	73.35	71.04	69.27

*Data based on a selected sample, containing a higher proportion of influenced subjects. Criterion for selection was a score of 60 or above on Questionnaire I.

high on Questionnaire I and declines on Questionnaires II and III. In the attractiveness group, agreement is high on Questionnaires I and II and declines on Questionnaire III. In the credibility group, changes from questionnaire to questionnaire are minimal. Analyses of variance clearly confirmed all the experimental predictions.

V. CONCLUSIONS

It would be premature to accept the hypotheses tested in this experiment as general principles that have been proved. The experiment does, however, lend considerable support to them. To the extent to which the hypotheses were substantiated, the experiment also gives support to the theoretical framework from which these hypotheses were derived. The mediating concepts of compliance, identification, and internalization seem to provide a unified and meaningful way of organizing the present experimental findings and of relating them to a more general conceptual framework.

The framework presented here can be applied directly to the analysis of the effects of various communications and other forms of social influence on attitudes and actions in the international sphere. In the study of public opinion, for example, it should help us identify some of the conditions which are likely to produce one or another of these processes and predict the subsequent histories and action implications of attitudes adopted under these sets of conditions. This framework may also be helpful in the study of the social influences which affect decision-making processes and negotiations on the part of various elites.

Some of the concepts presented here might be useful not only for the study of change but also for the analysis of existing attitudes and their motivational bases. Let us take, for example, people's attitudes toward their own country's system of government. Even if we look only at those individuals who have favorable attitudes, various distinctions suggest themselves. For some individuals, acceptance of their system of government may be based largely on compliance: They may go along with the accepted norms in order to avoid social ostracism or perhaps even persecution. For others, attitudes toward their government may be largely identification-based: Their relationship to their own nation and its major institutions may represent an essential aspect of their identity, and acceptance of certain political attitudes and beliefs may serve to maintain this relationship and their self-definition which is anchored in it. For a third group of individuals, belief in the country's system of government may be internalized: They may see this political form as fully congruent and integrated with their value systems and likely to lead to a maximization of their own values. Our evaluation of the meaning of "favorable attitudes" on the part of a particular individual or group or subpopulation and our prediction of the consequences of these attitudes would certainly vary with the motivational processes that underlie them. The conditions under which these attitudes are likely to be changed, the kinds of actions to which they are likely to lead, and the ways in which they are likely to affect reactions to particular events will be different, depending on whether these attitudes are based on compliance, identification, or internalization.

NOTES

1. A detailed description of the theoretical framework and of the experiment reported here is in preparation and will be published elsewhere.
2. A similar distinction, between four processes of conformity, was recently presented by Marie Jahoda (1956).

REFERENCES

Festinger, L. An analysis of compliant behavior. In M. Sherif & M. O. Wilson (Eds.), *Group relations at the crossroads*. New York: Harper, 1953.

French, J. R. P., Jr. A formal theory of social power. *Psychological Review*, 1956, **63**, 181–194.

Jahoda, M. Psychological issues in civil liberties. *American Psychologist*, 1956, **11**, 234–240.

Kelman, H. C. Attitude change as a function of response restriction. *Human Relations*, 1953, **6**, 185–214.

Kelman, H. C. *Social influence and personal belief: A theoretical and experimental approach to the study of behavior change*. New York: Wiley, in preparation.

Socrates on Conformity

I think it better, my good friend, that my lyre should be discordant and out of tune, and any chorus I might train, and that the majority of mankind should disagree with and oppose me, rather than that I, who am but one man, should be out of tune with and contradict myself.

As cited in *Gorgias*, 482b–c, trans. W. D. Woodhead, in *The Collected Dialogues of Plato*, Edith Hamilton and Huntington Cairns, Eds. New York: Pantheon Books, Inc., 1961.

ROBERT B. CIALDINI
JOYCE E. VINCENT
STEPHEN K. LEWIS
JOSÉ CATALAN
DIANE WHEELER
BETTY LEE DARBY

Reciprocal Concessions Procedure for Inducing Compliance:
The Door-in-the-Face Technique

The foot-in-the-door technique has been investigated by Freedman and Fraser (1966) as a procedure for inducing compliance with a request for a favor. They demonstrated that obtaining a person's compliance with a small request substantially increases the likelihood of that person's compliance with a subsequent, larger request. Freedman and Fraser sugest that the mediator of the foot-in-the-door effect is a shift in the self-perception of the benefactor. After performing or agreeing to perform an initial favor, a person "may become, in his own eyes, the kind of person who does this sort of thing, who agrees to requests made by strangers, who takes action on things he believes in, who cooperates with good causes. . . . The basic idea is that the change in attitude need not be toward any particular person or activity, but may be toward activity or compliance in general." Thus, one effective way to obtain a favor is to begin by making a *minimal* first request which is sure to produce *compliance* and then to *advance* to a larger favor (the one which was desired from the outset). It may well be, however, that an equally effective method for getting a favor done involves the exact opposite procedure. What would be the result of making an *extreme* first request which is sure to be *rejected* and then asking for a more *moderate* second favor (the one which was desired from the outset)? There are two lines of evidence suggesting that such a technique would be efficacious in producing compliance with the second request.

The first sort of evidence comes from work investigating the concept of reciprocation. Gouldner (1960) maintains that a norm of reciprocity exists in all societies. Gouldner states the norm of reciprocity in its simple form as: "You

Abridged from "Reciprocal Concessions Procedure for Inducing Compliance: The Door-in-the-Face Technique" by Robert B. Cialdini, Joyce E. Vincent, Stephen K. Lerwis, José Catalan, Diane Wheeler and Betty Lee Darby from *Journal of Personality and Social Psychology*, vol. 31, 1975. Copyright © 1975 by the American Psychological Association. Reprinted by permission.

should give benefits to those who give you benefits.'' (p. 170) There is considerable experimental evidence attesting to the workings of such a rule in our culture (e.g., Brehm & Cole, 1966; Goranson & Berkowitz, 1966; Pruitt, 1968; Regan, 1971; Wilke & Lanzetta, 1970). In each case, receipt of a favor has been shown to increase the likelihood that the favor will be returned, although not necessarily in kind. While Gouldner (1960) speaks of the norm of reciprocity almost exclusively in terms of the reciprocation of benefits and services, it seems likely that a norm for reciprocity governs other types of social exchange also. Specifically, we would like to postulate a reciprocal concessions corollary to the general norm of reciprocity: ''You should make concessions to those who make concessions to you.'' Such a rule can be seen as having an important societal function. Very often in social interaction participants begin with requirements and demands which are unacceptable to one another. In order for the interaction to continue and hence for common goals to be achieved, compromise must be struck. *Mutual* concession is crucial. If there is no implicit prescription that retreat from an initial position by one participant should be reciprocated by the other participant, then it is unlikely that compromise attempts would be initiated and, consequently, that the interaction would continue. However, given a principle for reciprocation of concessions, an interaction participant could instigate compromise attempts with little fear of exploitation by his partner.

Evidence for the existence of a reciprocal concessions relationship in our society can be seen in numerous terms and phrases of the language: ''give and take,'' ''meeting the other fellow halfway,'' etc. Much more compelling, however, are the data which come from a number of studies of negotiation behavior. An experiment by Chertkoff and Conley (1967) demonstrated that the number of concessions a subject makes in a bargaining situation is significantly affected by the number of his opponent's concessions; more frequent concessions by the opponent elicited more frequent concessions from the subject. In a somewhat similar context, Komorita and Brenner (1968) had subjects bargain as buyers against opponent-sellers. In one condition, the opponent initially proposed what was a perfectly equitable selling price and refused to move from that price throughout the course of the negotiations; in other conditions, the opponent began with an extreme offer and then gradually retreated from that price as bargaining progressed. The consistent result was that the former condition elicited the least amount of yielding on the part of the subjects. Komorita and Brenner conclude that, ''in a bargaining situation, if one party wishes to reach an agreement at a 'fair' price, clearly a strategy of making an initial offer at that level and remaining firm thereafter is not an effective means of reaching an agreement'' (p. 18). In sum, it seems that the likelihood of a concession by one party is positively related to the occurrence of a concession by another party.

Let us now return to the original question, ''How might we enhance the probability that another will comply with our request for a favor?'' The analysis above suggests that if we were to begin by asking for an extreme favor which was sure to be refused by the other, and then we were to move to a smaller request, the other would feel a normative strain to match our concession with one of his own. Since the situation is such that the other's response to our request involves an essentially dichotomous choice—yes or no—the only available reciprocation route for him would be to move from his position of initial noncompliance to one of compliance. So, by means of an illusory retreat from our initial position, we should be able to obtain another's agreement to the request that we desired from the outset.

In line with the formulation we have proposed, two things are crucial to the success of such a procedure. First, our original request must be rejected by the target person; once this has occurred, the target will have taken a position and an apparent concession on our part will pressure him to meet us halfway and hence to yield to our smaller request. Second, the target must perceive that we have conceded in some way. Thus, the size of our second favor must be unambiguously smaller than that of the first; only then can the action of a reciprocal concessions norm come into play.

EXPERIMENT 1

In order to test the effectiveness of this procedure for inducing compliance, an experiment was conducted. It was expected that a person who followed a refused initial request with a smaller request would obtain more agreement to the smaller request than a person who made *only* the smaller request. Such a result could be explained, however, in a way quite apart from the theoretical account we have proposed. Rather than through the action of a reciprocal concessions mechanism, the superiority of the technique we have described could be seen as occurring through the action of a contrast effect. Exposure to an initial, large request could cause subjects to perceive a subsequent, smaller request as less demanding than would subjects who had never been exposed to the large request; consequently, the former type of subject might be expected to comply more with the critical request. It was necessary, therefore, to include in our experimental design a condition which differentiated these two theoretical explanations.

One point of departure for the two accounts lies in the requirement of the reciprocal concessions explanation for the target's refusal of and the requester's moderation of the initial, larger favor. The contrast effect explanation does not demand this sequence of refusal and moderation; rather, it requires only that the target person be previously exposed to the larger request. An experiment was performed, then, which included three conditions. In one condition, subjects were asked to perform a favor. In a second condition, subjects were asked to perform the critical favor after they had refused to perform a larger favor. In a final condition, subjects heard the larger favor described to them before they were asked to perform the critical one.

METHOD

Subjects

Subjects were 72 people of both sexes who were moving along university walkways during daylight hours. Only those individuals who were walking alone were selected, and no subjects were selected during the 10-minute break period between classes.

Procedure

A subject meeting the conditions above was approached by a student-experimenter[1] who initiated interaction by introducing him- or herself as being with the County Youth Counseling Program. At this point, the experimenter made (for the Youth Counseling Program) either an extreme request followed by a smaller request or made just the smaller request.

The extreme request asked subjects to perform as counselors to juvenile delinquents for a period of at least two years. Specifically, the experimenter said:

> We're currently recruiting university students to work as voluntary, nonpaid counselors at the County Juvenile Detention Center. The position could require two hours of your time per week for a minimum of two years. You would be working more in the line of a Big Brother (Sister) to one of the boys (girls) at the detention home. Would you be interested in being considered for one of these positions?

The smaller request asked subjects to perform as chaperones for a group of juvenile delinquents on a two-hour trip to the zoo. Specifically, the experimenter said:

> We're recruiting university students to chaperone a group of boys (girls) from the County Juvenile Detention Center on a trip to the zoo. It would be voluntary, nonpaid, and would require about two hours of one afternoon or evening. Would you be interested in being considered for one of these positions?

Subjects were randomly assigned to one of three conditions.

Rejection-moderation condition. Subjects in this condition heard the experimenter first make the extreme request. After subjects refused the large request, the experimenter said, "Well, we also have another program you might be interested in then." At this point the experimenter made the smaller request.

Smaller request only control. Subjects in this condition were asked by the experimenter only to perform the smaller request.

Exposure control. In this condition the experimenter first described the extreme and then the smaller favor and requested that the subjects perform *either* one. Specifically, subjects in the exposure only control heard the experimenter give the standard introduction and then say:

> We're currently recruiting university students for two different programs. In the first, we're looking for voluntary, nonpaid counselors to work at the County Juvenile Detention Center. The position would require two hours of your time per week for a minimum of two years. You would be working more in the line of a Big Brother (Sister) to one of the boys (girls) at the detention center. In the other program, we're looking for university students to chaperone a group of boys (girls) from the detention center on a trip to the zoo. It would also be voluntary, nonpaid, and would require two hours of one afternoon or evening. Would you be interested in being considered for either of these two programs?

No subject during the course of the experiment ever agreed to perform the initial, large favor. However, when a subject agreed to the smaller request, the experimenter took his or her name and phone number. The experimenter promised to call if the subject was needed but explained that "there is a chance that you won't be called because of the large number of people who have already volunteered to help.'' At this point, the experimenter thanked the subject and moved on.

Predictions

Two predictions derived from the reciprocal concessions model were made. First, it was expected that the subjects in the rejection-moderation condition would comply with the smaller request more than would subjects in the two control conditions. Second, it was predicted that the amount of compliance with the smaller request would not differ between the two controls.

RESULTS

No subject in the present experiment agreed to perform the extreme favor. The percentage of subjects who complied with the smaller request in each of the treatment conditions can be seen in Table 1.

. . . Comparing the compliance rates of the two control groups, no difference was found. Testing the combined control conditions against the rejection-moderation condition produced a highly significant difference. . . .

Additional analyses investigating the extent to which the pattern of results above was affected by such factors as the sex of the subject and the identity of the experimenter provided no statistic which approached conventional levels of significance; the same pattern obtained for all three experimenters and for male and female subjects. In all, then, it seems that the only factor which enhanced the amount of agreement to the smaller request was the procedure of moving to the smaller request *after* the larger request had been refused.

DISCUSSION

It is clear from the findings above that making an extreme initial request which is sure to be rejected and then moving to a smaller request significantly increases the probability of a target person's agreement to the second request. Moreover, this phenomenon does not seem mediated by a perceptual contrast effect; simply exposing the target to the extreme request beforehand does not affect compliance.

While the results of this first experiment lend some support to the reciprocal concessions explanation, they do not, of course, necessarily confirm the validity of the interpretation. If we are to gain confidence in such a model, additional predictions derivable from it must be proposed and demonstrated. To this end, it was decided to replicate and extend our findings in a second experiment.

TABLE 1. Percentage of Subjects Complying with the Smaller Request

Treatment	% Compliance
Rejection-moderation condition	50.0
Exposure control	25.0
Smaller request only control	16.7

Note. The *n* for each condition = 24.

EXPERIMENT 2

The reciprocal concessions formulation we have described suggests that a target person feels pressure to change from his initial position of noncompliance after it is seen that the requester has changed from his own initial position. It is not enough that the target has been asked to comply with a large then a smaller request, the target must perceive the request for the smaller favor as a concession *by the requester*. If this is in fact the case, a target person who is asked an extreme favor by one individual and a smaller favor by some other individual in a second interaction context should not experience a reciprocation-mediated tendency to agree to the smaller request. The second requester should not be perceived as conceding and thus, according to our model, the target should not be spurred to reciprocate via compliance. On the other hand, if, as in Experiment 1, the requests are made by the same person, compliance with the smaller request should be enhanced.

To test the importance of the perception of concession, an experiment was conducted which included three conditions. In one condition, subjects were asked to perform a favor by a single requester. In a second condition, subjects were asked by a single requester to perform the critical favor after they had refused to perform a larger favor for that requester. In the third condition, subjects were asked to perform the critical favor by one requester after they had refused to perform a larger favor for a different requester. An additional benefit of this third condition was that it afforded another test of the perceptual contrast explanation for the obtained effect and thus provided a conceptual replication of one aspect of Experiment 1.

METHOD

Subjects

Subjects were 58 males who were selected for participation in a fashion identical to that of Experiment 1.

Procedure

A subject meeting the conditions above was approached by two student-experimenters, one male and one female; we call them Experimenters A and B, respectively. Experimenter A initiated interaction by introducing both himself and Experimenter B to the subject. At this point, a second male experimenter (Experimenter C) who was apparently an acquaintance of Experimenter B, approached the group and engaged Experimenter B in conversation about an upcoming exam they both would be taking. This procedure uniformly distracted the subject's attention for a second, so Experimenter A waited for the subject to turn back to him. Here the three treatment conditions of the study differed.

Rejection-moderation condition. Subjects in this condition next heard Experimenter A ask for the extreme favor. The extreme favor was the same as that used in Experiment 1. After the subject had refused to comply, Experimenter A made the smaller request, which in this experiment asked subjects to chaperone a group of "low-income children" to the zoo. Specifically, he said:

Oh. Well. I'm also with the Campus Volunteer Service Organization in another program that has nothing to do with the Juvenile Detention Center. It involves helping to chaperone a group of low-income children on a trip to the zoo. We can't give you any money for it, but it would only involve about two hours of one afternoon or evening. Would you be willing to help us with this?

Two requester control.   The procedures of this condition were similar to those of the rejection-moderation condition except that, upon refusal of the extreme request, Experimenter A thanked the subject and walked away from the group with Experimenter B; this left Experimenter C alone with the subject. At this point, Experimenter C made the smaller request. He prefaced the request by saying,

> Excuse me, I couldn't help overhearing you say that you would not be able to be a counselor to juvenile delinquents for two years. [If a subject had given a reason for refusing the extreme request, Experimenter C mentioned that he had overheard the stated reason as well.[2]] But maybe you can help *me*. My name is __, and I'm with the Campus Volunteer Service Organization in a program that has nothing to do with the Juvenile Detention Center. [The remainder of the request was identical to that made in the rejection-moderation condition.]

Smaller request only control.   The procedures of this condition were similar to those of the rejection-moderation condition except that the extreme request was not made. The events in this condition were as follow: Experimenters A and B approached the subject; Experimenter A introduced himself and Experimenter B; Experimenter C joined the group and engaged Experimenter B in conversation; Experimenter A made the smaller request. It should be noted that in this and both other conditions the roles of Experimenter A and Experimenter C were alternated between the two male experimenters of the study.

Predictions

The predictions of the present experiment were similar to those of Experiment 1. It was expected, first, that the two control conditions would not differ from one another in amount of compliance with the smaller request. Second, it was thought that the rejection-moderation condition would produce more compliance with the smaller request than would the controls.

The experimenters in this instance were not aware of the nature of these predictions; in fact, they were led by the principal investigator to expect opposite results. As in Experiment 1, the experimenters were undergraduate research assistants. Because of evidence indicating that undergraduate experimenters have in the past produced results consistent with prediction via experimenter expectancy effects (Rosenthal, 1966) or conscious data fixing (Azrin, Holz, Ulrich, & Goldiamond, 1961), a test of such explanations for the obtained effect in Experiment 1 seemed in order. Hence, the experimenters of Experiment 2 were told that the principal investigator was predicting that the smaller request only control would produce the most compliance. This would supposedly be so because of an "irritation or reactance tendency in people who have been asked for favors twice in succession." If the pattern of results nonetheless appeared as predicted by the reciprocal concession formulation, experimenter bias could no longer be offered as a possible explanation for the superiority of the rejection-moderation condition.

TABLE 2. Percentage of Subjects Complying with the Smaller Request in Experiment 2.

Treatment	% Compliance
Rejection-moderation condition	55.5
Two requester control	10.5
Smaller request only control	31.5

Note. The *n* for the rejection-moderation condition = 20; the *n* for each of the two control conditions = 19.

RESULTS

Three subjects in Experiment 2 complied with the extreme request, two in the rejection-moderation condition and the other in the two requester control. These subjects were removed from the analysis and replaced by three other subjects.[3] The percentage of subjects who complied with the smaller request in each of the treatment conditions of Experiment 2 can be seen in Table 2.

. . . [Comparing] the amounts of compliance with the small request with the two control conditions, no conventionally significant difference occurred. Testing the rejection-moderation condition against the combined control conditions did produce a clearly significant difference. . . .

DISCUSSION

It appears from the results of Experiment 2 that the target's perception of concession by the requester is a crucial factor in producing compliance with the smaller request. Only when the extreme and the smaller favors were asked by the same requester was compliance enhanced. This finding provides further evidence for a reciprocal concessions mediator of the rejection-then-moderation effect. It seems that our subjects increased the frequency of assent to the smaller request only in response to what could be interpreted as concession behavior on the part of the requester; such assent, then, would seem best viewed as reciprocal concession behavior.

It might be noted that compliance in the two requester control was inhibited relative to that in the small request only control. This finding replicates quite closely a result obtained by Snyder and Cunningham (1975) and fits very well with evidence suggesting that in most cases, people are quite consistent in their responses to requests for favors (Freedman & Fraser, 1966; Snyder & Cunningham, 1975). Unless there was a pressure to reciprocate a concession, 89.5% of the subjects in our experiment who said, "No" to an initial request said, "No" to a subsequent one.

EXPERIMENT 3

While the data of Experiments 1 and 2 are wholly consistent with the reciprocal concessions formulation, an alternative explanation for these results is applicable as well. It may have been that the heightened compliance in our rejection-moderation conditions was due to the fact that only in these conditions did one requester persist in making a second request after his first had been refused. Perhaps subjects in these conditions acquiesced to the critical, zoo trip request not because of pressure to reciprocate a concession but because they were dunned into accession by a tenacious requester or because they wanted to avoid the requester's perception of them as having a generally antisocial or unhelpful nature.

In order to test this type of explanation, a third experiment was performed. Included in Experiment 3 was a procedure in which subjects were asked to perform an initial favor and then were asked by the same requester to perform a second favor (the critical request) of *equivalent* size. Since the proposal of an equivalent second favor does not constitute a concession on the part of the requester, the reciprocal concessions model would predict no increased compliance with the critical request from this procedure. However, if the persistance of a single requester is the mediator of enhanced compliance, then such a procedure should produce heightened agreement to perform the critical request. A second function of Experiment 3 was to provide a conceptual replication of Experiment 2. As in Experiment 2, one group of subjects received two requests but should not have construed the second request as a concession on the part of the person who made it. In Experiment 2, the perception of concession was avoided by having a second requester make the smaller, critical request; in Experiment 3, it was done by making the initial request equivalent in size to the critical one. For both procedures, the results should be similar—no enhancement of compliance.

METHOD

Subjects

Subjects were 72 people of both sexes who were selected for participation in a fashion identical to that of Experiments 1 and 2.

Procedure

A subject meeting the conditions above was approached by a student-experimenter in a fashion identical to that of Experiment 1.[4] Subjects were randomly assigned to one of three conditions.

Rejection-moderation condition. Subjects in this condition were treated identically to subjects in the comparable condition of Experiment 1; that is, after hearing and rejecting an extreme request (to perform as a counselor to a juvenile delinquent for a minimum of two years), a subject heard the same requester make a smaller request (to perform as a chaperone for a group of juvenile delinquents on a two-hour trip to the zoo).

Smaller request only control. Subjects in this condition were treated identically to subjects in the comparable condition of Experiment 1; that is, a subject heard the requester make only the smaller request to chaperone a group of juvenile delinquents on a trip to the zoo.

Equivalent request control. Subjects in this condition heard a requester initially request that they perform as chaperones for a group of juvenile delinquents on a two-hour trip to the city museum; after the subjects responded to this first request, the experimenter then requested that they chaperone a group of juvenile delinquents on a two-hour trip to the zoo.

TABLE 3. **Percentage of Subjects Complying with the Smaller Request in Experiment 3.**

Treatment	% Compliance
Rejection-moderation condition	54.1
Equivalent request control	33.3
Smaller request only control	33.3

Note. The *n* for each condition = 24.

Predictions

As in the previous experiments, it was predicted on the basis of the reciprocal concessions model that, first, the two control conditions would not differ from one another in amount of compliance with the critical request (the zoo trip) and, second, that the rejection-moderation condition would produce more compliance with the critical request than would the controls.

RESULTS

No subject in Experiment 3 complied with the extreme request in the rejection-moderation condition. However, eight subjects complied with the initial request in the equivalent request control. The percentage of subjects who complied with the critical request in each of the treatment conditions of Experiment 3 can be seen in Table 3.

. . . [Contrasting] the two control conditions, no significant difference resulted. Testing the rejection-moderation condition against the combined controls, a marginally significant difference occurred. Two features of the data from this experiment argue against the interpretation that a requester's persistence in making requests accounts for the superiority of the rejection-moderation condition. First, the equivalent request control, which involved successive requests from the same requester, produced exactly the same amount of compliance as the smaller request only control. Second, of the eight subjects who agreed to perform the critical request in the equivalent request control, only one had refused to perform the similar-sized initial request. Clearly then, it is not the case that a persistent requester induces compliance to a second request solely through the act of making a second request. Indeed, in the equivalent request control, subjects were stoutly consistent in the nature of their responses to the two requests. Twenty-two of the 24 subjects in that group responded similarly to both requests.

GENERAL DISCUSSION

Taken together, the findings of Experiments 1, 2, and 3 seem to support the reciprocal concessions model. Each experiment indicated that proposing an extreme request which is rejected and then moving to a smaller request increases compliance with the smaller request. The results of Experiment 1 suggested that the target person's rejection of the initial, extreme request is crucial to the effectiveness of this technique. Through his refusal to perform the large favor, the target puts himself in a position from which virtually his only possible retreat is accession to the smaller request. Thus when the requester moves from his extreme proposal to a smaller one, the target must agree to the second proposal in order to relieve any felt pressure for reciprocation of concessions. As was shown in Experiment 1, if movement to a smaller request occurs without the target's initial rejection of the extreme request, compliance with the smaller request will not be significantly enhanced. Experiment 1 demonstrated further, as did Experiment 2, that merely exposing a target person to an extreme request does not increase the likelihood of his compliance with a subsequent smaller request; such results tend to disconfirm a perceptual contrast explanation of the phenomenon. Experiments 2 and 3 demonstrated the importance of concession. Simply presenting a target person with a smaller request after he had rejected a larger one or simply presenting a target person with a second request of equivalent size, does not increase agreement to the second request. Only when the proposal of the second favor can be considered a concession on the part of the requester is compliance increased.

Several aspects of the phenomenon we have investigated suggest that its use would be highly functional for someone in need of a favor. First, it is clear that the effect is quite a powerful one for inducing compliance. Averaging over all three studies and comparing against the small request only control conditions, we were able to double the likelihood of compliance through the use of the rejection-then-moderation procedure. The strength of this procedure is further evidenced when it is realized that it is working in a direction counter to any tendency for the target to be consistent in his responses to requests for favors. It should be remembered that Freedman and Fraser (1966) found such a tendency for consistency to be a potent one in their foot-in-the-door study, and we found a similar tendency in the two requester control of Experiment 2 and the equivalent request control of Experiment 3. Seemingly, then, the size of the effect is such that it overwhelmed a strong propensity in our subjects for constancy in their reactions to compliance requests.

Second, the technique does not limit a requester to the receipt of small favors. It is only necessary that the critical request be *smaller* than the initial one for a reciprocal concessions mechanism to come into play. Evidence that a requester can use this technique to gain assent to a substantial request can be seen in the data of Experiment 1. The smaller request in that study might well be seen, objectively, as an extreme one in itself; it asked subjects to be responsible for an unspecified number of juvenile delinquents of unspecified age in a public place for a period of two hours outdoors in winter.[5] Only 16.7% of our population was willing to agree to such a request when it was the only one made. Yet, the proposal of this request after the rejection of a still more extreme favor produced 50% compliance.

Another benefit of the rejection-then-moderation procedure is that its force seems to derive from the existence of a social norm. Thus, a requester wishing to use the procedure need have little reward or coercive power over his target to be effective.

A final advantage of a compliance induction procedure which uses concessions involves the feelings of the target person toward the outcome of the interaction. Benton, Kelley, and Liebling (1972) present evidence suggesting that not only will someone who applies such a procedure be quite effective in obtaining favorable payoffs for himself but that the person to whom it is applied will feel more responsible for and satisfied with the outcome. In an allocation of resources situation, subjects faced a bargaining opponent who intransigently demanded the maximum payoff for himself, intransigently demanded a moderately favorable payoff for himself, or retreated from the maximum payoff demand to the moderate payoff demand. In each condition, failure to reach an allocation agreement resulted in a loss of all money by both participants. It was found that the retreat strategy produced the highest average earning for the opponent. Moreover, not only did subjects concede the greatest payoffs to an opponent using this tactic, they felt significantly more responsible for and satisfied with the outcome than did subjects faced with an intransigent opponent. The results of this study when coupled with those of our experiments suggest some intriguing implications. One who feels responsible for the terms of an agreement should be more likely to meet his commitments concerning that agreement. Thus, someone who uses concession to produce compliance with a request for a favor is likely to see the favor actually performed. Second, one who feels fairly satisfied with the outcome of an interaction with another person should be willing to enter into interaction with that person again. Thus, the target person of a rejection-then-moderation procedure may well be vulnerable to subsequent requests by the same requester. In all, then, it appears that the rejection-then-moderation procedure can be an extremely valuable technique for the elicitation of compliance.

A note of caution should probably be interjected at this point lest we make too much of the potential implications of the present findings. It is the case that the rejection-then-moderation procedure has been shown to work under a fairly limited set of conditions. The extent to which the effect is generalizable to other contexts and situations remains to be seen. For example, we have tested the effectiveness of the procedure only in situations in which the interaction was face-to-face, the interactants were of the same sex, and the requests were prosocial in nature. Moreover, it would be well to remember that, while the present research appears to support a reciprocal concessions interpretation of the effect, it in no way ultimately confirms that interpretation. Other explanations may exist which account completely for the data of this study; and to the extent that they do exist, they should be tested in subsequent work.

Future research on the reciprocal concessions procedure might also profitably investigate the nature of the concept of concession. In the present studies, a concession by a requester was operationalized as moderation from a large request to a smaller one. Involved in such moderation, however, are two separate components: the target will no doubt perceive the move from the large to the smaller request as *more* desirable for himself but *less* desirable for the requester and his cause. While these two aspects of concession usually occur together, there is no good reason to assume that both are necessary for the enhancement of compliance. It may be the proposal of a more desirable arrangement for the target—rather than the proposal of a less desirable arrangement for the requester—that is the crucial, compliance-producing aspect of concession; or the opposite may be the case. Stated otherwise, a concession involves two normally correlated but conceptually separate features: the granting of a more favorable situation to one's interaction partner and the surrendering of a more favorable position for oneself. It remains for further investigation to determine whether the aspect of concession which induces compliance involves the granting of something, the surrendering of something, or both.

NOTES

1. The experimenters were three college age students, one female and two male. Experimenters approached only subjects of the same sex as themselves.
2. A replication of Experiment 2 was subsequently performed by the authors. The only difference between the original and replicated versions was that in the replication Experimenter C's performance in the two requester control did not include a claim that he had overheard the target's conversation with Experimenter A. The data of the two versions of Experiment 2 were virtually identical.
3. It was necessary to discard the data of the original three subjects because of the likelihood that their responses to the second request would be mediated by a foot-in-the-door effect rather than a reciprocal concessions effect; thus our results would have been artificially inflated in the direction of prediction.
4. In the present experiment there were four experimenters, three female and one male. Experimenters approached only subjects of the same sex as themselves.
5. Only Experiment 1 was conducted in the winter of the year. Experiments 2 and 3 were conducted in the spring or summer which may account for the somewhat higher compliance rates in the small request only controls of these experiments.

REFERENCES

Azrin, N. H., Holz, W., Ulrich, R., & Goldiamond, I. The control of the content of conversation through reinforcement. *Journal of the Experimental Analysis of Behavior*, 1961, **4**, 25–30.

Benton, A. A., Kelley, H. H., & Liebling, B. Effects of extremity of offers and concession rate on the outcomes of bargaining. *Journal of Personality and Social Psychology*, 1972, **24**, 73–83.

Brehm, J. W., & Cole, A. H. Effect of a favor which reduces freedom. *Journal of Personality and Social Psychology*, 1966, **3**, 420–426.

Chertkoff, J. M., & Conley, M. Opening offer and frequency of concession as bargaining strategies. *Journal of Personality and Social Psychology*, 1967, **7**, 185–193.

Freedman, J. L., & Fraser, S. Compliance without pressure: The foot-in-the-door technique. *Journal of Personality and Social Psychology*, 1966, **4**, 195–202.

Goranson, R. E., & Berkowitz, L. Reciprocity and responsibility reactions to prior help. *Journal of Personality and Social Psychology*, 1966, **3**, 227–232.

Gouldner, A. W. The norm of reciprocity: A preliminary statement. *American Sociological Review*, 1960, **25**, 161–178.

Komorita, S. S., & Brenner, A. R. Bargaining and concession making under bilateral monopoly. *Journal of Personality and Social Psychology*, 1968, **9**, 15–20.

Pruitt, D. G. Reciprocity and credit building in a laboratory dyad. *Journal of Personality and Social Psychology*, 1968, **8**, 143–147.

Regan, D. T. Effects of a favor and liking on compliance. *Journal of Experimental Social Psychology*, 1971, **1**, 627–639.

Rosenthal, R. *Experimenter effects in behavioral research*. New York: Appleton-Century-Crofts, 1966.

Snyder, M., & Cunningham, M. R. To comply or not comply: Testing the self-perception explanation of the "foot-in-the-door" phenomenon. *Journal of Personality and Social Psychology*, 1975, **31**, 64–67.

Wilke, H., & Lanzetta, J. T. The obligation to help: The effects of amount of prior help on subsequent helping behavior. *Journal of Experimental Social Psychology*, 1970, **6**, 488–493.

We think as we do, mainly because other people think so.

Samuel Butler, *Note-Books*, p. 328.

PHILIP MEYER

If Hitler Asked You to Electrocute a Stranger, **Would You?**

In the beginning, Stanley Milgram was worried about the Nazi problem. He doesn't worry much about the Nazis anymore. He worries about you and me, and, perhaps, himself a little bit too.

Stanley Milgram is a social psychologist, and when he began his career at Yale University in 1960 he had a plan to prove, scientifically, that Germans are different. The Germans-are-different hypothesis has been used by historians, such as William L. Shirer, to explain the systematic destruction of the Jews by the Third Reich. One madman could decide to destroy the Jews and even create a master plan for getting it done. But to implement it on the scale that Hitler did meant that thousands of other people had to go along with the scheme and help to do the work. The Shirer thesis, which Milgram set out to test, is that Germans have a basic character flaw which explains the whole thing, and this flaw is a readiness to obey authority without question, no matter what outrageous acts the authority commands.

The appealing thing about this theory is that it makes those of us who are not Germans feel better about the whole business. Obviously, you and I are not Hitler, and it seems equally obvious that we would never do Hitler's dirty work for him. But now, because of Stanley Milgram, we are compelled to wonder. Milgram developed a laboratory experiment which provided a systematic way to measure obedience. His plan was to try it out in New Haven on Americans and then go to Germany and try it out on Germans. He was strongly motivated by scientific curiosity, but there was also some moral content in his decision to pursue this line of research, which was, in turn, colored by his own Jewish background. If he could show that Germans are more obedient than Americans, he could then vary the conditions of the experiment and try to find out just what it is that makes some people more obedient than others. With this understanding, the world might, conceivably, be just a little bit better.

But he never took his experiment to Germany. He never took it any farther than Bridgeport. The first finding, also the most unexpected and disturbing finding, was that we Americans are an obedient people: not blindly obedient, and not blissfully obedient, just obedient. "I found so much obedience," says Milgram softly, a little sadly, "I hardly saw the need for taking the experiment to Germany."

There is something of the theatre director in Milgram, and his technique, which he learned from one of the old masters in experimental psychology, Solomon Asch, is to stage a play with every line rehearsed, every prop carefully selected, and everybody an actor except one person. That one person is the subject of the experiment. The subject, of course, does not know he is in a play. He thinks he is in real life. The value of this technique is that the experimenter, as though he were God, can change a prop here, vary a line there, and see how the subject responds. Milgram eventually had to change a lot of the script just to get people to stop obeying. They were obeying so much, the experiment wasn't working—it was like trying to measure oven temperature with a freezer thermometer.

The experiment worked like this: If you were an innocent subject in Milgram's melodrama, you read an ad in the newspaper or received one in the mail asking for volunteers for an educational experiment. The job would take about an hour and pay $4.50. So you make an appointment and go to an old Romanesque stone structure on High Street with the imposing name of The Yale Interaction Laboratory. It looks something like a broadcasting studio. Inside, you meet a young, crew-cut man in a laboratory coat who says he is Jack Williams, the experimenter. There is another citizen, fiftyish, Irish face, an accountant, a little overweight, and very mild and harmless-looking. This other citizen seems nervous and plays with his hat while the two of you sit in chairs side by side and are told that the $4.50 checks are yours no matter what happens. Then you listen to Jack Williams explain the experiment.

It is about learning, says Jack Williams in a quiet, knowledgeable way. Science does not know much about the conditions under which people learn and this experiment is to find out about negative reinforcement. Negative reinforcement is getting punished when you do something wrong, as opposed to positive reinforcement which is getting rewarded when you do something right. The negative reinforcement in this case is electric shock. You notice a book on the table, titled, *The Teaching-Learning Process*, and you assume that this has something to do with the experiment.

Then Jack Williams takes two pieces of paper, puts them in a hat, and shakes them up. One piece of paper is supposed to say, "Teacher" and the other, "Learner." Draw one and you will see which you will be. The mild-looking accountant draws one, holds it close to his vest like a poker player, looks at it, and says, "Learner." You look at yours. It says, "Teacher." You do not know that the drawing is rigged, and both slips say "Teacher." The experimenter beckons the mild-mannered "learner."

"Want to step right in here and have a seat, please?" he says. "You can leave your coat on the back of that chair . . . roll up your right sleeve, please. Now what I want to do is strap down your arms to avoid excessive movement on your part during the experiment. This electrode is connected to the shock generator in the next room.

"And this electrode paste," he says, squeezing some stuff out of a plastic bottle and putting it on the man's arm, "is to provide a good contact and to avoid a blister or burn. Are there any questions now before we go into the next room?"

You don't have any, but the strapped-in "learner" does.

"I do think I should say this," says the learner. "About two years ago, I was at the veterans' hospital . . . they detected a heart condition. Nothing serious, but as long as I'm having these shocks, how strong are they—how dangerous are they?''

Williams, the experimenter, shakes his head casually. ''Oh, no,'' he says. ''Although they may be painful, they're not dangerous. Anything else?''

Nothing else. And so you play the game. The game is for you to read a series of word pairs: for example, blue-girl, nice-day, fat-neck. When you finish the list, you read just the first word in each pair and then a multiple-choice list of four other words, including the second word of the pair. The learner, from his remote, strapped-in position, pushes one of four switches to indicate which of the four answers he thinks is the right one. If he gets it right, nothing happens and you go on to the next one. If he gets it wrong, you push a switch that buzzes and gives him an electric shock. And then you go to the next word. You start with 15 volts and increase the number of volts by 15 for each wrong answer. The control board goes from 15 volts on one end to 450 volts on the other. So that you know what you are doing, you get a test shock yourself, at 45 volts. It hurts. To further keep you aware of what you are doing to that man in there, the board has verbal descriptions of the shock levels, ranging from ''Slight Shock'' at the left-hand side, through ''Intense Shock'' in the middle, to ''Danger: Severe Shock'' toward the far right. Finally, at the very end, under 435- and 450-volt switches, there are three ambiguous X's. If, at any point, you hesitate, Mr. Williams calmly tells you to go on. If you still hesitate, he tells you again.

Except for some terrifying details, which will be explained in a moment, this is the experiment. The object is to find the shock level at which you disobey the experimenter and refuse to pull the switch.

When Stanley Milgram first wrote this script, he took it to fourteen Yale psychology majors and asked them what they thought would happen. He put it this way: Out of one hundred persons in the teacher's predicament, how would their break-off points be distributed along the 15-to-450-volt scale? They thought a few would break off very early, most would quit some place in the middle and a few would go all the way to the end. The highest estimate of the number out of one hundred who would go all the way to the end was three. Milgram then informally polled some of his fellow scholars in the psychology department. They agreed that very few would go to the end. Milgram thought so too.

''I'll tell you quite frankly,'' he says, ''before I began this experiment, before any shock generator was built, I thought that most people would break off at 'Strong Shock' or 'Very Strong Shock.' You would get only a very, very small proportion of people going out to the end of the shock generator, and they would constitute a pathological fringe.''

In his pilot experiments, Milgram used Yale students as subjects. Each of them pushed the shock switches, one by one, all the way to the end of the board.

So he rewrote the script to include some protests from the learner. At first, they were mild, gentlemanly, Yalie protests, but, ''it didn't seem to have as much effect as I thought it would or should,'' Milgram recalls. ''So we had more violent protestation on the part of the person getting the shock. All of the time, of course, what we were trying to do was not to create a macabre situation, but simply to generate disobedience. And that was one of the first findings. This was not only a technical deficiency of the experiment, that we didn't get disobedience. It really was the first finding, that obedience would be much greater than we had assumed it would be and disobedience would be much more difficult than we had assumed.''

As it turned out, the situation did become rather macabre. The only meaningful way to generate disobedience was to have the victim protest with great anguish, noise, and vehemence. The protests were tape-recorded so that all the teachers ordinarily would hear the same sounds and nuances, and they started with a grunt at 75 volts, proceeded through a ''Hey, that really hurts,'' at 125 volts, got desperate with, ''I can't stand the pain, don't do that,'' at 180 volts, reached complaints of heart trouble at 195, an agonized scream at 285, a refusal to answer at 315, and only heartrending, ominous silence after that.

Still, sixty-five percent of the subjects, twenty- to fifty-year-old American males, everyday, ordinary people, like you and me, obediently kept pushing those levers in the belief that they were shocking the mild-mannered learner, whose name was Mr. Wallace, and who was chosen for the role because of his innocent appearance, all the way up to 450 volts.

Milgram was now getting enough disobedience so that he had something he could measure. The next step was to vary the circumstances to see what would encourage or discourage obedience. There seemed very little left in the way of discouragement. The victim was already screaming at the top of his lungs and feigning a heart attack. So whatever new impediment to obedience reached the brain of the subject had to travel by some route other than the ear. Milgram thought of one.

He put the learner in the same room with the teacher. He stopped strapping the learner's hand down. He rewrote the script so that at 150 volts the learner took his hand off the shock plate and declared that he wanted out of the experiment. He rewrote the script some more so that the experimenter then told the teacher to grasp the learner's hand and physically force it down on the plate to give Mr. Wallace his unwanted electric shock.

''I had the feeling that very few people would go on at that point, if any,'' Milgram says. ''I thought that would be the limit of obedience that you would find in the laboratory.''

It wasn't.

Although seven years have now gone by, Milgram still remembers the first person to walk into the laboratory in the newly rewritten script. He was a construction worker, a very short man. ''He was so small,'' says Milgram, ''that when he sat on the chair in front of the shock generator, his feet didn't reach the floor. When the experimenter told him to push the victim's hand down and give the shock, he turned to the experimenter, and he turned to the victim, his elbow went up, he fell down on the hand of the victim, his feet kind of tugged to one side, and he said, 'Like this, boss?' Zzumph!''

The experiment was played out to its bitter end. Milgram tried it with forty different subjects. And thirty percent of them obeyed the experimenter and kept on obeying.

"The protests of the victim were strong and vehement, he was screaming his guts out, he refused to participate, and you had to physically struggle with him in order to get his hand down on the shock generator," Milgram remembers. But twelve out of forty did it.

Milgram took his experiment out of New Haven. Not to Germany, just twenty miles down the road to Bridgeport. Maybe, he reasoned, the people obeyed because of the prestigious setting of Yale University. If they couldn't trust a center of learning that had been there for two centuries, whom could they trust? So he moved the experiment to an untrustworthy setting.

The new setting was a suite of three rooms in a run-down office building in Bridgeport. The only identification was a sign with a fictitious name: "Research Associates of Bridgeport." Questions about professional connections got only vague answers about "research for industry."

Obedience was less in Bridgeport. Forty-eight percent of the subjects stayed for the maximum shock, compared to sixty-five percent at Yale. But this was enough to prove that far more than Yale's prestige was behind the obedient behavior.

For more than seven years now, Stanley Milgram has been trying to figure out what makes ordinary American citizens so obedient. The most obvious answer— that people are mean, nasty, brutish and sadistic—won't do. The subjects who gave the shocks to Mr. Wallace to the end of the board did not enjoy it. They groaned, protested, fidgeted, argued, and in some cases, were seized by fits of nervous, agitated giggling.

"They even try to get out of it," says Milgram, "but they are somehow engaged in something from which they cannot liberate themselves. They are locked into a structure, and they do not have the skills or inner resources to disengage themselves."

Milgram, because he mistakenly had assumed that he would have trouble getting people to obey the orders to shock Mr. Wallace, went to a lot of trouble to create a realistic situation.

There was crew-cut Jack Williams and his grey laboratory coat. Not white, which might denote a medical technician, but ambiguously authoritative grey. Then there was the book on the table, and the other appurtenances of the laboratory which emitted the silent message that things were being performed here in the name of science, and were therefore great and good.

But the nicest touch of all was the shock generator. When Milgram started out, he had only a $300 grant from the Higgins Fund of Yale University. Later he got more ample support from the National Science Foundation, but in the beginning he had to create this authentic-looking machine with very scarce resources except for his own imagination. So he went to New York and roamed around the electronic shops until he found some little black switches at Lafayette Radio for a dollar apiece. He bought thirty of them. The generator was a metal box, about the size of a small footlocker, and he drilled the thirty holes for the thirty switches himself in a Yale machine shop. But the fine detail was left to professional industrial engravers. So he ended up with a splendid-looking control panel dominated by the row of switches, each labeled with its voltage, and each having its own red light that flashed on when the switch was pulled. Other things happened when a switch was pushed. Besides the Zzumphing noise, a blue light labeled "voltage energizer" went on, and a needle on a dial labeled "voltage" flicked from left to right. Relays inside the box clicked. Finally, in the upper left-hand corner of the control panel was this inscription, engraved in precise block letters:

SHOCK GENERATOR TYPE ZLB

DYSON INSTRUMENT COMPANY

WALTHAM, MASS.

OUTPUT: 15 VOLTS–450 VOLTS

One day a man from the Lehigh Valley Electronics Company of Pennsylvania was passing through the laboratory, and he stopped to admire the shock generator.

"This is a very fine shock generator," he said. "But who is this Dyson Instrument Company?" Milgram felt proud at that, since Dyson Instrument Company existed only in the recesses of his imagination.

When you consider the seeming authenticity of the situation, you can appreciate the agony some of the subjects went through. It was pure conflict. As Milgram explains to his students, "When a parent says, 'Don't strike old ladies,' you are learning two things: the content, and, also, to obey authority. This experiment creates conflicts between the two elements."

Here is a partial transcription from one of the experiments. The naive "teacher" is a heavyset, worried-looking man with prematurely grey hair. He is wearing a polo shirt. He is very polite. He has just pushed the 180-volt lever. A hidden camera is recording the performance.

LEARNER (who, from the teacher's point of view is heard but not seen, an offstage voice): Ow, I can't stand the pain. Don't do that. . . .

TEACHER (pivoting around in his chair and shaking his head): I can't stand it. I'm not going to kill that man in there. You hear him hollering?

EXPERIMENTER: As I told you before, the shocks may be painful, but—

TEACHER: But he's hollering. He can't stand it. What's going to happen to him?

EXPERIMENTER (his voice is patient, matter-of-fact): The experiment requires that you continue, Teacher.

TEACHER: Aaah, but, unh, I'm not going to get that man sick in there— . . . know what I mean?

EXPERIMENTER: Whether the learner likes it or not, we must go on, through all the word pairs.

TEACHER: I refuse to take the responsibility. He's in there hollering!

EXPERIMENTER: It's absolutely essential that you continue, Teacher.

TEACHER (indicating the unused questions): There's too many left here, I mean, Geez, if he gets them wrong, there's too many of them left. I mean who's going to take the responsibility if anything happens to that gentleman?

EXPERIMENTER: I'm responsible for anything that happens to him. Continue please.

TEACHER: All right. (Consults list of words.) The next one's "Slow—walk, truck, dance, music." Answer, please. (A buzzing sound indicates the learner has signaled his answer.) Wrong. A hundred and ninety-five volts. "Dance." (Zzumph!)

LEARNER: Let me out of here. My heart's bothering me! (Teacher looks at experimenter.)

EXPERIMENTER: Continue, please.

LEARNER   (screaming): Let me out of here, you have no right to keep me here. Let me out of here, let me out, my heart's bothering me, let me out! (Teacher shakes head, pats the table nervously.)

TEACHER: You see, he's hollering. Hear that? Gee, I don't know.

EXPERIMENTER: The experiment requires. . . .

TEACHER   (interrupting): I know it does, sir, but I mean—hunh! He don't know what he's getting in for. He's up to 195 volts! (Experiment continues, through 210 volts, 225 volts, 240 volts, 255 volts, 270 volts, delivered to the man in the electric chair, at which point the teacher, with evident relief, runs out of word-pair questions.)

EXPERIMENTER: You'll have to go back to the beginning of that page and go through them again until he's learned them all correctly.

TEACHER: Aw, no. I'm not going to kill that man. You mean I've got to keep going up with the scale. No sir. He's hollering in there. I'm not going to give him 450 volts.

EXPERIMENTER: The experiment requires that you go on.

TEACHER: I know it does, but that man is hollering in there, sir.

EXPERIMENTER   (same matter-of-fact tone): As I said before, although the shocks may be painful. . . .

TEACHER   (interrupting): Awwww. He—he—he's yelling in there.

EXPERIMENTER: Start with "Blue," please, at the top of the page. Continue, please, Teacher. Just go ahead.

TEACHER   (concentrating intently on list of words in front of him, as if to shut everything else out): "Blue—boy, girl, grass, hat." (Buzz indicates answer.) Correct. "Night—day, sky, job, chair. (Buzz) Wrong. The answer is "day." Two hundred and eighty-five volts. (Zzumph!)

LEARNER: Ohhhuhhoohhh!

EXPERIMENTER: Continue, please.

TEACHER: "Fat—man, lady, tub, neck." Answer, please. (Buzz) Wrong. The answer is "neck." Three hundred volts. (Zzumph!)

LEARNER: Ohhh. I absolutely refuse to answer any more. (Shouting urgently, now) Let me out of here. You can't hold me here. Get me out. Get—me—out—of—here.

EXPERIMENTER: Continue. The next word is "Green," please.

TEACHER: "Green—grass, hat, ink, apple." (Nothing happens. No answering buzz. Just gloomy silence.)

TEACHER: I don't think he is going to answer.

EXPERIMENTER: If the learner doesn't answer in a reasonable time, about four or five seconds, consider the answer wrong. And follow the same procedures you have been doing for wrong answers. Say "Wrong," tell him the number of volts, give him the punishment, read him the correct answer. Continue, please.

TEACHER: "Green—grass, hat, ink, apple." Answer, please. (More silence. Teacher just sits there.)

EXPERIMENTER: Go on with the procedure, please, Teacher.

TEACHER: Three hundred and fifteen volts. The answer is "ink." (Zzumph!)

LEARNER: Ohh. Ooohh.

TEACHER (relieved to hear response): Next one. . . .

LEARNER: I absolutely refuse to answer.

TEACHER: You got to. You get a shock if you don't answer. (Experiment continues with learner refusing to answer, and, finally, failing even to grunt or groan. At 375 volts, the teacher stands up. Has he had enough? Will he break off the experiment? Will he disobey?)

TEACHER: I think something's happened to that fellow in there. I don't get no answer. He was hollering at less voltage. Can't you check in and see if he's all right, please?

EXPERIMENTER (same detached calm): Not once we've started. Please continue, Teacher.

TEACHER (sits down, sighs deeply): "Cool—day, shade, water, paint." Answer, please. Are you all right in there? Are you all right?

EXPERIMENTER: Please continue, Teacher. Continue, please. (Teacher pushes lever. Zzumph!)

TEACHER (swiveling around in his chair): Something's happened to that man in there. (Swiveling back) Next one. "Low—dollar, necklace, moon, paint." (Turning around again) Something's happened to that man in there. You better check in on him, sir. He won't answer or nothing.

EXPERIMENTER: Continue. Go on, please.

TEACHER: You accept all responsibility.

EXPERIMENTER: The responsibility is mine. Correct. Please go on. (Teacher returns to his list, starts running through words as rapidly as he can read them, works through to 450 volts.)

TEACHER: That's that.

EXPERIMENTER: Continue using the last switch on the board, please. The four-fifty switch for each wrong answer. Continue, please.

TEACHER: But I don't get no anything!

EXPERIMENTER: Please continue. The next word is "White."

TEACHER: Don't you think you should look in on him, please.

EXPERIMENTER: Not once we've started the experiment.

TEACHER: But what if something has happened to the man?

EXPERIMENTER: The experiment requires that you continue. Go on, please.

TEACHER: Don't the man's health mean anything?

EXPERIMENTER: Whether the learner likes it or not. . . .

TEACHER: What if he's dead in there? (Gestures toward the room with the electric chair.) I mean, he told me he can't stand the shock, sir. I don't mean to be rude, but I think you should look in on him. All you have to do is look in the door. I don't get no answer, no noise. Something miight have happened to the gentleman in there, sir.

EXPERIMENTER: We must continue. Go on, please.

TEACHER: You mean keep giving him what? Four hundred fifty volts, what he's got now?

EXPERIMENTER: That's correct. Continue. The next word is "White."

TEACHER (now at a furious pace): "White—cloud, horse, rock, house." Answer, please. The answer is "horse." Four hundred and fifty volts. (Zzumph!) Next word, "Bag—paint, music, clown, girl." The answer is "paint." Four hundred and fifty volts. (Zzumph!) Next word is "Short—sentence, movie. . . ."

EXPERIMENTER: Excuse me, Teacher. We'll have to discontinue the experiment.

(Enter Milgram from camera's left. He has been watching from behind one-way glass.)

MILGRAM: I'd like to ask you a few questions. (Slowly, patiently, he dehoaxes the teacher, telling him that the shocks and screams were not real.)

TEACHER: You mean he wasn't getting nothing? Well, I'm glad to hear that. I was getting upset there. I was getting ready to walk out.

(Finally, to make sure there are no hard feelings, friendly, harmless Mr. Wallace comes out in coat and tie. Gives jovial greeting. Friendly reconciliation takes place. Experiment ends.)*

Subjects in the experiment were not asked to give the 450-volt shock more than three times. By that time, it seemed evident that they would go on indefinitely. "No one," says Milgram, "who got within five shocks of the end ever broke off. By that point, he had resolved the conflict."

Why do so many people resolve the conflict in favor of obedience?

Milgram's theory assumes that people behave in two different operating modes as different as ice and water. He does not rely on Freud or sex or toilet-training hang-ups for this theory. All he says is that ordinarily we operate in a state of autonomy, which means we pretty much have and assert control over what we do. But in certain circumstances, we operate under what Milgram calls a state of agency (after agent, *n* . . . one who acts for or in the place of another by authority from him; a substitute; a deputy—*Webster's Collegiate Dictionary*). A state of agency, to Milgram, is nothing more than a frame of mind.

"There's nothing bad about it, there's nothing good about it," he says. "It's a natural circumstance of living with other people. . . . I think of a state of agency as a real transformation of a person; if a person has different properties when he's in that state, just as water can turn to ice under certain conditions of temperature, a person can move to the state of mind that I call agency . . . the critical thing is that you see yourself as the instrument of the execution of another person's wishes. You do not see yourself as acting on your own. And there's a real transformation, a real change of properties of the person."

To achieve this change, you have to be in a situation where there seems to be a ruling authority whose commands are relevant to some legitimate purpose; the authority's power is not unlimited.

But situations can be and have been structured to make people do unusual

*Copyright 1965 by Stanley Milgram. From the film OBEDIENCE, distributed by the New York University Film Library.

things, and not just in Milgram's laboratory. The reason, says Milgram, is that no action, in and of itself, contains meaning.

"The meaning always depends on your definition of the situation. Take an action like killing another person. It sounds bad.

"But then we say the other person was about to destroy a hundred children, and the only way to stop him was to kill him. Well, that sounds good.

"Or, you take destroying your own life. It sounds very bad. Yet, in the Second World War, thousands of persons thought it was a good thing to destroy your own life. It was set in the proper context. You sipped some saki from a whistling cup, recited a few haiku. You said, 'May my death be as clean and as quick as the shattering of crystal.' And it almost seemed like a good, noble thing to to, to crash your kamikaze plane into an aircraft carrier. But the main thing was, the definition of what a kamikaze pilot was doing had been determined by the relevant authority. Now, once you are in a state of agency, you allow the authority to determine, to define what the situation is. The meaning of your action is altered."

So, for most subjects in Milgram's laboratory experiments, the act of giving Mr. Wallace his painful shock was necessary, even though unpleasant, and besides they were doing it on behalf of somebody else and it was for science. There was still strain and conflict, of course. Most people resolved it by grimly sticking to their task and obeying. But some broke out. Milgram tried varying the conditions of the experiment to see what would help break people out of their state of agency.

"The results, as seen and felt in the laboratory," he has written, "are disturbing. They raise the possibility that human nature, or more specifically the kind of character produced in American democratic society, cannot be counted on to insulate its citizens from brutality and inhumane treatment at the direction of malevolent authority. A substantial proportion of people do what they are told to do, irrespective of the content of the act and without limitations of conscience, so long as they perceive that the command comes from a legitimate authority. If, in this study, an anonymous experimenter can successfully command adults to subdue a fifty-year-old man and force on him painful electric shocks against his protest, one can only wonder what government, with its vastly greater authority and prestige, can command of its subjects."

This is a nice statement, but it falls short of summing up the full meaning of Milgram's work. It leaves somequestions still unanswered.

The first question is this: Should we really be surprised and alarmed that people obey? Wouldn't it be even more alarming if they all refused to obey? Without obedience to a relevant ruling authority there could not be a civil society. And without a civil society, as Thomas Hobbes pointed out in the seventeenth century, we would live in a condition of war, "of every man against every other man," and life would be "solitary, poor, nasty, brutish and short."

In the middle of one of Stanley Milgram's lectures at C.U.N.Y. recently, some mini-skirted undergraduates started whispering and giggling in the back of the room. He told them to cut it out. Since he was the relevant authority in that time and that place, they obeyed, and most people in the room were glad that they obeyed.

This was not, of course, a conflict situation. Nothing in the coeds' social upbringing made it a matter of conscience for them to whisper and giggle. But a case can be made that in a conflict situation it is all the more important to obey. Take the case of war, for example. Would we really want a situation in which every participant in a war, direct or indirect—from front-line soldiers to the people who sell coffee and cigarettes to employees at the Concertina barbed-wire factory in Kansas—stops and consults his conscience before each action? It is asking for an awful lot of mental strain and anguish from an awful lot of people. The value of having civil order is that one can do his duty, or whatever interests him, or whatever seems to benefit him at the moment, and leave the agonizing to others. When Francis Gary Powers was being tried by a Soviet military tribunal after his U-2 spy plane was shot down, the presiding judge asked if he had thought about the possibility that his flight might have provoked a war. Powers replied with Hobbesian clarity: "The people who sent me should think of these things. My job was to carry out orders. I do not think it was my responsibility to make such decisions."

It was not his responsibility. And it is quite possible that if everyone felt responsible for each of the ultimate consequences of his own tiny contributions to complex chains of events, then society simply would not work. Milgram, fully conscious of the moral and social implications of his research, believes that people should feel responsible for their actions. If someone else had invented the experiment, and if he had been the naive subject, he feels certain that he would have been among the disobedient minority.

"There is no very good solution to this," he admits, thoughtfully. "To simply and categorically say that you won't obey authority may resolve your personal conflict, but it creates more problems for society which may be more serious in the long run. But I have no doubt that to disobey is the proper thing to do in this [the laboratory] situation. It is the only reasonable value judgment to make."

The conflict between the need to obey the relevant ruling authority and the need to follow your conscience becomes sharpest if you insist on living by an ethical system based on a rigid code—a code that seeks to answer all questions in advance of their being raised. Code ethics cannot solve the obedience problem. Stanley Milgram seems to be a situation ethicist, and situation ethics does offer a way out: When you feel conflict, you examine the situation and then make a choice among the competing evils. You may act with a presumption in favor of obedience, but reserve the possibility that you will disobey whenever obedience demands a flagrant and outrageous affront to conscience. This, by the way, is the philosophical position of many who resist the draft. In World War II, they would have fought. Vietnam is a different, an outrageously different situation.

Life can be difficult for the situation ethicist, because he does not see the world in straight lines, while the social system too often assumes such a God-given, squared-off structure. If your moral code includes an injunction against all war, you may be deferred as a conscientious objector. If you merely oppose this particular war, you may not be deferred.

Stanley Milgram has his problems, too. He believes that in the laboratory situation, he would not have shocked Mr. Wallace. His professional critics reply that in his real-life situation he has done the equivalent. He has placed innocent and naive subjects under great emotional strain and pressure in selfish obedience to his quest for knowledge. When you raise this issue with Milgram, he has an answer ready. There is, he explains patiently, a critical difference between his naive subjects and the man in the electric chair. The man in the electric chair (in the mind of the naive subject) is helpless, strapped in. But the naive subject is free to go at any time.

Immediately after he offers this distinction, Milgram anticipates the objection. "It's quite true," he says, "that this is almost a philosophic position, because we have learned that some people are psychologically incapable of disengaging themselves. But that doesn't relieve them of the moral responsibility."

The parallel is exquisite. "The tension problem was unexpected," says Milgram in his defense. But he went on anyway. The naive subjects didn't expect the screaming protests from the strapped-in learner. But they went on.

"I had to make a judgment," says Milgram. "I had to ask myself, was this harming the person or not? My judgment is that it was not. Even in the extreme cases, I wouldn't say that permanent damage results."

Sound familiar? "The shocks may be painful," the experimenter kept saying, "but they're not dangerous."

After the series of experiments was completed, Milgram sent a report of the results to his subjects and a questionnaire, asking whether they were glad or sorry to have been in the experiment. Eighty-three and seven-tenths percent said they were glad and only 1.3 percent were sorry; 15 percent were neither sorry nor glad. However, Milgram could not be sure at the time of the experiment that only 1.3 percent would be sorry.

Kurt Vonnegut, Jr., put one paragraph in the preface to *Mother Night*, in 1966, which pretty much says it for the people with their fingers on the shock-generator switches, for you and me, and maybe even for Milgram. "If I'd been born in Germany," Vonnegut said, "I suppose I would have *been* a Nazi, bopping Jews and gypsies and Poles around, leaving boots sticking out of snowbanks, warming myself with my sweetly virtuous insides. So it goes."

Just so. One thing that happened to Milgram back in New Haven during the days of the experiment was that he kept running into people he'd watched from behind the one-way glass. It gave him a funny feeling, seeing those people going about their everyday business in New Haven and knowing what they would do to Mr. Wallace if ordered to. Now that his research results are in and you've thought about it, you can get this funny feeling too. You don't need one-way glass. A glance in your own mirror may serve just as well.

My opinion, my conviction, gains infinitely in strength and success, the moment a second mind has adopted it.

Novalis, Fragment, trans. Thomas Carlyle.

CHARLAN NEMETH

The Role of an Active Minority in Intergroup Relations

. . . For decades, many researchers have defined majority/minority disagreements in a "small group" from the point of view of the majority. Originating with Asch's (1955) series of ingenious experiments, influence processes between a majority and a minority have often been viewed unidirectionally. Influence occurs because the minority abdicates its position and moves in the direction of the initial majority. The alternative is that the minority remains independent. The possibility that a minority may have a system of answers of its own—that the minority may attempt to influence the majority (and possibly succeed)—could not be observed or investigated, given the paradigm that has often been used.

Let us consider the original Asch paradigm, which has formed the basis for hundreds of studies on conformity. Subjects are shown a standard line and three comparison lines and are simply asked to judge which of the comparison lines is equal in length to the standard line. A group of three to seven confederates agree on an incorrect answer. The question is whether or not a subject will agree with this erroneous majority judgment or trust the judgment of his own senses. Asch's original studies show that approximately 35% of the judgments were in agreement with the erroneous majority, whereas subjects were rarely incorrect when making their judgments alone.

This powerful process, termed the *conformity process*, has been widely investigated by social psychologists. Each new study has introduced information on the conditions under which, and the reasons why, a subject will conform to an erroneous majority or remain independent. However, the paradigm has remained fairly constant. Even when the question of an ally has been investigated, this minority of two (one confederate and one subject) has been investigated in such a way that the only possible outcomes of the experiment are conformity or independence (or, possibly, anticonformity). For consensus to be achieved, it has to revolve around the majority. Since the majority is composed of experimental confederates, there is no possibility of compromise or of minority influence. Thus, the paradigm forces influence to be construed from the point of view of the majority and the maintenance of the status quo.

This orientation can also be found in the tendency to equate the minority position with deviance. If one promotes cooperation and agreement as a desirable end state, the notion of a minority as deviant offers a value judgment as to how consensus should be acheived. Deviants, by resisting, disallow group locomotion and maintain discomfort by insisting on a different position. The question of influence then becomes how to check these deviants, and the usual answer is to influence them or reject them.

That the majority has such tools at its disposal is not under question. Schachter's (1951) study, for example, shows that majority members communicate frequently to a "deviant" in an attempt to influence him; if unsuccessful, they reject him sociometrically. And it turns out that subjects in a minority are not unaware of such tools at the hands of the majority. Such considerations have been found to weigh heavily in the minds of minority individuals when deciding whether or not to conform. Asch's subjects, for example, report concerns over being different—about "sticking out like a sore thumb." And the minority is also prone to uncertainty about whether or not their position is correct when faced with a unanimous majority. Assuming that truth lies in numbers, as in the slogan "Forty million Frenchmen can't be wrong," many members of the minority in Asch's studies came to the conclusion that "I am wrong, they are right," and conformed accordingly.

Powerful as this conformity process may be, clearly it is not the only basis for agreement. The dissensions in the political arena of the 1960s made many of us aware that a small but vocal minority can sway majority opinion. As we reflect on the discoveries in the sciences, and the profound impact of individuals such as Galileo and Freud, we also recognize the importance of minority influence—of the process of social change as well as social control. While the conformity research has been very important in our understanding of social control, it has given us little information on the processes of social change, partly because the complexities of the interaction between a majority and a minority have been obscured. We have not learned about the ways in which each party shapes and reacts to the other— especially, the ways in which the initial minority may influence, as well as be influenced by, the majority.

MINORITY INFLUENCE

As a needed corrective to the emphasis on social control and the conformity process, several researchers have recently attempted to investigate the process by which a minority can influence a majority (Moscovici & Faucheux, 1972; Moscovici & Nemeth, 1974). In contemplating this phenomenon, these theorists have had to deal with the issue of the basis for influence. The conformity literature had already documented that the basis for influence by a majority on a minority is dependency. The minority is dependent on the majority for approval (or, at least, not disapproval); this has been termed *normative influence*. The minority is also dependent on the majority for information about reality; this has been termed *informational influence*.

With regard to the possibility of minority influence on the majority, it is clear from the outset that the minority lacks the numerical strength to successfully invoke either normative or informational influence at the beginning. If people are concerned about rejection as a result of disagreement, they will fare better resting with the majority than attempting to court minority acceptance. If consensus defines social reality and if others' judgments are taken as evidence about that reality, again there are more judgments in agreement with one's own when one is a member of the majority. Thus, at least in the beginning, it appears that the minority has little chance of prevailing. The majority is unlikely to collapse at the first recognition of a minority in disagreement with them.

Given this seeming initial powerlessness of the minority, the question remains: how does a minority exert influence? There are those unique cases in which a minority has peculiar resources, prestige, status, or power that can aid its members in their influence attempts. However, this is not the usual, or at least not the most interesting, situation. The situation at issue here is one involving peers, in which a minority of individuals takes a position in disagreement with that held by a majority. The existing literature suggests that this minority will be held in derision and that attempts will be made to influence its members to accept the position held by the majority; we maintain, however, that there are situations in which this minority can shape and influence the position held by the majority.

In an attempt to discover a possible basis for minority influence, we (Moscovici & Nemeth, 1974) have hypothesized that it may lie in the behavioral style of the minority—that is, the orchestration and patterning of their behavior as they attempt to persuade the majority. Further, the minority has some, though few, advantages. As previous research (such as Schachter, 1951) has shown, the minority, by virtue of being in the minority, gains the attention of the majority members. A good deal of communication is directed toward the minority members in attempts at persuasion. While this has been construed as pressure, which indeed it is, it also provides a focus of attention: the minority has the floor. With appropriate behavioral styles, the minority can then clarify and expound its position, thus paving the way for potential influence.

As a starting point, we have suggested that a behavioral style of *consistency* is necessary (if not sufficient) for minority influence. If the minority continues to insist on its position, if it consistently maintains this position in the face of real or imagined majority pressure, then it poses its position as an alternative. And it is precisely because people prefer, and possibly need, consensus to define social reality that such insistence on an alternative position creates the conflict necessary for social influence. As another starting point, we assume that consensus will revolve around the most stable anchor. Though, initially, the majority may assume that consensus rests with their own position, they may come to learn through the consistency and insistence of the minority that stability may be found in a consensus established around the minority position.

Such an emphasis on consistency over time in the presentation of the minority position has its counterpart in the conformity literature. Numerous studies (such as Asch, 1955) have shown that the power of the majority in the conformity setting depends on its unanimity, not on its sheer numbers. Thus, a unanimous majority of three is more powerful than a majority of five with one dissenter. And it turns out that the dissenter need not agree with the minority; that is, subjects do not need social support per se to remain independent. The break in unanimity of the majority is the important variable for weakening the conformity process. Thus, unanimity may provide a stable anchor to which the subject can move.

However, now we are considering the potential importance of stability over time rather than over numbers of people. If the minority maintains its position, then it is possible that at least some majority members may become uncertain and change their position. If such a shift occurs (by even one member), the majority is weakened, and the group may move to the more stable anchor provided by the minority.

RESEARCH ON MINORITY INFLUENCE

Starting with this hypothesis regarding the importance of consistency over time, Moscovici, Lage, and Naffrechoux (1969) conducted an experiment in which subjects were asked to indicate the color of a slide they were shown and to estimate its brightness on a 5-point scale. Six subjects estimated the color and brightness in sequence, and they were asked to make their judgments 36 times (6 slides presented 6 times each). The stimuli were slides on which two different types of filters were mounted. One permitted the passage of a beam of light of the dominant wavelength in the blue scale; the other was a neutral filter which reduced light intensity in certain proportions. The important point is that the subjects (who had been tested to make sure they had normal color vision) saw blue stimuli. Of these six individuals, two were paid confederates who were instructed to say that they saw green on the 36 trials. Thus, in the experimental condition, two confederates posed a minority norm: they saw green where everyone else saw blue, and they were consistent from trial to trial. The results showed that the naïve subjects in this condition called the stimulus green 8.42% of the time, whereas subjects in the control conditions reported green only 0.25% of the time—a difference that was statistically significant.

In a second condition, the confederates were inconsistent. They called the stimulus green 24 times and called it blue 12 times; the dispersion of ''blue'' answers was randomized. Subjects in this condition called the stimuli green only 1.25% of the time, a percentage not significantly different from the control.

Thus, this experiment provides evidence that the minority is much more influential when it maintains its position over time; in fact, when inconsistent, the minority exerted no influence. Results of the second part of the experiment provide even more compelling evidence for the ability of the minority to exert influence. Hypothesizing that some subjects might have maintained the majority position verbally while, in fact, being shaken and influenced by the minority, subjects were given a blue-green designation threshold task made up of 16 discs in the blue-green zone of Farnsworth's perception test. Three discs from each end of the blue and green scale were unambiguous; they were clearly blue or green. The other ten might have appeared ambiguous. Subjects were asked to call each disc blue or green. Of the 40 subjects who were exposed to the consistent minority espousing the ''green'' position, 3 subjects polarized: they called more green stimuli ''blue'' than did the control subjects. The other 37, however, showed a modification of their perceptual code consistent with the social influence of the minority: they called more blue stimuli ''green'' than did the control subjects.

This experiment was an important first step in understanding the impact of minorities, in that it provided a paradigm and a convincing demonstration of the phenomenon. Further, it pointed to the importance of maintenance of position by the minority in order to exert influence. The notion of maintenance of position, however, appears to be more subtle than the simple repetition used by the confederates in this experiment. Moscovici et al. (1969) emphasized the conflict engendered by the disagreement, hypothesizing that ''by insisting on his answer, a minority will not only engender a conflict, but will intensify the conflict, because it posed its own judgments and opinion as having the same value, as being equivalent to those of the majority'' (p. 367). In a subsequent experiment, Nemeth, Swedlund, and Kanki (1974) offered the hypothesis that it was not intensification of the conflict created by repetition that allowed for minority influence; rather, it was the *perception* that the minority had a position of which it was firmly convinced that was the necessary condition for minority influence. Such perceptions, they theorized, can be created by a consistent *pattern* of judgments. One can maintain a position without dogmatically repeating it. One can show an unwillingness to concede in more subtle ways than repetition. Further, when a property of the situation or stimulus changes, a minority can change its position (and, in fact, should, if it is credible) without suffering any loss in the perception that it has a position of which it is firmly convinced.

In their experiment, Nemeth et al. used basically the same paradigm as Moscovici et al. Two confederates posed a minority position to 4 naïve subjects. The stimuli were slides that differed in luminosity but were all pure blue in color. Here, the researchers took advantage of the differences in perceptions of brightness in legislating the responses of the confederates. In three of the experimental conditions, the confederates did not manifest repetition. They said that they saw the color as green on 50% of the trials and as green-blue on 50% of the trials. In one of these three conditions (the Random condition), these responses were given according to a memorized, predetermined random order. In the other two conditions, these responses were patterned according to the perceived brightness of the slides. In one of these conditions, the 14 slides (50%) that were brightest were called green-blue, and the 14 slides that were least bright were called green. In the other condition, this pattern was reversed: the 14 brightest slides were called green, and the other 14 slides were called green-blue. These two conditions represented the Correlated condition. In the other two experimental conditions, the confederates maintained their position by straight repetition. In one of these conditions (straight green), confederates said they saw green on every trial; in the other condition (straight green-blue), confederates said that they saw green-blue on every trial. A control condition was also run in which naïve subjects gave their judgments.

Results indicated that the Correlated condition produced the most influence ($\overline{X}$ = 5.84). Though not significantly more effective than a repetitious green-blue response ($\overline{X}$ = 4.00), it was significantly more effective than a repetitious green response ($\overline{X}$ = .69). Perhaps the most interesting finding came from a comparison among the three conditions in which confederates gave 50% ''green'' responses and

50% "green-blue" responses. Recall that in one of these conditions, the responses were randomly associated with the slides, whereas in the other two conditions, the responses were patterned with the perceived brightness of the slides. Both correlated conditions were significantly more effective in producing minority influence ($\overline{X}$ = 5.84) than was the random condition ($\overline{X}$ = .06). Further, the correlated conditions produced perceptions that the confederates were more sure in making their judgments, more organized, and more trusted than did the random condition.

Thus, this experiment provides evidence that the *patterning* of the judgments and the perceptions created from such patterns may be the basis for influence. Even though nonrepetitive, the minority in the correlated conditions were at least as effective as in any repetitive pattern. Further, they maintained the perception of being as sure of themselves and of having as good a color judgment as in any other condition. Without such patterning (that is, in the random condition), they were seen as much less sure of their judgments, less organized, and less trusted.

This experiment again underscores the importance of consistency on the part of the minority: they need to be seen as organized and sure of their position. But it is not necessary that they intensify the conflict by constantly repeating their position. What appears to be important is the creation of the perception that they have a position in which they are confident.

Such an analysis underscores the basic contention (for example, Moscovici & Faucheux, 1972; Moscovici & Nemeth, 1974) that the minority, by their behavioral style, can exert influence. They come into the situation with no particular status, resources, or power. In fact, by virtue of being a minority, they may well be initially suspect. But it is possible to attract attention, to draw to oneself the perception of possessing a committed alternative to the prevailing view. And this research demonstrates that the majority, far from being all-powerful, is susceptible to persuasion from a committed minority.

While these studies demonstrate the importance of consistency of position, the theorizing based on this research has also emphasized the importance of perceived *confidence*. In suggesting that it is the unwillingness to capitulate and the resistance to conformity pressure that conveys the stability of the minority position, we have implied that it is not passive consistency that aids the minority in its influence attempts but, rather, the maintenance of a position with confidence. Thus, behavioral styles that heighten the perception of confidence should increase the minority's effectiveness.

A study by Nemeth and Wachtler (1974) clarifies the importance of particular behavioral acts of confidence that, together with maintenance of position, increase the effectiveness of the minority position. Moreover, their study was conducted in a discussion (rather than a judgment) setting—a setting closer to the real-life counterpart of two groups in opposition, where each is committed to its own point of view and where discussion and interchange as well as pressure are allowed. Nemeth and Wachtler used a jury simulation, in which subjects were to decide on compensation for a victim in a personal-injury case. Pretesting indicated that most subjects would opt for approximately $15,000 compensation and that practically no one would take a position of less than $8,000. After hours of careful presentation, the researchers devised a series of arguments that would be appropriate for any discussion of this case; they had a confederate memorize these arguments and give them from memory in the deliberation. The position he espoused was compensation of $3,000—a position markedly different from that of the five naïve subjects who deliberated the case with him. In all conditions, the confederate maintained this position, giving only the memorized arguments and paraphrases thereof.

The behavioral act of confidence was drawn from previous research involving seating arrangements around a rectangular table. Numerous studies have attested to the importance of sitting at the head of a rectangular table for influence. However, these studies have generally confounded the taking of this seat with its occupation. As a result, some researchers (for example, Strodtbeck & Hook, 1961) have concentrated on the occupation aspect and have interpreted the importance of this seating arrangement in terms of visual accessibility. Such accessibility, they contend, allows for more verbal interchange as well as more influence attempts. Nemeth and Wachtler, however, offered the hypothesis that it is the taking of the head seat, rather than its simple occupation, that aids influence attempts, because such an act may well foster a perception of confidence on the part of that individual.

In their study, Nemeth and Wachtler separated these variables by either instructing each individual to sit in a given chair or by allowing the seating arrangements to be made by choice. The confederate espousing the minority position either chose or was assigned to the head seat, or he chose or was assigned to one of two side seats. In all conditions, he remained steadfast in his position of $3,000, and the arguments that he offered in support of his position were constant. Findings indicated that the *choice* of the head seat was the most effective action. In this condition, the confederate was significantly more effective in inducing the other subjects to lower their judgments of compensation to the victim. Choice or occupation of a side seat or the simple occupation of the head seat were not effective mechanisms for influence.

Two points should be made regarding these findings. The first is that simple acts promoting the perception of confidence appear to aid the minority in its influence attempts. By and large, the confederate choosing the head seat was seen as more consistent and confident. And he exerted the most influence. The second point to be remembered is that it is only in the Chosen Head seat condition that the minority was effective. In contrast to the judgment studies previously reported, simple maintenance of position was not, in and of itself, effective in creating minority influence. While consistency and maintenance of position still appears to be a necessary condition for minority influence, this study also demonstrates that it need not be sufficient.

One reason why it was more difficult for the minority to exert influence in this study is that the subjects comprising the majority were very committed to their position. Their anger at the confederate, their persistence in communicating counterarguments, and their frustration throughout the interchange were very evident. Another aspect is that subjects in this study learned, by means of the discussion, that they indeed formed a group; they were in basic agreement and in total disagreement with the minority position proposed. Lest we forget, the minority has an uphill battle in changing the judgments of a cohesive majority. But the studies indicate that, with the appropriate behavior style—in particular, a style that fosters perceptions of consistency and confidence—the minority can and does exert influence. In this study, when the confederate chose the head seat and maintained his position of $3,000, naïve subjects tended to move their judgments closer to his. Further, they lowered their judgments of compensation on a totally new personal-injury case subsequent to the deliberation.

Up to this point, we appear to have emphasized consistency and confidence— that is, particular behavioral styles—as though the quality of the arguments or the reasonableness of the position did not matter. It is undoubtedly clear to the reader that minority influence might have been much more difficult, if not impossible, to achieve had the minority in the judgment studies espoused a position of "red," for example, to the blue slides rather than "green." There are undoubtedly outer bounds to what can even be considered, but these bounds are probably much wider than one might expect. In many ways, the Nemeth and Wachtler study using the jury simulation demonstrated the ability of a minority to prevail even when his position was initially considered ludicrous to the majority. However, it should be clear that the reasonableness of the position itself is a factor to be considered in addition to behavioral style.

One recent study (Nemeth, Wachtler, & Endicott, 1977) has investigated the perception of presumed correctness as well as confidence with regard to minority influence. The variable that was manipulated to effect these perceptions was size of minority. In the previous studies, the minority consisted of either one or two individuals. In this study, that variable was manipulated, keeping the size of the majority constant at six. Either one, two, three, or four confederates offered the position of "green-blue" consistently to the blue sides. Perhaps surprisingly, it was found that all four conditions were effective in inducing minority influence, but that they did not differ significantly from one another. However, there appear to be different reasons for the essentially equal influence that was exerted. As the size of the minority increased, the majority was *more* likely to perceive the minority as having good color judgment and as more likely to be correct. At the same time, as the size of the minority increased, the majority was *less* likely to perceive the minority as confident and sure of its position. The best predictor of the influence scores was the sum of these two perceptions: competence and confidence.

It seems intuitively plausible that the greater the number of people espousing the minority position, the more likely one is to assume that they may be correct. However, there is a trade-off. The greater the number of people in the minority, the *less* likely one is to assume that each is sure of his position. It is as though the naïve subjects in the majority understand the pressures toward conformity. When they see a person espousing a minority position with a number of allies, they assume that he need not be so committed to, nor so confident of, his position as when he has only a single ally or stands alone. This, of course, is consistent with the evidence on conformity: an individual alone is susceptible to conformity, whereas if he has even one ally, he is more likely to remain independent.

TOWARD A BROADER CONCEPTION OF INFLUENCE

The studies described in the preceding section represent some first steps toward an understanding of the minority's influence on the majority and, as such, provide a perspective on the intergroup nature of the interaction between majority and minority. However, as in the conformity literature, these studies have tended to define influence in the fairly narrow sense of winning or prevailing. Thus, the question has been: how, for what reasons, and under what circumstances can the minority persuade the majority to adopt the minority viewpoint?

Influence, more broadly construed, can refer to the reassessment of a given position and to the adoption of third alternatives—alternatives not specifically promoted by the minority, but adopted as a result of the interaction between majority and minority. In fact, it appears that a strong and insistent minority can exert considerable influence on a majority, though not necessarily in the direction of the position espoused. And some recent evidence indicates that the minority can, as a result, offer a creative contribution to the problem-solving abilities of the majority. Further, this contribution appears to be much more in the province of minority influence than conformity. . . .

. . . We need to preserve the basic intergroup processes between majority and minority in order to understand social influence—which includes social change as well as social control. Toward this end, the work on minority influence has provided a needed corrective to a literature that has concentrated on the elimination of conflict rather than the creative contribution that conflict can provide. Further, it is a corrective to assumptions that the minority is necessarily an obstacle to group functioning. To the extent that this research has challenged the tendency to make a priori judgments on the value of cohesiveness and smooth group functioning and has forced, instead, a consideration of the dynamic interactions between majority and minority, it has served a useful purpose.

However, it is also clear that many of the studies reported here do not involve natural majorities and minorities in interaction. Their corrective to the literature has taken the form of pointing to a reciprocal process—minority influence—that could not be detected by means of the paradigms utilized in the conformity studies. Like the conformity research, however, these studies have tended to hold one group constant. In this case, the minority is composed of experimental confederates, and their judgments and behaviors are manipulated in order to observe the impact on the naïve subjects who comprise the majority. Ultimately, of course, we need to understand the processes that occur between the two groups in interaction. Minority influence, like conformity, is one possible outcome of the interaction between majority and minority. The studies from these literatures help us to understand the potential consequences of majorities and minorities in interaction. Yet, they do not enable us to understand the complexities of the interaction that may occur naturally; they do not tell us when the process will go to conformity, to minority influence, or possibly to compromise or polarization.

Recently, we have conducted some studies involving simulations of jury deliberations in which we have attempted to preserve the dynamic between natural majorities and minorities (Nemeth, 1976; Nemeth, Endicott, & Wachtler, 1976).

As this research was addressed primarily to questions relating to the law, however, the results regarding majority/minority interactions were secondary and are suggestive rather than definitive.

In these studies, six individuals deliberated a criminal case involving a charge of first-degree murder. By means of pretesting, these six individuals were chosen such that we knew beforehand that the initial ballot would split 4–2. In half the groups, the minority of two would vote "guilty"; in the other half, the minority of two would espouse the position of "not guilty." The six individuals actually believed the positions they espoused. Thus, we had a confrontation between a natural majority and a natural minority who were asked to agree on a decision—that is, a verdict. Confirming what we know from court statistics, our studies illustrated the decided advantage of the initial majority: in a large number of deliberations, the verdict coincided with the position held by the initial majority. When the minority prevailed, it was most likely to occur when they took the position of "not guilty." This is undoubtedly because it is easier to convince others that they have a reasonable doubt than to convince them beyond a reasonable doubt.

More pertinent to the nature of the influence processes between majority and minority, it was found that the amount of talking and, in particular, the number of comments made . . . giving information and giving opinions, was related to influence. As an illustration of this, we found that we could predict over 97% of the verdicts by means of simply coding and summing the number of comments made for one position as opposed to the other. Utilizing a procedure suggested by L. Richard Hoffman, we kept a running account of every comment uttered in terms of whether it was pro-prosecution or pro-defense. When the cumulative sum for comments favoring one position exceeded the number of comments favoring the other position by 7, we found that we could predict all but one of the verdicts: the actual verdict was the position favored by the most comments rather than by the most persons.

The interaction dynamics that result in this predictor variable are not clearly understood. However, it seems reasonable to assume that the number of comments favoring one position reflects a commitment to that position. Those strongly committed to their position would be likely to reiterate comments supporting that position; those who were becoming uncertain or "giving up" might utter fewer comments in support of their position.

Thus, again, we find a corroboration of the importance of persistence of position for influence. In this experiment, each member of the minority of two needed to talk at least twice as much as each member of the majority of four to keep the minority position viable. Either position could prevail, whether it was held by the initial majority or minority, if that party created a situation in which the number of comments favoring their position exceeded the number of comments in opposition to it by at least 7.

How the groups create such a situation favoring their own position is undoubtedly complex. The dependent variable reflects but, at the same time, masks the subtle processes of influence, the nature of groups in interaction. When one opinion prevailed, it was clear that the process was far more complicated and subtle than simple maintenance of position by the proponents of that position. But, though I could recognize the complexities, I found that I could not clearly specify them. It is with this awareness of the complexities that we do not tap that I now flounder as I come to the end of an exercise that has observed all the necessary rituals of scientific writing. Perhaps it is time for some realistic comments on the contribution of this research.

REFLECTIONS

Although we have pointed to and demonstrated an interesting phenomenon, I believe that the complexity and intricacy of groups in interaction still elude us. Let me first indicate what I think are the contributions of the research reported in this paper. I still believe that the work on minority influence has been a needed corrective to the literature on social influence. I think it points to the basic interaction *between* majority and minority and that it shows us the potentially creative contribution of conflict. Further, it is an interesting phenomenon in and of itself. Yet, like its predecessors, the research is hampered by conceptual and methodological limitations. The conceptualizations are univariate or, at times, broadly multivariate. Yet, the sum and even the interaction of these variables somehow misses the flow of human process and communication.

This conclusion would be reached each time I sat down to watch the videotapes of the jury-deliberation study. Even in these ad hoc groups, I was often awed and impressed by the booming, buzzing complexity (bordering on confusion for the observer) of these groups in interaction. For example, I would often notice special "moments" in the life of a given group. Sometimes this occurred after a particularly impassioned speech by one individual, a speech full of right, reason, and human values, one whose timing was perfect. At that moment, there was a shift, a breakthrough, a moment of change. We recognize such moments, and the individuals within the groups recognize it. Yet, we are not equipped to make a molecular reduction of these moments. We do not capture the complexity and intricacy of these and many other subtle aspects of groups in interaction that deal with the flow of change. These remain challenges for social psychology.

Another set of challenges is posed by a consideration of the role of reason in social influence. . . . The reassessment, the search for correctness, and the ultimate finding of nonobvious solutions [are] gratifying as experimental results. On the other hand, there is ample evidence, much of it indicated by the early studies in minority influence, to show the importance of dominance, of manipulation, of the weaving of a charismatic web that may have little to do with right, reason, or human values. To define and conceptualize these difficult, often obscure, terms is perhaps the first task. The second is to determine the situations in which reason and values prevail from those in which influence is dictated by emotional trappings and strategic considerations. To capture and understand these complexities is, I think, mandatory for a comprehension of social influence.

REFERENCES

Asch, S. Opinions and social pressure. *Scientific American*, 1955, **193**, 31–35.

Moscovici, S., & Faucheux, C. Social influence, conformity bias and the study of active minorities. In L. Berkowitz (Ed.), *Advances in experimental social psychology* (Vol. 7). New York: Academic Press, 1972.

Moscovici, S., Lage, E., & Naffrechoux, M. Influence of a consistent minority on the responses of a majority in a color perception task. *Sociometry*, 1969, **32**, 365–380.

Moscovici, S., & Nemeth, C. Social influence II: Minority influence. In C. Nemeth (Ed.), *Social psychology: Classic and contemporary integrations*. Chicago: Rand McNally, 1974.

Nemeth, C. Interactions between jurors as a function of majority vs. unanimity decision rules. *Journal of Applied Social Psychology*, 1976.

Nemeth, C., Endicott, J., & Wachtler, J. From the '50s to the '70s: Women in jury deliberations. *Sociometry*, 1976.

Nemeth, C., Swedlund, M., & Kanki, B. Patterning of the minority's responses and their influence on the majority. *European Journal of Social Psychology*, 1974, **4**, 53–64.

Nemeth, C., & Wachtler, J. Creating the perceptions of consistency and confidence: A necessary condition for minority influence. *Sociometry*, 1974, **37**, 529–540.

Nemeth, C., Wachtler, J., & Endicott, J. Increasing the size of the minority: Some gains and some losses. *European Journal of Social Psychology*, 1977.

Strodtbeck, F. L., & Hook, L. H. The social dimensions of a twelve-man jury table. *Sociometry*, 1961, **24**, 397–415.

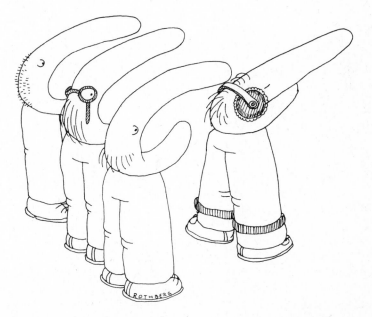

4

Loving and Liking

The very basis of social psychology has to do with people coming together and interacting. We do this not only to accomplish things in pairs and in groups, but for the sheer enjoyment of being with one another. But what is the nature of that social bond? Why are some people more enjoyable to be with than others? How do people go about seeking friendships and maintaining close relationships? These questions and others are the basis for the articles in this section.

While these issues are of great importance for understanding interpersonal relationships, they also begin to touch upon our deeper emotions like love and hate, the "soft side" of human affairs. Because these topics have been thought to defy any kind of "scientific analysis," in the past they have been left to the domain of novelists, poets, and songwriters. Even within psychology, these were considered to be in the realm of the clinician and counselor, but to be well outside of the expertise of the psychological researcher.

Yet more recently, social psychologists have come to realize that a careful and critical analysis of the questions around attraction and relationships are not only possible but necessary. While there may always be some element that cannot be tapped by research about human relationships, there is still no reason to believe that we cannot begin to use our research skills to understand how relationships develop, what purposes they serve, and why some fail while others prosper.

Zick Rubin, Professor of Psychology at Brandeis University, has been one of the most creative and imaginative researchers in this area. The research he reports on in his book *Liking and Loving: An Invitation to Social Psychology* (which is summarized in one of the readings in this section) represents a major step in conceptualizing and attempting to measure interpersonal sentiments. Consistent with the interests that he expressed in our conversation that we need to study a broad range of relationships, his most recent book touches upon a very different kind of relationship, and is called *Children's Friendships*. In our conversation, we touched upon a number of issues including the similarities among different kinds of relationships and the need to go about studying attraction using a variety of methods. A particularly interesting suggestion that he made was that the problems of many adult relationships (i.e., marriage) may be traced to the typical kinds of relationships that children form. That is, while boys and girls are rarely "best friends," we usually expect husbands and wives to be able to work in those roles.

A CONVERSATION WITH ZICK RUBIN

Brandeis University

KRUPAT: *What shall we call our topic? I guess the term interpersonal attraction is the most popular I'm familiar with.*
RUBIN: I would prefer to talk about "social relationships."
KRUPAT: *What's the difference?*
RUBIN: In practice, research on "interpersonal attraction" turns out to be research about one individual's attitude about another—how favorably or unfavorably one person evaluates or feels about another. This is one important aspect of the relationships people form, but we need to study relationships more fully. This includes looking not only at feelings of attraction, but at the development of relationships. How do pairs develop over time, in their particular social, cultural and historical contexts? Also, social psychologists have not given much attention to specific sorts of relationships, such as those between friends, between parents and children, and between husbands and wives. These are the things that we ought to be looking at.
KRUPAT: *But once you define things so broadly, can't that also bring problems? You and I are friends, we have one kind of relationship. You and your wife have a different kind, you and your sons have another, and the relationship between you and Ronald Reagan is still another. Can we use the same set of principles and concepts to understand all of these?*

RUBIN: Well, the last one I consider outside the scope of this topic, but the first three are certainly within it. We need to describe and understand particular sorts of relationships, such as parent-child relationships, friendship, and marriage, in their own terms. But I think it will turn out that some of the same general concepts are relevant to understanding all these different relationships.

KRUPAT: *Like what for instance?*

RUBIN: One general approach is to consider, on the one hand, the various needs people have that can be satisfied only by relationships with other people; and to examine, on the other hand, the entire network of relationships that people are likely to have. Then we can try to understand which relationships are serving which needs and why particular relationships seem to be specialized in a way that will serve certain sorts of needs. This is the approach that Robert Weiss, a social psychologist here in Boston, has taken in writing about the provisions of social relationships. For example, we seem to have a need for attachment from the time that we're infants. It's a feeling of security, a sense of place, of "this is where I feel comfortable." The prototype is the infant who is attached to its primary caretakers—in most families, the mother and to some extent the father. But then as adults, our attachments seem to shift to a sexual or romantic partner, often in marriage. In addition to this need for attachment, we seem to need other sorts of relationships that provide a sense of community or social integration, to be with people with whom we can compare ourselves and with whom we can share our concerns. These needs are commonly provided by friends. The different sorts of relationships cannot substitute for one another. Different relationships have different functions.

KRUPAT: *This sort of approach seems to make a lot of sense. But since it is an intelligent approach, why isn't it more popular?*

RUBIN: It's popular with me. But perhaps some of the questions that need to be asked sometimes don't get asked because they seem so obvious: What are relationships good for? What's a father, or a baby, or a lover good for? I think these are questions that deserve to be taken seriously. One way of doing this is by looking at people who *lack* particular relationships. Studying the problems of lonely people is an important way of gaining insight into the provisions of relationships. Recently there has been an explosion of research on loneliness.

KRUPAT: *Still, given any particular need or kind of relationship, how do people pick and choose? In the case of an infant, I'm not aware that any would reject a mother who satisfies its basic needs. But adults certainly do select, and find one person more satisfying than another.*

RUBIN: It's a good question, and one that is hard to answer in general terms. The basis on which you choose your wife might be different from the basis on which I choose my wife. And we both might be choosing on rather different bases from which our parents chose their partners. But in all cases there are "marketplace" principles at work. Each person is trying to find the most rewarding partner that he can, given his own social assets. On the whole people who are smarter, richer, better looking, more charming, or otherwise blessed will end up marrying other people who have the same general level of valued characteristics.

KRUPAT: *But how can you measure these things to know if someone has found another person "of equal value?"*

RUBIN: There are some things in our culture that one could put some general value on, while there are other things that are more idiosyncratic. People don't agree completely on who is better looking or who is more entertaining. So the analogy to an economic marketplace breaks down to some extent because we don't have anything quite like the common currency of money in the social domain.

KRUPAT: *You've talked about the "marketplace" and putting a "value" on another person. Wouldn't some people say, "How can you talk about love and tender feelings in such crass terms?" Yet I assume that you are simply making explicit some things that happen between people in real life that they don't like to acknowledge. Any person who has ever been to a dance can undoubtedly remember making the very sort of mental calculations that you're talking about.*

RUBIN: People often do react violently to the idea that people select friends or spouses by measuring their value in the marketplace and trying to get the best deal that they can. It can sound crass, but it isn't meant to be. Sometimes we talk about "rewards" or "value" in a relationship. When we say that a person likes another person because "He's a very rewarding person" or "She's a very valuable person," what we're saying is that the person gets satisfaction from that person, is stimulated by that person, that "I feel secure with him" or "She makes me feel good about myself." We're talking about rewards that you are obtaining from someone else. And if the relationship is going to survive, the chances are that you are providing rewards to that other person in return. These rewards and exchanges are not crass sorts of things. They are the rewards of warm, close, fulfilling relationships.

KRUPAT: *Let's get back to ways of finding out about relationships. As you've suggested, there are so many elements to consider—different people, different relationships, different values, and so on. How do you go about studying relationships once you realize and accept their complexities?*

RUBIN: My feeling is that we need to pursue several different strategies at the same time. One useful approach is to conduct quantitative studies that try to get at aspects of relationships very precisely. But what we can get at most precisely often does not turn out to be very deep or very rich. Among the most precise studies of interpersonal attraction are those which explore subjects' first impressions of hypothetical other people—people who are described to the subjects but whom they never actually meet. As you can see, such research stays at a rather superficial level. It's what George Levinger and Diedrick Snoek [see Levinger's article in this section] call Level

1 of social relationships—the one-way evaluation of one person by another person.

KRUPAT: *That's fine—as far as it goes. But does quantitative research have to stop at that point?*

RUBIN: Anne Peplau, Chuck Hill, and I have relied heavily on quantitative questionnaire data to study the development of dating couples' relationships over a period of two years. We have studied the similarities and differences between members of pairs which survive and those which don't. There are also some researchers who are doing highly precise studies of interaction between pairs of people—trying to code in great detail what might be happening over the course of a half hour or so.

KRUPAT: *Still, I detect in your voice a tone of reservation about this approach.*

RUBIN: You detect accurately.

KRUPAT: *Why the reservation?*

RUBIN: To penetrate the richness of relationships, I think that social psychologists must augment their quantitative approach with a return to methods that have been used the most by anthropologists, journalists, and novelists. We need to find out as much as we can about particular relationships by observing people and interviewing them. We need to move toward understanding and generalization by wrestling with materials from people's lives and trying to make sense of them.

KRUPAT: *Now that I hear you talk about studying relationships of all different kinds, it helps clear up for me some of the possible links between your recent work on the friendships of children and your earlier work on young adult couples. Do any of the things you are learning about kids relate to things you noticed about adults?*

RUBIN: I spent time a couple of years ago observing the developing friendships of three-year-olds in nursery school. I was struck by the extent to which these friendships seemed to serve many of the same functions as adult relationships. In some cases the children seem to be quite attached to one another and provide a sense of security for each other. In other cases children were using friends as people to compare themselves to and chart their own growth against. In some cases friends served as guides and as teachers for one another.

KRUPAT: *How do children pick their friends? For instance, do little boys prefer to play with other boys or does that not matter to them?*

RUBIN: Children's friendships tend to be highly sex-segregated—boys play with boys and girls play with girls. This tends to be the case even in nursery schools that try to be nonsexist and even among kids whose parents are quite liberated with respect to their attitudes about sex roles. And the sex segregation gets more and more pronounced as children get older. By the time children are in the fourth or fifth grade it is common for all of a boy's friends to be other boys and all of a girl's friends to be other girls. I think this is something that leaves a certain sort of legacy for us as we become adults.

KRUPAT: *What kind of legacy do you mean?*

RUBIN: Adult men and women do not typically have very many friends of the opposite sex, other than in sexual or romantic relationships—which may be a rather different sort of thing. And this difficulty in forming friends across sex lines may trace back to the sex segregation of childhood.

KRUPAT: *That's interesting. Society suggests that to be "normal," your one deepest and most complete relationship is with someone of the opposite sex. The heterosexual ideal is thought of to be so "natural," yet from what you've said it is anything but that.*

RUBIN: Yes. In American society today, husbands and wives are often expected to be "best friends," as well as lovers and partners in running a family. But this expectation may place considerable strain on marriages, especially because we have little practice in cross-sex friendship. These contradictory experiences and demands may be one of the reasons that the failure ratio of marriages today is so very high.

KRUPAT: *Is there any way to improve this state of affairs? Are there ways that spouses can increase their chances of being friends—and staying friends?*

RUBIN: One clue may come from the fact that people who get married younger are more likely to get divorced than people who get married older. The older people may have had a better chance to evaluate their own needs, as well as to get to know each other, before getting married. But there is no easy answer to your question. No matter how well you know your spouse ahead of time, how many interests you share, and how well suited you may be to one another, it is very hard to be sure that as the two of you change, as you go through the passages of life, you can change in sufficient synchrony with one another so that whatever sharing there is will continue to be there. I hope that research by social scientists can help us learn more about these issues.

KRUPAT: *It would almost seem that whether or not we have any good answers, it would be important just to specify what dimensions of relationships are important, even to let people know what questions to ask in the first place.*

RUBIN: Yes. But some people don't like us to. Often people seem to have an aversion to being too analytical about their relationships, to being too *rational* about them. You know, love is supposed to be *irrational*. The romantic ideal which still is conveyed to young people—in *Young Romance*-type comic books, soap operas, movies, and so on—has the image of love striking unpredictably, irrationally, out of the blue, in a way that is beyond your control. But I think that people might do better to give up just a little bit of the mystery, and to be a little bit more thoughtful about the formation of their relationships. We certainly advocate very careful consideration of a career, about what the rewards and costs are going to be, what the fringe benefits are, what age when we can retire, what is the chance of unemployment and so on. Friendship and love are no less important.

AN INTRODUCTION TO THE READINGS

The articles in this section help emphasize that relationships vary greatly in intensity and kind, and touch upon some of the bases on which they are formed. In the first paper, George Levinger presents an interesting conceptual overview of the area, considering relationships in terms of three levels of human relatedness. He draws a distinction among *unilateral awareness*, where one person is aware of another but they do not begin to interact; *surface contact*, where people meet and exchange some feelings or information; and *mutuality*, where people communicate more deeply and become "we" rather than "you and I." Levinger presents research examples of each of these kinds of relationships and suggests that we need to develop more complete ways of studying the ways in which people are related to one another.

The second paper, by Zick Rubin, shares with Levinger's a common interest in finding ways of studying deeper relationships. Rubin distinguishes between the concepts of liking and loving, but also goes an important step further in trying to develop and assess a self-report measure of romantic love. In order to do this, he first assembled a group of items which might tap feelings toward a boyfriend or girlfriend versus those which were related to a platonic friend. He then had dating couples respond to his scale in relationship to one another and also participate in an experiment. Among the many interesting findings he reports, is that on the average, men and women *love* each equally but that the women *like* their partners more than they are liked in return.

The third paper, by Elaine Hatfield and her colleagues, is aimed at investigating relationships at an earlier and therefore more superficial level of interaction. Looking at students' ratings of potential partners, the authors try to throw some light on a popular conception that the woman who is hard to get is a desirable "catch." The researchers performed five experiments to see if they could confirm this idea only to have all five fail. It was not until a sixth experiment that they found that someone who is *too* hard to get may be seen as cold or threatening, and that a combination of factors is necessary to understand this phenomenon. This research demonstrates once again that when we look more closely at an apparently simple aspect of social behavior, we are likely to discover interesting and subtle complexities. Moreover, it is only by this sort of careful inspection that we can gain a really accurate and complete picture of why people act the way they do toward others.

The final brief selection is by the highly regarded columnist James Reston of the *New York Times*. In it he responds to Senator William Proxmire's bestowing of the Golden Fleece Award to the National Science Foundation for funding research on love. While Reston readily admits that he is not sure that we will ever discover the "mystery" of love, he strongly reiterates the position taken by Zick Rubin that regardless of whether we can see immediate or obvious payoffs, efforts in this direction represent money and time well spent.

A Three-Level
Approach to Attraction:
Toward an Understanding
of Pair Relatedness

The good life is one inspired by love and guided by knowledge. . . . Although both love and knowledge are necessary, love is in a sense more fundamental, since it will lead intelligent people to seek knowledge, in order to find out how to benefit those whom they love.

Bertrand Russell (1957, p. 56)*

LEVELS OF HUMAN RELATEDNESS

In your lifetime, you will come into contact with only a small fraction of the world's several billion people. The rest you will never meet. That condition of "no contact" constitutes the zero point for any individual's existing social relations.

Beyond that point, three levels of relations may develop between two persons: (*a*) a unilateral awareness, where one person has some attitude toward the other, without any sense of reciprocation or interaction; (*b*) a bilateral surface contact, where interaction either is fleeting, or is governed primarily by the participants' social roles; or (*c*) a mutual relationship, where two persons respond to each other to some degree as unique individuals. At the third level, the two individuals have some past joint experience and future anticipation.

Figure 1 (adapted from Levinger & Snoek, 1972) depicts these three levels graphically. Note that Level 3 is conceived as a continuum. Its base line is a Level 2 surface contact; its ultimate realization is the total interpenetration of two human beings, as defined by their joint attitudes, joint behavior, and joint property.

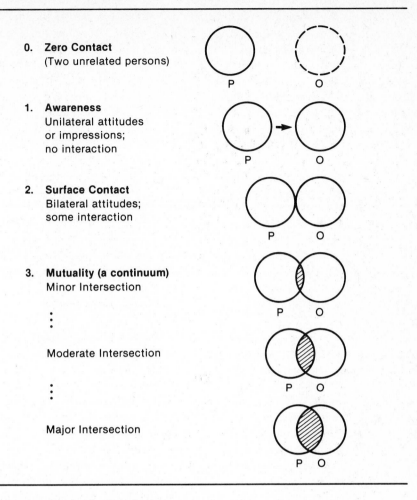

0. Zero Contact
(Two unrelated persons)

1. Awareness
Unilateral attitudes
or impressions;
no interaction

2. Surface Contact
Bilateral attitudes;
some interaction

3. Mutuality (a continuum)
Minor Intersection

⋮

Moderate Intersection

⋮

Major Intersection

FIGURE 1. Levels of pair relatedness.

The levels of relationship shown in Figure 1 may be considered as a series of potential stages in the development of interpersonal relationships. Let us now examine each of the three general levels of relatedness.

A. Unilateral Awareness (Level 1)

As I write this, I glance outside my window into the dusk and see a stranger walking past. He is silhouetted in the light of a street lamp. His image is that of a college student, a bit on the stocky side, carrying a stack of books. He walks slowly and deliberately up the path, his eyes fixed on the ground ahead of him. I see him as a representative of other students on campus; beyond that impression, I experience little sense of knowing him.

The largest portion of our relations with others consists of such momentary impressions of which the perceived other is not aware. And in social psychology, the bulk of research on person perception or impression formation pertains to subject–target encounters, where limited information is provided about an other as a perceptual object. It is not assumed that the subject will ever meet the other whom he evaluates. The subject's view is one of *unilateral awareness* and has little significance for either creating or maintaining a longer association.

At this level of unilateral awareness (Level 1), the other is likely to be seen entirely in terms of his or her external characteristics:

. . . The psychological processes here closely resemble a person's appraisal of other non-human aspects of his environment. The Other tends to be viewed as a combination of attributes, which evoke positive or negative reactions according to how much they either further one's goals or confirm one's own values [Levinger & Snoek, 1972, p. 6].*

Attraction to a stranger: an illustration. Much attraction research has dealt with the person's perception of a stranger. In the tradition of research on impression formation (see Anderson, 1965; Asch, 1946; Kelley, 1950; Tagiuri, 1969; Woodworth, 1938), the following experimental format has become popular:

A subject comes to the laboratory, having weeks earlier completed a questionnaire about his attitudes toward a variety of interesting items. He is told that the study is investigating '' . . . the extent to which one person can form valid judgments about another person just by knowing a few of his attitudes [Byrne, 1971, p. 51].'' The subject then receives a completed form, containing another subject's responses to the same items he had earlier responded to himself; the subject tries to indicate his best judgment of the other's personal characteristics, including how much he thinks he would like the other.

In this study, one subject receives information about a stranger whose responses to the questionnaire form are identical to his own; another subject in the same experiment finds drastic dissimilarity in the stranger's completed questionnaire. The results are that the first stranger is rated high in attractiveness; the second stranger is rated rather low.

This is a typical finding from experiments conducted during the past decade by Byrne and his collaborators (Byrne, 1971). The finding that attraction to another varies directly with his or her perceived similarity has been extended widely to comparisons among subjects who differ in age, in nationality, or in mental diagnosis; and among stimulus persons who differ in characteristics such as race, status, sex, or physical attractiveness. To explain the effects of similarity on attraction Byrne and others have posited principles linked to reinforcement theory. . . . In the terminology of our present framework, the methodological format of their research spotlights one person's unilateral awareness of a noninteracting social object.

*Levinger, George, and Snoek, J. Diedrick. *Attraction in relationship: A new look at interpersonal attraction.* (Morristown, N.J.: General Learning Press.) © 1972 General Learning Corporation.

B. Surface Contact (Level 2)

A person's reciprocal contacts range from surface into depth, from the trivial meeting to the profound attachment. A surface contact can occur in two ways, either as a transitory first meeting or as a segmental role relation. Transitory meetings take place in cafeterias, at bus stops, at large parties. They also occur in the typical dyadic experiment of the social psychologist. One person meets another and receives limited information about him, while also providing limited information to the other about himself. Within this context, impressions are formed about the other individual and about the self–other relation.

A segmental role relation involves a person's interaction with people whom he meets repeatedly, but with whom he exchanges little more than a token "hello." The bus driver, the building custodian, the colleague in the office down the hall—these are people a teacher may see often, but with whom he or she usually has minimal contact. Each day I show the bus driver my identification card and he glances at it, we nod to each other, and I pass by him. Other surface relations go further. But the actors' words and actions remain governed primarily by their socially defined roles. Interaction at this surface level transmits little information about the unique individuals who enact the roles.

To the extent that actors in surface contact play their roles uniquely, they may transmit information that helps others decide whether or not to go forward in the relationship. If, for example, I were to discover that my bus driver is an avid chess player, the two of us might some day break out of our usual roles and enter into a mutually involving encounter over a chess board. Surface interaction is useful for learning whether the other is a person whom one would like to get to know better, to share more with, or to build a mutual relationship with (see Thibaut & Kelley, 1959, Chapter 5).

Surface contacts: a research example. The situations social psychologists create for studying pairs experimentally usually involve surface contacts. Two strangers meet, their responses are monitored over a short time period; then conclusions are drawn. Though investigators thus are enabled to devise tightly controlled experiments, the format limits the generality of their conclusions. A variable that is particularly important for affecting attraction in surface meetings will not necessarily have the same impact for deeper relationships.

With respect to the effect of similarity on attraction, for instance, it is easy to manipulate information about a stranger's similarity in a first meeting. But it is quite difficult to study the effects of such similarity in existing relationships. It is simple to illustrate that another's similarity exerts a substantial influence on one's liking for him in a short-term laboratory dyad, but very difficult to demonstrate within a long-term dating or roommate relationship (Levinger, 1972).

As an example of research at Level 2, consider the field study done some years ago at the University of Minnesota (Walster, Aronson, Abrahams, & Rottmann, 1966):

Incoming freshman girls and boys were invited to take part in a computer dance during Welcome Week. When they registered for the dance, participants in the study were given a variety of psychological tests, their physical attractiveness was rated, and a variety of other measures were obtained. Altogether, 327 couples came to the dance—having been matched merely so that no girl was taller than her male partner. During an intermission, the dates rated their feelings toward each other. What measures or indices would distinguish between those partners who felt strongly attracted versus those who were weakly attracted to their matched date? What test scores would differentiate between compatible and incompatible couples?

Contrary to the investigators' expectations, none of the psychological measures differentiated significantly. Of all the measures obtained before the dance, the only important determinant of liking for the partner was the partner's *physical attractiveness*. This determined how much one liked one's date, how much one wanted to date him or her again, and whether or not the male decided to ask the female to go out again. (However, it did *not* predict the actual frequency of further dates together.)

If these computer dates are considered to be examples of "surface contacts," then it is not surprising that the other's physical appearance was the only variable that exerted a significant effect. The pairs typically met at the dance itself and were together for hardly more than 2 hours on a noisy dance floor. Dates, therefore, had little opportunity to react to more than superficial characteristics.

Berscheid and Walster (1972) have reviewed various additional studies showing that good looks elicit favorable attitudes and behavior in a wide variety of interpersonal settings. It remains unclear, however, under what conditions initial impressions of a "beautiful person" are outweighed by subsequent interaction with him or her; or how an "ugly" person may gradually or suddenly become attractive for reasons other than a change in physical appearance. Consider this striking autobiographical excerpt from Nikos Kazantzakis:

> When I was five years old, I was taken to some woman, vaguely a teacher, to learn how to draw *i*'s and kouloúria on the slate. . . . She was a simple peasant type, short and fattish, a little humpbacked, with a wart on the right side of her chin. . . . At first, I wanted nothing to do with her. I liked neither her breath nor her hump. But then, though I don't know how, she began to be transformed little by little before my eyes: The wart disappeared, her back straightened, her flabby body grew slim and beautiful, and finally after a few weeks, she became a slender angel wearing a snow-white tunic and holding an immense bronze trumpet. . . . Angel and Madame Teacher had become one [Kazantzakis, 1965, p. 42].*

This excerpt illustrates how a small boy's valuation of his teacher eventually went beyond her outer appearance, how his feelings were captured by what he saw as her inner worth. His changing feelings are an example of the development of a deeper interpersonal relationship.

C. Mutuality (Level 3)

Some pairs move from role-directed surface contact toward sharing a more personal relationship. The development of a Level 3 pairing implies the expansion of person—other (P–O) interdependence beyond that of a transient encounter, or one based on externally structured roles. The P–0 relationship is mutual to the extent that the partners possess shared knowledge of each other, assume responsibility for furthering each other's outcomes, and share private norms for regulating their association. The bond between P's and O's lives—suggested graphically by the size of the P–O intersections in Figure 1—represents the investment of the partners' joint efforts and joint experiences.

Various characteristics of dyadic relationships at Level 3 have been detailed elsewhere (Levinger & Snoek, 1972, pp. 8–11). But two processes must be emphasized here: the first process pertains to interpersonal discovery and disclosure, the second to the investment that the partners have put into their common bond.

Mutual disclosure.   Strangers tend to communicate about peripheral matters; their discussion is confined to topics such as the weather, their social backgrounds, and to their relatively public attitudes. If a relationship develops further, though, participants will disclose increasingly more about their unique selves and will share emotionally significant attitudes or feelings. Self–other attraction thus has been found to be associated significantly with degree of self-disclosure (Jourard, 1959; Taylor, 1968). And, while routine "friendly relations" are not usually conducive to intimate revelation, "close friendship" seems to require the exchange of intimate information (Kurth, 1970, p. 140).

Another aspect of mutual discovery involves the partners' "shared awareness" (Friedell, 1969). At Level 3, two persons not only know much about one another, but each one further knows what the other knows about him. Still further, each knows that the other knows that he knows it; and so on. In the intimate dyad, then, there is a spiral of shared assumptions.

Mutual investment.   Disclosure is only one important process in the development and maintenance of pair mutuality. A second process refers to behavior coordination and emotional investment (see Thibaut & Kelley, 1959; Levinger, Senn, & Jorgensen, 1970). As two persons get to know each other, they learn how to accommodate to each others' responses and preferences. And, as a relationship unfolds, each partner takes increasing pleasure from the other's satisfaction. The deeper the relationship, the larger is its cargo of joint experiences and shared feelings. As the intersection between two people's lives grows, the distinction between "I" and "you" lessens and merges into a larger "we." An ultimate merging would be characterized by the following quote from the ninth-century Mohammedan mystic, Sari-al-Sakadi: " . . . perfect love exists between two people only when each addresses the other with the words, 'O myself!' [as quoted in Kazantzakis, 1965, p. 370]."

Determinants of attraction to a "steady partner": research at level 3.   Compared to the many experimental studies at Levels 1 and 2, there are few studies of the determinants of attraction or change in attraction in long-term relationships. There are several reasons for this paucity of research. For one thing, it is not possible to create Level 3 relationships artificially in the way that it is possible to synthesize superficial relations. Furthermore, deep relationships are complex, and it is more difficult to disentangle the causal variables. A brief examination of two field studies will illustrate the complexity of research at Level 3:

> Both studies employed the same method. Large samples of college dating couples were approached in the fall of the school year (Time$_1$) and asked to participate in research on "seriously attached couples." In each couple, both partners filled out lengthy questionnaires concerning their personal backgrounds, values, and personality characteristics; they also rated the current relationship with their "steady." Six or seven months later (Time$_2$) the participants responded once more, this time answering questions about possible changes in their relationship during the intervening half year. The central aim was to uncover Time$_1$ differences between couples who "progressed" toward a closer relationship and those who did not "progress" during the succeeding interval.
>
> The first study, done at Duke University by Kerckhoff and Davis (1962), found that high Time$_1$ value agreement facilitated progress primarily among couples with a relatively "short" relationship (one shorter than 18 months). In contrast, complementarity of personal needs facilitated progress mainly by those couples who had been going together for a "long" time.
>
> The second study, done with college couples at state universities in Massachusetts and Colorado, by Levinger *et al.* (1970), failed to replicate the Kerckhoff and Davis findings on the respective contributions of value consensus and need complementarity. In this study, the strongest predictors of relationship progress were the partners' Time$_1$ involvement in their pairing, their own prediction of future progress, and the amount of their past joint activity.

On the basis of their 1962 study, Kerckhoff and Davis proposed a theory of "filtering factors" to explain the determinants of progress in dating relationships. It suggested that

. . . early in a relationship, similarity in backgrounds and interests encourages partners to come to know each other; somewhat later, similarity in attitudes or values becomes salient to the development of a couple's bond; still later, deeper aspects of "need" fit are the most salient determinants of further progress [paraphrased in Levinger *et al.*, 1970, p. 428].

Varying versions of a filter theory have been suggested by other writers. Despite our own failure to replicate Kerckhoff and Davis 1962 findings, I remain impressed by their suggestion that a filter theory will account for changes in the determinants of attraction in pairs who progressively increase their closeness. Nevertheless, our failure to repeat the earlier results underscores problems of conducting generalizable research in this area. The differences between the 1962 and the 1970 findings can be attributed to a variety of causes: historical drift in dating patterns, changes in personal needs or values, differences in geographical or cultural locale, or unidentifiable errors in one or both of the two studies (Levinger *et al.*, 1970, pp. 436–38). In any case, it is obviously difficult to conduct longitudinal studies *in natura*—to choose the strategic variables, to find adequate measures, and to obtain appropriate samples.

Compounding such difficulties is the inadequacy of current definitions of stages or levels of relationship. For example, Kerckhoff and Davis (1962) divide their total sample into two groups of ostensibly differing bond strengths on the basis of how long the partners had been going together. Yet sheer chronological length of a relationship is only a meager index of its depth; in the Levinger *et al.* study, *length* of relationship was not found to be significantly correlated with a couple's degree of involvement. (Below, I discuss other approaches toward defining the depth dimension of dyadic relations.)

A "third dimension" of pair relatedness. Can we consider the history of a pair's interaction as the third dimension of its relatedness? Can we conceive of the number and variety of its actual and potential joint behavior repertoires as one aspect of the relationship's depth? Viewed this way, contacts that have neither a past nor a future would be considered one- or two-dimensional.

In a unilateral P–O contact (Level 1), P sees only his own possible actions—for example, approach or avoidance—with regard to the passive O whom he evaluates. In a minimal surface contact at Level 2, both actors' behavior repertoires are relevant. If a relationship expands into Level 3, the number and the importance of the dyadic outcome matrices increase. Figure 2 graphically displays the contrast

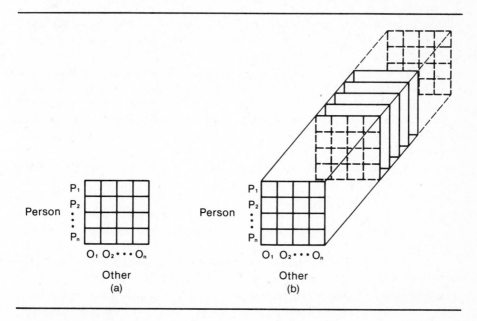

FIGURE 2. Dyadic outcome matrices shown in two and in three dimensions: (a) Level 2: surface contact (two dimensional); (b) Level 3: deep relationship (three dimensional).

between a single two-actor outcome matrix and the infinitely expansible collection of matrices available to a deeper dyadic relationship.

The matrix at the left of Figure 2 contains only one set of behavior options for each of the two partners. It exemplifies the matrices used by exchange theorists (see, for example, Thibaut & Kelley, 1959) and by game theorists (for example, Rapoport, 1966). The collection of matrices shown at the right of Figure 2 describes the multiple possibilities that exist in real-world pair relationships, where the interactors can relate to each other in situations other than their current one. While a first contact may indeed contain only a single matrix of dyadic outcomes, the continuation of an interrelation entails the increase of the actual and the potential store of dyadic situations. And two pairs whose relationship has equal depth may differ considerably in the distribution of their behavior contingencies.

Dyadic behavior contingencies of couples varying in degree of interpersonal involvement: pilot study. A 1972 pilot study by Mack illustrates the potential variety of pair behavior, engaged in by some couples, but not by others. Mack's purpose was to ascertain what behaviors are believed to be associated with different degrees of intimacy in heterosexual couples. To this end, 84 undergraduates at the University of Massachusetts were asked how likely it is that couples at four different degrees of involvement would engage in each of 52 different joint activities. Mack's four categories of pair involvement were described as follows: (*a*) "casually acquainted"; (*b*) "good friends, but not in love"; (*c*) "couples who are 'romantically attracted' without being fully committed"; and (*d*) "couples who are 'very much in love,' and are entirely committed to continue the relationship."

For each of these four categories of involvement, each judge rated how likely it was that a couple at that depth would engage in each of 13 possible couple behaviors (see the examples of such behaviors in Table 1). Judges were instructed as follows:

> Estimate how likely it is that such couples will engage in each of the listed behaviors. In other words, considering 100 such couples, how many of them (from 0 through 100) would you expect to do any particular behavior together? We are interested in what you believe to be true, not what you think is socially correct or proper.

Table 1 presents findings for a few of the 52 behaviors rated by Mack's subjects. Some behaviors, such as "smile at each other," were believed likely to be performed by almost all reasonably well-met pairs, and the ratings did not discriminate among different degrees of relatedness. At the opposite extreme, behaviors such as "refuse to date other persons" were believed to indicate a degree of exclusivity appropriate for only the deepest category of pair bonds.

Behaviors shown in Table 1 showed other sorts of discriminability. Holding each other's hands, for example, was seen as unlikely among the casually acquainted and less than typical among mere good friends, but it was perceived as highly and almost equally probable among couples in the two deepest categories. Parallel patterns were found for behaviors such as giving back rubs, preparing meals together, and trying to be alone with the other person. In contrast, activities such as staying up late to talk together, or confiding in the other, discriminated mainly

TABLE 1. Perceived Probabilities That Each Activity Is in Repertoire of Male-Female College Couples Varying in Interpersonal Involvement.

Activity	Type of couple			
	Casually acquainted	Good friends, not in love	Romantically attracted	Much in love, fully committed
Communication:				
smile at each other	89[a]	98	95	98
stay up late and talk	52	78	79	79
confide in each other	26	69	76	94
Physical contact:				
stand close to one another	51	79	90	93
hold hands	18	44	82	93
give "back rubs"	12	36	76	86
Joint actions:				
study together	55	65	74	82
watch TV together	57	82	79	89
go to parties together	29	61	84	93
prepare meals together	21	47	70	85
go camping together	13	43	54	74
live together	10	33	61	88
have sexual intercourse	3	28	61	79
Shared ownership:				
collect items together	36	51	61	75
exchange clothing	20	43	53	75
Exclusive commitment:				
try to be alone with other	13	25	76	85
refuse to date other persons	3	7	29	90

[a]Mean percentage of couples at each degree of involvement estimated "to engage in each of the listed behaviors." (The raters were 84 college students.)

between the casually acquainted and couples in the later three categories of intimacy.

Mack's study offers a method for ascertaining how various behaviors are perceived to differentiate among varying degrees of relatedness. The results shown in Table 1, however, pertain only to a particular population of judges (that is, University of Massachusetts undergraduates) rating the relations among heterosexual pairs of their peers. Mack's results do not necessarily apply to judges or to judged couples from a different culture or of different ages. For instance, while in United States college circles today it is generally expected that pairs of 19-year-olds who are in love will hold hands, the presence or absence of the same behavior is not necessarily an indicator of whether or not a pair of 49-years-olds is strongly or weakly attached. The meaning of behaviors must always be considered with reference to the situation in which they occur: where, with whom, and why.

A second limitation of Mack's findings is that they merely reflect impressions or stereotypes. They do not describe the actual behavior of differentially related pairs. The following section is concerned with the mapping of actual behavior differences among real couples who vary in relatedness.

BEHAVIORAL INDICES OF RELATEDNESS

Selective Perceptual Distortion

The typical subject in the perceptual illusion room designed by Adelbert Ames at Princeton University distorts the size of other persons whom he observes moving around the room. This effect is particularly pronounced when the subject has never seen the other person before. When spouses observe their own partner, however, they show a significantly smaller perceptual distortion than when they are looking at strangers (Wittreich, 1952).

Mutual Eye Gazing

A pair of subjects—one male, the other female—arrive in the psychological laboratory. Seated across from each other at a table, they discuss a human relations case. Observers in adjoining rooms monitor the couple's eye-gazing behavior. It is found that strongly-in-love pairs focus more upon one another's eyes simultaneously than do weakly-in-love couples (Rubin, 1970).

"Peak" and "Scallop" Effects

Imagine that a group of subjects sits around a large table, and that subjects around the table follow each other in pronouncing strange words or syllables. Later, when the individual participant is asked to recall the responses of each one who spoke, he is found to have good recall of his own responses ("peak" effect), but to have relatively poor recall of the responses by those nearby subjects who responded 9 sec either before or after he took his own turn ("scallop" effect).

In a memory experiment with dating couples based on this finding, sets of 12 couples participated in the same verbal memory test. Members of each couple were seated directly across the table from each other in the circle of 24 subjects. The dating partners were found to have almost as high a peak and scallop effect for their mate as for themselves. The size of the effect was associated significantly with subjects' degree of involvement in their pairing; strongly involved partners appeared to experience almost as much stage fright for their mate as for themselves. Another, less novel, finding of this study was that pair involvement was strongly correlated with the pairs' mutual touching behavior before and after the memory task (Brenner, 1971).

Painting as a Pair

Two people are given a large piece of paper and each receives a brush and two colors of acrylic paint. The paper is empty, except for a fold line down the middle. Some pairs paint two separate pictures, respecting each other's territory on the opposite side of the sheet. Other pairs paint a single picture with one unified theme, considering the entire sheet to be pair territory. Some pairs share their paint colors, others do not. Some couples stand very close and/or show much physical touching, others do not. Which of these indices is associated with the partners' self-report of emotional involvement?

In a recent exploratory study of this question, touch and proximity were clearly associated with pair involvement, paint sharing was less so. In this study, contrary to expectation, joint painting was not associated with emotional togetherness; strangers were almost equally likely to paint a unified picture as were intimate couples (DeLamarter & Levinger, 1973).

In each of the preceding experiments, researchers attempted to ascertain empirically the differences between established and ad hoc pairings. In these illustrative studies, certain indices distinguished very clearly—such as touching behavior in the studies of Brenner (1971) and DeLamarter and Levinger (1973). Other indices showed only a barely significant association with depth of relation— such as perceptual distortion (Wittreich, 1952), mutual looking (Rubin, 1970), or using one another's paint colors (DeLamarter & Levinger, 1973). . . .

This chapter began with a quote from Bertrand Russell, suggesting that love is fundamental to the good life. Russell proposed various definitions of love, ranging on a continuum from contemplative association of a passive other to vibrant interactive involvement—from, shall we say, the beginning to the end of love. Attraction researchers may choose between further mapping the delimited area near the first pole of Russell's continuum and trying to define the uncharted terrain of love "at its fullest." My treatment here has explored a few of the problems confronting those who would choose the latter alternative.

REFERENCES

Anderson, N. H. Adding versus averaging as a stimulus combination rule in impression formation. *Journal of Experimental Psychology*, 1965, **70**, 394–400.

Asch, S. E. Forming impressions of personality, *Journal of Abnormal and Social Psychology*, 1946, **41**, 258–290.

Berscheid, E., & Walster, E. Beauty and the best. *Psychology Today*, 1972, **5**, 42–46, 74.

Brenner, M. Caring, love, and selective memory. *Proceedings of the Annual Convention of the American Psychological Association*, 1971, **6**, 275–276.

Byrne, D. *The attraction paradigm*. New York: Academic Press, 1971.

DeLamarter, S. K., & Levinger, G. Painting in pairs: Exploring measures of pair relatedness. Unpublished technical report, 1973.

Friedell, M. F. On the structure of shared awareness. *Behavioral Science*, 1969, **14**, 28–39.

Jourard, S. M. Self-disclosure and other-cathexis. *Journal of Abnormal and Social Psychology*, 1959, **59**, 428–431.

Kazantzakis, N. *Report to Greco*. New York: Simon & Schuster, 1965.

Kelley, H. H. The warm-cold variable in first impressions of persons. *Journal of Personality*, 1950, **18**, 431–439.

Kerckhoff, A. C., & Davis, K. E. Value consensus and need complementarity in mate selection. *American Sociological Review*, 1962, **27**, 295–303.

Kurth, S. B. Friendship and friendly relations. In G. J. McCall, M. M. McCall, N. K. Denzin, G. D. Suttles, & S. B. Kurth (Eds), *Social relationships*. Chicago, Illinois: Aldine, 1970.

Levinger, G. Little sand box and big quarry: Comments on Byrne's paradigmatic spade for research on interpersonal attraction. *Representative Research in Social Psychology*, 1972, **3**, 3–19.

Levinger, G., Senn, D. J., & Jorgensen, B. W. Progress toward permanence in courtship: A test of the Kerckhoff–Davis hypotheses. *Sociometry*, 1970, **33**, 427–443.

Levinger, G., & Snoek, J. D. *Attraction in relationship: A new look at interpersonal attraction*. New York: General Learning Press, 1972.

Rapoport, A. *Two-person game theory*. Ann Arbor, Michigan: University of Michigan Press, 1966.

Rubin, Z. Measurement of romantic love. *Journal of Personality and Social Psychology*, 1970, **16**, 265–273.

Russell, B. What I believe. In *Why I am not a Christian*. New York: Simon & Schuster, 1957.

Sommer, R. *Personal space*. Englewood Cliffs, New Jersey: Prentice-Hall, 1969.

Taguiri, R. Person perception. In G. Lindzey & E. Aronson (Eds), *Handbook of social psychology*. Vol. 3. Reading, Massachusetts: Addison-Wesley, 1969.

Taylor, D. A. The development of interpersonal relationships: Social penetration processes. *Journal of Social Psychology*, 1968, **75**, 79–90.

Thibaut, J. W., & Kelley, H. H. *The social psychology of groups*. New York: Wiley, 1959.

Walster, E., Aronson, V., Abrahams, D., & Rottmann, L. Importance of physical attractiveness in dating behavior. *Journal of Personality and Social Psychology*, 1966, **4**, 508–516.

Wittreich, W. J. The Honi Phenomenon: A case of selective perceptual distortion. *Journal of Abnormal and Social Psychology*, 1952, **47**, 705–712.

Woodworth, R. S. *Experimental psychology*. New York: Holt, 1938.

ZICK RUBIN

Liking and Loving

Love, what is it? Answ. 'Tis very much like light,
a thing that everybody knows, and yet
none can tell what to make of it.

—Ladies Dictionary (1694)

Setting out to devise measures of love is like setting out to prepare a gourmet dish with a thousand different recipes but no pots and pans. The recipes for love abound. Throughout history poets, essayists, novelists, philosophers, theologians, psychologists, sociologists, and other men and women of goodwill have written more about love than about virtually any other topic. The index to my edition of Bartlett's *Familiar Quotations* lists 769 references to ''love,'' second only to ''man'' with 843. But whereas the nature of love has long been a prime topic of discourse and debate, the number of behavioral scientists who have conducted empirical research on love can be counted on one's fingers. And, until recently, the tools with which such research might have been conducted have not existed.

The state of our knowledge about interpersonal attraction has advanced considerably in the past two decades, but primarily through research on liking rather than research directly concerned with love. And while liking and loving are surely close relatives, they are by no means identical. The bridge between research on liking and the extensive writings on love remains to be built.

Here I will report on my own initial endeavor to help build this bridge. My goal was to develop and validate a self-report measure of romantic love. By the adjective ''romantic,'' I do not wish to connote all the trappings of the romantic ideal of the Middle Ages. I use the word simply to distinguish the sort of love that may exist between unmarried, opposite-sex partners from such other related forms as love between children and their parents, close friends, and men and God. The fact that the same word, *love*, may be applied to all of these sorts of relationships must be more than linguistic accident. There are undoubtedly important common elements among these overtly different manifestations. As a starting point for my research, however, it seemed wiser to restrict my attention to a single context.

Abridged from Zick Rubin, *Liking and Loving: An Invitation to Social Psychology*, New York: Holt, Rinehart and Winston, 1973, pp. 211–225, with permission of the author and the publisher.

EROS AND AGAPE

To anchor my attempt to measure love at one end with the work of the "liking researchers," I decided from the start to conceptualize love as an attitude that a person holds toward a particular other person. As such, love—like liking—is an invisible package of feelings, thoughts, and behavioral predispositions within an individual. But I also assumed that the content of this attitude is not the same as that of liking, even extremely strong liking. To determine the content of the attitude to be called love I would have to look elsewhere, to the many prescriptions provided through history.

"How do I love thee? Let me count the ways," declared Elizabeth Barrett Browning, thereby alluding to the most basic form of measurement. My first problem was to decide which ways to count. What Shakespeare defined as "a spirit all compact of fire" has been defined by others in such diverse ways as a "centrifugal act of the soul" (Ortega y Gassett), "a sickness full of woes" (Samuel Daniel), and "not ever having to say you're sorry" (Erich Segal). For Freud, love is a push from within, produced by the sublimation of overtly sexual impulses. For Plato it is a pull from ahead, engendered by the search for the ultimate good. "There are so many sorts of love," Voltaire wrote, "that one does not know where to seek a definition of it." In the midst of all of these conceptions and varieties, however, one dimension stands out as central. This is the opposition of love as *needing* and love as *giving*.

The equation of love with a physical or emotional need can be traced back at least as far as Sappho's symptomatology of love-sickness, offered in the sixth century B.C. The defining features of love, in terms of this conception, are powerful desires to be in the other's presence, to make physical contact, to be approved of, to be cared for. In its most extreme form the love-need appears as a passionate desire to possess and to be fulfilled by another person, corresponding to what the Greeks called *eros*. In more contemporary psychological terms, we can identify the need conception of love with *attachment*, as exemplified by the bonds formed between infants and their parents.

In apparent contrast to the conception of love as a cluster of needs is the conception of love as giving to another person. This is the aspect of love emphasized in the New Testament, epitomized by St. John's declaration, "God is love." Contemporary psychological definitions also depict the lover as the ultimate altruist. For Erich Fromm, "Love is the active concern for the life and growth of that which we love."[1] According to Harry Stack Sullivan, "When the satisfaction or the security of another person becomes as significant to one as is one's own satisfaction or security, then the state of love exists."[2] Love as giving corresponds to what the Greeks called *agape* and to what I will call *caring*.

It can be argued that attachment is a less mature form of love than caring. Whereas infants develop strong attachments toward their parents, for example, caring is a phenomenon that typically does not appear until somewhat later in life. (In Sullivan's view, people first learn to care about others in the context of childhood friendships.) Abraham Maslow associates attachment with people's "deficiency needs" for acceptance and approval. He suggests that "love hunger is a deficiency disease exactly as is salt hunger or the avitaminoses," and, as such, is an immature form of love. People who have reached a higher state of "self-actualization," in Maslow's framework, have already satisfied their deficiency need for love. D-love ("D" for "Deficiency") is replaced by B-love ("B" for "Being"), which is less needful and dependent, and more autonomous and giving.[3]

Maslow's analysis of love implies that attachment and caring stand opposed to one another, and that the more there is of one the less there will be of the other. But it is doubtful that such an opposition corresponds to the actual nature of love relationships. It seems more likely that as a couple's relationship becomes increasingly close, it will be associated with both increased attachment and increased caring. Clinical psychologist David Orlinsky suggests, for example, that attachment and caring merge to form a "dual feeling-impulse," which may be equated with love.[4]

Rather than equate love with attachment or with caring, therefore, I would consider both to be basic components of love. Both attachment and caring remain essentially *individual* conceptions, however, referring to inclinations within one person's mind or heart. But there is also an aspect of love that can only be attributed to the relationship between two people, rather than to the two parties individually. Martin Buber makes this point when he talks about the "I–Thou" relationship:

> Love does not cling to an I, as if the Thou were merely its "content" or object; it is *between* I and Thou. Whoever does not know this . . . does not know love, even if he should ascribe to it the feelings that he lives through, experiences, enjoys, and expresses.[5]

It seems useful, therefore, to postulate a third component of love, which refers to the bond or link between two people. This component may be manifest most clearly by close and confidential communication between two people, through nonverbal as well as verbal channels. I will call this third component *intimacy*.

Before constructing a measure of love, it was important to have an idea of how it might be distinguished from liking. In most of the existing research the evaluative component of liking is typically given greatest emphasis. A "likable" person is someone who is viewed as good or desirable on a number of dimensions. In our predominantly "task-oriented" society, the critical dimensions often seem to be task-related ones. We like people who are intelligent, competent, and trustworthy—the sorts of people whom we are disposed to work with or to vote for (as in "I Like Ike").

What would we expect to be the empirical relationships between one person's love and his liking for another person? One would certainly expect at least a moderately positive evaluation of another person to be a prerequisite for the establishment of attachment, caring, and intimacy. Thus, it would be surprising if liking and loving were not at least moderately correlated with one another. But whereas liking and loving may have much in common, we would hesitate to equate the two phenomena. People often express liking for a person whom they would not claim to love in the least. In other instances they may declare their love for someone whom they cannot reasonably be said to like very well.

A starting assumption in my attempt to develop self-report scales of liking and loving, therefore, was that they should represent moderately correlated, but nevertheless distinct, dimensions of one person's attitude toward another person. My study consisted of three stages. First, I constructed parallel self-report scales of liking and loving that met the requirements of the starting assumption. Second, I examined the ways in which the scores of members of dating couples on each of the two scales related to a variety of other things about them, including their plans for marriage. Third, I proceeded to assess the usefulness of the love scale in predicting people's subsequent behavior and the course of their relationships. I will describe each of these steps in the following sections.

PUTTING LOVE ON A SCALE

The first step in scale construction was to make up seventy statements reflecting aspects of one person's attitudes toward a particular other person. The items spanned a wide range of thoughts, feelings, and behavioral predispositions—for example, "How much fun is _____ to be with?" "How much do you trust _____?" "To what extent are you physically attracted to _____?" "How much does _____ get on your nerves?" As a check upon my own initial intuitions, I asked a number of friends and acquaintances of both sexes to sort the items into "liking" and "loving" sets, based on their own understandings of the meaning of the two terms. After making revisions suggested by these raters' judgments, I asked 198 undergraduates at the University of Michigan to indicate how much they agreed with each statement in terms of their feelings toward their boyfriend or girlfriend (if they had one), and again in terms of their feelings toward a "platonic friend" of the opposite sex. I then subjected these ratings to a statistical technique called factor analysis, which serves to indicate which sets of items form internally consistent clusters. This procedure led to the specification of two nine-item scales,* one of love and the other of liking (see Table 1).

On the whole, the content of the two scales corresponds closely to the conceptions of liking and loving outlined in the previous section. The love scale includes items that seem to tap the postulated components of attachment (e.g., "If I were lonely, my first thought would be to seek _____ out"); caring (e.g., "One of my primary concerns is _____'s welfare"); and intimacy (e.g., "I feel that I can confide in _____ about virtually everything"). The items on the liking scale focus on the favorable evaluation of the other person on such dimensions as adjustment, maturity, and good judgment. The close fit between the scales and the preceding conceptual discussion is not accidental. Rather, my own working definitions of liking and loving were to a large extent given focus by the results of the scale-development procedure.

I now had two paper-and-pencil scales with a reasonable degree of what psychological testers call "face validity"; that is, the content of each scale approximated people's understandings of what liking and loving should mean. Such face validity did not necessarily imply that the scales would be of any use, however. If,

---

*The original love and liking scales each contained thirteen items. They were later condensed to the current nine-item versions.

TABLE 1.   Love-Scale and Liking-Scale Items.

Love Scale
1. I feel that I can confide in _____ about virtually everything.
2. I would do almost anything for _____.
3. If I could never be with _____, I would feel miserable.
4. If I were lonely, my first thought would be to seek _____ out.
5. One of my primary concerns is _____'s welfare.
6. I would forgive _____ for practically anything.
7. I feel responsible for _____'s well-being.
8. I would greatly enjoy being confided in by _____.
9. It would be hard for me to get along without _____.

Liking Scale
1. I think that _____ is unusually well-adjusted.
2. I would highly recommend _____ for a responsible job.
3. In my opinion, _____ is an exceptionally mature person.
4. I have great confidence in _____'s good judgment.
5. Most people would react favorably to _____ after a brief acquaintance.
6. I think that _____ is one of those people who quickly wins respect.
7. _____ is one of the most likable people I know.
8. _____ is the sort of person whom I myself would like to be.
9. It seems to me that it is very easy for _____ to gain admiration.

for example, people tended to respond to the items in ways they thought would "look good," rather than in terms of their real feelings, then the scales might measure social anxiety rather than liking and loving. The next step, therefore, was to test the scales out, in the context of ongoing dating relationships.

LOVE'S CORRELATES

My subjects for this trial run were 182 dating couples at the University of Michigan.* The modal couple consisted of a junior man and a sophomore woman who had been dating for about one year. Some of the couples had been going together for as long as six or seven years, however, while others had been dating for only a few weeks. About 20 percent of the couples reported that they were engaged.

During the sessions, boyfriends and girlfriends were asked not to sit near one another. Each partner filled out the questionnaire individually. They were assured that their responses would be kept confidential, and that their partners would not be given access to their responses. The questionnaire included the love and liking

---

*By 1968–1969, when I conducted the study, it had already become somewhat outmoded for college students to "date." Continuing and casual contacts between the sexes, often facilitated by residential proximity in apartments or dormitories, have to a large extent replaced the traditional pattern in which boy phones girl days or weeks in advance to invite her to a movie, football game, or fraternity party. In spite of the decline of the date, however, exclusive or semi-exclusive relationships between unmarried men and women still thrive on American campuses. One of the major functions of these relationships, although it is not universally subscribed to, continues to be the selection of marriage partners. For lack of a better word ("opposite-sex relationships" is too pedantic; "boy-girl relationships," too patronizing), I continue to refer to these liaisons as "dating relationships" and to the principals as "dating couples."

scales, to be completed first with respect to one's partner and later with respect to a close same-sex friend. In each case the respondent indicated how much he agreed or disagreed with each item by placing a check on the continuous scale. For example:

1. I feel that I can confide in _____ about virtually everything.

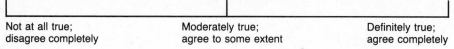

Not at all true;   Moderately true;   Definitely true;
disagree completely   agree to some extent   agree completely

With the help of a clear plastic ruler these responses were later converted to numbers from 1 to 9, to be used in analyzing the data. The questionnaire also called for a variety of other pieces of information about the subjects and their relationships, which I will say more about as I present some results.

The statistical analysis of the questionnaire data began with an examination of the internal structure of the liking and love scales. As desired, each of the two scales proved to be internally consistent; that is, in each case its component items were highly intercorrelated. Also in accord with my starting assumption, the correlation between liking and loving scores was only moderate. The correlation between men's love and liking scores for their girlfriends was .56, and the correlation between women's love and liking scores for their boyfriends was .36.*

Although the general pattern of intrascale versus interscale correlations emerged as I had hoped it would, the finding that love and liking were more highly related to one another among men than among women was unexpected. It is possible that this difference is a consequence of the distinctive specializations of the two sexes. In most societies, men tend to be the task specialists, while women tend to be the social–emotional specialists. By virtue of their specialization in matters involving interpersonal feelings, women may develop a more finely tuned and more discriminating set of interpersonal sentiments than men do. Whereas men may often blur such fine distinctions as the one between liking and loving, women may be more likely to experience and express the two sentiments as being distinct from one another.

Further insight into the nature of liking and loving for the two sexes was derived from a comparison of their average love and liking scores for their dating partners and their same-sex friends. These averages are presented in Table 2. Unsurprisingly, the students reported loving their partners much more than their friends, while the gap between liking for partners and liking for friends was narrower. Less obvious and more informative are the comparisons between the scores of men and women. As Table 2 reveals, the average love scores of men for their girlfriends and of women for their boyfriends were virtually identical. But women *liked* their boyfriends significantly more than they were liked in return. This

*The size of the correlation between any two measures indicates how closely people's relative standing on the first measure corresponds to their relative standing on the second. A correlation of 1.00 indicates a perfect correspondence, while a correlation of 0 indicates that the two measures are totally unrelated. Increasing values of a correlation from 0 to 1 indicates increasing degrees of correspondence between the two measures. As a rough rule of thumb we can consider correlations smaller than .30 to be ''small,'' those between .30 and .70 to be ''moderate,'' and those of .70 or greater to be ''large.''

TABLE 2. Average Love and Liking Scores for Dating Partners and Same-Sex Friends.

	Women	Men
Love for partner	90.57	90.44
Liking for partner	89.10	85.30
Love for friend	64.79	54.47
Liking for friend	80.21	78.38

result seems to reflect contemporary sex roles and stereotypes. The liking scale is "sex-biased" in that it asks the respondent to size up his partner on such stereotypically male characteristics as maturity, intelligence, and good judgment. It asks whether the respondent would recommend the partner for a responsible job. It seems, in other words, to be getting at a task-related sort of liking. It is doubtful that the men in our sample were in fact more responsible, more intelligent, or endowed with better judgment than their girlfriends. Nevertheless, it is generally considered to be more appropriate for men than for women to excel on these dimensions, and the obtained results conform precisely to these cultural expectations.

Table 2 also shows that when respondents evaluated their same-sex friends, there was no tendency for men to be liked more than women. Thus, the data do not support the conclusion that men are generally more "likable" than women, but only that they are liked more in the context of dating relationships. The pattern of liking scores suggests that the dating relationship, instead of obliterating stereotypical differences between the sexes, may in fact perpetuate them by emphasizing role and status discrepancies. This pattern is in accord with the feminist critique of traditionally structured male-female relationships as fortifying the favored position of the male and reemphasizing the subservient position of the female.

An additional finding shown in Table 2 is that women tended to love their same-sex friends more than men did. It is indeed more common for female friends than for male friends to speak of themselves as "loving" one another, a linguistic fact that may reflect substantive differences in the nature of men's and women's same-sex friendships. Evidence from several surveys suggests that while women do not typically have more same-sex friends than men, women's friendships tend to be more intimate, involving more spontaneous joint activities and more exchanging of confidences.[6] Men's special difficulties in establishing intimate relationships with other men are underlined by the love-scale results. The male role, for all its task-related "likability," may limit the ability to love.[7] Loving for men may often be channeled into a single opposite-sex relationship, whereas women may be more able to experience and express attachment, caring, and intimacy in other relationships as well.

Another approach toward assessing the validity of the love and liking scales was to examine their correlations with other measures. One of the items included on the questionnaire was "Would you say that you and _____ are in love?" to be answered by circling "yes," "no," or "uncertain." Slightly over two-thirds of both men and women answered affirmatively, with only about 10 percent of each sex reporting that they were not in love and the remaining 22 percent of each sex pleading uncertainty. The correlations between love scores and this "in love" index were reasonably high: .61 for women and .53 for men. The correlations between liking scores and the "in love" index were considerably lower: .29 for women and .36 for men. Thus, the love scale, even though it nowhere includes the word "love" itself, tapped a sentiment that was distinctively related to the students' own categorization of their relationships.

The partners were also asked to estimate the likelihood they would eventually marry one another, on a probability scale ranging from 0 to 100 percent. The average estimate by women was about 50 percent and by men 45 percent. The correlations between love scores and estimates of marriage likelihood were substantial: .60 for women and .59 for men. The correlations between liking scores and marriage likelihood estimates were much lower: .33 for women and .35 for men. Once again the obtained pattern of correlations is reasonable. In societies like our own with a "love pattern" of mate selection, the link between love and marriage is strongly emphasized by parents, mass media, and other socializing agents. The link between liking and marriage, on the other hand, is too often a well-kept secret. In the next phase of my study I proceeded to put the love scale to a more difficult test, going beyond the questionnaire to direct observations of couples' behavior.

THE GLANCE OF EYE TO EYE

It is well-known folk wisdom that people who are in love spend inordinate amounts of time gazing into each others' eyes. Not all such truisms are in fact true, but there is reason to believe that this one may be. Sociologists and song-writers alike have noted that eye contact plays, as Erving Goffman puts it, "a special role in the communication life of the community.[8] This is because eye contact serves as a mutually understood signal that the communication channel between two people is open. Georg Simmel eloquently described sociological function of eye contact in his *Soziologie*:

> The union and interaction of individuals is based upon mutual glances. This is perhaps the purest and most direct reciprocity that exists anywhere. . . . So tenacious and subtle is this union that it can only be maintained by the shortest and straightest line between the eyes, and the smallest deviation from it, the slightest glance aside, completely destroys the unique character of this union. . . . The totality of social relations of human beings, their self-assertion and self-abnegation, their intimacies and estrangements, would be changed in unpredictable ways if there existed no glance of eye to eye. This mutual glance between persons, in distinction from the simple sight or observation of the other, signifies a wholly new and unique union between them.[9]

Social scientists have speculated about the developmental and evolutionary origins of the social functions of eye contact. One developmental psychologist concluded, for example, that "not physical, but visual contact is at the basis of human sociability."[10] Another reported that "the nature of the eye contact between a mother and her baby seems to cut across all interactional systems and conveys the intimacy or 'distance' characteristic of their relationship as a whole."[11] On the evolutionary level Konrad Lorenz has, in his characteristic analogical style, noted convergences between the functions of eye contact among humans and among lower animals:

As he makes his proposal, the male [jackdaw] glances continually toward his love but ceases his efforts immediately if she chances to fly away; this however she is not likely to do if she is interested in her admirer. . . . He casts glowing glances straight into his loved one's eyes, while she apparently turns her eyes in all directions other than that of her ardent suitor. In reality, of course, she is watching him all the time, and her quick glances of a fraction of a second are quite long enough to make her realize that all his antics are calculated to inspire her admiration: long enough to let "him" know that "she" knows.[12]

Whatever its origins, eye contact provides a channel through which intimate feelings can be directly expressed. Conversely, when two people do not feel close to one another, eye contact at close quarters is extremely difficult to sustain.

To test the prediction that love and eye contact would be positively related, I invited dating couples who had previously completed the questionnaire to take part in a laboratory experiment. While the two partners sat across a table from one another, waiting for the experiment to begin, they were observed through a one-way mirror by two assistants. Whenever the man looked at the woman's face, one observer, strategically stationed behind the woman, pressed a button that activated a clock recorder. Whenever the woman looked at the man's face, the second observer pushed a button that activated a second clock recorder. Whenever the two observers were pushing their buttons simultaneously, a third clock recorder was activated. The third clock provided the most important of the measures obtained, because it indicated the amount of *simultaneous* looking engaged in by the two partners.

To provide the clearest test of my prediction, I included in the laboratory session only those couples in which both partners were "strong lovers" (both had scored above the median on the love scale) or in which both were "weak lovers" (both had scored below the median). The results indicated that the "strong love" couples indeed made significantly more eye contact than the "weak love" couples did. This finding was certainly not a surprising one. But it added considerably to my confidence that the love scale measured something that went beyond mere question-naire-checking. Importantly, the difference between "strong love" and "weak love" couples did not emerge with respect to the sheer quantity of looking-at-each-other by the two partners, as recorded on the first and second clocks, but only with respect to mutual eye contact, as recorded on the third clock. "Weak love" boyfriends and girlfriends were as likely as "strong love" partners to look at one another unilaterally, but "strong love" boyfriends and girlfriends were more likely to look at one another simultaneously.

Eye contact was also measured in two additional experimental conditions. These conditions again compared "strong lovers" and "weak lovers," but the subjects were paired with *other people's* boyfriends and girlfriends rather than with their own partners. These conditions were included to take into account the possibil-ity that "strong lovers" are the sort of people who find it easy to maintain eye contact not only with their partners, but with other people in general. Such a possibility is suggested by Erich Fromm's analysis of love. "Love is not primarily a relationship toward a particular person," Fromm maintains. "It is . . . an *orienta-tion of character* which determines the relatedness of a person toward the world as a whole, not toward one 'object' of love. . . . If I truly love one person I love all persons, I love the world, I love life.''[13] Thus one might conjecture that when two ''strong lovers'' encounter one another, even though they have never before met, they still might find it relatively easy to communicate intimately and to sustain considerable eye contact. Two ''weak lovers,'' on the other hand, might find such intimacy much harder to achieve.

The obtained data did not support this suggestion, however. When the dyads consisted of opposite-sex strangers, the ''strong lovers'' did not make significantly more eye contact than the ''weak lovers.'' Thus, the pattern of results was more congruent with a conception of love as an attitude toward a particular person than as an orientation toward all mankind. There may still be considerable truth in Fromm's analysis. As codified in Eleanor of Aquitaine's Court of Love, ''the man in love becomes accustomed to performing many services gracefully for everyone.''[14] But the behavioral implications of this conception of love may be offset by the equally compelling truth that when two people are in love with one another, they have fewer emotional resources left for others. Freud wrote, ''The more [two people] are in love, the more completely they suffice for one another.''[15] Or, as the popular song has it, ''I only have eyes for you.''

NOTES

1. Erich Fromm, *The Art of Loving*, Bantam ed. (New York: Harper & Row, 1956), p. 22.
2. Harry Stack Sullivan, *Conceptions of Modern Psychiatry*, 2d ed. (New York: Norton, 1953), pp. 42–43.
3. Abraham H. Maslow, ''Deficiency Motivation and Growth Motivation,'' in Marshall R. Jones (Ed.), *Nebraska Symposium on Motivation, 1955* (Lincoln: University of Nebraska Press, 1955).
4. David Orlinsky, ''Love Relationships in the Life Cycle: A Developmental Interpersonal Perspective,'' in Herbert A. Otto (Ed.), *Love Today: A New Exploration* (New York: Association
5. Martin Buber, *I and Thou* (New York: Scribner's, 1970), p. 66.
6. Studies comparing women's and men's same-sex friendships include Elizabeth Douvan and Joseph Adelson, *The Adolescent Experience* (New York: Wiley, 1966), chap. 6; and Alan Booth, ''Sex and Social Participation,'' *American Sociological Review*, 1972, **37**, 183–192.
7. For insights into these limitations of the male role, see Joseph Pleck and Jack Sawyer (Eds.), *Men and Masculinity* (Englewood Cliffs, N.J.: Prentice-Hall, Inc. Spectrum Books, 1974).
8. Erving Goffman, *Behavior in Public Places* (New York: Free Press, 1963), p. 92.
9. Georg Simmel, *Soziologie*, as cited in Robert E. Park and Ernest W. Burgess, *Introduction to the Science of Sociology*, 2d ed. (Chicago: University of Chicago Press, 1924), p. 358.
10. Harriet L. Rheingold, ''The Effect of Environmental Stimulation upon Social and Exploratory Behavior in the Human Infant,'' in B. M. Foss (Ed.), *Determinants of Infant Behavior*, vol. 1 (New York: Wiley, 1961).
11. Kenneth S. Robson, ''The Role of Eye-to-Eye Contact in Maternal–Infant Attachment,'' *Journal of Child Psychology and Psychiatry*, 1967, **8**, 13–25.
12. Konrad Lorenz, *King Solomon's Ring* (New York: Crowell, 1952), pp. 156–157.
13. Fromm, pp. 38–39.
14. Andreas Capellanus, *The Art of Courtly Love*, trans. by John Jay Parry (New York: Columbia University Press, 1941).
15. Sigmund Freud, ''Group Psychology and the Analysis of the Ego,'' in *The Standard Edition of the Complete Psychological Works of Sigmund Freud*, vol. 18 (London: Hogarth, 1955), p. 140.

ELAINE HATFIELD
G. WILLIAM WALSTER
JANE PILIAVIN
LYNN SCHMIDT

"Playing Hard To Get":
Understanding An Elusive Phenomenon

According to folklore, the woman who is hard to get is a more desirable catch than is the woman who is overly eager for alliance. Socrates, Ovid, Terence, the *Kama Sutra*, and Dear Abby all agree that the person whose affection is easily won is unlikely to inspire passion in another. Ovid (1963), for example, argued:

> Fool, if you feel no need to guard your girl for her own sake, see that you guard her for mine, so I may want her the more. Easy things nobody wants, but what is forbidden is tempting. . . . Anyone who can love the wife of an indolent cuckold, I should suppose, would steal buckets of sand from the shore [pp. 65–66].

When we first began our investigation, we accepted cultural lore. We assumed that men would prefer a hard-to-get woman. Thus, we began our research by interviewing college men as to why they preferred hard-to-get women. Predictably, the men responded to experimenter demands. They explained that they preferred hard-to-get women because the elusive woman is almost inevitably a valuable woman. They pointed out that a woman can only afford to be "choosy" if she is popular—and a woman is popular for some reason. When a woman is hard to get, it is usually a tip-off that she is especially pretty, has a good personality, is sexy, etc. Men also were intrigued by the challenge that the elusive woman offered. One can spend a great deal of time fantasizing about what it would be like to date such a woman. Since the hard-to-get woman's desirability is well recognized, a man can gain prestige if he is seen with her.

An easy-to-get woman, on the other hand, spells trouble. She is probably desperate for a date. She is probably the kind of woman who will make too many demands on a person; she might want to get serious right away. Even worse, she might have a "disease."

In brief, nearly all interviewees agreed with our hypothesis that a hard-to-get woman is a valuable woman, and they could supply abundant justification for their prejudice. A few isolated men refused to cooperate. These dissenters noted that an

Abridged from "Playing Hard to Get: Understanding an Elusive Phenomenon" by Elaine Hatfield, G. William Walster, Jane Piliavin and Lynn Schmidt from *Journal of Personality and Social Psychology*, vol. 26, 1973. Copyright © 1973 by the American Psychological Association. Reprinted by permission.

elusive woman is not always more desirable than an available woman. Sometimes the hard-to-get woman is not only hard to get—she is *impossible* to get, because she is misanthropic and cold. Sometimes a woman is easy to get because she is a friendly, outgoing woman who boosts one's ego and insures that dates are "no hassle." We ignored the testimony of these deviant types.

We then conducted five experiments designed to demonstrate that an individual values a hard-to-get date more highly than an easy-to-get date. All five experiments failed.

THEORETICAL RATIONALE

Let us first review the theoretical rationale underlying these experiments.

In Walster, Walster, and Berscheid (1971) we argued that if playing hard to get does increase one's desirability, several psychological theories could account for this phenomenon:

1. Dissonance theory predicts that if one must expend great energy to attain a goal, he is unusually appreciative of the goal (see Aronson & Mills, 1959; Gerard & Mathewson, 1966; Zimbardo, 1965). The hard-to-get date requires a suitor to expend more effort in her pursuit than he would normally expend. One way for the suitor to justify such unusual effort is by aggrandizing her.

2. According to learning theory, an elusive person should have two distinct advantages: (*a*) Frustration may increase drive—by waiting until the suitor has achieved a high sexual drive state, heightening his drive level by introducing momentary frustration, and then finally rewarding him, the hard-to-get woman can maximize the impact of the sexual reward she provides (see Kimball, 1961, for evidence that frustration does energize behavior and does increase the impact of appropriate rewards). (*b*) Elusiveness and value may be associated—individuals may have discovered through frequent experience that there is more competition for socially desirable dates than for undesirable partners. Thus, being "hard to get" comes to be associated with "value." As a consequence, the conditioned stimulus (CS) of being hard to get generates a fractional antedating goal response and a fractional goal response which leads to the conditioned response of liking.

3. In an extension of Schachterian theory, Walster (1971) argued that two components are necessary before an individual can experience passionate love: (*a*) He must be physiologically aroused; and (*b*) the setting must make it appropriate for him to conclude that his aroused feelings are due to love. On both counts, the person who plays hard to get might be expected to generate unusual passion. Frustration should increase the suitor's physiological arousal, and the association of "elusiveness" with "value" should increase the probability that the suitor will label his reaction to the other as "love."

From the preceding discussion, it is evident that several conceptually distinct variables may account for the hard-to-get phenomenon. In spite of the fact that we can suggest a plethora of reasons as to why playing hard-to-get strategy might be an effective strategy, all five studies failed to provide any support for the contention that an elusive woman is a desirable woman. Two experiments failed to demonstrate that outside observers perceive a hard-to-get individual as especially "valuable."

Three experiments failed to demonstrate that a suitor perceives a hard-to-get date as especially valuable.

Walster, Walster, and Berscheid (1971) conducted two experiments to test the hypothesis that teenagers would deduce that a hard-to-get boy or girl was more socially desirable than was a teenager whose affection could be easily obtained. In these experiments high school juniors and seniors were told that we were interested in finding out what kind of first impression various teenagers made on others. They were shown pictures and biographies of a couple. They were told how romantically interested the stimulus person (a boy or girl) was in his partner after they had met only four times. The stimulus person was said to have liked the partner ''extremely much,'' to have provided no information to us, or to like her ''not particularly much.'' The teenagers were then asked how socially desirable both teenagers seemed (i.e., how likable, how physically attractive, etc., both teenagers seemed). Walster, Walster, and Berscheid, of course, predicted that the more romantic interest the stimulus person expressed in a slight acquaintance, the less socially desirable that stimulus person would appear to an outside observer. The results were diametrically opposed to those predicted. The more romantic interest the stimulus person expressed in an acquaintance, the *more* socially desirable teenagers judged him to be. Restraint does not appear to buy respect. Instead, it appears that ''All the world *does* love a lover.''

Lyons, Walster, and Walster (1971) conducted a field study and a laboratory experiment in an attempt to demonstrate that men prefer a date who plays hard to get. Both experiments were conducted in the context of a computer matching service. Experiment III was a field experiment. Women who signed up for the computer matching program were contacted and hired as experimenters. They were then given precise instructions as to how to respond when their computer match called them for a date. Half of the time they were told to pause and think for 3 seconds before accepting the date. (These women were labeled ''hard to get.'') Half of the time they were told to accept the date immediately. (These women were labeled ''easy to get.'') The data indicated that elusiveness had no impact on the man's liking for his computer date.

Experiment IV was a laboratory experiment. In this experiment, Lyons et al. hypothesized that the knowledge that a woman is elusive gives one indirect evidence that she is socially desirable. Such indirect evidence should have the biggest impact when a man has no way of acquiring *direct* evidence about a coed's value or when he has little confidence in his own ability to assess value. When direct evidence is available, and the man possesses supreme confidence in his ability to make correct judgments, information about a woman's elusiveness should have little impact on a man's reaction to her. Lyons et al. thus predicted that when men lacked direct evidence as to a woman's desirability, a man's self-esteem and the woman's elusiveness should interact in determining his respect and liking for her. . . .

The dating counselor then told subjects that the computer had assigned them a date. They were asked to telephone her from the office phone, invite her out, and then report their first impression of her. Presumably the pair would then go out on a date and eventually give us further information about how successful our computer matching techniques had been. Actually, all men were assigned a confederate as a date. Half of the time the woman played hard to get. When the man asked her out she replied:

> Mmm [slight pause] No, I've got a date then. It seems like I signed up for that Date Match thing a long time ago and I've met more people since then—I'm really pretty busy all this week.

She paused again. If the subject suggested another time, the confederate hesitated only slightly, then accepted. If he did not suggest another time, the confederate would take the initiative of suggesting: "How about some time next week—or just meeting for coffee in the Union some afternoon?" And again, she accepted the next invitation. Half of the time, in the easy-to-get condition, the confederate eagerly accepted the man's offer of a date.

Lyons et al. predicted that since men in this blind date setting lacked direct evidence as to a woman's desirability, low-self-esteem men should be more receptive to the hard-to-get woman than were high-self-esteem men. Although Lyons et al.'s manipulation checks indicate that their manipulations were successful and their self-esteem measure was reliable, their hypothesis was not confirmed. Elusiveness had no impact on liking, regardless of subject's self-esteem level.

Did we give up our hypothesis? Heavens no. After all, it had only been disconfirmed four times.

By Experiment V, we had decided that perhaps the hard-to-get hypothesis must be tested in a sexual setting. After all, the first theorist who advised a woman to play hard to get was Socrates; his pupil was Theodota, a prostitute. He advised:

> They will appreciate your favors most highly if you wait till they ask for them. The sweetest meats, you see, if served before they are wanted seem sour, and to those who had enough they are positively nauseating; but even poor fare is very welcome when offered to a hungry man. [Theodota inquired] And how can I make them hungry for my fare? [Socrates' reply] Why, in the first place, you must not offer it to them when they have had enough—but prompt them by behaving as a model of Propriety, by a show of reluctance to yield, and by holding back until they are as keen as can be; and then the same gifts are much more to the recipient than when they're offered before they are desired [see Xenophon, 1923, p. 48].

Walster, Walster, and Lambert (1971) thus proposed that a prostitute who states that she is selective in her choice of customers will be held in higher regard than will be the prostitute who admits that she is completely unselective in her choice of partners.

In this experiment, a prostitute served as the experimenter. When the customer arrived, she mixed a drink for him; then she delivered the experimental manipulation. Half of the time, in the hard-to-get condition, she stated, "Just because I see you this time it doesn't mean that you can have my phone number or see me again. I'm going to start school soon, so I won't have much time, so I'll only be able to see the people that I like the best." Half of the time, in the easy-to-get condition, she did not communicate this information. From this point on, the prostitute and the customer interacted in conventional ways.

The client's liking for the prostitute was determined in two ways: First, the prostitute estimated how much the client had seemed to like her. (i.e., How much did he seem to like you? Did he make arrangements to return? How much did he pay you?) Second, the experimenter recorded how many times within the next 30 days the client arranged to have subsequent sexual relations with her.

Once again we failed to confirm the hard-to-get hypothesis. If anything, those clients who were told that the prostitute did not take just anyone were *less* likely to call back and liked the prostitute less than did other clients.

At this point, we ruefully decided that we had been on the wrong track. We decided that perhaps all those practitioners who advise women to play hard to get are wrong. Or perhaps it is only under very special circumstances that it will benefit one to play hard to get.

Thus, we began again. We reinterviewed students—this time with an open mind. This time we asked men to tell us about the advantages *and* disadvantages of hard-to-get *and* easy-to-get women. This time replies were more informative. According to reports, choosing between a hard-to-get woman and an easy-to-get woman was like choosing between Scylla and Charybdis—each woman was uniquely desirable and uniquely frightening.

Although the elusive woman was likely to be a popular prestige date, she presented certain problems. Since she was not particularly enthusiastic about you, she might stand you up or humiliate you in front of your friends. She was likely to be unfriendly, cold, and to possess inflexible standards.

The easy-to-get woman was certain to boost one's ego and to make a date a relaxing, enjoyable experience, but unfortunately, dating an easy woman was a risky business. Such a woman might be easy to get, but hard to get rid of. She might "get serious." Perhaps she would be so oversexed or overaffectionate in public that she would embarrass you. Your buddies might snicker when they saw you together. After all, they would know perfectly well why you were dating *her*.

The interlocking assets and difficulties envisioned when they attempted to decide which was better—a hard-to-get or an easy-to-get woman—gave us a clue as to why our previous experiments had not worked out. The assets and liabilities of the elusive and the easy dates had evidently generally balanced out. On the average, then, both types of women tended to be equally well liked. When a slight difference in liking did appear, it favored the easy-to-get woman.

It finally impinged on us that there are *two* components that are important determinants of how much a man likes a woman: (*a*) How hard or easy she is for him to get; (*b*) How hard or easy she is for *other men* to get. So long as we were examining the desirability of women who were hard or easy for everyone to get, things balanced out. The minute we examined other possible configurations, it becomes evident that there is one type of woman who can transcend the limitations of the uniformly hard-to-get or the uniformly easy-to-get woman. If a woman has a reputation for being hard to get, but for some reason she is easy for the subject to get, she should be maximally appealing. Dating such a woman should insure one of great prestige; she is, after all, hard to get. Yet, since she is exceedingly available to the subject, the dating situation should be a relaxed, rewarding experience. Such a *selectively* hard-to-get woman possesses the assets of both the easy-to-get and the hard-to-get women, while avoiding all of their liabilities.

Thus, in Experiment VI, we hypothesized that a selectively hard-to-get woman (i.e., a woman who is easy for the subject to get but very hard for any other man to get) will be especially liked by her date. Women who are hard for everyone—including the subject—to get, or who are easy for everyone to get—or control women, about whom the subject had no information—will be liked a lesser amount.

METHOD

Subjects were 71 male summer students at the University of Wisconsin. They were recruited for a dating research project. This project was ostensibly designed to determine whether computer matching techniques are in fact more effective than is random matching. All participants were invited to come into the dating center in order to choose a date from a set of five potential dates.

When the subject arrived at the computer match office, he was handed folders containing background information on five women. Some of these women had supposedly been "randomly" matched with him; others had been "computer matched" with him. (He was not told which women were which.)

In reality, all five folders contained information about fictitious women. The first item in the folder was a "background questionnaire" on which the woman had presumably described herself. This questionnaire was similar to one the subject had completed when signing up for the match program. We attempted to make the five women's descriptions different enough to be believable, yet similar enough to minimize variance. Therefore, the way the five women described themselves was systematically varied. They claimed to be 18 or 19 years old; freshmen or sophomores; from a Wisconsin city, ranging in size from over 500,000 to under 50,000; 5 feet 2 inches to 5 feet 4 inches tall; Protestant, Catholic, Jewish, or had no preference; graduated in the upper 10%–50% of their high school class; and Caucasians who did not object to being matched with a person of another race. The women claimed to vary on a political spectrum from "left of center" through "moderate" to "near right of center"; to place little or no importance on politics and religion; and to like recent popular movies. Each woman listed four or five activities she liked to do on a first date (i.e., go to a movie, talk in a quiet place, etc.).

In addition to the background questionnaire, three of the five folders contained five "date selection forms." The experimenter explained that some of the women had already been able to come in, examine the background information of their matches, and indicate their first impression of them. Two of the subject's matches had not yet come in. Three of the women had already come in and evaluated the subject along with her four other matches. These women would have five date selection forms in their folders. The subject was shown the forms, which consisted of a scale ranging from "definitely do *not* want to date" (-10) to "definitely want to date" ($+10$). A check appeared on each scale. Presumably the check indicated how much the woman had liked a given date. (At this point, the subject was told his identification dating number. Since all dates were identified by numbers on the forms, this identification number enabled him to ascertain how each date had evaluated both him and her four other matches.)

The date selection forms allowed us to manipulate the elusiveness of the woman. One woman appeared to be uniformly hard to get. She indicated that though she was willing to date any of the men assigned to her, she was not enthusiastic about any of them. She rated all five of her date choices from $+1$ to $+2$, including the subject (who was rated 1.75).

One woman appeared to be uniformly easy to get. She indicated that she was enthusiastic about dating all five of the men assigned to her. She rated her desire to date all five of her date choices $+7$ to $+9$. This included the subject, who was rated 8.

One woman appeared to be easy for the subject to get but hard for anyone else to get (i.e., the selectively hard-to-get woman). She indicated minimal enthusiasm for four of her date choices, rating them from $+2$ to $+3$, and extreme enthusiasm ($+8$) for the subject.

Two women had no date selection forms in their folders (i.e., no information women).

Naturally, each woman appears in each of the five conditions.

The experimenter asked the man to consider the folders, complete a "first impression questionnaire" for each woman, and then decide which *one* of the women he wished to date. (The subject's rating of the dates constitutes our verbal measure of liking; his choice in a date constitutes our behavioral measure of liking.)

The experimenter explained that she was conducting a study of first impressions in conjunction with the dating research project. The study, she continued, was designed to learn more about how good people are at forming first impressions of others on the basis of rather limited information. She explained that filling out the forms would probably make it easier for the man to decide which one of the five women he wished to date.

The first impression questionnaire consisted of three sections:

1. *Liking for various dates.* Two questions assessed subject's liking for each woman: "If you went out with this girl, how well do you think you would get along?"—with possible responses ranging from "get along extremely well" (5) to "not get along at all" (1)—and "What was your overall impression of the girl?"—with possible responses ranging from "extremely favorable" (7) to "extremely unfavorable" (1). Scores on these two questions were summed to form an index of expressed liking. This index enables us to compare subject's liking for each of the women.

2. *Assets and liabilities ascribed to various dates.* We predicted that subjects would prefer the selective woman, because they would expect her to possess the good qualities of both the uniformly hard-to-get and the uniformly easy-to-get woman, while avoiding the bad qualities of both her rivals. Thus, the second section was designed to determine the extent to which subjects imputed good and bad qualities to the various dates.

This section was comprised of 10 pairs of polar opposites. Subjects were asked to rate how friendly–unfriendly, cold–warm, attractive–unattractive, easy-going–rigid, exciting–boring, shy–outgoing, fun-loving–dull, popular–unpopular, aggressive–passive, selective–nonselective each woman was. Ratings were made on a 7-point scale. The more desirable the trait ascribed to a woman, the higher the score she was given.

3. *Liabilities attributed to easy-to-get women:* The third scale was designed to assess the extent to which subjects attributed selected negative attributes to each woman. The third scale consisted of six statements:

> She would more than likely do something to embarrass me in public.
> She probably would demand too much attention and affection from me.
> She seems like the type who would be too dependent on me.
> She might turn out to be too sexually promiscuous.
> She probably would make me feel uneasy when I'm with her in a group.
> She seems like the type who doesn't distinguish between the boys she dates. I probably would be "just another date."

Subjects were asked whether they anticipated any of the above difficulties in their relationship with each woman. They indicated their misgivings on a scale ranging from "certainly true of her" (1) to "certainly not true of her" (7).

The experimenter suggested that the subject carefully examine both the background questionnaires and the date selection forms of all potential dates in order to decide whom he wanted to date. Then she left the subject. (The experimenter was, of course, unaware of what date was in what folder.)

The experimenter did not return until the subject had completed the first impression questionnaires. Then she asked him which woman he had decided to date.

After his choice had been made, the experimenter questioned him as to what factors influenced his choice. Frequently men who chose the selectively easy-to-get woman said that "She chose me, and that made me feel really good" or "She seemed more selective than the others." The uniformly easy-to-get woman was often rejected by subjects who complained "She must be awfully hard up for a date—she really would take anyone." The uniformly hard-to-get woman was once described as a "challenge," but more often rejected as being "snotty" or "too picky."

At the end of the session, the experimenter debriefed the subject and then gave him the names of five actual dates who had been matched with him.

RESULTS

We predicted that the selectively hard-to-get woman (easy for me to get but hard for everyone else to get) would be liked more than women who were uniformly hard to get, uniformly easy to get, or neutral (the no information women). We had no prediction as to whether or not her three rivals would differ in attractiveness. The results strongly support our hypothesis.

Dating Choices

When we examine the men's choices in dates, we see that the selective woman is far more popular than any of her rivals. (See Table 1.) Nearly all subjects preferred to date the selective woman. When we compare the frequency with which her four rivals (combined) are chosen, we see that the selective woman does get far more than her share of dates. . . .

We also conducted an analysis to determine whether or not the women who are uniformly hard to get, uniformly easy to get, or whose popularity is unknown, differed in popularity. We see that they did not. . . .

TABLE 1. Men's Choices in a Date.

Item	Selectively hard to get	Uniformly hard to get	Uniformly easy to get	No information for No. 1	No information for No. 2
Number of men choosing to date each woman	42	6	5	11	7

Liking for the Various Dates

Two questions tapped the men's romantic liking for the various dates: (a) "If you went out with this woman, how well do you think you'd get along?" and (b) "What was your overall impression of the woman?" Scores on these two indexes were summed to form an index of liking. Possible scores ranged from 2 to 12.

. . . The data again provide strong support for the hypothesis that the selective woman is better liked than her rivals.

Additional Data Snooping

We also conducted a second [test] to determine whether the rivals (i.e., the uniformly hard-to-get woman, the uniformly easy-to-get woman, and the control woman) were differentially liked. The data indicate that the rivals are differentially liked. The uniformly hard-to-get woman seems to be liked slightly less than the easy-to-get or control women. . . .

To make it abundantly clear that the main result is that the discriminating woman is better liked than each of the other rivals, we performed an additional analysis, pitting each of the rivals separately against the discriminating woman. In these analyses, we see that the selective woman is better liked than the woman who is uniformly easy to get, than the woman who is uniformly hard to get, and finally, than the control women. . . .

Thus, it is clear that although there are slight differences in the way rivals are liked, these differences are small, relative to the overwhelming attractiveness of the selective woman.

Assets and Liabilities Attributed to Dates

We can now attempt to ascertain *why* the selective woman is more popular than her rivals. Earlier, we argued that the selectively hard-to-get woman should occupy a unique position; she should be assumed to possess all of the virtues of her rivals, but none of their flaws.

The virtues and flaws that the subject ascribed to each woman were tapped by the polar–opposite scale. Subjects evaluated each woman on 10 characteristics.

We expected that subjects would associate two assets with a uniformly hard-to-get woman: Such a woman should be perceived to be both "selective" and "popular." Unfortunately, such a woman should also be assumed to possess three liabilities—she should be perceived to be "unfriendly," "cold," and "rigid." Subjects should ascribe exactly the opposite virtues and liabilities to the easy-to-get woman: Such a woman should possess the assets of "friendliness," "warmth," and "flexibility," and the liabilities of "unpopularity" and "lack of selectivity." The selective woman was expected to possess only assets: She should be perceived to be as "selective" and "popular" as the uniformly elusive woman, and as "friendly," "warm," and "easy-going" as the uniformly easy woman. Our hypothesis is confirmed. The selective woman is rated most like the uniformly hard-to-get woman on the first two positive characteristics; most like the uniformly easy-to-get woman on the last three characteristics.

For the reader's interest, the subjects' ratings of all five women's assets and liabilities are presented in Table 2.

TABLE 2. Men's Reactions to Various Dates.

Item	Type of date			
	Selec-tively hard to get	Uni-formly hard to get	Uni-formly easy to get	No infor-mation
Men's liking for dates	9.41[a]	7.90	8.53	8.58
Evaluation of women's assets and liabilities				
Selective[b]	5.23	4.39	2.85	4.30
Popular[b]	4.83	4.58	4.65	4.83
Friendly[c]	5.58	5.07	5.52	5.37
Warm[c]	5.15	4.51	4.99	4.79
Easy-going[c]	4.83	4.42	4.82	4.61
Problems expected in dating	5.23[d]	4.86	4.77	4.99

[a]The higher the number, the more liking the man is expressing for the date.
[b]Traits we expected to be ascribed to the selectively hard-to-get and the uniformly hard-to-get dates.
[c]Traits we expected to be ascribed to the selectively hard-to-get and the uniformly easy-to-get dates.
[d]The higher the number the *fewer* the problems the subject anticipates in dating.

Comparing the Selective and the Easy Women

Scale 3 was designed to assess whether or not subjects anticipated fewer problems when they envisioned dating the selective woman than when they envisioned dating the uniformly easy-to-get woman. On the basis of pretest interviews, we compiled a list of many of the concerns men had about easy women (e.g., "She would more than likely do something to embarrass me in public.").

We, of course, predicted that subjects would experience more problems when contemplating dating the uniformly easy woman than when contemplating dating a woman who was easy for *them* to get, but hard for anyone else to get (i.e., the selective woman).

Men were asked to say whether or not they envisioned each of the difficulties were they to date each of the women. Possible replies varied from 1 (certainly true of her) to 7 (certainly not true of her). The subjects' evaluations of each woman were summed to form an index of anticipated difficulties. Possible scores ranged from 6 to 42.

. . . [The data indicate that] the selective woman engendered less concern than the uniformly easy-to-get woman. If the reader is interested in comparing concern engendered by each woman, these data are available in Table 2.

The data provide clear support for our hypotheses: The selective woman is strongly preferred to any of her rivals. The reason for her popularity is evident. Men ascribe to her all of the assets of the uniformly hard-to-get and the uniformly easy-to-get women, and none of their liabilities.

Thus, after five futile attempts to understand the "hard-to-get" phenomenon, it appears that we have finally gained an understanding of this process. It appears that a woman can intensify her desirability if she acquires a reputation for being hard-to-get and then, by her behavior, makes it clear to a selected romantic partner that she is attracted to him.

In retrospect, especially in view of the strongly supportive data, the logic underlying our predictions sounds compelling. In fact, after examining our data, a colleague who had helped design the five ill-fated experiments noted that, "That is exactly what I would have predicted" (given his economic view of man). Unfortunately, we are all better at postdiction than prediction.

REFERENCES

Aronson, E., & Mills, J. The effect of severity of initiation on liking for a group. *Journal of Abnormal and Social Psychology*, 1959, **67**, 31–36.

Berger, E. M. The relation between expressed acceptance of self and expressed acceptance of others. *Journal of Abnormal and Social Psychology*, 1952, **47**, 778–782.

Gerard, H. B., & Mathewson, G. C. The effects of severity of initiation and liking for a group: A replication. *Journal of Experimental Social Psychology*, 1966, **2**, 278–287.

Hays, W. L. *Statistics for psychologists*. New York: Holt, Rinehart, 1963.

Kimball, G. A. *Hilgard and Marquis' conditioning and learning*. New York: Appleton-Century-Crofts, 1961.

Lyons, J., Walster, E., & Walster, G. W. Playing hard-to-get: An elusive phenomenon. University of Wisconsin, Madison: Author, 1971. (Mimeo)

Morrison, D. F. *Multivariate statistical methods*. New York: McGraw-Hill, 1967.

Ovid. *The art of love*. Bloomington: University of Indiana Press, 1963.

Rosenberg, M. *Society and the adolescent self image*. Princeton, N.J.: Princeton University Press, 1965.

Rosenfeld, H. M. Social choice conceived as a level of aspiration. *Journal of Abnormal and Social Psychology*, 1964, **68**, 491–499.

Walster, E. Passionate love. In B. I. Murstein (Ed.), *Theories of attraction and love*. New York: Springer, 1971.

Walster, E., Walster, G. W., & Berscheid, E. The efficacy of playing hard-to-get. *Journal of Experimental Education*, 1971, **39**, 73–77.

Walster, E., Walster, G. W., & Lambert, P. Playing hard-to-get: A field study. University of Wisconsin, Madison: Author, 1971. (Mimeo)

Xenophon. *Memorabilia*. London: Heinemann, 1923.

Zimbardo, P. G. The effect of effort and improvisation on self persuasion produced by role-playing. *Journal of Experimental Social Psychology*, 1965, **1**, 103–120.

Proxmire On Love

Senator William Proxmire of Wisconsin has discovered that the National Science Foundation is spending $83,000 a year out of the Federal Treasury to find out why people fall in love, and he wants it stopped. Not the love but the spending. "Biggest boondoggle of the year," he says. "I don't want the answer."

This is not like our old buddy Bill. He is normally a sensible and even a romantic type himself, a physical fitness buff who jogs to the Capitol in the morning and spends most of his time there digging out the facts, but he wants romantic love to remain a mystery.

Mr. Proxmire is a modern man who believes that government should help people with their problems. He is a land-grant college man, and will vote any amount of money for basic research on the dangers of natural selection in animals, and on how to get the best bulls and cows together on the farms of Wisconsin, but he is against basic research on the alarming divorce rate or break-up of the human family in America. You have to assume he was kidding.

The National Center for Health Statistics of the Department of Health, Education and Welfare has just reported that there were 970,000 divorces in the United States in 1974, compared to 913,000 in 1973, and 479,000 in 1965. The *rate* of population growth in the United States is down over the last decade, but in 1974, the excess of births over deaths was still up by over a million and a quarter, while the rate of marriages was down and the rate of divorces up.

All the National Science Foundation was suggesting, and the Federal Government was financing, was a modest inquiry into these statistics. Why this increase in divorce, this decrease in marriage, this disbelief in the family as the basis of American life?

Were the expectations of married life unreasonably high? Were the assumptions of courtship, and of economic security an enduring reality or a trap? What was romantic love anyway—a basis for secure family and national life, or a dangerous illusion?

With these questions in mind, the National Science Foundation was given $83,000 to see whether it could come up with any answers or at least clues, and the burden of research fell on Ellen Berscheid, a professor of psychology at the University of Minnesota. When Senator Proxmire spoiled this $83,000 item as chairman of the Senate Appropriations subcommittee in charge of the National Science Foundation's budget, he almost blew his new hair do. "Get out of the love-racket," he told the foundation.

Obviously, he had a point. The reasons why people fall in love, or think they do, will always be a mystery, and many people, like Mr. Proxmire, probably "don't want the answer." But if the sociologists and psychologists can get even a suggestion of the answer to our pattern of romantic love, marriage, disillusion, divorce—and the children left behind—it could be the best investment of Federal money since Mr. Jefferson made the Louisiana Purchase.

Professor Berscheid thinks the illusions about romantic love, the confusion between infatuation and enduring love, are precisely what we have to understand if we are to deal with the consequences of the pill, the rejection of marriage, broken marriages, and abandoned and morally confused children.

It is the illusion of romantic love among the young that leads to broken marriages, she says, and broken families, which in turn contribute to the disorientation, instability, disunity and even violence of American life. Therefore, she concludes, research on how and why young men and women marry is fundamental, even if the researchers never find the answers.

Professor Berscheid hasn't gone far enough into her inquiries to pronounce or even indicate conclusions. But she does think she has found an illusion among the young: namely, that in married life, love and hostility are opposites; that if there is love there cannot be hate or even hostility, whereas her researches so far suggest that love and hostility, sometimes even hate, often exist together.

Mr. Proxmire, who has had some experience with life, would probably agree; but he saw what seemed to be an obvious boondoggle in the budget, and he attacked it as a budgetary swindle. It was good politics but probably bad history, for the world is being transformed now, not by political leaders, but by the fertility of the human mind and body, by the creation of life at the beginning and the prolongation of life at the end.

The politicians don't quite know how to find the jobs, schools, houses, food, fuel and transportation to deal with this torrent of people and problems. Therefore, the social scientists have to think about why new life is created in the first place, where the pill, and the concepts of romantic love, easy sex, marriage and divorce fit into the life of the nation.

"I don't want to know the answer," about why people fall in love, marry or don't, Senator Proxmire says in what was probably one of his few careless public statements. But a lot of other people want the answer studied, even if "romantic love" and why people marry remain a mystery, as they undoubtedly will.

5

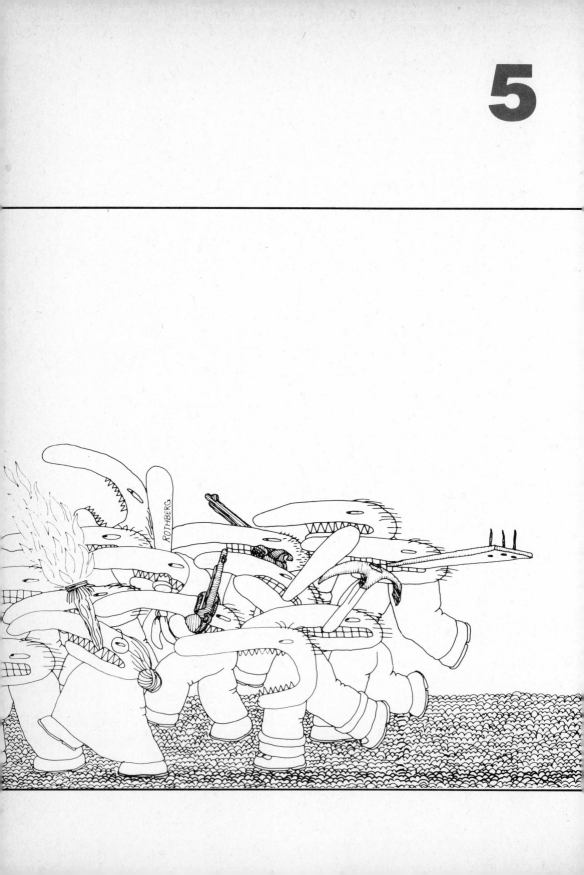

Aggression and Violence

The topic of violence is as old as the story of Cain and Abel, and people have tried to understand both the causes and consequences of violence since the earliest of times. Among many different approaches to an understanding of violence and aggression, two that have received very wide attention include the psychoanalytic approach of Sigmund Freud and the ethological approach of Konrad Lorenz. While these approaches differ in many ways, both tend to emphasize the instinctive or innate quality of aggressive behavior, and to suggest that such behavior is inevitable in humans and animals.

A social psychological approach to aggressive behavior, while not necessarily denying the human being's innate capacity for aggression, has a somewhat different orientation. Here, we are concerned chiefly with the ways in which violence results from the interaction between the individual and the social environment. We study when, why, and how an individual or group will act violently toward another individual or group—whether the type of violence be verbal insult, physical attack, murder, riot, or nuclear war.

Robert Baron, a social psychologist who has contributed greatly to this field, is currently Program Director of the National Science Foundation's Division of Social and Developmental Psychology. He has written a number of textbooks in psychology and social psychology and is the author of *Human Aggression* in addition to numerous articles in the field. We talked about certain of the basic issues in defining aggression, about the need for different strategies for studying it and about the many variables which can cause aggression. Dr. Baron pointed out that once we accept the complexity of this phenomenon, it makes easy and simple-minded suggestions for controlling and eliminating violence hard to accept. However, he does suggest at least two ways by which we may be able to at least lower the level of violence in our society.

A CONVERSATION WITH
ROBERT A. BARON

National Science Foundation

KRUPAT: *I think it would be best if we could start out with a definition of our topic, which is aggression. Just what does that term mean to you?*

BARON: What I mean by it and what I think most other researchers in this area mean by it is behavior that is directed toward the goal of harming or injuring another living being—especially another living being who is motivated to avoid that kind of treatment.

KRUPAT: *I notice that you included the fact that the behavior has to be directed toward hurting. Can I assume that in order to call an act aggressive it has to be intentional?*

BARON: This is a problem that researchers and scholars in this area have wrestled with for decades: Whether or not it is necessary to include a notion of intent or intention to harm in the definition of aggression. This turns out to be a very complicated issue. On the one hand, if you introduce the notion of intent, you have the problem of measuring it. How can you tell whether someone really meant to hurt or whether it was accidental? On the other hand, if you leave out the notion of intention, you get into binds such as these. For example, any accidental harm to another person would have to be viewed as aggression. Also, any behavior which attempts to harm another person but fails would not be considered aggression. If I aim a gun at you, shoot and miss, but you're not aware of that fact, then my action would not be considered aggression unless you consider my intentions. So I think that most scholars in this area feel that you have to include intention, even though it is complicated and somewhat messy.

KRUPAT: *When you refer to harm or injury, does that have to be physical or can we talk about more subtle ways of hurting others?*

BARON: That is a good point. Human beings can seek to hurt other people and succeed in doing so in many different ways. Physical harm is just one dimension in this respect. We often inflict verbal pain or psychological pain on other people. All of these could be considered aggression.

KRUPAT: *How about if I inflict pain on your property, of course not literally, but if I destroy something of yours?*

BARON: If you damage some prize possession of mine, I would see that as an act of aggression. The hurt is ultimately to me as the possessor of it.

KRUPAT: *Assuming that it was* meant *to upset you.*

BARON: That's right. If it's an accident, then you're just careless. But since we are talking about damage to property, let me briefly qualify something. The ultimate goal in your mind when you damage my property has to be in harming me, in some kind of psychic glee that I would be hurt by the destruction of my possessions. If all you are doing is destroying for the fun of it, and unfortunately that does seem to be the case for some people who break glass and throw rocks, I wouldn't see that as aggression.

KRUPAT: *But if a group of kids spotted an abandoned car and started tearing it to pieces, wouldn't many people talk about that as "getting out their aggressive urges"?*

BARON: There is an important distinction between the emotions that often accompany aggression and the behavior that we as social psychologists label aggression. In attacking a car, especially if the kids think it is abandoned and just a hunk of steel sitting on the street, what you have is emotional relief or an expression of an emotional reaction, not something I would call aggression.

KRUPAT: *But isn't it sometimes hard to know one from the other?*

BARON: It is. The problem is that the motoric component, the behaviors involved, are identical, but the motivations are different. I think that we have to focus on people's motives or intentions, again not because we prefer to, but if we don't, things get even worse.

KRUPAT: *Since we are talking about motivations, let me expand the issue and ask you why people do act aggressively. Are we born with aggressive urges? Is it conditioned by society?*

BARON: That's the proverbial $64 question. In some ways it is unanswerable, and in other ways you can address it to a reasonable extent. I think back over the last 30 to 40 years when people talked about the roots of human violence or the origins of human aggression. They tended to focus on one particular cause, to choose sides and stick very closely to one camp or another. For example, you had people in the Freudian tradition who felt that aggression is innate, part of our human nature. They believed that there is nothing we can do to get rid of it, all we can do is control it. On the other hand, you had pure environmentalists who felt that aggression stems entirely from external, environmental conditions and perhaps from past social learning experiences that are taught by society. According to this group, people learn that it is appropriate to aggress in certain situations and under certain conditions. I think that as empirical evidence has accumulated and as more and more has been learned about human aggression, it has become clear that neither of these views really is very accurate. Instead, human aggression stems from a tremendous number of different factors—and now I am relying very much on empirical data—everything from unpleasant environmental conditions such as crowding, noise, heat, air pollution, unpleasant aromas— through internal states and individual differences. I visualize that if someone were to ask me for a list of all the variables that influence aggression or act as sources of aggression, I could take a scroll, throw it out on the floor, and it would just keep on rolling. The number of variables is almost infinite. Understanding aggression is a very complicated task and that's a problem. Ultimately, we would like to be able to prevent and control aggression, and that is difficult because it springs from so many different sources.

KRUPAT: *To me it seems refreshing to hear you considering the multiple causes of aggression rather than focusing on one exclusively. Is that necessarily typical of all modern aggression research?*

BARON: I think this is one unique contribution that social psychologists can make. Because of our interest in social behavior, we are primed to look for and take account of causes of aggression where perhaps members of other disciplines would not. We look for causes of aggression in the physical and the social environment as well as causes within the individual.

KRUPAT: *Okay. Then where specifically would you start looking in the social environment, for example?*

BARON: In the social environment, it turns out that there are many causes. They range from direct provocation where one person insults or somehow physically provokes another through social pressure. For example, the presence of an audience that is calling for retaliation or aggression can increase such behavior. There is also evidence that certain forms of thwarting or frustration which are produced by others can facilitate aggression. So if other people stand in the way of our reaching certain valued goals, under some conditions this may produce aggression. I should also mention modeling effects, specifically those in the mass media. In other words, if we are exposed to other people acting in an aggressive manner or responding to provocation aggressively, as we are quite often in films or TV shows, that can also serve as a social cause of aggression.

KRUPAT: *Now that you have raised the issue, could you comment on the issue of television and violence. Just what is the relationship between aggression in the media and aggression in the population? Should I turn off the TV if my kids start watching a show that has violence in it?*

BARON: There is a tremendous amount of attention focused on this issue partly because of its social relevance and partly because it involves the concern that many adults have about what is shaping the behavior and future values of our children. Most of the research does seem to suggest that if youngsters are exposed to a steady diet of televised or film violence, or even violence in the stories and books that they read, this can have a stimulating effect on their own tendencies to aggress. I might note that that seems to stem from three basic mechanisms. First, there is what is known as observational learning. Kids can learn new ways of harming others by observing these kinds of actions on television or in films. Second, there is what we call a disinhibitory effect, where kids can have their inhibitions against engaging in aggression reduced. In other words, if children are exposed to violence in the mass media, they may soon pick up the notion that this is an acceptable form of behavior, not something that should be inhibited or restrained. The third thing is that they may experience a desensitization effect in that exposure to aggression and the consequences of aggression, signs of pain and suffering on the part of victims for example, lose their impact. As a result kids may not respond in an emotional sense as much as they did before prolonged exposure to such cues. Together, these kinds of effects point in the direction of a stimulating effect flowing from exposure to televised or filmed violence.

KRUPAT: *And yet hasn't it been very difficult to clearly demonstrate or "prove" viewing violence in the media causes people to act more violently as a result?*

BARON: That's true. Obviously, it is difficult to disentangle the separate factors that might lead a particular individual to aggress in a particular situation. In addition many of the early studies of televised violence and its impact were criticized on what seem to be telling grounds. Many of these used specially prepared films of a child attacking a plastic Bobo doll, and many people wondered whether the results of those studies could transfer to actual televised violence, the kind that is shown on the TV screen every night. Recently, there have been long-range field studies in which children have been exposed to steady diets of either violent or nonviolent TV programs or films over a period of several weeks. The actual behavior of these children vis-à-vis other children in the course of their daily lives has been studied and the same kind of effect seemed to occur: exposure to film or media violence facilitated aggression in actual face-to-face encounters.

KRUPAT: *But in interpreting these studies aren't there many other factors to consider? For instance, isn't there the problem that parents who allow or encourage their children to watch a lot of TV violence are themselves people who practice various forms of aggression in the home? So it might be the parents who the children are modeling as well as or instead of the TV.*

BARON: I agree that there are many kinds of effects such as the one you just mentioned. We would want to consider what else is different in the home of a child who is permitted to watch a good deal of violence versus the home in which a child is not. But before we go any further, let me make one important comment about the results of these studies. I have been indicating that several lines of research seem to point toward an increase in aggression stemming from exposure to the media violence. But I want to hasten to add that the effect that I have mentioned seems to be relatively small. It is not the kind of effect where if the kid is exposed to lots of violence on television that he or she becomes a raving, homicidal maniac, or something of that nature. The effect is there, and it has been shown repeatedly with different methodologies and different subject populations, but it is minor, and I want to emphasize that exposure to televised violence, film violence, or media violence in general is just one of the many, many factors that predispose people to aggression.

KRUPAT: *Then if aggression is such a complex thing—if it can occur for so many different reasons under so many different circumstances, how should we go about studying it? Much of the social psychological research is laboratory oriented, yet some people ask how you can study why nations go to war and people kill each other in the lab. What are your feelings about methodological strategies?*

BARON: I think this is a phenomenon that has to be studied with a multipronged approach, and although much of my work has been in the laboratory, I see myself as someone who is really eclectic in this regard. You need to study aggression in a systematic way in the laboratory where you get the advantage of control over the relevant variables. You also need to study it by direct observation out in the real world to see if the variables and relationships in fact do act in a similar manner out there. I think we can also gain perspective by looking at archival data, records of past events to see when riots and crimes have occurred, how criminals got into the kinds of behavior patterns they show. So you need a wide range of approaches to understand aggression, but this is a problem because people are often trained in a particular discipline and tend to adopt a particular strategy to study a given phenomenon.

KRUPAT: *I was thinking in particular of what gets called in the lab "the effect of thermal environment on aggression" or what gets called a good deal more simply in urban ghettos "the long, hot summer" effect.*

BARON: I might be biased, of course, because this is research I've been doing, but I think that is a perfect illustration of the multipronged approach we have to take to study an important phenomenon such as aggression. Let me mention what we did. We were interested in this particular case in studying the notion that extreme heat makes people irritable and therefore contributes to major outbreaks of aggression such as those which occur during riots. In fact some people feel that heat may trigger riots and that's why they occur during the summer months. To get at that question we did a number of different kinds of studies. First, we did a series of laboratory studies in which we systematically varied the temperature to see whether this made subjects irritable, and whether it made them more ready to respond to provocation. Then we did some field research where we went out and observed people in the real world. For instance, we observed drivers in cars that were air conditioned and not air conditioned on warm days to see whether in fact their behavior was different. And then we went back and looked at the weather bureau reports to tell us when riots actually did occur. What we found in all three lines of research was pretty much the same thing. Up to a point, and that point is somewhere in the mid-to-upper 80s, heat does make people irritable and more aggressive. But beyond that point people seem to get less aggressive. So in answer to the question: is there a long, hot summer effect, our answer is yes, but only up to a point. Riots are probably less likely to occur when it is 98 degrees than when it is 88 degrees.

KRUPAT: *I find that fascinating. I've always been impressed at not only how the lab and real-world findings back each other up, but also at how the results demonstrate that the relationship is not as simple as we might have assumed. But let me change our focus a bit. Instead of looking at the perpetrators of aggression for the moment, what do we know about the targets of aggression? Why is one person or one object chosen over another?*

BARON: That is an important question too, and again it seems that many factors play a role. At one extreme, there is the notion that when people are strongly enough provoked they will take it out on any available, convenient person. But that extreme seems to be relatively rare, although there is some indication that such effects exist. At the other extreme are cases in which individuals very carefully choose their victims. While both of these extremes seem to exist, in the middle ground there are situations in which a particular individual is chosen as a target for aggression because he or she shares certain characteristics with a group that an individual dislikes. For example, this is where racial or ethnic prejudice may play a role. Related to that are effects that Leonard Berkowitz and his colleagues have been studying on the nature of association with aggression. Apparently if an individual is associated either with past instances of aggression or is in some other way linked with aggressive acts and aggressive behavior, that person may pick up what is called aggressive cue value. As a result the person may serve as a stimulus to aggression, even if he or she has done nothing to provoke the person who is doing the aggressing.

KRUPAT: *But if, as you say, there are so many different factors which determine who becomes a target and so many factors which affect whether a person acts aggressively in the first place, how can we ever begin to deal with them and reduce the level of aggression in our society?*

BARON: It is a problem. If you go back to the times before we were aware of or sensitive to all the potential causes, it seemed as if there might be a simple way to prevent or control it. In particular people talked about catharsis, or blowing off steam in safe, nonharmful activities, and punishment as the two most effective ways of controlling aggression. But as the list of variables that seem to facilitate aggression has lengthened, it has become increasingly clear that we are going to need a multipronged approach to *controlling* aggression just as we need one to *study* aggression. Since aggression stems from many different causes, it can only be controlled by many different methods.

KRUPAT: *Can you recommend certain strategies that you feel are likely to work?*

BARON: There has been an upsurge in research on control, and I think there are a number of interesting approaches that have been suggested. Let me just talk about two of them. One general approach is known or described as a cognitive approach to the control of aggression. Essentially, it draws on the very basic notion that people think and interpret the world in very active ways. If we can somehow change individuals' interpretations of the world around them, this may be a way of reducing aggression. Let me give you a specific instance. If another person acts in a provocative manner toward you, either you can become angry and perhaps engage in some form of aggression or retaliation against that person; or under some conditions you may perceive that the provocative behavior stemmed from some reasonable cause, in which case you may be much less likely to become angry or aggress. There is a considerable amount of research that points to the notion of what is called mitigating circumstances as something which would sharply reduce the effects of provocation and therefore reduce aggression. If you know that the other person is acting provocatively towards you because he or she is very uptight, very unhappy, ill, or something of that nature, then you are very much less likely to get angry and aggress.

KRUPAT: *It sounds to me as if that approach is tied very directly to attribution theory and the matter of determining the causes of someone else's behavior.*

BARON: That's right. Attributions lie at the heart of this approach. We somehow have to get people to avoid perceiving malevolence behind the behavior of others in situations where it isn't present. Obviously there are situations where it is present and the cognitive reinterpretation might be less effective.

KRUPAT: *Which would get us to Technique Number Two.*

BARON: Yes. A second technique that has been investigated is one that is based on a very simple notion known as incompatible responses. The basic idea here is that it is impossible or at least very difficult to be angry and act aggressively, and at the same time to experience some emotional state or behavioral tendencies that are incompatible with aggression and anger. A number of variables have been studied. Humor is one that is found to be very effective. If an individual has been angered or provoked and then somehow can be gotten to laugh or feel amusement, this seems to be very effective in reducing aggression. Another one is empathy. When a person is angry and then somehow can be induced to feel kinship or some relationship or sympathy with the potential victim, that may be a way of reducing aggression.

KRUPAT: *I can certainly see how these two emotions are basically incompatible. But just because they are, isn't it unlikely that they will occur in someone who is angered and potentially likely to aggress?*

BARON: Right, but the basic notion here is not for it to come from within the individual. It is unlikely that a person feeling angry would begin to chuckle because of internal cues. The idea is that in a tense situation other people would produce the stimuli that lead to a humorous reaction. For instance, at a tense meeting where people's tempers are beginning to fray, a humorous comment can often get things off that track pointing toward aggression.

KRUPAT: *Can you think of other examples where that approach might be useful?*

BARON: Actually, people who study rape and rape prevention have mentioned to me that the notion of incompatible responses seems quite applicable to their interests. In a recent book on rape, there is a good instance of this. A woman who had gotten off a subway train in an isolated region was being followed by a man who intended to rape her. She suddenly turned around and asked him for help because she was afraid to walk down the street alone. This man then walked her to her door without ever touching her, totally puzzled at his inability to rape her. When I related this instance at a talk I gave recently, a woman in the audience raised her hand and reported a similar instance. Her sister, who is apparently a very humorous person, was accosted by someone, and even in a situation like this couldn't refrain from joking. It was a cold winter night and the rapist, who was wearing a fur coat, told her to lie down on the pavement. She began to joke, asking him how he expected her to lie down when it was so cold. She began to joke about other things and asked him for his fur coat. He gave it to her and apparently got tremendously frustrated because he was incapable of raping her. Eventually he ran off and left her alone. I am not trying to suggest that all females should try this, but there does seem to be a tie-in here between incompatible responses and prevention of rape—which is basically an aggressive, not a sexual act.

KRUPAT: *Some people would say however, that the best way to protect ourselves against muggers and rapists and crooks is to be stronger than they are, to arm ourselves and prevent aggression by letting the other person know that we will hit back. Can aggression ever be a "good" thing?*

BARON: We do have to be careful about letting our value, which is to reduce and prevent aggression as much as possible, bias a pragmatic approach to human relations. There are some cases where after all is said and done the only way to respond is with counter-aggression. It would be a wonderful world if there were no initial aggressors or people who engage in aggression without provocation. But given that such people exist, I would be reluctant to recommend against *ever* engaging in some form of counter-aggression. Self-defense is such a case. Hopefully we can minimize those situations where responding with aggression is necessary, but I don't think we can ever eliminate them entirely. Still, what happens when one responds by physically retaliating is that this provokes the initial aggressor, and you get a mounting intensity of aggression back and forth between two people or two groups or two countries. So while there may be some times when there is no other choice in responding to aggression, I would say that in most instances almost any other form of behavior would be more effective than responding in kind.

AN INTRODUCTION TO THE READINGS

The articles in this section report on a number of different approaches to aggression. However, consistent with the interests of social psychologists, they focus largely on the situational or environmental factors that lead a person to act more or less aggressively. In the first article in this section, Robert Baron and Victoria Ransberger report on the effects-of-temperature research referred to in our conversation. Using data collected on 102 violent outbreaks during the years 1967 to 1971, Baron and Ransberger looked at the timing of riots and the temperature before, during, and after them. Their data are extremely clear. They indicate that the number of outbreaks increases as the temperature rises, but only up to the mid-80s. Beyond that, incidents decrease. Moreover, before the outbreaks, temperatures are generally on the rise and during them they remain relatively high. While we recognize that heat is not the cause of ghetto riots but rather one factor that facilitates the outbreak of violence, the relationship that is pointed out between *temper* and *temper*ature is an interesting and important one.

The next article by John P. Murray looks at another possible influence of aggression in our culture, television. Murray reviews a number of studies cited by the Surgeon General's Scientific Advisory Committee on Television and Social Behavior. He notes the sheer prevalence of aggressive acts depicted on television and suggests that the balance of research points toward the conclusion that TV violence does encourage viewer violence. While there are others who are not in total agreement with Murray about these negative effects of TV violence, most would agree with his "plea for more beneficial and useful forms of television content."

The third article further documents the effect that the media may have on aggressive behavior, in this case sexual violence against women. This paper reports on two studies that use different methodologies, but lead to similar conclusions. In the first, Edward Donnerstein had subjects watch erotic, violent, or nonviolent films and then gave them the opportunity to deliver shocks to another person whom they believed to be a subject in the experiment. In the second, Neil Malamuth and James Check had subjects go to the movies (some with violent sexual content and others without) and later tested them on their attitudes toward rape and sexual violence. Both studies indicate that violence and sex depicted in the popular media may have serious negative effects, and that these effects are especially strong for males.

The final selection offers some compelling evidence that when people act violently, they may do so largely because situational pressures cause them to. Philip Zimbardo, Craig Haney, and W. Curtis Banks set up a mock prison at Stanford University and placed a group of normal college students in this "jail." Randomly, they assigned half to be prisoners and the other half to be guards. Although the study was planned to run two weeks, the shocking cruelty of the guards led the investigators to call it off after only six days. Their findings argue against the position that violent *people* make for violent prisons; it is rather the case that poor conditions and violent *expectations* lead to violent behavior. The students assigned to be guards acted aggressively because the situational pressures in the role of guard called for that behavior and allowed them to be violent, not because they were any more personally aggressive than those who acted as prisoners. This research suggests that if we desire less violence we should attempt to *re-define* situations to make "helping" the name of the game and not "hurting." If we could do that, institutions such as prisons can be made places where people are made whole, rather than degraded and dehumanized.

ROBERT A. BARON
VICTORIA M. RANSBERGER

Ambient Temperature and the Occurrence of Collective Violence: The "Long, Hot Summer" Revisited

During the late 1960s and early 1970s, a wave of dangerous riots and civil disturbances swept through the United States and several other nations. Not surprisingly, many different factors—ranging from continued social injustice through provocative actions by police—were suggested as possible causes of these events (U. S. Riot Commission, 1968). One variable that often received considerable attention in this respect in the mass media, however, was ambient temperature. Newspaper, radio, and television accounts of these frightening events often suggested that uncomfortable heat played a crucial role in their initiation. More specifically, such descriptions suggested that prolonged exposure to temperatures in the high 80s or 90s (degrees Fahrenheit) had shortened tempers, increased irritability, and so set the stage for the outbreak of collective violence.

In general, these suggestions rested largely on informal observation. Two indirect types of empirical evidence, however, were sometimes marshaled in their support. First, the results of several laboratory studies (Griffitt, 1970; Griffit & Veitch, 1971) pointed to the conclusion that consistent with "common knowledge," individuals did in fact become more irritable, prone to outbursts of temper, and negative in their reactions to others under uncomfortably hot than under confortably cool environmental conditions. Second, systematic observation revealed that a large proportion of the serious instances of collective violence occurring in major cities during the late 1960s did in fact take place during the hot summer months, when heat-wave or near heat-wave conditions prevailed (U. S. Riot Commission, 1968; Goranson & King, Note 1).

Together, these findings seemed to provide support for the existence of an important link between ambient temperature and aggression. They did not, however, provide any direct information concerning the shape or nature of this function.

The authors wish to express their appreciation to Robert W. Horton for his assistance in collection of a portion of the data and to Andrew Schettino for his aid in conducting statistical analyses. The final draft of this manuscript was prepared during the first author's tenure as Visiting Professor of Psychology, Princeton University.

Yet, despite this fact, serious discussions of this possible heat–aggression relationship (e.g., U. S. Riot Commission, 1968) often suggested that it is linear in nature. That is, it was implicitly assumed, if not overtly stated, that at least through temperature levels normally experienced in natural settings (i.e., the mid- to upper 90s), the likelihood of outbreaks of collective violence increases with corresponding increments in ambient temperature.

While this suggestion of a linear relationship between ambient temperature and overt aggression may well have been a reasonable "first guess" several years in the past, the findings of recent laboratory investigations now point to another possibility. Specifically, the results of these studies (Baron, 1972, 1978; Baron & Bell, 1975, 1976) suggest that the relationship between ambient temperature and overt aggression may actually be curvilinear in form. Briefly, these findings suggest that up to some determinable point, increments in temperature induce corresponding increments in negative affect (i.e., feelings of irritation, annoyance, or discomfort) among potential aggressors and that these, in turn, enhance the dominance—and therefore likelihood—of outbreaks of overt aggression. Beyond some point, however, further increments in ambient temperature may serve to induce such high levels of subjective discomfort among individuals that responses incompatible with overt aggression (e.g., attempts to minimize one's discomfort) become increasingly prepotent. As a result, the likelihood of aggressive actions toward others may actually be reduced. In short, the results of recent laboratory studies point to the possibility that all other factors being equal, the relationship between ambient temperature and the occurrence of instances of collective violence may be curvilinear in nature.

While the parametric data necessary for precisely estimating the inflection point of this function are currently lacking, existing evidence (e.g., Baron, 1978; Bell & Baron, 1976) points to the possibility that it may occur in the mid- to upper 80s. That is, it seems possible that up to this point, increments in temperature are accompanied by increments in the likelihood of collective violence, but that beyond it, further increments in temperature are accompanied by actual reductions in the frequency of such events. The present investigation was specifically designed to examine these suggestions. That is, it sought to determine (a) whether the relationship between ambient temperature and the likelihood (i.e., frequency) of collective violence is indeed curvilinear in nature and (b) whether, as proposed here, the inflection point of this function occurs in the mid- to upper 80s.

Given the nature of the variables and hypotheses under investigation, it was deemed appropriate to adopt an archival strategy of research. Thus, records of instances of collective violence and ambient temperature were consulted to determine whether, as suggested earlier, the frequency of such outbreaks would be found to increase with ambient temperature through the mid-80s but then to decrease sharply with further increments in temperature beyond this level.

A second major purpose of the present investigation involved examination of the possibility that the outbreak of collective violence is related, in some manner, to shifts or changes in ambient temperature. Data gathered by Goranson and King (Note 1) in a previous investigation suggest that riots and similar disturbances are most likely to occur following periods of sharply rising temperatures. Thus, there is some indication that the relatively sudden onset of uncomfortable heat may play a "triggering" or facilitating role in this respect. Unfortunately, the data reported by Goranson and King were restricted to events occurring within a single year. In view of this fact, it seemed useful to expand upon these earlier findings by examining a somewhat broader sample of collective violence. Thus, the present study examined changes in temperature across the days preceding, during, and following 102 separate riots occurring during the 5-year period 1967–1971. On the basis of the findings reported by Goranson and King, it was tentatively predicted that ambient temperature would increase in the days preceding the outbreak of collective violence, would remain relatively high during its occurrence, and would then decrease in the days following its termination.

METHOD

Overview

Since the investigation was primarily archival in nature, data collection involved two major steps. First, it was necessary to identify individual instances of collective violence occurring during the target period (1967–1971). And second, it was necessary to obtain information concerning the temperatures prevailing on the dates and in the locations involved. Once this information has been obtained, appropriate statistical analyses were performed to determine (a) whether the frequency of instances of collective violence varied with ambient temperature in the curvilinear manner predicted and (b) whether any systematic changes in temperature could be noted across the days preceding collective violence, during its occurrence, and following its termination.

Procedure

Identification of instances of collective violence.   Two archival sources were used to identify individual instances of collective violence: *Report of the National Advisory Commission on Civil Disorders* (U. S. Riot Commission, 1968) and *Violence in the U. S.*, Volume 2 (Parker, 1974). In examining both sources, we classified events as instances of collective violence only if they encompassed all of the following characteristics: (a) the occurrence of fires, looting, or rock throwing; (b) persistence of the events for at least 1 day; (c) participation by sizable crowds of individuals; and (d) the necessity for intervention by law-enforcement authorities (state police, National Guard, or federal troops). Thus, only relatively serious civil disorders were selected for further study.

Through the application of these criteria, 102 separate instances of collective violence occurring in the United States during the years 1967–1971 were identified. Of these, 16 may reasonably be viewed as directly related to the assassination of Martin Luther King on April 4, 1968: 14 occurred within a few days of his death, and 2 others took place on or within a few days of the anniversary of his assassination, in April, 1969. Because these disturbances were apparently closely related to a special (and tragic) historical event, it was deemed appropriate to consider them separately, as well as combined with the other instances of collective violence uncovered (see below).

. . . The instances of collective violence selected for further study were widely distributed in terms of geographic locale. Indeed, all geographic regions of the United States were represented in this respect. Further, there was no apparent relationship between general climatic conditions in these areas and the frequency of riots recorded. For example, the largest number of disturbances (30) occurred in the East North-Central Region (Wisconsin, Michigan, Illinois, Indiana, and Ohio), an area not usually identified with excessive environmental heat, whereas a much smaller number (4) occurred in the West South-Central Region (Texas, Oklahoma, Arkansas, and Louisiana), an area characterized by a considerably warmer overall climate.

Climatological (temperature) data. Maximum ambient temperatures occurring in the geographic location of each incident of collective violence were obtained for (a) the 7 days preceding the outbreak of these events, (b) the 1-5 days on which collective violence took place, and (c) the 3 days following its termination. These data were obtained from the 1967–1971 volumes of *Climatological Data* (Environmental Data Service, U. S. Department of Commerce).

RESULTS

Frequency of Collective Violence as a Function of Ambient Temperature

The frequency of instances of collective violence (i.e., serious riots) occurring in each of 16 different temperature ranges during the 5-year target period is represented in Figure 1. (Note that data for all 102 riots considered and for the 86 riots not related to the death of Martin Luther King are represented in separate functions.)

Inspection of this figure lends support to the suggestion of a curvilinear relationship between ambient temperature and the incidence of collective violence. That is, consistent with initial predictions, the frequency of such events increases with ambient temperature through approximately the mid-80s but then decreases sharply with further increments in temperature beyond this level. . . .

Inspection of Figure 1 also suggests that as anticipated, the greatest frequency of instances of collective violence occurred when temperatures attained moderately, but not extremely, uncomfortable levels. Thus, considering all riots, 38 (37.25%) took place when temperatures were in the range of 81°–90°F, whereas only 9 (8.8%) occurred when temperatures were in the range of 91°–100°F. Correspondingly, considering the 86 riots not related to the assassination of Martin Luther King, 38 (44.19%) took place when temperatures were in the range of 81°–90°F, whereas only 9 (10.46%) occurred when they were in the range of 91°–100°F. In sum, the analyses performed suggested that ambient temperature and the occurrence of collective violence are curvilinearly rather than linearly related and that contrary to suggestions based on informal observation, such events are much more likely to take place in the presence of moderate rather than extreme environmental heat.

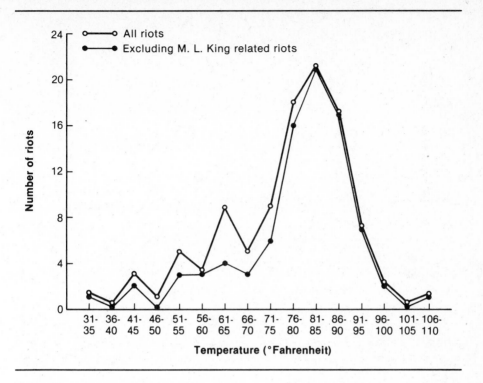

FIGURE 1. Frequency of collective violence (riots) as a function of ambient temperature.

Changes in Ambient Temperature Across Riot and Nonriot Days

The mean maximum temperature recorded on each of the 7 days preceding collective violence, on the 1st day of its occurrence, and on the 3 days following its termination are presented in Figure 2. Again, data for all riots and for those not related to the assassination of Martin Luther King are presented separately. Inspection of these data suggests that in both cases, ambient temperature rose during the preriot period but then dropped during the days following civil disturbances. This pattern, however, appears to be somewhat stronger or more clear-cut with respect to the 86 incidents not directly linked to the death of Martin Luther King.

Inspection of Figure 2 also suggests that ambient temperature was somewhat higher across the period considered when riots related to the assassination of Martin Luther King are excluded. Given the fact that all of these latter events occurred in early April, this finding is far from surprising and does not seem to merit further, detailed attention.

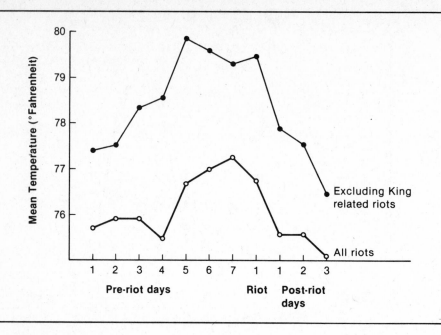

FIGURE 2. Mean maximum ambient temperature on 7 days preceding collective violence, on the 1st day of its occurence, and on 3 days following its termination.

To examine the two sets of data presented in Figure 2 more closely, separate repeated measures analyses were performed upon each. Taken as a whole, the results of all of the analyses performed suggest that as indicated by Figure 2, ambient temperature increased during the days preceding collective violence but then decreased during the period following its termination.[1]

Turning next to the data for all riots, we find a somewhat weaker pattern of results. It appeared that temperature showed a similar curvilinear trend over days. This pattern of findings, however, was less clear-cut than was the case when riots related to the death of Martin Luther King were eliminated. . . .

Incidence of Collective Violence by Season of the Year

To examine the suggestion that instances of collective violence are more likely to occur during the warm summer months than at other times of the year, the frequency of such events during summer (June, July, August), fall (September, October, November), winter (December, January, February), and spring (March, April, May) was examined. The proportion of riots occurring during each of these

1. It should be noted that examination of the data for each of the years considered revealed identical patterns of findings. That is, ambient temperature rose during the preriot period and then dropped following the conclusion of collective violence.

seasons was as follows: summer, .558; fall, .105; winter, .116; spring, .221.[2] An analysis performed upon these data revealed that as anticipated, riot frequency did in fact vary significantly across season. Thus, further evidence for the observation that riots are more likely to occur during the warm summer months than at other times of the year was obtained.

Ambient Temperature and Public Celebrations

Because it seemed possible that other types of collective behavior might be related to ambient temperature in a manner similar to that of riots, one additional form of such activity, public celebrations, was also examined.[3] It was reasoned that such celebrations are analogous to riots in several important respects (e.g., both involve the participation of large numbers of individuals and both involve the performance of vigorous motor activities). Examination of back issues of newspapers and magazines suggested that such events were relatively rare except in connection with sports activities. In view of this fact, we decided to focus on public celebrations occurring in relation to victories in major athletic contests. Specifically, attention was focused on events occurring in the hometowns of the victors (during 1967–1971) of the following events: the Rose, Sugar, Orange, and Cotton Bowl games; the Super Bowl game; the World Series; the National Basketball Association play-offs; and the National Hockey League Stanley Cup play-offs. In this manner, 58 public celebrations were identified. Examination of the ambient temperatures prevailing at the time of such events failed to yield a pattern of findings analogous to those for the occurrence of collective violence. That is, the frequency of public celebrations was not significantly related to ambient temperature. In fact, such events seemed to be relatively uniformly distributed across a wide range of temperatures, with 17.25% occurring in the range of 31°–40°F, 22.41% in the range of 41°–50°F, 13.79% in the range of 51°–60°F, 24.14% in the range of 61°–70°F, and 20.69% in the range of 71°–80°F. Thus, in contrast to the findings for collective violence, there was no indication that public celebrations of this type were more likely to take place at certain temperatures than at others. Instead, it appeared that such activities were more closely related to particular events (e.g., the victorious arrival of the home team) and occurred in connection with these stimuli regardless of prevailing ambient temperatures.

DISCUSSION

The results of the present investigation provide support for the hypothesis of a curvilinear relationship between ambient temperature and the outbreak of collective

2. Riots directly related to the assassination of Martin Luther King—all of which took place during the month of April—were omitted from this analysis. When such events are considered, the corresponding proportions for each season are as follows: summer, .471; fall, .088; winter, .098; spring, .422.

3. The authors wish to offer their thanks to Anthony G. Greenwald for suggesting this intriguing possibility.

violence. As predicted, the frequency of serious civil disorders increased with ambient temperature through the mid-80s but then decreased sharply with further increments in environmental heat beyond this level. Thus, in contrast to the "common sense" suggestion of a simple linear relationship between heat and aggression presented in many TV, newspaper, and magazine reports, the present findings point to the existence of a somewhat more complicated, curvilinear link between these factors.

One Potential Explanation for the Curvilinear Relationship Between Ambient Temperature and Collective Violence

While the specific mechanisms underlying this apparent curvilinear function are undoubtedly quite complex, the results of several recent laboratory studies point to one possible explanation for its existence (e.g., Baron, 1977, 1978; Baron & Bell, 1975, 1976; Rotton et al., in press). Briefly, these investigations suggest that the curvilinear relationship between temperature and the occurrence of overt aggression noted here may be underlaid, at least in part, by a corresponding curvilinear function between negative affect (i.e., subjective discomfort) and such behavior. More specifically, they suggest that up to some determinable point, increments in negative affect—whether induced by environmental heat, unpleasant smells, crowding, or other aversive conditions—serve to enhance the dominance or likelihood of hostile actions by potential aggressors. Beyond this point, however, further increments in negative affect may actually lead to reductions in aggressive tendencies, as responses incompatible with such behavior (e.g., attempts to minimize one's discomfort or to escape from the unpleasant situation) become prepotent. Put more simply, it appears that up to some determinable level, increments in subjective discomfort cause individuals to become increasingly irritable or annoyed, thus enhancing the likelihood that they will respond aggressively to provocation, the presence of aggressive models, or other aggression-evoking conditions (cf. Baron & Lawton, 1972). Beyond this point, however, they experience such high levels of discomfort that responses incompatible with aggression become prepotent, and the likelihood of such behavior is reduced.

These theoretical considerations are, in a general sense, consistent with the finding that outbreaks of collective violence are much more likely to occur in the presence of moderately uncomfortable temperatures than in the presence of extreme environmental heat. Further, as noted earlier, they are supported by the findings of previous laboratory studies (cf. Bell & Baron, 1976). Despite these facts, however, it would certainly be premature to conclude that this mechanism underlies or accounts for the curvilinear relationship between ambient temperature and the occurrence of collective violence observed in the present investigation. Collective violence is a highly complex form of behavior and, as such, is undoubtedly influenced by many variables absent from, or actively controlled in, laboratory settings. For example, it seems possible that several different factors that vary concomitantly with ambient temperature (e.g., the number of people out on the street in urban areas; consumption of some types of alcoholic beverages) may exert important effects on the initiation of riots and related disorders. Similarly, it is possible that prolonged exposure to extreme heat—a condition not readily or ethically produced in laboratory studies—may induce direct physiological reactions that in and of themselves lower the likelihood of all forms of strenuous physical activity, including overt aggression. In view of such considerations, further research is clearly needed before firm conclusions regarding the basis for the present findings can be established. The apparent consistency between the results of the present archival investigation and those of previous laboratory studies, however, suggests that it may prove fruitful, in future research, to direct at least some attention to the potential mediating role of negative affect with respect to the relationship between ambient temperature and collective violence.

Frequency of Occurrence of Ambient Temperatures in Various Ranges

At this point, one potential source of ambiguity with respect to the present data should be considered. Specifically, it might be suggested that the relatively high frequency of instances of collective violence in the presence of temperatures in the low to mid-80s stems from the fact that such environmental conditions are simply more common than others (i.e., occur on a greater number of days during the year). To the extent that this is the case, the function plotted in Figure 1 would be somewhat artifactual in nature. Such an argument is not, however, supported by relevant climatological data. In almost every region of the United States, lower temperatures are far more common during the course of the year than those in the mid- to upper 80s. And even during the warmest summer months (July and August) temperatures of 81°–85°F are no more common or frequent than those in ranges associated with a lower frequency of collective violence. Perhaps this latter fact is best illustrated by examination of the appropriate records for those regions of the nation in which dangerous riots were most common during the period in question (the East North-Central, South Atlantic, and Middle Atlantic States). In the case of the East North-Central Region, temperatures of 76°–80°F, 81°–85°F, and 86°–90°F were recorded on 29.0%, 27.9%, and 22.6% of the days, respectively. In the case of the South Atlantic Region, temperatures of 81°–85°F, 86°–90°F and 91°–95°F were recorded on 17.7%, 30.9%, and 30.9% of the days, respectively. And in the case of the Middle Atlantic Region, temperatures in the ranges of 76°–80°F, 81°–85°F, and 86°–90°F were recorded on 23.3%, 26.1%, and 21.3% of the days, respectively.[4] Together, these data suggest that temperatures of 81°–85°F were not more common than those in other ranges; indeed, in two of the three regions examined, they were actually less frequent during the summer months than temperatures in other ranges associated with a lower incidence of collective violence. In view of this fact, an interpretation of the present findings based solely on the

4. These data were based on temperatures recorded in the following cities: Cincinnati, Gary, Milwaukee, Detroit (East North-Central Region); Pittsburgh, Buffalo, Newark (Middle Atlantic Region); Newport News, Orangeburg, Tampa, Baltimore (South Atlantic Region).

suggestion that temperatures in the low to mid-80s are far more common than others during the summer months does not seem to be supported.[5]

Changes in Ambient Temperature Across Riot and Nonriot Days

A second major finding of the present research deserving of careful attention is the observed pattern of changes in ambient temperature across the days preceding, during, and following instances of collective violence. As will be recalled, the present data indicate that ambient temperature rose during the 7 days preceding the outbreak of collective violence, seemed to remain relatively high (and stable) during the occurrence of such events, and then decreased following their termination. This pattern of findings is quite similar to that reported by Goranson and King (Note 1) with respect to the riots occurring during a single year. Thus, taking the results of both investigations into account, it appears to be a fairly stable phenomenon. While these findings are, of course, purely observational in nature, they seem to suggest that shifts in ambient temperature may play a role in the outbreak of collective violence. Specifically, it may well be that exposure to increasing environmental warmth produces corresponding increments in subjective discomfort (i.e., negative affect) among potential aggressors and so enhances the likelihood that they will respond aggressively to provocation or other external factors. As a result, the likelihood of instances of collective violence may then be increased.

In the absence of direct experimental evidence concerning such suggestions, they should be viewed as only tentative in nature. Further, the possibility that factors related to rising temperatures, rather than increasing warmth itself (e.g., an increasing number of persons out on the street), are crucial should not be overlooked. Indeed, additional research designed to examine such possibilities appears to be necessary. For the present, it is only reasonable to conclude that variations in ambient temperature both precede and follow instances of collective violence and may well play a role in their occurrence.

Before concluding, we should draw attention to several limitations of the present research. First, it should be recalled that the present study focused on serious rather than minor instances of civil disorder. As a result, generalization of the obtained findings should be restricted only to the former class of events. Second, all of the riots examined took place within the boundaries of the United States. While there are no strong grounds for assuming that different findings would

5. Additional evidence against the view that the present findings are attributable to a relatively high incidence of temperatures in the low to mid-80s is provided by examination of the temperatures occurring on the same dates as riots and in the same cities where such events took place but in different (nonriot) years. Three findings with respect to these data are of special interest. First, it was observed that temperatures of 81°–85°F occurred on a lower percentage of nonriot days (16.66%) than riot days (21.56%). Second, it was noted that temperatures of 81°–85°F were *not* more common on nonriot days than temperatures in other ranges. In fact, considering all riots, temperatures of 76°–80°F and 86°–90°F actually occurred slightly more frequently on such days (17.65%) than temperatures of 81°–85°F (16.66%). Finally, as might be expected, relatively cool temperatures (i.e., below 80°F) were more common on nonriot days (34.88%) than on riot days (25.58%). Together, these findings cast further doubt on the suggestion that the present findings stemmed solely from a high frequency of occurrence of temperatures in the low to mid-80s.

be obtained in other nations or geographic settings, independent evidence on this issue is lacking. Finally, it should be stressed that the present data are purely archival in nature and, as a result, suffer from certain problems often associated with such information. For example, while a high degree of confidence may be placed in the accuracy of records of ambient temperature, somewhat less confidence can be attached to the reliability of the eyewitness accounts on which selection of the 102 disorders was, of necessity, based. In the face of these and other limitations, and despite their apparent consistency with previous laboratory findings (cf. Baron, 1978), the present results should be interpreted with a considerable degree of caution. Even taking such restrictions into account, however, the results seem to point to two practical—and potentially important—implications. First, they suggest that instances of collective violence are most likely to occur in the presence of moderate, rather than extreme, environmental warmth. And second, they suggest that such events frequently follow periods of gradually rising temperatures. To the extent that these generalizations are confirmed in further research, they may help to specify the circumstances under which instances of collective violence are most likely to take place. And such information, in turn, may be of considerable use to civil authorities in their attempts to prevent or minimize these events.

NOTE

1. Goranson, R. E., & King, D. *Rioting and daily temperature: Analysis of the U. S. riots in 1967.* Unpublished manuscript, York University, Ontario, Canada, 1970.

REFERENCES

Baron, R. A. Aggression as a function of ambient temperature and prior anger arousal. *Journal of Personality and Social Psychology*, 1972, **21**, 183–189.

Baron, R. A. *Human aggression.* New York: Plenum Press, 1977.

Baron, R. A. Aggression and heat: The "long, hot summer" revisited. In A. Baum, S. Valins, & J. Singer (Eds.), *Advances in environmental research* (Vol. 1). Hillsdale, N.J.: Erlbaum, 1978.

Baron, R. A., & Bell, P. A. Aggression and heat: Mediating effects of prior provocation and exposure to an aggressive model. *Journal of Personality and Social Psychology*, 1975, **31**, 825–832.

Baron, R. A., & Bell, P. A. Aggression and heat: The influence of ambient temperature, negative affect, and a cooling drink on physical aggression. *Journal of Personality and Social Psychology*, 1976, **33**, 245–255.

Baron, R. A., & Lawton, S. F. Environmental influences on aggression: The facilitation of modeling effects by high ambient temperatures. *Psychonomic Science*, 1972, **26**, 80–82.

Bell, P. A., & Baron, R. A. Aggression and heat: The mediating role of negative affect. *Journal of Applied Social Psychology*, 1976, **6**, 18–30.

Environmental Data Service. *Climatological data.* Washington, D.C.: U. S. Department of Commerce, 1967–1971.

Griffitt, W. Environmental effects on intrapersonal affective behavior: Ambient effective temperature and attraction. *Journal of Personality and Social Psychology*, 1970, **15**, 240–244.

Griffitt, W., & Veitch, R. Hot and crowded: Influence of population density and temperature on interpersonal affective behavior. *Journal of Personality and Social Psychology*, 1971, **17**, 92–98.

Parker, T. *Violence in the U. S.* (Vol. 2). New York: Facts on File Publications, 1974.

Rotton, J., Frey, J., Barry, T., Milligan, M., & Fitzpatrick, M. Modeling, malodorous air pollution, and interpersonal aggression. *Journal of Applied Social Psychology*, in press.

United States Riot Commission. *Report of the national advisory commission on civil disorders.* New York: Bantam Books, 1968.

JOHN P. MURRAY

Television and Violence:
Implications of the Surgeon General's Research Program

The magnitude of television's involvement in our daily lives is rather impressive. Recent census figures estimate that 96% of the households in the United States contain at least one television set; many have two or more. In families where there are young children, the television ownership rate approaches total saturation—99%. Moreover, the data available from broadcast rating services indicate that American television sets are turned on for an average of approximately six hours each day. The obvious implication of these rather dry statistics is that virtually every person in the United States has access to television, and some are watching for a considerable length of time. These facts, coupled with the common observation that our youngest citizens are among the heaviest users, have fostered serious concern about television's potential impact on the attitudes, values, and behavior patterns of this vast audience. This concern has been expressed not only by legislators but also by parents, teachers, and a wide range of mental health professionals involved with the growth and development of children.

Throughout television's quarter-of-a-century broadcast history, various commissions and committees have questioned its impact. In the early 1950s, the National Association of Educational Broadcasters surveyed the program content of stations in four major cities (Los Angeles, New York, New Haven, and Chicago) and reported that ''crime and horror'' drama accounted for 10% of all programming broadcast in these cities.

The first Congressional inquiry was launched in 1954 by Senator Estes Kefauver, Chairman of the Subcommittee to Investigate Juvenile Delinquency. As a result of testimony presented in this committee, it was concluded that televised crime and brutality could be potentially harmful to young children. Broadcasters were then urged to take appropriate action to reduce the level of violence portrayed in their programming. A subsequent survey of program content, undertaken by the same Senate subcommittee in 1961, indicated an increase in the level of televised violence over that observed in the 1950s. An additional survey conducted in 1964 again indicated no diminution in the level of portrayed violence. As Chairman of these later hearings, Senator Thomas Dodd noted:

> Not only did we fail to see an appreciable reduction of violence in the new shows, but we also found that the most violent shows of the 1961–62 season have been syndicated and are now being reshown on independent networks and stations [U.S. Senate, 1964, p. 3731].

The committee concluded that, despite its laudable achievement in the fields of education and entertainment, television has also functioned as "a school for violence."

In 1969, the Mass Media Task Force of the National Commission on the Causes and Prevention of Violence concluded, on the basis of a review of existing research, that there was sufficient justification to call for a general reduction in the level of televised violence. The Commission particularly stressed the need to eliminate violence portrayed in children's cartoon programming. The Violence Commission also recommended continued evaluation of television programming, research on the long-term cumulative effects of viewing televised violence, and an analysis of the broad range of television's impact on society (Baker & Ball, 1969).

In response to this mounting concern, Senator John O. Pastore, Chairman of the Subcommittee on Communications of the Senate Commerce Committee, asked the Secretary of Health, Education, and Welfare to request the Surgeon General to conduct a study of the impact of televised violence. In requesting the Surgeon General's participation, Senator Pastore noted the recent success of the Smoking and Health Study and indicated that he considered television violence to be a similar public health question. As a result of this request, the Surgeon General's Scientific Advisory Committee on Television and Social Behavior, composed of 12 behavioral scientists, was appointed in June 1969. At the same time, $1 million was allocated for research funds, and a staff at the National Institute of Mental Health was appointed to coordinate the research program. During the following two years, a total of 23 independent research projects were conducted by scholars at a number of universities and research institutes. The resulting set of approximately 60 reports and papers was reviewed by the Advisory Committee during the late summer and fall of 1971, and the Committee's report, entitled "Television and Growing Up: The Impact of Televised Violence," was presented to the Surgeon General on December 31, 1971. The Advisory Committee report and five volumes of research reports were published early in 1972.

The studies in this program were focused on three major research questions concerning (a) the characteristics of television program content: (b) the characteristics of the audience (Who watches what? For how long?); and (c) the potential impact of televised violence on the attitudes, values, and behavior of the viewer. Within this framework, let us turn first to the research findings that bear on the nature of the stimulus—the characteristics of television programs viewed in American homes.

TELEVISION CONTENT

One study, conducted by George Gerbner (1972) at the Annenberg School of Communications, was addressed to an analysis of the content of prime time (7:30–10:00 p.m. on weekdays and 9:00–11:00 a.m. on Saturday) television programming broadcast during one week in October for the years 1967, 1968, and 1969. Observers recorded all instances of violence defined by "the overt expression of physical force against others or self, or the compelling of action against one's will on pain of being hurt or killed." The results indicated the following:

1. The level of violence did not change from 1967 to 1969. In each of the three years, violent episodes occurred at the rate of five per play or eight episodes per hour, with 8 out of every 10 plays containing some form of violence.

2. Lethal violence (killing) *did* decline over the measured years from 2 in 10 leading characters involved in killing in 1967; to 1 in 10 in 1968; to 1 in 20 in 1969.

3. The level of violence portrayed in programs especially designed for children—cartoons (already the leading violent program format in 1967)—became increasingly violent in 1969. As Gerbner (1972) pointed out: "Of all 95 cartoon plays analyzed during the three annual study periods, only two in 1967 and one each in 1968 and 1969 did not contain violence [p. 36]."

On the average, in 1967, one hour of cartoons contained *three* times as many violent episodes as one hour of adult programming. However, in 1969, one hour of cartoons contained *six* times as many violent episodes as an adult hour.

A more recent study, conducted by F. Earle Barcus (1971) at Boston University, was focused on the content of Saturday morning children's programs during the 1971 season. Barcus reported findings that parallel Gerbner's: 71% of all segments had at least one instance of human violence and 3 out of 10 dramatic segments were "saturated" with violence.

In one sense, these statistics are merely body counts, significant perhaps, but to "understand" televised violence one must look at the qualitative aspects: the time, place, or setting and the characteristics of the aggressors and victims. In the world of television, violence tends to occur in the past or future; in places other than the United States; and frequently in remote, uninhabited, or unidentifiable areas. The means to commit violence are usually weapons, with guns being the most favored weapon. The agents of this violence are usually humans; however, the prevalence of nonhuman agents has increased each year from 1967 to 1969. The consequences of all this violence are almost negligible. Punching, kicking, biting, even shooting, do not seem to result in much suffering. As Gerbner (1972) pointed out:

> Pain and suffering were so difficult to detect that observers could not agree often enough to make the results acceptable. There was no doubt that no painful effect was shown in over half of all violent episodes [p. 41].

Who commits all this mayhem? And who are the unlucky recipients? We noted earlier that the agents of most of the violence are humans—so, too, are the victims. But the aggressors and the victims, the powerful and the weak, the killers and the killed, do not share many common characteristics. Indeed, as Gerbner lyrically indicated: "The shifting sands of fate have piled a greater burden of victimization on women [p. 50]." The aggressors are more likely to be male, American, middle-upper class, unmarried, and in the "prime of life."

Approximately 70% of all leading characters studied by Gerbner were involved in some form of violence (either as an aggressor or a victim). Of those involved in killing, the odds are two to one in favor of the leading character being a killer rather than being the one killed. Moreover, the odds were also seven to one that the killer would *not* be killed in return.

How "real" is this violence? Some researchers have suggested that, in a statistical sense, it is very *un*real. For example, content analyses show that violence in the *television* world occurs between total strangers, but crime statistics indicate that lethal violence in the *real* world is likely to be perpetrated by persons known to the victim. A study conducted by David Clark and William Blankenburg (1972) at the University of Wisconsin failed to find a clear relationship between the level of televised violence broadcast each year and an environmental crime index based on the FBI Uniform Crime Reports. What they were able to demonstrate is that the level of broadcast violence has fluctuated from 1953 to 1969 and seems to run in cycles reaching a peak every four years. In addition, if the audience applauded violent television programs during one season, the viewers were likely to receive an increased dosage during the following season. Thus, Clark and Blankenburg were able to demonstrate a significant correlation between the number of high-violence programs available during a given season and the average Nielsen rating of that type of program during the preceding season.

What are the implications of these content analyses? Foremost is that violence is inherent in television drama and, according to Gerbner (1972), appears to be used to define power and status. In another study, conducted by Cedric Clark (1972) at Stanford University, the author concludes that some members of our society are regularly denied power and status by being continually cast in the role of the helpless victim. Indeed, Clark suggests that the portrayal of specific groups, such as blacks or women, in powerless roles is a form of violence against society.

The overwhelming conclusion that can be drawn from these content analyses is that violent behavior is a common theme in many of the television programs viewed in American homes. Keeping this fact in mind, let us turn next to the topic of viewing.

VIEWING PATTERNS

Who watches television? Virtually everyone does. It was noted earlier that some studies have estimated that the television set is turned on for an average of more than six hours each day. However, it would be a mistake to leave the impression that everyone views extensively. True, almost every home has a television set, but the patterns of use vary according to age, sex, and the family's socioeconomic level. There are, of course, some general guidelines concerning the extent of viewing, such as younger children view more than older children; women more than men; and persons from lower income homes more than middle and upper income families. With regard to children, the developmental pattern is one of onset of television viewing at 1½–2 years of age, followed by extensive television viewing during preschool and early elementary school years, which is followed by a sharp decline in viewing as the youngster approaches adolescence. Indeed, the extent and duration of viewing remain low from adolescence to early adulthood. For adults, the peak life-span viewing periods occur for persons in their late twenties through early thirties and the elderly.

An idealized curve demonstrating the extent of television viewing across all ages would identify three primary clusters of viewers: young children, young adults, and elderly persons. The most parsimonious explanation for these clusters is the lack of alternative activities: young children have limited physical mobility outside the home; young adults are more likely to be married and have families with young children; and elderly persons frequently report a restricted range of outside activities due to physical limitations.

Our research program has been focused on only one of these three groups: young children. Although this seemed reasonable in terms of limited resources, future research should not neglect the elderly viewer. At present, one can only speculate about the experiences of a person who is physically separated from his or her family, alone and lonely, whose only regular visitor is Johnny Carson.

With regard to children's viewing, we have already suggested that they are among the heaviest users of television. Indeed, several studies (Lyle & Hoffman, 1972a, 1972b; Murray, 1972) have demonstrated that young children spend between two and three hours watching television each day, and they watch more on weekends than during the week. On the average, preschoolers spend approximately half of an adult's workweek sitting in front of the television set.

What kinds of programs do they watch? Universally, the youngest children prefer cartoons and situation comedies to other types of television fare. There is a definite sequence of change in preference patterns during childhood, beginning with cartoons and shifting to situation comedies (e.g., *I Love Lucy*) and child adventure (e.g., *Lassie*), and then to action/adventure programs (e.g., *Hawaii Five-O* and *Mod Squad*). It should *not* be assumed, however, that very young children are only exposed to relatively nonviolent programming. Indeed, we have already noted that cartoons are among the most violent programs on television. Moreover, the three studies cited above, which asked parents to keep a diary of the programs viewed by their children, indicated that even preschoolers spent almost half of their viewing time watching action/adventure programs such as *Mannix*, *Mod Squad*, and the *FBI*.

IMPACT OF TELEVISED VIOLENCE

Given the fact that there is a considerable amount of violence portrayed on television and that large segments of our society are routinely exposed to such material, one may legitimately question the impact of such programming. In this regard, a considerable body of prior research on imitative behavior (Bandura, 1969), as well as accumulated folk wisdom, has led to the conclusion that children *can* learn from observing behavior of others. The "others" may be their fellow playmates, parents, teachers, or the repairman who visits the child's home. Thus, the boy or girl who mimics the teacher's voice and the youngster who pretends to be the plumber who repaired the family's kitchen sink yesterday are generally considered living proof of this thesis. Can one extend this line of reasoning to include television as one of the "others" from whom a child is likely to learn specific behaviors? (For recent reviews, see Murray, Nayman, & Atkin, 1972; Weiss, 1969.) We know that there have been isolated incidents in which a child has attempted to replicate behavior he has just observed on television—occasionally with tragic consequences. But what about the youngster who is merely surly or inconsiderate toward his brothers and sisters, excessively aggressive or disruptive on the playground, or hostile and cynical about the value of trust and love in interpersonal relationships? Can these, too, be related to the behaviors the child has observed on the television screen? Perhaps. However, the basic question to which several studies in this program were addressed was, Are children who view televised violence more aggressive than those who do not view such fare? With this question in mind, let us look at some of the findings.

One study, conducted by Aletha Stein and Lynette Friedrich (1972) at the Pennsylvania State University, assessed the effect of exposing preschool children to a "diet" of either antisocial, prosocial, or neutral television programming. The antisocial programs consisted of *Batman* and *Superman* cartoons; prosocial programs were composed of segments of *Misteroger's Neighborhood*; and neutral programming consisted of children's travelogue films. The children were observed throughout a nine-week period which consisted of two weeks of previewing, four weeks of television exposure, and three weeks of follow-up. All observations were conducted while the children were engaged in their daily activities in the nursery school. The observers recorded various forms of behavior that could be described as prosocial (i.e., helping, sharing, cooperative play, tolerance of delay) or antisocial (i.e., arguing, pushing, breaking toys). The overall results indicated that children who were adjudged to be initially somewhat more aggressive became significantly more aggressive as a result of viewing the *Batman* and *Superman* cartoons. On the other hand, the children who viewed 12 episodes of *Misteroger's Neighborhood* became significantly more cooperative, willing to share toys and to help other children.

In another study, Robert Liebert and Robert Baron (1972), at the State University of New York at Stony Brook, assessed young children's willingness to hurt another child after viewing either aggressive or neutral television programming. The aggressive program consisted of segments drawn from *The Untouchables*, while the neutral program featured a track race. The main findings indicated that the children who viewed the aggressive program demonstrated a greater willingness to hurt another child. The experimental setting provided a situation in which a child could press a button that would either HELP or HURT a child in another room. The youngest children who had viewed the aggressive program pressed the HURT button earlier and for a longer period of time than did their peers who had viewed a track race. Moreover, when the children were later observed during the free-play period, those who had viewed *The Untouchables* exhibited a greater preference for playing with weapons and aggressive toys than did the children who had watched the neutral programming.

In a related study, Paul Ekman (1972) and his associates at the Langley Porter Neuropsychiatric Institute filmed the facial expressions of the children in the Liebert and Baron study and attempted to relate the child's emotional expression while viewing to later hurting or helping behavior. The results indicated that young boys whose facial expressions depicted positive emotions of happiness, pleasure, interest, or involvement while viewing *The Untouchables* were more likely to make hurting responses than were the boys whose facial expressions indicated displeasure or disinterest in such television fare.

An additional series of studies conducted by Aimee Leifer and Donald Roberts (1972) at Stanford University further explored the impact of televised violence in relation to the child's understanding of the motivations and consequences for the portrayed violent acts. The results indicated that as the child grows older, he is more likely to understand the portrayed motives and consequences, but such increased understanding does not seem to modify his postviewing aggressive behavior. Indeed, when a number of variables were assessed, the best predictor of subsequent aggressive behavior was the amount of violence portrayed in the program viewed: children who had viewed the more violent programs produced significantly more aggressive responses.

The several studies we have discussed thus far have demonstrated some immediate, short-term effects of viewing televised violence. But one may justifiably question the long-range cumulative impact of viewing violence. In this regard, a number of studies in this research program attempted to relate the child's program preference and viewing patterns to the viewer's perception of violence and attitudes concerning the use of violence or force to resolve conflicts. Bradley Greenberg and Thomas Gordon (1972) have suggested, on the basis of a series of studies conducted at Michigan State University, that watching violence on television sensitizes the viewer to perceive more violence in the world around him and increases the likelihood that the viewer will espouse attitudes favorable toward the use of violence as a means of resolving conflicts. Moreover, Steven Chaffee and his associates (Chaffee & McLeod, 1971; McLeod, Atkin, & Chaffee, 1972a, 1972b) at the University of Wisconsin and Jennie McIntyre and James Teevan (1972) at the University of Maryland have noted that there is a consistent and reliable relationship between preference for and viewing of violent television programs and engaging in aggressive or delinquent acts.

Perhaps the most crucial study in this regard was one conducted by Monroe Lefkowitz and his colleagues (Lefkowitz, Eron, Walder, & Huesmann, 1972) at the New York State Department of Mental Hygiene. This study is of particular importance because it was designed to investigate the development of aggressive behavior in children by studying the same boys and girls over a 10-year period, at ages 8 and 18. Ten years ago, the investigators obtained several measures of each child's aggressive behavior and related these to his or her preference for violent television programs (see Eron, 1963). Now, 10 years later, when the subjects were one year out of high school, the investigators obtained similar measures of program prefer ences and aggressive behavior. For boys, the results indicated that preference for violent programs at age 8 was significantly related to aggressive and delinquent behavior at age 18. For girls, this relationship was in the same direction but was less strong. Thus, one general interpretation of the results of this study is that preferring violent television at age 8 is at least one cause of the aggressive and antisocial behavior these young men displayed 10 years later.

The conclusions that can be drawn from the results of this series of studies are threefold. First, there is considerable violence portrayed on the television screen. And such violence tends not to mirror societal violence, but rather is used as a dramatic punctuation mark—a definer or arbiter of power and status among the performers in each dramatic episode. Second, young children view a considerable amount of television, in the course of which they are exposed to a considerable amount of televised violence. Third, there are a number of studies which point to the conclusion that viewing televised violence causes the viewer to become more aggressive. Indeed, the Surgeon General's Scientific Advisory Committee on Television and Social Behavior (1972) summarized its interpretation of this point as follows:

> Thus, there is a convergence of the fairly substantial experimental evidence for *short-run* causation of aggression among some children by viewing violence on the screen and the much less certain evidence from field studies that extensive violence viewing precedes some *long-run* manifestations of aggressive behavior [p. 10].

Thus, the major implication of the results of this research program is the clear need for a reduction in the level of violence portrayed on television. At the same time it is equally important to encourage broadcasters to modify the balance of programming in favor of prosocial content. Indeed, the recommendations stemming from this research program are not merely negative sanctions against televised violence but rather a plea for more beneficial and useful forms of television content.

REFERENCES

Baker, R. K., & Ball, S. J. *Mass media and violence: A staff report to the National Commission on the Causes and Prevention of Violence*. Washington, D.C.: U.S. Government Printing Office, 1969.

Bandura, A. Social learning theory of identificatory processes. In D. A. Goslin (Ed.), *Handbook of socialization theory and research*. Chicago: Rand McNally, 1969.

Barcus, F. E. *Saturday children's television: A report of TV programming and advertising on Boston commercial television*. Boston: Action for Children's Television, 1971.

Chaffee, S., & McLeod, J. Adolescents, parents, and television violence. Paper presented at the annual meeting of the American Psychological Association, Washington, D.C., September 1971.

Clark, C. Race, identification, and television violence. In G. A. Comstock, E. A. Rubinstein, & J. P. Murray (Eds.), *Television and social behavior*. Vol. 5. *Television's effects: Further explorations*. Washington, D.C.: U.S. Government Printing Office, 1972.

Clark, D. G., & Blankenburg, W. B. Trends in violent content in selected mass media. In G. A. Comstock & E. A. Rubinstein (Eds.), *Television and social behavior*. Vol. 1. *Media content and control*. Washington, D.C.: U.S. Government Printing Office, 1972.

Ekman, P., Liebert, R. M., Friesen, W., Harrison, R., Zlatchin, C., Malmstrom, E. J., & Baron, R. A. Facial expressions of emotion while watching televised violence as predictors of subsequent aggression. In G. A. Comstock, E. A. Rubinstein, & J. P. Murray (Eds.), *Television and social behavior*. Vol. 5. *Television's effects: Further explorations*. Washington, D.C.: U.S. Government Printing Office, 1972.

Eron, L. Relationship of TV viewing habits and aggressive behavior in children. *Journal of Abnormal and Social Psychology*, 1963, **67**, 193–196.

Gerbner, G. Violence in television drama: Trends and symbolic functions. In G. A. Comstock & E. A. Rubinstein (Eds.), *Television and social behavior*. Vol. 1. *Media content and control*. Washington, D.C.: U.S. Government Printing Office, 1972.

Greenberg, B. S., & Gordon, T. F. Children's perceptions of television violence: A replication. In G. A. Comstock, E. A. Rubinstein, & J. P. Murray (Eds.), *Television and social behavior*. Vol. 5. *Television's effects: Further explorations*. Washington, D.C.: U.S. Government Printing Office, 1972.

Lefkowitz, M., Eron, L., Walder, L., & Huesmann, L. R. Television violence and child aggression: A follow up study. In G. A. Comstock & E. A. Rubinstein (Eds.), *Television and social behavior*. Vol. 3. *Television and adolescent aggressiveness*. Washington, D.C.: U.S. Government Printing Office, 1972.

Leifer, A. D., & Roberts. D. F. Children's reponses to television violence. In J. P. Murray, E. A. Rubinstein, & G. A. Comstock (Eds.), *Television and social behavior*. Vol. 2. *Television and social learning*. Washington, D.C.: U.S. Government Printing Office, 1972.

Liebert, R. M., & Baron, R. A. Short-term effects of televised aggression on children's aggressive behavior. In J. P. Murray, E. A. Rubinstein, & G. A. Comstock (Eds.), *Television and social behavior*. Vol. 2. *Television and social learning*. Washington, D.C.: U.S. Government Printing Office, 1972.

Lyle, J., & Hoffman, H. R. Children's use of television and other media. In E. A. Rubinstein, G. A. Comstock, J. P. Murray (Eds.), *Television and social behavior*. Vol. 4. *Television in day-to-day life: Patterns of use*. Washington, D.C.: U.S. Government Printing Office, 1972. (a)

Lyle, J., & Hoffman, H. R. Explorations in patterns of television viewing by preschool-age children. In E. A. Rubinstein, G. A. Comstock, & J. P. Murray (Eds.), *Television and social behavior*. Vol. 4. *Television in day-to-day life: Patterns of use*. Washington, D.C.: U.S. Government Printing Office, 1972. (b)

McIntyre, J., & Teevan, J. Television and deviant behavior. In G. A. Comstock & E. A. Rubinstein (Eds.), *Television and social behavior*. Vol. 3. *Television and adolescent aggressiveness*. Washington, D.C.: U.S. Government Printing Office, 1972.

McLeod, J., Atkin, C., & Chaffee, S. Adolescents, parents, and television use: Adolescent self-report measures from Maryland and Wisconsin samples. In G. A. Comstock & E. A. Rubinstein (Eds.), *Television and social behavior*. Vol. 3. *Television and adolescent aggressiveness*. Washington, D.C.: U.S. Government Printing Office, 1972. (a)

McLeod, J., Atkin, C., & Chaffee, S. Adolescents, parents, and television use: Self-report and other-report measures from the Wisconsin sample. In G. A. Comstock & E. A. Rubinstein (Eds.), *Television and social behavior*. Vol. 3. *Television and adolescent aggressiveness*. Washington, D.C.: U.S. Government Printing Office, 1972. (b)

Murray, J. P. Television in inner-city homes: Viewing behavior of young boys. In E. A. Rubinstein, G. A. Comstock, & J. P. Murray (Eds.), *Television and social behavior*. Vol. 4. *Television in day-to-day life: Patterns of use*. Washington, D.C.: U.S. Government Printing Office, 1972.

Murray, J. P., Nayman, O. B., & Atkin, C. K. Television and the child: A comprehensive research bibliography. *Journal of Broadcasting*, 1972, **26**(1), 21–35.

Stein, A., & Friedrich, L. K. Television content and young children's behavior. In J. P. Murray, E. A. Rubinstein, & G. A. Comstock (Eds.), *Television and social behavior*. Vol. 2. *Television and social learning*. Washington, D.C.: U.S. Government Printing Office, 1972.

Surgeon General's Scientific Advisory Committee on Television and Social Behavior. *Television and growing up: The impact of televised violence*. Washington, D.C.: U.S. Government Printing Office, 1972.

United States Senate, Committee on the Judiciary. Effects on young people of violence and crime portrayed on television. Part 16. *Investigation of juvenile delinquency in the United States, July 30, 1964*. Washington, D.C.: U.S. Government Printing Office, 1964.

Weiss, W. Effects of the mass media of communication. In G. Lindzey & E. Aronson (Eds.), *The handbook of social psychology*. (2nd ed.) Reading, Mass.: Addison-Wesley, 1969.

ROBERT TROTTER

Sex and Violence:
Pornography Hurts

Sexual attacks against women—our newspapers, magazines, novels, movies and television shows are full of such incidents. Considering the long history and continued prevalence of this kind of violence, it might seem that little can be done to curb it. But the situation may not be so bleak. Social scientists are beginning to pinpoint the many factors associated with violence, and the National Institute of Mental Health recently has concluded that an understanding of the conditions that lead to sexual attacks against women should be a major goal of research. . . .

Pornography and its possible role as a causative factor in eliciting violent behavior against women is one of the many areas currently being investigated. And the findings contradict much previous research. Ten years ago, the Presidential Commission on Obscenity and Pornography concluded that there was no relationship between exposure to erotic presentations and subsequent aggression, particularly sexual crimes. This conclusion was attacked by some researchers at the time and has been attacked by many (especially feminists) since. Now researchers are reevaluating the data, reexamining the question and finding solid evidence that at least one kind of pornography is responsible for attitudinal and behavioral changes that result in increased aggression by men against women. The type of pornography in question is called aggressive-erotic. It contains explicit sexual violence against women, and in recent years it has been produced and shown with increasing frequency. Two research projects, each taking a different approach to the study of sexually violent material, are among those described. . . .

Edward Donnerstein of the University of Wisconsin in Madison conducted one of the experiments. In order to examine the effects of aggressive-erotic material on male aggression toward females, 120 male college students were either angered or treated neutrally by either a male or female confederate of the experimenter. The subjects then were shown either a neutral, erotic or aggressive-erotic film. Several minutes later they were given an opportunity to deliver electric shocks to the fingertips of the original male or female confederate—as part of what they were told was a study of the effects of stress on learning. The subjects were unaware of the true purpose of the research, and they did not realize that the films they had seen

"Sex and Violence: Pornography Hurts" by Robert Trotter, *Science News*, September 13, 1980. Reprinted with permission from *Science News*, the weekly news magazine of science. Copyright 1980 by Science Service, Inc.

were part of the same experiment. Debriefings following the experiment, says Donnerstein, indicate that the subjects really had been tricked by the rather complex research design.

The results showed that exposure to an aggressive-erotic film increased aggressive behavior (giving shocks) to a level higher than for the erotic film. These findings were even more pronounced in subjects who had previously been angered by the confederates. When angered subjects were paired with a male, the aggressive-erotic film produced no more aggression than did the erotic film. When paired with a female, however, the subjects displayed an increase in aggression only after viewing the aggressive-erotic film.

Donnerstein's study and others like it find consistent results, but they are open to criticism on several counts—the artificiality of the laboratory setting, and the aggression is seen only immediately after exposure to violent pornography. "There clearly exists a need to assess the effects of mass media stimuli that fuse sexuality and violence outside the laboratory context," say Neil M. Malamuth and James V. Check of the University of Manitoba in Winnipeg. And that's what they have done.

Hundreds of students were sent to the movies as part of an experiment to test the effects of exposure to films that portray sexual violence as having positive consequences. The movies they saw were not pornography, just everyday sex and violence. They included *Swept Away* (a violent male sexual aggressor and a woman who learns to crave sexual sadism find love on a deserted island) and *The Getaway* (a woman falls in love with the man who raped her in front of her husband, then both taunt the husband until he commits suicide). The control films used, *A Man and a Woman* and *Hooper*, show tender romance and nonexplicit sex.

Within a week of viewing the movies, an attitude survey was administered to all students in the introductory psychology sections from which the subjects had been signed up for the experiment. The students did not know that the survey had anything to do with the films they had seen, but embedded within the survey were questions relating to acceptance of interpersonal violence, acceptance of the rape myth (that women enjoy being raped) and adversarial sexual beliefs. Subjects rated from "strongly agree" to "strongly disagree" statements such as "A man is never justified in hitting his wife" and "Many women have an unconscious wish to be raped and may then unconsciously set up a situation in which they are likely to be attacked."

The results of the survey indicated that exposure to the films portraying violent sexuality increased male subjects' acceptance of interpersonal violence against women. A similar (though nonsignificant) trend was found for acceptance of rape myths. For females the trend was in the opposite direction. Women exposed to violent-sexual films tended to be slightly less accepting of interpersonal violence and of rape myths than were control subjects. "The present findings," say the researchers, "constitute the first demonstration in a nonlaboratory setting . . . of relatively long-term effects of movies that fuse sexuality and violence."

Why do these findings differ from those of several years ago? Check says that "what's in the pornography is the important factor." Recent findings still suggest that nonviolent pornography has no immediate negative effects (though long-term effects have not been studied), but the new pornography is much more violent.

Donnerstein agrees: "We're looking at different material now. . . . 10-year-old pornography is very bland in comparison." Also, he adds, the women's movement affected us. "Women raised the question, and now social scientists have the responsibility of proving or disproving." And what we have found comes as no surprise, he adds. Many studies, such as those with children and televised violence, have shown similar effects. Now it has been found with violence in pornography, "Everyone finds the same results, no matter what measures they use. . . . There are no discrepant data here at all."

PHILIP ZIMBARDO
CRAIG HANEY
W. CURTIS BANKS

A Pirandellian Prison

The quiet of a summer morning in Palo Alto, California, was shattered by a screeching squad car siren as police swept through the city picking up college students in a surprise mass arrest. Each suspect was charged with a felony, warned of his constitutional rights, spread-eagled against the car, searched, handcuffed and carted off in the back seat of the squad car to the police station for booking.

After fingerprinting and the preparation of identification forms for his "jacket" (central information file), each prisoner was left isolated in a detention cell to wonder what he had done to get himself into this mess. After a while, he was blindfolded and transported to the "Stanford County Prison." Here he began the process of becoming a prisoner—stripped naked, skin-searched, deloused and issued a uniform, bedding, soap and towel.

The warden offered an impromptu welcome:

> As you probably know, I'm your warden. All of you have shown that you are unable to function outside in the real world for one reason or another—that somehow you lack the responsibility of good citizens of this great country. We of this prison, your correctional staff, are going to help you learn what your responsibilities as citizens of this country are. Here are the rules. Sometime in the near future there will be a copy of the rules posted in each of the cells. We expect you to know them and to be able to recite them by number. If you follow all of these rules and keep your hands clean, repent for your misdeeds and show a proper attitude of penitence, you and I will get along just fine.

There followed a reading of the sixteen basic rules of prisoner conduct.

> *Rule Number One:* Prisoners must remain silent during rest periods, after lights are out, during meals and whenever they are outside the prison yard. *Two:* Prisoners must eat at mealtimes and only at mealtimes. *Three:* Prisoners must not move, tamper, deface or damage walls, ceilings, windows, doors, or other prison property. . . . *Seven:* Prisoners must address each other by their ID number only. *Eight:* Prisoners must address the guards as 'Mr. Correctional Officer. . . . *Sixteen:* Failure to obey any of the above rules may result in punishment.

Abridgement of "A Pirandellian Prison" by Philip Zimbardo, Craig Haney, and W. Curtis Banks in *The New York Times Magazine*, April 8, 1973. © 1973 by The New York Times Company. Reprinted by permission.

By late afternoon these youthful "first offenders" sat in dazed silence on the cots in their barren cells trying to make sense of the events that had transformed their lives so dramatically.

If the police arrests and processing were executed with customary detachment, however, there were some things that didn't fit. For these men were now part of a very unusual kind of prison, an experimental mock prison, created by social psychologists to study the effects of imprisonment upon volunteer research subjects. When we planned our two-week-long simulation of prison life, we sought to understand more about the process by which people called "prisoners" lose their liberty, civil rights, independence and privacy, while those called "guards" gain social power by accepting the responsibility for controlling and managing the lives of their dependent charges.

Why didn't we pursue this research in a real prison? First, prison systems are fortresses of secrecy, closed to impartial observation, and thereby immune to critical analysis from anyone not already part of the correctional authority. Second, in any real prison, it is impossible to separate what each individual brings into the prison from what the prison brings out in each person.

We populated our mock prison with a homogeneous group of people who could be considered "normal-average" on the basis of clincial interviews and personality tests. Our participants (10 prisoners and 11 guards) were selected from more than 75 volunteers recruited through ads in the city and campus newspapers. The applicants were mostly college students from all over the United States and Canada who happened to be in the Stanford area during the summer and were attracted by the lure of earning $15 a day for participating in a study of prison life. We selected only those judged to be emotionally stable, physically healthy, mature, law-abiding citizens.

This sample of average, middle-class, Caucasian, college-age males (plus one Oriental student) was arbitrarily divided by the flip of a coin. Half were randomly assigned to play the role of guards, the others of prisoners. There were no measurable differences between the guards and the prisoners at the start of the experiment. Although initially warned that as prisoners their privacy and other civil rights would be violated and that they might be subjected to harassment, every subject was completely confident of his ability to endure whatever the prison had to offer for the full two-week experimental period. Each subject unhesitatingly agreed to give his "informed consent" to participate.

The prison was constructed in the basement of Stanford University's psychology building, which was deserted after the end of the summer-school session. A long corridor was converted into the prison "yard" by partitioning off both ends. Three small laboratory rooms opening onto this corridor were made into cells by installing metal barred doors and replacing existing furniture with cots, three to a cell. Adjacent offices were refurnished as guards' quarters, interview-testing rooms and bedrooms for the "warden" (David Jaffe) and the "superintendent" (Zimbardo). A concealed video camera and hidden microphones recorded much of the activity and conversation of guards and prisoners. The physical environment was one in which prisoners could always be observed by the staff, the only exception being when they were secluded in solitary confinement (a small, dark storage closet, labeled "The Hole").

Our mock prison represented an attempt to simulate the psychological state of imprisonment in certain ways. We based our experiment on an in-depth analysis of the prison situation, developed after hundreds of hours of discussion with Carlo Prescott (our ex-con consultant), parole officers and correctional personnel, and after reviewing much of the existing literature on prisons and concentration camps.

"Real" prisoners typically report feeling powerless, arbitrarily controlled, dependent, frustrated, hopeless, anonymous, dehumanized and emasculated. It was not possible, pragmatically or ethically, to create such chronic states in volunteer subjects who realize that they are in an experiment for only a short time. Racism, physical brutality, indefinite confinement and enforced homosexuality were not features of our mock prison. But we did try to reproduce those elements of the prison experience that seemed most fundamental.

We promoted anonymity by seeking to minimize each prisoner's sense of uniqueness and prior identity. The prisoners wore smocks and nylon stocking caps; they had to use their ID numbers; their personal effects were removed and they were housed in barren cells. All of this made them appear similar to each other and indistinguishable to observers. Their smocks, which were like dresses, were worn without undergarments, causing the prisoners to be restrained in their physical actions and to move in ways that were more feminine than masculine. The prisoners were forced to obtain permission from the guard for routine and simple activities such as writing letters, smoking a cigarette or even going to the toilet; this elicited from them a childlike dependency.

Their quarters, though clean and neat, were small, stark and without esthetic appeal. The lack of windows resulted in poor air circulation, and persistent odors arose from the unwashed bodies of the prisoners. After 10 P.M. lockup, toilet privileges were denied, so prisoners who had to relieve themselves would have to urinate and defecate in buckets provided by the guards. Sometimes the guards refused permission to have them cleaned out, and this made the prison smell.

Above all, "real" prisons are machines for playing tricks with the human conception of time. In our windowless prison, the prisoners often did not even know whether it was day or night. A few hours after falling asleep, they were roused by shrill whistles for their "count." The ostensible purpose of the count was to provide a public test of the prisoners' knowledge of the rules and of their ID numbers. But more important, the count, which occurred at least once on each of the three different guard shifts, provided a regular occasion for the guards to relate to the prisoners. Over the course of the study, the duration of the counts was spontaneously increased by the guards from their initial perfunctory 10 minutes to a seemingly interminable several hours. During these confrontations, guards who were bored could find ways to amuse themselves, ridiculing recalcitrant prisoners, enforcing arbitrary rules and openly exaggerating any dissension among the prisoners.

The guards were also "deindividualized." They wore identical khaki uniforms and silver reflector sunglasses that made eye contact with them impossible. Their symbols of power were billy clubs, whistles, handcuffs and the keys to the cells and the "main gate." Although our guards received no formal training from us in how to be guards, for the most part they moved with apparent ease into their roles. The media had already provided them with ample models of prison guards to emulate.

Because we were as interested in the guards' behavior as in the prisoners', they were given considerable latitude to improvise and to develop strategies and tactics of prisoner management. Our guards were told that they must maintain "law and order" in this prison, that they were responsible for handling any trouble that might break out, and they were cautioned about the seriousness and potential dangers of the situation they were about to enter. Surprisingly, in most prison systems, "real" guards are not given much more psychological preparation or adequate training than this for what is one of the most complex, demanding and dangerous jobs our society has to offer. They are expected to learn how to adjust to their new employment mostly from on-the-job experience, and from contacts with the "old bulls" during a survival-of-the-fittest orientation period. According to an orientation manual for correctional officers at San Quentin, "the only way you really get to know San Quentin is through experience and time. Some of us take more time and must go through more experiences than others to accomplish this; some really never do get there."

You cannot be a prisoner if no one will be your guard, and you cannot be a prison guard if no one takes you or your prison seriously. Therefore, over time a perverted symbiotic relationship developed. As the guards became more aggressive, prisoners became more passive; assertion by the guards led to dependency in the prisoners; self-aggrandizement was met with self-deprecation, authority with help-lessness, and the counterpart of the guards' sense of mastery and control was the depression and hopelessness witnessed in the prisoners. As these differences in behavior, mood and perception became more evident to all, the need for the now "righteously" powerful guards to rule the obviously inferior and powerless inmates became a sufficient reason to support almost any further indignity of man against man:

GUARD K: During the inspection, I went to Cell 2 to mess up a bed which the prisoner had made and he grabbed me, screaming that he had just made it, and he wasn't going to let me mess it up. He grabbed my throat, and although he was laughing I was pretty scared. . . . I lashed out with my stick and hit him in the chin (although not very hard), and when I freed myself I became angry. I wanted to get back in the cell and have a go with him, since he attacked me when I was not ready.
GUARD M: I was surprised at myself . . . I made them call each other names and clean the toilets out with their bare hands. I practically considered the prisoners cattle, and I kept thinking: I have to watch out for them in case they try something.
GUARD A: I was tired of seeing the prisoners in their rags and smelling the strong odors of their bodies that filled the cells. I watched them tear at each other on orders given by us. They didn't see it as an experiment. It was real and they were fighting to keep their identity. But we were always there to show them who was boss.

Because the first day passed without incident, we were surprised and totally unprepared for the rebellion that broke out on the morning of the second day. The prisoners removed their stocking caps, ripped off their numbers and barricaded themselves inside the cells by putting their beds against the doors. What should we do? The guards were very much upset because the prisoners also began to taunt and curse them to their faces. When the morning shift of guards came on, they were upset at the night shift who, they felt, must have been too permissive and too lenient. The guards had to handle the rebellion themselves, and what they did was startling to behold.

At first they insisted that reinforcements be called in. The two guards who were waiting on standby call at home came in, and the night shift of guards voluntarily remained on duty (without extra pay) to bolster the morning shift. The guards met and decided to treat force with force. They got a fire extinguisher that shot a stream of skin-chilling carbon dioxide and forced the prisoners away from the doors; they broke into each cell, stripped the prisoners naked, took the beds out, forced the prisoners who were the ringleaders into solitary confinement and generally began to harass and intimidate the prisoners.

After crushing the riot, the guards decided to head off further unrest by creating a privileged cell for those who were "good prisoners" and then, without explanation, switching some of the troublemakers into it and some of the good prisoners out into the other cells. The prisoner ringleaders could not trust these new cellmates because they had not joined in the riot and might even be "snitches." The prisoners never again acted in unity against the system. One of the leaders of the prisoner revolt later confided:

> If we had gotten together then, I think we could have taken over the place. But when I saw the revolt wasn't working, I decided to toe the line. Everyone settled into the same pattern. From then on, we were really controlled by the guards.

It was after this episode that the guards really began to demonstrate their inventiveness in the application of arbitrary power. They made the prisoners obey petty, meaningless and often inconsistent rules, forced them to engage in tedious, useless work, such as moving cartons back and forth between closets and picking thorns out of their blankets for hours on end. (The guards had previously dragged the blankets through thorny bushes to create this disagreeable task.) Not only did the prisoners have to sing songs or laugh or refrain from smiling on command; they were also encouraged to curse and vilify each other publicly during some of the counts. They sounded off their numbers endlessly and were repeatedly made to do pushups, on occasion with a guard stepping on them or a prisoner sitting on them.

Slowly the prisoners became resigned to their fate and even behaved in ways that actually helped to justify their dehumanizing treatment at the hands of the guards. Analysis of the tape-recorded private conversations between prisoners and of remarks made by them to interviewers revealed that fully half could be classified as nonsupportive of other prisoners. More dramatic, 85 percent of the evaluative statements by prisoners about their fellow prisoners were uncomplimentary and deprecating. . . .

In less than 36 hours, we were forced to release prisoner 8612 because of extreme depression, disorganized thinking, uncontrollable crying and fits of rage. We did so reluctantly because we believed he was trying to "con" us—it was unimaginable that a volunteer prisoner in a mock prison could legitimately be suffering and disturbed to that extent. But then on each of the next three days another prisoner reacted with similar anxiety symptoms, and we were forced to terminate them, too. In a fifth case, a prisoner was released after developing a psychosomatic rash over his entire body (triggered by rejection of his parole appeal by the mock parole board). These men were simply unable to make an adequate adjustment to prison life. Those who endured the prison experience to the end could be distinguished from those who broke down and were released early in only one dimension—authoritarianism. On a psychological test designed to reveal a person's authoritarianism, those prisoners who had the highest scores were best able to function in this authoritarian prison environment.

If the authoritarian situation became a serious matter for the prisoners, it became even more serious—and sinister—for the guards. Typically, the guards insulted the prisoners, threatened them, were physically aggressive, used instruments (night sticks, fire extinguishers, etc.) to keep the prisoners in line and referred to them in impersonal, anonymous, deprecating ways: "Hey, you," or "You [obscenity], 5401, come here." From the first to the last day, there was a significant increase in the guards' use of most of these domineering, abusive tactics.

Everyone and everything in the prison was defined by power. To be a guard who did not take advantage of this institutionally sanctioned use of power was to appear "weak," "out of it," "wired up by the prisoners," or simply a deviant from the established norms of appropriate guard behavior. Using Erich Fromm's definition of sadism as "the wish for absolute control over another living being," all of the mock guards at one time or another during this study behaved sadistically toward the prisoners. Many of them reported—in their diaries, on critical-incident report forms and during post-experimental interviews—being delighted in the new-found power and control they exercised and sorry to see it relinquished at the end of the study.

Some of the guards reacted to the situation in the extreme and behaved with great hostility and cruelty in the forms of degradation they invented for the prisoners. But others were kinder; they occasionally did little favors for the prisoners, were reluctant to punish them, and avoided situations where prisoners were being harassed. . . .

Still, the behavior of these good guards seemed more motivated by a desire to be liked by everyone in the system than by a concern for the inmates' welfare. No guard ever intervened in any direct way on behalf of the prisoners, ever interfered with the orders of the cruelest guards or ever openly complained about the subhuman quality of life that characterized this prison.

Perhaps the most devastating impact of the more hostile guards was their creation of a capricious, arbitrary environment. Over time the prisoners began to react passively. When our mock prisoners asked questions, they got answers about half the time, but the rest of the time they were insulted and punished—and it was not possible for them to predict which would be the outcome. As they began to "toe the line," they stopped resisting, questioning and, indeed, almost ceased responding altogether. There was a general decrease in all categories of response as they learned the safest strategy to use in an unpredictable, threatening environment from which there is no physical escape—do nothing, except what is required. Act not, want not, feel not and you will not get into trouble in prisonlike situations.

Can it really be, you wonder, that intelligent, educated volunteers could have lost sight of the reality that they were merely acting a part in an elaborate game that would eventually end? There are many indications not only that they did, but that, in addition, so did we and so did other apparently sensible, responsible adults.

Prisoner 819, who had gone into a rage followed by an uncontrollable crying fit, was about to be prematurely released from the prison when a guard lined up the prisoners and had them chant in unison, "819 is a bad prisoner. Because of what 819 did to prison property we all must suffer. 819 is a bad prisoner." Over and over again. When we realized 819 might be overhearing this, we rushed into the room where 819 was supposed to be resting, only to find him in tears, prepared to go back into the prison because he could not leave as long as the others thought he was a "bad prisoner." Sick as he felt, he had to prove to them he was not a "bad" prisoner. He had to be persuaded that he was not a prisoner at all, that the others were also just students, that this was just an experiment and not a prison and the prison staff were only research psychologists. A report from the warden notes, "While I believe that it was necessary for *staff* [me] to enact the warden role, at least some of the time, I am startled by the ease with which I could turn off my sensitivity and concern for others for 'a good cause.' "

Consider our overreaction to the rumor of a mass escape plot that one of the guards claimed to have overheard. It went as follows: Prisoner 8612, previously released for emotional disturbance, was only faking. He was going to round up a bunch of his friends, and they would storm the prison right after visiting hours. Instead of collecting data on the pattern of rumor transmission, we made plans to maintain the security of our institution. After putting a confederate informer into the cell 8612 had occupied to get specific information about the escape plans, the superintendent went back to the Palo Alto Police Department to request transfer of our prisoners to the old city jail. His impassioned plea was only turned down at the last minute when the problem of insurance and city liability for our prisoners was raised by a city official. Angered at this lack of cooperation, the staff formulated another plan. Our jail was dismantled, the prisoners, chained and blindfolded, were carted off to a remote storage room. When the conspirators arrived, they would be told the study was over, their friends had been sent home, there was nothing left to liberate. After they left, we would redouble the security features of our prison making any future escape attempts futile. We even planned to lure ex-prisoner 8612 back on some pretext and imprison him again, because he had been released on false pretenses! The rumor turned out to be just that—a full day had passed in which we collected little or no data, worked incredibly hard to tear down and then rebuild our prison. Our reaction, however, was as much one of relief and joy as of exhaustion and frustration. . . .

But perhaps the most telling account of the insidious development of this new reality, of the gradual Kafkaesque metamorphosis of good into evil, appears in excerpts from the diary of one of the guards, Guard A:

Prior to start of experiment: As I am a pacifist and nonaggressive individual I cannot see a time when I might guard and/or maltreat other living things.

After an orientation meeting: Buying uniforms at the end of the meeting confirms the gamelike atmosphere of this thing. I doubt whether many of us share the expectations of "seriousness" that the experimenters seem to have.

First Day: Feel sure that the prisoners will make fun of my appearance and I evolve my first basic strategy—mainly not to smile at anything they say or do which would be admitting it's all only a game. . . . At Cell 3 I stop and setting my voice hard and low say to 5486, "What are you smiling at?" "Nothing, Mr. Correctional Officer." "Well, see that you don't." (As I walk off I feel stupid.)

Second Day: 5704 asked for a cigarette and I ignored him—because I am a nonsmoker and could not empathize. . . . Meanwhile since I was feeling empathetic towards 1037, I determined not to talk with him . . . after we had count and lights out [Guard D] and I held a loud conversation about going home to our girl friends and what we were going to do to them.

Third Day (preparing for the first visitors' night): After warning the prisoners not to make any complaints unless they wanted the visit terminated fast, we finally brought in the first parents. I made sure I was one of the guards on the yard, because this was my first chance for the type of manipulative power that I really like—being a very noticed figure with almost complete control over what is said or not. While the parents and prisoners sat in chairs, I sat on the end of the table dangling my feet and contradicting anything I felt like. This was the first part of the experiment I was really enjoying. . . . 817 is being obnoxious and bears watching.

Fourth Day: . . . The psychologist rebukes me for handcuffing and blindfolding a prisoner before leaving the [counseling] office, and I resentfully reply that it is both necessary security and my business anyway.

Fifth Day: I harass "Sarge" who continues to stubbornly overrespond to all commands. I have singled him out for special abuse both because he begs for it and because I simply don't like him. The real trouble starts at dinner. The new prisoner (416) refuses to eat his sausage . . . we throw him into the Hole ordering him to hold sausages in each hand. We have a crisis of authority; this rebellious conduct potentially undermines the complete control we have over the others. We decide to play upon prisoner solidarity and tell the new one that all the others will be deprived of visitors if he does not eat his dinner. . . . I walk by and slam my stick into the Hole door. . . . I am very angry at this prisoner for causing discomfort and trouble for the others. I decided to force-feed him, but he wouldn't eat. I let the food slide down his face. I didn't believe it was me doing it. I hated myself for making him eat but I hated him more for not eating.

Sixth Day: The experiment is over. I feel elated but am shocked to find some other guards disappointed somewhat because of the loss of money and some because they are enjoying themselves.

We were no longer dealing with an intellectual exercise in which a hypothesis was being evaluated in the dispassionate manner dictated by the canons of the scientific method. We were caught up in the passion of the present, the suffering, the need to control people, not variables, the escalation of power and all of the unexpected things that were erupting around and within us. We had to end this experiment. So our planned two-week simulation was aborted after only six (was it only six?) days and nights.

Was it worth all the suffering just to prove what everyone knows—that some people are sadistic, others weak and prisons are not beds of roses? If that is all we demonstrated in this research, then it was certainly not worth the anguish. We believe there are many significant implications to be derived from this experience, only a few of which can be suggested here.

The potential social value of this study derives precisely from the fact that normal, healthy, educated young men could be so radically transformed under the institutional pressures of a "prison environment." If this could happen in so short a time, without the excesses that are possible in real prisons, and if it could happen to the "cream-of-the-crop of American youth," then one can only shudder to imagine what society is doing both to the actual guards and prisoners who are at this very moment participating in that unnatural "social experiment."

The pathology observed in this study cannot be reasonably attributed to preexisting personality differences of the subjects, that option being eliminated by our selection procedures and random assignment. Rather, the subjects' abnormal social and personal reactions are best seen as a product of their transaction with an environment that supported the behavior that would be pathological in other settings, but was "appropriate" in this prison. Had we observed comparable reactions in a real prison, the psychiatrist undoubtedly would not have been able to attribute any prisoner's behavior to character defects or personality maladjustment, while critics of the prison system would have been quick to label the guards as "psychopathic." This tendency to locate the source of behavior disorders inside a particular person or group underestimates the power of situational forces. . . .

During a series of encounter debriefing sessions immediately after our experiment, we all had an opportunity to vent our strong feelings and to reflect upon the moral and ethical issues each of us faced, and we considered how we might react more morally in future "real life" analogues to this situation. Year-long follow-ups with our subjects via questionnaires, personal interviews and group reunions indicate that their mental anguish was transient and situationally specific, but the self-knowledge gained has persisted.

For the most disturbing implication of our research comes from the parallels between what occurred in that basement mock prison and daily experiences in our own lives—and we presume yours. The physical institution of prison is but a concrete and steel metaphor for the existence of more pervasive, albeit less obvious, prisons of the mind that all of us daily create, populate and perpetuate.

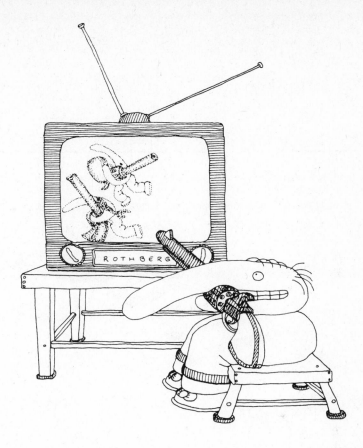

A Disposition Toward Fighting

*To fight is a radical instinct: if men have nothing else
to fight over they will fight over words, fancies, or
women, or they will fight because they dislike each
other's looks, or because they have met walking in
opposite directions. To knock a thing down, especially if it is cocked at an arrogant angle, is a deep
delight to the blood.*

George Santayana
From *The Life of Reason*, published by Charles
Scribner's Sons, 1922.

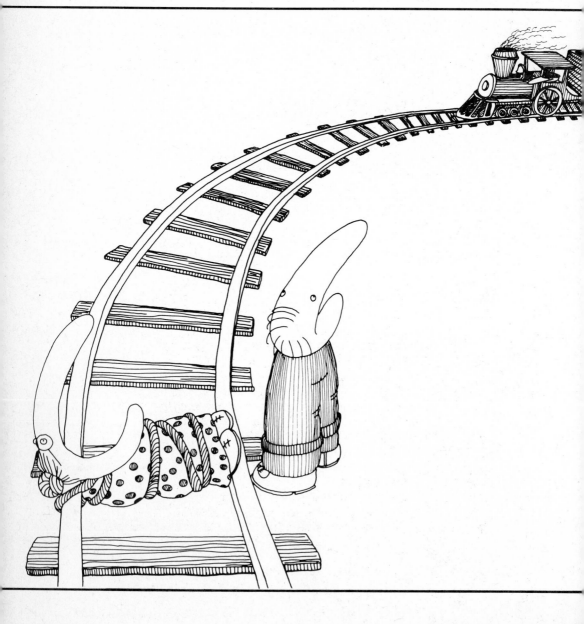

6

Altruism and Aid

If, as you began to read this, you heard a scream for help, what would you do? Each of us would like to think that we would do the right thing and go to help. Yet, almost every day we hear another story about bystander apathy toward people in need of help. We, as potential helpers or needers of help, are naturally concerned about knowing why help is offered under certain circumstances and not under others.

The reasons that have been given for failure to help have been numerous. Some psychologists have expressed the extreme view that witnessing violence without helping satisfies latent sadistic needs; others have laid the blame on apathy and the depersonalization of society. Some have pointed to the nature of helping norms in our culture, and still others have based their explanations on the rewards and costs associated with helping.

John Darley, Professor of Psychology at Princeton University, was teaching at New York University in 1964 when he heard the widely circulated reports of the murder of a young woman in the borough of Queens—a murder which thirty-eight people witnessed without doing anything to help the victim. He and Bibb Latané, then teaching at Columbia University, were highly concerned about the incident, and the two decided to work together in seeking reasons for the bystanders' apathy.

As a result of their research, they have concluded that when help is needed, there is not necessarily strength in numbers. That is, once a person has noticed and decided that there is an emergency, the presence of others may diffuse responsibility and may actually deter individual action. Darley and Latané research, which in turn has stimulated much additional research on this topic, brought them the Socio-Psychological Prize of the American Association for the Advancement of Science in 1968, and is summarized in their book, *The Unresponsive Bystander: Why Doesn't He Help?* (Latané and Darley, 1970).

During our conversation, Dr. Darley discussed his own research in relation to other explanations of helping behavior. He recommended the use of both laboratory and field techniques in studying helping behavior, and talked about some practical plans for increasing helping that are currently being tried. I began our discussion by probing for some basic definitions.

A CONVERSATION WITH
JOHN M. DARLEY

Princeton University

KRUPAT: *The first thing, if we're going to talk about helping behavior, is to ask you why helping behavior is within the domain of what we call social psychology in the first place? What is it and how does it belong?*

DARLEY: There are two possible answers, I suppose. The first is that it is an important social problem, and that is the sort of problem any social psychologist wants to be concerned about. But second, and I think this is the reason why I feel comfortable attacking it, is that it is a topic to which our social psychological theories are relevant, or at least ought to be. For instance, certain of our theories, developed around the conformity research of Solomon Asch, have turned out to account for some aspects of helping behavior.

KRUPAT: *But when you talk about helping behavior, are you referring to the same thing other researchers have called altruism? Or just how do these terms fit together?*

DARLEY: *Altruism* is a word that is usually reserved for helping another person under conditions in which we can see no benefits and probably some cost to the helper for doing so. However, some people have argued that even though others may not see any reward when an individual helps another, there still might be internal rewards he gives himself, so an apparently altruistic act does not prove the existence of "true" altruism. I've shied away from the debate about whether there is any such thing as altruism, and have contented myself with talking about helping other people in situations where one doesn't have much contact with the other person in advance and there don't seem to be any huge rewards for helping.

KRUPAT: *But, regardlelss of what you call it, "altruism" or just plain "helping," obviously this is not a new topic of study. Can you account for all the recent interest in this area? How did you get interested in it?*

DARLEY: First of all, let me make it clear that the work I have done on helping was done jointly with Bibb Latané, who was at Columbia at the time we began this work. Certainly the precipitating event for us all was the murder of a young lady in New York, the now famous Kitty Genovese case that the *New York Times* picked up. A young lady was murdered, but sadly that's a rather typical incident. What was atypical was that thirty-eight people in her apartment building watched out their windows while this happened, and none of them did much in the way of helping. Bibb and I were having dinner together one night shortly thereafter. Everybody was talking about it and so were we. And, as we started to talk about it, we began to realize that this was something that could be analyzed in terms of the theories we knew and were teaching. We probably sketched out the experiments on a table-cloth that day.

KRUPAT: *I guess the simplest question is: Why didn't they help? That's obviously a very big question, I realize.*

DARLEY: Well, again two points need to be made. First, I don't think we'll ever know for sure why those *specific* people didn't help. It's important to distinguish what a social psychologist does from what a social historian might do. What we psychologists do is to look at an incident and analyze it to develop hypotheses about the general problem, but we don't necessarily think we've explained the incident once we've finished with our studies.

Given that caveat, though, I suspect the reason that people in general don't help is greatly because they're influenced by the people around them. That is, the fact that shocks us about emergencies is that we look at the relationship between the bystander and the victim, and we say, "He's callously ignoring the victim, or choosing not to help him." But, if we look at what goes on between the networks of bystanders, we begin to be able to see explanations for their failure to act. One explanation is that when *many* people are present, any *one* person feels less responsible for helping, so that crowds diffuse the responsibility of any crowd member. One can always say, "I bet somebody here is better trained, like the police, etc."—and thus rationalize inaction.

The second reason, which is true at least in our culture, is that when one of us sees an emergency he first tries to figure out exactly what's happening. It's only in the clear light of hindsight that we know an event was an emergency. Actually, when a potential emergency occurs, a witness has to figure out what is happening; and, in our culture, it is traditional to maintain a poker face until you yourself have figured out what is going on. So, if I see you looking at an emergency with a poker face, I'm prone to think, "He knows something I don't know. There's nothing wrong here; otherwise he wouldn't be poker-faced; he'd be running around." And you see me doing the same; so, we each define the event as no emergency for the other.

KRUPAT: *But still, in the first place, why don't we each do the opposite? That is, why don't we each jump immediately, spot that the other is unnerved, worried, and therefore both leap into action?*

DARLEY: Sometimes we do that, but it depends on the characteristics of the emergency. In a study I did with Alan Teger and Larry Lewis, we found that if the emergency is a loud crash and the two subjects can see each other, each sees the other startled and they go ahead and respond to the situation as if it were an emergency. If they can't see each other when the emergency occurs, if they don't see that initial startle reaction, then each models inaction for the other, and neither is likely to react.

KRUPAT: *Actually, it's a lot easier to do nothing than to do something.*

DARLEY: There are a lot of reasons to worry about doing something. We all know stories about doctors getting sued for trying to help.

KRUPAT: *Then maybe when we ask, "Why don't people help?" we are asking the wrong question. Should we be asking instead, "Why should anybody* help?"

DARLEY: That, I think, is exactly the critical direction for research to go in. There's been some discussion about why people do help, and social psychologists' initial answer has been helping norms. That is, we are all taught about the Golden Rule, but don't seem to apply it very clearly to our situations.

KRUPAT: *But if norms are rules which define proper and improper social behavior, are you implying that there are no rules that relate to helping, or that they don't explain this type of behavior?*

DARLEY: For instance, one ought to help an epileptic; the norms ought to be equally strong, no matter how many people are present. Yet, the number of people present *does* make a difference to whether one helps. Dan Batson and I recently did a study looking at whether norms do govern people's helping behavior. All of our subjects were theology students who were supposed to give a sermon, and some were made to feel in a hurry and others were not. For some of these subjects, we attempted to make the helping norm extremely salient. That is, they were either in a hurry or not to give a sermon on the parable of the Good Samaritan. The others were on their way to give a sermon on a helping-irrelevant topic. In order to get to their talk they had to pass down an alleyway where there was a man (our confederate) lying by the side groaning and coughing. What we found was that whether or not individuals were in a hurry made a greater difference to their helping behavior than did our attempted manipulation of normative relevance. Berkowitz has recently also found, to put the conclusion conservatively, less behavioral effects of normative manipulations than we would initially have expected.

KRUPAT: *Then, am I right to say that it seemed to be more important what the nature of the situation was, rather than how strong the norm was in the person's mind?*

DARLEY: Yes, and there's another fact that we should recognize about the way we use norms in our society. What we do is to teach people, after the fact, to account for their behavior in normative terms. However, we ought to realize that our behavior may be determined in *other* ways *before* the fact.

Let me give you a concrete example. Friends of ours have two children, a daughter and also a baby. Naturally, at one point the daughter bit the baby, because she was angry at the baby. Fair enough, older children should be angry at younger children; they're taking their resources.

But, there was the father witnessing all this and ready to punish the daughter. Being a rational-oriented father, he said, "Why did you do that?" and an interesting exchange occurred.

If the child can get her behavior under norms—if she can account for it in normative terms—then it is acceptable. This is difficult to do with the case of biting the baby, but she was ingenious, saying, 'The baby bit me first."

At that point the father pointed out the baby has no teeth, and punished her anyway. So it didn't work in this instance, but it shouldn't mask the general truth that more actions are rationalized after the fact on normative grounds than ever were committed for normative reasons. Explanations of an act after the fact are often quite different from the motivations for doing the act in the first place.

KRUPAT: *But then, if we reject norms as explaining helping, what are we left with?*

DARLEY: I'm afraid that you're right. Once we've criticized norms, we can't substitute any really solid alternatives for why people help. One possibility is a kind of sympathy explanation. You help other people when you feel their human condition, are touched by their plight, and therefore want to restore them to some normal state. Harvey Hornstein and Morton Deutsch are working on a similar kind of idea that they call "promotive tension." You cooperate with other people when you feel you share their goals, so that when you feel you are (in Hornstein's terms) in a "we group" with other people, you will help those in the group.

KRUPAT: *I admit that it seems very difficult to locate the basic motives for helping. But are there differences, at least, between the kinds of people who help and the kind who don't? Can you distinguish or predict who will be a helper on the basis of personal characteristics or background?*

DARLEY: I think there are differences, although Latané and I have resisted talking on those terms because we think it's all too easy to say nonhelpers are different in personality. In a way that is the equivalent of saying: "They are moral defectives and we, good people that we are, would have helped." As far as personality differences go, in terms of the standard scales we have available—such as those concerning alienation, social responsibility, and so on—we, as well as others, have found that these scales don't seem to predict actual helping in experimental situations. So the more obvious type of personality statements some people would make don't seem to hold up very well when they are actually tested.

But there are other personal differences among people besides psychologists' "personality" variables. One such difference has to do with where a person has grown up, in a small town or a big city. This is because many of the determinants of helping that we have found, such as the fact that you are more likely to help a person whom you are acquainted with, apply to the small town–big city distinction. In New York, for instance, you are dealing mostly with strangers. Also, sadly, you see so many people in trouble that you can't help everyone, so you adapt and tend not to help at all. Another personal difference is how much ambiguity you can tolerate in a situation prior to deciding what you're going to do. This is important because emergencies are often quite ambiguous as you are experiencing them. So, I think there are differences, although I do think that still the specific help-needing situation is a larger determinant than people are initially likely to think.

KRUPAT: *How about going beyond individual differences and talking about relationships between people? For instance, Piliavan, Rodin, and Piliavin explored whether being of the same sex or race of a person needing aid affected helping. Do you think this is an important determinant of help-giving?*

DARLEY: I don't think that a variable like shared race or shared sex with a victim would *automatically* make you a helper. The important thing is if you feel, in Hornstein's terms, this kind of "we" feeling with him. This might happen because you are a girl college student in a previously all-male college recently gone coed. Or, if you are of the same race in a sea of faces of another race, then indeed I suspect you would feel an increased desire to help the other person.

KRUPAT: *We've been talking now for some time about the results of your and others' research, and some conclusions people have drawn from them. In terms of working in this type of area, I notice that you have gone back and forth quite a bit between laboratory and field experimental situations. What's the purpose of doing both, as you see it? What can you pull out of the one that you can't get from the other?*

DARLEY: Well, the great strength of the laboratory study is that you can control for alternative explanations of your results, so that if you're doing a theory-testing operation, you will often set up an artificial situation. Lab settings are often criticized as being artificial, but I think that misunderstands their purpose. They ought to be artificial; that is, they ought to be relevant to a test of one postulate of a theory in a way that rules out all of the other potentially causal factors that are usually confounded with that. So that if they're not artificial, in *that* sense, they're not much worth doing. A field study, on the other hand, gives you a much better feel for the working of forces much stronger than you can create in laboratory settings. And it removes your subject from the whole set of demands placed upon him merely by the fact that he knows he is being studied.

The awful possibility in the laboratory experiment is that you are not studying the behavior of your subject; you're studying his *psychology*. That is, he is telling you what he thinks you expect, what he thinks the "usual and normal person" does when confronted with the stimulus, instead of simply acting. In field experiments, the problem is considerably ameliorated. That is why we want to go back and forth between the two.

I think it would probably be roughly accurate to say that you're not sure about the importance of an effect-causing variable until you've picked up the external validity, the external generalizability, from a field study. But as for internal validity, that one gets from a laboratory study. Sadly, psychologists have their biases, so that most of us are prone to stick with one form or the other because we're more comfortable with the certainties of experiments or with the practicalities of field studies.

KRUPAT: *And yet, what do we do when certain of the results of our field studies disagree with our lab studies? For instance, the Piliavin, Rodin, and Piliavin study, where a man collapsed in the subway, seemed to disconfirm the diffusion-of-responsibility hypothesis. The more people who were around, the more help was offered.*

DARLEY: Actually, there's not as much inconsistency between our ideas and this study as some people have seen. We made a somewhat different statement about helping which is distinguished from a stronger statement. Our statement is: The more people present, the less likely any *one* person is to help. The stronger statement would be: The more people present, the less likely you are to get help from the entire group. The second is not necessarily so. That is, even if any one of five people are only 50-percent likely to help, if you work out the mathematics you are almost certain to get help from at least one person. So, first of all, in the Piliavin study, in which the number of people available to help was quite high, we would also expect help from at least one person. And second, since some of the people, at least, were facing each other when the startling emergency of a man falling over occurred, their faces may have signaled their definitions of the situation to one another, and therefore the group inhibition process we talked about earlier did not take place.

KRUPAT: *But are you concerned that since you and Bibb Latané are so closely identified with the diffusion hypothesis you may be called upon to defend it to the death against others?*

DARLEY: As of yet, that hasn't come up; and I hope we wouldn't do that. Latané and I suggested, and a reasonable number of studies done on the emergency situation have shown, that the ambiguity of the event and the number of people present are determinants of whether one responds to it oneself. By and large, that generalization has become confirmed, and it has been intelligently extended in research by Bickman and Korte, who have shown that it's not simply how many other persons are present that determine any one individual's likelihood of response, but how many other persons are present *and* are available to help.

KRUPAT: *Now that you mention about how to ask for help, sometimes I've wondered as I look at some of the helping literature, what I would do to get help if I needed it. A friend once suggested that if attacked he would call out the name of a specific person to try to focus helping pressures on him. Also, some students of mine have suggested yelling "Fire" instead of "Help," and that way people might be more likely to get involved. One student had a unique idea. She said if she were attacked, she would pick up the nearest rock, but instead of throwing it at her attacker she would heave it through somebody's window. As a result, the police would be called, although the motive would be self-interest rather than helping.*

DARLEY: On your analysis, you get help in passing. The act performed by another person to help himself will also help you. A clever suggestion, but is it a serious one? Here is another possibility: In a suburb of Chicago which used to have a high rate of mugging and crime, many of the residents now have police whistles. The instruction simply is: When you hear potential trouble, blow your whistle. In this manner trouble can be localized quite quickly. That, in a way, is training to overcome diffusion, and it seems to be quite successful.

KRUPAT: *I agree that's a useful idea, but I must admit that I don't think the original idea is quite as frivolous as it might appear if we are cynical about people as helpers. When you yell "Fire," the person will help you to help himself, so to speak. Perhaps that's the only reason for which a person will help.*

DARLEY: My impression is, looking back over a good many experiments, that very few of our subjects are concerned only with helping themselves. By and large, they do seem to be concerned with getting help for other people, even when there is no obvious payoff to themselves for doing so.

KRUPAT: *But still, the title of your book is* The Unresponsive Bystander: Why Doesn't He Help? *The implication seems obvious that, in most cases, he doesn't help as much as you think he ought to.*

DARLEY: Certainly he doesn't help as often as an outside observer who is not aware of the specific circumstances thinks he should.

KRUPAT: *Then, how can we change things; what can we do that will make for a society of helpers?*

DARLEY: Well, a reasonable number of people are trying important practical things that are consistent with (I hardly want to say follow from) our research: suicide prevention centers, hot lines, whistle experiments in Chicago, the Bell Telephone Company making it possible to call the police without having to find a dime. So there are a reasonable number of specific practical things we can suggest.

But a second level of suggestion involves becoming more aware of the social processes that affect all of us. We can become more aware that we can be victims of conformity pressures, and being aware of that, we can deal with it and can overcome it. But these are not inevitable processes. That is, knowing that we pick up our definitions of events from other people, when confronted with ambiguity we can say, "Wait a minute. You and I are both confused about this, I think. If you are, let's talk about it and let's see what we ought to do in response." And social psychologists can teach about these processes to people, if people can only sit through our lectures.

AN INTRODUCTION TO THE READINGS

This section begins with the report of a study undertaken by Perry London and his colleagues, who asked themselves why people would risk their lives to save others. Specifically, they wanted to see if it were possible to identify a set of traits shared by non-Jews who had helped save Jews in Nazi Germany during World War II. Through intensive interviews, the researchers did find a set of characteristics that were more or less common to these people. It was not that they were especially warm or sympathetic to Jews, nor that they were particularly anti-Nazi; rather, they were generally adventurous, they were socially marginal, and they strongly identified with an extremely moral parent.

While the London study does suggest that the identification of some characteristics of helpers may eventually be possible, traditional paper-and-pencil measures have not so far been successful. As a result, we are led, once again, to the investigation of situational as well as individual determinants of helping behavior. The Latané and Darley article reviews a series of their now-classic studies—studies that were motivated by a question directly opposite to the one London began with. They asked: Why is it that people do *not* help? And their findings indicate that people may fail to help for one of the following reasons: because they fail to notice the event; because they fail to define the situation as an emergency; or because they fail to take personal responsibility for action. Contradictory to the notion that there is safety in numbers, the evidence of Latané and Darley suggests that the presence of other people may actually deter any *single* individual from acting. Their research demonstrates that the presence of others may sometimes lead people away from defining the situation as one requiring action, and may also diffuse the responsibility for action among observers to an emergency. That is, any given individual may feel less of a personal necessity to intervene, believing that "someone else will do it" or "If he won't, why should I?"

In the next paper, Daniel Batson and his colleagues addressed another set of issues that John Darley raised in our conversation, phrasing their question in terms of the Parable of the Good Samaritan. In an experiment, they had half of their subjects feel as if they ought to be in a hurry to get to another place and half not in a hurry. In addition, subjects felt that others were either highly dependent on them to arrive or not. On the way, all subjects encountered an experimental confederate moaning, coughing, and generally in need of aid. The dilemma: Whether to stop and help one person in immediate need of aid at the expense of many others who are highly dependent on you. Based on their findings, the authors suggest that often it is the case of conflicting demands, not callousness that helps explain a person's decision not to help.

The final paper deals with helping somewhat differently—not from the perspective of the giver but from the perspective of the potential recipient. Experimenters in the research by Ellen Langer and Robert Abelson approached people in the street and asked for a favor. They offered either a legitimate excuse ("Could you mail something for me, I have to catch a train") or an illegitimate one ("I have to go to Macy's"). In addition, they either used a victim-oriented approach (directing attention to their *own* need) or one that was target oriented (directed toward the "duty" of the potential helper). They found that in order to get the most help, it is not enough to have a legitimate reason for needing aid, but that it is also important for attention to be drawn to one's need.

PERRY LONDON

The Rescuers:
Motivational Hypotheses About Christians Who Saved Jews From the Nazis

The study I am going to describe was never completed, and since the sample involved was small and specialized and the data obtained from it were broad and complex, they were never formally analyzed. Even so, the history of the study, its problems, its potentials, and the hypotheses to which it led, all seemed so provocative and germane to understanding altruism that we felt it would be worth reporting despite its anecdotal limitations. Essentially a personality research project, its aim was to find out if there are stable traits of character connected with the extremely altruistic acts such as those in which the Christians in Nazi-occupied Europe risked their lives trying to save Jews. . . .

The idea for the study originated in the mind of Rabbi Harold Schulweis of Oakland, California; and James H. Bryan of Northwestern University, Robert Kurtzman of the Jerusalem Municipality, David Rosenhan of Swarthmore College, and I did the study collaboratively.

Our initial goal was to identify Christians who had, to one degree or another, risked their lives in an effort to rescue Jews from the Nazis all over Europe. We then wanted to see if we could, in the course of interviewing them, identify some stable personality traits or characteristics which might be related to altruism. If we succeeded in isolating such traits, we hoped to undertake a number of systematic studies to compare different kinds of altruistic behavior in different social contexts, to compare altruistic with other kinds of interpersonal behavior, and eventually to sneak up on a general understanding of the personal and situational dynamics of social deviance. The study of the rescuers seemed ideally suited to launch all of this, not so much because of its inherent drama and historical interest as because of its inherent complexity and the demands it placed on us for confronting important problems of theory and method. . . .

Our strategy for the pilot study was quite straightforward. We developed a standardized interview schedule, and began seeking out rescuers and rescued people who had moved to the United States. We did a number of interviews in this country, but Kurtzman did most of them in Israel. Although many of those we contacted were reluctant to grant us an interview at first, all of them finally agreed to talk to us and, once they started talking, willingly gave us the information we sought. We ended up with tape-recorded interviews of 27 rescuers and 42 rescued people, all of whom had emigrated from Europe since 1945. These people may be consistently different in important characteristics from rescuers who stayed in Europe. Thus, we cannot generalize from this sample to the majority of those who aided Jews during World War II. The following discussion, then, concerns a limited, albeit interesting, population of rescuers.

THE INTERVIEWING PATTERN

Our interview schedules were constructed in a way that allowed them to be used across several different samples, to be coded for quantitative analysis, and to yield a maximum of biographical information, as well as to tap attitudes and values. . . . The general pattern of the interviews, in all cases, was to begin by asking the subject to tell, in his own words, what the relevant incidents were, then to inquire about the background events that led to them, and only parenthetically to ask about personal details, attitudes, and seemingly incidental aspects of the individual's experience which would fill in the information we were seeking about personality characteristics. The interviewer worked with a detailed checklist of subject areas, all of which had to be completed before he could terminate the session (or series), and none of which had to be taken in any special order. From the subject's own point of view, therefore, much of the personal information he communicated was spontaneous, and the setting, despite checklists and tape recorders, was friendly and informal. From the interviewer's point of view, he was able to approach sensitive material obliquely and tactfully, without being secretive or deceptive and without sacrificing questions that he needed to ask, or making the subject feel uncomfortable or "like a guinea pig." Since all the rescuers available to us for the pilot study had already experienced some publicity, they were understandably sensitive on these scores.

The limited extent of the study prevented us from drawing "conclusions," but it did not stop us from gaining "impressions," two sets of which deserve communication. The first, derived from the variety of material revealed in our interviews, concerns the enormous complexity of defining altruism and studying it meaningfully. The second, deduced from apparent consistencies in the material, suggests to us some hypotheses about personality traits that may predispose people to altruistic acts.

DEFINITION OF ALTRUISM

Almost from the beginning it was clear that no easy criterion existed for deciding what kind of rescues to consider altruistic actions. In some cases, an individual's rescue effort was a small part of an underground organization's activity which involved little personal risk to the rescuer. In others, rescue efforts involved life-or-death risks, sometimes so often that they became almost routine for the rescuer. In still a third type of case the rescuer began helping someone in a relatively safe or minor way and, as circumstances changed, found himself embroiled in major ways because there was no longer a safe or easy alternative.

We often think of altruism in terms of relatively simple motives and acts, defining an altruist as one who confers a benefit on someone else without profit to himself, or without intention of profiting from his act, or with positive motives to be helpful. The behavior of rescuers cannot easily be classified by any simplistic definition, however. Some were paid a great deal of money for their efforts, usually in connection with essential parts of their operations, such as buying forged papers, food, or arms, or bribing officials. Some spent fortunes and were left destitute as a result. Some who had almost nothing to begin with shared it with good grace—or without.

In all of the behavioral categories indicated, motives were still less easily classified than were activities—because motives change, because they were conflicting, or because they were obscure. Some rescuers undertook the work deliberately and with benevolence aforethought, in utter secrecy sometimes, and with no possibility of outside help; others began it as an incidental part of other work, responding essentially to social pressure to participate and to social reinforcement for doing so; still others "fell in" to the rescue business thoughtlessly, mistakenly, or for irrelevant or selfish reasons. Some rescuers were fanatically religious, others were devout atheists. Some were deeply affiliated with Jews, others were anti-Semitic. And on and on.

It is difficult to estimate how often initial involvement with rescue work was confounded with a misunderstanding of the risks involved or of how long it might be necessary to continue taking them, but it was not a rare event in our sample. The most famous rescuer we interviewed, a German who devoted himself for almost 4 years to this work at fantastic personal cost and saved about 200 people, reported his initiation into the business with retrospective good humor, as follows: "I was believing in 1942 that the war will be another year. It cannot be any longer. It's impossible. I was then a rich man, I had about 300,000 or 400,000 marks, and I started with one person, then six people, from there to 50, then 100. . . . People came to me—maybe they like my looks—I don't know what it was—asking me very bluntly and very frankly, 'Will you save me?' "

It began, for him, when his secretary came to him, said that the Germans were going to kill her Jewish husband, and asked for help. He thought at first that she was crazy, and told her, "Germans don't do things like that!" But she was convinced that they were going to kill all the Jews in town so, although he felt it was not true, he agreed to let her husband stay in his office over the weekend. Through this act of compassion he found himself in the business of rescue. Once he found that the Jews' fears were justified, he was pulled in deeper and deeper. He had access to resources that few others had, he had compassion for his hapless clients, and he had the personal resources of wit, tenacity, and courage to remain with it for years.

There were several such cases on a small scale, where a rescuer had taken someone for a few nights until some underground organization would transport them over the border or they could otherwise escape. The pickup or the opportunity to leave never came and the rescuer's choice was turning the people over to the Nazis, which meant death, or keeping them—hiding the adult, passing the child off as his own.

PERSONALITY TRAITS OF RESCUERS

Even though starting to do rescue work may have been a function of situational variables or miscalculations, sticking with it for long periods of time usually was not. In the course of our interviews, we formulated three hypotheses about structural personality traits which would seem to be related to altruistic behavior. These characteristics were: (a) A spirit of adventurousness, (b) an intense identification with a parental model of moral conduct, and (c) a sense of being socially marginal.

Fondness for Adventure

Almost all the rescuers interviewed, regardless of where they came from and of what they did to fall into our sample, seemed to possess a fondness for adventure. They had not only a desire to help, but also a desire to participate in what were inherently exciting activities. For example, we interviewed a man from the Netherlands who responded to a question about his recreational preferences by describing what had been his favorite adolescent hobby—racing motorcycles, especially over narrow boards on top of deep ditches. His work as a rescuer in the Dutch underground was a fairly tame job, but he and his friends had a sort of extracurricular hobby of putting sugar in the gas tanks of German army trucks. This was not part of any organized sabotage, just something they did for fun. His daughter was present during the interview, and he asked her if she remembered the underground jobs that she had done. Since she had been about 5 years old at the time she did not remember much, so he described for us how she had carried papers hidden under loaves of bread on her bicycle from one part of town to another. They assumed, apparently correctly, that the Germans would not stop a little girl on a bicycle. Had they discovered the nature of her errand, they might have killed her and her family. In telling about these episodes, the father did not dwell much on the danger involved; he described them as great adventures. If thoughts about the danger occurred to him, as they surely must have, then either they did not faze him or he had long since forgotten that aspect of the events.

A number of people described in varying degrees their general adventurousness. One East European rescuer spontaneously described a sort of private anti-Fascist campaign he conducted in several places after World War II, evidently blowing up the property of assorted extreme right-wing organizations and apparently becoming much sought after by the police.

The German rescuer mentioned earlier had been a Nazi party member in 1934, was thrown out for denouncing a local party leader (not for ideological reasons but because he didn't like him and "had something on him" he could make public), and successfully avoided the draft—something quite rare in Germany in World War II. His civilian skills were important to the German war effort, and this put him in a position where he was able to develop an elaborate rescue operation which involved an underground railroad 1000 kilometers long and included many phony branch offices of his railroad engineering business. Most of this was accomplished after he had a severe heart attack from which he never completely recovered.

Along with the efficiency and genius of this man went a wild adventurous streak, perhaps best illustrated, in a story well documented by the Polish government, by his colorful rescue of a Polish underground leader from jail. He did this by walking into the place and telling the jailers that he had secret verbal orders to take the man; they were too secret to be written and from too high a source to be questioned, implying that the orders came from Hitler. The jailers let him take the man out. Asked how he worked up the nerve for this scheme, he gleefully told the interviewers, "You have to understand the German mentality! I know, I'm a German, and you have to know how to talk to Germans. You have to be authoritative and you have to bluff them, and that's what I did!"

Two other personal characteristics that our subjects seemed to share gave rise to a single hypothesis. We observed, first of all, that almost all the rescuers tended to have very strong identifications with parents, usually more with one parent than with the other, but not necessarily with the same-sex parent. Second, the parent with whom they had the strong identification tended to be a very strong moralist— not necessarily religious, but holding very firm opinions on moral issues and serving as a model of moral conduct.

Identification With A Moralizing Parent

The strong identification with a moralizing parent is clear in the interview with the German rescuer. "I come from a poor family. My mother came from Hesse which was mainly small farmers. . . . I believe that is part of my personality. You inherit something from your parents, from the grandparents. My mother said to me when we were small, and even when we were bigger, she said to me—she ran the family, my mother, and my father was number two; he could not speak so much in front of people—'Regardless of what you do with your life, be honest. When it comes the day you have to make a decision, make the right one. It could be a hard one. But even the hard ones should be the right ones.' I didn't know what it means. . . ."

He went on to talk about his mother in glowing terms, about how she had told him how to live, how she had taught him morals, and how she had exemplified morality for him. Asked if she was a member of a church, "Sure, we had to be," he said. "Protestant?" we asked. "Lutheran Protestant—that is another thing. Protest is Protestant. I protest. Maybe I inherit it from way back . . . my mother . . . always in life she gave me so much philosophy. She didn't go to high school, only elementary school, but so smart a woman, wisdom, you know. It is born in you. . . ."

When he later described his father at greater length, he said his father was weak and incapable of raising the children, that his father did not set the moral standards for the family, and that his father's moral posture was not significant for the family, only his mother's.

Social Marginality

The final characteristic we noted often among our rescuers was social marginality. The German, for example, grew up in Prussia, but his mother was from Hesse and spoke a different German dialect than that common in Prussia. He said that he always felt friendless. His family was nominally Lutheran, but his mother refused to go to church, although his father went—probably the reverse of a typical German family's religious habits. His mother had no political affiliation, but was a fierce anti-Nazi. He himself grew up stuttering (a habit of which he successfully cured himself). Apparently these experiences in marginality served him well when he had to work in isolation for 4 years. His rescue work was originally in Russia, and his underground network eventually spread into Western Europe, involving hundreds of people without his ever revealing his activities to more than two people other than those he actually rescued.

Social marginality and intense identification with one parent were not always obviously related to each other. A Belgian woman who spent years in Nos Petits, the Belgian underground, came from a family that lived for generations in the same house in the same town, characteristics we found among many in our sample. This woman so strongly identified with her father and in describing her family talked so glowingly and at such length about him that the interviewer had the impression her mother was dead. At some point he asked outright if her mother "was also living at home." She answered, "Yes. My father was in business before the great depression, he was sort of a self-made man, very bright man. He had a lot of social confidence. That was the atmosphere at home." She made no other reference to her mother. Her social marginality did not involve her relationship with her parents, however, but her intense personal involvement with Jews.

The strong parental identification does not seem to have been related to any gender link. Another rescuer we interviewed was a Seventh Day Adventist minister who very strongly identified with his father, also an Adventist minister from the Netherlands, a country where almost everyone is either Calvinist or Catholic. Seventh Day Adventists were very marginal socially and not always treated kindly in Holland; his father spent considerable time in jail. Although this minister described himself as mildly anti-Semitic, like his father, during the war he organized a very effective and large-scale operation for rescuing Dutch Jews. The reason he gave for doing so was simply that it was a Christian's duty.

Some kind of active moralism seemed characteristic of all the rescuers and usually was related to parental morality rather than to a specific kind of ideology. The Dutch minister saw himself as motivated by a transcendental religious doctrine, the German and Belgian rescuers by clearly social kinds of morality, but all were acting out roles which their moral parental models would have lauded on the same grounds.

The same general attributes seem to pertain to other rescuers, even when described only briefly. There was a Polish woman who hid two girls from the Nazis throughout the war. During the war she picked up a Russian prisoner and hid him too. She was of peasant origin, self-educated, a devout, informed Roman Catholic, extremely honest and exacting of herself and others. She was a schoolteacher, rather unpopular because she set high standards, was critical of others, intolerant of the slightest hypocrisy, and an independent thinker. In history classes, for example, she eschewed false patriotism and was even critical of Polish national unity—a very unusual stand in Poland. In Communist Poland, therefore, she preferred teaching at the elementary level to avoid voicing her views. She was against the communist regime, and, although she was appreciative of the universal education available, she complained that students in postwar Poland lacked interest and discipline and were indifferent to values. Her husband, like his father and sister, was an Anthropopathist. She told us she was a practicing religionist because this expressed her nonconformity and gave her a challenge. Although in many opinions quite liberal, she was a person of puritanical and Spartan habits, with low tolerance for physical weakness and pampering.

A final example is a woman whose father was a miner; he foresaw the massacre of the Jews and became involved in helping save some. He was supposedly killed in a mine accident, but was possibly murdered. His daughter and wife carried on this man's work after his death. The daughter, whom we interviewed, had been in bad health, but with the great responsibilities she assumed— including an increasing risk to her life—her health improved. She even replaced her father in the mines. When we talked to her, she told us that she believed the holocaust happened because the Jews did not keep the laws of the Bible, and that the destruction visited upon them would soon engulf other people. She had a fanatical belief in a God of rewards and punishments, and felt that her reward for helping the Jews was improved health. Later she suffered a mental breakdown, during which she quoted passages from the Old Testament to prove that man suffers for his own misdeeds.

SUMMARY

In summary, it seemed to us that a zest for adventure and the workings of chance both were important in the initiation of rescue behavior, but that, in all of those we interviewed, strong identification with a very moralistic parental model and the experience of social marginality gave people the impetus and endurance to continue their rescue activities. This identification did not seem to be related to extraordinary warmth or closeness in family relationships, to general adequacy of parental models, or to the rescuer's social competence; it seemed, in fact, to be more often positively related to social marginality. I should point out again that all of the people we interviewed were a long way from their native country at the time we talked to them, and perhaps rescuers who did not emigrate were not marginal people. Not all of our sample, moreover, expressed feelings of marginality though circumstances often were such that the interviewer could not help but infer it. What was expressed directly most often was the admiration for a parent or adherence to his strong moralistic opinions.

The gaps in our data are so great that we cannot even conjecture about the generality of our hypotheses. The situations which favored or inhibited rescue work in different countries of Europe and at different times should have been separately considered. Differences in Nazi policy or ability to implement it, the sentiments of the civilian population toward the Jews, the effectiveness of resistance movements, even the physical terrain were all interacting factors in the survival or destruction of the Jews and, to some extent, in the initiation or success of rescue work. We lacked means to sample separately by these categories, or to learn who died, or where, in rescue work, or to probe who perhaps did not persist in it and finally betrayed their clients. The original design of the study was to compare among people still living in each country representative samples of rescuers, nonparticipants, and known collaborators. Our initial thought was that, in terms of personality characteristics, we might find the same general traits among collaborationists and rescuers; that is, we would find similarities among people whose behavior was deviant in either direction from general social reactions to Nazi occupation. None of this was possible for us to do, though a number of excellent documentation centers in Europe, Israel, and America make the work of identification and location quite feasible.

One must not forget, however, how small the total population of rescuers was to begin with. The complete survey we had hoped to do could only have emphasized the gruesome truth that while most people in Nazi-occupied Europe did not collaborate with the Germans in the massacre of the Jews, neither did they take active steps to prevent or interfere with it. This very fact gives the tiny ''saving remnant'' an importance entirely disproportionate to their numbers. Their capacity for individual action on behalf of fellow men and in the face of social isolation or of lethal peril is a hopeful augur for preserving human dignity and decency in a steadily more complex and imperiled world.

BIBB LATANÉ
JOHN M. DARLEY

Social Determinants of Bystander Intervention in Emergencies

Almost 100 years ago, Charles Darwin wrote: "As man is a social animal, it is almost certain that he would . . . from an inherited tendency be willing to defend, in concert with others, his fellowmen; and be ready to aid them in any way, which did not too greatly interfere with his own welfare or his own strong desires" (*The Descent of Man.*). Today, although many psychologists would quarrel with Darwin's assertion that altruism is inherited, most would agree that men will go to the aid of others even when there is no visible gain for themselves. At least, most would have agreed until a March night in 1964. That night, Kitty Genovese was set upon by a maniac as she returned home from work at 3:00 A.M. Thirty-eight of her neighbors in Kew Gardens came to their windows when she cried out in terror; but none came to her assistance, even though her stalker took over half an hour to murder her. No one even so much as called the police.

Since we started our research on bystander response to emergencies, we have heard about dozens of such incidents. We have also heard many explanations: "I would assign this to the effect of the megalopolis in which we live, which makes closeness very difficult and leads to the alienation of the individual from the group," contributed a psychoanalyst. "A disaster syndrome," explained a sociologist, "that shook the sense of safety and sureness of the individuals involved and caused psychological withdrawal from the event by ignoring it." "Apathy," others claim. "Indifference." "The gratification of unconscious sadistic impulses." "Lack of concern for our fellow men." "The Cold Society." These explanations and many more have been applied to the surprising failure of bystanders to intervene in emergencies—failures which suggest that we no longer care about the fate of our neighbors.

But can this be so? We think not. Although it is unquestionably true that the witnesses in the incidents above did nothing to save the victim, "apathy," "indifference," and "unconcern" are not entirely accurate descriptions of their reactions. The 38 witnesses of Kitty Genovese's murder did not merely look at the scene once and then ignore it. Instead they continued to stare out of their windows at what was going on. Caught, fascinated, distressed, unwilling to act but unable to turn away, their behavior was neither helpful nor heroic; but it was not indifferent or apathetic either.

Actually, it was like crowd behavior in many other emergency situations; car accidents, drownings, fires, and attempted suicides all attract substantial numbers of people who watch the drama in helpless fascination without getting directly involved in the action. Are these people alienated and indifferent? Are the rest of us? Obviously not. It seems only yesterday we were being called overconforming. But why, then, do we not act?

Paradoxically, the key to understanding these failures of intervention may be found exactly in the fact that so surprises us about them: so many bystanders fail to intervene. If we think of 38, or 11, or 100 individuals, each looking at an emergency and callously deciding to pass by, we are horrified. But if we realize that each bystander is picking up cues about what is happening and how to react to it from the other bystanders, understanding begins to emerge. There are several ways in which a crowd of onlookers can make each individual member of that crowd less likely to act.

DEFINING THE SITUATION

Most emergencies are, or at least begin as, ambiguous events. A quarrel in the street may erupt into violence or it may be simply a family argument. A man staggering about may be suffering a coronary, or an onset of diabetes, or he simply may be drunk. Smoke pouring from a building may signal a fire, but on the other hand, it may be simply steam or air-conditioner vapor. Before a bystander is likely to take action in such ambiguous situations, he must first define the event as an emergency and decide that intervention is the proper course of action.

In the course of making these decisions, it is likely that an individual bystander will be considerably influenced by the decisions he perceives other bystanders to be taking. If everyone else in a group of onlookers seems to regard an event as nonserious and the proper course of action as nonintervention, this consensus may strongly affect the perceptions of any single individual and inhibit his potential intervention.

The definitions that other people hold may be discovered by discussing the situation with them, but they may also be inferred from their facial expressions or behavior. A whistling man with his hands in his pockets obviously does not believe he is in the midst of a crisis. A bystander who does not respond to smoke obviously does not attribute it to a fire. An individual, seeing the inaction of others, will judge the situation as less serious than he would if alone.

But why should the others be inactive? Probably because they are aware that other people are also watching them. The others are an audience to their own reactions. Among American males, it is considered desirable to appear poised and collected in times of stress. Being exposed to the public view may constrain the actions and expressions of emotion of any individual as he tries to avoid possible ridicule and embarrassment. Even though he may be truly concerned and upset about the plight of a victim, until he decides what to do, he may maintain a calm demeanor.

If each member of a group is, at the same time, trying to appear calm and also looking around at the other members to gauge their reactions, all members may be led (or misled) by each other to define the situation as less critical than they would if alone. Until someone acts, each person sees only other nonresponding bystanders and is likely to be influenced not to act himself. A state of "pluralistic ignorance" may develop.

It has often been recognized that a crowd can cause contagion of panic, leading each person in the crowd to overreact to an emergency to the detriment of everyone's welfare. What we suggest here is that a crowd can also force inaction on its members. It can suggest by its passive behavior that an event is not to be reacted to as an emergency, and it can make any individual uncomfortably aware of what a fool he will look for behaving as if it is.

Where There's Smoke, There's (Sometimes) Fire[1]

In this experiment we presented an emergency to individuals either alone or in groups of three. It was our expectation that the constraints on behavior in public combined with social influence processes would lessen the likelihood that members of three-person groups would act to cope with the emergency.

College students were invited to an interview to discuss "some of the problems involved in life at an urban university." As they sat in a small room waiting to be called for the interview and filling out a preliminary questionnaire, they faced an ambiguous but potentially dangerous situation. A stream of smoke began to puff into the room through a wall vent.

Some subjects were exposed to this potentially critical situation while alone. In a second condition, three naive subjects were tested together. Since subjects arrived at slightly different times, and since they each had individual questionnaires to work on, they did not introduce themselves to each other or attempt anything but the most rudimentary conversation.

As soon as the subjects had completed two pages of their questionnaires, the experimenter began to introduce the smoke through a small vent in the wall. The "smoke," copied from the famous Camel cigarette sign in Times Square, formed a moderately fine-textured but clearly visible stream of whitish smoke. It continued to jet into the room in irregular puffs, and by the end of the experimental period, it obscured vision.

All behavior and conversation were observed and coded from behind a one-way window (largely disguised on the subject's side by a large sign giving preliminary instructions). When and if the subject left the experimental room and reported the smoke, he was told that the situation "would be taken care of." If the subject had not reported the smoke within 6 minutes from the time he first noticed it, the experiment was terminated.

The typical subject, when tested alone, behaved very reasonably. Usually, shortly after the smoke appeared, he would glance up from his questionnaire, notice the smoke, show a slight but distinct startle reaction, and then undergo a brief period of indecision, perhaps returning briefly to his questionnaire before again staring at the smoke. Soon, most subjects would get up from their chairs, walk over to the vent and investigate it closely, sniffing the smoke, waving their hands in it, feeling its temperature, etc. The usual Alone subject would hesitate again, but finally would walk out of the room, look around outside, and, finding somebody there, calmly report the presence of the smoke. No subject showed any sign of panic; most simply said: "There's something strange going on in there, there seems to be some sort of smoke coming through the wall . . . ." The median subject in the Alone condition had reported the smoke within 2 minutes of first noticing it. Three-quarters of the 24 people run in this condition reported the smoke before the experimental period was terminated.

Because there are three subjects present and available to report the smoke in the Three Naive Bystanders condition, as compared to only one subject at a time in the Alone condition, a simple comparison between the two conditions is not appropriate. We cannot compare speeds in the Alone condition with the average speed of the three subjects in a group because, once one subject in a group had reported the smoke, the pressures on the other two disappeared. They could feel legitimately that the emergency had been handled and that any action on their part would be redundant and potentially confusing. Therefore, we used the speed of the first subject in a group to report the smoke as our dependent variable. However, since there were three times as many people available to respond in this condition as in the Alone condition, we would expect an increased likelihood that at least one person would report the smoke by chance alone. Therefore, we mathematically created "groups" of three scores from the Alone condition to serve as a baseline.

In contrast to the complexity of this procedure, the results were quite simple. Subjects in the three-person-group condition were markedly inhibited from reporting the smoke. Since 75% of the Alone subjects reported the smoke, we would expect over 98% of the three-person groups to include at least one reporter. In fact, in only 38% of the eight groups in this condition did even one person report. Of the 24 people run in these eight groups, only one person reported the smoke within the first 4 minutes before the room got noticeably unpleasant. Only three people reported the smoke within the entire experimental period. Social inhibition of reporting was so strong that the smoke was reported faster when only one person saw it than when groups of three were present.

Subjects who had reported the smoke were relatively consistent in later describing their reactions to it. They thought the smoke looked somewhat "strange." They were not sure exactly what it was or whether it was dangerous, but they felt it was unusual enough to justify some examination. "I wasn't sure whether it was a fire, but it looked like something was wrong." "I thought it might be steam, but it seemed like a good idea to check it out."

Subjects who had not reported the smoke were also unsure about exactly what it was, but they uniformly said that they had rejected the idea that it was a fire. Instead, they hit upon an astonishing variety of alternative explanations, all sharing the common characteristic of interpreting the smoke as a nondangerous event. Many thought the smoke was either steam or air-conditioning vapors, several thought it was smog, purposely introduced to simulate an urban environment, and two actually suggested that the smoke was a "truth gas" filtered into the room to induce them to answer the questionnaire accurately! Predictably, some decided that "it must be some sort of experiment'' and stoically endured the discomfort of the room rather than overreact.

The results of this study clearly support the prediction. Groups of three naive subjects were less likely to report the smoke than solitary bystanders. Our predictions were confirmed—but this does not necessarily mean that our explanation of these results is the correct one. As a matter of fact, several alternative explanations center around the fact that the smoke represented a possible danger to the subject himself as well as to others in the building. For instance, it is possible that the subjects in groups saw themselves as engaged in a game of ''chicken'' in which the first person to report would admit his cowardliness. Or it may have been that the presence of others made subjects feel safer, and thus reduced their need to report.

To rule out such explanations, a second experiment was designed to see whether similar group inhibition effects could be observed in situations where there is no danger to the individual himself for not acting. In this study, male Columbia University undergraduates waited either alone or with a stranger to participate in a market research study. As they waited they heard a woman fall and apparently injure herself in the room next door. Whether they tried to help and how long they took to do so were the main dependent variables of the study.

The Fallen Woman[2]

Subjects were telephoned and offered $2 to participate in a survey of game and puzzle preferences conducted at Columbia by the Consumer Testing Bureau (CTB), a market research organization. When they arrived, they were met at the door by an attractive young woman and taken to the testing room. On the way, they passed the CTB office, and through its open door they were able to see a desk and bookcase piled high with papers and filing cabinets. They entered the adjacent testing room, which contained a table and chairs and a variety of games, and they were given questionnaires to fill out. The representative told subjects that she would be working next door in her office for about 10 minutes while they were completing the questionnaire, and left by opening the collapsible curtain which divided the two rooms. She made sure that subjects were aware that the curtain was unlocked and easily opened and that it provided a means of entry to her office. The representative stayed in her office, shuffling papers, opening drawers, and making enough noise to remind the subjects of her presence. Four minutes after leaving the testing area, she turned on a high-fidelity stereophonic tape recorder.

The Emergency. If the subject listened carefully, he heard the representative climb up on a chair to reach for a stack of papers on the bookcase. Even if he were not listening carefully, he heard a loud crash and a scream as the chair collapsed and she fell to the floor. ''Oh, my God, my foot . . . I . . . I . . . can't move . . . it. Oh . . . my ankle,'' the representative moaned. ''I . . . can't get this . . . thing . . . off me.'' She cried and moaned for about a minute longer, but the cries gradually got more subdued and controlled. Finally she muttered something about getting outside, knocked over the chair as she pulled herself up and thumped to the door, closing it behind her as she left. The entire incident took 130 seconds.

The main dependent variable of the study, of course, was whether the subjects took action to help the victim and how long it took them to do so. There were actually several modes of intervention possible: A subject could open the screen dividing the two rooms, leave the testing room and enter the CTB office by the door, find someone else, or most simply, call out to see if the representative needed help. In one condition, each subject was in the testing room alone while he filled out the questionnaire and heard the fall. In the second condition, strangers were placed in the testing room in pairs. Each subject in the pair was unacquainted with the other before entering the room and they were not introduced.

Across all experimental groups, the majority of subjects who intervened did so by pulling back the room divider and coming into the CTB office (61%). Few subjects came the round-about way through the door to offer their assistance (14%), and a surprisingly small number (24%) chose the easy solution of calling out to offer help. No one tried to find someone else to whom to report the accident.

Since 70% of Alone subjects intervened, we should expect that at least one person in 91% of all two-person groups would offer help if members of a pair had no influence upon each other. In fact, members did influence each other. In only 40% of the groups did even one person offer help to the injured woman. Only eight subjects of the 40 who were run in this condition intervened. This response rate is significantly below the hypothetical baseline. Social inhibition of helping was so strong that the victim was actually helped more quickly when only one person heard her distress than when two did.

When we talked to subjects after the experiment, those who intervened usually claimed that they did so either because the fall sounded very serious or because they were uncertain what had occurred and felt they should investigate. Many talked about intervention as the "right thing to do" and asserted they would help again in any situation.

Many of the noninterveners also claimed that they were unsure what had happened (59%), but had decided that it was not too serious (46%). A number of subjects reported that they thought other people would or could help (25%), and three said they refrained out of concern for the victim—they did not want to embarrass her. Whether to accept these explanations as reasons or rationalizations is moot—they certainly do not explain the differences among conditions. The important thing to note is that noninterveners did not seem to feel that they had behaved callously or immorally. Their behavior was generally consistent with their interpretation of the situation. Subjects almost uniformly claimed that in a "real" emergency they would be among the first to help the victim.

These results strongly replicate the findings of the Smoke study. In both experiments, subjects were less likely to take action if they were in the presence of others than if they were alone. This congruence of findings from different experimental settings supports the validity and generality of the phenomenon; it also helps rule out a variety of alternative explanations suitable to either situation alone. For example, the possibility that smoke may have represented a threat to the subject's personal safety and that subjects in groups may have had a greater concern to appear "brave" than single subjects does not apply to the present experiment. In the present experiment, nonintervention cannot signify bravery. Comparison of the two experiments also suggests that the absolute number of nonresponsive bystanders may not be a critical factor in producing social inhibition of intervention; pairs of strangers in the present study inhibited each other as much as did trios in the former study.

Other studies we have done show that group inhibition effects hold in real life as well as in the laboratory, and for members of the general population as well as college students. The results of these experiments clearly support the line of theoretical argument advanced earlier. When bystanders to an emergency can see the reactions of other people, and when other people can see their own reactions, each individual may, through a process of social influence, be led to interpret the situation as less serious than he would if he were alone, and consequently be less likely to take action.

These studies, however, tell us little about the case that stimulated our interest in bystander intervention: the Kitty Genovese murder. Although the 38 witnesses to that event were aware, through seeing lights and silhouettes in other windows, that others watched, they could not see what others were doing and thus be influenced by their reactions. In the privacy of their own apartments, they could not be clearly seen by others, and thus inhibited by their presence. The social influence process we have described above could not operate. Nevertheless, we think that the presence of other bystanders may still have affected each individual's response.

DIFFUSION OF RESPONSIBILITY

In addition to affecting the interpretations that he places on a situation, the presence of other people can also alter the rewards and costs facing an individual bystander. Perhaps most importantly, the presence of other people can reduce the cost of not acting. If only one bystander is present at an emergency, he carries all of the responsibility for dealing with it; he will feel all of the guilt for not acting; he will bear all of any blame others may level for nonintervention. If others are present, the onus of responsibility is diffused, and the individual may be more likely to resolve his conflict between intervening and not intervening in favor of the latter alternative.

When only one bystander is present at an emergency, if help is to come it must be from him. Although he may choose to ignore them out of concern for his personal safety, or desire "not to get involved," any pressures to intervene focus uniquely on him. When there are several observers present, however, the pressures to intervene do not focus on any one of the observers; instead, the responsibility for intervention is shared among all the onlookers and is not unique to any one. As a result, each may be less likely to help.

Potential blame may also be diffused. However much we wish to think that an individual's moral behavior is divorced from considerations of personal punishment or reward, there is both theory and evidence to the contrary. It is perfectly reasonable to assume that under circumstances of group responsibility for a punishable act, the punishment or blame that accrues to any one individual is often slight or nonexistent.

Finally, if others are known to be present, but their behavior cannot be closely observed, any one bystander may assume that one of the other observers is already taking action to end the emergency. If so, his own intervention would only be redundant—perhaps harmfully or confusingly so. Thus, given the presence of other onlookers whose behavior cannot be observed, any given bystander can rationalize his own inaction by convincing himself that "somebody else must be doing something."

These considerations suggest that even when bystanders to an emergency cannot see or be influenced by each other, the more bystanders who are present, the less likely any one bystander would be to intervene and provide aid. To test this suggestion, it would be necessary to create an emergency situation in which each subject is blocked from communicating with others to prevent his getting information about their behavior during the emergency.

A Fit to be Tried[3]

A college student arrived in the laboratory, and was ushered into an individual room from which a communication system would enable him to talk to other participants (who were actually figments of the tape recorder). Over the intercom, the subject was told that the experimenter was concerned with the kinds of personal problems faced by normal college students in a high-pressure, urban environment, and that he would be asked to participate in a discussion about these problems. To avoid embarrassment about discussing personal problems with strangers, the experimenter said, several precautions would be taken. First, subjects would remain anonymous, which was why they had been placed in individual rooms rather than face-to-face. Second, the experimenter would not listen to the initial discussion himself, but would only get the subject's reactions later by questionnaire.

The plan for the discussion was that each person would talk in turn for 2 minutes, presenting his problems to the group. Next, each person in turn would comment on what others had said, and finally there would be a free discussion. A mechanical switching device regulated the discussion, switching on only one microphone at a time.

The emergency.   The discussion started with the future victim speaking first. He said he found it difficult to get adjusted to New York and to his studies. Very hesitantly and with obvious embarrassment, he mentioned that he was prone to seizures, particularly when studying hard or taking exams. The other people, including the one real subject, took their turns and discussed similar problems (minus the proneness to seizures). The naive subject talked last in the series, after the last prerecorded voice.

When it was again the victim's turn to talk, he made a few relatively calm comments, and then, growing increasingly loud and incoherent, he continued:

> I er I think I I need er if if could er er somebody er er er er er er er give me a little er give me a little help because I er I'm er er h-h-having a a a a real problem er right now and I er if somebody could help me out it would er er s-s-sure be good . . . because er there er er a cause I er I uh I've got a a one of the er sie . . . er er things coming on and and and I could really er use some help so if somebody would er give me a little h-help uh er-er-er-er-er c-could somebody er er help er uh uh uh (choking sounds) . . . . I'm gonna die er er I'm . . . gonna die er help er er seizure (chokes, then quiet).

The major independent variable of the study was the number of people the subject believed also heard the fit. The subject was led to believe that the discussion group was one of three sizes: a two-person group consisting of himself and the victim; a three-person group consisting of himself, the victim and the other person; or a six-person group consisting of himself, the victim, and four other persons.

The major dependent variable of the experiment was the time elapsed from the start of the victim's seizure until the subject left his experimental cubicle. When the subject left his room, he saw the experimental assistant seated at the end of the hall, and invariably went to the assistant to report the seizure. If 5 minutes elapsed without the subject's having emerged from his room, the experiment was terminated.

Ninety-five percent of all the subjects who ever responded did so within the first half of the time available to them. No subject who had not reported within 3 minutes after the fit ever did so. This suggests that even had the experiment been allowed to run for a considerably longer period of time, few additional subjects would have responded.

Eighty-five percent of the subjects who thought they alone knew of the victim's plight reported the seizure before the victim was cut off; only 31% of those who thought four other bystanders were present did so. Every one of the subjects in the two-person condition, but only 62% of the subjects in the six-person condition ever reported the emergency. . . .

Subjects, whether or not they intervened, believed the fit to be genuine and serious. "My God, he's having a fit," many subjects said to themselves (and we overheard via their microphones). Others gasped or simply said, "Oh." Several of the male subjects swore. One subject said to herself, "It's just my kind of luck, something has to happen to me!" Several subjects spoke aloud of their confusion about what course of action to take: "Oh, God, what should I do?"

When those subjects who intervened stepped out of their rooms, they found the experimental assistant down the hall. With some uncertainty but without panic, they reported the situation. "Hey, I think Number 1 is very sick. He's having a fit or something." After ostensibly checking on the situation, the experimenter returned to report that "everything is under control." The subjects accepted these assurances with obvious relief.

Subjects who failed to report the emergency showed few signs of the apathy and indifference thought to characterize "unresponsive bystanders." When the experimenter entered the room to terminate the situation, the subject often asked if the victim was all right. "Is he being taken care of?" "He's all right, isn't he?" Many of these subjects showed physical signs of nervousness; they often had trembling hands and sweating palms. If anything, they seemed more emotionally aroused than did the subjects who reported the emergency.

Why, then, didn't they respond? It is not our impression that they had decided not to respond. Rather, they were still in a state of indecision and conflict concerning whether to respond or not. The emotional behavior of these nonresponding subjects was a sign of their continuing conflict, a conflict that other subjects resolved by responding.

The fit created a conflict situation of the avoidance-avoidance type. On the one hand, subjects worried about the guilt and shame they would feel if they did not help the person in distress. On the other hand, they were concerned not to make fools of themselves by overreacting, not to ruin the ongoing experiment by leaving their intercoms, and not to destroy the anonymous nature of the situation, which the experimenter had earlier stressed as important. For subjects in the two-person condition, the obvious distress of the victim and his need for help were so important that their conflict was easily resolved. For the subjects who knew that there were other bystanders present, the cost of not helping was reduced and the conflict they were in was more acute. Caught between the two negative alternatives of letting the victim continue to suffer or rushing, perhaps foolishly, to help, the nonresponding bystanders vacillated between them rather than choosing not to respond. This distinction may be academic for the victim, since he got no help in either case, but it is an extremely important one for understanding the causes of bystanders' failures to help.

Although subjects experienced stress and conflict during the emergency, their general reactions to it were highly positive. On a questionnaire administered after the experimenter had discussed the nature and purpose of the experiment, every single subject found the experiment either "interesting" or "very interesting" and was willing to participate in similar experiments in the future. All subjects felt that they understood what the experiment was all about and indicated that they thought the deceptions were necessary and justified. All but one felt they were better informed about the nature of psychological research in general.

CONCLUSION

We have suggested two distinct processes which might lead people to be less likely to intervene in an emergency if there are other people present than if they are alone. On the one hand, we suggested that the presence of other people may affect the interpretations each bystander puts on an ambiguous emergency situation. If other people are present at an emergency, each bystander will be guided by their apparent reactions in formulating his own impressions. Unfortunately, their apparent reactions may not be a good indication of their true feelings. It is possible for a state of "pluralistic ignorance" to develop, in which each bystander is led by the apparent lack of concern of the others to interpret the situation as being less serious than he would if alone. To the extent that he does not feel the situation is an emergency, he will be unlikely to take any helpful action.

Even if an individual does decide that an emergency is actually in process and that something ought to be done, he still is faced with the choice of whether he himself will intervene. Here again, the presence of other people may influence him—by reducing the costs associated with nonintervention. If a number of people witness the same event, the responsibility for action is diffused, and each may feel less necessity to help.

"There's safety in numbers," according to an old adage, and modern city dwellers seem to believe it. They shun deserted streets, empty subway cars, and lonely dark walks in dark parks, preferring instead to go where others are or to stay at home. When faced with stress, most individuals seem less afraid when they are in the presence of others than when they are alone.

A feeling so widely shared should have some basis in reality. Is there safety in numbers? If so, why? Two reasons are often suggested: Individuals are less likely to find themselves in trouble if there are others about, and even if they do find themselves in trouble, others are likely to help them deal with it. While it is certainly true that a victim is unlikely to receive help if nobody knows of his plight, the experiments above cast doubt on the suggestion that he will be more likely to receive help if more people are present. In fact, the opposite seems to be true. A victim may be more likely to get help, or an emergency be reported, the fewer the people who are available to take action.

Although the results of these studies may shake our faith in "safety in numbers," they also may help us begin to understand a number of frightening incidents where crowds have heard but not answered a call for help. Newspapers have tagged these incidents with the label, "apathy." We have become indifferent, they say, callous to the fate of suffering of others. Our society has become "dehumanized" as it has become urbanized. These glib phrases may contain some truth, since startling cases such as the Genovese murder often seem to occur in our large cities, but such terms may also be misleading. Our studies suggest a different conclusion. They suggest that situational factors, specifically factors involving the immediate social environment, may be of greater importance in determining an individual's reaction to an emergency than such vague cultural or personality concepts as "apathy" or "alienation due to urbanization." They suggest that the failure to intervene may be better understood by knowing the relationship among bystanders rather than that between a bystander and the victim.

NOTES

1. A more complete account of this experiment is provided in Latané and Darley (1968). Keith Gerritz and Lee Ross provided thoughtful assistance in running the study.
2. This experiment is more fully described in Latané and Rodin (1969).
3. Further details of this experiment can be found in Darley and Latané (1968).

REFERENCES

Darley, J. M., and Latané, B. Bystander intervention in emergencies: Diffusion of responsibility. *Journal of Personality and Social Psychology*, 1968, **8**, 377–383.

Latané, B., & Darley, J. M. Group inhibition of bystander intervention. *Journal of Personality and Social Psychology*, 1968, **10**, 215–221.

Latané, B., & Rodin, J. A lady in distress: Inhibiting effects of friends and strangers on bystander intervention. *Journal of Experimental Social Psychology*, 1969, **5**, 189–202.

Outside of a Small Circle of Friends

Look outside the window, there's a
woman being grabbed.
They dragged her to the bushes, and
now she's being stabbed.
Maybe we should call the cops and try
to stop the pain,
But Monopoly is so much fun, I'd hate
to blow the game.
And I'm sure it wouldn't interest anybody outside of a small circle of friends.

Riding down the highway, yes, my
back is getting stiff.
Thirteen cars have piled up—they're
hanging on a cliff.
Maybe we should pull them back with
our towing-chain,
But we gotta move, and we might get
sued, and it looks like it's gonna rain.
And I'm sure it wouldn't interest anybody outside of a small circle of friends.

Sweating in the ghetto with the Pan-
thers and the poor.
The rats have joined the babies who
are sleeping on the floor.
Now, wouldn't it be a riot if they really
blew their tops,
But they got too much already, and
besides we got the cops.
And I'm sure it wouldn't interest anybody outside of a small circle of friends.

There's a dirty paper using sex to
make a sale.
The Supreme Court was so upset they
sent him off to jail.

Maybe we should help the fiend and
take away his fine,
But we're busy reading Playboy and
The Sunday New York Times.
And I'm sure it wouldn't interest any-
body outside of a small circle of friends.

Smoking marijuana is more fun than
drinking beer,
But a friend of ours was captured; and
they gave him thirty years.
Maybe we should raise our voices, ask
somebody why;
But demonstrations are a drag,
besides we're much too high.
And I'm sure it wouldn't interest anybody outside of a small circle of friends.

Look outside the window, there's a
woman being grabbed.
They dragged her to the bushes, and
now she's being stabbed.
Maybe we should call the cops and try
to stop the pain,
But Monopoly is so much fun, I'd hate
to blow the game.
And I'm sure it wouldn't interest anybody outside of a small circle of friends.

Phil Ochs

C. DANIEL BATSON
PAMELA J. COCHRAN
MARSHALL F. BIEDERMAN
JAMES L. BLOSSER
MAURICE J. RYAN
BRUCE VOGT

Failure to Help When in a Hurry:
Callousness or Conflict?

Darley and Batson (1973) reported data indicating that individuals in a hurry were less likely to help someone in possible need. It is not clear, however, why those in a hurry help less. Perhaps they are more intensely goal-oriented than persons with time on their hands. Attending to a narrower cognitive map (Tolman, 1948), they may be less likely to process goal-irrelevant information (Milgram, 1973; Schroder, Driver, & Streufert, 1967). As a result, they may fail to recognize others' needs. Or, harried and concerned with being on time, individuals in a hurry may be consumed with self-concern (Berkowitz, 1970; Duval & Wicklund, 1972), and so be less empathic (Krebs, 1975). They may recognize others' needs but care less about them.

These arguments suggest that acceleration of our pace of life may have serious implications for prosocial behavior. We may become increasingly callous, less likely to recognize others' suffering or to care about reducing it. But there is another possibility. If, as in Darley and Batson's (1973) simulation of the parable of the Good Samaritan, a person is hurrying because someone is depending on him to get to a particular place quickly, he is caught in a bind. Does he stop and offer aid to a stranger who seems to be in need and, by stopping, risk failing to reach his destination on time? Or does he ignore the stranger and respond to the needs of those who are counting on him to hurry?

Faced with this zero-sum conflict, he may be forced to decide who needs his help most. Like the White Rabbit in *Alice's Adventures in Wonderland*, he may be late for a very important date. If so, when confronted with a person in need, he may decide he must continue on his way. If the date is less important, however, he may decide to stop and help.

This analysis suggests a very non-traditional interpretation of the parable of the Good Samaritan. Conflict over how to be most helpful could account for the apparent callousness of the mythical priest and Levite. As social and religious leaders, they likely had more people counting on their prompt arrival in Jerusalem than did the lowly Samaritan. They might have ignored the needs of the man who fell among thieves, not because they were unhelpful but because they wished to help in a way that would provide the greatest good for the greatest number.

METHOD

Procedure. Building upon this reasoning, an experiment was designed to assess the effect of the importance of the appointment to which one is hurrying upon willingness to help. Forty male undergraduates participated in a study ostensibly concerned with man-machine interactions. While on the way to another building to interact with a computer, subjects encountered a male undergraduate "victim" slumped on the stairs, coughing and groaning. The dependent variable was whether subjects sought to help the victim. The independent variables were hurry and importance of the computer appointment. Subjects were randomly assigned to conditions. Some subjects were told they must hurry to be on time for their computer interaction (high hurry); others were told they would be early and would have to wait (low hurry). Some were told that because the experimenter's deadline for completing the research had been moved up, their computer interaction data were of vital importance to the experimenter (high importance); others were told that because the deadline had been moved back their data were not essential (low importance).

Predictions. It was predicted that the importance of their computer interaction data would affect the likelihood of subjects in a hurry stopping to offer aid to the victim. Subjects told that they must hurry and that the experimenter was counting on their data were not expected to stop. Subjects not told to hurry or told that their data were not essential were. Thus, the rate of helping was expected to be lower in the high hurry-high importance condition than in the other three conditions. In these latter conditions, the rate of helping was expected to be uniformly high. This predicted pattern of results, if obtained, would support the contention that being in a hurry per se does not reduce the likelihood of noticing needs or of empathizing; it instead confronts one with a zero-sum conflict over how to respond.

RESULTS

First, it was necessary to determine whether the manipulations were effective. Whenever he was not busy debriefing a previous subject, an assistant timed how long it took subjects to cover the distance from the first building to the victim on the stairs of the second building. Subjects in the low hurry condition averaged 189.0 seconds; subjects in the high hurry condition, 126.7 seconds. This difference was highly significant. Effects on speed of the importance manipulation and the hurry $\times$ importance interaction did not approach significance. . . .

To check the effectiveness of the importance manipulation, subjects were asked on a questionnaire, "How important is the data that you can provide?" Responses were on a scale from not at all important (1) to extremely important (8).

TABLE 1. Percentage of Subjects Who Offered Help in Each Experimental Condition.

	Low Hurry	High Hurry
Low Importance	80%	70%
High Importance	50%	10%

Note.—$n = 10$ in each experimental condition.

The mean response on this question for low importance subjects was 5.20; the mean for high importance subjects was 6.35. This difference was significant. . . .

Since the manipulations appeared generally effective, attention was turned to the influence they had on subjects' helping responses. Table 1 presents the number of subjects in each experimental condition who helped. . . .

. . . Inspection of the frequency of helping in each experimental condition revealed that, as predicted, the high hurry-high importance condition differed dramatically from the other three. In this condition only 1 out of 10 subjects (10.0%) helped. In the other three conditions, from 5 to 8 out of 10 helped. The frequency of helping in the high hurry-high importance condition differed significantly from the frequency in each of the other three conditions. Comparisons between the other three conditions revealed no significant differences.

DISCUSSION

As predicted, the importance for others of his appointment affected the likelihood of an individual in a hurry offering help to a person in possible need. When others were not counting on him, being in a hurry did not seem to deter him from helping; 8 of 10 helped when not in a hurry, 7 of 10 when in a hurry. When others were counting on him, however, the likelihood of helping was affected by being told he must hurry; 5 of 10 helped when not in a hurry, 1 of 10 when in a hurry.

Two observations should be made about these results. First, we successfully replicated the Darley and Batson (1973) hurry effect. The percentages of helping in our high importance conditions closely parallel those reported by Darley and Batson: 63% of their low hurry subjects and 10% of their high hurry subjects helped. (The event to which their subjects were hurrying was important.)

Second, it is important to note that the difference in frequency of helping between the high and low importance subjects did not seem attributable to differential impact of the hurry manipulation. It might be imagined that subjects told they must hurry to an important event would hurry more than those told they must hurry to a less important event. But this did not seem to be the case. Speed scores revealed no significant difference in hurry between the two importance conditions and no interaction between the hurry and importance manipulation. Indeed, the small speed differences that appeared between the importance conditions were in the opposite direction: in both the high and low hurry conditions, low importance subjects tended to reach Building B slightly faster than did high importance subjects.

Alternatively, one might imagine that the low importance manipulation would annoy or anger subjects. They had come at night to participate in an experiment only to learn that their data were not really needed. Resentment might be especially strong when subjects in the low importance condition were then told they must hurry. But responses of subjects in this condition show no evidence of anger or resentment. These subjects hurried as fast as subjects in the high hurry-high importance condition and they displayed a high rate of helping (70%). In retrospect, it seems likely that receipt of the promised experimental credit may have mitigated any resentment. Each subject in each condition got what he came for.

Faced with the dilemma of (a) stopping to help and thereby missing an appointment or (b) passing someone in possible need, subjects apparently decided who needed their help most and acted accordingly. Consistent with Berkowitz' (Berkowitz & Daniels, 1963) notion of dependency eliciting helping behavior, if the experimenter was heavily dependent on them they tended to keep going (only 1 of 10 stopped). If he was not, they tended to stop and offer aid (7 of 10 stopped). These responses differed significantly. . . .

Although the evidence is admittedly indirect, subjects' helping responses indicated that being in a hurry did not by itself reduce concern or compassion. For in one condition those in a hurry displayed considerable help. Instead, it appeared that subjects in a hurry chose whom to help, the victim or the experimenter who was counting on them to be somewhere quickly. Conflicting demands, not callousness, appeared to account for the tendency for those in a hurry not to stop and help someone in possible need.

Should, then, the unhelpful Priest and Levite in the parable of the Good Samaritan be exonerated? Not on the basis of the present study, because the specific nature of the conflict to which subjects were responding remains unclear. While they may have experienced an altruistically motivated approach-approach conflict over how to be most helpful, there is another possibility. They may have experienced a selfishly motivated avoidance-avoidance conflict. Subjects may have been choosing between facing guilt for not helping the victim and facing chastisement for ruining the experiment. Having been told that the experimenter desperately needed their data, subjects may have been most concerned about what the experimenter would do to them if they stopped to help the victim. Ambiguity over the nature of the conflict suggests that we direct our future inquiry inward, to an analysis of the factors an individual considers in deciding whom to help. Does one consider the consequences for the people in need, for oneself, or both?

REFERENCES

Berkowitz, L. The self, selfishness, and altruism. In J. Macaulay and L. Berkowitz (Eds) *Altruism and helping behavior*. Academic, 1970.

Berkowitz, L., & Daniels, L. R. Responsibility and dependency. *Journal of Abnormal and Social Psychology*, 1963, **66**, 429–437.

Darley, J. M., & Batson, C. D. "From Jerusalem to Jericho": A study of situational and dispositional variables in helping behavior. *Journal of Personality and Social Psychology*, 1973, **27**, 100–108.

Duval, S. & Wicklund, R. A. *A theory of objective self-awareness*. New York: Academic, 1972.

Krebs, D. Empathy and altruism. *Journal of Personality and Social Psychology*, 1975, **32**, 1134–1146.

Langer, E. J., & Abelson, R. The semantics of asking a favor: How to succeed in getting help without really dying. *Journal of Personality and Social Psychology*, 1972, **24**, 26–32.

Milgram, S. The experience of living in cities. *Science*, 1970 **167**, 1461–1468.

Schroder, H. M., Driver, M. J., & Streufert, S. *Human information processing*. New York: Holt, 1967.

Winer, B. J. *Statistical principles in experimental design* (2nd ed.). New York: McGraw-Hill, 1971.

ELLEN J. LANGER
ROBERT P. ABELSON

The Semantics of Asking a Favor:
How to Succeed in Getting Help Without Really Dying

A number of laboratory and field studies of bystander behaviors suggest that helping behavior in fortuitous social encounters is extremely sensitive to seemingly trivial situational influences. In laboratory studies of reactions to emergencies (Darley & Latané, 1968; Latané & Darley, 1968; Latané & Rodin, 1969), the frequency of helping behavior sharply declines as the number of bystanders increases. Field research on the effects of social models (Byran & Test, 1967; Hornstein, 1970; Hornstein, Fisch, & Holmes, 1968) demonstrates the very marked but variable influence of models who engage in altruistic behavior, In a series of recent experiments, Staub (1970, 1971) found casual, arbitrary rules permitting or prohibiting entry into a certain location to exert an overwhelming influence on whether or not aid is given to a victim appealing for help from within such a location.

This study broadens the exploration of factors controlling helping by considering the way the request for help is phrased in relation to the favor asked. There are both theoretical and practical reasons for studying semantic factors in appeals for help. We would like to show that the wording of an appeal exerts a strong influence on the probability that help will be given, and that these variations in probability can be explained by the way in which the appeal gives a "definition of the situation" (McHugh, 1968) to the potential helper. Since the specific wording of an appeal is a very easy factor to manipulate in field studies of helping, it is a potentially very useful independent variable if it can be shown to have theoretical coherence. Atheoretical exploratory studies by Darley and Latané (1970) have already suggested the empirical power of simple appeal wording in influencing the probability of helping behavior, and an interesting field study by Katz and Danet (1966) has shown that different types of people tend naturally to use different appeal wordings in attempting to influence a social agency.

In what ways can appeals for help be phrased so as to convey the meaning of an ambiguous distressing situation to a target person, a potential helper? We conceptualize the problem of the person seeking help—the victim—as one of creating a familiar stimulus context within which the target person will play the part of the helper by virtue of past experience with similar situations.

One familiar situation arises when the target person feels sorry for the victim and helps because of sympathy for her[1] needy condition. To occasion such a setting, the victim should presumably emphasize her state of urgent personal need. Any appeal which quickly conveys this state we refer to as "victim oriented." The victim dwells on her condition with the intent of evoking empathy from the target person. Examples of simple phrases with victim-oriented properties are: "I'm hurt"; "I'm suffering"; "What a mess I'm in!"; etc.

In an alternative type of appeal, sympathy is unnecessary, and emphasis is placed on the duty or responsibility of the target person to help the victim. Such an appeal we call "target oriented." The implication is that the target person helps the victim because she is called upon to do so, and the situation does not readily permit a convenient alternative. Following such an appeal, help might be given begrudgingly. It is often a chore to perform a favor dutifully, as most people know from childhood experience. Simple examples of target-oriented phrases are "Do something for me"; "Can you give a hand?"; "Would you do me a favor?"; etc.

Many naturally occurring pleas for help may combine elements of both victim- and target-oriented appeals. From the point of view of the target person in a transient encounter with the victim, however, it seems likely that the *first phrase or two of the appeal cues the appropriate reference*. The necessity for prompt reaction one way or the other by the target person will tend to yield a primacy effect for the victim's appeal style: If victim-oriented appeals come first, then the target person faces an invitation to act empathically; if target-oriented appeals come first, then the target person's option is whether or not to behave dutifully.

The probability of giving help will of course depend on the favor asked as well as the appeal used. In the experiments to be reported, favors were varied along the dimension of *legitimacy*. The reason for this choice was the likelihood that the two appeal types would be differentially successful depending on the legitimacy of the favor asked. If the victim merits legitimate concern by virtue of the convincingness of her plight, then an appeal stressing her need should be extremely appropriate, more so than a bland call to duty. Thus, our first hypothesis: When the victim asks a legitimate favor, her chances of receiving help are relatively greater if she begins her appeal with victim-oriented phrases than with target-oriented phrases.

Conversely, if the victim makes an illegitimate or presumptuous request, then the opportunity for the target person to engage in empathic behavior is denied. When people feel that undue advantage is being taken of them, they are not likely to behave sympathetically toward the "nervy" individual responsible. However, sympathy is not a prerequisite for dutiful behavior. Thus, our second hypothesis: When the victim asks an illegitimate favor, her chances of receiving help are relatively less if she begins her appeal with victim-oriented phrases than with target-oriented phrases. . . .

An empirical test was carried out in two separate field experiments varying in numerous specifics such as the locale, the favor asked, and the identity of the confederate.

---

[1]Since in the experiments to be described below both the target person and the victim are female, we arbitrarily use the pronoun "her" throughout.

EXPERIMENT I

Method

The experiment took place at an indoor shopping center in New Haven, Connecticut. A white female, aged 22, stationed before each trial at the top of a well-trafficked stairway, feigned a knee injury and asked help from the first companionless female ascending or descending the stairway. The "victim" requested that the target person (subject) make a telephone call for her. If the target person complied, she went to use the phone that was in full view at the bottom of the stairs, dialed the number the victim had given her, received no answer, and proceeded back up the stairs. As the target person reapproached the victim, one of the victim's friends (the experimenter) arrived and offered to drive the victim to her destination, thereby relieving the target person of her responsibility.

The victim (naive to the major purpose of the experiment) was equipped with a bag from which she would randomly select a slip with the appeal to be used for that particular trial. On the back of the slip, the confederate noted whether or not the subject had complied. She waited until the previous target person was out of sight before resuming her station by the stairway.

There were 20 subjects run in each of four conditions that differed only in the victim's request for help. The following display presents the four different appeals.

Condition 1: Victim oriented, legitimate
 My knee is killing me, I think I sprained it. Would you do something for me?
 Please do me a favor and call my *husband* and ask him to pick me up.

Condition 2: Target oriented, legitimate
 Would you do something for me? Please do me a favor and call my *husband* and ask him to pick me up. My knee is killing me, I think I sprained it.

Condition 3: Victim oriented, illegitimate
 My knee is killing me, I think I sprained it. Would you do something for me?
 Please do me a favor and call my *employer* and tell him I'll be late.

Condition 4: Target oriented, illegitimate
 Would you do something for me? Please do me a favor and call my *employer* and tell him I'll be late. My knee is killing me, I think I sprained it.

It should be pointed out here the victim-oriented appeal (Condition 1) differs from the target-oriented appeal (Condition 2) only in the *word order* of the request. The same relationship exists between Conditions 3 and 4. The major difference between Conditions 1 and 3 or 2 and 4 is whether the object of the request was the victim's husband or her employer. Our assumption was that a request to call the victim's husband would be seen as legitimate, but that a request to call the victim's employer to "tell him I'll be late" would smack of malingering and be regarded as relatively illegitimate.

Results

To be regarded as helping, the target person had to descend the stairs, dial the number, and return upstairs with the dime and the message that there was no answer. In fact, all those who began this response sequence followed it through to its conclusion. Table 1 compares the number of people helping the victim in each of the four conditions. Of those people asked to call the victim's husband, 70% complied when the appeal began with a statement of the victim's suffering, as opposed to only 30% when it began with the introduction "Would you do something for me?" However, when the object of the requested phone call was the victim's employer rather than her husband, the effectiveness of the different word orders was slightly reversed. In this case only 35% of those approached with a victim-oriented plea helped as opposed to 50% of those approached with the target-oriented appeal. This pattern of results is consistent with the predictions made. . . .

EXPERIMENT II

When the results of the first experiment were discussed with colleagues, it soon became apparent that many interpretations of the "husband" versus "employer" manipulation could be devised as alternatives to our "legitimacy" explanation. We endeavored to meet this line of argument in two ways.

The first step was to provide evidence that the level of legitimacy would indeed be perceived differently for husband and employer requests. A brief questionnaire was administered to 16 respondents, mainly students, approached in a Yale library. The questionnaire presented 11 situations of favor asking which the respondent was asked to rate and then rank on legitimacy. The two crucial items were: "A female in a shopping center asks a stranger to call her husband to pick her up because she hurt her knee." and "A female in a shopping center asks a stranger to call her employer to tell him she'll be late because she hurt her knee." Thirteen of the 16 respondents ranked the first request as more legitimate than the second. For a number of reasons this supportive evidence is somewhat weak, but it is reassuring that the perceptions of naive individuals corresponded to our own intuition about the legitimacy variable.

The more convincing step was to design a second experiment in which the legitimacy variation would be much more obvious and compelling. Rather than varying the interpersonal nature of what the target person was asked to do (calling the husband versus calling the employer), we varied the quality of the excuse the victim gave for asking a single favor.

TABLE 1. Frequency of Helping Behavior in Experiment I.

Favor	Appeal	
	Victim oriented	Target oriented
Legitimate	14 (70%)	6 (30%)
Illegitimate	7 (35%)	10 (50%)

Note.—n = 20 per cell.

Method

The experiment was conducted near the downtown New Haven, Connecticut, Post Office. On each trial our confederate (white female, aged 44) approached the first companionless female passerby with a request to mail a bulky envelope. This request was either victim oriented or target oriented. The legitimate excuse for the mailing request was that the victim had to catch a train, and the illegitimate excuse was that she intended to go shopping. Although the appeals for help differed from those of Experiment I, the relationships among the four new conditions were the same, as shown in the following display.

Condition 1: Victim oriented, legitimate
   I'm in a terrible state, and I need this mailed. Would you do something for me? Do me a favor and bring this to the Post Office. *I have to catch a train.*

Condition 2: Target oriented, legitimate
   Would you do something for me? Do me a favor and bring this to the Post Office. I'm in a terrible state, and I need this mailed. *I have to catch a train.*

Condition 3: Victim oriented, illegitimate
   I'm in a terrible state, and I need this mailed. Would you do something for me? Do me a favor and bring this to the Post Office. *I have to go to Macy's.*

Condition 4: Target oriented, illegitimate
   Would you do something for me? Do me a favor and bring this to the Post Office. I'm in a terrible state, and I need this mailed. *I have to go to Macy's.*

A shopping bag containing twenty 9 × 12 inch stamped addressed envelopes was held by the experimenter inside a store next to the Post Office. The address on the randomly selected envelope (addressed to E. Langer or E. J. Langer, zip code or no zip code) defined the condition. After each trial, the confederate returned to the store for a new envelope for the next subject, and the experimenter noted the results of the previous trial.
   There were 20 subjects approached in each of the four conditions.

Results

Table 2 displays the number of people giving help in each of the four conditions. In percentages, 80% complied with the appeal by the hurried train catcher when the

TABLE 2. Frequency of Helping Behavior in Experiment II.

	Appeal	
Favor	Victim oriented	Target oriented
Legitmate	16 (80%)	11 (55%)
Illegitimate	4 (20%)	9 (45%)

Note.—*n* = 20 per cell.

first phrase mentioned her distress, as opposed to 55% when the appeal began with "Would you do something for me?." On the other hand, when the confederate was in a hurry to go shopping, the appeal beginning with her distress succeeded only 20% of the time, whereas the target-oriented appeal had a 45% success rate. . . .

Pooling results for the two appeal types, 67.5% complied with the legitimate request versus 32.5% for the illegitimate request. This difference . . . supports the assumption that catching a train is a better excuse than going shopping for asking someone to mail an envelope for you.

As in Experiment I, there was no main effect of appeal type. Overall, exactly 50% of the target women complied with both victim- and target-oriented pleas.

DISCUSSION

The two reported experiments demonstrate that the way an appeal for help is phrased in relation to the favor asked is a very important determiner of whether help is given. We had hypothesized that the two categories of appeals—victim oriented and target oriented—differed in their cue properties directing the potential helper toward one or another definition of the situation and the appropriate response sequence. A close examination of these cue properties in light of the experimental results is in order.

A composite picture of the overall results of the two experiments may be obtained by adding the compliance frequencies for each of the four experimental cells with the outcome shown in Table 3. This, of course, is a rough procedure, since there are qualitative dissimilarities in the kind of appeals made and the manner of varying legitimacy in Experiments I and II; nevertheless, the composite picture tends to smooth statistical irregularities and to be quite suggestive. . . .

There is good reason why the type of favor should make little or no difference when the appeal is target oriented. Such an appeal, by throwing the burden of decision immediately on the helper (e.g., "Would you do me a favor?"), forces her to review her own situation and mood before she even knows what the favor is. Attention is shifted away from the specifics of the favor to personal considerations for the target person: Does she have the time to do a favor, does she feel in the mood, will she win the gratitude of the victim? The target person may not adequately process characteristics of the favor such as its legitimacy because she is too preoccupied with her own decision. This is the implication of the lack of a legitimacy effect on target-oriented appeals. One might think that postponement of decision in response to the request "Would you do me a favor?" would be available

TABLE 3. Frequency of Helping Behavior—Both Experiments

Favor	Appeal	
	Victim oriented	Target oriented
Legitimate	30 (75%)	17 (42%)
Illegitimate	11 (27%)	19 (47%)

Note.—$n = 20$ per cell.

through the frank response "It depends." This rejoinder is often used among casual friends, and it is interesting that it was not employed by the target strangers in our experiments. Possibly there is inhibition of this ungracious orientation to a stranger. However, it may not be appropriate to invoke this speculation in our situation, since the phrase "Would you do something for me?" was used rhetorically, with no pause for the target to reply directly without interrupting.

The two victim-oriented cells in Table 3 display quite a different picture. When the favor is legitimate, there is 75% compliance, but when, illegitimate, only 27.5% compliance—a differential effect of almost 50%! When the appeal is victim oriented, the attention of the target is presumably focused on the characteristics of the victim and her state of need. Our culture teaches that one should, whenever possible, comply with legitimate requests to help the needy. But there is also a strong cultural imperative ("rugged individualism") that people should not let others take illegitimate advantage of them. Therefore, we are called on to discriminate sharply between deserving and undeserving victims. Our target sample shows strong behavioral differentiation indeed when the appeal is victim oriented.

It is noteworthy that the appeal manipulation worked very well despite the fact that the words used in the two conditions were exactly the same except for the order reversal. (See displays in text). One would expect a primacy effect for appeals in our situations: A single communicator was used, and there were no interpolated pauses, both conditions favoring primacy (cf. Hovland, Mandell, Campbell, Brock, Luchins, Cohen, McGuire, Janis, Feierabend, & Anderson, 1957, pp. 133–135). Nonetheless, the extent of the effect is perhaps remarkable. The second member of each appeal sequence appears not to have had much influence at all, though there could have been a slight tendency to damp the effects of the first member. One wonders, therefore, what would have happened had the victim-oriented phrases been omitted altogether following the target-oriented overture, and vice versa. Would the interaction have been even stronger? We do not know. It is also possible that the inclusion of the second member served as "filler," preventing the target person from interrupting, and that this feature tended to enhance the effects of the opening phrases. Thus, omission of the filler might weaken the obtained interaction.

The victim versus target orientation may also be a useful distinction to make in the study of interpersonal attraction and impression formation—for example, does the user of a victim-oriented approach suffer a status loss? These lines of speculation are among many along which the present experimental findings may be pursued empirically.

REFERENCES

Bryan, J. H., & Test, M. A. Models and helping: Naturalistic studies in aiding behavior. *Journal of Personality and Social Psychology*, 1967, **6**, 400–407.

Darley, J. M., & Latané, B. Bystander intervention in emergencies: Diffusion of responsibility. *Journal of Personality and Social Psychology*, 1968, **8**, 377–383.

Darley, J. M., & Latané, B. Norms and normative behavior: Field studies of social interdependence. In J. Macauley & L. Berkowitz (Eds.), *Altruism and helping behavior*. New York: Academic Press, 1970.

Hornstein, H. A., Fisch, E., & Holmes, M. Influence of a model's feelings about his behavior and his relevance as a comparison on other observer's helping behavior. *Journal of Personality and Social Psychology*, 1968, **10**, 222–226.

Hornstein, H. A. The influence of social models on helping. In J. Macauley & L. Berkowitz (Eds.), *Altruism and helping behavior*. New York: Academic Press, 1970.

Hovland, C. I., Mandell, W., Campbell, E. H., Brock, C., Luchins, A. S., Cohen, A. R., McGuire, W. J., Janis, I. L., Feierabend, R. L., & Anderson, N. H. *The order of presentation in persuasion*. New Haven, Conn.: Yale University Press, 1957.

Katz, E., & Danet, B. Petitions and persuasive appeals: A study of official-client relations. *American Sociological Review*, 1966, **31**, 811–821.

Latané, B., & Darley, J. M. Group inhibition of bystander intervention. *Journal of Personality and Social Psychology*, 1968, **10**, 215–221.

Latané, B., & Rodin, J. A lady in distress: Inhibiting effects of friends and strangers on bystander intervention. *Journal of Experimental Social Psychology*, 1969, **5**, 189–202.

McHugh, P. *Defining the situation: The organization of meaning in social interaction*. New York: Bobbs-Merrill, 1968.

Staub, E. A child in distress: The influence of nurturance and modeling on children's attempts to help. *Journal of Personality and Social Psychology*, 1970, **14**, 130–141.

Staub, E. Helping a person in distress: The influence of implicit and explicit "rules" of conduct on children and adults. *Journal of Personality and Social Psychology*, 1971, **17**, 137–144.

7

ROTHBERG

Male and Female

Our society is full of popular stereotypes and generalizations about what men and women are like—and how they came to be that way. Yet when we take a careful look at them, some of our beliefs about similarities and differences between men and women require a good deal of reexamination.

When we talk about the woman in America, we are talking of a person who plays a certain role or set of roles. She is a housewife (perhaps), a mother (perhaps), a lawyer or a doctor (perhaps)—and not necessarily in that order. She is extremely happy (perhaps) or possibly she is outraged; more likely she is somewhere in between. But she is a woman and that means not only that she is physically different from a man, but also that she is psychologically different. This is the result of socialization pressures she has been exposed to, values she has come to espouse, and the opportunities and constraints she has met and is meeting. In addition, while there has been a tendency to look at *women's* roles and to talk about *women's* liberation, it is equally important to recognize that as the experiences, opportunities, and expectations concerning women change, these have important implications for men as well.

This section is organized around the social psychological factors that affect both sexes in relationship to their actions, their self-concepts, and their personalities. This topic was chosen because it is a clear instance of how social psychological principles help us to understand something that is of great personal as well as social significance.

Rhoda Unger, Associate Professor of Psychology at Montclair State College, is one of a growing number of bright female professionals having an important impact on the field. She is particularly interested in the confusion that often exists between environmentally versus physiologically determined aspects of male and female behavior, an issue highlighted in her recent book *Female and Male: Psychological Perspectives*. Our conversation began with this issue and got into the complexity of conceptualizing individuals and their behaviors in terms of masculinity and femininity. We concluded with a discussion of whether *real* social change has taken place in recent years and what the goal of such change might be.

Rhoda Unger

A CONVERSATION WITH
RHODA UNGER

Montclair State College

KRUPAT: *It seems that there are so many terms to consider when we discuss ideas and research having to do with men and women. Can you clarify some things for me concerning the implications of using words like* gender *and* sex *or* masculine *and* feminine?

UNGER: First of all, I should say that there is absolutely no consensus on this. Anything I say would be my own opinion. The psychology of women as a field has been in existence since 1973 as an official part of the organizational structure of APA [the American Psychological Association]. That term made the most sense politically, but it was never generally accepted. We still discuss the idea of changing it except we can't find an alternative that suits everybody.

KRUPAT: *What do you consider wrong with it?*

UNGER: Mostly, what I and others don't like about it is the idea that people who study women study *only* women. In fact, one of the things many of us have objected to in the study of psychology in general was that it was really the psychology of men. Most of us study both sexes in one way or another, or certainly use materials that are relevant to both sexes. In a book I published recently, the last line is something like: What I would really like to do is encourage a psychology of people, sex unspecified. I think that's really the direction we're going.

KRUPAT: *But if you had to choose an alternative term, what would you select?*

UNGER: I would prefer the psychology of sex and gender mostly because that's about as general as you can get.

KRUPAT: *What do you mean by the difference between sex and gender? And why bother to make the distinction?*

UNGER: I would regard "sex" as those aspects of males and females that are biologically and physiologically given. "Gender" refers to all other aspects that I would think of as being socially learned or at least environmentally determined. Some of my students get terribly confused and I tell them that the quick way to remember is that when you're talking about male and female you are talking about "sex." When you are talking about masculine and feminine you're talking about "gender." Essentially the reason for making the distinction has to do with the way that people explain the origin of differences between the sexes. That is, when we talk about sex differences, the assumption is that there is some sort of biologically determined factor involved. The real problem is the use of description as explanation.

KRUPAT: *I can certainly accept the need to be careful about assuming that when we observe differences between races or sexes that it's because they were "born" that way. But then which differences between men and women are biologically determined and which ones are socially learned?*

UNGER: Well, I guess the best answer is that I don't know, and I'm not sure that anybody at this point can really answer that question. The reason for this, and the most recent research is even stronger on this point, is that the environments of males and females are so different right from birth that we haven't got enough information on people of both sexes raised in identical environments to find out. The variability is just too high in terms of environment.

KRUPAT: *Then is it possible that we will ever find out? Obviously there are ethical problems in doing real experimental research. Are there other ways?*

UNGER: One of the things that we need a lot more of is cross-cultural work. Of course that's a common complaint among psychologists in general, that psychologists tend to limit their studies to the United States or maybe Western Europe. What we need are societies where the assumptions about what is appropriate to each sex and gender are different than the assumptions we have here. There's a little bit of work, for example, that shows that in India the premenstrual syndrome has a quite different symptomology than it has in the United States. Now that doesn't rule out the possibility of some sort of biological causality, but it says that at least the form it takes is different where the culture is different.

KRUPAT: *Well, then, let's take one step backwards and let me ask you just what similarities and differences there are between men and women regardless of what caused them.*

UNGER: There is a line that I love to use: Men and women are most similar in their beliefs about their own differences. As a cognitive social psychologist, I think that the belief in the differences between male and female and the assumption that you are either one or the other controls a great deal of behavior for people. It's very rare to find a situation that is what you might call sex-blind.

KRUPAT: *Except that little boys and little girls act in different ways before they have very strong self-concepts. Just how early can it all start?*

UNGER: About the first point that you can study any sort of concepts that kids have at all would be about two when they start becoming verbal. You find the two concepts that have been learned are good–bad and boy–girl. So you could argue that in fact their behavior is being controlled from the time they can form a self-concept at all by those two kinds of assumptions. Another issue is: How much does other people's behavior which differentiates between the two sexes before they have these self-concepts affect their eventual ways of acting? There are studies showing that parents are treating little boy and girl infants differently before they get out of the hospital nursery. So if you've been treated differently even before you know what you are, the question is how much of a difference will that make.

KRUPAT: *In what ways do parents start treating their children differently that early?*

UNGER: Ross Parke has done studies in hospital nurseries. What he finds is that parents look at boy children more, they pay more attention to them, and they walk around with them more. Simply more attention is paid to boy children, especially if they're the first child. There are fewer sex differentiations between later-born children. Boys and girls who are first children are apparently the most intensively socialized. So oldest boys are most masculine and oldest girls are most feminine. Also there are the studies by Phyllis Katz and her associates about baby X. By taking the same child and giving people the label half the time that it's a boy and half the time it's a girl, she finds that different adjectives are used to describe the child. And Michael Lewis has done a variety of studies showing that from 6 months on there's a lot more proximal stimulation for girls than there is for boys. Mothers talk to their little girl infants more, they smile at them, they coo at them. They have more distant behavior towards the boys. Now this could account for why in our society girls talk earlier than boys do. The argument is usually differential maturation of the nervous system, which of course it could be. But we don't know the role of the environment in accentuating this differentiation.

KRUPAT: *That's interesting. And I guess that differential treatment is something which happens even when people are consciously aware of trying not to raise their children in sexist sorts of ways. As an example I think of my brother's children. His son loves tools and enjoys running and banging into things, while his daughter loves to get dressed up. They certainly aren't consciously aware of influencing them in these ways.*

UNGER: Yes, but we have two girls who are quite different in the same way. Our older one loves gadgets. Her idea of getting a gift is a penknife. And she is athletically inclined. It's counter to a lot of things in our family. My husband and I are not very sports minded. The younger one loves Barbie dolls. So that here are two girls who are very different and I cannot see where the influence came from. One of the things we as psychologists—and I don't mean just in terms of people interested in sex and gender but as psychologists in general—have not explored very much is the whole role of temperament which seems to be something present at birth. I could be wrong, but I have a feeling that one of the things the psychology of women will do is to increase the interest in individual differences again.

KRUPAT: *Do you mean individual differences within sex groupings?*

UNGER: Yes. One of the ways we may be able to understand a lot of our supposed sex differences is to look at real differences within a sex—at aggressive versus unaggressive girls and the same for boys.

KRUPAT: *But when you start talking about aggressive and unaggressive boys or girls, it sounds like we're getting into an area that we touched on briefly before, but never really got into, the idea of masculinity versus femininity. What do these things mean?*

UNGER: Discussing masculine–feminine represents for me a funny problem. I don't regard gender as being a dichotomy, and I think by using these terms the way we do we increase the belief that it is a dichotomy.

KRUPAT: *But still, aren't there certain traits or ways of behaving that traditionally have been typical or appropriate for one group versus another?*

UNGER: I think I would prefer to say they are normative or expected. It is perfectly true for our society that more females are "feminine" and more males are "masculine." And I would argue that this is largely because sex is a socially desirable characteristic, and a good deal of sex-and-gender effects are really simple adaptations to what is normal and nondeviant.

KRUPAT: *But, specifically, what does a woman do when she is acting in a feminine manner?*

UNGER: Simply, to be nonthreatening, receptive, sensitive, concerned about other people rather than herself. These are fairly standard ways of acting, and there is research suggesting that they are in fact more acceptable. My own anecdotal evidence is that those women psychologists who combine a feminine style with what you might call competence, which we always think of as being masculine, are more successful in terms of having their ideas accepted.

KRUPAT: *So being masculine is what? Competent? Aggressive?*

UNGER: Yes. Also assertive and opinionated. And I don't mean it in a necessarily negative way. I'm probably more masculine in style than feminine.

KRUPAT: *Well, can you be both? Doesn't this raise the issue of androgyny that Sandra Bem and others have discussed? Just what is meant by this?*

UNGER: It goes back to the earliest scales having to do with masculinity and femininity and the assumption that they were polar opposites. So that if somebody behaved in ways you might consider to be feminine, the way the scales were set up this automatically made that person be nonmasculine. The two things were considered to be opposite. The androgyny scales assume that masculine and feminine characteristics are independent of each other and that someone doesn't automatically become less masculine by being more feminine or vice versa. So, an androgynous person is regarded as somebody who has fairly sizable numbers of both masculine and feminine characteristics.

KRUPAT: *Do you consider this way of viewing things an important step in thinking about sex and gender?*

UNGER: I think that there are some very good things about androgyny and some bad ones. The good thing is the idea that you can separate biological sex from psychological sex, which I call gender. So that, yes, it's possible for males to have feminine qualities and females to have masculine ones. Another nice thing about androgyny is that it says that both kinds of characteristics are socially desirable. For instance, it's not weak to be feminine. Both Arnold Kahn and Virginia O'Leary have found that when people are given stories involving males crying, they are not considered socially undesirable. In fact, people admire them for being able to show their feelings. The problem with the androgyny scales that are current is that we're really working with separate traits rather than with some sort of an integration of them. So far, nobody has really talked about behaviors which don't really have words for them. The only thing current in psychology for someone that has two kinds of opposite traits in integration would be passive-aggressive. We all know what a passive-aggressive is. It's possible that what we need to do is to invent some words and get away from the whole idea of masculine and feminine, but I'm not prepared to do that yet.

KRUPAT: *I seem to hear you saying that androgyny is not the ultimate answer.*

UNGER: The problem is that, like fear of success, it was grabbed at as being the savior of all, and it got very popular. As soon as someone comes up with a scale, there's so much nonsense published correlating it to everything in the world without any conceptual framework that it's extremely difficult to find the valuable insights without having to go through all the trash. The people who are most enthusiastic about it are the clinicians because they think that being androgynous is somehow equivalent to being mentally healthy.

KRUPAT: *And, obviously, I assume it's not that simple.*

UNGER: There are a lot of problems. First of all androgynous males and females turn out to have somewhat different characteristics. Also, it's hard to distinguish between masculine females and androgynous females. If that's true, then femininity is actually unimportant, and I don't think that anybody wants to accept that as a possibility. In addition, something that Janet Spence found out early which has never gotten the attention that I would like, and I think is fascinating, is that the relationship between self-rated characteristics, which essentially is what androgyny is, and the use of sex-role stereotypes is zero. In other words, people could score as being very androgynous, and still be very stereotypic in their judgments about *other* people. As a social psychologist I think that is important. If that is really true, it means we could train a whole generation to be androgynous and not change the society one bit in terms of its degree of sexism.

KRUPAT: *It's funny that you should raise the issue of change because that's the next thing I wanted to ask you about anyway. The women's movement was a rather new thing in the '60s. It had time to mature and gain force in the '70s. Now in the '80s, do you think things have changed a lot since then? Will they change in the future?*

UNGER: I wish they would change, but I really don't think this is happening. This past year I team-taught a course with an historian and it helped me to realize how very important it is for people in this area to remember history. In the '20s we went through the same kind of wave of feminism. If you read some of the early feminist psychologists they deal with these same issues. They were saying the same things, and they were actually getting evidence to support the kinds of things that we are supporting today. But it was completely forgotten. I think we're about to get into another wave of conservatism. Look at the 1980 Republican platform. The problem is for the psychology of women to gain what I would call legitimacy.

KRUPAT: *In what sense do you mean?*

UNGER: We have it in some ways as being part of the APA organizational structure. But on the other hand, you'll hardly ever see a job ad for somebody who has expertise in the psychology of women. You also find that when a course like that is taught at an institution, it is frequently taught by a graduate student or a young female faculty member who has no training in the area. The assumption is that the fact that you are a woman is sufficient expertise to enable you to teach the course. I have an analogy for that one, and that is that you should have schizophrenics teaching all abnormal psych courses. But the point is that the course is not regarded as having a data base the way a respectable psychology course does, and therefore it is easily disposed of when money gets tight or the person who taught it leaves.

KRUPAT: *Beyond the politics of the study of sex roles, what are your feelings on the impact of all this on society as a whole. For instance, I often think of television as mirroring changes in public attitudes and orientations. In the '50s you had the scatterbrained woman-child, in* I Love Lucy. *In the '60s and '70s, you had a more career-oriented, competent type much like Mary Tyler Moore. I can't think of a good example in the most recent times. Have* real *changes taken place?*

UNGER: The only changes that I see on TV are that the stereotypes have become somewhat more subtle. There have been many studies of sex-role stereotypes in the media. They find, for example, that in the soap operas there are just as many women as men. Yet what is also found is that the women do all the talking in the domestic areas, but in the hospitals, even though as many women are supposed to be physicians, it's the men who do all the talking. So rather than not representing equal numbers of men and women, in subtle ways they say certain things about what you expect men and women to do. In TV cartoons, there is an excellent study by Sternglanz and Serbin about the characteristics of heroines versus heroes. The researchers first started out with the most popular cartoons for children and couldn't analyze them because there weren't enough popular cartoons that had women as main characters. So they finally started to study those cartoons that did have women as main characters, and found that almost all of them had magical powers of some sort. This is very interesting because it says that the only way a woman in our society can influence things is indirectly, in ways where you don't let anybody else know what you are doing.

It's a terrible role model for a child because what is she going to do when she grows up and discovers that being a witch is not a viable career?

KRUPAT: *Are there any optimistic notes to sound? Or are there any major or really important changes you've noticed over the years?*

UNGER: There is one in particular I can think of. Helen Hacker, a feminist sociologist who was way ahead of her time, wrote a paper in the late '40s called "Women as a Minority Group." I remember hearing a talk she gave five or six years ago in which she said that the only way that women and men would ever become equal is if women had to work. I remember being appalled by that. I thought, "How could she say that? Everyone should have a choice, whether a man or a woman." I realize that she was right because you have a situation today where many women do have to work, and I think that has had the greatest influence on sex roles of anything in our society in the last 30 or 40 years. For one thing, it's changed our entire view of childbearing.

KRUPAT: *Childbearing? Or do you mean child rearing?*

UNGAR: Childbearing—women who have remained in the work force, and especially women who think of their jobs as careers as opposed to simply ways of making money are postponing childbirth. Scanzoni, a sociologist, has found that husbands tend to go along with what their wives want in this area. So that women are having children much later, and this also results in people having smaller families on the average. Talk about things having major social implications, this probably has the largest of all.

KRUPAT: *We've talked about a good many things, but as a last issue, I did want to raise something about a phrase you just used. You said, "if men and women would ever become equal." That seems like a funny term to me. Do you mean "separate but equal," "different but equal," or what?*

UNGER: I think that's a good question and we have to be very careful about that. When we say equal we don't necessarily mean the same. There's no reason why two men who are equal should be the same. I think that's a misconception about feminism or maybe it's a way of attacking feminism— the idea that all women have to be a certain type of person. What some feminists want, and I know this is what I am talking about, is the freedom of choice. But real choice. That is, if you are socialized to have relatively low self-esteem and a feeling that you don't control your own destiny, and you are put in situations where it's productive to feel this way as many women are, then you don't really have free choice. Men don't have free choice either. Men have to achieve. I think someone has said that masculinity is measured by the size of the paycheck. Men are not free to choose *not* to work or to be nurturant and concerned about relationships. Women are not free to choose those kinds of things which give them joy outside the home. What I am really saying and what most reasonable feminists would say is that choice should be based on what people want knowing the alternatives, not through pre-programming based upon their external genitalia.

AN INTRODUCTION TO THE READINGS

The articles in this section explore a variety of approaches to matters of sex and gender. In the first article, Kay Deaux looks at an issue raised in our conversation: How should we conceptualize and measure masculinity and femininity? She points out that masculinity and femininity are not necessarily opposite ends of a single dimension but rather separate characteristics that may *both* be part of the same individual. Referring to the work of Sandra Bem on androgyny, she notes that this concept may hold a great deal of promise in allowing us to look at the behavior of men and women in a new way, but also points out (as did Unger) that this is only one element in the total consideration of differences and similarities between the sexes.

In the next paper, Carol Tavris and Carole Offir consider the position that differences between the sexes result from the fact that boys and girls are differentially socialized. Research in this tradition is aimed at demonstrating that from the time they are born, the personalities and self-images of girls are shaped by social forces so as to make them less confident and less successful when they grow up. Tavris and Offir cite numerous studies on self-esteem, the need for achievement, and the fear of success among women that support this position, yet point to the limitations of this approach as well. They suggest that while socialization pressures and resulting personality differences are important, there are other important forces which help explain the differences in status and achievement between men and women.

As if to support the position taken by the previous authors, the next article, by Susan Darley, attempts to explain the differences in career achievement using a different set of concepts. Leaning heavily on role theory, Darley suggests that it is not the personalities of women that account for their differing levels of success, but rather the social norms and expectations which allow for or require success in certain areas and certain situations. For example, Darley neatly points out that men hardly ever compete to see who can maintain a clean house, yet they typically vie for promotions in the office with great vigor. On the other hand, women rarely discuss sports competitively, but they often do compete about which one has the cleaner laundry or the fluffier rice. The question for women, according to Darley, is how to integrate roles that in our society today have competing demands and expectations.

The final article by Barbara Katz, explores the effect of sex-role socialization and normative expectations, but from the flip side—the perspective of *men*. Katz points out that while the female role is limiting in many ways, society places certain restrictions on men that are often more subtle but are equally limiting in other ways. The message is that what we have is not a matter of men's *versus* women's interests, but that the movement known as "women's liberation" is really one that can have liberating effects for people of both sexes.

Women, Men, and Androgyns

Everyone is partly man and partly woman.

Virginia Woolf

The truth is, a great mind must be androgynous.

Samuel Coleridge

MEASURING MASCULINITY AND FEMININITY

In the most general sense, masculinity and femininity are considered to be relatively stable traits of the individual, rooted in anatomy, physiology, and early experience.[1] Furthermore, it is assumed that, although there will be a certain number of exceptions, most biological males will be high in psychological masculinity, and most biological females will be high in psychological femininity. These assumptions are very clearly rooted in the development of questionnaires designed to measure masculinity and femininity. Masculinity is what men typically do, and femininity is what women typically do. . . .

. . . In nearly every scale that has been developed over the past several decades, test constructors have assumed that masculinity and femininity represent the opposite ends of a single dimension. In other words, if a particular characteristic is not masculine, then it must be feminine. This assumption is reflected in most of the M–F scales that have been developed. Generally, people are given a choice between two responses. Selecting one of these responses will result in a point scored for masculinity, while the choice of the other response will add a point to the femininity score. The fewer masculine items a person agrees with, the more feminine that person is considered, and vice versa.

Recently, psychologists have begun to question these assumptions. Is it reasonable to assume that masculinity and femininity represent a single dimension? Does a person have to be either masculine *or* feminine? Or can a person be both masculine and feminine, combining characteristics of both sexes in a single person? Phrased in another way, is it possible for people to be androgynous?

THE DEVELOPMENT OF ANDROGYNY

Biologists have known for years that men and women possess quantities of both male and female hormones. The balance between the hormones is different for men and women, but both kinds are present in the male and in the female body. Perhaps psychologically there can be a parallel coexistence. Writers for centuries have suggested that such a coexistence is possible. Plato, in presenting a myth of sexuality in the *Symposium*, described beings who were half male and half female. Many years later, Samuel Coleridge asserted that the great mind is an androgynous mind, combining both masculine and feminine traits. More recently, Carolyn Heilbrun has argued that the concept of androgyny can be found in major literary works throughout the centuries, and she buttresses her arguments with quotes from Aristophanes through Shakespeare to Virginia Woolf.[2]

Within the field of psychology, Sandra Bem deserves the major credit for directing the attention of investigators to the concept of androgyny.[3] People, she suggests, are not as limited as the earlier conceptions of masculinity and femininity would suggest. According to this early research, the world is made up of masculine males, feminine females, and sex-reversed deviants. Bem, along with a growing number of other investigators,[4] believes that androgyny is a meaningful concept. Men and women may have both masculine and feminine characteristics. A person may be both assertive and yielding, both instrumental and expressive. While the earlier methods of measuring masculinity and femininity could not uncover this type of person, Bem believes that androgyns are alive and well in 20th-century life.

To measure androgyny, Bem constructed two separate scales—one that measures masculine characteristics and one that measures feminine characteristics.[5] Each scale consists of 20 personality characteristics that are considered desirable in our culture. The masculinity scale contains, for example, such items as "competitive," "self-reliant," and "analytical." On the femininity scale are items like "affectionate," "sensitive to the needs of others," and "yielding." Bem's first important finding was that these two scales are independent of one another. Earlier investigators had assumed that a person who is high on masculinity will necessarily be low on femininity, and they constructed their questionnaires in such a way that their assumption was automatically true. Because Bem used two separate scales, however, she was able to test the assumption that masculinity and femininity are the mirror image of each other. Her results showed that they are not. In statistical terms, the correlation between the two scales approximated zero. What this means is that a person who scores high on femininity may be high, medium, or low on masculinity, and vice versa. Knowing a person's score on one scale gives you no ability to predict that person's score on the other scale.

Androgyny, as defined by Bem, is reflected in the balance between a person's score on these two scales. If a person's scores on the two scales are relatively equal, then that person is considered androgynous. Both masculine and feminine characteristics are endorsed in approximately equal proportions. For example, an androgynous person might say that he or she was competitive, independent, and athletic but also loyal, shy, and understanding. Such a self-description would tend to indicate a balance between masculine and feminine characteristics. Other individuals might show a much greater difference in their endorsement of items on the masculinity and femininity scales. A person who agreed with a large number of items on the masculinity scale but who felt very few items on the femininity scale were accurate self-descriptions would be considered masculine sex-typed. A feminine sex-typed person would be one who agreed with many of the items on the femininity scale and very few on the masculinity scale. In her initial work, Bem found that approximately 50% of the California college students that she tested could be considered traditionally sex-typed feminine females or masculine males. More than a third of the people in her sample, however, were androgynous—showing a relatively equal balance between masculine and feminine traits. The remainder of her sample were considered sex-reversed—women who scored much higher on the masculinity scale than on the femininity scale and men who scored higher on femininity than on masculinity.

Accepting Bem's notion of masculinity and femininity as two separate dimensions, University of Texas psychologists Janet Spence, Robert Helmreich, and Joy Stapp have advocated an alternative conception of androgyny.[6] These investigators argue that, while masculinity and femininity represent two separate sets of characteristics, a simple balance between these characteristics does not guarantee androgyny. For example, someone who felt he or she had few masculine characteristics and also had few feminine characteristics would be androgynous by Bem's definition, in that there would be a balance between the two sets of traits. In contrast, Spence and her colleagues would argue that only those persons who had a high percentage of both masculine and feminine traits would be truly androgynous. Theoretically, this latter conception is surely closer to the ideas of Plato, Coleridge, and Heilbrun, pointing to a person who has developed skills in both arenas rather than withdrawing from both.[7] We'll return to this distinction, but let's first consider the relevance of androgyny for behavior.

WHY ANDROGYNY?

It is certainly of some interest to know that masculinity and femininity are independent of one another: that both men and women can have either masculine or feminine characteristics or have both at the same time. Probably the more interesting question, however, is what are androgynous people like? Are there advantages to being androgynous as opposed to being more traditionally sex-typed? Sandra Bem leaves no doubt about her opinion; she considers androgyny the more positive state. In support of her contention, she has reviewed much of the earlier literature on sex-typing and finds considerable evidence to suggest that strong sex-typing may not be the best state of affairs. For example, a review of the literature shows that boys and girls who show stronger cross-sex typing (boys with some feminine traits and girls with some masculine traits) are generally higher in intelligence and show more creativity.[8] Some other evidence reviewed by Bem suggests that highly sex-typed girls express more anxiety and show lower psychological adjustment. Results for boys are not as clear, but at the least they do not give strong evidence that sex-typing is best.[9]

An even stronger case for the value of both masculine and feminine traits has recently been presented by Spence, Helmreich, and Stapp.[10] These investigators looked at the relationship between sex-role identification and self-esteem and found that for both men and women high scores on both the masculine and the feminine items were associated with high self-esteem. In contrast, those people who indicated a low proportion of both masculine and feminine traits were characterized by low self-esteem, supporting the view of these investigators that an even balance is not enough. Traditionally sex-typed persons, in comparison, were midway between these two groups in terms of self-esteem. Spence and her colleagues also report that individuals high on both masculine and feminine characteristics may have different backgrounds from more sex-typed individuals. For example, they have found that androgyns received more honors and awards during their school years, dated more, and were sick less often than were sex-typed individuals.[11]

Beyond these differences in background and self-esteem, Sandra Bem has suggested that the androgynous person may be capable of functioning effectively in a wider variety of situations than the sex-typed individual can. For example, in a situation in which assertiveness and independence are required, a masculine sex-typed person should be more effective than a feminine sex-typed person. However, if Bem's theorizing is true, the androgynous male or female should be able to function just as effectively in such a situation as the masculine person. In similar manner, we would expect that, in a situation calling for warmth and emotional expressiveness, feminine persons would be more effective than masculine persons. Again, Bem would predict that the androgynous person would also be able to do well in this situation. Thus, Bem would argue that the androgynous person has a wider range of capabilities. Depending on what the situation requires, the androgynous person can show masculine assertiveness or feminine warmth and should be equally effective in both situations. The sex-typed person, in contrast, is more restricted, being limited to doing well only in those situations where the requirements are consistent with the person's own sex-typed characteristics.

In her first test of these theoretical predictions, Bem set up two different situations that presumably had different kinds of requirements.[12] The first situation was a typical conformity experiment. Subjects in this experiment were told that they were participating in a study of humor. Each student was asked to look at a series of cartoons and rate each cartoon for its funniness. However, before giving his or her own rating, each student heard two other subjects give their opinions of the cartoon's humor. Relying on the early studies that showed greater female conformity . . . , Bem predicted that in this type of conformity situation, both sex-typed men and androgynous men and women would show less conformity than would sex-typed women. Her predictions proved to be correct. Feminine males and females conformed on an average of 23 out of 36 possible trials, while both masculine subjects and androgynous subjects (males and females) showed less conformity, following the group's opinions on less than half of the total trials.

Bem then applied the same kind of reasoning to a second task, this time one in which women would be expected to be more facile. In this second situation, subjects were given the opportunity to play with a small kitten, and the experimenters recorded how long each subject did this. The expectation was that both feminine sex-typed persons and androgynous persons would play with the kitten longer than would masculine sex-typed persons. Among the men, Bem found some support for her predictions. Feminine and androgynous men did play with the kitten more than did masculine men. For women, however, the results were a bit confusing. The androgynous women played with the kitten quite a bit, but the feminine women did not; in fact, these latter women played with the kitten much less than did masculine women.

In later studies, Sandra Bem and her colleagues have found some evidence that when given a series of choices sex-typed individuals are more likely to select own-sex behaviors and avoid cross-sex behaviors.[13] Yet once again, these findings were much clearer among the men than they were for the women.

Bem's failure so far to find unambiguous support for the connection between androgyny and behavior is certainly not uncommon in the early stages of research. While some of the findings are promising, it is clear that we are only beginning to tap the top of an iceberg that may prove to be much larger (and much more complicated) as the research continues. A more fundamental difficulty may lie in Bem's conception of androgyny. Logically, there is no reason to expect someone who possesses few masculine or feminine traits to behave in either terribly masculine or feminine ways. Such persons may in fact be more neutral in all their behaviors. In contrast, if we adopt a notion of androgyny as representing only those people who are high in both masculinity and femininity, then Bem's predictions about the behavior of androgynous people should hold true.

Androgyny is an exciting concept and deserves much more attention by investigators in the future. Intuitively, it makes a great deal of sense to think that people can combine masculine and feminine traits and be free to use either type according to the situation. As many recent commentators have suggested, it might be good if men could express emotions, disclose their feelings with other people, and worry less about dominating all people in all situations. At the same time, many have argued that women should be able to be more assertive, to strive for achievement in the marketplace, and to be independent enough to avoid total reliance on others. If the early theorizing is true, an androgynous person could be all of these things.

Yet even with this alternative conception, some questions remain. What kinds of predictions could we make, for example, in a situation where either a masculine or feminine response may be appropriate? In many of the social settings we have studied, there is not necessarily a better or worse strategy. Men and women have frequently been found to differ, but the labels of good or bad cannot be so readily applied. What would our androgynous person do in these settings? Androgyny may prove very useful in our understanding of some behavior in some settings. However, the concept may be most useful in conjunction with, rather than as a replacement of, our accumulated knowledge of the behavior of women and men.

NOTES

1. Anne Constantinople, "Masculinity-Femininity: An Exception to a Famous Dictum?," *Psychological Bulletin*, 1973, **80**, 389–407. (This article provides an extensive discussion of the validity of various M-F scales.)
2. Carolyn G. Heilbrun, *Toward a Recognition of Androgyny* (New York: Knopf, 1973).
3. Sandra L. Bem, "The Measurement of Psychological Androgyny," *Journal of Consulting and Clinical Psychology*, 1974, **42**, 155–162.
4. A similar conception of the benefits of androgyny has been presented by Jeanne H. Block ("Conceptions of Sex Role: Some Cross-Cultural and Longitudinal Perspectives," *American Psychologist*, 1973, **28**, 512–526.).
5. Bem, op. cit.
6. Janet T. Spence, Robert Helmreich, and Joy Stapp, "Ratings of Self and Peers on Sex-Role Attributes and Their Relation to Self-Esteem and Conceptions of Masculinity and Femininity," *Journal of Personality and Social Psychology*, in press; also Janet T. Spence, personal communication, 1975.
7. In fairness to these investigators, it should be acknowledged that they are less interested in the concept of androgyny per se and more interested in the dualism of masculinity and femininity. They would argue that on some occasions a single dimension may be most predictive, while a combination of the two would be a better predictor on other occasions.
8. Eleanor E. Maccoby, "Sex Differences in Intellectual Functioning," in E. E. Maccoby (ed.), *The Development of Sex Differences* (Stanford, Calif.: Stanford University Press, 1966).
9. Sandra L. Bem, "Psychology Looks at Sex Roles: Where Have All the Androgynous People Gone?" (paper presented at UCLA Symposium on Women, May 1972).
10. Spence, Helmreich, and Stapp, op. cit.
11. A more basic and fascinating question concerns the origin of androgyny. Why do some boys and girls become androgynous, while others develop more traditionally sex-typed traits? Janet Spence and her colleagues are beginning to investigate the connections between the masculinity and femininity of parents and their children, but the results are unfortunately still in a very preliminary stage.
12. Sandra L. Bem, "Sex-Role Adaptability: One Consequence of Psychological Androgyny, *Journal of Personality and Social Psychology*, 1975, **31**, 634–643.
13. Sandra L. Bem and Ellen Lenney, "Sex-Typing and the Avoidance of Cross-Sex Behavior," *Journal of Personality and Social Psychology*, in press.

CAROL TAVRIS
CAROLE OFFIR

Some Consequences of Socialization

By the time they are three or four, children tend to choose sex-typed toys, activities, and games. Boys especially are likely to prefer "boy-toys" and avoid "girl-toys" like the plague (Maccoby and Jacklin 1974). Their sense of masculinity at this tender age, and perhaps later, seems to hinge on not being like girls.

By the time they enter kindergarten, children have a pretty good idea of what is going to be expected of them as adults—they know for sure that boys can be firemen and policemen and girls can be teachers and nurses. An undergraduate student, Linda Ollison, asked twenty-nine kindergarten girls and twenty-nine boys a revealing question: "What do you think is the most important job in the world?" Boys and girls alike listed policeman, fireman, and doctor, while girls added teacher. Then Ollison asked, "Do you think you could do that when you grow up?" and found that the boys were much more optimistic. Twenty of the twenty-nine boys answered yes compared to twelve of the twenty-nine girls. Further, only six boys conceded that a girl could do the most important job in the world, but twenty-two girls said that a boy could do the work.

The messages of socialization, overt and subtle, teach children what toys are okay to play with and which jobs are all right to aim for. The lessons hit home within the first few years of a child's life. But that's the way it has been in virtually every society in history. Why now are so many people arguing that separate-but-equal treatment of children, as of blacks, is discriminatory and unfair?

One answer is that the messages about the sexes are out of synch with reality, and that both girls and boys should learn about the variety of roles they will be expected to play in their lives—as spouses, parents, employees, students. Nine out of ten girls born today will work for a substantial period of their lives, but most grow up to believe (incorrectly) that marriage will be their permanent, full-time job. Another answer is that the current system of socialization has two negative consequences for women: females grow up thinking that they are not quite as good as males, or maybe that they are not worth very much at all; and they suppress or

Abridged from *The Longest War* by Carol Tavris and Carole Offir, © 1977 by Harcourt Brace Jovanovich, Inc. Reprinted by permission of the publisher.

deflect the motivation to strive and succeed. To many writers, the resulting sex differences in self-esteem and achievement motivation account for the greater prevalence of males in politics, business, science, and art. To be creative you have to be confident; to advance in your field you need some drive and energy. If socialization squelches a girl's ambitions and self-regard as it encourages a boy's, the implications for sex differences in social status and personal happiness are serious.

SELF-ESTEEM VS. SELF-DISLIKE

"I never yet knew a tolerable woman to be fond of her own sex," wrote Jonathan Swift, who wasn't terribly fond of either men or women. Indeed, many women throughout history have been willing to proclaim the inferiority of their sex. "I'm glad I'm not a man," confessed Madame de Staël, "for if I were, I'd be obliged to marry a woman." One of the early goals of the women's movement was to banish the longstanding belief that women don't like themselves or each other very much, that a "real woman" prefers to spend her time with men and gets her self-esteem vicariously, through the man she loves. These efforts, like the "black is beautiful" movement, were aimed at least in part at creating a self-fulfilling prophecy—at encouraging women to like their own sex.

Psychologists have tried to find out whether females really have lower self-esteem than males, usually by asking people to rate their own self-regard. The results are not what you might expect. After surveying a slew of self-esteem studies with children and college students (and a few with older adults), Maccoby and Jacklin concluded that females feel no worse about themselves than men do. This conclusion may be premature. Self-esteem is another personality trait that is hard to measure. People do not like to admit dissatisfaction with themselves or their lives; they may insist that they are happy as larks even when they are suffering from psychosomatic disorders brought on by stress and anxiety. . . . So we need to consider other evidence.

1. Females envy males more than males envy females. More females than males suspect that the grass is greener on the other side of the fence and say they have fantasized about being a member of the other sex. The belief that males have more fun arises early in life. When Ollison asked her kindergartners, "If you could, would you rather be a girl [boy]?" twenty-eight of the twenty-nine boys said they would rather fight than switch, but six of the girls were ready to change. Of course, such results don't necessarily mean that females think males are inherently superior; children of both sexes may simply perceive that it's a man's world and want to join. It's possible, though, that envy leads to a belief that males really are more valuable human beings, that a man's destiny matters more than a woman's.

2. Many women hold other women in low esteem and devalue their intellectual competence. It takes time to learn this attitude. When Ollison asked her kindergartners whether boys or girls are smarter, two-thirds of each sex replied that their own sex was smarter. Not one girl conceded that a boy could have the edge on

intelligence. But when Ollison asked whether mommies or daddies are smarter, she heard a portent of things to come: over half of the girls replied that daddies were smarter.

By the time they are grown, some females are prejudiced against their sex. Philip Goldberg (1968) asked college women to rate several short articles for persuasive impact, profundity, and overall value, and their authors for writing style, professional competence, and ability to sway the reader. Half of the women got articles purportedly written by men (for example, John T. McKay) and half got the same articles signed by women (for example, Joan T. McKay). The women consistently gave higher marks to articles allegedly written by men. Another study, which asked people to rate a male or female painter, had similar results (Pheterson, Kiesler, and Goldberg 1971). However, some recent variations on the Goldberg study got mixed results. One study (M. B. Morris 1970) found that women gave higher ratings to articles written by *women*. Another (H. Mischel 1974) found that high-school and college students of both sexes tended to rate male authors higher in male-dominated fields, but female authors higher in female-dominated fields. Yet another study found that raters were unaffected by the sex of the author or the topic of the article (Levenson et al. 1975). Apparently antifemale bias is on the wane, has gone underground, or both. Probably people are more sensitive than they once were about openly expressing a low opinion of women (or blacks or Chicanos), but their inner feelings do not always keep pace with public statements. These feelings show up when, for example, they avoid consulting a female (or black or Chicano) doctor or lawyer.

Many psychologists believe that when people disparage the group they belong to they reveal a hatred of themselves. Self-disparagement is not uncommon among minorities, who are exposed to the same cultural images of their groups as the majority is; there are anti-Semitic Jews and white-supremacist blacks. Helen Mayer Hacker (1951), in a classic essay on women as a minority group, observed twenty-five years ago, "Like those minority groups whose self-castigation outdoes dominant group derision of them, women frequently exceed men in the violence of their vituperations of their sex."

3. Females have less self-confidence than males. In several studies, college students have predicted how well they will do at some particular task. Men are consistently more confident than women about their performance, and they are also more satisfied with themselves after completing the job. This is true even when the task is one at which women do just as well as men, such as anagrams (Feather 1968, 1969). Similarly, if you ask students to estimate their grades for the next term, men usually expect to do at least as well as they have in the past, and perhaps better, while women expect to do worse. In one typical study, female college students predicted lower course grades than males did, despite the fact that actually the women's grades turned out to be slightly higher than the men's (Crandall 1969; see also Deaux 1976).

Of course, it's possible that what we have here is merely a case of feminine modesty and male bravado. But an important line of research suggests a different explanation, based on differences in the way the sexes interpret success. When you do well at something, you can react in various ways. You may believe you did well because you're competent, because you worked very hard, because the task was easy, or because luck was on your side that day. Psychologists find that many people consistently favor one sort of explanation over another. Those who attribute success to their own ability or effort are said to have an *internal locus of control*. Those who attribute success to the ease of the task or the fickle finger of fate are said to have an *external locus of control*. During childhood the sexes do not differ in this regard, but by college age more women than men have an external locus of control (Rotter and Hochreich 1973, cited in Frieze 1975; also Simon and Feather 1973).

Kay Deaux, Leonard White, and Elizabeth Farris (1975) had the imaginative idea of observing what kind of games men and women sought out at a county fair. As they predicted, the women went for games of luck (Bingo), while the men liked games of skill (ring tosses). Intrigued, they set up their own fair in the laboratory and found again that 75 percent of the men chose to play a skill game while 65 percent of the women chose a luck game. Why? Expectancy seems to be the key, the researchers believe. Women thought they would do better in a game of luck and men thought they would succeed more often in a game of skill.

Ability is something you can count on, but luck is not; it's here today, gone tomorrow. If women have learned to attribute their success to luck, that could explain why they feel more insecure than men do about their future performance (Frieze 1975). To make matters worse, some studies (though not all) find that women feel that their lives are externally controlled only when it comes to success. When they fail, they suddenly turn internal, blaming their poor showing on a lack of ability. These women are caught: if they do well, they sacrifice the credit, but if they bomb, they shoulder the blame. Sooner or later a woman in this situation is likely to decide that if at first she doesn't succeed, she might as well forget it.

THE ACHIEVEMENT MOTIVE

The differences between men and women in their evaluation of their abilities suggests another explanation for sex differences in status and power. It is that girls do not acquire the same drive to achieve, to meet a personal standard of excellence, that many boys do. Psychologists usually regard the need to achieve as a stable disposition that a child acquires early in life. Some years ago David McClelland and his colleagues developed the Thematic Apperception Test (TAT) to assess how strong an achievement motive a person has. The TAT is a series of ambiguous pictures, and the person taking the test is asked to make up a story about each one. The stories are scored for themes related to achievement, using a carefully defined scoring system. Suppose a picture showed a middle-aged man talking to a younger man. A person who said that the young man was trying to convince his boss to try a new system to increase the company's productivity would get a higher need-for-achievement score than one who said a father and son were discussing the fun they had on a fishing trip.

Achievement-motivation theory, as originally formulated, said that people with a strong need to achieve would want to do well in situations requiring intelligence and leadership (McClelland et al. 1953). If you put them in such a situation and gave them the TAT, the number of achievement fantasies should shoot up. This prediction turned out to be true—for men, but not for women. Indeed, TAT scores were usually related to actual achievement—especially school grades—for men, but not for women. The research with women kept confounding the theory. The response of psychologists was like that of the proverbial man who dropped his wallet in a dark street but searched for it beneath a street light because he could see better there: they stopped studying women. In 1958 an 873-page compilation of the research on achievement and related motives appeared; research on females was confined to a single footnote (Atkinson 1958).

In the sixties, psychologist Matina Horner (1969) turned a searchlight on the dark street men had ignored. She argued that women, unlike men, have a motive to *avoid* success, a fear that achievement will have disastrous consequences. Because women learn that achievement (especially intellectual achievement) is aggressive, and therefore masculine, they worry that they will be less feminine if they compete. Anxiety about this conflict makes women feel defensive if they do achieve and may prevent them from achieving in the first place. Able men do not have this problem because achievement and the masculine role go hand in hand.

To test her theory, Horner asked ninety female undergraduates to tell a story based on the following sentence: "After first-term finals, Anne finds herself at the top of her medical school class." Eighty-eight men responded to the same sentence, but about John. When Horner scored the stories, she found that most of the men (90 percent) were comfortable about John's success and saw a rosy future for him. "John is a conscientious young man who worked hard," wrote one male. "John continues working hard and eventually graduates at the top of his class."

But a majority of the stories written by women (65 percent) contained images that reflected what Horner called a fear of success (FOS). The most common theme was that Anne's academic success would bring her social rejection. She would be unpopular, unmarried, and lonely. Another was that Anne would feel unfeminine. One young woman saw particularly dire consequences for Anne: "Anne starts proclaiming her surprise and joy. Her fellow classmates are so disgusted with her behavior that they jump on her in a body and beat her. She is maimed for life." Some stories solved Anne's "problem" by having her drop out of medical school to marry a successful doctor or to enter a more "feminine" field, such as social work.

Next Horner compared the way students performed on tests when they worked alone or in a competitive group. Men tended to do better when they were competing with others, as did women whose stories about Anne did not show fear of success. Most women who showed high fear of success (77 percent) did better when they worked alone. Horner concluded that a psychological barrier of anxiety blocks achievement for many bright women.

When Horner published her work, a chorus of "Aha's!" went up throughout the land. Researchers thought they now understood why women had been ruining their studies. College women had a reason for their uncertain career plans. Journalists announced that an explanation had been found for women's low status in the world of work: the fault lay not in the stars but in women themselves. They might want to achieve, but they also wanted to be feminine, and the two motives were as incompatible as oil and water.

In the years that followed, dozens of follow-up studies were done all over the country and the world—Yugoslavia, Italy, Norway, the West Indies. The more data that came in, the more it appeared that the matter of women's lack of achievement was not quite solved. Criticisms of Horner's work began to appear (Tresemer 1974; Condry and Dyer 1976; Shaver 1976).

One problem is that men often show as much "fear of success" as women, and sometimes more. David Tresemer reviewed dozens of studies and found a remarkable range of results. In forty-five experiments, the proportion of women who wrote fear-of-success themes varied from 11 percent to 88 percent, with a median of 47 percent. In the twenty-two experiments that included men, the proportion of men who wrote fear-of-success themes varied from 22 percent to 85 percent, with a median of 43 percent—not significantly different from the median for women. In fourteen studies, men showed *more* fear of success than women did. One of these is especially important because it was an exact duplication of Horner's work. The study, by Lois Hoffman (1974), was conducted at the same university, in the same room, at the same time of year, with a similar male experimenter and similar students. Slightly more males than females (77 percent to 65 percent) wrote fear-of-success themes.

So the "motive to avoid success" is not limited to women. But the sexes do seem to regard the perils of achievement differently. Women associate success with social rejection; men question the value of success in the first place. They wonder whether hard work really pays off. In their stories, John may drop out of medical school to write a novel or take a 9-to-5, blue-collar job. Or John may find that his victory is a Pyrrhic one: "He graduates with honors and hates being a doctor. He wonders what it was all for." "It's great for his parents, but he doesn't give a shit" (Hoffman 1974). Anne suffers by becoming unpopular and dateless, but John suffers by dropping dead prematurely (Robbins and Robbins 1973).

New interpretations argue that the stories about Anne and John reflect not deep-seated motives but realistic attitudes—an assessment of the consequences of conforming or not conforming to social convention. In this view, it is not success that women fear but deviation from traditional roles. Studies that ask both sexes to write stories about John and Anne find that men and women recognize that female achievement is unusual, and that it frequently brings down punishment on the head of the achiever. In fact, men are sometimes more disturbed by Anne's number-one status than women are—they write more negative themes about her than women write about either Anne or John. So perhaps women are right to worry about the consequences of doing better than men; if they step too far toward the front of the line, they may arouse the worst in some males.

To avoid the consequences of being number one, women may turn to achievement in "safe" areas such as homemaking, philanthropy, or civic work. Or they may choose to do their work well but not to aim for public recognition or positions of power—the "woman behind the throne" sidestep. If this speculation is true, then women's fear-of-success scores should be lower when the cue is less threatening than Anne at the head of her class in medical school. And indeed, fear-of-success imagery does drop if women are given the story line, "After first-term finals, Anne finds herself at the top of her class" (Alper 1974), or if the story states that half of Anne's medical-school classmates are women (Katz 1973).

John Condry and Sharon Dyer (1976) offer a nice analogy to show that fear-of-success themes may reflect an understanding of social realities rather than fear of achievement. Suppose you gave people a description of an interracial couple who had just gotten married and were about to set up housekeeping in rural Georgia. You ask them to write a story about what will happen to this couple. If you took each story that mentioned negative consequences and labeled it "fear of interracial marriage," you would be making a serious mistake. The people who predicted bad things for the couple would not necessarily be afraid or bigoted; they might just know which way the racist wind blows.

The assumption that fear-of-success motives affect a person's actual performance has also been questioned. Some studies support Horner's finding that women with this motive do worse in competition with men than when they work by themselves. Other research finds the opposite pattern. When the motive affects performance, its impact is usually rather small. Tresemer points out that the women in Horner's group who were most likely to show fear of success were honors students. "If the people who show FOS imagery are the ones who get good grades," he says, "just how deeply debilitating is it?" On the other hand, perhaps even more women would be high achievers in school if it were not for fear of success. Also, school achievers do not always achieve after graduating.

Researchers still disagree about whether fear of success has actually kept anyone from succeeding in a career. But even if worry about being different does not actually block achievement, it may cause women to feel ambivalent and guilty about their accomplishments and create considerable personal anguish.[2] When women compete in male-dominated professions, they may rein in their ambitions and play down their achievements. Or they may suffer from psychosomatic ailments due to emotional strain (see Shaver 1976). Their conflict will be especially painful if they have been punished for competing in the past, as by losing a man they loved.

EVALUATING THE LEARNING PERSPECTIVE

Hardly anyone denies that children are raised differently depending on their sex. Socialization takes place in many ways through inadvertent as well as deliberate rewards and punishments, and through language, media messages, and adult examples. Sometimes the only way to experience the ubiquity of sex-role images in this society is to immerse oneself in another culture. China, for example, shakes up one's expectations. You see a soldier, rifle on back, walking along; you pass him and discover he is a woman carrying not only a gun but a baby. You attend a surgical operation and see two men and two women working on a patient. The women are the doctors; the men, the nurses.

In studying how socialization creates sex differences, however, many researchers have tried to stuff real people into rigid stereotypes, which don't fit flesh-and-blood human beings very well. They lose sight of the fact, as Mischel observes, that "there are many different acceptable ways of being a boy or girl, and even more diverse ways of being a man or woman." The learning perspective itself allows for this range of behavior, but the demands of the laboratory often force researchers to narrow their horizons. . . .

Another issue raised by the learning perspective is the common assumption that basic attitudes, abilities, and traits are set rather firmly in childhood. Just as most psychologists have paid little attention to variation within sex roles, they have also tended to ignore changes in people's behavior and personalities during adulthood. The learning approach does not rule out the possibility of adult changes; social-learning theory, in particular, stresses that as rewards change, so will a person's behavior. But in practice, researchers and laymen often think that adults are not really able to choose freely what path they will follow—their course was established in those "formative years."[3] The conclusion, therefore, is that if you want to teach children to conform, or *not* to conform, you'd better get them young. Thus Sandra and Daryl Bem (1976) write:

> The free will argument [of role choice] proposes that a 21-year-old woman is perfectly free to choose some other role if she cares to do so; no one is standing in her way. But this argument conveniently overlooks the fact that the society which has spent twenty years carefully marking the woman's ballot for her has nothing to lose in that twenty-first year by pretending to let her cast it for the alternative of her choice. Society has controlled not her alternatives, but her motivation to choose any but one of those alternatives (p. 184).

Psychologists are starting to reconsider this belief. Adult experiences matter too, as any adult who has ever changed careers or marriages or returned to school can testify. Take the matter of self-esteem. Overall, women probably have lower self-esteem than men. But self-esteem, like any other personality trait, can change with time and place. Paul Mussen (1962) found this shift in a study of adolescent boys. Those who had highly masculine job interests liked themselves better, had more self-confidence, and were better "adjusted" according to psychological tests than boys who had less traditional, more feminine interests. Observers rated the masculine teenagers as more carefree, contented, and relaxed. This makes sense: boys who buck their peers in adolescence risk some bad times and heavy social pressure. But because Mussen's data came from a longitudinal study, he was able to take the rare step of seeing what happened to the boys when they reached their late thirties. He found that the boys who had been very masculine as teenagers now were *less* self-confident and self-accepting than the "feminine" boys.

Parents do shape their children's behavior and attitudes, of course, but adult role models can mitigate or even reverse the effects of childhood models. Elizabeth

Tidball (1973) found that the number of faculty women at a college is an excellent predictor of how many career women the school will produce. Ironically, in this heyday of efforts to integrate schools, women's colleges produce more ambitious, less traditional graduates.

The learning perspective explains women's second-class status by pointing to the different personality traits that men and women acquire as they grow up. It acknowledges but does not emphasize the influence of social norms and institutions on people. To the question, "Why do most women hold low-ranking jobs?" this perspective answers, "Because women have acquired certain traits—fear of success, dependence, sociability, noncompetitiveness—that limit their aspirations and their abilities." Sociologist Jessie Bernard (1975) summarizes the views of feminist critics who observe that defenders of the status quo can say, "Sorry, girls, too bad you haven't got what it takes; you're afraid of success and all that. I know it isn't your fault; I know it's the way you were socialized as a child; you'd be just as superior as I am if you had played with trucks instead of dolls. But what can I do about it, after all?"

Today the cradle-to-grave approach to human development is becoming increasingly popular. There may be no point at which we can say of a person, "She lived happily (or miserably) ever after." And some critics of the learning approach point out that whatever their childhood experiences, people grow up to face a world that assigns different (and discriminatory) roles to women and men. According to them, personality differences do not wholly explain status differences. One must also understand the social roles that adults are expected to play and the value society places on those roles. Parents and the media do not get their ideas about how boys and girls should behave from thin air. Where do these ideas come from? Many writers, Jessie Bernard notes, feel that "emphasis on socialization merely offers an easy out; it does not open doors." A thousand more studies on the development of personality differences will not give us the whole answer to the lesser status of women. We need rather to attack "the institutional structure which embalms these differences in the form of discrimination against women. The name of the game is power."

NOTES

1. Women don't always choose luck explanations. Deaux studied men and women in top management positions and asked them how they got there. Obviously a successful manager can't attribute her or his position to luck. Yet even here women were reluctant to say "I'm really good, that's how." They tended to say hard work and effort were the reasons, while men invoked ability as well as effort (Deaux 1976).
2. Black college women seem less likely than their white sisters to feel conflict between achievement and femininity, and they get lower fear-of-success scores (Weston and Mednick 1970). There is a problem in this study, though, because only highly motivated members of minority groups tend to go to college.
3. An early goal of social-learning theorists was to translate some of Freud's ideas and explain some of his observations in learning-theory terms. Freud's emphasis on early childhood was rarely questioned.

REFERENCES

Alper, Thelma G. 1974. Achievement motivation in college women: a now-you-see-it-now-you-don't phenomenon. *American psychologist* 29:194–203.

Atkinson, John W. ed. 1958. *Motives in fantasy, action, and society: a method of assessment and study.* Princeton, New Jersey: Van Nostrand.

Bem, Sandra L., and Bem, Daryl J. 1976. Case study of a nonconscious ideology: training the woman to know her place. In *Female psychology: the emerging self.* ed. Sue Cox, pp. 180–90. Chicago: Science Research Associates.

Bernard, Jessie. 1975. *Women, wives, mothers: values and options.* Chicago: Aldine.

Condry, John, and Dyer, Sharon. 1976. Fear of success: attribution of cause to the victim. *Journal of social issues* 32(3):63–83.

Crandall, Virginia J. 1969. Sex differences in expectancy of intellectual and academic reinforcement. In *Achievement-related motives in children*, ed. Charles P. Smith, pp. 11–45. New York: Russell Sage Foundation.

Deaux, Kay. 1976. Ahhh, she was just lucky. *Psychology today* 10 (December):70ff.

Feather, N.T. 1968. Change in confidence following success or failure as a predictor of subsequent performance. *Journal of personality and social psychology* 9:38–46.

———. 1969. Attribution of responsibility and valence of success and failure in relation to initial confidence and task performance. *Journal of personality and social psychology* 13:129–44.

Frieze, Irene Hanson. 1975. Women's expectations for and causal attributions of success and failure. In *Women and achievement: social and motivational analyses*, eds. Martha T. Shuch Mednick, Sandra Schwartz Tangri, and Lois Wladis Hoffman, pp. 158–71. New York: Halsted Press.

Goldberg, Philip. 1968. Are women prejudiced against women? *Trans-action* 5 (April):28–30.

Hacker, Helen Mayer. 1951. Women as a minority group. *Social forces* 30 (October):60–69.

Hoffman, Lois Wladis. 1974. Fear of success in males and females: 1965 and 1971. *Journal of consulting and clinical psychology* 42:353–58.

Horner, Matina S. 1969. Fail: bright women. *Psychology today* 3 (November):36–38ff.

Katz, M. L. 1973. *Female motive to avoid success: a psychological barrier or a response to deviancy?* Princeton, New Jersey: Educational Testing Service.

Levenson, Hanna; Burford, Brent; Bonno, Bobbie; and Davis, Loren. 1975. Are women still prejudiced against women? a replication and extension of Goldberg's study. *Journal of pyschology* 89:67–71.

McClelland, David C.; Atkinson, John W.; Clark, Russell A.; and Lowell, Edgar L. 1953. *The achievement motive.* New York: Appleton-Century-Crofts.

Maccoby, Eleanor Emmons, and Jacklin, Carol Nagy. 1974. *The psychology of sex differences.* Stanford, California: Stanford University Press.

Mischel, Harriet. 1974. Sex bias in the evaluation of professional achievements. *Journal of educational psychology* 66:157–66.

Morris, M. B. 1970. Anti-feminism: some discordant data. Paper read at annual meeting of the Pacific Sociological Association.

Mussen, Paul H. 1962. Long-term consequences of masculinity of interests in adolescence. *Journal of consulting psychology* 26:435–40.

Ollison, Linda. 1975. Socialization: women, worth, and work. Unpublished paper. San Diego State University, San Diego.

Pheterson, Gail I.; Kiesler, Sara B.; and Goldberg, Philip A. 1971. Evaluation of the performance of women as a function of their sex, achievement, and personal history. *Journal of personality and social psychology* 19:114–18.

Robbins, Lillian, and Robbins, Edwin. 1973. Comment on "Toward an understanding of achievement-related conflicts in women." *Journal of social issues* 29(1):133–37.

Shaver, Phillip. 1976. Questions concerning fear of success and its conceptual relatives. *Sex roles* 2:305–20.

Tidball, M. Elizabeth. 1973. Perspective on academic women and affirmative action. *Educational record* 54:130–35.

Tresemer, David. 1974. Fear of success: popular, but unproven. *Psychology today* 7(March):82–85.

I Am Woman

I am woman, hear me roar
In numbers too big to ignore,
And I know too much to go back to
pretend
'Cause I've heard it all before
And I've been down there on the floor,
No one's ever gonna keep me down
again. Oh,

You can bend but never break me
'Cause it only serves to make me
More determined to achieve my final
goal.
And I come back even stronger,
Not a novice any longer,
'Cause you've deepened the conviction
in my soul. Oh,

I am woman, watch me grow
See me standing toe to toe
As I spread my lovin' arms across the
land.
But I'm still an embryo
With a long, long way to go
Until I make my brother understand. Oh,

Chorus
Yes, I am wise but it's wisdom born of
pain.
Yes, I paid the price but look how
much I gained.
If I have to I can do anything.
I am strong,
I am invincible,
I am woman.

Helen Reddy and Ray Burton

"I Am Woman" words by Helen Reddy,
music by Ray Burton. Copyright ©
1971 IRVING MUSIC, INC. & BUG-
GERLUGS MUSIC CO. (BMI) All
Rights Reserved. International Copyright Secured. Reprinted by
permission.

I Am Woman, You Are Man

1st Chorus
I am woman, you are man.
I am smaller, so you can be taller
than.
You are softer to the touch.
It's a feeling I like feeling very much.
You are someone I've admired.
Still our friendship leaves something
to be desired.
Does it take more explanation than
this?
I am woman, you are man.
I am woman, you are man, let's kiss.

Bob Merrill and Jule Styne

From "You are Woman, I am Man" by
Bob Merrill and Jule Styne. Copyright
© 1963 & 1964 by Bob Merrill & Jule
Styne. International Copyright Secured.
ALL RIGHTS RESERVED. Used by
permission of Chappell & Co., Inc.

SUSAN A. DARLEY

Big-Time Careers for the Little Woman:
A Dual-Role Dilemma

Impressive data support the contention that men and women show differential career achievement (Epstein, 1970). Historically this apparent difference has suggested to some (Freud, 1927) that women are genetically inferior to men; to others (Horner, 1972), that women have deficient personalities as a result of early socialization. (See Condry & Dyer, 1976, for a discussion of this issue.) This paper contends that to understand women's apparent lack of achievement we might do better to analyze social rather than genetic or personality variables. While allowing for genetic contributions to sex differences and for the fact that boys and girls are indeed socialized differently from an early age, the following analysis is based on the belief that the importance and the influence of biological and personality variables have been overstated, and that variables stemming from the more immediate social situations in which adult men and women find themselves have been relatively understated.

ROLE BEHAVIOR

The particular nature of a given social situation, including the expectations of real or imagined other people, can shape the kind of behavior that will be displayed. Some expectations may relate to the individual's sex, so that different kinds of behavior will be expected of men than of women, and for the most part people's behavior conforms to such sex-role expectations. When a person fails to behave role-appropriately, she/he violates role expectations and is likely to meet with disapproval and perhaps outright hostility from others. By such social sanctions one tends to learn to avoid roles that are inappropriate. While Horner (1972) suggests that women develop a motive to avoid success through rewards and punishments received during childhood, the alternative proposed here extends through adulthood the implicit social reinforcement focus of Horner's thinking and avoids the assumption of personality traits. Here it is suggested instead that in a particular situation

Abridged from "Big-Time Careers for the Little Woman: A Dual-Role Dilemma" by Susan A. Darley from *Journal of Social Issues*, vol. 32, no. 3, 1976. Copyright © 1976 by The Society for the Psychological Study of Social Issues. Reprinted by permission.

women will choose to avoid behaviors that might make them appear to be filling a male-appropriate rather than female-appropriate role; and conversely, that men will choose not to display behaviors which would, in a particular situation, be generally expected of women. This hypothesis suggests that men would not competitively or aggressively clean house and that as a rule women would not competitively or aggressively discuss sports. On the other hand, it might explain why men vie avidly for office space and promotions in the office hierarchy, while women compete equally vigorously for cleaner laundry and fluffier rice.

My working hypothesis, then, is that qualities like competitiveness, assertiveness, and competence are not uniquely possessed by men either by virtue of genetics, anatomy, or early socialization. They are characteristic of both men and women but will be displayed by the two sexes in different kinds of situations. Unlike Horner's model, it is not assumed here that women as compared to men have a general disposition to avoid success, but rather that both sexes will avoid success when such success conflicts with social norms relating to sex role, and both will seek success when the norms allow for or require success (Howe & Zanna, Note 1).

ROLE CLARITY AND STABILITY

So far we have been discussing behavior in terms of sex role as though these roles are defined equally clearly for men and women and, in both cases, clearly enough that the behaviors appropriate to each role may be determined with ease and lack of ambiguity. If this were true, one would expect that men and women would have the same general kind of role choices to make and that qualitatively the consequences of these choices would be essentially similar. There are some suggestions in the literature, however, that this may not be the actual state of affairs; and if it is not, perhaps we have uncovered a second factor deriving from a role theory approach that might help explain achievement differences between men and women. That is, it may not be only the kind of behaviors demanded by the different sex roles that lead to differences in achievement, but also differences in the clarity and consistency with which these sex-role demands are defined.

It has been hypothesized by Rose (1951), for example, that "the social changes accompanying the industrial revolution left the middle-class urban woman's roles relatively less specific and less definite than those of comparable men and hence her pre-adult expectations are less adequate" (p. 69). Sarbin and Allen (1968) make a similar observation, using women's role expectations of marriage as an example. The obligations and responsibilities of wifehood are not validly depicted in movies and popular magazines nor are they clear simply from observing the behavior of one's parents, especially when such observations are made from the perspective of a child. As a result, it is difficult for girls to prepare adequately for the role of wife, and often they come into the role with vague and unrealistic ideas about what will be required or expected of them. According to Sarbin and Allen, boys grow up with a relatively clear and accurate picture of a husband's role.

The problem stems not so much from lack of role models—for certainly little girls have more opportunity to observe the daily life and work of their mothers than do little boys that of their fathers—as from the disparity between what our formal system of education is designed to prepare children to do as adults and what, in fact, they will likely be doing as adults. In school, children are taught academic and vocational skills which presumably prepare them for job responsibilities as adults. As former U.S. Education Commissioner S. P. Marland has recently written, "whether we acknowledge it or not, our society expects our schools and colleges to equip young men and women for successful entry into the world of work" (cited in *Newsweek*, 1974). And in our schools, girls follow the same general curricula as boys and are even encouraged to excel. In fact, they often outperform the boys on such measures of academic success as grades (Maccoby, 1966).

Having completed the educational gamut, however, girls are typically encouraged not to use directly the skills they have learned but rather to abandon them for a new set of skills—housekeeping, childcare, and husband tending—skills which are not typically an important part of public education. Boys, on the other hand, are encouraged if not actually pushed into using their marketable skills. To the extent that this is true, the educational preparation is more compatible with the activities involved in the stereotypic adult-male role than it is with the stereotypic adult-female role. Thus, it may be not only the career woman who faces an ambiguous role situation for which much of her experience and training have been inadequate but also the homemaker. Before analyzing the role problems confronting a career woman, then, let's turn briefly to the more traditional but far from simple role situation with which a housewife-mother must cope.

THE ROLE OF HOMEMAKER

Before the industrial revolution, the roles of housewife and mother were relatively clearly defined in terms of keeping the hearth and ministering to the needs of children and husband. In earlier days, too, formal education outside the home was neither as widespread nor as intensive for girls as for boys. The activities involved in homemaking were relatively unambiguous, and the role training received by girls in childhood was more consistent with the traditional adult-female role than it is at present.

Today too the criteria for a well-kept hearth are not so clearly related to the personal efforts of the individual homemaker. Many essential services are provided by outside personnel and institutions, and with the development of almost limitless household appliances, the work of running a household has become more mechanical. In this sense, perhaps, the domestic role of homemaker has become less challenging.

On the other hand, most of the evidence (Linder, 1970; Morgan, Sirageldin, & Baerwaldt, 1966) suggests that despite modern conveniences, running a home has not become less time-consuming. Built-in obsolescence makes tracking down repair services a constant chore for homemakers, and the fact that the repairs are often costly and only to be accomplished by the intervention of experts may make the role of homemaker a more frustrating experience than ever.

And what of the role of mother? The explosion of books, articles, and television talk shows on the subject of motherhood suggests that the expectations for this role are almost without limit, stunningly unclear, and highly variable. Is a good mother permissive or firm or both? Is she a friend to her children or an advisor or both? Should she provide a lot of structure for them or allow them to schedule their own patterns of eating, sleeping, and play? "What's a mother to do?" a cliché plaint, aptly reflects the state of affairs in matters of motherhood. Note that what is expected of a good father is also unclear, but the parent role is not generally taken to be as salient for a man as it is for a woman.

In one sense, the activities involved in the role of parent, like that of house-worker, may be diminishing. With the increase in day-care facilities and organized after-school programs, a parent's physical presence is not as necessary as it once was for the proper care of young children. Again, like the homemaker role, however, a parent's job has probably increased in complexity, despite or perhaps because of the fact that more and more aspects of the role have been taken over by outside institutions and personnel.

With their children at school relatively early in life, many women turn to active involvement in community affairs. This aspect of the woman's role, i.e., voluntary involvement in community good works, however, is only partially institutionalized and perhaps as a result is accompanied by what Parsons (1942) has called "marks of strain and insecurity" (p. 612). Also, the possible social rewards to be gained for activity in this area are moderate at best; volunteerism is not a highly regarded pursuit and in fact has come under increasing attack from the feminist movement as exploitative.

A woman's lot, therefore, even if she restricts herself to the traditional and socially acceptable roles of wife, mother, and community volunteer is not an easy one, nor is it rich in extrinsic rewards. The strains and insecurities with which it is marked, however, are probably no greater, and perhaps less, than those facing the woman who seeks to combine the traditional role with that of career person.

THE DUAL-ROLE WOMAN: HOMEMAKER AND CAREER PERSON

Both Maccoby (1963) and Horner (1972) have emphasized the incompatibility between qualities traditionally associated with the role of wife-mother (e.g., nurturance, emotionality, responsiveness to people rather than ideas) and qualities associated with the role of achiever in the occupational and professional world (e.g., aggressiveness, rationality, and independence). A woman who exhibits such achievement-oriented characteristics in her career, or even simply by virtue of having a career, is usually considered to be fulfilling a socially inappropriate sex role and thus will most likely experience some anxiety and possibly some real social sanctions as well.

As difficult as the satisfactory performance of either the housewife-mother role or the career-woman role may be, the satisfactory performance of the two in conjunction appears almost impossible. Certainly, there are a myriad of practical and logistical problems that make the combination difficult and often exhausting. Furthermore there are as yet no clear-cut norms for such a combination of roles, and one would expect that women who attempt such a combination experience many strains and insecurities indeed.

Perhaps this would not be the case if performance in one role had no implications for performance in a different role, but . . . such generalization does occur. The generalization is mediated by inferences made by an observer about an individual's personality. People are likely to infer, for example, that a successful career woman has an aggressive, competitive nature, rather than that she is simply capable of behaving in an aggressive, competitive way when her immediate role requires such behavior. People interpret behavior as reflecting stable underlying traits of the behaving individual. This is the same kind of inference that Horner makes in her theory, and it is an inference which often works against women. If the fact that a woman succeeds at a career implies that she has a tough, contentious, hard-driving nature, it also implies, given current stereotypes, that she must not be a good mother—for insofar as anything is clear about what a good mother should be, this set of qualities, taken as personality traits, does not describe the ideal. In fact, these traits are often assumed to be the opposite of the ideal mother and of the ideal wife.

The strains and insecurities associated with the combined role of wife/mother and career woman, then, derive in part from the tendency for people to make inferences about an individual's personality from his/her behavior. Whether or not a woman combining the two roles is aware of the inferences being made about her, she suffers the effects. If she is unaware of them, she is nonetheless likely to be derogated as a mother and thus treated less cordially by her neighbors, and also likely to be taken less seriously at work, in which case her performance on the job may actually be impaired. If though, as is often the case, she is aware of the kinds of inferences, i.e., personality judgments, that are being made about her, the self-doubt and internal tension she must sustain are further increased.

One case in which such inferences are probably not made should be mentioned: the case of the wife/mother who has no choice but to work. These women may not be negatively sanctioned for working, perhaps because the fact that they work does not imply a set of nonfeminine personality characteristics, nor does it suggest that they have rejected the traditional female role. The assumption can easily be made that these women would not freely choose to work if conditions did not force them to it. It is only women who *choose* to work who are violating role expectations and whose personalities are assumed to be warped. If a woman has to work, for example, if she is widowed or living separately from her husband, it is usually the man who is negatively sanctioned and who is assumed to have a defective personality. If, on the other hand, a woman works because she enjoys it, she is usually assumed to be somehow lacking in the womanly qualities that make for good wives and mothers.

In addition to the negative inferences that dual-role women may face, there are also problems that stem from the particular nature of the spouse/parent and occupational roles that may work against career success in women. Sarbin and Allen (1968) have provided a theoretical conceptualization of role conflict that may elucidate what some of these problems might be and help explain apparent sex differences in career achievement. They describe two kinds of roles, ascribed and achieved, and differentiate them primarily in terms of the degree of choice one exercises in entering them. Ascribed roles, of which the role of parent is an example, are attained by virtue of one's inherent characteristics or by virtue of one's necessary relationship to another person. One may choose to have children, for instance, but if one has them, one is a parent regardless of how one acts. Achieved roles, on the other hand, are usually attained through processes like training, personal achievement, or election. Sarbin and Allen hypothesize that roles that are predominantly ascribed differ from those that are predominantly achieved in terms of the range of valuations that may be assigned to the respective role enactments or performances. Specifically, they suggest that valuations for poor or nonperformance of achieved roles are at or near the neutral point; whereas proper or good enactments of such roles may be very positively evaluated and marked by real rewards, e.g., Pulitzer prizes, military medals. Possible evaluations for achieved roles, then, are assumed to range from neutral to highly positive. For ascribed roles, like mother or father, however, the range is from negative for poor or nonperformance to neutral for proper role enactment. Mothers, for example, are not generally rewarded for enacting the parent role well, but they are severely judged if they fail. Note that fathers who work to support their families are simultaneously filling two roles, one that is ascribed and one that is achieved. If they are economically unsuccessful or achieve less than their class background demands, they may be evaluated quite negatively. The Sarbin and Allen hypothesis would hold, however, that it is the fact that they are fathers, i.e., failing in their ascribed role, that accounts for the negativity and not the simple fact that they did poorly on the job, i.e., failure in their achieved role. The hypothesis suggests that a man who fails to achieve at work but who is not responsible for supporting a family will be only mildly sanctioned.

Sarbin and Allen hypothesize further that there is a tendency for the standards used in evaluating ascribed roles to be more ambiguous than those used in evaluating achieved roles. It's not nearly as clear what a good parent is, or does, as it is what a successful job holder is or does. So the rewards, even though only moderate for proper fulfillment of ascribed roles, are probably more difficult to come by than are those for proper fulfillment of achieved roles. Even though the clearer standards for achieved roles make failure in these roles relatively unambiguous, the sanctions for such failure are mild compared to the sanctions applied for poor performance of ascribed roles.

Sarbin and Allen also point out, "Perhaps for the male the occupational role is most salient and central, while the mother role seems to have similar saliency for most females" (p. 539). If this is true, and it does seem to be a fairly widespread assumption, then men are clearly more likely to be positively evaluated in the performance of their characteristic role since this role happens to be an achieved one. The situation for women, unfortunately, is just the reverse; not only are the possible rewards available to them for good performance of their salient role less striking, but also the possible punishments are greater than they are for men. The Sarbin and Allen analysis also lends support to the point made earlier about the lack of clarity associated with the traditional female role. Since the salient role for women is the parent role, an ascribed role, the standards they must meet will be more ambiguous than those for men, whose salient role is an achieved one.

It is possible to analyze in these terms the case of women who try to combine both kinds of roles, the ascribed role of parent and the achieved role of job holder. If it is correct that good mothers are assumed to be rather less good as job holders or conversely that a woman who is a success in her occupation is assumed to be necessarily lacking as a mother, then it is clear that working women are in an unresolvable conflict. They cannot reap whatever positive evaluations might accrue to them because of good performance on the job when such performance implies poor performance in their ascribed role as mothers. And failure to fulfill ascribed roles has the potential for being severely punished. The implicit moral to women is don't try such a combination, you simply can't win. On the other hand, a man who is successful at his work not only gains positive evaluation in that role but at the same time is highly evaluated in his ascribed roles of father and husband. One really can't help feeling that the "game," such as it is, is rigged.

Although the ascribed vs. achieved role analysis suggests that women have a more difficult role situation to resolve than do men, note that the reference is to extrinsic rewards and sanctions and almost exclusively to how people other than the individual role occupant evaluate his/her activities. The intense and profoundly personal experience of parenting, however, has intrinsic rewards (and anxieties) that may far exceed whatever external trappings of success or failure the career world has to offer.

Whatever the intrinsic pleasures and pains involved in the parent role, how-ever, men who have careers and for whom the parent role is as salient as it is for women, i.e., dual-role men, find themselves in a role conflict every bit as difficult as that described for dual-role women. In fact, the situational approach suggests that the conflict for men might be even worse than for women. After all, a man who devotes a lot of time and emotional energy to domestic activities will be doubly sanctioned. Not only is he violating sex-role expectations, but also he is pursuing a kind of activity that is not generally highly regarded in our culture. This double-sanction effect may account in part for the apparent fact that more women are currently crossing sex-role boundaries to enter careers than are men to expand and develop activities in the domestic domain.

The issue of choice may play an important part in creating strains for dual-role women and in creating the apparent difference between men and women in terms of professional or occupational achievement. Rose (1951) reports:

> The modern woman has a choice between "career" and marriage, or she can work out some combination of them almost by herself. Since she has a choice, she may later question whether the goals she chose are the ones she "really" wants. A man has no such choice facing him: He must get an occupation. . . . Other people measure his success in terms of achievements in his occupation whereas even if a woman is a success in what she sets out to do, public acclaim will not be at all universal. (p. 70)

POSSIBLE SOLUTIONS TO DUAL-ROLE CONFLICT IN WOMEN

Let us assume, then, that women who seek to combine a career with wifehood and motherhood are confronted with an ambiguous situation. On the face of it, they have a great deal of free choice about the role combination. The standards that must be met, however, are contradictory, i.e., to be good in one role implies relative failure in the other, and the ranges of evaluations associated with each of the combined roles are different. It is probably safe to assume that this kind of role conflict may well inhibit occupational and professional achievement in women and that to realize fully their achievement potential, women must somehow resolve the conflict. How might such resolution be accomplished?

One useful strategy for dual-role women is to seek to compare their performance in the two roles with relevant others, most often other people who are in the same kind of situation. Festinger (1954) has postulated that all people will seek to compare their opinions and abilities with people who are similar to themselves. This hypothesis has been examined in many investigations (Schachter, 1959; Wrightsman, 1960; Radloff, 1966; Zanna, Goethals, & Hill, 1975), and has received considerable support.

Unfortunately, for the career/wife-and-mother there are still not many other mothers or wives in the office with whom she can compare her performance on the job, and there are still not many women in her neighborhood who leave their homes and children every day to pursue careers. There simply aren't many relevant others with whom these women can compare themselves in either of the two roles, and the self-evaluative information they get therefore will not be very stable. The information must be frequently verified and validated, and it is in the effort to gain such validation, which can only be obtained in social contexts, that women may appear to be more dependent and affiliative than men. Because the role requirements of having a career and being a good husband and father are not contradictory and because most husbands and fathers have careers and many men with careers are also husbands and fathers, men can evaluate their role performances and their attitudes far more easily and reliably than can women. For men, an occasional check is sufficient; for women, it is not.

The drive for evaluation, as postulated by Festinger (1954), "is a force acting on persons to belong to groups, to associate with others. And the subjective feelings of correctness in one's opinions and the subjective evaluations of adequacy of one's performance on important abilities are some of the satisfactions that persons attain in the course of these associations with other people" (pp. 135–136). But the chances are that dual-role women often find less satisfaction in any one social-comparison encounter than do men, mainly because the relevant other for a woman is usually less relevant than is the relevant other for a man. Most of the woman's colleagues are likely to be men, which makes them dissimilar on an important dimension; and of the few colleagues that are women, not all will be married or have children, and so they too may be importantly different and thus not ideal social-comparison referents. On the other hand, many of the woman's evaluators for her enactment of the wife-mother role will not be career women and so will not understand the full range of responsibilities and role demands that she must meet. They too are less than perfect social-comparison referents.

Women who try to combine the traditional feminine role of wife and mother with a career are caught between two reference groups which have conflicting values and standards for self-appraisal of their members. In their discussion of the research reported in *The American Soldier*, Merton and Kitt (1950) consider the patterns of self-evaluation that are often displayed by people who "are subject to multiple reference groups operating at cross-purposes" (p. 63). One pattern involves a compromise self-appraisal, intermediate between the evaluation of the two conflicting reference groups. A second alternative when two membership groups exert opposing pressures for self-evaluation is for the individual to adopt a third group for social-comparison purposes. Additional possibilities suggested by Lazarsfeld, Berelson, and Gaudet (1948) "range all the way from individual neurotic reactions, such as inability to make a decision at all, to intellectual solutions which might lead to new social movements" (p. xxii).

Whatever the solution, however, an individual who tries to maintain membership simultaneously in two groups whose values are contradictory is likely to engender hostility from both groups. As Merton and Kitt (1950) point out: "What the individual experiences as estrangement from a group of which he is a member tends to be experienced by his associates as repudiation of the group, and this ordinarily evokes a hostile response" (p. 93). While the deviant may at first receive considerable attention and communication from other group members (Festinger, 1950; Schachter, 1951), the tendency for the group to reject the individual will increase as the person orients him/herself toward outgroup values, either verbally or in his/her behavior. And of course for an individual who from the outset maintains some affiliation with each of two opposing groups, such orientation is constant. Each group is continuously being threatened by the individual's membership in the other. Women who seek to combine the traditional feminine role with a career are bound to be viewed as deviants within each of their role-reference groups.

What options are open to a woman contemplating both family and career? She can, for instance, give up professional aspirations and decide to stay home where, supposedly, she belongs and to devote herself exclusively to her husband and children; or she can forswear a family and devote herself entirely to a career. Since in the latter case she is failing to fill the role that is considered most appropriate for women in current American society, she is likely to suffer various negative social sanctions. Still, if she adopts the standards of an appropriate career-oriented reference group, she may receive enough social support within her profession or occupation to withstand the general pressures to conform to traditional role expectations.

For women who do not want to give up either the opportunities for self-development and the monetary and other tangible rewards involved in a career or the satisfactions of family life, the situation is more complicated but perhaps not as bleak as it might appear. If the number of women choosing to combine previously contradictory roles increases, a third kind of reference group will emerge and will validate the combined role choice. It will also be a source of stable social-comparison information for group members. And as self-evaluation becomes more stable for these women, their behavior may appear to become more independent since they will no longer have to check with as many and as conflicting social-comparison referents. Their status in the social order will become less deviant, certainly in a statistical sense but also perhaps in a social sense. Finally, as their status becomes more acceptable, women who combine family life and careers may have less energy bound up in internal conflict and more energy available to channel into their work. Thus they may more visibly achieve in areas currently reserved for men. If women, in other words, can free themselves from the kind of role conflict outlined in this paper, their apparent overdependence on others for social support and their seemingly nonachieving "natures" may be revealed as largely or wholly epiphenomenal.

NOTE

1. Howe, K. G., & Zanna, M. P. *Sex-appropriateness of the task and achievement behavior*. Paper presented at the meeting of the Eastern Psychological Association, New York, April 1975.

REFERENCES

Condry, J., & Dyer, S. Fear of Success: Attribution of cause to the victim. *Journal of Social Issues*, 1976, **32**(3).

Epstein, C. F. *Woman's place: Options and limits in professional careers*. Berkeley: University of California Press, 1970.

Festinger, L. Informal social communication. *Psychological Review*, 1950, **57**, 271–282.

Festinger, L. A theory of social comparison processes. *Human Relations*, 1954, **7**, 117–140.

Freud, S. Some psychological consequences of the anatomical distinction between the sexes. *International Journal of Psychoanalysis*, 1927, **8**, 133–142.

Horner, M. Achievement-related conflicts in women. *Journal of Social Issues*, 1972, **28**(2), 157–175.

Lazarsfeld, P. F., Berelson, B., & Gaudet, H. *The people's choice*. New York: Columbia University Press, 1948.

Linder, S. *The harried leisure class*. New York: Columbia University Press, 1970.

Maccoby, E. Women's intellect. In S. M. Farber & R. H. L. Wilson (Eds.), *The potential of women*. New York: McGraw-Hill, 1963.

Maccoby, E. Sex differences in intellectual functioning. In E. E. Maccoby, *The development of sex differences*. Stanford, CA: Stanford University Press, 1966.

Merton, R. K., & Kitt, A. S. Contributions to the theory of reference group behavior. In R. K. Merton & P. F. Lazarsfeld (Eds.), *Continuities in social research: Studies in the scope and method of "The American Soldier."* Glencoe, Ill.: Free Press, 1950.

Morgan, J. N., Sirageldin, I. A., & Baerwaldt, N. *Productive Americans*. Ann Arbor: University of Michigan Press, 1966.

Newsweek, November 1974, p. 112.

Parsons, T. Age and sex in U.S. social structure. *American Sociological Review*, 1942, **7**, 604–616.

Radloff, R. Social comparison and ability evaluation. In B. Latané (Eds.), *Studies in social comparison*. New York: Academic Press, 1966.

Rose, A. M. The adequacy of women's expectations for adult roles. *Social Forces*, 1951, **30**, 69–77.

Sarbin, T. R., & Allen, V. L. Role theory. In G. Lindzey & E. Aronson (Eds.), *The handbook of social psychology* (Vol. 1). Reading, Mass.: Addison-Wesley, 1968.

Schachter, S. Deviation, rejection, and communication. *Journal of Abnormal and Social Psychology*, 1951, **46**, 190–207.

Schachter, S. *The psychology of affiliation*. Stanford: Stanford University Press, 1959.

Wrightsman, L. S., Jr. Effects of waiting with others on changes in level of felt anxiety. *Journal of Abnormal and Social Psychology*, 1960, **61**, 216–222.

Zanna, M. P., Goethals, G. R., & Hill, J. F. Evaluating a sex-related ability: Social comparison with similar others and standard setters. *Journal of Experimental Social Psychology*, 1975, **11**, 86–93.

BARBARA J. KATZ

Women's Lib Auxiliaries?

The word "brother" is taking on a new meaning.

   Men Against Cool, a Chicago group

The men are on the march. But it's a quiet, decidedly uncoordinated march, so hidden from view that one must listen very carefully to hear its stirrings. It's the first, faltering footsteps of a men's liberation movement.

Men's liberation? That's right. In cities, suburbs, and small towns as diverse as Fresno, Calif., Lawrence, Kan., and Fort Lee, N.J., an estimated 300 men's groups now meet regularly to explore the ways in which sex-role stereotypes limit and inhibit them. In heart-of-the-country places like Oberlin, Ohio; Lansing, Mich.; and Iowa City, Iowa, conferences on such topics as "the new masculine consciousness" attract hundreds of participants. And once in a while, in sophisticated urban centers like New York City and Chicago, small groups of men demonstrate against the "crippling sex-role training" found in children's books and the "exploitation of the insecurities of men" practiced by Playboy king Hugh Hefner.

Some men put their new views into print in publications like Brother: A Forum for Men against Sexism, published in Berkeley, Calif. Some are writing books: At least five books on men's liberation are now in the works. Others form organizations, like Boston's Fathers for Equal Justice, to try to dispel what they regard as a widespread view of men—particularly divorced men—as bystanders unconcerned with the rearing of their children. Others act as individuals, like the teacher from New York City who has successfully challenged a school policy denying men the right to take child-care leaves.

Generally, though, the men taking part in this new movement—mostly white, middle-class, and in their mid-20s to mid-50s—are more introspective than political. Most have become involved in response to the women's movement: At first defensive under female questioning of accepted sex roles, they soon came to question these roles themselves.

Unlike the members of the women's movement, however, they have not yet formulated a widely accepted set of social and political goals, nor produced a highly visible structure to fight for these goals. Some would even deny they are members of a "movement." Eschewing rhetoric, they explore their concerns about the traditional male sex role on an intensely personal level, usually within groups of from 6 to 10 members.

In a brightly lit, comfortable living room in North Arlington, Va., four men, one of them with his 3-month-old son on his knee, are "rapping." Jean, a 37-year-old sandy-haired, craggy-faced lawyer, is talking:

I was brought up in a family where traditionally the males keep everything to themselves. You grin and bear it and never recognize that there are any problems. Or if there is a problem, you just take a deep breath, throw back your shoulders, and say, "I'm a big guy and I'm just gonna live through it and override it."

Competitive pressures are something else I've always felt strongly—"Get in there and compete and work your 10-hour days and work every week end." I've always done a lot of that, sort of following the road map that others have laid out, neglecting my family and my personal desires in the process. I'm trying to get out of both these binds now, but it's not that easy to change the rules after playing the game the old way for so long.

" 'Getting ahead' and 'staying cool'—these have been the two main prescriptions of the male role in our society," says Joseph Pleck, a psychology instructor at the University of Michigan and a frequent speaker at men's conferences. "But it's becoming clear to many of us that many of our most important inner needs cannot be met by acting in the ways we have been expected to act as men."

Dr. Robert Gould, a psychiatrist at New York's Metropolitan General Hospital and speaker at a recent men's conference at Oberlin College, agrees: "It's more difficult to appreciate men's distress, since they have the dominant role in society, but their role is just as rigidly defined and stereotyped."

The idealized male sex-role, Gould explains, is to be tough, competitive, unfeeling, emotionally inexpressive, and masterful—"to come as close as possible to satsfying the John Wayne image." But trying to play that role exacts its price. Says Gould: "By striving to fulfill the role society sets forth for them, men repress many of their most basic human traits. They thus cut off about half their potential for living."

Men's consciousness-raising, or "rap," groups are one tool for increasing that potential. In these groups, men simply try to talk honestly about their lives to other men—a new experience for many—and to raise the questions that have begun to bother them.

Why, the men ask, aren't men supposed to express emotions? Why must men never reveal weakness? Why can't men be more than "buddies" with one another, sharing their feelings, not just their views on sports, women, and work? Why can't men touch one another, the way women do, without being thought homosexual?

Why must men be the sole or major breadwinner? Why must they always assume the dominant role with women? Why must they prove their "manliness" by "putting down" or "beating out" the next guy? Why must men always strive to "get ahead" instead of just enjoying their work? Why aren't men supposed to have too much to do with children, even their own?

Warren Farrell, who teaches "sexual politics" at American University and heads the National Organization for Women's task force on the "male mystique," believes that men's groups are "the basic instrument of the men's liberation movement." Farrell . . . travels around the country lecturing on men's liberation and after each talk invites members of the audience to become the nucleus of a new group. "So far we've formed at least 50 groups this way," he says. So great is the demand for men's groups, he says, that he and other concerned men are now planning a national conference to train group "facilitators."

Why this sudden concern for men's liberation? Most men in the movement today credit the growing strength of the women's liberation movement. For every woman rethinking *her* role, they say, there's probably a man somewhere rethinking *his*.

> In a small, pleasant living room in Berwyn, Ill., a Chicago suburb, eight men, one with a 7-month-old daughter, and four cats of mixed descent sit in the overstuffed furniture and sprawl on the floor. Bowls of turkey soup—made by one of the men—and jugs of wine and apple juice are passed around. George, a tall, gangly, 47-year-old Unitarian minister, is talking:
>
> When my wife got involved in the women's movement several years ago, her thinking and questioning about her role started having an effect on both our lives. I saw I had to start dealing with some of the issues she was raising.
>
> When I first joined a group, about four years ago, we did some "guilt-tripping" at first—flagellating ourselves for the ways we were oppressing women—but we soon moved on to sharing other problems. We soon came to see that it wasn't just the women in our lives who were having problems and whom we were having problems relating to, but we also had problems within ourselves, and problems relating to each other. We discovered that in some way we had been dehumanized, and we came to want to find out what it means to be a male human being.

But is the move toward greater awareness only a process of raising questions? No, reply the men who've stayed with it. There are answers and gains.

For some men, it's meant their first close male friendships. For others, it's meant a lessening of competitive pressure and a greater recognition of the importance of personal and family desires.

For Jean, the Virginia lawyer trying to emerge from his double bind, it's meant "being able to show more emotion with our little daughter" and a willingness to take "an enormous amount of time off of work—even at the risk of cutting his salary—to help his wife through a difficult pregnancy.

For George, the Chicago minister, it's meant a "net energy gain" from the support provided by "people I really dig." It's meant being able to share the most personal of concerns with peers who understand and share his concerns—even his emotional struggle over the "finality" of the vasectomy he's considering.

For Mark, a 40-year-old burglar-alarm specialist in Chicago, it's meant being able to view his wife "more as an equal partner, a whole person, a friend. Before I saw her primarily as a mother and housekeeper, and I was always playing the big protector, the big man around the house. That's really a pretty crummy role, and besides, you can't have a really open relationship with a servant. It's been a lot nicer lately.''

And for Jeff, a 26-year-old advertising executive in Deale, Md., it's meant the discovery that "vulnerability isn't necessarily a bad thing," and that "crying is a tremendous release." It's also enabled him to face that fact that, although successful at his job, he doesn't like what he's doing. "It's so easy to get caught up in simply doing what you're trained to do, what you're expected to do, even if you know it's not what you really want," he says. Jeff is planning to switch to an entirely different field—ecological architecture.

Liberation, these men say, does not mean that men will be "liberated" from the need to work or to share family responsibilities. It does mean becoming aware of what they see as the subtle ways they are forced into doing things because they must satisfy society's expectations of "what it takes to be a man."

Those who have given some thought to men's liberation say there are two major obstacles to overcome if one is to "unlearn" those expectations: The first is recognizing and unlearning the underlying contempt they say most men feel for women; the second is questioning the male "hierarchy of values."

"Men learn from the time they're boys that the worst possible thing is to be considered feminine—a 'sissy,' " says Warren Farrell. "The male's fear that he might be thought of as a female—with all the negative implications that carries— has been the central basis of his need to prove himself 'masculine.' A more positive image of women frees a man to come in contact with the so-called feminine parts of his personality and allows him to start displaying human emotions without fear of being called feminine."

The male "hierarchy of values," with its emphasis on competition and "success," is so ingrained in our society that "it takes a revolution in one's thinking to see what it's about," says psychiatrist Robert Gould. "In American society, success has nothing to do with how you live your life," he says, "but with whether you satisfy American values of what success is—wealth, power, and status. One learns very early that if you're bigger and stronger and louder, you'll win all the marbles. One seldom questions whether what is given up in the process of winning the marbles—meaningful relationships with people, enjoyment of work for its own sake—is worth it."

The men taking part in the men's movement *are* doing that questioning. But their movement is small and, while growing, not yet at the pace of the women's movement. Some, like Jim, a 33-year-old reporter in Washington, D.C., believe "the real guts of this is in the children we bring up.

"Surely our impact, for good or ill, is going to have an impact on them," he says. "We're not going to find exact answers to all our questions immediately, but certainly we're setting a different example from what we had."

8

Environment and City

Throughout this book our concern has been with the social nature of the individual, and how the individual is affected by forces within the social environment. We have talked about the "environment" in a general way as a setting in which people react to the pressures, expectations, and evaluations of others, but for the most part we have failed to directly observe and study individuals in the *actual* contexts and environments in which they live and interact with others.

At the present time, we have become far more aware of major effects of ecological and environmental variables on our behavior and have come to realize that the *social* environment encompasses the *physical* environment as well. There is little doubt that physical living conditions have strong implications for interpersonal relations and social behavior. As a result, we are now asking questions about the effects of crowding, the nature of privacy, and most significantly, we have begun to look at the effects of the urban setting upon individual behavior and patterns of interaction.

Harold Proshansky, President of the Graduate School and University Center, City University of New York, is a social psychologist long respected for his work in the environmental field. In the book (coauthored with William Ittelson, Leanne Rivlin, and Gary Winkel) *An Introduction to Environmental Psychology*, 1974), he has helped define a growing area of interest.

In our conversation, Dr. Proshansky commented upon a wide range of issues associated with urban life, reflecting the belief that social, political, and economic factors must all be considered when trying to describe the city, its inhabitants, and their future. He described a number of ways in which people in large cities differ from other people, and suggested that much research is needed to discover how these differences come about. Moreover, he felt that a certain *type* of research is necessary—research which actively involves social scientists with their environments on a working, living basis.

A CONVERSATION WITH HAROLD PROSHANSKY

The City University of New York

KRUPAT: *If we're going to talk about the social individual as an urban individual, maybe we'd better start off by seeing if we can define what urban means. As a social psychologist, could you define a city? What is one, and what are its defining characteristics?*

PROSHANSKY: Let me first respond to that question in a textbookish sense. The city, in modern times, is an organization of large numbers of individuals engaged in a variety of human activities in systematic and meaningful ways that represent the achievement of both the values and purposes of a given society. That sounds somewhat pretentious, so let me say it in simpler terms: The city is a set of human activities concentrated in a given geographical area in order to provide the dimensions of human life that characterize what we call organized society.

KRUPAT: *If I'm correct then, the city is people, it is activity—not just land. But, then the question is: Why is something like the city worth studying in and of itself? What is special to the behavior of individuals that the city contributes as a setting?*

PROSHANSKY: First, urbanism and the city is not *a* way of life; it is increasingly becoming *the* way of life. To that, you must tie modern technology. If technological advances continue, they increase the probability of more and more people living in greater concentrations, because technology allows us to integrate, organize, and carry out a variety of activities involving many, many people. So, it would seem that urbanism is the key to understanding complex industrial society. And part of urbanism is change, with the rate of change proceeding at an increasingly accelerated rate. If all this is true, then understanding human behavior—particularly social behavior and social interaction—must take place in the broader context of what I would call the urban setting. If you want to understand social interaction and social process, then you must study that social interaction and social process produced where large numbers of individuals work together, play together, carry out activities together on increasingly impersonal terms.

KRUPAT: *Now, you've touched upon a great many possible aspects or explanations of why and how the city affects people in various ways. You've mentioned numbers, concentration, patterns of organization, etc. For you, is there one key variable which is important in how the city affects the individual in his everyday life, or do you believe it is just a whole wealth of things impinging on the person?*

PROSHANSKY: I do think there is a key. I believe that what affects all of us who are city dwellers (now, I don't mean a city of 50,000 people; I mean to talk about large urban centers) are the highly *impersonal* and structure-defined activities and role relationships that we experience. In the city, where I work I don't know everybody; where I ride I don't know everybody; yet sometimes I end up being more "intimate" with a man on an extremely crowded train than I am with my own family. How I meet the requirements of government are highly impersonal, and if we now add to that the computer and the IBM card and information processing, I think that the city has become that place where the individual becomes shaped like a manufactured product. Maintaining the human element in this setting depends on one's skill in selecting out of all this something that represents the other values in human life which are not work, transportation, or success, but have to do with love, interpersonal relationships, aesthetic feelings, and so on.

KRUPAT: *But haven't big government, the computer, and the IBM card found their ways out of the big city? Just what is the* critical *difference between this monster we call the great urban center and whatever the term is which is its opposite?*

PROSHANSKY: I think, unfortunately, that any attempt to sharply demarcate a city from whatever is a noncity grows increasingly difficult. It used to be that a small community had properties that were so radically different from the larger city that it was not difficult to list them. First, the numbers of people and the size of the schools; therefore, the way in which education and health practices were organized. The general practitioner didn't disappear because specialization forced him out. The whole nature of doctors in city complexes changed as it became more and more difficult for a doctor to have his fifty patients and handle them on a personal basis with the resources available, such as transportation.

The discrimination between urban and nonurban areas becomes less clear because everything has become large-scale. Coca-Cola is international and the telephone is in the rural area, and there are regional transportation systems and statewide universities. What has happened is that size and remoteness have practically disappeared as dimensions by which we can distinguish the city from the noncity—and urbanism is all over the place. Sure, I can take you to a small mountain village in Tennessee, but even there, the inputs of technology are so great that the differences have decreased considerably.

KRUPAT: *But at the other extreme, to what extent can we generalize even about large cities and their effects upon their inhabitants? I once lived in New York, but now I live in Boston. They're two major urban centers, and yet it's like living in two different worlds to me.*

PROSHANSKY: I suspect that what your experience reflects is not so much a difference in the inherent structures or basic properties of these two or any two large cities—Boston has large numbers of people, a complex educational system, a complex transportation system, and lots of other things New York has. But, still, its geographical structure is different, and its problems are different. At this point, you can ask: To what degree does the city frustrate and impede the individual? How many areas of Boston can you walk around free of fear, free of the threat of mugging or rape compared to New York? But while cities offer varying amounts of frustration, they also offer variety and freedom of choice in varying degrees. So, while the good and the bad vary in degrees and may lead to very different feelings in New York or Montreal or London or Paris, much of how large cities affect their inhabitants remains constant.

KRUPAT: *But then, maybe we've come to the most important issue, at least as I see the value of discussing the city. What exactly are the effects of the city on its people and their* behavior? *Are city people really different than noncity people? It would seem that this is the question which social psychologists ought to be able to relate to and add to our knowledge of, beyond what the purely sociological literature has already accumulated.*

PROSHANSKY: Well, I haven't really read all of the sociological books, although I have read a fair amount about city life; but I regard all of the early demographic material as useless. At this point, a good deal of the most interesting things I've read have been anecdotal, and I can only theorize about the psychological effects of living in big cities and what cities do to people.

To begin: I think without any doubt in my mind that a large city creates a difference in *pace*. I've experienced it; I've measured it in certain ways; and I believe it's true. In Ann Arbor, Michigan, when people want to get from one place to another, they have no "rapid" transit system. Everyone has adjusted to the simple notion that you can get from one part of town to another by car. Distances are shorter, the possibilities of traffic jams are much more remote, and the pace is slower.

What does *pace* mean? Let's take a simple fact: After you've controlled for all the other relevant variables such as age and class, the number of coronaries is six times greater in New York than in Albuquerque, New Mexico. I've lived there and I can tell you that the pace is very different.

KRUPAT: *I can agree with your Ann Arbor example. Coming to the Midwest from New York, I could never understand how people could wait in lines with the patience they did. I was in too much of a hurry to tolerate waiting. Undergraduate girls from places like New York mentioned that they were often embarrassed on dates when they found they were walking five or six steps ahead of the escorts from small towns.*

PROSHANSKY: If you've ever lived in England, as I have, you suddenly realize that you're jumping up and down and you're not quite sure why you're in a hurry. Finally, you realize this, and by God, you adjust. And suddenly you find that you like it.

KRUPAT: *OK, I wholeheartedly agree that cities speed up the pace of life; and some of the apparent consequences, such as brusqueness and intolerance, are not too hard to imagine. Are there other differences?*

PROSHANSKY: Let me give you a second factor, and I don't think one has to be a brilliant theorist to say this. The large city creates in many ways what I call "the diversity of experience." There are more people, more stores, more schools, more strange people, more museums, more kinds of entertainment. If a new fad suddenly starts out, I don't care what it is, it's more likely to find itself in New York than in Saddle River, New Jersey. My guess is that the city dweller makes greater demands on his environment for novelty; and indeed he expects more of it because he's been given more of it.

Let me best identify this by what happened many years ago to my son shortly after we had moved from New York to Ann Arbor. He came home from school on the second day of classes and told me, "Gee, it's a funny class. I was one of the three new kids; I got introduced to all the others; and they elected me president."

I said, "They elected you president—how could they do that, they don't know you from Adam!"

"Well," he said, "they asked me about New York in the morning and then they had elections in the afternoon. I told them about the subway, about crossing streets so wide they had two traffic islands, and about being on top of the Empire State Building—so they elected me president."

He didn't use the words, but it was clear that they felt he was someone with broader horizons and a greater diversity of experience.

KRUPAT: *OK, so we have pace and now also diversity. The first effect most people feel is somewhat negative, and clearly the second is a positive aspect of the city's effect upon its people. How about the fact you mentioned earlier, that life among such large numbers of people gives one a feeling of anonymity?*

PROSHANSKY: I believe anonymity is definitely a third major effect, but I don't regard it as a negative characteristic, and I believe it's been misinterpreted. It's just that there are too many people to know and it becomes natural to be living in a world full of strangers—there's no other way to do it. What evolves is a sense that one can only establish privacy and a sense of wholeness in a relationship with *some* people by being as impersonal as possible with *other* people. It is not that city people dislike other people; it's just too difficult to be related to all of them.

I would call this feature "tried and tested and required anonymity in personality." It isn't that the New Yorker is really all that cold and gruff; but if you take the pace, take the diversity, and you take the fact that there are that many people, you just have to break through them. You can't be expected to smile and say hello to everyone because you'd have to smile and say hello for six hours just to get from one block to the other.

KRUPAT: *What you've said sounds very much in line with many of the ways Milgram has described the "overloaded" city person in a selection in this section. Basically then, the city person acts the way he does toward strangers because there are too many, but it is important to remember that among friends he can be warm, personal, and caring.*

PROSHANSKY: I think some of the things Milgram emphasizes are different from mine, but I certainly do agree with him in general. Anonymity doesn't have a negative quality about it because it's the only way you can function. It happens to involve what the limits of human interaction are.

But now, let me point out another thing the city does. Large metropolitan centers tend to produce what I call the "diversity of groups." By this I mean that if the city is as complicated as it is and one has to select and define the world, it becomes easier to draw lines around particular groupings of people. Particular ethnic groups, racial groups, religious groups, gay groups, or whatever, became the basis for organizing people. I think the structure and organization of cities really support the concept of cultural pluralism; and this is fine, except for one thing. Once you begin to add other factors, such as the economic and political, it is not just cultural pluralism that you have. Instead, it's cultural antagonism. And then you have problems.

KRUPAT: *Are you saying that because of all these other aspects of the city, people need to simplify by applying labels to people so that they can select out the familiar from the unfamiliar, friend from foe?*

PROSHANSKY: That's a good point, and this is the reason for stereotypes, neighborhoods, territories—anything that establishes a reality and a familiarity to the world. You can be secure within your group, but when you have to step out, then all the labels and identifying features become quite crucial.

KRUPAT: *There are endless other questions I could ask about the effects of the city, but I think it might be useful to pursue a somewhat different line of thought. When you began listing the psychological (or social psychological) effects of the city, you began by saying that you could only theorize. It would seem as if we don't have a lot of good, hard data in an area where there's so much information needed and so much to be gained. I've read that you believe that the place to start is not in the laboratory. If not there, how can we gain the sorts of knowledge we need to understand the city, its people, and its processes—and just possibly improve it as a result?*

PROSHANSKY: Well, let me answer that one quite explicitly and with less hesitancy than some of the more difficult questions you've asked. Let me start by saying that the worst way to find out about the city is to replicate it not just in the laboratory, but with any kind of model. It seems to me that the methodology involved here is that you must begin with Step 1. That is, one has to define some problem. You can't just say, "I want to study the city." You have to be able to specify a problem of exploration such as: What is the effect of living in an apartment dwelling compared to a one-family residence; how does one organize educational experiences for large numbers of people?

I think we know beans about people in cities. We've written books; we've talked about it; but we have no data. Therefore, to me one basic approach is to leave it intact and not distort the phenomenon in any way. That means no fake crowds, no fake little houses. It also means that observation and other nonobtrusive measures become our basic tools. Also, if you want to study a phenomenon, you'd better get to know your topic. If you want to learn about mass transportation and its effects upon people, then you had better study transportation systems before you define any specific hypothesis, such as "Riding on the subway every day does X." And, in addition to all this, I feel very strongly that no research about the city can be successful unless the methodology includes the researcher who, to use an expression, signs himself up permanently.

Let me illustrate what I mean. The former police commissioner of New York, a very intelligent and sympathetic man, said to me, "We do want research on police-community relations, but I don't want the kind of research that you social scientists have done in the past. If you want to understand the negative and positive aspects of the police in relation to the community, you come in and you *stay*. This means that you can't come in and grab a piece, think you have it, run back and dirty up the situation and say you've studied it. You will understand what we're like, you'll be able to formulate problems, and moreover, you will have consequences for change if you, the policeman, the community member, and the government are all part of the same process." What he was suggesting was really an advanced version of what we call "living action research," and I'm convinced that he is right.

KRUPAT: *But, let's say for the moment that we have discovered some important things and we have some relevant answers. How can we go about applying them? How likely is it that people will be willing to use our knowledge?*

PROSHANSKY: If people have asked you because they've got a severe problem and you can provide an answer that will change or save their lives, they will change. If I can show a guy how to go ten blocks without being hit over the head, there's no question he's going to listen. Unfortunately, many of the social problems we have are not raised for us in as simple terms as that. Besides, what a government may perceive as a problem is not necessarily perceived by a group of people as a problem. But, in instances such as the commissioner described, where people are slowly involved, become part of the process, and can see consequences for a change, my guess is that changes will occur. Still, that's no guarantee of being useful, because even then people seldom examine *other* consequences of a proposed change. For instance, if giving up smoking means not getting cancer, that's great. But, if it means getting ulcers or overeating, somebody is going to have to deal with that.

What I really believe is that change in any significant sense can only come out of the members of society, not out of the behavioral sciences. All we can do is offer an approach and hope to provide answers to understand a problem. In cases where we do produce significant insights which should lead to change, our job becomes one of making the findings available and to encourage; but change itself is a product of society, of the government, of the citizens. Beyond that, we should stop, and to the extent we insist that changes occur, we are simply being citizens, politicians, and influencers; we are no longer in the role of behavioral scientists.

KRUPAT: *But up to this point I'm still not sure how much you feel we need change or how likely it is to occur. In your opinion, should we be optimistic or pessimistic about the future of the city—or, more correctly, of the indi-vidual in the urban setting?*

PROSHANSKY: There are a couple of ways I could answer that. On a kind of fantasy level I could say, let's forget about politics, Nixon, Watergate, Russia, China, and the most single obvious truth that everything is interrelated.

A colleague of mine has said, "Suppose we cleaned up the city of all its dirt, made the subways noiseless, removed the smog, and increased the amount of space; would this then be a good city or a city to live in?" There may still be aspects to the design and organization of cities and their conse-quences that we know little about. But even within this context, I see things getting worse and not better, for this reason. Technology goes faster and faster, and I see no significant evidence of planning—just constant expan-sion. Technology seems to lead us by the nose. Most often we neither plan nor think of maintaining the human element. In effect, we don't run the city; the city runs us.

KRUPAT: *Then I believe there is one final and important question. Is there any way we can run the cities rather than vice versa? Is there some way we can make the city more human or perhaps even more humane?*

PROSHANSKY: Sometimes we think we have planned and considered— for instance, when an architect designs a building—but the whole concept of the human element is left out. But let's not even go into that. The fact is, we never go back to find out. We never ask what the building is doing. We never evaluate: Is this physical setting doing what we intended it to do? If it isn't, why isn't it? Second (and also crucial), in our planning we are like medicine was twenty-five years ago. We always plan with intended consequences, but we never give thought to unintended consequences. For instance, will that antibiotic also cause havoc in other parts of the body? The way we deal with our cities, our schools, our roads can also have unintended consequences. That road may get everyone from one end of town to the other in thirty minutes instead of two hours, but it may also do lots of other things to people that are seldom thought about.

It takes a new kind of planning, a planning which says that we don't introduce major changes until we have a good grasp of their consequences, both intended and unintended. Still, that's an intellectual response. My gut reaction is that the only way we can get a handle on the city and ourselves is that there has to be a fundamental change in the values and priorities of American society. The New York City school system could stand on its head and whistle Dixie and no matter what it says, unless we tear up the present program and start taking money out of the till that we put into going to the moon, the problems of minority group members, poor people, and poor reading scores will always plague us.

I know this begins to sound more like advocacy than an objective, social science-type answer, but unless there is this fundamental shift about the values of human life, the city will only become more unmanageable. Someone around here decided that the Hudson River must be made clean. Over a period of ten years and a cost of well beyond a billion dollars, it will be done. But it is interesting. When they make up their minds, when they shift the priority of costs, they manage to do it. I have no doubt that with a radical approach we can get a handle on the city.

AN INTRODUCTION TO THE READINGS

The articles in this section bring together a number of important positions and statements on the effects of environmental variables in general and urban settings in particular. In the first paper, Irwin Altman offers a clear and concise review of the concept of crowding. He points out, among other things, that crowding must be differentiated from density, and that whether crowding results from having "too many people" or "too little space" may have different effects on the individual. In reviewing a good deal of both field and experimental studies of crowding, Altman demonstrates the way that different methodologies may suggest different conclusions. He also notes that both approaches are necessary if we are to fully understand why and when people feel crowded and how they react to such situations.

The second article, by Stanley Milgram, whose work on obedience was described in an earlier section, attempts to build a social psychology of the actual experience of city life. Pointing out that the urbanite is constantly involved with other people, Milgram suggests that the way to understand the urban experience is to see it as a matter of overload: too much to see, too much to do, too much to pay attention to. Within the framework of this single concept of overload, Milgram discusses research on social responsibility, anonymity, and urban role behavior. He then goes beyond this overload model to discuss research aimed at describing and explaining the distinctive atmospheres and behaviors of people in different large cities.

The third article is an excerpt from Kevin Lynch's classic book *The Image of the City*. Like Milgram, Lynch focuses on perceptual elements of the city, but as an urban planner, his interests are somewhat different. He addresses the questions of how people form a mental image of a city and why such an image is important. Lynch suggests that a city which helps create a clear image allows people to navigate through it with a minimum of difficulty, gives people a sense of security and freedom and provides them with images which they can share with others. The job of the planner is to help structure cities so that they are, in Lynch's terms, legible and imageable.

The next article is from Jane Jacobs' *The Death and Life of Great American Cities*. Jacobs' position is that cities are very different from small towns, not only in the quantity of people but also in the quality of life and the patterns of interaction that evolve. In commenting on the nature of city life, she points to the fact that when there are great numbers of people living near one another, they must set up mechanisms that guarantee their privacy. People may be friendly or familiar with many others in an extremely casual and superficial way, yet they will still maintain a very limited set of private close relationships. This article points out that urban people learn to develop specialized patterns of interaction, in this case by distinguishing between public and private space in order to protect themselves against feelings of overload and crowding. It would be an interesting exercise to bring together the issues in the four articles in this section in considering how to make city life more humane. How can we utilize the concepts of crowding and density, overload, mental images, and public and private interaction to help accentuate the positive and eliminate the negative in urban living?

IRWIN ALTMAN

The Nature and Meaning of Crowding

What is meant by the term "crowding"? In everyday usage there are many situations in which people say "I am crowded" or "This place is crowded." For example,

> At a football game where the stands are filled or in a theater where there are no empty seats.
> As one squeezes into a packed elevator.
> A popular beer hall on Saturday night.
> The downtown area of a large city at lunchtime.
> A large family who lives in a small home or apartment.

In some of these examples crowding does not necessarily imply an undesirable or stressful situation. In fact, sometimes the presence of many people is expected or even sought. For example, as long as one has a seat, a crowd at a football game or at a theater adds to the pleasure of the event. A crowded party also provides an exciting atmosphere, with many interaction opportunities. And the visitor to a large city often feels the positive excitement of being with others. Even a crowded elevator is not always aversive, as long as one isn't in it too long. To press the point further, some of these examples demonstrate that *too little* crowding may be unpleasant. For example, who would want to be in an empty football stadium or theater or at a poorly attended party? Thus some degree of density or contact with others is often desirable. Yet other examples in the very same settings show how crowding can be negative:

> A theatergoer faces long lines trying to purchase refreshments at intermission.
> Football fans leaving the stadium are jostled, can move only slowly toward parking lots, and must inch their way home in bumper-to-bumper traffic.
> The packed elevator stops floor by floor, and people push their ways on and off.
> People shove their way toward the bar in a crowded beer hall.
> The residents of an urban area wait to cross the street with droves of other people, struggle in lines to buy lunch, and are jostled in subways day by day and year after year.
> A member of a large family living in a small apartment must dress and undress in the presence of others, wait in line for the bathroom, and share a bed with others.

These examples illustrate that crowding is not a simple concept. It has been applied to large populations, such as cities, and to relatively small groups at parties and in homes. It has even been used to portray a relationship between two persons, as captured by the phrase "You crowd me!" To understand crowding, therefore, requires an unraveling of its dimensions and a recognition that it is a complex idea. Moreover, the term is used in a variety of situations—where people want more physical space, where they are blocked from desired resources (for example, waiting in a long line for some service), where they are intruded on by others, and where they are in short- versus long-term situations of high density (for example, an elevator rather than a crowded ghetto or home). These examples point to a few dimensions of crowding, such as space availability, access to resources, intrusion, and duration of contact with others. In addition, our examples illustrate the optimization and dialectic qualities of crowding, discussed earlier in relation to privacy. The presence of others provides positive gratifications; yet there are circumstances in which the presence of others is negative. Furthermore, there is an interplay of forces in which other people can be simultaneously positively and negatively gratifying. For example, city life involves considerable positive stimulation—a variety of cultural, economic, and political resources that can be tapped, making life a rich experience. Yet these very qualities can be negative. People are subject to intrusion, noise, difficulty in gaining access to resources, and the impersonality of others (Simmel, 1950; Wirth, 1938; Milgram, 1970).

At the root of my analysis lies a central theme—that crowding is an *interpersonal* process, at the level of people interacting with one another in pairs or in small groups. While it is proper and necessary to study crowding at the large-scale level of cities or nations, my emphasis is in understanding aspects of crowding that involve ongoing social interaction among people.

SOME DISTINCTIONS BETWEEN CROWDING AND DENSITY

The differences between the terms "crowding" and "density" are not always made clear. Sometimes the terms are used synonymously, to reflect the physical idea of number of people per unit of space. And, even in that case, the unit of space is not always the same but covers the range from people per acre of land, people per census tract, people per room in homes, dwelling units per acre of land, and the like. As I shall discuss later, these different indicators of density may not yield identical effects on behavior.

Recently, Stokols (1972a, 1972b) brought the distinction between density and crowding into sharp focus. He limited density to a strictly physical meaning—the number of people per unit of space. Crowding, on the other hand, is a psychological concept, with an experiential, motivational base. In his terms:

> The experience of crowding, thus, can be characterized as a motivational state directed toward the alleviation of perceived restriction and infringement, through the augmentation of one's space supply, or the adjustment of social and personal variables so as to minimize the inconveniences imposed by spatial limitation [p. 276].

Several points are worth highlighting about Stokols' approach. First, crowding is a personal, subjective reaction, not a physical variable. Second, it is a motivational state that often results in goal-directed behavior, to achieve some end or to relieve discomfort. Third, crowding centers around a feeling of too little space. Density, on the other hand, is strictly a physical quality with no inherent psychological meaning; it is merely a measure of people per unit of space.

Stokols stated that density is a necessary though not sufficient condition for the feeling of being crowded. That is, increased numbers of people per unit of space is an important prior condition for a feeling of crowding, but it is not always wholly sufficient to create that feeling. For example, one can be with a group of friends and not feel crowded, but can be with the same-size group of strangers and feel quite crowded. Thus certain other conditions such as amount and arrangement of space, noise, glare, and the like might interact with conditions of high density to trip off feelings of crowding. Similarly, social factors such as competition, interference from others, or power struggles can combine with density to affect feelings of crowding. Finally, personality and past experiences may interact with spatial density. As discussed later, my distinction between density and crowding is quite compatible with Stokols', although I will not emphasize feelings of spatial imitation as strongly.

Stokols also distinguished between *nonsocial crowding*, whereby physical factors alone generate feelings of inadequate space (for example, a space capsule), and *social crowding*, whereby the feeling of crowding comes primarily from the presence of too many other people. In addition, Stokols noted the difference in molecular and molar crowding. That is, feelings of crowding can be associated with large-scale, urban populations (molar crowding). But there is also a microlevel of analysis concerned with individual, small-group, and interpersonal events. The final distinction concerns subjective states of crowding and stress. Stokols observed that all feelings of crowding involve stress—either psychological or physiological. Psychological stress includes feelings of cognitive inconsistency (discrepancy between a person's desire for space and the amount of space actually available) and emotional imbalance (infringement, alienation from others). Physiological stress includes rises in blood pressure or hormone secretions.

Somewhat similar ideas have been offered by others. Esser (1972) described crowding as a mental state with a stress component, and he also emphasized the link between psychological and physiological processes. He hypothesized that feelings of crowding stem from a disharmony between the central nervous system and stimulus conditions. For example, feelings of crowding can derive from novel or strange situations, which involve a link with the neocortex (the most evolutionarily advanced brain area) through perceptual information processing and expectancy judgments. Or crowding can involve the biologically older part of the brain, the reticular system, when basic needs for territory are frustrated by population concentration and density.

Desor (1972) also emphasized social aspects of crowding and defined it as " . . . receiving excess stimulation from social sources." Other writers also pointed to the stimulus overload aspect of crowding (Rapoport, 1972; Wohlwill,

1974; Milgram, 1970). Implicit in this approach is the idea that crowding represents more interaction than what was desired. In my terms, crowding exists when various privacy-regulation mechanisms fail to produce a match between desired and achieved levels of privacy, with less privacy resulting than was desired.

Varieties of Density

Relatively little attention has been given, until recently, to the concept of density (Michelson, 1970; Zlutnick & Altman, 1972; Day & Day, 1973). The most general meaning of the term has been number of people per unit of space. In sociological studies conducted since the 1920s, a variety of density indicators have been related to social behavior. These have included number of people per city, number of people per census tract, number of people per dwelling unit, number of rooms per dwelling unit, number of buildings per neighborhood, and so on. Several recent studies, to be described in more detail later, indicate quite clearly that these various indicators of density have very different relationships with crowding (Galle, Gove, & McPherson, 1972; Marsella, Escudero, & Gordon, 1970; Booth & Welch, 1973). In these studies little relationship existed between various measures of social pathology such as crime or mental health and the more molar indicators of density such as number of people per acre or per community. The main findings indicated that micromeasures of density (for example, high numbers of people in homes) were associated with various kinds of social problems. Thus being in a densely populated neighborhood has different implications than being in a home with many people. Not that one is more important than the other, only that they are different and cannot be lumped together and called the same thing—"high density."

A differentiated approach to density analysis is summarized in Figure 1. It combines two levels of density—inside housing-unit density and outside housing-unit density (Zlutnick & Altman, 1972). Inside density refers to the number of people per unit of space within a residence, whereas outside density refers to the number of people per unit of space in a larger spatial unit, such as a street or census tract. From this two-factor framework a variety of living situations can be identified. Typical suburban living involves a small number of people inside residences and a small number of people outside residences in the immediate community. At the other extreme is the big-city ghetto, which often has a high concentration of people both inside and outside homes. Rural areas are often characterized by high densities within a home (primarily among poor people) but few people immediately outside the home (neighbors are remote from one another). The east-side luxury area of New York, on the other hand, has apartments with relatively small numbers of people inside but high concentrations of people in the outside neighborhood and city. While one can speculate about the effects of such density profiles, I can illustrate here only that density is a complex concept that may require more than a unidimensional approach. Therefore, to speak of all "low-density" situations as similar is an oversimplification. . . .

Several writers distinguish between *social density* and *spatial density* (Hutt & Vaizey, 1966; Loo, 1973a, 1973b; McGrew, 1970). Spatial density involves comparisons of same-size groups in different-size spaces—for example, a six-person

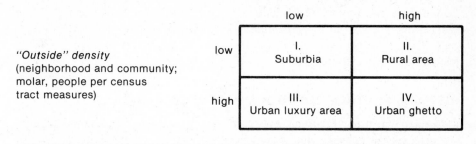

"Inside" density
(within residential units;
molecular,
people per room measures)

		low	high
"Outside" density (neighborhood and community; molar, people per census tract measures)	low	I. Suburbia	II. Rural area
	high	III. Urban luxury area	IV. Urban ghetto

FIGURE 1. Some Density Profiles. From "Crowding and Human Behavior," by S. Zlutnick & I. Altman, in J. F. Wohlwill & D. H. Carson (Eds.), *Environment and the Social Sciences: Perspectives and Applications.* Copyright 1972 by the American Psychological Association. Reprinted by permission.

group in a large versus a small room. Social density involves constant-size space but different numbers of people—for example six- versus twelve-person groups in the same-size room. Loo (1973a) speculated that different outcomes might occur in social- and spatial-density conditions, particularly if group composition shifts, as when a group in a constant space adds new members (social density). She contended that this may introduce problems of absorbing newcomers, not merely problems of space limitations per person. Thus if you are in a stable social group and decide to add several new members, there is apt to be a period of adjustment, not only to absorb the newcomers physically and spatially but to weave them into the social fabric of the group. Growing organizations in a fixed space who must add employees may face problems of absorption in both physical and social terms. And the rate at which population density increases will also make a difference. One person added to a group at a time is a quite different matter from a large influx of new members added all at once. On the other hand, a group whose space becomes limited but whose membership is constant may perceive the high density to be due to an external source, and members may not react to the issue as a group problem. Thus if a fixed-sized office group is squeezed into a smaller space (spatial density increases), they may see the problem as one imposed on them by management and respond differently than if the increased spatial density were caused by their own actions.

Day and Day (1973) raised other considerations in relation to population density. They called for attention to such factors as geographical features of population distribution. For example, a "dispersed agricultural" arrangement, in which farm land is spread equally over a geographical area, is different from a "coastal" arrangement, in which the same number of farms are packed along a coastline and the interior is not used. And these arrangements are in turn different from a "strip" arrangement, in which farms center around one area (perhaps along a river), and other parts of the land are unused. In these examples, the same average population concentration can be very differentially dispersed over a fixed area, which will obviously have different implications for the lives of the people. Day and Day also argue that one must have an understanding of transportation systems in such areas, residential-commercial mixes of functions, and a host of other variables.

In summary, we must pay attention not only to differences between crowding and density but also to the potentially rich meaning of each of these concepts considered separately and to the possibility that varieties of each may have different relationships to social processes. . . .

HISTORICAL STAGES OF RESEARCH ON CROWDING

Research on crowding began about five decades ago, as population in the Western world increased, as cities and technology grew, and as the social and behavioral sciences gained stature and turned toward the analysis of various social problems. Historically, two streams of research can be distinguished—one in sociology and the other in psychology. Within each tradition, there are some early-phase studies and some later-phase studies, distinguished by the sophistication of their methodological strategies.

Early Correlational-Sociological Studies

Th earliest work on crowding was done by sociologists who, beginning in the 1920s, tried to identify social outcomes of population density and indicators of social pathology, such as mental health and disease, crime, and various forms of social disorganization. For example, Schmid (1969, 1970) found high population densities and high crime rates in ghettos and central-city areas of Minneapolis and Seattle and a progressive decrease in the less populated surrounding suburbs. In Honolulu, Schmitt (1957) found a high correlation between population density, juvenile delinquency, and adult crime. Many other studies confirmed this type of relationship in other cities (Bordua, 1958; White, 1931).

Correlational data for mental illness and density yielded similar results. Faris and Dunham (1965) reported a decreasing incidence of mental illness from city centers outward to suburbs. Lantz (1953) found a higher incidence of mental illness in military officers from densely populated areas. Similar data on suicide were obtained by Cavan (1928), Schmid (1955), and Sainsbury (1956). Citation of additional studies could go on at length, but further examples can be obtained in a review by Michelson (1970).

Several characteristics of these earlier studies are worth noting. First, this research is correlational in methodological strategy. That is, studies examined statistical covariations between population density and social-pathology indicators, based on records and archives. While most of these investigations found moderate associations between density and social pathology, it cannot be concluded that density *caused* social disorganization. In many of these studies alternative explanations could have accounted for the correlations. For example, pure density is not the only variable that distinguishes the center of a city from its suburbs. Factors such as the inhabitants' physical well-being, economic status, health facilities, and education are only a few variables that often differ in central-city and suburban areas, and these factors might be related to social pathology. Thus the fact that two variables correlate in no way guarantees causation. Therefore, while these studies are suggestive, they do not justify hard conclusions about the effect of density on various social outcomes.

A second feature of early studies is that density was treated in a relatively undifferentiated fashion. Typical measures of density included people per acre, people per census tract, people per nation, and structures per acre or per census tract—all of which are relatively large geographical units. Only occasionally were measures based on people or families per dwelling unit or other small social units. And various measures of density were not compared systematically. Reading this literature gives the impression that researchers had a nontheoretical, pragmatic approach to density and crowding and explored such measures because they were available, quantitative, and seemingly rigorous.

A third feature of this early phase of research was its emphasis on social-system *outcomes* rather than on social *processes*. Crime rates, mental-health disorders, death, and disease are, in a sense, outcomes or final end products of a long history of social experience. Early studies did not examine what happened between people in high- and low-density situations on a day-to-day basis. They could only vaguely infer about ongoing social interaction as people coped with high and low density. Furthermore, their approach to crowding was to treat it as a broad social-system problem rather than as an individual or microinterpersonal phenomenon. Their interest seemed to be on how the whole society was affected by crowding, with only secondary concern for how individuals and families coped with and responded to population concentrations.

Later Correlational-Sociological Studies

Beginning in the 1960s sociological studies shifted their methodological strategy in several ways. A classic study was conducted by Galle, Gove, and McPherson (1972) in Chicago. They viewed population density in a more differentiated fashion than previously and studied how closely the density measure came to actual interpersonal processes. Their framework included (1) number of persons per room in a dwelling unit (the smallest and most directly interpersonal level of density), (2) number of rooms per housing unit, (3) number of housing units per structure (for example, apartments per apartment house), and (4) number of residential structures per acre (the least directly interpersonal measure). Thus they made different types of density indicators explicit, with the most microlevel one being relatively "close" to interpersonal relations. A second feature of their approach concerned the problem in prior research of the obscuring effects of ethnic background, socioeconomic status, and other variables on the relationship between density and social pathology. In this study, such factors were statistically controlled. Their results illustrate the value of a differentiated approach to density. The highest correlations occurred between *people per room* and social pathology indicators of mortality, fertility, public assistance, and juvenile delinquency. Thus the density measures that reflected social interaction most closely (people in a room) were the important ones. Galle and associates interpreted their results in terms of ongoing social processes that might have occurred in densely populated homes. For example, ill persons may not have obtained the quiet privacy they needed to recover, yielding higher mortality rates; higher fertility may have resulted, in part, from difficulties in using birth-control techniques in dense homes; and children may have received less attention in larger families and may have had to rely more on peers for guidance, thereby contributing to juvenile delinquency. While these were only post hoc interpretations, they reflect a focus on social processes that may have mediated density-pathology relationships. Thus this study attempted to get closer to ongoing social interaction rather than treat population concentration as a vague producer of ultimate outcomes.

Other recent studies also moved in these directions, giving more attention to different levels of analysis of population concentration. For example, Marsella, Escudero, and Gordon (1970) examined the impact of persons per dwelling unit in Manila on psychosomatic symptomatology; Mitchell (1971) analyzed the relationship between number of families per dwelling unit and marital satisfaction in Hong Kong; and Booth and Welch (1973) examined the relationship between density, health, and aggression in 65 countries.

In summary, recent sociological studies have taken a more sophisticated approach and emphasized (1) the differentiated analysis of density, with more attention given to the interpersonal, microlevel of density, (2) the interpersonal social processes that occur in high-density conditions rather than the broad social outcomes alone, and (3) the control of underlying variables that might account for density-pathology relationships.

Early Experimental-Psychological Studies

A second stream of research on crowding is different in several ways from the sociological approach. First, it is experimental and laboratory oriented, involving subjects who are often strangers and who enter social groups solely for the purpose of the study. Second, group members interact for relatively short periods of time compared with persons in sociological studies. Third, subjects in many experimental studies work on tasks developed for the specific setting, rather than those that are a part of the ongoing and natural aspects of their everyday lives. Fourth, this research style emphasizes manipulation and control of variables. An atempt is made to vary certain things, such as density, and to control other variables, such as sex, age, and testing conditions in order to permit reasonably strong inferences about cause-effect relationships.

Laboratory-oriented research on crowding began only in the last decade, with probably about two dozen studies reported at the time of this writing. Thus psychologists came late to the problem of crowding. There are two good examples of early experimental studies. Griffitt and Veitch (1971) gave subjects information about a stranger who presumably had attitudes similar to or different from their own. They were then placed in small or large groups. The room was an environmental chamber in which half the groups were in a cool, pleasant setting and the other half functioned in a hot, uncomfortable environment. The results indicated that people liked the hypothetical stranger more in the uncrowded and cooler environment, based on responses to a rating scale. Freedman and his associates (1971) examined the impact of room size and group size on individual performance on a variety of intellectual tasks, such as word formation, object use, memory, and concentration, and on a group-discussion task. There were no differences in performance as a function of density.

These and similar studies reflect early experimental approaches to the issue of crowding, comparable to the early phase of correlational research. In these studies, the concept of density was treated in a relatively undifferentiated fashion. Although the Freedman investigation varied both spatial and social density, many early studies did not. Moreover, many early experimental studies emphasized end products or outcomes, such as performance success, rather than social processes. For example, in the Freedman study, there was no analysis of how people attacked problems or how they gradually came to develop feelings about others. Rather, such studies examined only final performance or final liking of others.

Another feature of early experimental studies is the absence of social interaction among people. Both the Freedman and associates (1971) and the Griffitt and Veitch (1971) studies emphasized the effects of density on people who worked alone, not as members of an interacting group. If more recent sociological studies say anything, it is that we should try to understand interpersonal processes, not just individual effects of density.

Later Experimental-Psychological Studies

There are signs that a more advanced stage of research in the psychological, experimental tradition is beginning to emerge. For example, Hutt and Vaizey (1966) examined the impact of different group sizes on children's aggressive behavior in a playroom. The important element of this study was its focus on *ongoing social process* rather than on only the ultimate outcomes. This feature has become more prevalent in other research also. For example, Freedman, Levy, Buchanan, and Price (1972) examined the impact of density on performance of tasks involving cooperation or competition between people and on degree of social punitiveness in a mock-jury situation; Loo (1973b) studied aggression and dominance in children's groups; Stokols, Rall, Pinner, and Schopler (1973) tapped social behaviors of laughing, hostility, and so on in various density arrangements.

We can also now begin to see a richer conception of density. For example, a number of studies have varied *both* room and group size to get at spatial- and social-density effects (Freedman et al., 1971; McGrew, 1970). And there now are more attempts to study the richness, differentiation, and articulation of environment. For example, Desor (1972) examined the effects of wall partitions, room shapes, door placements, and other factors on willingness of subjects to place simulated figures in a room mock-up. Rohe and Patterson (1974) varied the richness of resources (number and variety of toys available to children) in different-size groups and studied the effect on aggressive behavior.

A recent program of research by Valins and Baum (1973) and Baum and Valins (1973) is important because it studied the longer-term implications of living in crowded environments on later social behavior. Dormitory residents who lived in a crowded corridor-room arrangement were compared with those in uncrowded suites. Residents in each living arrangement served as subjects and were directed to a waiting room where a confederate was seated. The results showed that crowded residents sat farther away from a confederate and spent less time looking at him or talking with him than did uncrowded residents, suggesting that dense living was associated with the mutual avoidance of social interaction—a kind of social-process cost. This type of study is important because it capitalizes on real-life crowding, it tracks effects on social process, and it works in a seminaturalistic situation.

An important issue concerns the relative strengths of correlational and experimental studies. Correlational studies have several advantages. They deal with factors such as mental health, mortality, and crime that involve the everyday lives of people. In addition, they reflect years of exposure to density, not minutes or hours. And the social groups are often real ones that have a long history and whose members are deeply involved with one another as families or neighbors. Such relationships are not easily produced in the laboratory.

On the other hand, experimental studies have several advantages not easily found elsewhere. The systematic manipulation and control of variables allows clearer inferences about cause-effect relationships involving density and behavior. By manipulating density directly and controlling other factors, it is easier to pinpoint ways in which behavioral changes are related to density. In correlational studies it is difficult to identify causal ties, and the possible contaminating role of unmeasured or unknown variables is greater. Another advantage of laboratory studies in that they allow *direct* examination of social processes. Because groups can be observed on the scene, measurement of aggression and other social behaviors is possible. This is not easily done in correlational studies. While these strategic approaches are not always categorically distinct, the strengths of the experimental laboratory study are generally the weaknesses of the correlational study, and vice versa. Elements of each strategy seem necessary to develop a full understanding of crowding, to generate and test out a range of hypotheses, to provide a kind of triangulation from different perspectives on the same issue, and to complement one another where questions cannot easily be dealt with in one setting or the other.

REFERENCES

Baum, A., & Valins, S. Residential environments, group size and crowding. *Proceedings, 81st Annual Convention, American Psychological Association*, 1973, 211–212.

Booth, A., & Welch, S. The effects of crowding: A cross-national study. Paper presented at American Psychological Association, Montreal, Canada, 1973.

Bordua, D. J. Juvenile delinquency and "anomie": An attempt at replication. *Social Problems*, 1958, **6**, 230–239.

Cavan, R. S. *Suicide*. Chicago: University of Chicago Press, 1928.

Day, A. T., & Day, L. H. Cross-national comparison of population density. *Science*, 1973, **181**, 1016–1023.

Desor, J. A. Toward a psychological theory of crowding. *Journal of Personality and Social Psychology*, 1972, **21**, 79–83.

Esser, A. H. A biosocial perspective on crowding. In J. F. Wohlwill and D. H. Carson (Eds.), *Environment and the social sciences: Perspectives and applications*. Washington, D.C.: American Psychological Association, 1972. Pp. 15–28.

Faris, R., & Dunham, H. W. *Mental disorders in urban areas* (2nd ed.). Chicago: Phoenix Books, 1965.

Freedman, J. L., Klevinsky, S., & Ehrlich, P. I. The effect of crowding on human task performance. *Journal of Applied Social Psychology*, 1971, **1**, 7–26.

Freedman, J. L., Levy, A. S., Buchanan, R. W., & Price, J. Crowding and human aggressiveness. *Journal of Experimental Social Psychology*, 1972, **8**, 528–548.

Galle, O. R., Gove, W. R., & McPherson, J. M. Population density and pathology: What are the relationships for man? *Science*, 1972, **176**, 23–30.

Griffitt, W., & Veitch, R. Hot and crowded: Influence of population density and temperature on interpersonal affective behavior. *Journal of Personality and Social Psychology*, 1971, **17**, 92–98.

Hutt, C., & Vaizey, J. J. Differential effects of group density on social behavior. *Nature*, 1966, **209**, 1371–1372.

Lantz, H. R. Population density and psychiatric diagnosis. *Sociology and Social Research*, 1953, **37**, 322–326.

Loo, C. M. Important issues in researching the effects of crowding on humans. *Representative Research in Social Psychology*, 1973, **4**(1), 219–227. (a)

Loo, C. M. The effect of spatial density on the social behavior of children. *Journal of Applied Social Psychology*, 1973, **2**(4), 372–381. (b)

Marsella, A. J., Escudero, M., & Gordon, P. The effects of dwelling density on mental disorders in Filipino men. *Journal of Health and Social Behavior*, 1970, **11**(4), 288–294.

McGrew, P. L. Social and spatial density effects on spacing behavior in preschool children. *Journal of Child Psychology and Psychiatry*, 1970, **11**, 197–205.

Michelson, W. *Man and his urban environment: A sociological approach*. Reading, Mass.: Addison-Wesley, 1970.

Milgram, S. The experience of living in cities. *Science*, 1970, **167**, 1461–1468.

Mitchell, R. Some social implications of higher density housing. *American Sociological Review*, 1971, **36**, 18–29.

Rapoport, A. Some perspectives on human use and organization of space. Paper presented at Australian Association of Social Anthropologists, Melbourne, Australia, May 1972.

Rohe, W., & Patterson, A. H. The effects of varied levels of resources and density on behavior in a day care center. Paper presented at Environmental Design Research Association, Milwaukee, Wis., 1974.

Sainsbury, P. *Suicide in London*. New York: Basic Books, 1956.

Schmid, C. Completed and attempted suicides. *American Sociological Review*, 1955, **20**, 273.

Schmid, C. Urban crime areas: Part I. *American Sociological Review*, 1969, **25**, 527–542.

Schmid, C. Urban crime areas: Part II. *American Sociological Review*, 1970, **25**, 655–678.

Schmitt, R. C. Density, delinquency and crime in Honolulu. *Sociology and Social Research*, 1957, **41**, 274–276.

Simmel, G. The metropolis and mental life. In K. W. Wolff (Ed. and trans.), *The sociology of George Simmel*. New York: The Free Press, 1950.

Stokols, D. On the distinction between density and crowding: Some implications for future research. *Psychological Review*, 1972, **79**(3), 275–278. (a)

Stokols, D. A social psychological model of human crowding phenomena. *American Institute of Planners Journal*, 1972, **38**, 72–83. (b)

Stokols, D., Rall, M., Pinner, B., & Schopler, J. Physical, social, and personal determinants of the perception of crowding. *Environment and Behavior*, 1973, **5**(1), 87–117.

Valins, S., & Baum, A. Residential group size, social interaction and crowding. *Environment and Behavior*, 1973, **5**(4), 421–440.

White, R. C. The relation of felonies to environmental factors in Indianapolis. *Social Forces*, 1931, **10**(4), 498–509.

Wirth, L. Urbanism as a way of life. *American Journal of Sociology*, 1938, **44**, 1–24.

Wohlwill, J. F. Human adaptation to levels of environmental stimulation. *Human Ecology*, 1974, **2**(2), 127–147.

Zlutnick, S., & Altman, I. Crowding and human behavior. In J. F. Wohlwill and D. H. Carson (Eds.), *Environment and the social sciences: Perspectives and applications*. Washington, D.C.: American Psychological Association, 1972. Pp. 44–60.

STANLEY MILGRAM

The Experience of Living in Cities

> When I first came to New York it seemed like a nightmare. As soon as I got off the train at Grand Central I was caught up in pushing, shoving crowds on 42nd Street. Sometimes people bumped into me without apology; what really frightened me was to see two people literally engaged in combat for possession of a cab. Why were they so rushed? Even drunks on the street were bypassed without a glance. People didn't seem to care about each other at all.

This statement represents a common reaction to a great city, but it does not tell the whole story. Obviously cities have great appeal because of their variety, eventfulness, possibility of choice, and the stimulation of an intense atmosphere that many individuals find a desirable background to their lives. Where face-to-face contacts are important, the city offers unparalleled possibilities. It has been calculated by the Regional Plan Association (in the *New York Times*, June 15, 1969) that in Nassau County, a suburb of New York City, an individual can meet 11,000 others within a 10-minute radius of his office by foot or car. In Newark, a moderate-sized city, he can meet more than 20,000 persons within this radius. But in midtown Manhattan he can meet fully 220,000. So there is an order-of-magnitude increment in the communication possibilities offered by a great city. That is one of the bases of its appeal and, indeed, of its functional necessity. The city provides options that no other social arrangement permits. But there is a negative side also, as we shall see.

Granted that cities are indispensable in complex society, we may still ask what contribution psychology can make to understanding the experience of living in them. What theories are relevant? How can we extend our knowledge of the psychological aspects of life in cities through empirical inquiry? If empirical inquiry is possible, along what lines should it proceed? In short, where do we start in constructing urban theory and in laying out lines of research?

Observation is the indispensable starting point. Any observer in the streets of midtown Manhattan will see (1) large numbers of people, (2) a high population density, and (3) heterogeneity of population. These three factors need to be at the root of any sociopsychological theory of city life, for they condition all aspects of our experience in the metropolis. Louis Wirth (1938), if not the first to point to

Abridgement of "The Experience of Living in Cities" by Stanley Milgram in *Science*, Vol. 167 (March 13, 1970), pp. 1461–1468. Copyright 1970 by the American Association for the Advancement of Science. Reprinted by permission.

A 51-minute film depicting the experiments described in this article is available to educational groups. It is entitled "The City and the Self" and is distributed by Time-Life Films.

these factors, is nonetheless the sociologist who relied most heavily on them in his analysis of the city. Yet, for a psychologist, there is something unsatisfactory about Wirth's theoretical variables. Numbers, density, and heterogeneity are demographic facts but they are not yet psychological facts. They are external to the individual. Psychology needs an idea that links the individual's *experience* to the demographic circumstances of urban life.

One link is provided by the concept of overload. This term, drawn from systems analysis, refers to a system's inability to process inputs from the environment because there are too many inputs for the system to cope with, or because successive inputs come so fast that input A cannot be processed when input B is presented. When overload is present, adaptations occur. The system must set priorities and make choices. A may be processed first while B is kept in abeyance, or one input may be sacrificed altogether. City life, as we experience it, constitutes a continuous set of encounters with overload, and of resultant adaptations. Overload characteristically deforms daily life on several levels, impinging on role performance, the evolution of social norms, cognitive functioning, and the use of facilities.

The concept has been implicit in several theories of urban experience. In 1903 George Simmel pointed out that, since urban dwellers come into contact with vast numbers of people each day, they conserve psychic energy by becoming acquainted with a far smaller proportion of people than their rural counterparts do, and by maintaining more superficial relationships even with these acquaintances. Wirth (1938) points specifically to "the superficiality, the anonymity, and the transitory character of urban social relations."

One adaptive response to overload, therefore, is the allocation of less time to each input. A second adaptive mechanism is disregard of low-priority inputs. Principles of selectivity are formulated such that investment of time and energy are reserved for carefully defined inputs (the urbanite disregards the drunk sick on the street as he purposefully navigates through the crowd). Third, boundaries are redrawn in certain social transactions so that the overloaded system can shift the burden to the other party in the exchange; thus, harried New York bus drivers once made change for customers, but now this responsibility has been shifted to the client, who must have the exact fare ready. Fourth, reception is blocked off prior to entrance into a system; city dwellers increasingly use unlisted telephone numbers to prevent individuals from calling them, and a small but growing number resort to keeping the telephone off the hook to prevent incoming calls. More subtly, a city dweller blocks inputs by assuming an unfriendly countenance, which discourages others from initiating contact. Additionally, social screening devices are interposed between the individual and environmental inputs (in a town of 5000 anyone can drop in to chat with the mayor, but in the metropolis organizational screening devices deflect inputs to other destinations). Fifth, the intensity of inputs is diminished by filtering devices, so that only weak and relatively superficial forms of involvement with others are allowed. Sixth, specialized institutions are created to absorb inputs that would otherwise swamp the individual (welfare departments handle the financial needs of a million individuals in New York City, who would otherwise create an army of mendicants continuously importuning the pedestrian). The interposition of institutions between the individual and the social world, a characteristic of all modern society, and most notably of the large metropolis, has its negative side. It deprives the individual of a sense of direct contact and spontaneous integration in the life around him. It simultaneously protects and estranges the individual from his social environment. . . .

In sum, the observed behavior of the urbanite in a wide range of situations appears to be determined largely by a variety of adaptations to overload. I now deal with several specific consequences of responses to overload, which make for differences in the tone of city and town.

SOCIAL RESPONSIBILITY

The principal point of interest for a social psychology of the city is that moral and social involvement with individuals is necessarily restricted. This is a direct and necessary function of excess of input over capacity to process. Such restriction of involvement runs a broad spectrum from refusal to become involved in the needs of another person, even when the person desperately needs assistance, through refusal to do favors, to the simple withdrawal of courtesies (such as offering a lady a seat, or saying ''sorry'' when a pedestrian collision occurs). In any transaction more and more details need to be dropped as the total number of units to be processed increases and assaults an instrument of limited processing capacity.

The ultimate adaptation to an overloaded social environment is to totally disregard the needs, interests, and demands of those whom one does not define as relevant to the satisfaction of personal needs, and to develop highly efficient perceptual means of determining whether an individual falls into the category of friend or stranger. The disparity in the treatment of friends and strangers ought to be greater in cities than in towns; the time allotment and willingness to become involved with those who have no personal claim on one's time is likely to be less in cities than in towns.

Bystander Intervention in Crises

The most striking deficiencies in social responsibility in cities occur in crisis situations, such as the Genovese murder in Queens. In 1964, Catherine Genovese, coming home from a night job in the early hours of an April morning, was stabbed repeatedly, over an extended period of time. Thirty-eight residents of a respectable New York City neighborhood admit to having witnessed at least a part of the attack, but none went to her aid or called the police until after she was dead. Milgram and Hollander, writing in *The Nation* (1964), analyzed the event in these terms:

> Urban friendships and associations are not primarily formed on the basis of physical proximity. A person with numerous close friends in different parts of the city may not know the occupant of an adjacent apartment. This does not mean that a city dweller has fewer friends than does a villager, or knows fewer persons who will come to his aid; however, it does mean that his allies are not constantly at hand. Miss Genovese required immediate aid from those physically present. There is no evidence that the

city had deprived Miss Genovese of human associations, but the friends who might have rushed to her side were miles from the scene of her tragedy.

Further, it is known that her cries for help were not directed to a specific person; they were general. But only individuals can act, and as the cries were not specifically directed, no particular person felt a special responsibility. The crime and the failure of community response seem absurd to us. At the time, it may well have seemed equally absurd to the Kew Gardens residents that not one of the neighbors would have called the police. A collective paralysis may have developed from the belief of each of the witnesses that someone else must surely have taken that obvious step.

Latané and Darley (1969) have reported laboratory approaches to the study of bystander intervention and have established experimentally the following principle: The larger the number of bystanders, the less the likelihood that any one of them will intervene in an emergency. Gaertner and Bickman of The City University of New York have extended the bystander studies to an examination of help across ethnic lines. Blacks and whites, with clearly identifiable accents, called strangers (through what the caller represented as an error in telephone dialing), gave them a plausible story of being stranded on an outlying highway without more dimes, and asked the stranger to call a garage. The experimenters found that the white callers had a significantly better chance of obtaining assistance than the black callers. This suggests that ethnic allegiance may well be another means of coping with overload: The city dweller can reduce excessive demands and screen out urban heterogeneity by responding along ethnic lines; overload is made manageable by limiting the "span of sympathy."

In any quantitative characterization of the social texture of city life, a necessary first step is the application of such experimental methods as these to field situations in large cities and small towns. Theorists argue that the indifference shown in the Genovese case would not be found in a small town, but in the absence of solid experimental evidence the question remains an open one.

More than just callousness prevents bystanders from participating in altercations between people. A rule of urban life is respect for other people's emotional and social privacy, perhaps because physical privacy is so hard to achieve. And in situations for which the standards are heterogeneous, it is much harder to know whether taking an active role is unwarranted meddling or an appropriate response to a critical situation. If a husband and wife are quarreling in public, at what point should a bystander step in? On the one hand, the heterogeneity of the city produces substantially greater tolerance about behavior, dress, and codes of ethics than is generally found in the small town, but this diversity also encourages people to withhold aid for fear of antagonizing the participants or crossing an inappropriate and difficult-to-define line.

Moreover, the frequency of demands present in the city gives rise to norms of noninvolvement. There are practical limitations to the Samaritan impulse in a major city. If a citizen attended to every needy person, if he were sensitive to and acted on every altruistic impulse that was evoked in the city, he could scarcely keep his own affairs in order.

Willingness to Trust and Assist Strangers

We now move away from crisis situations to less urgent examples of social responsibility. For it is not only in situations of dramatic need but in the ordinary, everyday willingness to lend a hand that the city dweller is said to be deficient relative to his small-town cousin. The comparative method must be used in any empirical examination of this question. A commonplace social situation is staged in an urban setting and in a small town—a situation to which a subject can respond by either extending help or withholding it. The responses in town and city are compared.

One factor in the purported unwillingness of urbanites to be helpful to strangers may well be their heightened sense of physical (and emotional) vulnerability—a feeling that is supported by urban crime statistics. A key test for distinguishing between city and town behavior, therefore, is determining how city dwellers compare with town dwellers in offering aid that increases their personal vulnerability and requires some trust of strangers. Altman, Levine, Nadien, and Villena of The City University of New York devised a study to compare the behaviors of city and town dwellers in this respect. The criterion used in this study was the willingness of householders to allow strangers to enter their home to use the telephone. The student investigators individually rang doorbells, explained that they had misplaced the address of a friend nearby, and asked to use the phone. The investigators (two males and two females) made 100 requests for entry into homes in the city and 60 requests in the small towns. The results for middle-income housing developments in Manhattan were compared with data for several small towns (Stony Point, Spring Valley, Ramapo, Nyack, New City, and West Clarkstown) in Rockland County, outside of New York City. As Table 1 shows, in all cases there was a sharp increase in the proportion of entries achieved by an experimenter when he moved from the city to a small town. In the most extreme case the experimenter was five times as likely to gain admission to homes in a small town as to homes in Manhattan. Although the female experimenters had notably greater success both in cities and in towns than the male experimenters had, each of the four students did at least twice

TABLE 1. Percentage of Entries Achieved by Investigators for City and Town Dwellings.

Experimenter	Entries achieved (%)	
	City*	Small town†
Male		
No. 1	16	40
No. 2	12	60
Female		
No. 3	40	87
No. 4	40	100

*Number of requests for entry, 100. †Number of requests for entry, 60.

as well in towns as in cities. This suggests that the city-town distinction overrides even the predictably greater fear of male strangers than of female ones.

The lower level of helpfulness by city dwellers seems due in part to recognition of the dangers of living in Manhattan, rather than to mere indifference or coldness. It is significant that 75 percent of all the city respondents received and answered messages by shouting through closed doors and by peering out through peepholes; in the towns, by contrast, about 75 percent of the respondents opened the door.

Supporting the experimenters' quantitative results was their general observation that the town dwellers were noticeably more friendly and less suspicious than the city dwellers. In seeking to explain the reasons for the greater sense of psychological vulnerability city dwellers feel, above and beyond the differences in crime statistics, Villena points out that, if a crime is committed in a village, a resident of a neighboring village may not perceive the crime as personally relevant, though the geographic distance may be small, whereas a criminal act committed anywhere in the city, though miles from the city dweller's home is still verbally located within the city; thus, Villena says, "the inhabitant of the city possesses a larger vulnerable space."

Civilities

Even at the most superficial level of involvement—the exercise of everyday civilities—urbanites are reputedly deficient. People bump into each other and often do not apologize. They knock over another person's packages and, as often as not, proceed on their way with a grumpy exclamation instead of an offer of assistance. Such behavior, which many visitors to great cities find distasteful, is less common, we are told, in smaller communities, where traditional courtesies are more likely to be observed.

In some instances it is not simply that, in the city, traditional courtesies are violated; rather, the cities develop new norms of noninvolvement. These are so well defined and so deeply a part of city life that *they* constitute the norms people are reluctant to violate. Men are actually embarrassed to give up a seat on the subway to an old woman; they mumble "I was getting off anyway," instead of making the gesture in a straightforward and gracious way. These norms develop because everyone realizes that, in situations of high population density, people cannot implicate themselves in each others' affairs, for to do so would create conditions of continual distraction which would frustrate purposeful action.

In discussing the effects of overload I do not imply that at every instant the city dweller is bombarded with an unmanageable number of inputs, and that his responses are determined by the excess of input at any given instant. Rather, adaptation occurs in the form of gradual evolution of norms of behavior. Norms are evolved in response to frequent discrete experiences of overload; they persist and become generalized modes of responding.

Overload on Cognitive Capacities: Anonymity

That we respond differently toward those whom we know and those who are strangers to us is a truism. An eager patron aggressively cuts in front of someone in a long movie line to save time only to confront a friend; he then behaves sheepishly. A man is involved in an automobile accident caused by another driver, emerges from his car shouting in rage, then moderates his behavior on discovering a friend driving the other car. The city dweller, when walking through the midtown streets is in a state of continual anonymity vis-à-vis the other pedestrians.

Anonymity is part of a continuous spectrum ranging from total anonymity to full acquaintance, and it may well be that measurement of the precise degrees of anonymity in cities and towns would help to explain important distinctions between the quality of life in each. Conditions of full acquaintance, for example, offer security and familiarity, but they may also be stifling, because the individual is caught in a web of established relationships. Conditions of complete anonymity, by contrast, provide freedom from routinized social ties, but they may also create feelings of alienation and detachment.

Empirically one could investigate the proportion of activities in which the city dweller or the town dweller is known by others at given times in his daily life, and the proportion of activities in the course of which he interacts with individuals who know him. At his job, for instance, the city dweller may be known to as many people as his rural counterpart. However, when he is not fulfilling his occupational role—say, when merely traveling about the city—the urbanite is doubtless more anonymous than his rural counterpart.

Limited empirical work on anonymity has begun. Zimbardo (1969) has tested whether the social anonymity and impersonality of the big city encourage greater vandalism than do small towns. Zimbardo arranged for one automobile to be left for 64 hours near the Bronx campus of New York University and for a counterpart to be left for the same number of hours near Stanford University in Palo Alto. The license plates on the two cars were removed and the hoods were opened, to provide "releaser cues" for potential vandals. The New York car was stripped of all movable parts within the first 24 hours, and by the end of 3 days was only a hunk of metal rubble. Unexpectedly, however, most of the destruction occurred during daylight hours, usually under the scrutiny of observers, and the leaders in the vandalism were well-dressed, white adults. The Palo Alto car was left untouched.

Zimbardo attributes the difference in the treatment accorded the two cars to the "acquired feelings of social anonymity provided by life in a city like New York," and he supports his conclusions with several other anecdotes illustrating casual, wanton vandalism in the city. In any comparative study of the effects of anonymity in city and town, however, there must be satisfactory control for other confounding factors: the large number of drug addicts in a city like New York; the higher proportion of slum-dwellers in the city; and so on.

Another direction for empirical study is investigation of the beneficial effects of anonymity. The impersonality of city life breeds its own tolerance for the private lives of the inhabitants. Individuality and even eccentricity, we may assume, can flourish more readily in the metropolis than in the small town. Stigmatized persons may find it easier to lead comfortable lives in the city, free of the constant scrutiny of neighbors. . . .

Role Behavior in Cities and Towns

Another product of urban overload is the adjustment in roles made by urbanites in daily interactions. As Wirth has said (1938): "Urbanites meet one another in highly segmental roles. . . . They are less dependent upon particular persons, and their dependence upon others is confined to a highly fractionalized aspect of the other's round of activity." This tendency is particularly noticeable in transactions between customers and individuals offering professional or sales services. The owner of a country store has time to become well acquainted with his dozen-or-so daily customers, but the girl at the checkout counter of a busy A & P, serving hundreds of customers a day, barely has time to toss the green stamps into one customer's shopping bag before the next customer confronts her with his pile of groceries.

Meier, in his stimulating analysis of the city (1962), discusses several adaptations a system may make when confronted by inputs that exceed its capacity to process them. Meier argues that, according to the principle of competition for scarce resources, the scope and time of the transaction shrink as customer volume and daily turnover rise. This, in fact, is what is meant by the "brusque" quality of city life. New standards have developed in cities concerning what levels of services are appropriate in business transactions (see Figure 1).

McKenna and Morgenthau, in a seminar at The City University of New York, devised a study (1) to compare the willingness of city dwellers and small-town dwellers to do favors for strangers that entailed expenditure of a small amount of

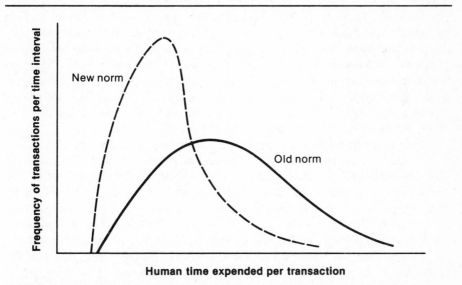

FIGURE 1. Changes in the demand for time for a given task when the overall transaction frequency increases in a social system.

[Reprinted from A Communications Theory of Urban Growth by R. L. Meier by permission of the M.I.T. Press, Cambridge, Massachusetts. Copyright 1962 by M.I.T. Press.]

time and slight inconvenience but no personal vulnerability, and (2) to determine whether the more compartmentalized, transitory relationships of the city would make urban salesgirls less likely than small-town salesgirls to carry out, for strangers, tasks not related to their customary roles.

To test for differences between city dwellers and small-town dwellers, a simple experiment was devised in which persons from both settings were asked (by telephone) to perform increasingly onerous favors for anonymous strangers.

Within the cities (Chicago, New York, and Philadelphia), half the calls were to housewives and the other half to salesgirls in women's apparel shops; the division was the same for the 37 small towns of the study, which were in the same states as the cities. Each experimenter represented herself as a long-distance caller who had, through error, been connected with the respondent by the operator. The experimenter began by asking for simple information about the weather for purposes of travel. Next the experimenter excused herself on some pretext (asking the respondent to "please hold on"), put the phone down for almost a full minute, and then picked it up again and asked the respondent to provide the phone number of a hotel or motel in her vicinity at which the experimenter might stay during a forthcoming visit. Scores were assigned the subjects on the basis of how helpful they had been. McKenna summarizes her results in this manner:

> People in the city, whether they are engaged in a specific job or not, are less helpful and informative than people in small towns; . . . People at home, regardless of where they live, are less helpful and informative than people working in shops.

However, the absolute level of cooperativeness for urban subjects was found to be quite high, and does not accord with the stereotype of the urbanite as aloof, self-centered, and unwilling to help strangers. The quantitative differences obtained by McKenna and Morgenthau are less great than one might have expected. This again points up the need for extensive empirical research in rural-urban differences, research that goes far beyond that provided in the few illustrative pilot studies presented here. At this point we have very limited objective evidence on differences in the quality of social encounters in city and small town.

But the research needs to be guided by unifying theoretical concepts. As I have tried to demonstrate, the concept of overload helps to explain a wide variety of contrasts between city behavior and town behavior: (1) the differences in role enactment (the tendency of urban dwellers to deal with one another in highly segmented, functional terms, and of urban sales personnel to devote limited time and attention to their customers); (2) the evolution of urban norms quite different from traditional town values (such as the acceptance of noninvolvement, impersonality, and aloofness in urban life); (3) the adaptation of the urban dweller's cognitive processes (his inability to identify most of the people he sees daily, his screening of sensory stimuli, his development of blasé attitudes toward deviant or bizarre behavior, and his selectivity in responding to human demands); and (4) the competition for scarce facilities in the city (the subway rush; the fight for taxis; traffic jams; standing in line to await services). I suggest that contrasts between city and rural behavior probably reflect the responses of similar people to very different situations, rather than intrinsic differences in the personalities of rural and city dwellers. The city is a situation to which individuals respond adaptively.

FURTHER ASPECTS OF URBAN EXPERIENCE

Some features of urban experience do not fit neatly into the system of analysis presented thus far. They are no less important for that reason. The issues raised next are difficult to treat in quantitative fashion. Yet I prefer discussing them in a loose way to excluding them because appropriate language and data have not yet been developed. My aim is to suggest how phenomena such as "urban atmosphere" can be pinned down through techniques of measurement.

The "Atmosphere" of Great Cities

The contrast in the behavior of city and town dwellers has been a natural starting point for urban social scientists. But even among great cities there are marked differences in "atmosphere." The tone, pacing, and texture of social encounters are different in London and New York, and many persons willingly make financial sacrifices for the privilege of living within a specific urban atmosphere which they find pleasing or stimulating. A second perspective in the study of cities, therefore, is to define exactly what is meant by the atmosphere of a city and to pinpoint the factors that give rise to it. It may seem that urban atmosphere is too evanescent a quality to be reduced to a set of measurable variables, but I do not believe the matter can be judged before substantial effort has been made in this direction. It is obvious that any such approach must be comparative. It makes no sense at all to say that New York is "vibrant" and "frenetic" unless one has some specific city in mind as a basis of comparison.

In an undergraduate tutorial that I conducted at Harvard University some years ago, New York, London, and Paris were selected as reference points for attempts to measure urban atmosphere. We began with a simple question: Does any consensus exist about the qualities that typify given cities? To answer this question one could undertake a content analysis of travel-book, literary, and journalistic accounts of cities. A second approach, which we adopted, is to ask people to characterize (with descriptive terms and accounts of typical experiences) cities they have lived in or visited. In advertisements placed in the *New York Times* and the *Harvard Crimson* we asked people to give us accounts of specific incidents in London, Paris, or New York that best illuminated the character of that particular city. Questionnaires were then developed, and administered to persons who were familiar with at least two of the three cities.

Some distinctive patterns emerged (cf. Abuza). The distinguishing themes concerning New York, for example, dealt with its diversity, its great size, its pace and level of activity, its cultural and entertainment opportunities, and the heterogeneity and segmentation ("ghettoization") of its population. New York elicited more descriptions in terms of physical qualities, pace, and emotional impact than Paris or London did, a fact which suggests that these are particularly important aspects of New York's ambiance.

A contrasting profile emerges for London; in this case respondents placed far greater emphasis on their interactions with the inhabitants than on physical surroundings. There was near unanimity on certain themes: those dealing with the tolerance and courtesy of London's inhabitants. One respondent said:

When I was 12, my grandfather took me to the British Museum . . . one day by tube and recited the *Aeneid* in Latin for my benefit. . . . He is rather deaf, speaks very loudly and it embarrassed the hell out of me, until I realized that nobody was paying any attention. Londoners are extremely worldly and tolerant.

In contrast, respondents who described New Yorkers as aloof, cold, and rude referred to such incidents as the following:

I saw a boy of 19 passing out antiwar leaflets to passersby. When he stopped at a corner, a man dressed in a business suit walked by him at a brisk pace, hit the boy's arm, and scattered the leaflets all over the street. The man kept walking at the same pace down the block.

We need to obtain many more such descriptions of incidents, using careful methods of sampling. By the application of factor-analytic techniques, relevant dimensions for each city can be discerned.

The responses for Paris were about equally divided between responses concerning its inhabitants and those regarding its physical and sensory attributes. Cafes and parks were often mentioned as contributing to the sense that Paris is a city of amenities, but many respondents complained that Parisians were inhospitable, nasty, and cold.

We cannot be certain, of course, to what degree these statements reflect actual characteristics of the cities in question and to what degree they simply tap the respondents' knowledge of widely held preconceptions. Indeed, one may point to three factors, apart from the actual atmospheres of the cities, that determine the subjects' responses.

1. A person's impression of a given city depends on his implicit standard of comparison. A New Yorker who visits Paris may well describe that city as "leisurely," whereas a compatriot from Richmond, Virginia, may consider Paris too "hectic." Obtaining reciprocal judgment, in which New Yorkers judge Londoners, and Londoners judge New Yorkers, seems a useful way to take into account not only the city being judged but also the home city that serves as the visitor's base line.

2. Perceptions of a city are also affected by whether the observer is a tourist, a newcomer, or a longer-term resident. First, a tourist will be exposed to features of the city different from those familiar to a long-time resident. Second, a prerequisite for adapting to continuing life in a given city seems to be the filtering out of many observations about the city that the newcomer or tourist finds particularly arresting; this selective process seems to be part of the long-term resident's mechanism for coping with overload. In the interest of psychic economy, the resident simply learns to tune out many aspects of daily life. One method for studying the specific impact of adaptation on perception of the city is to ask several pairs of newcomers and old-timers (one newcomer and one old-timer to a pair) to walk down certain city blocks and then report separately what each has observed.

Additionally, many persons have noted that when travelers return to New York from an extended sojourn abroad they often feel themselves confronted with "brutal ugliness" (Abelson, 1969) and a distinctive, frenetic atmosphere whose contributing details are, for a few hours or days, remarkably sharp and clear. This period of fresh perception should receive special attention in the study of city atmosphere. For, in a few days, details which are initially arresting become less easy to specify. They are assimilated into an increasingly familiar background atmosphere which, though important in setting the tone of things, is difficult to analyze. There is no better point at which to begin the study of city atmosphere than at the moment when a traveler returns from abroad.

3. The popular myths and expectations each visitor brings to the city will also affect the way in which he perceives it (see Strauss, 1968). Sometimes a person's preconceptions about a city are relatively accurate distillations of its character, but preconceptions may also reinforce myths by filtering the visitor's perceptions to conform with his expectations. Preconceptions affect not only a person's perceptions of a city but what he reports about it.

The influence of a person's urban base line on his perceptions of a given city, the differences between the observations of the long-time inhabitant and those of the newcomer, and the filtering effect of personal expectations and stereotypes raise serious questions about the validity of travelers' reports. Moreover, no social psychologist wants to rely exclusively on verbal accounts if he is attempting to obtain an accurate and objective description of the cities' social texture, pace, and general atmosphere. What he needs to do is to devise means of embedding objective experimental measures in the daily flux of city life, measures that can accurately index the qualities of a given urban atmosphere.

Experimental Comparisons of Behavior

Roy Feldman (1968) incorporated these principles in a comparative study of behavior toward compatriots and foreigners in Paris, Athens, and Boston. Feldman wanted to see (1) whether absolute levels and patterns of helpfulness varied significantly from city to city, and (2) whether inhabitants in each city tended to treat compatriots differently from foreigners. He examined five concrete behavioral episodes, each carried out by a team of native experimenters and a team of American experimenters in the three cities. The episodes involved (1) asking natives of the city for street directions; (2) asking natives to mail a letter for the experimenter; (3) asking natives if they had just dropped a dollar bill (or the Greek or French equivalent) when the money actually belonged to the experimenter himself; (4) deliberately overpaying for goods in a store to see if the cashier would correct the mistake and return the excess money; and (5) determining whether taxicab drivers overcharged strangers and whether they took the most direct route available.

Feldman's results suggest some interesting contrasts in the profiles of the three cities. In Paris, for instance, certain stereotypes were borne out. Parisian cab drivers overcharged foreigners significantly more often than they overcharged compatriots. But other aspects of the Parisians' behavior were not in accord with American preconceptions: In mailing a letter for a stranger, Parisians treated foreigners significantly better than Athenians or Bostonians did, and, when asked to mail letters that were already stamped, Parisians actually treated foreigners better than they treated compatriots. Similarly, Parisians were significantly more honest than

Athenians or Bostonians in resisting the temptation to claim money that was not theirs, and Parisians were the only citizens who were more honest with foreigners than with compatriots in this experiment.

Feldman's studies not only begin to quantify some of the variables that give a city its distinctive texture but they also provide a methodological model for other comparative research. His most important contribution is his successful application of objective, experimental measures to everyday situations, a mode of study which provides conclusions about urban life that are more pertinent than those achieved through laboratory experiments.

TEMPO AND PACE

Another important component of a city's atmosphere is its tempo or pace, an attribute frequently remarked on but less often studied. Does a city have a frenetic, hectic quality, or is it easygoing and leisurely? In any empirical treatment of this question, it is best to start in a very simple way. Walking speeds of pedestrians in different cities and in cities and towns should be measured and compared. William Berkowitz of Lafayette College has undertaken an extensive series of studies of walking speeds in Philadelphia, New York, and Boston, as well as in small and moderate-sized towns. Berkowitz writes that "there does appear to be a significant linear relation between walking speed and size of municipality, but the absolute size of the difference varies by less than ten percent."

Perhaps the feeling of rapid tempo is due not so much to absolute pedestrian speeds as to the constant need to dodge others in a large city to avoid collisions with other pedestrians. (One basis for computing the adjustments needed to avoid collisions is to hypothesize a set of mechanical manikins sent walking along a city street and to calculate the number of collisions when no adjustments are made. Clearly, the higher the density of manikins the greater the number of collisions per unit of time, or, conversely, the greater the frequency of adjustments needed in higher population densities to avoid collisions.)

Patterns of automobile traffic contribute to a city's tempo. Driving an automobile provides a direct means of translating feelings about tempo into measurable acceleration, and a city's pace should be particularly evident in vehicular velocities, patterns of acceleration, and latency of response to traffic signals. The inexorable tempo of New York is expressed, further, in the manner in which pedestrians stand at busy intersections, impatiently awaiting a change in traffic light, making tentative excursions into the intersection, and frequently surging into the street even before the green light appears. . . .

CONCLUSION

I have tried to indicate some organizing theory that starts with the basic facts of city life: large numbers, density, and heterogeneity. These are external to the individual. He experiences these factors as overloads at the level of roles, norms, cognitive functions, and facilities. These overloads lead to adaptive mechanisms which create the distinctive tone and behaviors of city life. These notions, of course, need to be examined by objective comparative studies of cities and towns.

A second perspective concerns the differing atmospheres of great cities, such as Paris, London, and New York. Each has a distinctive flavor, offering a differentiable quality of experience. More precise knowledge of urban atmosphere seems attainable through application of the tools of experimental inquiry.

REFERENCES

Abelson, P. *Science*, 1969, **165**, 853.

Abuza, N. Harvard University. The Paris-London-New York questionnaires. Unpublished manuscript.

Altman, D., Levine, M., Nadien, M., & Villena, J. Graduate Center, The City University of New York. Unpublished research.

Berkowitz, W. Personal communication.

Feldman, R. E. Response to compatriot and foreigner who seek assistance. *Journal of Personality and Social Psychology*, 1968, **10**, 202–214.

Gaertner, S., & Bickman, L. Graduate Center, The City University of New York. Unpublished research.

Latané, B., & Darley, J. M. Bystander "apathy." *American Scientist*, 1969, **57**, 244–268.

McKenna, W., & Morgenthau, S. Graduate Center, The City University of New York. Unpublished research.

Meier, R. L. *A communications theory of urban growth*. Cambridge, Mass.: M.I.T. Press, 1962.

Milgram, S., & Hollander, P. The murder they heard. *Nation*, 1964, **198**, No. 25, 602–604.

Simmel, G. *The sociology of George Simmel*, Wolff, K. H. (Ed.). New York: Macmillan, 1950.

Strauss, A. L. (Ed.) *The American city: A sourcebook of urban imagery*. Chicago: Aldine, 1968.

Wirth, L. Urbanism as a way of life. *American Journal of Sociology*, 1938, **44**, 1–24.

Zimbardo, P. G. Paper presented at the Nebraska Symposium on Motivation, 1969.

KEVIN LYNCH

The Image of the Environment

Looking at cities can give a special pleasure, however commonplace the sight may be. Like a piece of architecture, the city is a construction in space, but one of vast scale, a thing perceived only in the course of long spans of time. City design is therefore a temporal art, but it can rarely use the controlled and limited sequences of other temporal arts like music. On different occasions and for different people, the sequences are reversed, interrupted, abandoned, cut across. It is seen in all lights and all weathers.

At every instant, there is more than the eye can see, more than the ear can hear, a setting or a view waiting to be explored. Nothing is experienced by itself, but always in relation to its surroundings, the sequences of events leading up to it, the memory of past experiences. Washington Street set in a farmer's field might look like the shopping street in the heart of Boston, and yet it would seem utterly different. Every citizen has had long associations with some part of his city, and his image is soaked in memories and meanings.

Moving elements in a city, and in particular the people and their activities, are as important as the stationary physical parts. We are not simply observers of this spectacle, but are ourselves a part of it, on the stage with the other participants. Most often, our perception of the city is not sustained, but rather partial, fragmentary, mixed with other concerns. Nearly every sense is in operation, and the image is the composite of them all.

Not only is the city an object which is perceived (and perhaps enjoyed) by millions of people of widely diverse class and character, but it is the product of many builders who are constantly modifying the structure for reasons of their own. While it may be stable in general outlines for some time, it is ever changing in detail. Only partial control can be exercised over its growth and form. There is no final result, only a continuous succession of phases. No wonder, then, that the art of shaping cities for sensuous enjoyment is an art quite separate from architecture or music or literature. It may learn a great deal from these other arts, but it cannot imitate them.

A beautiful and delightful city environment is an oddity, some would say an impossibility. Not one American city larger than a village is of consistently fine quality, although a few towns have some pleasant fragments. It is hardly surprising, then, that most Americans have little idea of what it can mean to live in such an environment. They are clear enough about the ugliness of the world they live in, and they are quite vocal about the dirt, the smoke, the heat, and the congestion, the chaos and yet the monotony of it. But they are hardly aware of the potential value of harmonious surroundings, a world which they may have briefly glimpsed only as tourists or as escaped vacationers. They can have little sense of what a setting can mean in terms of daily delight, or as a continuous anchor for their lives, or as an extension of the meaningfulness and richness of the world.

LEGIBILITY

This book will consider the visual quality of the American city by studying the mental image of that city which is held by its citizens. It will concentrate especially on one particular visual quality: the apparent clarity or "legibility" of the cityscape. By this we mean the ease with which its parts can be recognized and can be organized into a coherent pattern. Just as this printed page, if it is legible, can be visually grasped as a related pattern of recognizable symbols, so a legible city would be one whose districts or landmarks or pathways are easily identifiable and are easily grouped into an over-all pattern.

This book will assert that legibility is crucial in the city setting, will analyze it in some detail, and will try to show how this concept might be used today in rebuilding our cities. As will quickly become apparent to the reader, this study is a preliminary exploration, a first word not a last word, an attempt to capture ideas and to suggest how they might be developed and tested. Its tone will be speculative and perhaps a little irresponsible: at once tentative and presumptuous. . . .

Although clarity or legibility is by no means the only important property of a beautiful city, it is of special importance when considering environments at the urban scale of size, time, and complexity. To understand this, we must consider not just the city as a thing in itself, but the city being perceived by its inhabitants.

Structuring and identifying the environment is a vital ability among all mobile animals. Many kinds of cues are used: the visual sensations of color, shape, motion, or polarization of light, as well as other senses such as smell, sound, touch, kinesthesia, sense of gravity, and perhaps of electric or magnetic fields. . . . Despite a few remaining puzzles, it now seems unlikely that there is any mystic "instinct" of way-finding. Rather there is a consistent use and organization of definite sensory cues from the external environment. This organization is fundamental to the efficiency and to the very survival of free-moving life.

To become completely lost is perhaps a rather rare experience for most people in the modern city. We are supported by the presence of others and by special way-finding devices: maps, street numbers, route signs, bus placards. But let the mishap of disorientation once occur, and the sense of anxiety and even terror that accompanies it reveals to us how closely it is linked to our sense of balance and well-being. The very word "lost" in our language means much more than simple geographical uncertainty; it carries overtones of utter disaster.

In the process of way-finding, the strategic link is the environmental image, the generalized mental picture of the exterior physical world that is held by an individual. This image is the product both of immediate sensation and of the memory of past experience, and it is used to interpret information and to guide . The need to recognize and pattern our surroundings is so crucial, and has such long roots in the past, that this image has wide practical and emotional importance to the individual.

Obviously a clear image enables one to move about easily and quickly: to find a friend's house or a policeman or a button store. But an ordered environment can do more than this; it may serve as a broad frame of reference, an organizer of activity or belief or knowledge. On the basis of a structural understanding of Manhattan, for example, one can order a substantial quantity of facts and fancies about the nature of the world we live in. Like any good framework, such a structure gives the individual a possibility of choice and a starting-point for the acquisition of further information. A clear image of the surroundings is thus a useful basis for individual growth.

A vivid and integrated physical setting, capable of producing a sharp image, plays a social role as well. It can furnish the raw material for the symbols and collective memories of group communication. A striking landscape is the skeleton upon which many primitive races erect their socially important myths. Common memories of the "home town" were often the first and easiest point of contact between lonely soldiers during the war.

A good environmental image gives its possessor an important sense of emotional security. He can establish an harmonious relationship between himself and the outside world. This is the obverse of the fear that comes with disorientation; it means that the sweet sense of home is strongest when home is not only familiar but distinctive as well.

Indeed, a distinctive and legible environment not only offers security but also heightens the potential depth and intensity of human experience. Although life is far from impossible in the visual chaos of the modern city, the same daily action could take on new meaning if carried out in a more vivid setting. Potentially, the city is in itself the powerful symbol of a complex society. If visually well set forth, it can also have strong expressive meaning.

It may be argued against the importance of physical legibility that the human brain is marvelously adaptable, that with some experience one can learn to pick one's way through the most disordered or featureless surroundings. There are abundant examples of precise navigation over the "trackless" wastes of sea, sand, or ice, or through a tangled maze of jungle.

Yet even the sea has the sun and stars, the winds, currents, birds, and sea-colors without which unaided navigation would be impossible. The fact that only skilled professionals could navigate among the Polynesian Islands, and this only after extensive training, indicates the difficulties imposed by this particular environment. Strain and anxiety accompanied even the best-prepared expeditions. . . .

It must be granted that there is some value in mystification, labyrinth, or surprise in the environment. Many of us enjoy the House of Mirrors, and there is a certain charm in the crooked streets of Boston. This is so, however, only under two conditions. First, there must be no danger of losing basic form or orientation, of never coming out. The surprise must occur in an over-all framework; the confusions must be small regions in a visible whole. Furthermore, the labyrinth or mystery must in itself have some form that can be explored and in time be apprehended. Complete chaos without hint of connection is never pleasurable.

But these second thoughts point to an important qualification. The observer himself should play an active role in perceiving the world and have a creative part in developing his image. He should have the power to change that image to fit changing needs. An environment which is ordered in precise and final detail may inhibit new patterns of activity. A landscape whose every rock tells a story may make difficult the creation of fresh stories. Although this may not seem to be a critical issue in our present urban chaos, yet it indicates that what we seek is not a final but an open-ended order, capable of continuous further development.

BUILDING THE IMAGE

Environmental images are the result of a two-way process between the observer and his environment. The environment suggests distinctions and relations, and the observer—with great adaptability and in the light of his own purposes—selects, organizes, and endows with meaning what he sees. The image so developed now limits and emphasizes what is seen, while the image itself is being tested against the filtered perceptual input in a constant interacting process. Thus the image of a given reality may vary significantly between different observers.

The coherence of the image may arise in several ways. There may be little in the real object that is ordered or remarkable, and yet its mental picture has gained identity and organization through long familiarity. One man may find objects easily on what seems to anyone else to be a totally disordered work table. Alternatively, an object seen for the first time may be identified and related not because it is individually familiar but because it conforms to a stereotype already constructed by the observer. An American can always spot the corner drugstore, however indistinguishable it might be to a Bushman. Again, a new object may seem to have strong structure or identity because of striking physical features which suggest or impose their own pattern. Thus the sea or a great mountain can rivet the attention of one coming from the flat plains of the interior, even if he is so young or so parochial as to have no name for these great phenomena.

As manipulators of the physical environment, city planners are primarily interested in the external agent in the interaction which produces the environmental image. Different environments resist or facilitate the process of image-making. Any given form, a fine vase or a lump of clay, will have a high or a low probability of evoking a strong image among various observers. Presumably this probability can be stated with greater and greater precision as the observers are grouped in more and more homogeneous classes of age, sex, culture, occupation, temperament, or familiarity. Each individual creates and bears his own image, but there seems to be substantial agreement among members of the same group. It is these group images, exhibiting consensus among significant numbers, that interest city planners who aspire to model an environment that will be used by many people.

Therefore this study will tend to pass over individual differences, interesting as they might be to a psychologist. The first order of business will be what might be called the "public images," the common mental pictures carried by large numbers of a city's inhabitants: areas of agreement which might be expected to appear in the interaction of a single physical reality, a common culture, and a basic physiological nature.

The systems of orientation which have been used vary widely throughout the world, changing from culture to culture, and from landscape to landscape. . . . The world may be organized around a set of focal points, or be broken into named regions, or be linked by remembered routes. Varied as these methods are, and inexhaustible as seem to be the potential clues which a man may pick out to differentiate his world, they cast interesting side-lights on the means that we use today to locate ourselves in our own city world. . . .

STRUCTURE AND IDENTITY

An environmental image may be analyzed into three components: identity, structure, and meaning. It is useful to abstract these for analysis, if it is remembered that in reality they always appear together. A workable image requires first the identification of an object, which implies its distinction from other things, its recognition as a separable entity. This is called identity, not in the sense of equality with something else, but with the meaning of individuality or oneness. Second, the image must include the spatial or pattern relation of the object to the observer and to other objects. Finally, this object must have some meaning for the observer, whether practical or emotional. Meaning is also a relation, but quite a different one from spatial or pattern relation.

Thus an image useful for making an exit requires the recognition of a door as a distinct entity, of its spatial relation to the observer, and its meaning as a hole for getting out. These are not truly separable. The visual recognition of a door is matted together with its meaning as a door. It is possible, however, to analyze the door in terms of its identity of form and clarity of position, considered as if they were prior to its meaning.

Such an analytic feat might be pointless in the study of a door, but not in the study of the urban environment. To begin with, the question of meaning in the city is a complicated one. Group images of meaning are less likely to be consistent at this level than are the perceptions of entity and relationship. Meaning, moreover, is not so easily influenced by physical manipulation as are these other two components. If it is our purpose to build cities for the enjoyment of vast numbers of people of widely diverse background—and cities which will also be adaptable to future purposes—we may even be wise to concentrate on the physical clarity of the image and to allow meaning to develop without our direct guidance. The image of the Manhattan skyline may stand for vitality, power, decadence, mystery, congestion, greatness, or what you will, but in each case that sharp picture crystallizes and reinforces the meaning. So various are the individual meanings of a city, even while its form may be easily communicable, that it appears possible to separate meaning from form, at least in the early stages of analysis. . . .

If an image is to have value for orientation in the living space, it must have several qualities. It must be sufficient, true in a pragmatic sense, allowing the individual to operate within his environment to the extent desired. The map, whether exact or not, must be good enough to get one home. It must be sufficiently clear and well integrated to be economical of mental effort: the map must be readable. It should be safe, with a surplus of clues so that alternative actions are possible and the risk of failure is not too high. If a blinking light is the only sign for a critical turn, a power failure may cause disaster. The image should preferably be open-ended, adaptable to change, allowing the individual to continue to investigate and organize reality: there should be blank spaces where he can extend the drawing for himself. Finally, it should in some measure be communicable to other individuals. The relative importance of these criteria for a ''good'' image will vary with different persons in different situations; one will prize an economical and sufficient system, another an open-ended and communicable one.

JANE JACOBS

The Use of Sidewalks: **Contact**

Reformers have long observed city people loitering on busy corners, hanging around in candy stores and bars and drinking soda pop on stoops, and have passed a judgment, the gist of which is: "This is deplorable! If these people had decent homes and a more private or bosky outdoor place, they wouldn't be on the street!"

This judgment represents a profound misunderstanding of cities. It makes no more sense than to drop in at a testimonial banquet in a hotel and conclude that if these people had wives who could cook, they would give their parties at home.

The point of both the testimonial banquet and the social life of city sidewalks is precisely that they are public. They bring together people who do not know each other in an intimate, private social fashion and in most cases do not care to know each other in that fashion.

Nobody can keep open house in a great city. Nobody wants to. And yet if interesting, useful and significant contacts among the people of cities are confined to acquaintanceships suitable for private life, the city becomes stultified. Cities are full of people with whom, from your viewpoint, or mine, or any other individual's, a certain degree of contact is useful or enjoyable; but you do not want them in your hair. And they do not want you in theirs either.

In speaking about city sidewalk safety, it is necessary that there should be, in the brains behind the eyes on the street, an almost unconscious assumption of general street support when the chips are down—when a citizen has to choose, for instance, whether he will take responsibility, or abdicate it, in combating barbarism or protecting strangers. There is a short word for this assumption of support: trust. The trust of a city street is formed over time from many, many little public sidewalk contacts. It grows out of people stopping by at the bar for a beer, getting advice from the grocer and giving advice to the newsstand man, comparing opinions with other customers at the bakery and nodding hello to the two boys drinking pop on the stoop, eying the girls while waiting to be called for dinner, admonishing the children, hearing about a job from the hardware man and borrowing a dollar from the druggist, admiring the new babies and sympathizing over the way a coat faded. Customs vary: In some neighborhoods people compare notes on their dogs; in others they compare notes on their landlords.

Most of it is ostensibly utterly trivial but the sum is not trivial at all. The sum of such casual, public contact at a local level—most of it fortuitous, most of it associated with errands, all of it metered by the person concerned and not thrust upon him by anyone—is a feeling for the public identity of people, a web of public respect and trust, and a resource in time of personal or neighborhood need. The absence of this trust is a disaster to a city street. Its cultivation cannot be institutionalized. And above all, *it implies no private commitments.*

I have seen a striking difference between presence and absence of casual public trust on two sides of the same wide street in East Harlem, composed of residents of roughly the same incomes and same races. On the old-city side, which was full of public places and the sidewalk loitering so deplored by Utopian minders of other people's leisure, the children were being kept well in hand. On the project side of the street across the way, the children, who had a fire hydrant open beside their play area, were behaving destructively, drenching the open windows of houses with water, squirting it on adults who ignorantly walked on the project side of the street, throwing it into the windows of cars as they went by. Nobody dared to stop them. These were anonymous children, and the identities behind them were an unknown. What if you scolded or stopped them? Who would back you up over there in the blind-eyed Turf? Would you get, instead, revenge? Better to keep out of it. Impersonal city streets make anonymous people, and this is not a matter of esthetic quality nor of a mystical emotional effect in architectural scale. It is a matter of what kinds of tangible enterprises sidewalks have, and therefore of how people use the sidewalks in practical, everyday life. . . .

To understand why drinking pop on the stoop differs from drinking pop in the game room, and why getting advice from the grocer or the bartender differs from getting advice from either your next-door neighbor or from an institutional lady who may be hand-in-glove with an institutional landlord—we must look into the matter of city privacy.

Privacy is precious in cities. It is indispensable. Perhaps it is precious and indispensable everywhere, but most places you cannot get it. In small settlements everyone knows your affairs. In the city everyone does not—only those you choose to tell will know much about you. This is one of the attributes of cities that is precious to most city people, whether their incomes are high or their incomes are low, whether they are white or colored, whether they are old inhabitants or new, and it is a gift of great-city life deeply cherished and jealously guarded.

Architectural and planning literature deals with privacy in terms of windows, overlooks, sight lines. The idea is that if no one from outside can peek into where you live—behold, privacy. This is simple-minded. Window privacy is the easiest commodity in the world to get. You just pull down the shades or adjust the blinds. The privacy of keeping one's personal affairs to those selected to know them, and the privacy of having reasonable control over who shall make inroads on your time and when, are rare commodities in most of this world, however, and they have nothing to do with the orientation of windows.

Anthropologist Elena Padilla, author of *Up from Puerto Rico*, describing Puerto Rican life in a poor and squalid district of New York, tells how much people know about each other—who is to be trusted and who not, who is defiant of the law and who upholds it, who is competent and well informed and who is inept and ignorant—and how these things are known from the public life of the sidewalk and its associated enterprises. These are matters of public character. But she also tells how select are those permitted to drop into the kitchen for a cup of coffee, how strong are the ties, and how limited the number of a person's genuine confidants, those who share in a person's private life and private affairs. She tells how it is not considered dignified for everyone to know one's affairs. Nor is it considered dignified to snoop on others beyond the face presented in public. It does violence to a person's privacy and rights. In this, the people she describes are essentially the same as the people of the mixed, Americanized city street on which I live, and essentially the same as the people who live in high-income apartments or fine town houses, too.

A good city street neighborhood achieves a marvel of balance between its people's determination to have essential privacy and their simultaneous wishes for differing degrees of contact, enjoyment or help from the people around. This balance is largely made up of small, sensitively managed details, practiced and accepted so casually that they are normally taken for granted.

Perhaps I can best explain this subtle but all-important balance in terms of the stores where people leave keys for their friends, a common custom in New York. In our family, for example, when a friend wants to use our place while we are away for a weekend or everyone happens to be out during the day, or a visitor for whom we do not wish to wait up is spending the night, we tell such a friend that he can pick up the key at the delicatessen across the street. Joe Cornacchia, who keeps the delicatessen, usually has a dozen or so keys at a time for handing out like this. He has a special drawer for them.

Now why do I, and many others, select Joe as a logical custodian for keys? Because we trust him, first, to be a responsible custodian, but equally important because we know that he combines a feeling of good will with a feeling of no personal responsibility about our private affairs. Joe considers it no concern of his whom we choose to permit in our places and why.

Around on the other side of our block, people leave their keys at a Spanish grocery. On the other side of Joe's block, people leave them at the candy store. Down a block they leave them at the coffee shop, and a few hundred feet around the corner from that, in a barber shop. Around one corner from two fashionable blocks of town houses and apartments in the Upper East Side, people leave their keys in a butcher shop and a bookshop; around another corner they leave them in a cleaner's and a drug store. In unfashionable East Harlem keys are left with at least one florist, in bakeries, in luncheonettes, in Spanish and Italian groceries.

The point, wherever they are left, is not the kind of ostensible service that the enterprise offers, but the kind of proprietor it has.

A service like this cannot be formalized. Identifications . . . questions . . . insurance against mishaps. The all-essential line between public service and privacy would be transgressed by institutionalization. Nobody in his right mind would leave his key in such a place. The service must be given as a favor by someone with an unshakable understanding of the difference between a person's key and a person's private life, or it cannot be given at all.

Or consider the line drawn by Mr. Jaffe at the candy store around our corner—a line so well understood by his customers and by other storekeepers too that they can spend their whole lives in its presence and never think about it consciously. One ordinary morning last winter, Mr. Jaffe, whose formal business name is Bernie, and his wife, whose formal business name is Ann, supervised the small children crossing at the corner on the way to P.S. 41, as Bernie always does because he sees the need; lent an umbrella to one customer and a dollar to another; took custody of two keys; took in some packages for people in the next building who were away; lectured two youngsters who asked for cigarettes; gave street directions; took custody of a watch to give the repair man across the street when he opened later; gave out information on the range of rents in the neighborhood to an apartment seeker; listened to a tale of domestic difficulty and offered reassurance; told some rowdies they could not come in unless they behaved and then defined (and got) good behavior; provided an incidental forum for half a dozen conversations among customers who dropped in for oddments; set aside certain newly arrived papers and magazines for regular customers who would depend on getting them; advised a mother who came for a birthday present not to get the ship-model kit because another child going to the same birthday party was giving that; and got a back copy (this was for me) of the previous day's newspaper out of the deliverer's surplus returns when he came by.

After considering this multiplicity of extra-merchandising services I asked Bernie, "Do you ever introduce your customers to each other?"

He looked startled at the idea, even dismayed. "No," he said thoughtfully. "That would just not be advisable. Sometimes, if I know two customers who are in at the same time have an interest in common, I bring up the subject in conversation and let them carry it on from there if they want to. But oh no, I wouldn't introduce them."

When I told this to an acquaintance in a suburb, she promptly assumed that Mr. Jaffe felt that to make an introduction would be to step above his social class. Not at all. In our neighborhood, storekeepers like the Jaffes enjoy an excellent social status, that of businessmen. In income they are apt to be the peers of the general run of customers and in independence they are the superiors. Their advice, as men or women of common sense and experience, is sought and respected. They are well known as individuals, rather than unknown as class symbols. No; this is that almost unconsciously enforced, well-balanced line showing, the line between the city public world and the world of privacy.

This line can be maintained, without awkwardness to anyone, because of the great plenty of opportunities for public contact in the enterprises along the sidewalks, or on the sidewalks themselves as people move to and fro or deliberately loiter when they feel like it, and also because of the presence of many public hosts, so to speak, proprietors of meeting places like Bernie's where one is free either to hang around or dash in and out, no strings attached.

Under this system, it is possible in a city street neighborhood to know all kinds of people without unwelcome entanglements, without boredom, necessity for excuses, explanations, fears of giving offense, embarrassments respecting impositions or commitments, and all such paraphernalia of obligations which can accompany less limited relationships. It is possible to be on excellent sidewalk terms with people who are very different from oneself, and even, as time passes, on familiar public terms with them. Such relationships can, and do, endure for many years, for decades; they could never have formed without that line, much less endured. They form precisely because they are by-the-way to people's normal public sorties.

"Togetherness" is a fittingly nauseating name for an old ideal in planning theory. This ideal is that if anything is shared among people, much should be shared. "Togetherness," apparently a spiritual resource of the new suburbs, works destructively in cities. The requirement that much shall be shared drives city people apart.

When an area of a city lacks a sidewalk life, the people of the place must enlarge their private lives if they are to have anything approaching equivalent contact with their neighbors. They must settle for some form of "togetherness," in which more is shared with one another than in the life of the sidewalks, or else they must settle for lack of contact. Inevitably the outcome is one or the other; it has to be; and either has distressing results.

In the case of the first outcome, where people do share much, they become exceedingly choosy as to who their neighbors are, or with whom they associate at all. They have to become so. A friend of mine, Penny Kostritsky, is unwittingly and unwillingly in this fix on a street in Baltimore. Her street of nothing but residences, embedded in an area of almost nothing but residences, has been experimentally equipped with a charming sidewalk park. The sidewalk has been widened and attractively paved, wheeled traffic discouraged from the narrow street roadbed, trees and flowers planted, and a piece of play sculpture is to go in. All these are splendid ideas so far as they go.

However, there are no stores. The mothers from nearby blocks who bring small children here, and come here to find some contact with others themselves, perforce go into the houses of acquaintances along the street to warm up in winter, to make telephone calls, to take their children in emergencies to the bathroom. Their hostesses offer them coffee, for there is no other place to get coffee, and naturally considerable social life of this kind has arisen around the park. Much is shared.

Mrs. Kostritsky, who lives in one of the conveniently located houses, and who has two small children, is in the thick of this narrow and accidental social life. "I have lost the advantage of living in the city," she says, "without getting the advantages of living in the suburbs." Still more distressing, when mothers of different income or color or educational background bring their children to the street park, they and their children are rudely and pointedly ostracized. They fit awkwardly into the suburbanlike sharing of private lives that has grown in default of city sidewalk life. The park lacks benches purposely; the "togetherness" people ruled them out because they might be interpreted as an invitation to people who cannot fit in.

"If only we had a couple of stores on the street," Mrs. Kostritsky laments. "If only there were a grocery store or a drug store or a snack joint. Then the telephone calls and the warming up and the gathering could be done naturally in public, and then people would act more decent to each other because everybody would have a right to be here."

Much the same thing that happens in this sidewalk park without a city public life happens sometimes in middle-class projects and colonies, such as Chatham Village in Pittsburgh for example, a famous model of Garden City planning.

The houses here are grouped in colonies around shared interior lawns and play yards, and the whole development is equipped with other devices for close sharing, such as a residents' club which holds parties, dances, reunions, has ladies' activities like bridge and sewing parties, and holds dances and parties for the children. There is no public life here, in any city sense. There are differing degrees of extended private life.

Chatham Village's success as a "model" neighborhood where much is shared has required that the residents be similar to one another in their standards, interests and backgrounds. In the main they are middle-class professionals and their families.[1] It has also required that residents set themselves distinctly apart from the different people in the surrounding city; these are in the main also middle class, but lower middle class, and this is too different for the degree of chumminess that neighborliness in Chatham Village entails.

The inevitable insularity (and homogeneity) of Chatham Village has practical consequences. As one illustration, the junior high school serving the area has problems, as all schools do. Chatham Village is large enough to dominate the elementary school to which its children go, and therefore to work at helping solve this school's problems. To deal with the junior high, however, Chatham Village's people must cooperate with entirely different neighborhoods. But there is no public acquaintanceship, no foundation of casual public trust, no cross-connections with the necessary people—and no practice or ease in applying the most ordinary techniques of city public life at lowly levels. Feeling helpless, as indeed they are, some Chatham Village families move away when their children reach junior high age; others contrive to send them to private high schools. Ironically, just such neighborhood islands as Chatham Village are encouraged in orthodox planning on the specific grounds that cities need the talents and stabilizing influence of the middle class. Presumably these qualities are to seep out by osmosis.

People who do not fit happily into such colonies eventually get out, and in time managements become sophisticated in knowing who among applicants will fit in. Along with basic similarities of standards, values and backgrounds, the arrangement seems to demand a formidable amount of forbearance and tact.

City residential planning that depends, for contact among neighbors, on personal sharing of this sort, and that cultivates it, often does work well socially, if rather narrowly, *for self-selected upper-middle-class people*. It solves easy problems for an easy kind of population. So far as I have been able to discover, it fails to work, however, even on its own terms, *with any other kind of population*.

The more common outcome in cities, where people are faced with the choice of sharing much or nothing, is nothing. In city areas that lack a natural and casual public life, it is common for residents to isolate themselves from each other to a fantastic degree. If mere contact with your neighbors threatens to entangle you in their private lives, or entangle them in yours, and if you cannot be so careful who your neighbors are as self-selected upper-middle-class people can be, the logical solution is absolutely to avoid friendliness or casual offers of help. Better to stay thoroughly distant. As a practical result, the ordinary public jobs—like keeping children in hand—for which people must take a little personal initiative, or those for which they must band together in limited common purposes, go undone. The abysses this opens up can be almost unbelievable.

For example, in one New York City project which is designed—like all orthodox residential city planning—for sharing much or nothing, a remarkably outgoing woman prided herself that she had become acquainted, by making a deliberate effort, with the mothers of every one of the ninety families in her building. She called on them. She buttonholed them at the door or in the hall. She struck up conversations if she sat beside them on a bench.

It so happened that her eight-year-old son, one day, got stuck in the elevator and was left there without help for more than two hours, although he screamed, cried, and pounded. The next day the mother expressed her dismay to one of her ninety acquaintances. "Oh, was that *your* son?" said the other woman. "I didn't know whose boy he was. If I had realized he was *your* son I would have helped him."

This woman, who had not behaved in any such insanely calloused fashion on her old public street—to which she constantly returned, by the way, for public life—was afraid of a possible entanglement that might not be kept easily on a public plane.

NOTE

1. One representative court, for example, contains as this is written four lawyers, two doctors, two engineers, a dentist, a salesman, a banker, a railroad executive, a planning executive.

The City: Pro and Con

Socrates: *Fields and trees teach me nothing, but the people in a city do.*

    Dialogues of Plato: Phaedrus, 230d

Cities give not the human senses room enough.

    Ralph Waldo Emerson, *Essays, Second Series: Nature*

If you would be known, and not know, vegetate in a village; if you would know, and not be known, live in a city.

    Charles C. Colton, *Lacon*, Vol. 1, l. 334

God made the country, and man made the town.

    William Cowper, *The Task*, Bk. 1, l. 749

from City for Sale

It was an ingenious idea and everyone was amazed that no one had thought of it before. The problem was to find the descendants of the Indians who had sold Manhattan to Peter Minuit in 1626.

The search was on, and finally the present chief of the tribe, who was working as a riveter on a new skyscraper in midtown Manhattan, was located. Three city officials climbed up the girders and began to speak while the Indian ate his lunch.

"Chief, we're here on behalf of the City of New York and we understand that your ancestors sold the island of Manhattan for $24."

The chief said, "That's true. The Dutch drove a hard bargain in those days. We were robbed."

"Well," said the second official, "we New Yorkers have always felt very bad about it and we want to make it up to you. How would you people like to buy the place back?"

"For how much?" the chief asked suspiciously.

"Twenty-four dollars."

"That's a lot of money," the chief said.

"We're willing to throw the Bronx, Brooklyn, Queens, and Staten Island in the package."

The chief stared down at the traffic jam below him.

"I don't think my people would be interested," he said.

"If it's a question of financing," the third official said, "you could give us four dollars down and four dollars a month."

Smoke and smog kept drifting up and the chief wiped his eyes with a red bandanna. "It isn't a question of the money. We just don't want it."

The first official said, "Chief, this is a golden opportunity for your people. Not only would you get all the land, but you'd have Lincoln Center, the Metropolitan Museum of Art, the Verrazano Bridge, and Shea Stadium."

The chief said, "White man speaks with forked tongue. Who gets the subway?"

"Why you do, of course."

"The deal's off," the chief said. . . .

While they were talking, police sirens sounded and three men down below came running out of a bank, guns blazing. . . .

The first official said, "It's obvious you don't know a good thing when you see it. We're sorry we even brought it up."

The three officials started their long climb down. Waiting nervously at the bottom was the Mayor.

"What did he say?" the Mayor wanted to know.

"No dice."

"I was afraid of that," he said. "Well, I'll have to think of something else."

Art Buchwald

Reprinted by permission of G. P. Putnam's Sons from *Son of the Great Society* by Art Buchwald. Copyright © 1965, 1966 by Art Buchwald.

9

Health and Illness

As social psychologists have brought their involvement into new areas, one major interest that has begun to emerge is that of health and health care. It is important to realize that this is not merely psychology's traditional relationship with *mental* health, but that we are coming to recognize more and more each day that people's physical health and well-being can be affected in both a positive and negative manner by their everyday life-styles and social relationships.

In one way, the emerging relationship of social psychology and physical health represents a rediscovery of the relationship between body and mind. Research has demonstrated that in addition to the traditionally recognized risk factors associated with heart disease such as family history and blood pressure, people with a hard-driving, competitive orientation toward life and work (called the Type-A pattern) have a higher rate of heart attacks. In addition, factors such as a person's level of social support have been linked to many health-related outcomes, including both the development of certain diseases and recovery from surgery or serious illness.

But more than the relationship of the body and mind of *one* person, social psychologists are concerned about a "meeting of minds"—about the interaction between doctor and patient or between patient and any number of health-care providers, including nurses, dentists, and pharmacists. It is all too easy to forget that health practitioners are human beings and that interactions with them are subject to the same difficulties of communication, stereotypes, and attributional biases as we have in any interpersonal situation. Moreover, the doctor and patient usually meet when there are problems—when the patient may be in pain and is likely to be uncertain, upset, and tense. There is considerable evidence that after spending much time, money, and effort to see a doctor, a large proportion of medical recommendations are not followed. For instance, what good is a powerful drug if patients forget or simply choose not to take it? It may be that the key to many health problems lies in the attitudes and interactions of *people* (whether healthy or sick, patient or practitioner) and that it will take medical science and social science together to solve them.

Having been a psychologist in a health setting for a number of years, George Stone is familiar with the problems and promise of psychology in health. He is Professor of Psychology at the University of California at San Francisco Medical Center and Director of the Graduate Group in Psychology. With Nancy Adler and Frances Cohen, he has edited the *Handbook of Health Psychology* and has been appointed the first editor of the newly founded journal, *Health Psychology*. Our conversation covered a range of topics relative to his interests, especially concerning the communication process in health settings. In addition, we discussed the kinds of roles that psychologists can play as they operate within the health system and deal day to day with health practitioners.

A CONVERSATION WITH GEORGE STONE

University of California

KRUPAT: *Whenever we think of psychology in relation to health, the typical association is* mental *health. Can you tell me what psychology has to do with* physical *health?*

STONE: As I see it, psychology is concerned with the study of what determines people's behaviors and their experience, and how we assess their behavior and experience. One of the things about which people behave and experience is health. They engage in behavior to protect and restore their health, they have ideas about health, they experience ill health and so on. All of those things are part of behavior of people, and when psychologists study it, they are studying health behavior.

KRUPAT: *Now that you've said it it sounds so obvious. Then let me ask* that question from the opposite side. Since psychology and health have such a natural link, why has it taken us so long to get involved in it?

STONE: Well, that is an interesting question. Actually, psychologists became involved in the health system very early. There was a symposium at the American Psychological Association in 1912 at which a number of famous psychologists including John Watson were talking about how to teach psychology to medical students. I presume that they were looking at the whole issue of psychology and health. Somehow, I think the notion of mental health so preoccupied psychologists that followed them that they forgot all about this other aspect of behavior. It has been very interesting to me, for example, that educational psychology started about the same time, and developed as a distinct field. Yet it wasn't really until 1969 or 70 that psychologists identified all those parts of the world concerned with health as being of sufficient interest and having enough in common to be recognized as an area for study.

KRUPAT: *When psychologists get involved in this area what do they become: health psychologists? medical psychologists? specialists in behavioral medicine? There are so many terms that it can get confusing.*

STONE: There are meaningful distinctions among these terms. It doesn't make sense to me to use those three terms interchangeably and have three different names for the same thing. I have a very strong set of views about this that I have been advocating. Other people have different views about it, but I can tell you what mine are. Health psychology, as I see it, is any aspect of psychology that is relevant to understanding health behavior and experiences that people have in relation to health and illness. From that point of view, health psychology is just as broad as all of psychology, except that it is looking at only those things concerned with health rather than at esthetic experience or political judgments, etc. In England, medical psychology has a meaning which is very much like what we call psychiatry here—it is the treatment of mental illness. In this country, I think medical psychology applies to what people who are trained as clinical psychologists do when they turn to the medical or the general health scene as opposed to the mental health scene. Although I am sure it will not disappear, I don't like the term medical psychology because it confuses issues by referring only to the profession of medicine, leaving out nursing, pharmacy, dentistry, and others. I think clinical psychologists have services to offer to dental patients or any other kinds of patients. Behavioral medicine seems to be that aspect of medicine that makes use of behavioral interventions such as biofeedback or behavior modification. These are techniques that psychologists have developed, but when they are applied to the treatment of medical problems, behavioral medicine may be practiced by physicians, nurses, or dentists as well as people trained as psychologists.

KRUPAT: *Maybe I'm just being picky, but I was curious about your use of the term "patient." I thought somehow that we as psychologists were trying to get involved with health issues that dealt with people in general and not just with people identified as patients.*

STONE: I have fallen into using the term "patient." For awhile I was rather self-consciously using the term "client," but I found this created more problems than it solved in talking with medical people. It would be nice to have a good, clean term that referred to people with whose health we were concerned, whether they had fallen sick, were taking preventive actions, were involved in rehabilitation or whatever. We are also interested in people who are neither patients nor clients, who are not engaged in seeking professional care. But there is really no word in our language to deal with people whose health is at issue. "People at risk" perhaps, but it is an awkward term.

KRUPAT: *Regardless of the terms we use then, once psychologists are recognized as being relevant to health matters, what can they do?*

STONE: It seems to me that among other things psychology is concerned with studying behavior and ways of altering behavior. So that to the extent that a person's behavior is contributing to health problems—and it can in many different ways—if we can identify the relationship between the behavior of the person and the outcome, then we can design ways of changing that behavior and contribute to reducing health problems.

KRUPAT: *But wouldn't many people say that the progress of health care and health research was doing just fine without social psychologists, that diseases are conquered by discovering vaccines and studying germs. What does all this have to do with the attitudes or interactions of people?*

STONE: Medicine has been very successful in the past 150 years. It has conquered many diseases which were scourges of the human race, mainly those that could be conquered by medical means and public health means. But public health measures at the level of draining swamps and cleaning up sanitation and things like that also have their psychological impacts. We can look around now and see public-health hazards: ozone in the stratosphere, sulphur dioxide in the atmosphere. In my view, these problems are going to require social psychologists to analyze what is taking place. How is it that people put up with these hazards in their environment? What can be done about it? I think up to now there have been efforts to ask this sort of question, but there has been relatively little effort to look at it as a psychological phenomenon.

KRUPAT: *There's no doubt that there is a role for the social psychologist in studying public attitudes and public-health practices, and getting involved in the making of policy. Yet, it is surprising for me to hear you mention this first since I realize that one of your major interests has been in studying behavior on a smaller scale, on the level of relations between doctors and patients.*

STONE: I have been interested in the topic of patient compliance, which is what I believe you are referring to. The term "patient compliance" already suggests part of the problem. It suggests that the patient is simply supposed to do what the doctor says. As psychologists look at this issue, they begin to question that point of view. Maybe "compliance" isn't what is needed, maybe something more active is needed.

KRUPAT: *I agree. It is interesting that this is the same term Kelman has used in a completely different context. Maybe patients shouldn't merely comply. Maybe they should be encouraged to "internalize" which, as you suggested, implies a more active role for the patient.*

STONE: If you look into the compliance literature, the earliest studies that you can find are about the mid '50s to late '60s when researchers first thought to ask empirically: Do people actually do what they are advised to do? The fact of the matter is that under most conditions they don't. By and large only about half of the recommendations made are followed and this is an enormous loss of medical resources. Most of that early work, by the way, was not done by psychologists.

KRUPAT: *And what contributions have psychologists made since then?*

STONE: Psychologists didn't really get involved in studying compliance in the health system until in the 1970s. I think they transformed the character of that field, raised new questions. Psychologists came with their tools of analysis and pointed out this is really a social psychological problem. There is an interpersonal exchange that is going on between doctor and patient.

KRUPAT: *Well then, what is wrong in many cases with the relationship between the patient and the provider?*

STONE: The way I look at it, the transaction is very complex. It generally consists of two people coming together, each with some kind of a notion of what the transaction is going to be about: what they are going to get and what they are going to give in the transaction. Characteristically in a health trans- action there is a problem to be solved. In rather general form, the solution is sought by patients giving information about their symptoms and what is going on, then there is some kind of processing of that information using the expertise of the provider. Out of that comes a recommended solution to the problem. So basically what you have is a social problem-solving situation in which each party has different parts of the solution. If you conceive of it that way, then you can begin to ask what could go wrong with the process. Well, one of the things that could go wrong is that the two participants are not trying to solve the same problem. They come together and the doctor thinks *this* is the problem while the patient thinks *that* is the problem. They are working on different things. The next thing to be done after they have come together is to communicate about what is going on, and they have to communicate in ways that are mutually intelligible. So even if they have some kind of agreement about what the problem is, they still have many different levels of possible difficulty in the communication. It may be just that they don't talk the same language—one is trained medically and the other is not, or maybe one speaks English and the other speaks Spanish.

KRUPAT: *Sometimes it might as well be.*

STONE: Yes. At another level, what goes wrong is that people come in with a medical problem or a health problem, but they also come with other agendas. Doctors have agendas about what is professionally appropriate, what's economical, and how much time they can spend with a patient.

Patients come in with agendas about who they are, and what kind of respect and consideration they are going to get from the doctor. Many times there are discrepancies between the agendas of the two participants that will divert them from the medical problem and get their attention on problems of self esteem, time, and other sorts of things.

KRUPAT: *Another complicating factor must be the fact that, for the patient especially, there is a good deal of fear and emotion. And while I'm sure most patients want their doctors to be calm, don't they sometimes seem too calm, almost aloof?*

STONE: Just because there is a lot of emotion involved in some of the situations that doctors and health providers have to face, they learn to do things to protect themselves from these excessive emotions. Otherwise they experience what is known as "burnout"; and in fact that is another of the topics that health psychologists are interested in. Sociologists have done research on the socialization of medical students, and part of what goes on is learning to distance oneself to some degree from these emotions. As a whole, our culture tries to keep things fairly cool and not let much emotion into everyday interactions. We tend to shy away and be fearful of emotional interactions, partly because we don't have comfortable skills or ways of dealing with them. So one of the things that seems to be very helpful when you are working with problems of communication between providers and patients is helping providers to be more comfortable with hearing and feeling emotions from other people.

So what you have is this transaction which is very complicated where lots of things can go wrong. We need to develop a good description of it and all of the different things that can go wrong with it so that we can watch the transaction and see how it is functioning. Kind of like a check-off list you might use if you were trouble-shooting a car. If we have a good map of what a health transaction looks like, we can see where the problem is and diagnose it.

KRUPAT: *Before you go any further, let me ask you to what extent you believe a doctor would make this same kind of analysis?*

STONE: You know, doctors are very well trained in problem solving. That is what medical education is largely about. But they are not trained to *think about* problem solving. The doctor probably doesn't think about that process any more than we think about walking, we just walk. Since they don't think about the way they are solving problems or about how they are communicating, they don't think about what is going wrong. That is where the psychologist comes in. The psychologist is trained to watch people and to notice the process of problem solving, not to solve medical problems.

KRUPAT: *It all makes so much sense to me once you say it, yet this kind of transaction has gone for so long without the close scrutiny you've just mentioned. How do doctors respond when you describe this to them?*

STONE: I am constantly practicing my way of describing it, but I would have to say that up to now it is hard to get doctors to comprehend what I am talking about. I have much better luck when I am talking to psychologists about it. I think that part of what psychologists need to do is learn how to talk to doctors; to learn about what is similar and what is different between psychologists and medically trained people and how we can communicate. In a sense, we have to engage in a transaction with the doctor, so we can also apply this model that I am talking about to our interactions with doctors. What is their agenda for coming and talking to a psychologist and what is my agenda for going and talking to a doctor? What kinds of things can go wrong with our conversations? We need to become conscious of our own interactions with the medical profession. I am still at the stage of trying to understand things and trying to figure out how to make it work better.

KRUPAT: *But once we figure out how to do it, who should we direct our knowledge towards? There are all sorts of health professionals, but then there are the people who receive the care. Assuming that we can't get to everyone simultaneously, what should we do to have the greatest impact?*

STONE: Personally, I think we should be addressing both providers and patients, but let me answer your question in terms of our own Health Psychology program. By virtue of being in a medical setting, we have access to providers, and therefore we have oriented ourselves more toward the providers than to the patients. The Public Health schools are more oriented toward educating the people and population. If we had to choose one or the other—doctors or patients—there is a trade-off. Doctors have to be educated more intensively, given more of a one-to-one kind of education. At the same time, two hundred thousand doctors account for just about all of the doctor-patient transactions with two hundred million people. On the other hand, the two hundred million people can be approached through the media, television, and so on. I think we should be educating both, that we have to educate them in different ways, and that both kinds of education are very important.

KRUPAT: *I guess if the problem is one of mutual understanding and communication, changing one without the other won't do.*

STONE: There was an interesting study reported not too long ago in which psychologists undertook to teach patients to ask more questions. The outcome of that was complex, but one of the results was that patients and doctors left the transactions less satisfied. They were both sort of irritated as a result of what the patients were taught, but the patients did better than a control group in keeping their appointments for the next four months.

KRUPAT: *On the other end of things, there are probably plenty of patients who would be equally unhappy if the doctor offered too much detail to them—people who want reassurance, not information. How is a doctor to know what each patient's needs are?*

STONE: That's a tough question, one that I found out about after I had been working in the area for a while. Initially, I had the notion that there was a right way to communicate, and what we needed to do was to teach everyone that way. As I began to get into it, it became clear that different people didn't want the same things out of the transactions and that we needed to back off. That is why I have doubts about teaching "skills." It seems to me that prior to teaching skills we need to help people to discover what their approach or stance is in relation to others.

KRUPAT: *Do you mean by this that we have to consider something broader than what to answer Person X when he or she asks a particular question?*

STONE: Yes. When I got into this, I started off by trying to do process ratings, looking at interactions and making very detailed notes about what was going on. I was going to figure out correlations between this kind of behavior and that. But the more I did this the more I began to believe that this is not where the variance is. The variance in the outcomes of these interactions is at a more abstract level in terms of how people are construing the relationship they are engaged in, in their self-attributions and their attributions about other people.

KRUPAT: *While I'm sure we could go on discussing issues of interpersonal relations in health care and their various effects, I'd like to raise a completely different issue simply because it seems that there are so many interesting areas concerning social psychology and health. What I'd like to ask you about is what has been called Type-A, or coronary-prone behavior. How is it that such a different topic falls within the same general arena?*

STONE: I do see that as a different domain, but one that is definitely within health psychology. Before we were talking about the social psychology of the treatment process. This example has to do with the psychosomatic element, to use the old term, or the relationship between people's behaviors, their internal states, and their bodily responses. This is an area where a tremendous amount of work is going on, and where social psychology is quite relevant. For instance, it is clear that it's not what *happens* to people as much as how they *interpret* what happens that affects the endocrine or the nervous system, which in turn produces heart disease or changes in resistance to bacteria. We know a lot about the bodily links, but less about the relationship between the circumstances and the interpretation of these circumstances.

KRUPAT: *But this is such a new and current issue. How is it that psychologists never pointed this out before?*

STONE: My answer to that has to do with my own history of health psychology. Anthropologists have been studying the meanings of illness ever since anthropology began but psychologists were trying to make things very simple. They were using very, very simple-minded models for what organisms were, using the metaphor of the reflex and things like that. But organisms are ever so much more complicated than that. It wasn't until we acknowledged this complexity and let the mind, attention, and consciousness back into psychology, from which they were excluded for 50 years, that we could begin to approach questions like this.

KRUPAT: *And now that we are into these matters, are we making an impact on people and their behaviors? Are the lessons we are learning filtering into public awareness?*

STONE: I suspect that if you went out on the streets of San Francisco and asked people about Type-A behavior that half of the people would know what you are talking about right now. It seems to me that there is a great deal of education that is going on through magazines and television and so on, and that people are becoming aware that the way they live affects their lives. People are stopping smoking. The sale of cigarettes in California is down again this year from the previous year. There has been a steady decline in recent years. People do listen to these messages; and when they are presented clearly, people respond.

KRUPAT: *Then as we get involved in getting people to quit smoking and getting public agencies to clean up the environment, to what extent are we acting as psychologists, that is as "objective researchers," and to what extent are we stepping out of that traditional role and becoming merely individual activists?*

STONE: That is a question I don't feel very comfortable in answering because I think that my position is a bit deviant. I feel that it is impossible for me as an individual to be objective. I have values and I live my values. I think that we need to distinguish between having values and an idea about the way we want the world to be, and letting those values color the data that we get in our research. If I allow my thoughts about the way I feel the world ought to be to influence my observations about the way the world really is, then I am going to get bad information and I am not being useful as a scientist. A lot of attention has been paid to experimenters' expectancies and wishes about how research is going to come out and how it actually comes out. We all know that there is a danger there, and we have to be clear about the danger, but I am not going to give up my values about the way that I want the world to look.

KRUPAT: *Certainly one value which nobody would argue with is the desire for good health and good health care. But one problem I have heard from some health-care providers is that all we do is to be critical. Are psychologists guilty of merely being outside observers and what some have called "doctor-baiting"?*

STONE: That is a very important question. I don't think psychologists are as much at fault as people in some of the other social and behavioral sciences who have gone in, looked at things, and come back and written a book for their field or the general public. I think that psychologists are much more integrated into the system, and they are much more oriented toward interventions. I think one of the big differences between psychologists and sociologists or anthropologists, for example, is that both sociologists and anthropologists have a stance of being objective, of observing and not letting their participation influence the system that they are looking at. Psychologists have been interventionists and "meddlers" from the very beginning. They get right in there. I think that is an advantage in overcoming the thing that you are pointing to because it encourages us to be collaborators with the doctors, rather than coming in and telling them what they are doing wrong. I'm sure there are some out there who are just making money, but I believe that most doctors want to do the best job they can. I think there is an enormous committment on their part. What is most appropriate for health psychologists is to enter into collaborative studies of these processes with physicians and for both to be happy when things come out better.

AN INTRODUCTION TO THE READINGS

The first article in this section, by Melvin Snyder and Steven Mentzer, notes that while we already have "a psychology of the patient," for a fuller understanding of the medical encounter we also ought to have a "psychology of the physician." Pointing out that two critical functions of physicians are to make judgments and to communicate with patients, they review the literature in these areas and demonstrate their relevance to physician behavior. They point out that doctors—as human beings—may be subject to errors in making diagnosis and treatment decisions and also have to learn to deal with conveying bad news to patients. They suggest that when we can replace speculation with the findings of research, it may be possible to train physicians to become aware of these potential pitfalls and thereby overcome them.

The next article is by Robin DiMatteo, a social psychologist who has been involved in the sort of training suggested by Snyder and Mentzer. Focusing upon the emotional aspects of the relationship between doctor and patient, DiMatteo suggests that we need "a science of the art of medicine." Reporting on a variety of studies, she concludes that an important factor in determining whether patients are satisfied and whether they follow treatment regimens is whether doctors pay attention to the socioemotional as well as the medical needs of their patients. DiMatteo especially suggests that doctors should be aware of what they are communicating nonverbally as well as what they say.

In the next article, by David Glass, the focus changes from the doctor and patient to the patient and his or her personality. In particular, Glass looks at what some have called the Type-A or coronary-prone pattern of behavior. The characteristics of a Type-A individual are those of the hard-working striver who feels the need to control events and reacts in frustration with hostility. Noting that Type-A behavior is one of the strongest predictors of recurring heart attacks, Glass discusses how a person's psychological reactions to stress create physiological responses in the body which might then lead to heart attacks.

Just as Glass points out how medical problems may be *caused* by certain behaviors and reactions, the final article, by Adam Smith, demonstrates how attitudes and orientations may help *cure* the body as well. Smith's article reports on the now famous self-cure of writer/editor Norman Cousins, whose main ingredients for cure seemed to be a positive outlook and heavy doses of laughter. The message of this article is not that of the Christian Scientist nor that of the quack cure, but rather that we should be less in reverence of "hard" (i.e., medical) facts and more open to the "soft" (i.e., personal and interpersonal) aspects of health and disease. As Smith says, "theory changes, the knowledge base keeps changing, but contact and compassion don't."

MELVIN L. SNYDER
STEVEN MENTZER

Social Psychological Perspectives on the Physician's Feelings and Behavior

When someone mentions psychology and medicine in the same breath, usually what comes to mind is mental illness, what many call behavior disorders. [This paper and others] on health and illness demonstrate a broader role in medicine for psychology with examples from social psychology. Social psychology relates to the plight of perfectly normal people who happen to feel ill or get cancer or respond to everyday stress. These papers demonstrate the value of a psychology of the patient. Might we also profit from a psychology of the physician?

There are a variety of issues that a psychology of the physician might elucidate. To mention a few: How does the physician feel when a treatment expected to produce a cure does not do so? How does the physician reconcile the demand to project warmth and reassurance with the need for an aloof objectivity? Just how important is warmth and reassurance? How do notoriously heavy workloads affect the physician's performance and health? Does the physician's status in society influence the quality of medical care? What is gained and what is lost psychologically by the increase in specialization?

We selected two issues for discussion. First, recent laboratory studies of judgment have found evidence for systematic bias in making predictions. These findings raise the possibility of such bias in medical judgment. Second, we consider the implications of the MUM effect—a reluctance to communicate bad news—for understanding physician's general unwillingness to inform the terminally ill of their prognosis.

The practice of medicine, while based on science, is an art requiring, among other things, good judgment. The physician hears the patient's complaint, conducts an examination, and decides what questions to ask and what tests to perform. Having diagnosed what is wrong, the physician decides how to treat it. Although these steps and their order are scarcely invariable, they illustrate the sorts of decisions the physician must make. While most decisions are routine, others are not. There are often times when a pattern of symptoms defies ready categorization and the physician may have to weigh the risks of a diagnostic procedure against the risks of taking action without the information it would provide. Sometimes the treatment for one ailment aggravates another one. In prescribing drugs, the physician must choose a medicine and a dosage that balance between maximizing effectiveness and minimizing risk. The physician must judge when the convalescing patient is sufficiently recovered to resume normal activities, weighing the dangers of relapse versus atrophy. The physician must make these judgments while taking into account such individual factors as the patient's general health, body build, temperament, stamina and tolerance for pain.

The rules that the physician learns do not cover all possible contingencies, and even when there is an appropriate rule, its application requires the exercise of judgment. Even a simple rule like "Do not use drug X when there are serious respiratory problems," requires an assessment of the extent of breathing difficulty and a consideration of the merits of alternative courses of action. As one young resident put it, "I thought everything was going to be fairly clear-cut, but it just isn't that way" (Knafl & Burkett, 1974, p. 399). As the physician resolves particular cases, simultaneously he or she probably also attempts to formulate new rules to improve treatment should the same problem arise again. Initially the rule may take the form of a hypothesis subject to confirmation or rejection as new evidence comes in. The assessment of hypotheses, like the resolution of specific cases, is a matter of judgment.

How does judgment develop? We scarcely know the details of the process, but we can point to two kinds of experience that are important. One observes the assessments made by experienced others and compares them to one's own judgments. Second, one can learn more directly. As another resident said, "You do a case and see what happens," (Knafl & Burkett, 1974, p. 399). One makes a diagnosis and prescribes a treatment, and the results provide feedback. Thus, one develops judgment through observation of others' judgments and through clinical experience.

How can the efficacy of such training be assessed? One way is to check whether those who develop expertise in this way agree with each other. We presume they do agree more often than not (Einhorn, 1972, 1974). Still, Lasagna (1976) reports disagreement among experts in a survey of recommendations for the use of drugs in various treatment programs. Lasagna suggests two reasons for these discrepancies. One is that physicians make different value judgments. He illustrates by noting that his colleagues take different stands on the risk-efficacy dimension. Coronary bypass surgery has a 5% mortality rate. Some physicians therefore advise against it; others believe the patient has nothing to lose. The second reason Lasagna gives is that physicians have different data bases. Some are more experienced with relevant cases.

Lasagna's points are well taken. There is, however, a way to account for disagreement among experts even if they have had equal exposure to relevant cases and even if their values are identical. The data experts have can differ simply according to the laws of chance. Consider an ailment for which there is no established treatment and from which 50% die and 50% recover. If an experimental treatment works once or twice, few will jump to a conclusion. But if in six cases it saves all but one, most of us would feel that we were on to something. Five out of six is an .833 batting average, outstanding in most any league. We are, however, forgetting that a player named chance is batting .500. In the language of statistics, five out of six is not significant.

Tversky and Kahneman (1971) report that many even have confidence when out of five occasions a positive result occurs four times, a result even further from significance. In a paper entitled "Belief in the law of small numbers," they note the believer tends to place "undue confidence in early trends" (p. 109). Who is the believer? One of their samples was the audience at a mathematical psychology meeting. They note that "Apparently, acquaintance with formal logic and with probability theory does not extinguish erroneous intuitions" (p. 109). How do they account for the tendency to take small samples so seriously? They suggest that people believe random samples, even small ones, must be representative of the population from which they are drawn. If there are five successes on the first six occasions we extrapolate that ratio and expect it to hold whether the sample is six, sixty or six thousand. In the informal testing of hypotheses that we all do, we may erroneously treat evidence that is consistent but inconclusive as definitive.

Unwarranted extrapolation from small samples can be explained in terms of Tversky and Kahneman's (1973) concept of availability. The idea is that people judge the probability of an event by the ease with which previous instances come to mind, that is how psychologically available they are. When five positive instances and one negative one have occurred the odds favor a positive case coming to mind first. There are several ways that an event may become psychologically available. Judgments of the percentage of males and females on an orally-presented list of famous people favored the sex with the relatively more famous members. Presumably subjects judged the list as a whole on the basis of the sex of those who came to mind, i.e., the more famous members. Similarly, physicians must find some of their patients more memorable than others. Conclusions may be drawn disproportionately on the basis of these more salient cases. The result could be a medicine of the memorable. Cases may be salient for a different reason. They stand out more if they fit a theory. Few of us, psychologists or physicians, follow Darwin's lead and write down each bit of evidence that contradicts our hypothesis.

One might expect that a false conclusion would get corrected when additional cases came along. While this certainly happens much of the time, Kahneman and Tversky (1971) suggest that the investigator can readily find explanations when new data seem to contradict old. If a treatment saves five out of six patients but only two of the next four, it is easy to think of a "reason", such as an exceptionally poor prognosis, to explain the failures. Desire to do so may be strong if one has already told colleagues or if one has published the discovery. The well-known process of dissonance reduction—justification of one's behavior—may ensue. In a similar vein, a hypothesis may serve as a self-fulfilling prophecy—an expectancy which leads to its own confirmation (Jones, 1977). For the physician this could mean either that the patient's reaction is misperceived as the predicted one or that the physician behaves so as to bring about the expected reaction in the patient. In either case we presume the physician is unaware of his or her role in constructing and shaping reality.

We are, of course, speculating. We are extrapolating from the psychological laboratory to the physician's office, the clinic, and the hospital. An anecdote may serve to illustrate the plausibility of our speculations and extrapolations (Note 1). During surgery a physician entered the operating room and spoke to the surgeon performing the operation. "Looks like you have got a bleeder, I give mine a shot of vitamin E. I've done it three times—every time there haven't been any problems." This anecdote raises several questions. What is the baseline level of bleeding in the sample selected? Is three cases enough to assess the effectiveness and reliability of the treatment? How are cases selected? Certainly the success rate could be subtly enhanced by selecting marginal cases who probably would have no problems anyway. We should also add that for all we know vitamin E may turn out to be just the thing for bleeding. The point isn't whether it is or not. The point is to discover the usual basis for drawing such conclusions, to determine how often they go astray and with what consequences and, if it seems warranted, to develop means for reducing error, e.g. by educating physicians about biases in judgment and by formalizing the decision process—perhaps with the aid of the computer—through the use of algorithms, Venn diagrams, utility curves, or regression equations (Elstein, 1976; Feinstein, 1974; Schwartz, Garry, Kassirer & Essig, 1973).

The other issue we wish to discuss also concerns judgment. It is the question of whether to tell the terminally ill (typically cancer patients) their prognosis. Here, we know more about what physicians actually do, and there is some indirect evidence concerning why they do it. Although no Gallup poll of physicians has been taken, samplings in various locales have found that physicians usually do not inform patients. A rough estimate is that 80% of the terminal patients are never told by their physician (Fitts and Ravdin, 1953; Life, 1972; Oken, 1961). It is curious, then, that surveys reveal that about 80% of the public say that they do want to know. Kelley and Friesen (1950) reported that 89% of cancer patients and 82% of noncancer patients preferred to know their diagnosis. Cappon (1962) asked various groups whether, if they were very sick, they would want to know whether they would die from the illness. The percentages saying yes were 67% of those who were in fact dying, 81% of somatic patients, 91% of nonpatients and 82% of psychiatric patients. Life (1972) magazine invited readers to answer a survey about medical care. 70% of the respondents said patients should be told about terminal illness. More recently in the winter quarter of 1978, the senior author conducted two classroom surveys at Dartmouth College. The percentages of students desiring to be informed of terminal illness were 88% and 94%. Why this discrepancy between the patient's desires and the physician's behavior? Oken (1961) found that physicians who remain silent often say the "patients really do not want to know regardless of what people say" (p. 1123). The physician at one time may have told a patient. The patient may have gotten upset or the physician may have inferred that the patient was upset (Cf. Snyder and Frankel, 1976). The physician therefore may have concluded that it is better not to tell. Tesser and Rosen (1975) suggest that this conclusion mistakes the patient's desire to avoid having the disease for a desire to avoid hearing about it. Certainly, no one wants to find out that she or he has cancer; nevertheless, if one does have it, it may be more distressing to suspect it and remain uncertain than to know. A variety of laboratory studies have shown people often prefer to be informed about uncertain outcomes, both positive and negative (e.g. Lanzetta & Driscoll, 1966).

> Hackett and Weisman (1962) quote a woman who had inquired about her headaches: When the doctor said it was probably nerves, she asked why she was nervous. He returned the question. She replied, "I am nervous because I have lost 60 pounds in a year, the Priest comes to see me twice a week, which he never did before, and my mother-in-law is nicer to me even though I am meaner to her. Wouldn't this make you nervous?" There was a pause. Then the doctor said, "You mean you think you are dying?" She said, "I do." He said, "You are." Then she smiled and said, "Well, I've finally broken the sound barrier; someone's finally told me the truth." (p. 122)

Tesser and Rosen (1975) place physician's unwillingness to inform terminal patients in the context of a more general phenomenon, a reluctance to deliver bad news. Working in the psychological laboratory, they have found evidence that several factors contribute to this reluctance. In one study they manipulated the apparent emotionality of the potential recipient of bad news and found subjects were less likely to tell if the recipient was emotional. Interestingly enough, physicians often explain not informing patients because of their emotional instability. Further reflection however, reveals that patient emotionality is an inadequate reason for silence about impending death. It fails because many, probably most, patients with terminal diagnoses find out anyway (Lasagna, 1970; Oken, 1961), for example, because of the drastic loss of weight or by the reactions of others. The patient receives verbal reassurances contradicted by smiles full of pity. Doubt is created and eventually the messages from the body and from others may change it into an unspeakable certainty. Is this the way the emotionally unstable should discover they are dying? Ironically, the physician's judgment of patient emotionality may appear to be confirmed in the manner of the self-fulfilling prophecy discussed above.

Glaser and Straus (1965) discuss various consequences of the patient and family knowing and not knowing. Unaware patients are denied the possibility of planning realistically for the time that remains and for the future of their survivors. They cannot tie up loose ends, end feuds, complete projects and so forth. They are also less likely to come to terms with death. Glaser and Straus (1965) note the tension that is created when the patient is unaware and the family knows but must pretend otherwise. When the patient and family both know, they can face the crisis together and perhaps provide mutual support.

Tesser and Rosen (1975) considered other explanations for reluctance to transmit bad news. Perhaps the communicator feels guilt or fears a negative evaluation. If either is so, one would expect less communication the more attractive the recipient. Guilt should be greater and so should concern about the recipient's reaction. In one study attractiveness of the recipient was varied by describing her as attitudinally similar and pleasant or as attitudinally dissimilar and unpleasant. It turned out that subjects told the bad news more readily when the recipient was attractive rather than unattractive. This finding weakens the hypotheses of guilt or fear of negative evaluation.

Tesser and Rosen (1971) found support for a hypothesis based on the need for the communicator to adopt a bad mood in order to deliver bad news. People do adopt such a mood when communicating bad news, and people already placed in a bad mood are likely to tell. One reason people in a good or average mood may not tell is to avoid incurring the psychological cost of adopting an appropriate mood. There is support for the relevance of this explanation to physicians. Saul and Kass (1969) note that informing terminal patients is one of the two experiences most threatening to medical students, the other being informing the family of a death. It is possible, then, that physicians who are reluctant to inform the terminal patient are acting out of concern for their own psychological state rather than that of the patient who eventually may find out anyway.

Earlier in discussing medical judgment, we speculated that physicians may sometimes jump to conclusions. Now we suggest that some are more concerned about their own emotions than their patients'. Of course, these speculations may prove to be unfounded. Much more evidence is needed. But we should like to point out that all we are really suggesting is that physicians are human. Who has not prematurely drawn a conclusion? Who has not been reluctant to inform another of bad news, that he or she has lost a job, missed a promotion or flunked a course? There is important work for social psychologists to do, not only in a psychology of the physician, but also more broadly in a psychology of medicine. There are at least two sorts of contributions that can be made. One is the application in medical contexts of social psychological concepts. We illustrated this by asking whether physicians' judgments can be illuminated using the concept of psychological availability and whether physicians' reluctance to inform the terminally ill can be understood as an instance of the MUM effect and thus explainable in the same way. To mention some other relevant concepts: risk-taking, achievement motivation, mechanisms for coping with stress, helplessness, unpredictability, norms, self-concept, self-awareness, persuasion, and self-disclosure.

The other contribution is the application in medical contexts of sophisticated human research methodology, for example, to resolve the issues raised by the application of concepts. Social psychologists are aware of the many possible sources of artifact that can invalidate conclusions based on human data: e.g., subject conformity to obvious hypotheses, unintended differential treatment of subjects in different conditions, self-presentation and face-saving. We also have learned to deal with these sorts of problems in various ways such as concealment of the hypothesis from the subject, concealment of the subjects' experimental condition from the experimentor, and controls for the social desirability of responses. We also know the power of random assignment of subjects to experimental conditions as a way to answer questions about causality.

The ethical issues raised in medical settings may even be more agonizing than those raised in the social psychological laboratory. But as Aronson (1976) has pointed out, when there is a potential benefit to society, the researcher may have an ethical obligation to go ahead. Prime candidates for research include issues on which physicians do not agree and policies based on tradition or unarticulated clinical experience.

To get down to specifics, we will use the two issues we selected for discussion. When physicians disagree on how to treat a particular ailment, a carefully designed interview might reveal whether differences are a consequence of the judgment biases discussed by Tversky and Kahneman (1974). If so, psychologists could then devise and evaluate educational programs to overcome the biases. Similarly with regard to informing the terminally ill, social psychologists could assess whether physicians are more likely to tell those who are likeable, as suggested by a laboratory study of the MUM effect (Tesser & Rosen, 1975) and as suspected by Glaser & Straus (1965).

And if we really wanted to know whether it is better to leave the terminally ill uninformed, an experiment could be done randomly assigning patients to be informed or not. Outcomes to be measured include longevity, anxiety, depression and the quality of social relationships. Of course, there are ethical issues surrounding the conduct of such research, but in the absence of a convincing rationale for the current predominant practice of not informing, perhaps it is unethical not to do the research. The general idea is to try to resolve dilemmas by replacing speculation with fact.

NOTE

1. H'Doubler, P. B. Jr. Personal communication, August 1977.

REFERENCES

Aronson, E. *The social animal* (2nd. ed.). San Francisco: W. H. Freeman, 1976.

Cappon, D. Attitudes of man towards the dying. *Canadian Medical Association Journal*, 1962, **87**, 693–700.

Einhorn, H. J. Expert measurement and mechanical combination. *Organizational Behavior and Human Performance*, 1972, **7**, 86–106.

Einhorn, H. J. Expert judgment: Some necessary conditions and an example. *Journal of Applied Psychology*, 1974, **59**, 562–571.

Elstein, A. S. Clinical judgment: psychological research and medical practice. *Science*, 1976, **194**, 696–700.

Feinstein, A. An analysis of diagnostic reasoning: III. The construction of clinical algorithms. *Yale Journal of Biology and Medicine*, 1974, **1**, 5–32.

Fitts, W. T. Jr., & Ravdin, I. S. What Philadelphia physicians tell patients with cancer. *Journal of the American Medical Association*, November 7, 1953, **153**, 901–904.

Glaser, B. G., Straus, A. L. *Awareness of dying*. Chicago: Aldine, 1965.

Hackett, T. P. & Weisman, A. D. The treatment of the dying. *Current Psychiatric Therapies*, 1962, **2**, 121–216.

Jones, R. A. *Self-fulfilling prophecies: social, psychological and physiological effects of expectancies*. Hillsdale, New Jersey: Lawrence Erlbaum Associates, 1977.

Kelly, W. D., & Friesen, S. R. Do cancer patients want to be told? *Surgery*, 1950, **27**, 822–826.

Knafl, K. & Burkett, G. Professional socialization in a surgical speciality: Acquiring medical judgment. *Social Science and Medicine*, 1975, **9**, 397–404.

Lanzetta, J. T., & Driscoll, J. M. Preference for information about an uncertain but unavoidable outcome. *Journal of Personality and Social Psychology*, 1966, **3**, 96–102.

Lasagna, L. Physicians behavior toward the dying patient. In O. G. Brim, H. E. Freeman, S. Levine, and N. A. Scotch (Eds.), *The dying patient*. New York: Russell Sage Foundation, 1970.

Lasagna, L. Consensus among experts: The unholy grail. *Perspectives in Biology and Medicine*, 1976, **19**, 537–548.

Life Magazine. Reader response: What do you think of your medical care. August 11, 1972, **73**(6), 38–39.

Oken, D. What to tell cancer patients. *Journal of the American Medical Association*, April 1, 1961, **175**, 1120–1128.

Saul, E. V. & Kass, T. S. Study of anticipated anxiety in a medical school setting. *Journal of Medical Education*, 1969, **44**, 526–532.

Schwartz, W. B., Garry, G. A., Kassirer, J. P., Essig, A. Decision analysis and clinical judgment. *American Journal of Medicine*, 1973, **55**, 459–472.

Snyder, M. L. & Frankel, A. Observer bias: A stringent test of behavior engulfing the field. *Journal of Personality and Social Psychology*, 1976, **34**, 857–864.

Tesser, A. & Rosen, S. The reluctance to transmit bad news. In L. Berkowitz (Ed.), *Advances in experimental social psychology*. Vol. 8. New York: Academic Press, 1975.

Tversky, A., & Kahneman, D. Belief in the law of small numbers. *Psychological Bulletin*, 1971, **76**, 105–110.

Tversky, A. & Kahneman, D. Availability: A heuristic for judging frequency and probability. *Cognitive Psychology*, 1973, **5**, 207–232.

Tversky, A., & Kahneman, D. Judgment under uncertainty: Heuristics and biases. *Science*, 1974, **185**, 1124–1131.

M. ROBIN DI MATTEO

A Social-Psychological Analysis of Physician-Patient Rapport:
Toward a Science of the Art of Medicine

Nearly every society has defined specific roles and status for the ill and their healers, and for many years the rights and duties of the individuals who occupy these roles have been examined by sociologists and anthropologists (King, 1962). In modern American society, the primary healing role is given to the physician. This professional role ranks highly in prestige and power, and demands technical competence, emotional neutrality, and a commitment to serving people (Parsons, 1951). Likewise, the sick person occupies a social role. Parsons (1958) has delineated the benefits to and obligations of the individual who is ill. He or she is relieved of normal social responsibilities, and is expected both to seek medical help and to profess a desire to get well. When the physician and patient are brought together on the health care stage, their interaction is not a mere enactment of script or a simple learned scenario. The interpersonal nature of the physician-patient relationship involves a highly charged affective component. This intensity results from the physician's access to the patient's body and intimate details of the patient's life, as well as from the considerable emotional dependency of people who are ill. The treatment of illness is partly a process of social influence (King, 1962; Fox, 1959; Bloom, 1963; Wilson and Bloom, 1972). The physician and patient bring to their interaction their characteristics, backgrounds and past experiences, and their personal attitudes, beliefs, and values. Albert Schweitzer said of this interaction: "It is our duty to remember at all times and anew that medicine is not only a science, but also the art of letting our own individuality interact with the individuality of the patient" (Strauss, 1968, p. 361).

During the past few decades, medicine has made more significant strides in the diagnosis and treatment of disease than in all the years of its long history. Medicine has begun performing treatment miracles and is now one of America's largest industries, accounting for about 9% of the gross national product (Hamburg and Brown, 1978). Yet, as Eisenberg (1977) has noted, "It is . . . curious that dissatisfaction with medicine in America is at its most vociferous just at a time when doctors have at their disposal the most powerful medical technology the world has yet seen. The 'old fashioned' general practitioner, with few drugs that really worked and not much surgery to recommend, is for some reason looking good to many people—in retrospect, at least'' (p. 235). Eisenberg has gone on to explain that . . . ''Present-day disenchantment with physicians, at a time when they can do more than ever in history to halt and repair the ravages of serious illness, probably reflects the perception by people that they are not being cared for. . . . The patient wants time, sympathetic attention, and concern for himself as a person'' (Eisenberg, 1977, p. 238).

A solution to these complaints is not likely to emerge naturally in today's health care system, for in order to maintain and further develop the technical excellence of modern medicine, medical students are selected primarily for their scientific abilities. Very little attention is paid to the depth of their interpersonal skills. In addition, present day medical training emphasizes the scientific aspects of patient care, with little recognition of what has been termed the ''Art of Medicine.'' Many modern physicians have developed a very narrow view of what is ''scientific'' and have come to believe that medicine is a much more specific science than it actually is. They seem to ignore ancient and modern evidence that patients' responses to their physicians are no less real than their responses to drugs and other treatments, and that patients benefit (or suffer) not only from the medications they are given but also from their physicians' behavior toward them (Eisenberg, 1977; Engel, 1977).

Compassion and an effective bedside manner were almost all that physicians had to offer their patients throughout much of the history of medicine. Thus, the early physicians emphasized the significance of the physician's manner and interpersonal sensitivity to patients. In the fourth century B.C. (1923 Translations) Hippocrates wrote of the physician-patient relationship: ''The patient, though conscious that his condition is perilous, may recover his health simply through his contentment with the goodness of the physician.'' Hippocrates wrote of the ways in which the physician must communicate this goodness. ''On entering [the sick person's room, the physician must] bear in mind [his] manner of sitting, reserve, arrangement of dress, decisive utterance, brevity of speech, composure, bedside manners, care, replies to objections, calm self-control . . . his manner must be serious and humane; without stooping to be jocular or failing to be just, he must avoid excessive austerity; he must always be in control of himself.'' In a similar vein, Sir William Osler advocated that ''The practice of medicine is an art, not a trade; a calling, not a business; a calling in which your heart will be exercised equally with your head'' (Osler, 1904). Frederick Shattuck, a prominent 20th century American physician, wrote in 1907 of what he perceived as a potentially serious gap between the developing science of medicine and what he knew as the art of medicine. He emphasized that disease is one phenomenon but the *diseased person* is another. The physician must have sympathy and empathy for his or her patient as well as gentleness and cheerfulness. He warned that concern for the newly developing scientific aspects of medicine should never replace compassionate medical care and treatment of the patient as a person both because of humanitarian concerns and because medical care without compassion may be ineffective.

In spite of this warning, however, as the body of technical medical knowledge grew there developed a sharp division between the physical care of the patient as science and the emotional care of the patient as interpersonal art. In 1963, Bloom proposed that the physician-patient relationship must now be seen as being composed of two independent dimensions: the "instrumental dimension," which emphasizes the purely technical aspects of the physician's treatment of the patient, and the "expressive dimension" which emphasizes the affective or socio-emotional components of the relationship.

The major purpose of this paper is to review evidence that these two components of the physician-patient relationship should still, as in the earlier days of medicine, be inseparable, and that focusing on one to the exclusion of the other results in ineffective medical care. However, with the help of sound basic and applied social psychological research, physicians can combine the two dimensions for more humane, more effective, and possibly more efficient (and, hence, less expensive) medical care delivery.

THE SIGNIFICANCE OF THE SOCIO-EMOTIONAL DIMENSION IN PATIENT CARE

It is obvious that the practice of medicine in modern times in a manner that emphasizes compassion and ignores technical expertise is quackery. It is not so obvious that the technical treatment of patients without attention to the socio-emotional dimension of the physician-patient relationship may result in equally serious problems. In recent years, a considerable amount of social psychological research has begun to examine the importance of the socio-emotional side of the physician-patient relationship. A brief review of this literature points to the overwhelming influence of this dimension on patient satisfaction with medical care, patient cooperation with medical regimens, and the actual outcome of treatment.

Patient Cooperation

A major unsolved problem in medicine today is patients' lack of cooperation (often called noncompliance) with medical regimens (Gillum and Barsky, 1974). Davis (1966) estimated that at least one-third of all patients fail to cooperate with doctors' orders. Studies have reported rates of noncooperation ranging from 15 to 93 percent. Research evidence suggests that a very important factor may be the failure of the physician to communicate effectively to the patient the correct information about the prescribed treatment (see Stone, 1979, for a detailed review of this informational aspect of communication). The evidence also suggests the necessity of affective communication—a kindness and concern that communicates to the patient that he or she is cared for as a person.

The socio-emotional dimension of the physician-patient relationship can significantly affect patient cooperation. In a study by Francis, Korsch, and Morris (1969), for example, lack of cooperation was related to the pediatrician's lack of sensitivity to, and subsequent failure to meet, the mother's expectations for her visit. Similarly, patients most likely to fail to keep appointments in an out-patient referral clinic tend to be those who feel that they have no doctor with whom they can talk (Alpert, 1964). Davis (1968a, 1968b) analyzed verbal communication from tape-recordings of doctor-patient interactions and determined the degree of patient cooperation by questioning patients and physicians and by content-analyzing medical records. Failure to cooperate was found to be high when the doctor behaved in an antagonistic manner. If the physician collected information from the patient and ignored the patient's need for feedback, the patient tended to be uncooperative. When the physician concentrated solely on an analysis of the patient's medical situation (ignoring the psychological), and on the expression of the physician's own opinions, lack of cooperation was also a likely outcome. On the other hand, if tension built up in the interaction was released through joking or laughing, the probability of patient cooperation with medical regimens was increased.

Other studies have shown that in a psychiatric intake interview, the reported anger of the psychiatric resident correlates negatively with the walk-in applicant's cooperation with recommendations for return to a second diagnostic interview (Salzman, Shader, Scott and Binstock, 1970). The cooperation of alcoholic patients with prescribed treatment regimens have been shown to be related to the communicated affect of their physicians toward alcoholics in general (Milmoe, Rosenthal, Blane, Chafetz, and Wolf, 1967).

In summary, then, it appears from correlational data that the socio-emotional dimension of the physician-patient interaction bears an important relationship to patients' cooperation with medical advice. The existing evidence tends to suggest that a patient's willingness to accept and follow the prescribed treatment regimen might be increased if the physician is sensitive to the patient's needs as a person, communicates caring, and develops rapport with the patient. (See Rodin and Janis, 1979, for an analysis of the development and consequences of a possible mediating mechanism in this relationship—the physician's referent power.)

The Outcome of Treatment

There is evidence that the quality of the interpersonal relationship between the physician and patient can significantly influence the outcome of treatments that may appear to depend solely upon technical factors. In one of the few experimental studies of this kind, Egbert, Battit, Welch, and Bartlett (1964) demonstrated the importance of effective anesthesiologist-patient communication. Surgical patients were randomly divided into two groups. Half of these patients were visited pre-operatively by their anesthesiologist and told about the post-operative pain they would experience and how to relax their muscles in order to reduce the pain. The other patients were told nothing about post-operative pain. After the first post-operative day the group of patients given the special visit and information required a significantly lower dosage of narcotics and their surgeons (blind to each patient's experimental condition) discharged experimental group patients from the hospital an average of 2.7 days earlier than those in the control group. While this result may have been due to any number of factors such as information, familiarity with the anesthesiologist before surgery, some unknown component of the one-to-one contact, or the patients' actual compliance with muscle relaxation techniques, the results did demonstrate that the physician's efforts to reach out to the patient with reassurance and information can influence the outcome of a technical procedure such as surgery.

Pain and illness are accompanied by a significant amount of anxiety, which can have important health-related consequences. For example, a patient's level of anxiety and fear before surgery can affect post-operative recovery (Janis, 1958; Langer, Janis and Wolfer, 1975). Confidence in the physician and the reduction of patient anxiety have been found to be inextricably intertwined. Confidence in the physician's technical expertise is significantly influenced by the patient's perception of the physician's affective behavior (Ben-Sira, 1976). Patients tend to judge the competence of their physicians in part by the degree of emotional support they receive. Confidence in their physicians, in turn, lowers the anxiety of patients, thus increasing the chance of more rapid recovery.

There is some evidence that the physician's interpersonal behavior toward the acutely ill patient can influence the patient's observable physiological condition. Järvinen (1955) found a significant increase in the number of sudden deaths among coronary patients during or shortly after ward rounds conducted by the medical staff. Ward rounds are nearly always conducted as a formal procedure with little regard for the patient as a person, but rather with attention to the patient as a "case." Järvinen suggested that this formal behavior on the part of the physicians serves to increase the fear and anxiety of patients to the point where it can reach a dangerously high level. Indeed, human interaction in a frightening, upsetting, or negative emotional context, has been found to have major effects on the cardiac rhythm and the electrical impulses of the hearts of cardiac patients (Lynch, Thomas, Mills, Malinow, and Katcher, 1974). This recognition of the physician's possible influence on the physiological condition of his or her patient highlights the importance of attending to effective bedside manner in medical practice.

Patient Satisfaction

Another important consequence of an effective socio-emotional relationship between physician and patient is the patient's own satisfaction with the care he or she receives. A number of studies reveal that patients clearly desire a good rapport and clear communication with their physicians, and that when they receive it, they are less likely to turn from the medical profession to quacks and charlatans or to bring medical malpractice suits against their physicians.

Koos (1955) surveyed a random sample of one thousand urban families, stratified on economic level, regarding their satisfaction with medical care. The greatest criticism of a majority of the respondents (64%) was about the nature of the physician-patient relationship they experienced. Similarly, a majority of Freidson's (1961) survey respondents felt that good medical care requires an interest in the patient as a person. More recently, Doyle and Ware (1977) found that physician conduct toward the patient was the strongest influence on satisfaction with medical care. Korsch, Gozzi, and Francis (1968) identified specific characteristics of physician-patient verbal interaction that contribute to patient satisfaction and dissatisfaction with medical care. Eight hundred patient visits to a pediatric walk-in clinic were studied by analysis of (a) a tape-recording of the doctor-patient (mother) interaction, and (b) a follow-up interview with the patient. Communication barriers such as the doctor's lack of warmth and friendliness, failure to take account of the patient's concerns and expectations from the medical visit, lack of a clear-cut explanation concerning diagnosis and causation of illness, and use of medical jargon, were all significant contributors to patient dissatisfaction.

Lack of physician-patient rapport may be one reason that terminally ill patients reject medical advice and seek out quacks and charlatans in the hope of cure. Cobb (1954) interviewed twenty cancer patients who rejected the medical establishment and sought help from nonmedical healers because of a lack of understanding and reassurance from their physicians, and a lack of sufficient information about what was being done for them. These patients, with a strong need for emotional support and sympathy, felt abandoned by their physicians. They misunderstood their prognoses and treatment regimens so they sought the help of nonmedical healers who offered understanding and hope. The multimillion dollar nonmedical "healing" industry tends to be patronized by patients who seek sympathy and attention not provided by their physicians.

The medical malpractice suit may be another result of the breakdown in the physician-patient relationship. In a study by Blum (1957, 1960), physicians who repeatedly experienced malpractice litigations were found to be rather insecure with patients, fearful of patients' anger, and both derogatory about patients as people and bothered by their emotions. Suit-prone physicians were unable to admit to themselves their own limitations of training or experience. When confronted by dissatisfied patients, they ignored them, dismissing their complaints as trivial. Being unable to face their own failures, these doctors seemed to punish their patients by indifference and rejection, and many patients responded with law suits to vent their dissatisfaction. While the medical malpractice suit usually reflects a patient's dissatisfaction with the results of technical treatment, frequently it is an expression of anger by the patient toward the physician who treated him or her. As Mechanic (1968) pointed out, "Much criticism of medicine in recent years and many medical malpractice suits against physicians reflect the impersonal nature of doctor-patient relationships and patients' doubts concerning the doctor's interest in their problems and the care and concern accorded to them" (p. 169). Vaccarino (1977) has suggested that many malpractice suits can be avoided with clear communication of caring and concern by physicians. Because the research up to now has been retrospective, this hypothesis has not been tested adequately. Sound prospective studies are needed in order to examine the impact of physician-patient rapport on malpractice litigation.

Many patients change primary care physicians because they are dissatisfied with the interpersonal treatment they receive. In an extensive survey reported in 1953, Gray and Cartwright found that a considerable number of adults in the United Kingdom's National Health Service changed physicians because of "inadequate treatment and attention." Patients terminated the physician-patient relationship if the doctor was too busy to talk with them or appeared to be uninterested in them as people. In a more recent survey in the United States, Kasteler, Kane, Olsen and Thetford (1976) found that patients' dislike of the doctor as a person, their dissatisfaction with the amount of time spent with them, and their perception of their physician's seeming lack of interest in them, significantly increased doctor-shopping behavior.

Thus, physicians' inability to satisfy their patients with meaningful affective behavior can contribute to the economic and human costs associated with health care delivery, such as extensive lack of patient cooperation with medical advice, seeking of nonmedical healers by seriously ill patients, extensive doctor-shopping, and an increasing incidence of malpractice litigation. Because of their potential for minimizing or eliminating these costs, programs to train physicians in the interpersonal aspects of the healing process should be developed without delay. The interpersonal aspects of patient care must balance and blend with the extensive, sophisticated training in the technological aspects of patient care. Both the recognition and implementation of this vital part of the physician's training is long overdue.

DEFINING THE AFFECTIVE COMPONENT OF THE PHYSICIAN-PATIENT RELATIONSHIP

. . . The physician's ability to communicate caring and concern to patients through verbal and nonverbal channels may be an essential addition to technical expertise in the effective delivery of medical care, for without the communication of positive affect, patients may have little confidence in their physicians (Ben-Sira, 1976). Patients' perceptions of the caring and concern, warmth, and positive feeling of their physicians can strongly influence their desire to continue the relationship (DiMatteo, Prince and Taranta, 1979) and their tendency to comply with physicians' orders (Francis, Korsch and Morris, 1969). In the communication of empathy, nonverbal cues have been found to be extremely important, possibly even more important than the verbal message itself (Haase and Tepper, 1972).

Friedman, DiMatteo, and Taranta (in press) report two studies conducted with medical house officers that measured directly their nonverbal expressiveness, and examined its relationship to patient satisfaction. In the two studies, a total of forty-seven medical residents were audiotaped and/or filmed while expressing (to a person who was simulating a patient) a number of verbally neutral sentences communicating various emotions. These emotions were Happiness, Sadness, Anger, and Surprise. These audiotapes and films were then edited and played back to large groups of raters or judges. The judges were asked to guess which emotion was being "sent" in each communication. The proportion of judges who correctly labelled the communication (for example, labelled the emotion Happiness when the physician was in fact trying to communicate Happiness) was taken as a measure of the physician's ability successfully to communicate the emotion to others. If a high percentage of the judges guessed correctly what the physician was "sending," or encoding, then the physician was a successful sender; if few understood his or her communications, the physician's nonverbal encoding skills were scored as poor. Patients' ratings of the physician's interpersonal behavior were collected, and these ratings were found to be moderately correlated with the "sending skill" scores. The results of both studies indicated that a physician's ability to communicate emotions through nonverbal channels of facial expression and voice tone was related to his or her patients' satisfaction with the interpersonal aspects of care.

These findings are consistent with social-psychological theories of social influence. For example, the patient may look to the physician for cues as to how he or she should respond to the medical situation and to what the patient should attribute emotional arousal. If the patient's anxiety is high regarding aspects of the treatment or details of the diagnosis, the physician can do much to communicate to the patient that the appropriate response should be calm and hopeful rather than a response fraught with panic, fear or hopelessness (see Friedman, 1979). A friendly physician who can communicate warmth and bring the receiver of a persuasive communication to like him or her will be more successful in changing attitudes (such as increasing compliance) than will someone who is not liked by the receiver of the message (see Rodin and Janis, 1979).

These notions are also closely aligned to Carl Rogers' (1957) specifications for effective counselling and psychotherapy: (a) the communication of warmth and unconditional positive regard to the client, (b) an understanding of the client's feelings and a communication of that understanding, and (c) the communication of genuineness and sincerity. The latter has been operationally defined by researchers on nonverbal communication, such as Friedman (in press), in terms of consistency between verbal and nonverbal cues. The physician's nonverbal sensitivity and expressiveness therefore, appear to be linked both theoretically and empirically, to patient satisfaction with medical treatment. Social psychologists are making headway toward more precise definitions of physician-patient rapport and the socio-emotional aspects of patient care. . . .

TOWARD A SCIENCE OF THE ART OF MEDICINE

Health care professionals, especially medical educators, will probably listen carefully to what social scientists have to say (Engel, 1977) about the "art of medicine" if the information is based upon methodologically sound research findings.

There is some sound evidence to suggest that nonverbal communication between the physician and the patient is especially important in the socio-emotional dimension of care. The physician must learn to read the patient's cues to emotion in facial expressions, body movements, and voice tone and must learn to use these same nonverbal channels in communicating with his or her patients. Social psychology has made great strides in this area of human behavior in recent years. Many principles of nonverbal communication have already been rigorously derived and tested. These principles, as well as many other axioms of human interaction, are now ready to be taught to physicians, and the success of this instruction is now ready to be evaluated rigorously.

The successful development of scientifically based training programs in the Art of Medicine holds, perhaps, the most significant promise of transforming an habitual, stereotyped scenario acted out by physician and patient into a fruitful interpersonal encounter. The improved quality of this interchange might be expected to have a significant positive impact on patients' emotional responses to treatment, and hence increase the actual effectiveness of this treatment. Enhanced affective communication in the physician-patient relationship might significantly increase patients' satisfaction with their care, and hence decrease the incidence of anger-induced rejection of the physician, and/or patient retaliation with malpractice litigation. Finally, physicians' increased responsiveness to patients' emotional reactions and needs, as well as physicians' enhanced abilities to communicate warmth, caring, and concern might significantly increase patients' understanding and acceptance of, as well as their motivation to cooperate with, prescribed treatment regimens. Investments in the development of training programs in the Art of Medicine might well produce immediate gains in the efficiency and effectiveness with which health care is delivered, and the cost-effectiveness of such programs might well become immediately evident. This is likely, however, only if these programs are firmly grounded in a rigorous science of human behavior and social interaction.

REFERENCES

Alpert, J. J. Broken appointments. *Pediatrics*, 1964, **34**, 127–132.

Ben-Sira, Z. The function of the professional's affective behavior in client satisfaction: A revised approach to social interaction theory. *Journal of Health and Social Behavior*, 1976, **17**, 3–11.

Bloom, S. W. *The doctor and his patient: A sociological interpretation*. New York: Russell-Sage Foundation, 1963.

Blum, R. H. *The psychology of malpractice suits*. San Francisco, CA: The California Medical Association, 1957.

Blum, R. H. *The management of the doctor-patient relationship*. New York: McGraw-Hill, 1960.

Cobb, B. Why do people detour to quacks? *The Psychiatric Bulletin*, 1954, **3**, 66–69.

Davis, M. S. Variations in patients' compliance with doctors' orders: Analyses of congruence between survey responses and results of empirical investigations. *Journal of Medical Education*, 1966, **41**, 1037–1048.

Davis, M. S. Physiologic, psychological, and demographic factors in patient compliance with doctors' orders. *Medical Care*, 1968, **6**, 115–122 (a).

Davis, M. S. Variations in patients' compliance with doctors' advice: An empirical analysis of patterns of communication. *American Journal of Public Health*, 1968, **58**, 274–288 (b).

DiMatteo, M. R., Prince, L. M., and Taranta, A. Patients' perceptions of physicians' behavior: Determinants of patient commitment to the therapeutic relationship. *Journal of Community Health*, in press.

Doyle, B. J. and Ware, J. E. Physician conduct and other factors that affect consumer satisfaction with medical care. *Journal of Medical Education*, 1977, **52**, 793–801.

Egbert, L. D., Battit, G. E., Welch, C. E., and Bartlett, M. K. Reduction of postoperative pain by encouragement and instruction of patients: A study of doctor-patient rapport. *New England Journal of Medicine*, 1964, **270**, 825–827.

Eisenberg, L. The search for care. *Daedalus*, 1977, **106**, 235–246.

Engel, G. L. The care of the patient: Art or Science? *The Johns Hopkins Medical Journal*, 1977, **140**, 222–232.

Fox, R. C. *Experiment perilous: physicians and patients facing the unknown*. Glencoe, Ill.: The Free Press, 1959.

Francis, V., Korsch, B. M., and Morris, M. J. Gaps in doctor-patient communication: Patients' response to medical advice. *New England Journal of Medicine*, 1969, **280**, 535–540.

Freidson, E. *Patients' views of medical practice*. New York: Russell-Sage Foundation, 1961.

Friedman, H. S. The interactive effects of facial expressions of emotion and verbal messages on perceptions of affective meaning. *Journal of Experimental Social Psychology*, in press.

Friedman, H. S. Nonverbal communication between patients and medical practitioners. *The Journal of Social Issues*, 1979, **35**(1).

Friedman, H. S., DiMatteo, M. R., and Taranta, A. A study of the relationship between individual differences in nonverbal expressiveness and factors of personality and social interaction. *Journal of Research in Personality*, in press.

Gillum, R. F. and Barsky, A. J. Diagnosis and management of patient noncompliance. *Journal of the American Medical Association*, 1974, **228**, 1563–1567.

Gray, P. G. and Cartwright, A. Choosing and changing doctors. *The Lancet*, 1953, *Dec. 19*, 1308.

Haase, R. F. and Tepper, D. T. Nonverbal components of empathic communication. *Journal of Counseling Psychology*, 1972, **19**, 417–424.

Hamburg, D. A. and Brown, S. S. The science base and social context of health maintenance: An overview. *Science*, 1978, **200**, 847–849.

Hippocrates. *Volume II: On Decorum and the Physician*, with English translation by W. H. S. Jones, London: William Heinemann, Ltd., 1923.

Janis, I. L. *Psychological stress: Psychoanalytic and behavioral studies of surgical patients*. New York: Wiley, 1958.

Järvinen, K. A. J. Can ward rounds be a danger to patients with myocardial infarction? *British Medical Journal*, 1955, **1**, 318–320.

Kasteler, J., Kane, R. L., Olsen, D. M., and Thetford, C. Issues underlying prevalence of "doctor-shopping" behavior. *Journal of Health and Social Behavior*, 1976, **17**, 328–339.

King, S. H. *Perceptions of illness and medical practice*. New York: Russell-Sage, 1962.

Koos, E. "Metropolis"—what city people think of their medical services. *American Journal of Public Health*, 1955, **45**, 1551–1557.

Korsch, B. M., Gozzi, E. K., and Francis, V. Gaps in doctor-patient communication. I: doctor-patient interaction and patient satisfaction. *Pediatrics*, 1968, **42**, 855–871.

Langer, E. J., Janis, I. L., and Wolfer, J. A. Reduction of psychological stress in surgical patients. *Journal of Experimental Social Psychology*, 1975, **11**, 155–165.

Lynch, J. J., Thomas, S. A., Mills, M. E., Malinow, K., and Katcher, A. H. The effects of human contact on cardiac arrhythmia in coronary care patients. *The Journal of Nervous and Mental Disease*, 1974, **158**, 88–99.

Mechanic, D. *Medical sociology: A selective view*. New York: The Free Press, 1968.

Milmoe, S., Rosenthal, R., Blane, H. T., Chafetz, M. L., and Wolf, I. The doctor's voice: Postdictor of successful referral of alcoholic patients. *Journal of Abnormal Psychology*, 1967, **72**, 78–84.

Osler, W. The master-word in medicine. In *Aequanimitas with other addresses to medical students, nurses, and practitioners of medicine*. Philadelphia, PA: Blakiston Co., 1904, 369–371.

Parsons, T. *The social system*. Glencoe, Ill.: The Free Press, 1951, 428–479.

Parsons, T. Definitions of health and illness in the light of American values and social structure. In E. G. Jaco (Ed.) *Patients, physicians and illness*. New York: The Free Press, 1958, 165–187.

Rodin, J. and Janis, I. L. The social power of health care practitioners as agents of change. *The Journal of Social Issues*, 1979, **35**(1).

Rogers, C. R. The necessary and sufficient conditions of therapeutic personality change. *Journal of Consulting Psychology*, 1957, **21**, 95–103.

Salzman, C., Shader, R., Scott, D. A., and Binstock, W. Interviewer anger and patient dropout in a walk-in clinic. *Comprehensive Psychiatry*, 1970, **11**, 267–273.

Shattuck, F. C. The science and art of medicine in some of their aspects. *Boston Medical and Surgical Journal*, 1907, **157**, 63–67.

Stone, G. Compliance and the role of the expert. *Journal of Social Issues*, 1979, **35**(1).

Strauss, M. B. (Ed.) *Familiar medical quotations*. Boston, Mass.: Little-Brown and Co., 1968.

Vaccarino, J. M. Malpractice: The problem in perspective. *The Journal of the American Medical Association*, 1977, **238**, 861–863.

Wilson, R. N. and Bloom, S. W. Patient-practitioner relationships. In H. E. Freeman, S. Levine, and L. G. Reeder (Eds.) *Handbook of medical sociology*, Englewood Cliffs, N.J.: Prentice-Hall, 1972, p. 315–339.

DAVID C. GLASS

Stress, Competition and Heart Attacks

A person who suffers a heart attack is most likely a victim of coronary heart disease, a disorder of the coronary arteries that may destroy parts of the heart muscle itself. The usual cause of coronary artery disease is atherosclerosis, commonly known as hardening of the arteries. More Americans die of this disease than any other single cause. An estimated one to three million Americans had heart disease in 1975; of these, close to 675,000 will die of it, 175,000 of them before they reach 65.

Researchers know the physical factors that make a person likely to develop heart disease. Such an individual is an older male who has high levels of cholesterol or other fats in his blood, high blood pressure, diabetes, parents who suffered heart disease, is fat, exercises little, and smokes at least a pack of cigarettes each day. But knowing all these factors that make atherosclerosis likely does not help us identify new victims of the disease. Most heart patients, for example, do not have excessive levels of cholesterol, only a few are hypertensive, and fewer still are diabetic. Experts do not agree that a person who shows these characteristics will necessarily have a heart attack. It is by no means clear that a fat old man who spends his days sitting in a chair and chain-smoking increases his risk of heart attack.

Because the physical facts alone provide little help, researchers have broadened their investigation to include psychological factors. Most have settled on stress and what they call "Type-A" behavior as the prime candidates for psychological causes of heart attacks. A person who shows Type-A behavior is highly competitive, feels pressured for time, and reacts to frustration with hostility. My research focuses on the interplay between the Type-A personality, life stress, and heart attack.

In order to classify people as Type A or Type B, I use their responses to questions about their ambitions, competitiveness, sense of being pressed for time, and hostile feelings. Type-A people, for example, are likely to set deadlines or quotas for themselves at work or at home at least once per week, while Type-B people do so only occasionally. A Type-A person brings his work home with him frequently, a Type-B almost never. The Type-A person is highly achievement-oriented and pushes himself to near capacity, while the Type-B person takes it easy. Hard-driving Type-A students earn more academic honors than their Type-B counterparts, though they are no more intelligent. The Type-A behavior pattern earns a person the rewards he seeks, but at a cost to his body that may be the death of him. Obviously, not all Type-A people have heart attacks, but there are certain times, especially when they come under severe stress, when their risk of heart attack is greatest.

Both medical research and popular lore implicate stressful events such as the sudden death of a spouse or loss of a job as causes of heart attacks. Recent research suggests the biological mechanisms responsible for this link. The immediate cause of a stress-induced heart attack, says one approach, is the build-up of cholesterol deposits on the walls of the arteries. These deposits form plaques, which narrow the vessels. Should these plaques decay and tear away from the artery walls, they form clots that close off the channels of one or more of the coronary arteries, already narrowed by plaques. The result is a heart attack.

Taxes and cholesterol. Stress can make such an attack likely by increasing levels of cholesterol in the bloodstream. During the first two weeks in April, for instance, as the income-tax deadline approaches, serum cholesterol levels in the blood of tax accountants shoot up from normal levels. As the deadline passes, their cholesterol levels fall sharply.

Another way stress can lead to heart attack is by increasing blood pressure. Blood passing through the arteries under high pressure increases the likelihood of tears in the arterial walls. It is around these tears that fatty deposits form plaques. These plaques are, in turn, more likely to tear away when blood pressure is high.

Still another route from stress to heart attack is through the body's general reactions to stress. When a person is under stress, his brain causes the release of the hormones adrenaline and noradrenaline, which help mobilize his body to cope with danger. But these hormones speed up blood clotting, thereby increasing the formation of arterial clots. At the same time, these hormones raise one's blood pressure, which can in turn lead to sudden bleeding in an arterial plaque and the formation of clots.

Hostile achievers. For all these reasons, stress makes the danger of heart attack more likely. For the person with Type-A behavior, this risk is even greater— in fact, a recent study shows that Type-A behavior is one of the strongest predictors of recurring heart attacks. Type-A people have higher cholesterol levels than their behavioral opposites, the more easygoing Type B's. In my own laboratory, I have found high cholesterol levels in extreme Type-A men as young as 19 years old. Though Type-A men do not have more hypertension than do Type B's, when their hostility—a key Type-A trait—is aroused, their blood pressure increases sharply. Further, the blood-clotting time of Type-A men is significantly faster than that of others, and some evidence shows they react to stress with greater noradrenaline secretion.

The push to achieve leads Type A's to press their bodies to the limits. I had students walk continuously on a motorized treadmill at increasingly sharp angles of incline until they gave up. As they walked, every few minutes they rated their level of fatigue. I then measured each student's aerobic capacity, to see how close each had pushed himself to his lungs' capacity to absorb oxygen. Type-A subjects on the treadmill reached 91.4 percent of their capacities, while Type B's reached only 82.8

percent. Even so, A's admitted to less fatigue than did B's. The hard-driving A's ignore or deny their body's tiredness in their struggle to attain their goals—in this case, a superior performance on a treadmill.

In sum, the Type-A person works hard and fast to succeed, and in striving toward his goals, he suppresses feelings, such as fatigue, that might interfere with his performance. Type A's get angry if someone or something gets in the way of their success. I submit that all these traits suggest a person who rises to master challenges out of a need to control his world.

Master of his fate.   The concept of control helps us to understand under which circumstances the Type-A person is more vulnerable to heart attack. If the Type-A person is highly concerned with controlling his environment, then he should be upset by threats to that control. He should be even more distressed when that threat is beyond his control, so that, try as he may, there is nothing he can do to master the situation.

I found preliminary support for my theory when I compared a group of men between 35 and 55 who were hospitalized for heart attack with a group of men hospitalized for other kinds of disease, and with a comparable group of healthy, nonhospitalized men. As would be expected, the heart-attack victims had stronger Type-A patterns than either of the other two groups. Of greater interest, though, were their scores on a Loss Index, a 10-item scale that asks a person to describe the incidence during the last year of stressful events in his life over which he had minimal control, such as the death of a loved one, being fired, or a large financial loss. Within the year preceding their illness, both hospitalized groups experienced more such losses than had the healthy group. Life events that leave a person feeling bereft and helpless can lead to disease. In the face of uncontrollable losses, a Type-A person is likely to have a heart attack, while one lower in Type-A traits will more often develop some other disease.

All of us are hit hard by life's losses, but the Type-A person may react to such loss with a heart attack. To see why this might be so, I looked more closely at the way in which the Type-A person reacts to stress. In one study, I watched how Type A's and Type B's handled a 12-burst series of very loud noise. Half the people in each group could cut off the noise if they mastered a tricky pattern of lever pressing; the other half could do nothing to escape the noise.

Immediately after the noise, each person was tested for his complex reaction time on a task that required him to respond to lights by lifting his finger from a telegraph key. The intervals between lights were relatively long, which we believed would make the Type A's impatient and thus slow their reactions. As we expected, B's were faster than A's after the session when escape was possible. But after the session when they could not escape the noise, the A's had faster reaction times than B's. I interpreted this to mean that A's are more threatened than B's by a form of stress they cannot control, and therefore compensate by restraining their impatience, which would normally interfere with fast performance.

A person who increases his efforts to master a situation he can never control is bound to be frustrated. To see how Type A's responded after lengthy exposure to uncontrollable stress, I used the same loud noise during two different sessions. In the first session, half the people could escape and half could not; in the second session everyone had a chance to learn to escape the noise. This time I tripled the length of time each person heard the noise, and varied the noise level so that half heard the loud noise, while the other half heard a softer sound.

Passive listeners. After the sessions, those people who were unable to escape reported they felt quite helpless compared to their counterparts who could stop the noise. Indeed, some of those who had been in the session where escape was impossible sat dejectedly through the second session when they could have escaped, listening passively to the noisy bursts without lifting a hand. Most of the helpless people were Type A's; being unable to escape hit them especially hard. Once they had been frustrated by loud noise they could not stop, Type A's who did escape took much longer to learn to shut off the noise, but B's performed equally well whether or not they had just been frustrated. A's became helpless or inefficient only when the noise was offensively loud; in the less stressful sessions with mild noise, it was the frustrated B's who later had a hard time learning to stop the sound. Under this less stressful situation, there was no difference among the A's. It took intense stress, plus a complete lack of control over its source, to make the A's later do poorly.

These complicated reactions seem to indicate that the Type-A person at first rises to any challenge. He tries hard to control a highly stressful situation, but when his best efforts fail, he feels helpless and his attempts to master it suffer. The death of someone close, the loss of a job, or a financial setback are all events that we can do little to remedy. Although life's tragedies are hard for anyone, they are particularly dangerous for the Type-A person. For him, they can spell heart attack—and even death.

Mind, Body and Laughter

Norman Cousins, former owner and editor of *Saturday Review*, well-known man of causes, had never told his own medical story when I talked to him about it five years ago. Such reticence was not characteristic of Norman, and what happened to him after the telling of his story reveals something of what is going on in people's attitudes toward the relationship of mind and body.

"Norman Cousins Laughs Himself Back" was what I called it in my book *Powers of Mind*. Briefly: Cousins had come back from a trip with a high fever. Heaviness in his legs and back became paralysis; he could barely move his neck and jaws. His sedimentation rate—the rate at which blood precipitates solids—was dangerously high. The tentative diagnosis was that of a collagen disease, a disintegration of the connective tissue between the cells. His physician told him to get his affairs in order, and one doctor left a note for another that said, "I'm afraid we may be losing Norman."

Cousins then announced that he was taking the responsibility for his own cure. He checked out of the hospital and into a hotel. He had read up on stress and vitamin C, and he took massive doses of that vitamin. And he laughed. He sent for and screened the Marx Brothers' movies and tapes of *Candid Camera*. "Ten minutes of belly laughter gave me an hour of pain-free sleep," Norman says. His sedimentation rate came down ten points at a time, and "the more I laughed, the better I got." His symptoms disappeared and he returned to work, making no mention of his unconventional and seemingly miraculous cure. It was ten years later that I printed it as an example of an uncharted, unexplained mind-body phenomenon. I tucked it between Stewart Alsop's cancer dream and a sober account from the *Archives of General Psychiatry* about a ten-year-old black girl who had been bleeding stigmatically and stopped on Good Friday. The Cousins story was not quite three pages long, but its appearance changed his life. He eventually got over three thousand letters and numerous invitations to speak at medical schools.

He wrote for the *New England Journal of Medicine* a more detailed account of his illness and his self-designed cure, which he has now expanded into a national best seller, *Anatomy of an Illness*. When *Saturday Review* went through a change of ownership, Cousins became a consultant, accepted a lectureship at the UCLA medical school and left New York, where he had been on the scene for forty years. He bought a contemporary hilltop home in Los Angeles, and he now teaches a course in medicine and values to seventy-five medical students at UCLA. Throughout the year he makes a circuit of medical schools, visits veterans' hospitals and sifts through invitations to speak at medical school commencements. Most recently, he decided, together with some people from Rand Corporation, to start a research project at UCLA on the influence of attitude on the autonomic nervous system.

Cousins is pleased that the curriculum committee at UCLA gives the same credit for his course that it gives for anatomy and physiology, the "harder stuff." "The irony is," he says, "that in a medical school, everything that isn't science is 'soft.' If you talk about the relationship between the physician and the patient, that's 'soft.' 'Hard' is what can be measured. And yet, if you take the physicians who are twenty-five years out of medical school, they find that much of the 'hard' stuff turns out not to be so hard. What happened to the infected-teeth theory of arthritis? Or to lobotomies? Or to tonsillectomies? Theory changes, the knowledge base keeps changing, but contact and compassion don't.

"I've been over and over my own case. Did the ascorbic acid help collagen formation? I certainly think so. What about the laughter? Well, oxygen deprivation is a common characteristic of every illness. So, if you want to be hard-nosed, you can say that laughter enhances respiration, oxygenates the blood, combats the levels of carbon dioxide—like internal jogging. What I'm teaching is that the successful practice of medicine eliminates arbitrary divisions. I told Franklin Murphy [the former chancellor of UCLA] and Sherman Mellinkoff, the medical school dean, that medical school students were well-trained but not well-educated. They knew the science of medicine but not the art of medicine. The art involves a respect for life, for the great mysteries, the imponderables, human potentiation."

I agree with Cousins: That list sounds magnificent but "soft" for a medical school—although you wouldn't get any proper medical school dean denying a respect for life or for imponderables. Nevertheless, medicine has gotten more and more mechanistic; nowadays there is a lot of talk about "health care delivery packages." Meanwhile, a movement loosely called holistic is growing in medicine: The physician takes the time to consider the whole patient—lifestyle, emotions and nutrition—so that he is not merely treating a specific symptom with a specific antidote.

"We've all grown up with externalization," Norman says. "An illness is what happens after you bump into a germ. The germ comes from outside. Then you take something from a bottle to fix it. But other people bump into germs and nothing happens. Their defenses work. Why do some defenses work when others don't? That's why I want to do research on attitudes. But the medical establishment looks askance at holistic medicine. Sometimes you can see why. I went to a holistic medical meeting, and it was replete with sideshows of astrology, numerology, pyramidology.

"Not every disease is reversible. But we don't know much about the biochemistry of the emotions. Fear, hate and rage produce bodily changes—why not positive feelings? The patient has to give it his best shot."

Norman shuffles through some papers. "Here's a physician from Denver with a patient who had cancer of the prostate that had metastasized to the skull, hips, spine—257 lesions altogether. How long could the guy live—three weeks, four weeks? His doctor told him, if you believe this cancer is terminal, it will be. You and I will go into a partnership. I'll give you everything medicine knows—surgery, estrogen, whatever is needed. I want *you* to have the best time of your life: Laugh, do what you want to do, begin to see it as funny.''

I know what the ending to that story will be. Norman sighs.

"Oh, yeah," he says, "I've heard the guy's alive, the lesions have mostly cleared, and I think somebody from the Stanford medical school is writing it up." Norman shrugs.

"The best doctors have always been artists," I suggest. "Maybe holistic medicine is something that was always practiced and has just been overshadowed by the advances in immunology and biochemistry."

Norman is handed a phone message, a long-distance call. A fifty-two-year-old woman in Florida with cancer of the colon has had a recurrence and wants to fly to California to see Norman. "No," he says, almost angry. "I'm not practicing medicine. There's a difference between emotional support and doctoring."

Before I left Los Angeles, Norman called me. "I'm not sure you should use any of that stuff we talked about."

"That's what you said the last time, and here you are."

"This is a very sensitive area," he said, still reticent.

"That's what you said last time."

Norman's uncharacteristic reticence is typical of many rational and intellectual people when venturing into the twilight mists of mind-body relationships. The faith of sophisticates goes to large electronic machines with computer printouts or cathode-ray tube terminals, attended by white-coated acolytes and lubricated by government grants. When it comes to talk about the mind, the machine can't make satisfying electronic sounds, can't get a grip on it.

Aldous Huxley once said of mind-body relationships that "the only attitude for a researcher in this ticklish field is that of an anthropologist living in the midst of a tribe of potentially dangerous savages. Go about your business quietly, don't break the taboos or criticize the locally accepted dogmas." On the other hand, there is a large and hungry audience for miracles, for simplistic solutions. The gullible fill the tents of faith healers and the pockets of the producers of nostrums.

And yet, even the medical establishment is now beginning to believe that there must be something to this business of attitude and belief, to the harnessed energy of the unconscious. Conservative churches sponsor the laying on of hands; the last such ceremony I attended was at the venerable Trinity Church, at the end of Wall Street. And, at the same time, cell technology develops. Psychiatrists and brain reseachers look not only for complexes with the names of Greek characters but also at the neurotransmitters and receptors in brain cells—chemicals that transmit impulses from cell to cell in the brain. The specific sites in brain cells upon which morphine and other opiates act have been identified, and researchers have also found that the brain contains its own opiatelike substances called enkephalin and endorphin, which act on receptors to block pain. Enkephalin and endorphin, the researchers speculate, may dull not only physical pain but psychological stress as well.

The discovery of the opiate receptors spurred the brain mappers to look for other natural substances in the receptor sites of brain cells. Several researchers have already claimed advances in improving and sharpening memory, even though no one yet is sure where memory resides in the brain.

My speculation is that the brain researchers will go on cataloging the body's own apothecary and why it does what it does and why it can resist some conditions yet surrender to others. In ten or fifteen years, the neuroscientists will have come up with some reasons why laughter and attitude have an effect, and these researchers will have dutifully assigned the appropriate natural substances to the appropriate parts of brain and body. They will consider Norman's insights and experiences curious, antiquated and charming, effective in a cumbersome way, just as the historians of science consider the old researchers into combustion, who thought a combustible released a substance called phlogiston when it burned. Norman's experience will have passed through bestsellerdom into the annals of the *Reader's Digest*. In the face of cell technology, the Freudian maps of the unconscious will seem to many like the old maps of Africa that supplied pictures of elephants in the white spaces that were unexplored.

And even then, I would also bet that mists will continue to obscure at least some of the relationships between mind and body.

Index

Behavior, 222–228
Swedlund, M., 146
Swift, J., 303
Synder, M., 24, 28, 29

Taguiri, R., 164
Taranta, A., 403
TAT. *See* Thematic Apperception Test
Tavris, C., 295, 302–310
Taylor, D. A., 167
Taylor, S. T., 26
Technology, effect of, on individuals, 330–337
Teevan, J., 228
Teger, A., 247
Television, 222–229; and aggression, 222–230; sex role stereotypes on, 293–294. *See also* Media
Temperature, effect of, on collective violence, 206, 211–221
Tepper, D. T., 403
Terwilliger, R. F., 85
Tesser, A., 392, 393, 394, 395
Tessler, R. C., 65, 67 n2
Test, M. A., 278
Thematic Apperception Test (TAT), 305–306
Thetford, C., 402
Thibaut, J. W., 165, 167, 170
Thurstone, L. L., 67
Tidball, E., 309–310
Time, conception of, 236
Tittle, C. R., 67
Tognacci, L. N., 64, 69
Totten, J., 27
Tresemer, D., 307
Trotter, R., 231–233
Tversky, A., 391, 395
Type 1 error, 36
Type 2 error, 36, 44

Ulrich, R., 123
Unger, R., 287–295
Unilateral awareness, 161, 162–164
U.S. Riot Commission, 211, 212, 213

Vaccarino, J. M., 402
Vaizey, J. J., 342, 347
Valins, S., 13, 347–348
Veitch, R., 211, 346, 347
Verbal contact, 40–41
Vernon, D. T. A., 64, 69
Videotape, laboratory use of, 26–27
Villena, J., 354
Vincent, J. E., 117–129
Violence. *See* Aggression
Vogt, G., 274–277

Voltaire, 176
Vonnegut, K., Jr., 141

Wachtel, P., 29
Wachtler, J., 147, 148, 149, 150
Walder, L., 228
Wallach, H., 26
Walster, E., 165, 166, 186, 187, 188
Walster, G. W., 185–195
Ware, J. E., 401
Warner, L. G., 64
Watson, J., 381
Wayne, J., 324
Weigel, R., 63, 64–74
Weiner, B., 13
Weisman, A. D., 393
Weiss, R. R., 91, 157
Welch, C. E., 400
Welch, S., 342, 346
West, S. G., 27
Wheeler, D., 117–129
White, L., 305
White, R. C., 344
Wicker, A. W., 64, 66, 72, 73
Wicklund, R. A., 27, 274
Wiegal, R. H., 64, 69
Wiesel, E., 77
Wilke, H., 118
Wilkins, C., 65
Wilson, R. N., 397
Winkel, G., 329
Wirth, L., 330, 340, 351, 357
Wittreich, W. J., 172, 173
Wohlwill, J. F., 341–342
Wolf, I., 400
Wolfer, J. A., 401
Wolosin, R. J., 29
Women (and men), 287–326; achievement motive in, 306–308; and career achievement, 313–322; dating selective v. easy, 185–195; and legitimacy of feminism, 292; roles of, 287; and self-image, 303–305; as victims of television violence, 224–225. *See also* Androgyny; Men, and women; Sexual violence
Woodworth, R. S., 164
Woolf, V., 297
Wrightsman, L. S., Jr., 320

Yarrow, P. R., 65

Zanna, M. P., 314, 320
Zimbardo, P., 1, 7, 55–63, 186, 210, 234–242, 356
Zlutnick, S., 342